JULIUS FIRMICUS MATERNUS

MATHESIS

EDITED AND TRANSLATED
FROM THE LATIN
BY

JAMES HERSCHEL HOLDEN, M.A.
Fellow of the American Federation of Astrologers

First printing: 2011

ISBN-10: 0-86690-619-3
ISBN-13: 978-0-86690-619-7

Cover Design: Jack Cipolla

Published by:
American Federation of Astrologers, Inc.
6535 S. Rural Road
Tempe, AZ 85285

www.astrologers.com

Printed in the United States of America

Table of Contents

TRANSLATOR'S PREFACE

This translation has a curious history. I first encountered the Latin text of the *Mathesis* in a library when I was only 16 years old, and I was immediately fascinated by it. I resolved to translate it into English. And eleven years later I began to translate it on 5 April 1954 using first the older Teubner edition by Sittl and then a photocopy of the newer edition by Kroll, Skutsch, and Ziegler. I translated Book I, which I completed in 1955, and then I translated Book V, Chapter 1, after which I typed what I had translated.[1] Then I began the translation of Book II, but I thought that possibly some of the MSS might provide better readings here and there.

With that in mind, I acquired microfilms of most of the extant MSS and began to collate them. I worked out the filiation of the MSS for Book I and was able to make a few improvements in the text. I revised a portion of the translation that I had already made, finished translating Book II, and began translating Book III and portions of Book IV, but I ceased work on it before I had completed those books. I then turned my attention to other projects. From time to time during the next two decades, I translated a few more chapters of the *Mathesis*, including some in Books V to VIII, but I stopped altogether in 1975 when Bram's translation of the Mathesis was published. That translation was less literal than my own, and it often ignored some words and phrases in the text, but it was eminently readable.

However, in later years I occasionally made some further revisions and translated some additional chapters, since I had noticed that Bram had not taken into account the collation of MS **N** and the addenda that were published in the reprint edition of the Teubner text that appeared in 1968. Hence, there were a number of places where the translation could be improved. I had also gained some additional insight into Firmicus's astrology from some studies that I had made in the Greek astrologers in the intervening years. In 1999, I extracted the significations of the planets in houses 2, 6, 8, and 12 from my then completed translation of Book III

[1]The beginning of this translation was thus close to 1,600 years after Firmicus sent the presentation copy of the *Mathesis* to his friend Mavortius. See below.

for inclusion in my paper "Four Evil Houses" that was published in the *A.F.A. Journal of Research*, vol. 11 (Winter 1999): 29-57.

Thereafter, beginning in the year 2000, I again reviewed the translations that I had made previously, transferred them to new word processor files, and began to extend them. And now, on August 13, 2006, I have completed the translation of the *Mathesis* (except for the Indices).

Firmicus and the Mathesis.

The MSS give the author's name as Julius Firmicus Maternus Junior, V.C. The letters V.C. stand for *Vir Clarissimus* 'Very Outstanding Man', a title that indicated senatorial rank. Firmicus tells us in the Preface to Book I of the *Mathesis* that he was a native of Sicily and a student of astrology. In a later book, he relates that he had been a lawyer, but that, worn out by years of dog-eat-dog legal contention, he had retired from the law courts.[1] He also relates in the Preface how he came to write the *Mathesis*.

Returning in winter from a lengthy trip, he encountered Quintus Flavius Maesius Egnatius Lollianus Mavortius in Campania, a region south of Rome. Mavortius was also a V.C. and a high Roman official.[2] The two men struck up an instant friendship, and, learning that his guest was knowledgeable about astrology, Mavortius asked Firmicus to write a book on astrology in Latin. It should be remembered that Horoscopic Astrology was a Greek science, and almost all the books were in Greek.[3] Mavortius would of course have known Greek, but it was a second language for him, and he evidently preferred to have a book on astrology in his own native Latin. Firmicus agreed to write the book, and the two men parted, although they kept in contact. Many years later, probably in 354 or 355, Firmicus finally finished the entire book and sent it to Mavortius.

---

[1]*Mathesis* IV Preface.

[2]It is uncertain exactly when Firmicus and Mavortius met, but it was during the time that Mavortius was Governor of the Province of Campania 328-335. This then would indicate the approximate time when Firmicus began writing the *Mathesis*.

[3]There is only one Latin book on astrology written prior to the 4th century that has come down to us. That is Marcus Manilius's *Astronomica*, which is more poetry than astrology, and of little value as a textbook. Even though one or two other treatises may have been written in Latin, Greek was the language of astrology.

Not much else is known for certain about Firmicus, other than the fact that he was also the author of a little book entitled *De errore profanarum religionum* 'The Error of Pagan Religions', which from internal evidence was apparently written around the year 346. It has come down to us in a single defective MS **Vaticanus Palatinus Latinus 165** of the 9th or 10th century. The *De errore* is a fierce denunciation of non-Christian religions. Similarities of vocabulary and literary style are sufficient to remove any doubt that the same man wrote both the *Mathesis* and the *De errore*. In the 19th century, that fact annoyed the Christian sentiments of scholars, so it was generally assumed that Firmicus wrote the *Mathesis* in the early 330's and then, having abandoned the pagan art of astrology, was converted to Christianity in the 340's and wrote the *De errore*.[1] This theory was challenged by Thorndike in the early years of the 20th century.[2] He pointed out the significant fact that Christianity is never mentioned in the *Mathesis*, and astrology is never mentioned in the *De errore*!

We should bear in mind that a lawyer might well argue either side of a case. Hence, there was no reason why Firmicus could not have written the *De errore* as a digression while working on the *Mathesis*.[3] In fact it appears that in the *Mathesis* he actually refers to the *De errore*, when he says "We contemn the Gods, so it seems, and we make public the sanctified and venerable ceremonies of religions with a desperate ardor of sacrilege."[4] And, while Firmicus may at first glance seem to be addressing Constantine the Great at the end of the Preface to the *Mathesis*, a careful

[1]This was the opinion of the eminent German historian Theodor Mommsen (1817-1903), who wrote at a time when astrology had been a dead science in continental Europe for two centuries. His prestige as a historian was sufficient to convince most younger scholars.

[2]See Lynn Thorndike, *History of Magic and Experimental Science* (New York: Columbia University Press, 1923-1958. 8 vols.), vol. 1, pp. 525-526. Thorndike cites a telling parallel by noting that in his last work, *The Consolation of Philosophy*, the famous Christian scholar and philosopher Boethius (480-524) talks a lot about "Phoebus, the moon, the universe, the sky, and the starry constellations" but never once mentions Christ or the Trinity! If we apply similar academic logic, we could therefore assert that in his last years Boethius abandoned Christianity and reverted to Paganism.

[3]If the scholars had known anything about astrology, they would have recalled that the great English astrologer William Lilly (1602-1681) was a devout Christian who entitled his master work *Christian Astrology* (London, 1647).

[4]*Mathesis* i 2.8. And if, as seems likely, this is indeed a reference to the *De errore*, then it puts the date of composition of that portion of the Preface to the year 346 or later.

reading will show that Constantine was already deceased and that Firmicus is merely expressing a wish for the continuation of the Constantinian dynasty.[1]

Firmicus also states explicitly that his composition of the book had been long delayed, and that he finally finished it when his friend Mavortius had become consul-elect and had written to him requesting it.[2] It is known that Mavortius was Consul in the year 355. Hence, there seems no reason to doubt that the *Mathesis* was not completed until 354 or 355, or nearly a decade after the date of the *De errore*, and twenty years after the date usually assigned to the *Mathesis* in most modern references.[3]

At the end of the *Mathesis*, Firmicus entrusts the book to Mavortius and requests that he hand it down to his sons. It is possible that it was that copy of the book, or a copy of that copy, that survived the centuries to become the source of the *archetype* of the MSS that have come down to us. But where that copy resided during the period from the fourth century to the tenth, we do not know. It may even have been in Spain, for the historian William of Malmesbury (c.1093-c.1143) records in his *Deeds of the English Kings*[4] that "we have read that Gerbert, when in Spain among the Saracens, studied astrology, namely . . . Ptolemy on the astrolabe . . . Julius Firmicus on fate." This was the scholar Gerbert of Aurillac (c.940-1003), who became Pope Sylvester II (reigned 999-1003). This is the first known mention of the *Mathesis* after its composition in the fourth century.

The famous monastery of Monte Cassino was sacked by the Saracens in 883, and probably most of the books in its library were destroyed. The surviving monks fled to nearby cities. But under their successors the monastery and library were rebuilt in the early tenth century, and in the tenth and eleventh centuries the monastery became a great center of learning. Many books were added to the library, brought from other mo-

---

[1]See the notes at the end of *Mathesis* i. 10.

[2]*Mathesis* i. 8 *Proconsuli itaque tibi et ordinario consuli designato promissa reddimus*... 'And so we are sending to you, the Proconsul and designated Ordinary Consul, the promised work...' Mavortius was designated Ordinary Consul for the year 355.

[3]But not by Otto Neugebauer, A *History of Ancient Mathematical Astronomy* (New York, Heidelberg, Berlin: Springer Verlag, 1975. 3 vols.), vol. 2, p. 943, who assigns Firmicus to 350 A.D.

[4]Cited by the Teubner editors in *Mathesis*, Teubner edition, vol. 2, p. III.

nastic libraries in Europe, and many copies of books were made at the library and transmitted to other libraries in Europe.[1] It is possible that the *archetype* of the *Mathesis* was acquired by the Monte Cassino library at that time. The *sub-archetype* **Ω** of the oldest MSS may have been copied from it in the eleventh century. And in the first half of the 12th century, the Monte Cassino librarian Peter the Deacon (1107-after 1159) mentions that he had copied astrology from "old books." And it seems likely that the "old books" that he copied were in fact the two volumes of the *archetype* of the *Mathesis*.

The oldest extant MSS of the Mathesis were written in the 11th century, but they contain only the first four books. MSS containing all eight books began to appear in the latter half of the 15th century after the discovery in 1429 at Monte Cassino by the peripatetic humanist Poggio Bracciolini (1380-1459) of what was evidently the copy that Peter the Deacon had made. Poggio wrote several letters to his friend and fellow humanist Niccolò Niccoli (1363-1437), librarian to the Medici at Florence: (1) "I have found a book[2] that contains Julius Frontinus *De aquaeductibus urbis*[3] and also Julius Firmicus *matheseos libri viii*, but its beginning is lacking the first book and also part of the second[4]; I don't know whether you have read this book, but I want you to write to me. I carried that volume [away] with me, so that I could copy out Frontinus's book."

---

[1]For a convenient history of the Monte Cassino library, see James Westfall Thompson, *The Medieval Library* (New York & London: Hafner Publishing Co, 1967), p. 169 ff.

[2] MS **Casinensis 361**, which is described in the catalogue made in 1532 as containing: *Scolia matheseos de astrologia incip Hec omnia que. . . Item Lib. psilmi Vegetii de militia incip Primus. Item Lib. Iulii Frontonis de aque ductu urbis Rome incip Cum omnis res. . .* This tallies with Poggio's description of the *Mathesis* portion of the MS as lacking the first book, for the paragraph that is found at the end of Book I in the older MSS PR, is at the beginning of Book II in some of the newer MSS, such as AH, and in several of them it begins *Hec omnia que…* (rather than *Nec omnia quae…* as in the older MSS).

[3]*The Aqueducts of the City of Rome*, a technical treatise on the aqueducts that brought water to the City of Rome and on the distribution system within the city. It was written by Sextus Julius Frontinus (c.40-103), who was Commissioner of the City Waterworks in 97 A.D. See the excellent book by the hydraulics engineer Clemens Herschel, *The two Books on the Water Supply of the City of Rome* (Boston: Dana Estes and Company, 1899), which contains a facsimile of the portion of MS **Cas. 361** containing the Latin text, an edition of the Latin text, an English translation, and an extensive commentary. (The later reprints of this book omit the facsimile of the MS.)

[4]The "missing part" of Book II probably refers to the internal gap, since both the beginning and end of the book were present.

Soon after, Poggio wrote, (2) "When we have come to Rome, I will send Julius Firmicus to you . . . the book is correct and with few faults, as it seems, with the exception of the lack of the first book."[1] In another letter, (3) "The book from Monte Cassino was requested of me, and so I am sending it back; for, as you know, I have copied out the *De aquaeductibus* that I was interested in. The remainder [of the volume] does not interest me very much; I will bear up doing without it." And in a final letter to Niccoli, some time later, he says, (4) "But do you also want Julius Firmicus? If the book had been mine, I would have sent it to you."[2] Note the discrepancy between letter (2) and letter (4); we cannot tell from these letters that he ever sent the book to Niccoli. But it is possible that Niccoli later sent someone to Monte Cassino to retrieve the Firmicus portion of the volume or to make a copy of it.

In fact, the volume that Poggio had found is still in the Monte Cassino library. And it is still the prime source for the *De aquaeductibus*, but it no longer contains the *Mathesis*. It was rebound in the 17th century. So apparently, someone had gone to the library subsequent to Poggio's visit in 1429, removed the portion of the volume that contained the *Mathesis*, and never returned it. See the discussion below for further details.

The Sources and Contents of the Mathesis.

Firmicus translated or paraphrased a number of Greek astrological treatises. He mentions more than a dozen astrological writers by name, among them Abram, Achilles, Aesculapius, Antiochus, Critodemus, Dorotheus, Fronto, Hanubius, Mercurius, Navigius, Nechepso, Orfeus, Petosiris, Porphyry, and Ptolemy. However, he usually does not mention the names of their books. And since most of their books have not come down to us, we cannot cite specific sources for most of the sections of the *Mathesis*.

However, it is worth noting that while Ptolemy is mentioned three times in the *Mathesis*, his *Tetrabiblos* is not mentioned, and Ptolemy himself is only mentioned as having approved the later version of *antiscia* (measured from the tropical longitudes of the solstices), which is not true. For in fact, the word *antiscion* is never mentioned in the *Tetrabiblos*, and in Book I, Chapter 15, of that work, he says "Again they

[1]The Latin text of this letter is cited by the Teubner editors in their edition of the *Mathesis*, vol. 2, p. IX.

[2]The Latin text of Poggio's first, second, and fourth letters is cited by Karl Sittl in the preface to the first Teubner edition (1894), pp. X-XI.

say that the parts which are equally removed from the same tropical sign, whichever it may be, are of equal power."[1] And he does not say "from the same solstice, whichever it may be." Thus, it is plain that Firmicus did not have a copy of the *Tetrabiblos*, but had merely seen Ptolemy's name mentioned in some other book. This is still another indication that Ptolemy's books were not generally available in the second and third centuries and were probably still hard to come by in the early fourth century.[2]

Much of the material in the *Mathesis* is found nowhere else in the surviving classical literature, or, if it is found, it is not found in such detail. Hence, Firmicus's Latin translations of the lost Greek originals are especially precious. For that reason, I have translated the text as literally as possible, and I have discussed questionable readings in the footnotes, sometimes choosing an alternative reading or suggesting an emendation of my own. I have also indicated all of the augmentations of the Latin text due to the singular manuscript **N**.

In addition I have added explanatory footnotes identifying the historical characters mentioned in Book I and elsewhere, since we can scarcely suppose that every reader of this translation has had a classical education. And, for the particular benefit of astrologers, I have added footnotes explaining some astrological matters that were familiar to classical astrologers but are not well known by modern astrologers.

The Manuscripts of the Mathesis.

The reader who is unfamiliar with how books that were written before the invention of printing have come down to us may be interested in the following information. The author, in this case Firmicus, would have written the original text with pen and ink in his own hand (probably in rustic capitals with no spaces between the words). Then, one or more copies would have been made by professional copyists for him to give to his friends. Each of those copies may have been subsequently copied to produce a second generation of copies. And of all the old copies that were

---

[1]Ptolemy, *Tetrabiblos*, ed. and trans. by F. E. Robbins (Loeb Classical Library, 1940), p. 77.

[2]As stated in my book, *A History of Horoscopic Astrology* (Tempe, Az.: A.F.A., Inc., 1996), p. 43 (2nd ed., 2006, p. 45), it seems likely that Ptolemy's books did not become available to the public until around 300 A.D. For example, his younger contemporary Vettius Valens (120 – c.175), who lived in Alexandria, Egypt, had never heard of him or his books! See also my paper "Claudius Ptolemy" in the *Journal of Research of the American Federation of Astrologers*, Vol. 13: 121-130 (2010).

made, one of them survived into the 8th or 9th century, when learning revived in Europe and many old MSS were copied in the new style of writing that came into use during the Carolingian period. Thus, in most cases, all the surviving copies of an ancient Latin book go back to a now lost copy made in the 8th or 9th century, which is called the *archetype.*

It is easily understood that each handwritten copy inevitably contained errors made by the copyist. These errors are of several sorts—words misspelled; words misplaced; words replaced by synonyms; words, lines, or whole pages accidentally omitted; deliberate changes made by the copyist when he thought he could improve the text; marginal notes copied into the text, etc. And the errors necessarily piled up, since each copy contained all the errors of the preceding copies, plus the new errors made by the current copyist. In addition, the binding of an old book sometimes became loose, allowing whole leaves or groups of leaves to fall out and be lost. Hence, the text present in any MS surviving today contains numerous errors, interpolations, and omissions.

The task of a modern editor is to try by studying several MSS to eliminate as many of the accumulated errors as possible, thereby producing a text that is better than that contained in any one of the extant MSS. The immediate goal is to restore the text contained in the *archetype*, and then to detect and correct the errors that were already present in it. Obviously, this is not entirely possible, so, in the best available modern printed text, there are words that do not appear to make proper sense, and may therefore be errors. And there are places where some words are obviously missing.

A translator, then, is sometimes faced with a defective word or passage in the text, and he may either accept the modern printed text as it stands or else investigate the variants contained in the individual MSS and use his own judgment to select a variant (or even to propose an emendation) different from the one chosen by the editors of the printed text. And in some cases it may be difficult or impossible to ascertain the correct reading of the original text. In making the present translation, I have critically examined the Latin text, and I have discussed in the footnotes any problems that I found. References to a page and line number are to the 1968 Teubner edition of the Latin text.

The text of the *Mathesis* is preserved in some 30 different MSS in European libraries. I have used the sigla of the latest Teubner edition (1968) for most of the MSS, some of which are:

Manuscripts Containing only Books I-IV.

M Montepessulanus scholae medicorum H 180, a parchment MS of the 11th century, but half of Book II is missing.

V Vaticanus 3425, a parchment MS of the 13th century; the last half of Book I is missing, but was supplied by a hand of the 15th century.

P Parisinus 7311, a parchment MS of the 11th century, which agrees closely with MS **R**.

R Vaticanus reginae 1244, a parchment MS of the 11th century; it is very carefully written, but most of Book I is missing.

Z Leidensis Vossiani Q 92, a parchment MS of the 12th or 13th century.

Q Parisinus 17867, a parchment MS of the 13th century, but portions of the MS are in a hand of the 15th century.

K Monacensis 560, a parchment MS of the 11th century, which leaves off half-way through Book II. Carelessly written, it has many errors and interpolations, but it preserves some true readings.

I Parisinus 7312 a paper MS of the 15th century.

S Escorialensis C IV 13 a vellum MS of the 13th century, very carelessly written, although at 3,22 in the Latin text it alone of the **Ω** family of MSS has the reading *totius* (probably the scribe saw *potius* and wrote *totius* by mistake).

Manuscripts Containing Books I-VIII.

A Norimbergensis V 60, a paper MS written in 1468. It belongs to the **Γ** family of MSS. In their edition, the Teubner editors noted the frequent agreement of MS **A** with the 1497 edition **v** (see below) by the siglum **A′**.

B Monacensis 49, a paper MS of the 16th century, poorly written, and particularly carelessly in Books VII and VIII

E Escorialensis N III 1, a paper MS of the 15th century.[1]

---

[1]The Teubner editors assigned the siglum **E** to MS **Vaticanus Urbinas lat. 263**, which I have designated as **U**.

F Phillipsianus 3374 a beautifully written MS of the 15th century.[1]

G Marcianus Ven. lat. VI 156, a paper MS written about 1464.

O Oxoniensis collegii Linc. Lat. 114 of the 15th century.

C Vaticanus lat. 2227, a paper MS of the 15th or the beginning of the 16th century, belonging to the **Δ** family of MSS; Kroll collated about 20 pages and concluded that it was negligently written.

D Vaticanus Palatinus lat. 1418, a carefully written paper MS of the 15th century; it belongs to the **Δ** family of MSS, but it has been extensively corrected in another hand, mostly to bring it into agreement with the **Γ** family of MSS; these corrections are indicated by the siglum **D²**. There is a lengthy lacuna in Book IV (des. p. 239,29 *deiectionibus*—inc. p. 256,1 *geniturae*) with no break in the text, but with an inserted marker and a marginal note by **D²**. Interestingly, this lacuna is of about the same length as the two lacunae in Books VI and VII that are only preserved in MS **N** (and partly in **W**).

U Vaticanus Urbinas lat. 263 (formerly 493), a parchment MS of the 15th century, belonging to the **Δ** family; it was beautifully written and decorated for the library of Frederick of Montefeltro (1422-1482), Duke of Urbino.

H Harleianus 2766, a paper MS of the 15th century, ff. 47. It contains the first book complete, most of the third book, and the second book down to (Teubner ed.) 49,13-15, where it leaves off with *in opportunis locis positi vel pisces. Na mala que decernunt.* The remainder of the page is vacant and a marginal note reads *nil deficit secundum exemplar Monticasinen* 'nothing is lacking according to the Monte Cassino exemplar'. **H** belongs to the **Δ** family and often agrees with **N**.

N Neapolitanus bibliothecae nationalis V A 17, a very handsome parchment MS written in the latter part of the 15th century, and copied from a MS of the **Δ** family, but apparently collated with the copy of the *archetype* made by Peter the Deacon, since it contains many singular readings, additions, and two lengthy supple-

[1]The Teubner editors assigned the siglum F to another MS, **Vindobonensis 3195**.

ments to Books VI and VII not found in the other MSS. There is a lacuna in Book IV (des. p. 252,30 *respiciente*—inc. 260,1 *genituraе dominum)* due to two leaves having been lost between ff. 85 & 86. Some notes were added by $\mathbf{N}^2$.

W Aldina Guelferbytana, a copy of the Aldine edition **a** (see below) containing many marginal notes and two long handwritten supplements to Books VI and VII made by some unknown scholar. These were published by the Wolfenbüttel librarian G. E. Lessing (1729-1781) in 1773. They agree closely with similar readings and supplements in MS **N**.

The Teubner Editors list several additional MSS that are known to have existed but are now lost.

From a consideration of the collations made by Sittl, by Kroll, Skutsch, and Ziegler, and some that I made myself, the MS tradition may have been as follows. The *archetype* was perhaps of the 9th or 10th century, and it was probably in two volumes, the first containing Books I-IV and the second containing Books V-VIII. Most likely its four or five hundred year old exemplar, had suffered substantial losses before the *archetype* was copied from it. There is a lacuna in Book II, another in Book III, and perhaps 2/3 of Book V is lost (some 80 chapters, amounting to 50 or 60 translated pages); and there are several lacunae in Book VIII.

During the 11th century, the *subarchetype* **Ω,** a copy of the first volume, was made.[1] From it, three copies were made, which we may call μ, π, and κ. Of these, π was the source of the 11th century MSS **PR**, which agree closely with each other, and also of the later MSS **ZQ**; μ was the source of MSS **M** and **V**; and κ, which was less faithfully copied than μ and π, was the source of MSS **KIS**.

The short MS **K** of the 11th century, which leaves off in the middle of Book II, is a poor copy of the lost MS κ. Several later MSS, such as **IS**, which contain most of Books I-IV display many of the same errors that

[1]It may be that volume 2 had been misplaced, or that for some reason only the first of the two volumes was copied. It is also possible that three independent copies μ, π, and κ were made of vol. 1 of the archetype, but that seems less likely. The Teubner editors propose a somewhat different scheme for the MS tradition (discussed below), including the assumption that volume 2 of the archetype was actually lost prior to the 11th century. But I think that this is unlikely.

are contained in MS **K,** so they evidently go back either directly or indirectly to κ. In general, the MSS of the κ family are less useful for establishing the text of the *Mathesis*, although occasionally they preserve a true reading not present in some of the others.

Subsequent to the 11th century, the first volume of the *archetype* suffered the loss of all of Book I of the *Mathesis*. Then, in the early 12th century, another copy of both volumes of the *archetype* was made by the famous Monte Cassino librarian, Peter the Deacon (1107-after 1159), and after that, the archetypal volumes were probably either deliberately discarded or subsequently lost. Peter's copy was preserved in a thick volume containing the *Mathesis*, Frontinus's *De aquaeductibus*, Vegetius's *De militia*, and some other short tracts. That volume, **Casinensis 361**, was preserved intact at Monte Cassino at least until the 15th century,[1] and it is still there, but it was rebound in the 17th century, and it no longer contains the *Mathesis*.

Something more should be said about the MS **Casinensis 361**. In the description of the MSS of the *De aquaeductibus* in the Loeb Classical Library edition, we read that **Casinensis 361** is a parchment MS and that:

> "It had seen hard usage before it came to the monastery, some leaves being torn and some chapters much mutilated. Poleni [1683-1761] places its date at the end of the thirteenth or the beginning of the fourteenth century, while the catalogue of the library of Monte Cassino assigns it to the end of the eleventh or the beginning of the twelth. Bücheler [1837-1908] thinks it belongs to the thirteenth rather than the eleventh. It is written in minuscules which were growing dim even when copied by Gattola [early 18th century]; today some parts of the manuscript are so obscure as to be difficult to read. Various portions were copied in red ink; the punctuation is erratic; sentences sometimes begin with capitals, again with small letters; no intervals are left between words except where the intention is to show that something is missing from the text; but in places where lacunae are found, the spaces left do not always seem proportioned to the words to be supplied."

[1]Possibly as late as 1532, since the library catalogue of that year mentions the *Mathesis* as being contained in **Casinensis 361**; but, as the Teubner editors note, the 1532 catalogue may simply have been copied from an earlier catalogue.

This is of course a description of the portion of MS **Casinensis 361** containing the *De aquaeductibus*, but the whole MS is believed to be the work of Peter the Deacon, so presumably some of the description should also apply to the missing section that formerly contained the *Mathesis*. Note the discrepant views as to the age of the MS. If indeed it was the work of Peter the Deacon, it must be of the 12th century. And the description of the writing is more in accord with the 12th century than with the 13th or 14th century.

However, Clemens Herschel (1842-1930) visited the monastery in November 1897 and examined MS **Casinensis 361** himself. He was told by the learned librarian of the time Ambrogio Monsignore Amelli that the body of the MS was in the writing of Peter the Deacon, and was consequently written in the 12th century. Herschel was also permitted to have the portion of the MS containing Frontinus's *De aquaeductibus* photographed. And in his book he has printed facsimiles of those 23 pages. We thus have an opportunity to examine the MS pages ourselves. This is what I saw:

> I note that some of the description quoted above does not apply. The MS did not come from somewhere else but was copied at Monte Cassino. I did not see any evidence of torn pages. The script is in a round Roman hand (not Beneventan as we might expect). It is neatly written with 50 lines to a page, and most of the writing is perfectly clear.[1] There are a few places where the letters are dim (and occasionally, illegible), but they are usually followed by bolder letters, so it seems possible that the pen was running out of ink, but the scribe kept on writing longer than he should have before stopping to dip his pen in the ink.
>
> The usual abbreviations common to both the 12th and 13th centuries appear, with the exception that the letter *e* does not have any mark to indicate that it represents *ae* (but the word *romae* in the title line actually has the *ae* spelled out). And it is notable that the letter *d* has a straight vertical ascender rather than the left curling ascender that was common in the 13th century.
>
> As noted in the previous description, there are generally no

[1]But it is possible that the facsimile pages reproduced from photographs are a little clearer than the MS pages themselves, since photography sometimes increases the contrast between light and dark, thereby enhancing faint markings and making them more legible.

spaces between words, and sentences sometimes begin with small letters. Red ink was used occasionally on 6 of the 23 pages (Clemens gives a list of the places and says that the ink was still bright red when he saw the MS in 1897), and he notes that page XX was written in a different hand (but one similar to the main hand). And most pages have occasional blank spaces left where the scribe was evidently unable to read his exemplar. Clemens concluded that the exemplar was written in uncials.

The **Casinensis 361** was found by Poggio in 1429, as mentioned above. At some time between 1429 and 1437 at the latest, someone made a copy which we will call **Ψ** of the *Mathesis* portion of the volume.[1] It appears to have been copied hurriedly, since in many places one or more lines were skipped, usually due to homoeoteleuton.[2] From it two copies were apparently made that the Teubner editors call Γ and Δ. The original copy **Ψ** was soon discarded or lost, and **Γ** and **Δ** also disappeared,[3] but not before they became the source of most of the surviving 15th and 16th century MSS. The missing Book I of the *Mathesis* was supplied in **Ψ** by copying the text of that book from MSS of the older family **Ω**; in particular, MS **V** seems to have been used to supply the missing text of the first half of Book I (at least down to page 21,5 in the Teubner text). The resulting text of **Ψ** contained a number of errors, some interpolations, and numerous lacunae, which passed to its two copies **Γ** and **Δ**, so that the quality of the preserved text of Books V-VIII is less than that of Books I-IV.

In general, the MSS derived from the **Γ** copy have fewer errors than those derived from the Δ copy; also, the copyist of **Γ** seems to have made

---

[1]Something similar happened in the case of the younger family of MSS of Manilius. In his edition Housman reports that Poggio found an old MS that must have been a copy (**β**) of the archetype. It was soon lost, but a carelessly made copy **M** (1417) survives, and amongst its numerous errors it contains many readings that are superior to those of the oldest surviving MS **L** (11th century), which was evidently derived more carefully from a different copy (**α**) of the archetype.

[2]There are 32 instances of homoeoteleuton ('same ending') in Books 5-8, but only 11 in Books 1-4, showing that **Ψ** was more carelessly copied than **Ω** was. This type of error arises from the copyists's eye accidentally skipping from a line ending in one word or phrase to the next line ending with that same word or phrase, and thereby omitting one or more lines following the first word or phrase.

[3]This was possibly due to the sacking of the Medici Library in late 1489 or early 1490. It may well be that the lost MSS **Ψ** and also possibly **Γ** and **Δ** were in that library and were destroyed. Other possibilities of destruction are the Bonfire of the Vanities by Savonarola in 1497 and the sacking of Rome in 1527.

some obviously needed corrections to what he found in **Ψ**.[1] Some family groupings of the numerous 15th century MSS are obvious, for example MSS **AFO** are closely related, so they appear to be copies of a lost MS **φ**, which was a copy of **Γ**, and MS **G** and two other MSS **BE** are copies of another lost MS **β** copied from **Γ**, but the exact relationships of all of them have not yet been worked out in detail.[2]

In the second half of the 15th century, the splendid MS **N** was copied from either **Δ** itself or from a MS of the **Δ** family. But apparently the copyist still had the old **Casinensis 361** MS at hand,[3] and as he wrote he compared it with his 15th century exemplar. Thus, MS **N** is composite, and while its basic text belongs to the **Δ** family and is not outstanding, it contains many exemplary readings in Books II-VIII,[4] as well as many short supplements to those books and two long supplements to Books VI and VII that are not found in any of the other MSS. A later hand **N²** has made some corrections (not always valid) and added a few marginal notes to **N**.

The two supplements of nearly 20 Teubner pages each that are contained in MS **N** (and partly in the handwritten leaves designated as **W**) present a problem. The Teubner editors suggest that an early copy was

---

[1]For example, in Book I there are more than two dozen places where **A′** has a better reading than **N** and the **Ω** family, but most of these involve only one or two letters, such as at 17,14 *animati* instead of *animatae* or at 23,22 *animus* instead of *animi*, so these are probably corrections made by the copyist of **A** himself. The only singular reading is at 26,8, where **A′** (and also **DH**) have the interpolation *Cimbrico* instead of *in illyrico*, a deliberate change possibly due to the copyist of **Ψ**'s knowledge of Roman history. By contrast, **N** has superior readings in Book I at only two places: at 6,25 *luxuriosis* instead of *luxuriosi* and at 11,7 *inscitia* instead of *inscientia* (but this may simply be due to **N**'s fortunate failure to expand an abbreviation properly).

[2]In his edition of the *Mathesis*, Prof. Monat presents a completely different *stemma codicum* that also shows MSS **O** and **G** as being copies of **B**, but if the dates of the MSS as assigned by the Teubner editors are correct, that is wrong, since **B** is assigned to the 16th century, while **O** and **G** are assigned to the 15th century. See my further remarks below.

[3]As said above, it seems likely that he had access to Peter the Deacon's copy that formerly was part of **Casinensis 361** before it was removed, or possibly he may even have found the remains of the archetype itself, but that seems less likely. But see the notes to Book 3, Chapter 3e, and Book 4, Chapter 13.

[4]Since **Casinensis 361** lacked Book I, MS **N** had no source for the exemplary readings and supplements it copied from it in Books II-VIII. In fact, since **N** was copied from a MS of the **Δ** family, in Book I it has more than a dozen readings in common with MS **V**, which seems to have been the source of Book I for Ψ and its copies **Γ** and **Δ**.

made of the *archetype* containing all eight books of the Mathesis, from which copy two sets of quaternions[1] containing the two passages in Books VI and VII subsequently fell out, and that this copy was the parent of what I call **Ψ**. The *archetype* itself prior to the 11th century had already lost some pages from Book II and all of Books V-VIII, and from that mutilated book **Ω** was copied. They also assume that still another old and fuller copy of the *archetype* was available to the copyist of MS **N**. The immediate source of the handwritten supplements in **W** is uncertain.

I suppose a third possibility is that Peter the Deacon's copy had lost the two quaternions before it was copied in the 15th century, and that the old exemplar used by Peter was still in the library at Monte Cassino and was found by the copyist of MS **N** but has since been lost; however, that seems very unlikely.

It seems to me more likely that the only surviving copy of the *archetype* in the 15th century was Peter the Deacon's 12th century copy that Poggio found in **Casinensis 361**, and that Niccoli arranged to have a copy **Ψ** made of it at some time between 1429 and 1437 that carelessly omitted the two lengthy passages in Books VI and VII, and that it was that copy that was the parent of **Γ** and **Δ**. The *Mathesis* was evidently in demand, for many copies were subsequently made of those MSS. And MS **Casinensis 361** evidently still contained the *Mathesis* at Monte Cassino, for MS **N** was collated with it, and MS **H** has a marginal note directly relating to it. So perhaps the *Mathesis* was still contained in **Casinensis 361** when its Catalogue was made in 1532, but it was subsequently removed for some reason.

Here then is my suggested filiation of some of the MSS mentioned above:

[1]A quaternion is a gathering of four sheets folded in the middle to form 8 leaves or 16 pages. These were held together and bound to the spine of the book by string. If the string broke or decayed with age, some or all of the 8 leaves could fall out of the book with careless handling.

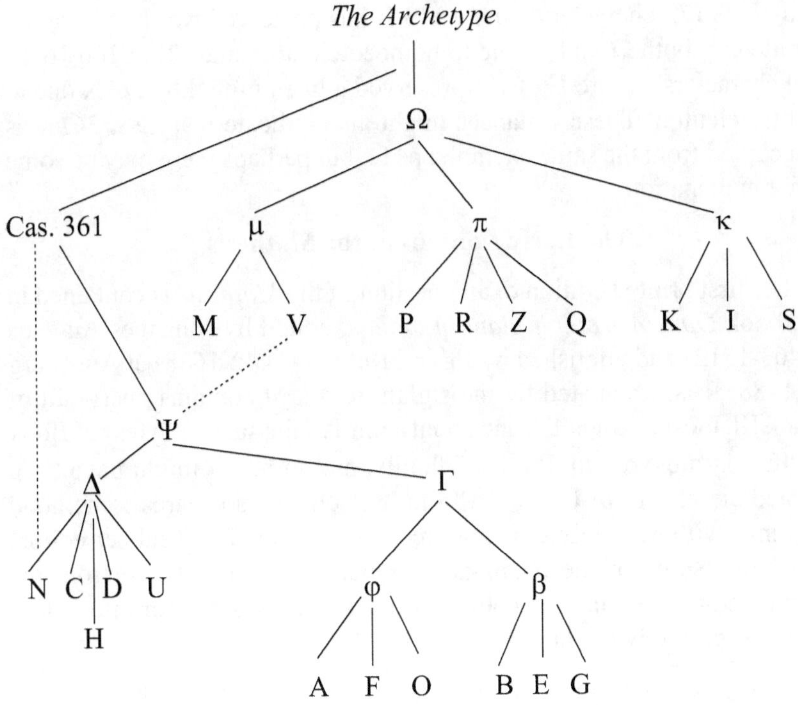

Those MSS indicated by Greek letters are postulated to have once existed, but are now lost. MSS **CDHUN** are all descended from **Δ**, but one or more of them may have been indirectly derived rather than copied directly from Δ as shown. And it is possible that some of the descendants of **Γ** are more indirectly derived than shown, but the two subgroups **φ** and **β** are distinct.

One possible difficulty with this stemma is that **Ψ** preserves the Latin text of 49,15-53,14, which is omitted by **Ω**. The Teubner editors think that this indicates that **Cas. 361** was not copied from the exemplar of **Ω** as my stemma shows, but was copied from another old copy of the *archetype*. However, it seems to me that the scribe of **Ω** may have accidentally skipped a leaf or two (after all, he omitted the last four books), or perhaps the leaves had fallen out of the *archetype* before **Ω** was copied, but were later restored before Peter made his copy.

Two other possible difficulties with this stemma are: (1) that there are two places in the text of the first four books: Teubner 44,1 (71 characters) and 58,23 (72 characters) where MS **N** has preserved two lines that are omitted by both **Ω** and **Ψ** due to homoeoteleuton; and (2) at 166,16-17 (49 characters) where **Γα** have preserved a line omitted by **ΩΔN** due to homeoteleuton. These instances might also indicate that **Cas. 361** was not copied from the same exemplar as **Ω**, but perhaps there may be some other explanation.

The Early Editions of the Mathesis.

The first printed edition of any portion of the *Mathesis* is contained in the book *Opus Astrolabij plani in tabulis*, edited by Johannes Angelus (1463-1512) and published by Erhard Ratdolt (1442-1528) at Augsburg in 1488. It is designated by the siglum **α**, and it contains nearly all of Book III, most of Book IV, and about a third of the surviving text of Book V. Its text most resembles the Γ family, and in fact it might have been copied directly from **Γ** or even from **Ψ** itself. It also shares some good readings with MS **N**, but their source is uncertain. The Teubner editors think that some of the readings in **N** may have been taken from the printed edition **α**, but this would put the date of MS **N** in or after 1488, which is probably too late.

Nine years later, in 1497, the first complete edition of the *Mathesis* was published at Venice. It is designated by the siglum **v**, and agrees fairly closely with MS **A** of the **Γ** family but it contains a number of correct emendations by its anonymous but learned editor. As mentioned above, the Teubner editors indicate the agreement of **v** with **A** by the siglum **A′**.

A year later, the Aldine edition, edited by a scholar who called himself Pescennius Franciscus Niger, was published at Venice. It is designated by the siglum **a**, and had as its base another MS of the **Γ** family, but one of lesser quality than MS **A**. However, it is remarkable for the large amount (20 of its 174 leaves) of spurious matter that it contains. Its editor, noting the lacunae in the previous edition **v**, claimed to have found a more complete MS that supplied all the missing matter. In fact, he merely wrote the supplements himself, throwing in a frequent *Mavortius, decus nostrum* to make them appear genuine; but his work is also betrayed by his Latinity, which is obviously not that of Firmicus. The text of that edition was reprinted at Reggio Emilia in 1503, and at Basel in 1533 and 1551. The astrologers and scholars who read the Aldine edition or one of its later reprints were not aware that the text was interpolated with spurious additions; nor were the lexicographers, who copied many of the strange interpolated words into their Latin dictionaries. As an example of Pescennius's interpolations, I have given a translation of his spurious additions to Book II, Chapter X in Appendix 1.

The Modern Editions of the Mathesis.

The first modern edition was produced by Karl Sittl (1862-1899) and published by Teubner in 1894. It contained only the first four books of the *Mathesis*. However, unsatisfied with the quality of that edition, Teubner invited Wilhelm Kroll (1869-1939) and Franz Skutsch (1865-1912) to re-edit the *Mathesis*. The first fascicle containing Books I-IV was published in 1897. The two editors continued their work, but after the premature death of Skutsch in 1912, Konrat Ziegler (1884-1974) joined Kroll, and the second fascicle containing the text of Books V-VIII was published in 1913; it also contained an *Appendix Praefationis* with a valuable collation of the printed text of Books I-IV with MS **N** and the printed book **α**, an *Addenda et Corrigenda* with additions and corrections to the text of both fascicles, and extensive indices of names and words in Books I-VIII. The two volume set was subsequently reprinted in 1968 with an *Addenda Addendis* prepared by the elderly surviving editor Konrat Ziegler. In addition to Ziegler's final emendations, it also contains proposed emendations by Geyza Némethy, Tage Wikström, and other scholars. All references in the present translation to page and line numbers of the Latin text refer to that Teubner edition.

From the collation of MS **N** and the first partial edition **α** (which was published from an unknown MS of good quality that sometimes agrees with **N**), it seems plain, as stated above, that the copyist of **N** had a MS of the **Δ** family before him, which he used as his usual source. But if my surmise is correct, he also had the MS **Casinensis 361**, and he collated the two MSS, copying what seemed to him to be the truer reading. He may not have done this as diligently as we would like, especially since the older MS was harder to read than the scion of **Δ**. Thus, while he copied many readings from the older MS, we cannot assume that he copied all of the potentially useful ones. He was acting as a critical editor, but he was probably not an outstanding scholar, and he may have judged wrongly in some places. Still, he preserved a large number of superior readings and additions. The Teubner editors found that many of those readings confirmed emendations that they or their predecessor Karl Sittl had proposed, and they adopted those and many other readings of **N** in the *Addenda et Corrigenda* at the end of fascicle 2 (pp. 546-555).

A new edition of the *Mathesis* has been prepared by Prof. Pierre Monat as *Firmicus Maternus / Mathesis* (Paris: Les Belles Lettres, 1992-1997. 3 volumes). It contains the Latin text and a French translation on facing pages. For example, there is an abbreviated apparatus to the Latin text with some footnotes below the translation and 25 pages of end notes in the first volume (but only an apparatus and a few pages of end notes in vols. 2 & 3). Prof. Monat has located an additional MS of the *Mathesis* not known to the Teubner editors, namely the **Florentianus S. Marco 198**, of the 13th century, which contains only the first four books of the *Mathesis* and thus belongs to the **Ω** family.

On p. 38 of the first volume of his work Prof. Monat presents a proposed *stemma codicum*. He represents the *archetype* by the siglum **Ω** (prior to the 8th century) and shows two 8th century copies that he calls **X** and **Ψ**. From **X** he shows three 11th century copies **MPR** and three 13th century copies **SQV**. Then from **Ψ** he shows two 11th century copies **Δ** and **Γ**, with 15th century copies **N** and **CDE** from **Δ**, and **ABGO** from **Γ**. He also indicates some transmission from **Ψ** to **N**. I think the early part of this is wrong! I believe my own *stemma codicum* as shown above is much closer to the truth.

The Present Translation.

The reader who wishes to compare my translation with the Latin text should obtain a copy of the Teubner edition mentioned above. I have also sometimes made reference to the earlier partial edition of the *Mathesis* by Karl Sittl, which contains some useful material not repeated in the later Teubner edition. I have, however, deviated from the chapter numbering of both of those editions. Instead, in Books I-IV, I have adopted the chapter numbering and titles shown in the Index, since it was presumably contained in the *archetype*. Whether Firmicus's original had chapter titles is uncertain. Nevertheless, I have adopted the numbers and titles shown in the Index. And where the MSS have inserted chapter titles that are not found in the Index, I have included them in angle brackets and distinguished them from the main chapter title by adding **a** or **b** or **c**, etc. Thus, the numbers and titles in this translation do not correspond directly with those in the Teubner edition. This change will annoy some readers, but it seemed reasonable to me. However, I have added the Teubner Chapter numbers in brackets after the chapter titles. In the case of Books V-VIII, I have proceeded somewhat differently as will be explained in the Note below the Index preceding those books.

In translating the Teubner text into English, I have carefully considered both the variant readings of the MSS given in the Apparatus, and also the lists of readings and emendations in the two Addenda at the end of fascicle 2 and the collations of MS **N** and the first partial edition **α**. I have accepted most of the readings of **N** adopted by the Teubner editors in the lists just mentioned, but in some places I have adopted readings of **N** or of other MSS that were not favored by them; these are commented on in the footnotes. Thus, I have in effect edited the Latin text. If I cite a MS reading that I judge to be common to all or most of the older **Ω** family of MSS, I use that siglum; and if I cite a reading that is common to all or most of the MSS of either the **Δ** or **Γ** families, I use those sigla, or if it is common to both of those families, I use the siglum **Ψ**.

As just mentioned, I have commented upon some places in the published Latin text that seem to me to be erroneous, and in a number of places I have proposed an emendation of my own to rectify the problem. I cannot hope that all of these are true, but at least they point up the problem and offer a possible correction. The Teubner editors' knowledge of Latin was of course superior to mine, but I have the advantage they did not possess of considering the text from both an astrologer's viewpoint and a translator's viewpoint. The editors present us with a text that they are content with (except for words commented on in the apparatus), and in effect they say to us: "We understand it, don't you?" But I am doing something that they did not do—namely, translating the text, which amounts to explaining as accurately as possible what the Latin means.

I have derived much benefit from the very comprehensive indices of words and names the editors Kroll and Ziegler placed at the end of fascicle 2 of the Teubner edition. And Franz Cumont's *L'Égypte des Astrologues* (Brussels: Fondation Égyptologique Reine Élisabeth, 1937) is an indispensable aid for clarifying the meaning of many Latin words describing occupations and social conditions in the classical world.[1] In that book and also in the apparatus to his edition of Rhetorius in the CCAG, Cumont carefully compared the text of Rhetorius's A*strological Compendium*[2] with Firmicus's *Mathesis*, since it is plain that both writers

---

[1]Cumont also gives a number of emendations of the text of the *Mathesis* on p. 249.

[2]The full title of Rhetorius's *Astrological Compendium* seems to have been *Explanation and Narration of the Whole Art of Astrology from the Treasury of Antiochus*, but in my translation of it (Tempe, Az.: A.F.A., Inc., 2009) and also here I refer to it by the shorter descriptive title.

used the same Greek sources in some places. This is especially noticeable in the significations of the Planets in the Houses as given in Book III of the *Mathesis* and in Chapter 57 of the *Compendium*. In that chapter, Rhetorius actually gives two sets of significations for each Planet; the second set is often quite similar to the significations given in the *Mathesis* but briefer. Those significations are probably from the lost work, the *Treasury*, of Antiochus of Athens (fl. c. 200 A.D.). By comparing Firmicus's Latin version and Rhetorius's Greek, it is possible to improve both texts.

Two other works that have been helpful are Adolf Berger's *Encyclopedic Dictionary of Roman Law* (Philadelphia: The American Philosophical Society, 1953) and Alexander Souter's *A Glossary of Later Latin to 600 A.D.* (Oxford: Oxford University Press, 1949).

One thing that must be borne in mind when translating the *Mathesis* is that much of it consists of translations from earlier Greek astrological treatises into Latin. Some of the statements in those treatises reflect social conditions in the Mediterranean world and especially in Egypt prior to the termination of the Egyptian kingdom in 30 B.C. Firmicus modernized some of the statements to reflect analogous conditions in the Roman Empire of the fourth century A.D., but he let others stand unchanged.

Another thing that should be mentioned is that the numerous statements of the effects of various horoscopic configurations seem to be partly derived from examples seen in actual horoscopes, while others seem to be based upon astrological theory. It is known that there were collections of horoscopes available to the ancient astrologers,[1] and of course each astrologer then as now made his own personal collection of charts. It is interesting to note that all social classes from the highest to the lowest are represented. We see references to configurations in the charts of kings, emperors, generals, judges, learned men, priests, business men, wealthy men and women, practitioners of all sorts of arts and skills, religious persons, athletes, freedmen, slaves, criminals, sufferers from various bodily defects or diseases, children who were exposed or

[1]Such collections were made by the Babylonian astrologers. And the names of two Greek compilers are known: Vettius Valens (120-c.175), and Antigonus of Nicaea, who wrote not earlier than the second century A.D. But Claudius Ptolemy mentions other older compilations in *Tetrabiblos* i. 21, where he says that the distribution of the terms according to the Egyptian method "is consistent with the nativities which have been recorded by them as examples" (Robbins's translation).

who died early, persons who died a violent death, persons notable for their various deviant sexual activities, and even animals.[1]

Since in almost no cases are the actual horoscopes given in detail, we cannot judge whether the astrological configurations cited were present in several charts or in only one. Nor can we know whether the configuration cited was the only one responsible for the signification mentioned. Therefore, the indications given may not always be generally applicable. We must also bear in mind that astrological influences manifest themselves differently in different social circumstances. And the social conditions of the classical world differed in many respects from those of the modern world.

My translation of the *Mathesis* is largely literal. I have avoided paraphrase where possible. I have also dulled Firmicus's style to some extent. He had a sizable vocabulary, and for stylistic reasons he used a number of synonyms of the more common words, but I have generally chosen the most common English rendering of a group and used it for all or most of the Latin synonyms (e.g. *collocatus* 'located' or 'placed' and *positus* 'put' or 'placed' are both sometimes translated as 'posited', a somewhat obsolescent but still useful astrological term). I have also translated some words by their equivalents in modern astrological terminology. An example is the word *locus* 'place', which most commonly means '(celestial) house'. Another is *domus* 'house', which I have usually translated as 'domicile', i.e. the sign that is ruled by a particular planet.

The words *radius* 'ray' and *radiatio* 'radiation' and their use in combination with verbs of seeing, I have rendered simply as the noun or verb 'aspect'. I have retained the term *testimonium* 'testimony', meaning an aspect from a planet in a certain position of significance. This useful term was in frequent use by the 17th and 18th century English astrologers, although it is now obsolete. In some cases I have inserted an 'and' or an 'or' or a 'to be' or a 'that' or a 'then' where the Latin omits them; I have also used the words 'person' and 'individual' to render Latin adjectives used as nouns, since in English we do not speak of 'a rich' or 'a sick'; and I have inserted the word 'Native' (i.e. 'the one who is born'), a now obsolescent English astrological term where it seemed to be needed.

In some places I have added one or more words in brackets to make the meaning of a phrase or sentence more understandable. Translations of

[1]Book 7, Chapter 7.

additions to the Latin text from various sources are enclosed in angle brackets. Places where it seems that some words have fallen out of the Latin text are indicated by dots, usually with a comment in a footnote. Words prefixed with a dagger † are words that are suspect and are commented on in a footnote. And where I was uncertain as to the meaning of the Latin text, I have stated the problem in a footnote. I have also mentioned some significant readings of different MSS in the footnotes, especially those of MS **N**. These may be helpful to future translators or editors of the *Mathesis*.

Firmicus mentions a number of occupations and titles that pertained to life in the Roman Empire. I have retained some of these in their Latin form with a footnote at their first occurrence to explain their significance; some examples are *praetor*, *consul*, *proconsul*, *tribune*, *grammarian*, *judge*, etc.[1] I have translated the frequent military term *dux*, literally 'leader',[2] as 'general', since it usually means an individual with the field command of a sizable military force. His subordinate commanders were *legates*, who were approximately equivalent in rank to our modern colonels.

I have also sometimes used the pronouns 'he, 'she', 'him', and 'her' referring to the Planets. Modern English-speaking astrologers usually refer to the Planets as 'it', but when two or three are mentioned in the same sentence, it seemed to me that using the masculine and feminine pronouns would make the referents more specific. I have usually not translated the ubiquitous Latin future perfect form of verbs as English future perfects, since that form is seldom used in English; rather, I have used the English present or past as seemed appropriate. And I have rendered the words *horoscopus* as ASC, *medium caeli* as MC (an abbreviation that Firmicus often uses), *occasus* 'setting' as DSC, and IMC (which Firmicus himself uses) for the 4th house cusp. All of these terms are familiar to astrologers.

The word *partiliter* is sometimes used in the astrological sense 'partilely', i.e. 'in that same degree', and at other times it seems merely to mean 'in that part', where 'part' may refer to a whole house; but there are also places where it seems to be an error for *pariter* 'together'. Two both-

[1]Neither of the last two occupations have the exact signification that the terms imply today. See the footnotes to their occurrence in the main text.

[2]Note the 20th century use of the literal translation by Benito Mussolini, *Il Duce*, and Adolf Hitler, *Der Fuehrer*, and the earlier title *Doge* of the head of the Venetian State, all of which meant simply the *Leader*.

ersome words are *ratio* 'reason' and *patrimonium* 'patrimony'; the former has many other meanings, such as 'theory', 'scheme', 'method', etc.; and the latter more often means 'personal assets', i.e. the personal wealth of an individual, be it large or small; but sometimes it does in fact refer to 'an inheritance', so I sometimes translate it one way and sometimes the other way.

I should also say something about the word *locus* when it is coupled with a specifier, such as *locus fortunae* or *locus patris*, literally 'the Place of Fortune' and 'the Place of the Father'. In these cases, the word *locus* has the signification 'House', since Firmicus sometimes instructs us to measure by degrees and to consider the *sign* in which the *last degree* of the measurement falls to be the *House* of the specified subject, but in other cases he merely instructs us to count by whole signs, which was probably the old way. This refers to the original "Sign-House" system of house division, in which each sign constituted a celestial house. But the Latin word for 'degree' is *pars*, and this gave rise to the term *pars fortunae*, etc., which in modern astrological terminology is the 'Part of Fortune'. However, I have decided to use 'part' only for the Part of Fortune and the Part of the Daemon (or Part of the Spirit) where the word 'degree' is actually mentioned.[1] For the others, I have translated *locus* as 'House', as in the 'House of the Father', etc. It seems to me that this is closer to Firmicus's intent.

Firmicus tried to write stylish Latin according to the standards of his day, and it sometimes seems flowery or unnecessarily redundant to us, but I have generally translated all of his words—unlike Bram, who often condenses statements that seemed to contain more or less synonymous words or to be unnecessarily lengthy by modern standards. For this reason, my translation is more wordy than Bram's, and to some extent more tedious to read. In passages where I had some doubt as to the meaning of the Latin text, I have considered both Bram's translation and also the French translation of Prof. Monat, and I have occasionally profited from their renderings of the Latin (as mentioned in the footnotes).

Aside from the defects of the Latin text, there are some words and phrases that can be translated in more than one way. I have tried to pick the most likely interpretation in such cases, but I cannot assume that I have always made the best choice.

---

[1]Which we see in *Mathesis* vi. 32, 45 & .46.

Finally, a word to the casual reader who would just like to skim the translation: Don't read the footnotes! They are there for the benefit of the reader who would like to get the most out of the translation and to have some assurance that the translator did his best. Those who merely want to get a quick overall impression of the *Mathesis* can ignore the footnotes.

Astrological Commentary.

In Book I of the *Mathesis*, Firmicus explains his reason for writing the book. He then gives the characteristics of the inhabitants of various countries, and he states that the planetary configurations of individuals can override them. Following that, he gives examples of fate to show how good things can happen to bad people, and how bad things can happen to good people. Finally, he stresses the fact that critics of astrology are uninformed persons who have never consulted an astrologer or acquired any knowledge of astrology. They are thus like a judge who would render a verdict without having seen any of the evidence! This was true in the fourth century, and unfortunately it is still true in the twenty-first century. Nothing has changed!

One particularly noteworthy feature of the *Mathesis* is the unique ethical code for astrologers set forth in the last chapter of Book II. It was the only thing of its kind prescribed in the older astrological community. It is thus comparable in significance to the Hippocratic Oath for Doctors. William Lilly (1602-1681) included an abbreviated and paraphrased version of it in his epistle 'To the Student in Astrology', which follows the 'Table of Contents' of his master work, *Christian Astrology* (1647), but he gave no mention of his source.[1]

Firmicus obviously had a sizable collection of Greek astrological treatises. Unfortunately, most of them have not come down to us, so we are grateful that Firmicus has left us Latin versions of substantial parts of them. In some places he has translated them word for word, but in other places he has paraphrased them, added his own explanations or comments, and even substituted the then current fourth century terminology for the earlier terminology, some of which reflected conditions in Egypt under the Ptolemies.

However, in some cases tracts in Greek and Latin are preserved that present obvious parallels to Firmicus's text. I have already mentioned the

[1]I noted this in my Master's Thesis, *William Lilly, Christian Astrologer* (Fort Worth: Texas Christian University, 1953).

Astrological Compendium of Rhetorius the Egyptian,[1] which offers significations of the planets in the houses of the horoscope that are similar (but much less detailed) to those in Book III of the *Mathesis*. The separations and applications of the Moon are found in part in the *Liber Hermetis*,[2] apparently a medieval Latin translation of several Greek texts that was made prior to the 13th century; however, the Latin translation only begins with the separation of the Moon from the Sun and its application to Mars. But figures similar to those given by Firmicus for the Full and Empty Degrees and the Masculine and Feminine Degrees in Book IV are embedded in Chapter XXV of the *Liber Hermetis*. They sometimes agree exactly, and at others times they differ; but they plainly go back to the same unknown Greek source.[3]

Firmicus also gives extensive material derived from books that are not mentioned by the other Greek astrologers whose works have come down to us. In particular we may mention the significations of the planets in the signs of the zodiac that are given in Book V and the excerpts from some treatise on the Barbaric Sphere that appear in Book VIII.

Books VI and VIII of the *Mathesis* contain significations of the fixed stars and constellations that appear to have been adapted from those given in Manilius's *Astronomica*, Book V.[4] But they were translated by

[1]This work was apparently written not long after 500 A.D. (not in the 7th century as David Pingree wrongly says). Most of it is edited in the *Catalogus Codicum Astrologorum Graecorum* (CCAG). Pingree has made a new edition, but it has not yet been published. I have translated what has been published plus a few chapters of the forthcoming publication of Pingree's edition that were kindly furnished to me by his current editor Stephan Heilen. My translation of Rhetorius was published in June 2009.

[2]This book is preserved in the unique Latin MS **Harleianus 3731** ff. 1-50, written in 1431, where it was discovered by the historian Lynn Thorndike (first mentioned in his *History of Magic and Experimental Science*, vol. 2 [1923]). It was edited a decade later and published with an elaborate German commentary by Wilhelm Gundel as *Neue astrologische Texte des Hermes Trismegistos* (Munich: Verlag der Bayerische, Akademie der Wissenschaften, 1936). Gundel noted that one of the chapters also appears in an Old French translation of the early 14th century, MS Parisinus fr. 613. This has recently been edited by Wolfgang Hübner in his *Grade und Gradebezirke der Tierkreiszeichen*, 2 vols. (Stuttgart & Leipzig: B. G. Teubner, 1995), vol. 1, pp. 37-91. Since some excerpts from Rhetorius's *Compendium* are contained in the *Liber Hermetis*, its date of composition must lie between the 6th and 14th centuries, most likely between the 12th and the 14th centuries.

[3]These are discussed in detail by Hübner, op. cit.

[4]I have identified the stars and given their longitudes and *paranatellonta* (for Alexandria) in footnotes. There are also tables of them in Appendices 3 and 4.

Manilius from some Greek original written not later than the first century B.C. Firmicus does not mention Manilius's name, so it seems likely that he only had Book V of the *Astronomica* and did not know who its author was.[1]

Books VI and VII of the Mathesis contain horoscopes and a large number of references to horoscopes derived from some earlier Greek works. Antigonus of Nicaea is known to have compiled a book of "notable nativities" in the second century A.D., and it is possible that Firmicus derived some of his citations from it, but since he does not mention Antigonus by name, he most likely used other sources. We must remember that all serious astrologers compile horoscopes of clients and notable persons; and if they write textbooks, they naturally refer to these as examples. Hence, many of the references to horoscopes are probably from Firmicus's own collection.

In Book VI, Chapters 3-27, Firmicus gives the significations of the mutual aspects of the planets, and the Teubner editors have cited parallel passages in Greek from an anonymous author (probably Anubio) whose text is edited from a 14th century MS in CCAG, vol. 2. Bram and Prof. Monat omitted these, but I have translated them in footnotes. He also explains how to calculate the Houses of various persons and conditions. And finally he gives detailed significations of the effects of the Planets in the standard system of symbolic progressions used by the Classical astrologers.

Book VIII contains Firmicus's translation of some treatise on the Barbaric Sphere. It offers prognostications for every *degree*[2] of the zodiac when it is on the ASC of a natal horoscope. This was in contrast to the *Myriogenesis*, which is stated to have given individual significations for every *minute* of every degree, a work that Firmicus intended to translate in 12 books! Nevertheless, his shorter list of prognostications gives us a valuable glimpse into the wealth of astrological detail that at least one ancient Greek astrologer had set forth.

I have followed Bram's lead and provided an Index of Occupations in Appendix 5—the larger part of the citations refer to Book VIII. And I have also provided an Index of the Causes of Death in Appendix 6, and an Index of Personal Characteristics in Appendix 7.

---

[1]Firmicus shows no knowledge of the first four books of the *Astronomica*.
[2]Unfortunately in several place there are lacunae in the Latin text.

It is interesting to note that Firmicus did not have Ptolemy's *Tetrabiblos*, which as I have contended elsewhere[1] did not become available to the astrological public before about 300 A.D. and must still have been hard to come by even fifty years later. However, since Ptolemy, like Firmicus, depended on earlier sources, some of the material in the *Mathesis* resembles the corresponding material in the *Tetrabiblos*, and we can occasionally improve the text of the *Mathesis* by comparing it with corresponding passages in the *Tetrabiblos*.

I might mention that Prof. Wolfgang Hübner's excellent new edition of the *Tetrabiblos* under the title *Apotelesmatika* (Stuttgart & Leipzig: B.G. Teubner, 1998) contains references to citations and parallel passages by later authors. And best of all, it contains a very useful Index of Greek Words. However, I have not given references to Hübner's edition but rather to Robbins's edition in the Loeb Classical Library, because the latter contains a facing English translation, which will be useful to those who do not know Greek. However, those who want detailed information on the Greek text and references to parallel passages in other classical authors should also consult Hübner's edition.

James Herschel Holden
Phoenix, Arizona 2006
Revised 18 February 2011

[1]See my *History of Horoscopic Astrology* (1996 ed., p. 43; and 2006 ed., p. 45) and my paper "Claudius Ptolemy" in the *A.F.A. Journal of Research*, vol. 13: 121-130. (Tempe, Az.: A.F.A., Inc., 2010).

Bibliography

Previous Translations of the Mathesis

Firmicus Maternus Matheseos lib. VIII.
trans. into German by Hagall Thorson
[said to be very rare; I recently discovered
a copy in the AFA Library at Tempe, but
I have not yet reviewed it]
Königsberg: Kalisch, 1927.

Ancient Astrology—Theory and Practice
trans. into English by Jean Rhys Bram
[with end notes, and a useful Index of Occupations,
an Index of Ancient Writers on Astrology, an extensive
bibliography, and a Glossary of Astrological Terms]
Park Ridge, N.J.: Noyes Press, 1975. xi,336 pp. 24 cm.

Firmicus Maternus. Mathesis.
ed. & trans. into French by Prof. Pierre Monat
[with an abbreviated apparatus, some footnotes, and end notes]
Paris: Les Belles Lettres, 1992-1997. 3 vols. 20 cm.

Other Works

Berger, Adolf
Encyclopedic Dictionary of Roman Law.
Philadelphia: The American Philosophical Society, 1953.

Cardan, Jerome
Claudii Ptolemaei Pelusiensis
Libri Quatuor.
De Astrorum Iudiciis cum expositione Hieronymi Cardani.
contained in: Volume 5 (pp. 93-368.) of Cardan's
Opera Omnia (Lyons: Huguetan & Ravaud, 1653) 10 vols.
New York & London: Johnson Reprint Corp., 1963. 10 vols. reprint in facs.

Catalogus Codicum Astrologorum Graecorum. [CCAG]
[detailed indexes of the MSS with some extracts edited;
Greek text with Latin prefaces and notes]
various editors
Brussels: various publishers, 1898-1953. 12 vols.

Cicero, Marcus Tullius
De natura deorum.
trans. by H. Rackham
Loeb Classical Library
Cambridge, Mass.; London, England: 1994. repr.

Cumont, Franz
L'Égypte des Astrologues.
[French text with indexes of Greek and Latin words]
Brussels: Fondation Égyptologique Reine Élisabeth, 1937. paper

Firmicus Maternus
Matheseos Libri VIII.
[Books I-IV only]
ed. Carolus Sittl
Leipzig: B. G. Teubner, 1894. xvi,246 pp.

Firmicus Maternus
Matheseos Libri VIII.
edd. W. Kroll, F. Skutsch, and K. Ziegler
Stuttgart: B. G. Teubner, 1968. 2nd ed. 2 vols.

Firmicus Maternus: The Error of Pagan Religions.
Ancient Christian Writers, No. 37.
trans. and annotated by Clarence A. Forbes, Ph.D.
[an excellent English translation of Firmicus's
De errore profanarum religionum with 565 end notes, an
Index of scriptural passages, and an Index of Authors]
New York, N.Y.: Newman Press, 1970. viii,251 pp.

Gundel, Wilhelm
Neue astrologische Texte des Hermes Trismegistos.
[The Latin text with a German translation and Commentary]
Munich: Verlag der Bayerische, Akademie der Wissenschaften, 1936. paper

Holden, James Herschel, M.A. FAFA
A History of Horoscopic Astrology
From the Babylonian Period to the Modern Age.
Tempe, Az.: A.F.A., Inc., 1996. 1st ed. paper xv,359 pp. diagrs. tables 22 cm.
Tempe, Az.: A.F.A., Inc., 2006. 2nd ed. paper xvii,378 pp. diagrs. tables 22 cm.

Holden, James Herschel
"Claudius Ptolemy" in
Journal of Research of the American Federation of Astrologers.
Tempe, Az.: A.F.A., Inc., 2010. Vol. 13: 121-130. paper 146 pp. 22 cm.

Herschel, Clemens
The two Books on the Water Supply of the City of Rome.
[with a facsimile of the fundamental MS Casinensis 361]
Boston: Dana Estes and Company, 1899.

Hübner, Wolfgang
Grade und Gradebezirker der Tierkreiszeichen.
[Degrees and Degree Areas of the Zodiac]
[vol I. edition of various texts; vol. II Commentary]
Stuttgart and Leipzig: B.G. Teubner, 1995. 2 vols. 265 and 272 pp. 24 cm.

Kidd, D. A., M.A.
Collins Latin Gem Dictionary.
[my favorite small dictionary]
London and Glasgow: Collins, 1972. repr.

Lewis, Charlton T., Ph.D.and Charles Short, LL.D
A Latin Dictionary.
Oxford: Clarendon Press, 1962. repr.

Lilly, William
Christian Astrology/ modestly/ Treated of in three Books.
[with a valuable bibliography of books on astrology]
London: John Partridge & Humphrey Blunden, 1647. [19],832,[20] pp.

Christian Astrology.
[with two appendices by Patrick Curry and Geoffrey Cornelius]
Exeter, England: Regulus Publishing Co., 1985. repr. in facs. with color portr.

Manilius, Marcus
Astronomicon.
ed. by A. E. Housman
Cambridge: University Press, 1937. 2nd edition 5 vols.

Manilius, Marcus
Astronomica.
ed. and translated into English by G. P. Goold
[with an excellent account of Manilius's astronomy and astrology and a select bibliography in the Preface; an appendix of readings different from those of A. E. Housman's Editio Minor; and an Index of words, names, and subjects.]
The Loeb Classical Library
Cambridge, Mass.: Harvard University Press;
London: William Heinemann Ltd., 1977. cxxii,388 pp. maps, tables, diagrs. 16 cm

Neugebauer, Otto
A History of Ancient Mathematical Astronomy.
New York, Heidelberg, Berlin: Springer Verlag, 1975. 3 vols.

Ptolemy's Tetrabiblos or Quadripartite …
Newly translated from the Greek Paraphrase of Proclus …
with Extracts from the Almagest … and his Centiloquy
by J. M. Ashmand.
[This is the translation that has most commonly been used
by English-speaking astrologers.]
London: Davis & Dickson, 1822.
London: W. Foulsham & Co., 1917. reprint.

Ptolemy, Claudius
Tetrabiblos.
ed. and translated into English by
F. E. Robbins, Ph.D./ University of Michigan
[An account of the principal MSS and the previous
editions in the Introduction, with the text in Greek
and the English translation on facing pages; and with
an English Index at the end]
The Loeb Classical Library
London: William Heinemann Ltd.;
Cambridge, Mass.: Harvard University Press, 1940. xxv,466 pp. 16 cm.

Ptolemaeus, Claudius
ΑΠΟΤΕΛΕΣΜΑΤΙΚΑ.
ed. by Wolfgang Hübner
[with a full account (in Latin) of the MSS and previous editions;
a stemma codicum, a bibliography; and a table of variant sigla;
the Greek text has a full apparatus, testimonia, references, and
an Index Verborum.]
Stuttgart and Leipzig: B.G. Teubner, 1998. lxxv,438,[2] pp. tables
diagrs.

Rhetorius the Egyptian
Astrological Compendium.
translated by James Herschel Holden, M.A. FAFA
Tempe, Az.: A.F.A., Inc., 2009. paper xx,223 pp. 22 cm.

Rhetorius, Qui dicitur.
Compendium Astrologicum.
Edited by Stephan Heilen and David Pingree
Munich & Leipzig: K. G. Saur Verlag, 2012. forthcoming

Souter, Alexander
A Glossary of Later Latin to 600 A.D.
Oxford: Oxford University Press, 1949.

Thompson, James Westfall
The Medieval Library.
New York & London: Hafner Publishing Co, 1967. repr.

Thorndike, Lynn
History of Magic and Experimental Science.
New York: Columbia University Press, 1923-1958. 8 vols.

Vettius Valens
Anthologiarum libri novem.
ed. by David Pingree
Leipzig: B. G. Teubner, 1986.

THE MATHESIS
BOOKS 1-4 INDEX

Here begin the chapters of the Books of Astrology of Julius Firmicus Maternus Junior, V.C.[1]

The first book has an essay on what astrology is.

The second book has [information] on the twelve signs.

[1]This Index is found in the oldest MSS of the **Ω** family and in a few of the 15th century MSS; hence, it was presumably in the archetype, since it lists chapters that were no longer present when **Ω** was copied, but it omits the last chapter of Book II, and it disagrees with the text in some details which will be noted subsequently. The numbering of the chapters does not agree with the numbering in the Teubner text, because there only the extant chapters are numbered. But in the present translation I have chosen to follow the Index of Books II-IV given above as closely as possible, giving the titles of the missing chapters, some indication of their contents, and stating that they are lost. Book II, Chapter 31 is omitted in the Index, but I have added it to the Index.

xiii. The configurations of the stars.
xiv. The characteristics of the stars and at what time they have what forces.
xv. When the stars are matutine and when they are vespertine.
xvi. The characteristics of the signs and their nature and rising times and which winds they are subject to.
xvii. The dodecatemoria.
xviii. The eight houses and the angles.
xix. The weak houses.
xx. The order of the houses.
xxi. The powers of the twelve houses.
xxii. The names of the twelve houses and what astrological significations are allotted to them.
xxiii. The quality of nativities.
xxiv. Oppositions, trines, squares, sextiles, and disjuncts.
xxv. Which parts of the body are attributed to which signs.
xxvi. Which God denotes how many years of life.
xxvii. The Ruler of the Times.
xxviii. The Division of Times.
xxix. The Division of the Year.
xxx. The numbers of the antiscions and their signification.
xxxi. What sort of life and what sort of practices astrologers ought to have.

The third book has this:

i. Man as an image of the world.
ii. The Nativity of the World.
iii. What the stars signify when they are individually placed in the houses.
iv. The conjunction of the Sun and Mercury.
v. The conjunction of Saturn and Mercury.
vi. The conjunction of Jupiter and Mercury.
vii. The conjunction of Mars and Mercury.
viii. The conjunction of Mercury and Venus.
ix. What the Moon does when it is placed in the individual houses with individual stars.

The fourth book has this:

i. The Moon is the greatest substance of the life of man.
ii. What the Moon denotes when it is applying to each star.
iii. The Moon when it applies to none, and which one it first comes to after an empty course; or from which it separates, and to which it applies; and what it does in each house; and when it separates from each star and moves then in empty course; and moving from none, to which it applies, or from which to which, and in what aspect it was.
iv. On finding the Place of Fortune, and, having found it, what it signifies.
v. The Place of the Daemon.
vi. Finding the Ruler of the Nativity.
vii. Having found the Ruler of the Nativity, what it does.
viii. What other stars do when they are joined to the Ruler of the Nativity.
ix. How the climacteric years are found.
x. When the climacteric years occur.
xi. The Givers of Actions.
xii. The empty and full places and their significations.
xiii. Which signs are masculine and which are feminine.
xiv. What the Moon denotes in which house and with which stars, and its separation.

THE MATHESIS
Book I.

Preface.

1. Long ago, Mavortius my friend,[1] I promised I would dedicate this little treatise to you, but for a long time a hesitant modesty restrained me and called me back with doubtful trepidation from the task of writing, for my frail talent could not conceive that it was capable of knowing anything it would judge fit for your ears.

2. For, when you were in charge of the Province of Campania, ennobling[2] yourself with the greatest dignity of honor through your meritorious administration of it, I chanced upon you, worn out [as I was] by the diversity of a long journey and numb from the winter snows. There you strove to relieve the debility of my weak and fatigued body with the most considerate and faithful alleviations of friendship.

3. Later, when my health, restored by your care and medication, had recalled me to my wonted condition, recollecting our past experiences in turn and calling to mind a variety of true stories, we related them.

4. After we talked of our activities and their progress, you questioned me, as you recall, about the situation of the whole of Sicily (where I live, and whence I am sprung), And with an evincing of true reason you in-

[1]Firmicus consistently adds the honorific *decus nostrum*, literally 'our ornament', to his friend's name, evidently to distinguish him as being the author's most highly placed friend. I have usually rendered it by the more common English phrase 'my friend', although 'my distinguished friend' would be closer to Firmicus's meaning. Prof. Monat notes that the same honorific was used by Horace to refer to his patron Maecenas.

[2]Reading **nobilitans* 'ennobling' rather than *nobilitas* 'nobility'. He was Governor of Campania 328-335.

quired about all those things that the old fables tell of. What Scylla and Charybdis[1] are. What the turbulent confusion of waters dashing together in the straits is, which the separate bodies of water bring together with a contrary collision of waves at certain times for a certain interval. What the fires do that burst forth from the summit of Mt. Etna. What their nature or substance is. From what source so many fires are exhaled and pass forth without any loss to the mountain. What sort of lake that is which appears near the bed of the river Symaethus,[2] whose name is Palicus,[3] which, befouled with a ghastly thickness, constantly bubbles and boils[4] with livid foam, and, with a sound like that of serpents,[5] hisses forth a noisy spewing.

5. Recalling with me also and inquiring about all the other things which literature both Attic and Roman had taught you from your earliest days concerning the admirable province of Sicily, at length you changed the subject of your conversation to the Sphere of Archimedes—thus showing me the wisdom and learning of your divine genius. What the nine spheres are. What the five zones are, which are colored by differing natures. What the twelve signs perform. What the ceaseless wandering of the five planets accomplishes. What the daily motion of the Sun and its yearly revolution accomplish. What the rapid motion of the Moon and the assiduous increases and diminutions of her light accomplish. Also, in how many revolutions that greater year which they speak of is completed—the one that restores the five planets, the Moon, and the Sun to their original places, which is completed in 1,461 years[6]. What causes the

---

[1]Scylla and Charybdis were the names of mythological sea monsters that attacked sailors. Scylla (the modern Scilla) is a headland projecting from the Italian coast into the Strait of Messina. Charybdis (the modern Galofalo is a whirlpool near the Strait of Messina. The passage through the Strait of Messina, ranging from 2 to 12 miles wide, separating Italy and Northern Sicily was very hazardous for ancient shipping, whence the ancient stories of sea monsters.

[2]The modern river Simeto, which rises west of Mt. Aetna and runs into the sea south of Catania.

[3]A small lake, said to be the Lago di Naftia 35 mi. SW of Catania and 4 mi. W of Palagonia. In ancient times, water spouts erupted from it, and its surface was disturbed by sulphureous gases. Today it has largely dried up, but it continues to give off carbon dioxide. However, this lake is not near the river Simeto, but rather the Caltagirone.

[4]Reading **effervescit* 'bubbles and boils' rather than *obatrescit* 'grows ever darker', an otherwise unattested Latin word. Cf. I. 7.17 (Teubner p. 23,17).

[5]Reading **serpentium convicio* 'sound of serpents' instead of *strepente coniugio* 'a sounding union'.

[6]The ancients had various estimates of the length of the "Great Year," but this

Milky Way and the eclipses of the Sun and Moon. Why the whirling rotation of the sky never causes the Big Bear to rise or set. What part of the Earth is subject to the north and what part to the south. What force suspends the earth itself in the middle with poise and balance. How great a space of land the ocean (which they call the Atlantic Ocean) encloses like an island with its surrounding waves.

6. When the facile instruction of your vivid description had conveyed all these things to me, Mavortius gem of good men, I too dared to offer something in the way of an unasked discourse. With the result that I promised I would set forth for you whatever the ancient sages and divine men of Egypt as well as the learned Babylonians have handed down to us concerning the force of the stars and their powers by the instruction of their divine doctrine.

7. And thus I was rash, as I knew I was, to make that promise. And, to tell you the truth, I often wished to be reprehended with severe reproof and to alter that which I had promised, if I might have been permitted to do so. But the encouragement given by your conversation diminished my temerity and urged me to begin what I have many times [since] set aside out of desperation. For when the governorship of all[1] the East had been handed over to you by the serene and venerable judgment of our lord and Emperor Constantine Augustus,[2] you lost no time in demanding from me that which I had promised you without your having asked for it.

8. And so I sent to you, the Proconsul[3] and designated Ordinary Consul[4] the promised work—praying and requesting indulgence for it, lest in

---

one is simply the number of Egytian years of 365 days that equals an integer number of years of 365.25 days, sc. 1460 years. That is, in 1461 Egyptian years the first day of the year (1 Thoth) would have rotated completely through the months of the 365.25 day year and returned to where it started. But the moon and planets would not have returned to their orginal places!

[1]The MSS have †*potius* 'rather' **Ω**, but the Teubner editors conjecture **totius* 'of all' = **S**, which I have adopted. However, **N** has *postea* 'afterwards', and Prof. Monat prefers that reading ('For afterwards when...the governorship of the East...')

[2]Not Constantine I (d. 337), but probably his son Constantius II (317-361), who, by an initial agreement with his brothers Constantine II (d. 340) and Constans I (d. 350) in 338, received the eastern portion of the Roman Empire. As Thorndike notes, the names Constantine and Constantius were easily confused by the copyists.

[3]A Proconsul was a man who had been a Consul and was later asigned to the governorship of a province.

[4]Mavortius was Ordinary Consul in the year 355. To attempt to reconcile that

this book the weight and pleasing quality of the perfect oration, the best treatments or grave and well-founded opinions might be required by the judgment and eloquence of your learning. I have but slight talent and a plain form of speech, and, what must truly be acknowledged, a very modest learning in astrology. All of which, though it frightened me with various desperation, I nevertheless entered upon the task of writing, so that, notwithstanding my being involved in these arduous and most difficult promises, I might not escape the most learned judgments of your wisdom, Lollianus.

Chapter 1.

1. And so, since we are involved in the opening part of this discourse and in the first parts of the principles themselves, we should do nothing more than reply to those who attempt to weaken the entire force of astrological science by manifold arguments. Those who think themselves able to destroy the whole body of philosophy and divine science in its entirety with their opinions and disputations—elevated as they are by the authority of their writing. Those who are motivated, as I believe and as is proved by the things themselves, not by any infirmity or falsity of the subject itself, but only by their desire of contradicting. So that things certain and definite, which we discern not alone by mind and reason, but which indeed we see with the glance and judgment of our own eyes, they oppose by argumentation [merely] arising from a contentious license.

2. For indeed, they try first of all to creep out of these very responses of the astrologers into their own excessively deep and subtle disputations, in order to destroy this whole science by some stratagem as it were. But the harder they fight, and the more they search for ways of persuading, so much the more vehemently and certainly do they confirm the truth of astrology.

3. For obviously there would be no truth to it unless they strained against it with such great forces of argument. Nor is there any reason to be surprised at this, since we know how great is their dissension among themselves over the nature of the Gods, and with what great arguments of

---

fact with his assignment of the composition of the *Mathesis* to the year 337, Mommsen was forced to conjecture that Mavortius's consulship had been promised to him by Constantine I but held up for nearly two decades until it was finally awarded by Constantius II. But that hardly seems likely.

disputation they try to overthrow the whole force of divinity. For some say there are <no>[1] Gods, others that they exist to be sure, but they restrict them to managing nothing at all. Others say that they both exist and undertake the care and management of our affairs. And in such great difference and dissension are all these critics involved, that it would be long and inappropriate to enumerate their several opinions, especially at this time when we have entered upon another task.

4. For some of them designate figures for the Gods according to their own judgment and assign them places; they also set up seats for them. And they declare that everything that is done and accomplished is ruled and governed by their judgment. Others say that they build nothing, care for nothing, and are free from all care of governing. And they assert all these things as something that invites the minds of their hearers to ready belief.

5. But those things that were said about the immortality of the soul by the divine Plato, and the things that were said by the very shrewd and diligent Aristotle, are manifestly contrary and contradictory, for they hold different opinions between themselves concerning good and evil.

6. The explanation of which things I think ought now to be passed over, for we have not entered upon this kind of disputation, nor have we formed our mind and counsel either to refute or to confirm these things. But we have just touched lightly on all these things in a short discussion, so that contentious comments of contradiction may be made known to all men by their own open study.

7. And so it is agreeable to consider those things that they say about astrology, and to take care to touch lightly upon all those things that they have said, in a short discussion. For, since it is our purpose to explain the substance of *Mathesis*[2] and astrology, we ought not to tarry longer in foreign subjects.

---

[1]Most of the MSS have *esse deos* 'there are Gods', but **A'** has *esse <non> deos* 'there are <no> Gods, which is probably correct. Firmicus had evidently read Cicero's *De Natura Deorum* 'The Nature of the Gods', in which the existence (*deos esse*) or non-existence of the Gods (*nullos esse*) and their relationship to the world and to man is discussed in great detail. Here, Paragraphs 3-7 summarize the topics discussed in Cicero's book.

[2]The Greek word means 'instruction' or 'education', especially in mathematics.

Chapter 2.

1. And so they first join together on the subject of the customs and colors of mankind, saying: that if customs and colors are bestowed on mankind by the configurations of the stars, and if the courses of the stars compose the lineaments of mortal bodies as if by some kind of picture or by some artifice, i.e. if the Moon makes white men, Mars red men, Saturn black men, why then are all those begotten in Ethiopia black, in Germany white, in Thrace red? Just as if the Moon and Mars do not have their own force and powers in Ethiopia. And in Germany and Thrace the planet Saturn lacks his own freedom of moulding.

2. With regard to the customs of mankind,[1] they add the following. If Saturn makes those who are cautious, serious, slow, avaricious, and taciturn; Jupiter, those who are mature, good, generous, and well-behaved; Mars, those who are cruel, treacherous, and warlike, the Sun, those who are religious, noble, and haughty; Venus, those who are voluptuous, charming, and handsome, and illustrious because of the honored magnificence of their charm[2]; Mercury, those who are artful, crafty, and trouble-making, with the mobilities of an aroused mind; the Moon, those who are sharp-witted, illustrious, refined, and excercising power through the respect of public approval; why then are certain races formed thus, so that they are well-known in a way from their own unity of customs?

3. The Scythians alone act with a cruelty of monstruous savagery; the Italians are made regal, always outstanding in their nobility; the Gauls are dull-witted; the Greeks fickle; the Africans underhanded, the Syrians avaricious; the Sicilians sharp-witted; the Asians always occupied with

---

[1]Here Firmicus describes the *typical* national of each of the countries he mentions. Ptolemy does something similar in *Tetrabiblos* II. 3 "The Familiarities between Countries and the Triplicities and Stars," and several earlier Greek writers stated what seemed to them to be the national characteristics of the inhabitants of various countries. It was not uncommon in giving an account of a country to give an account of the customs of the people who lived there, sometimes linking the customs to the nature of the climate and terrain, thus anticipating what the Germans call *Geopolitik*, which is discussed by Ellsworth Huntington (1876-1948) in his book *Season of Birth* (New York: J. Wiley & Sons, 1938). Nowadays, ascribing characteristics of any sort to nationals or races would be called by the pejorative term "racial profiling," although generalization of that sort is useful and as old as the human race.

[2]The Latin *honesto gratiae splendore fulgentes* describes that outstanding combination of physical beauty and personal magnetism, that is sometimes described in English as "throwing off sparks."

voluptuous[1] pleasures, the Spaniards preposterous with their exalted spirit of boastfulness?

4. For the reason that Jupiter never mitigates the ferocity of the Scythians, neither will the Sun ever deny world rulership to the Italians. Nor does the planet Saturn impose any weight on the fickleness of the Greeks. Nor is the lascivity of the Asians corrected by the sober moderation of Jupiter. Nor will the sharpness of the Sicilians ever be blunted by the frigid rising of Saturn. Nor is the avarice of the Syrians tempered by the lascivious aspects of Venus. Nor does the salutary planet Jupiter hold back the malicious comments of the Africans and their deceitful minds. Nor will Saturn's dull light[2] be able to inhibit the boastfulness of the Spaniards. Nor will the most wise planet Mercury arouse the dullness of the Gauls.

5. But the one of these [arguments] that is the most powerful, and the one that is vehemently thrown against us, is the concluding one. Because they say that all the duties of virtues are removed from human affairs by the institution of this art. If temperance, fortitude, prudence, and justice are to be ascribed to the decrees of the stars rather than to our own will, then, if anyone shall break the bond of society and respect, and if he shall neglect the laws of agreed-upon human conduct and shall hand himself over wholly to ferocity and perfidy, then he may securely ascribe to the stars his crime and the perverse desires of his mind.

6. He is unjust, he is dishonest, he is malevolent, he is irreligious—because a bad configuration of Mercury with Mars caused these defects. Why should we strengthen our souls by the practice of fortitude? Why with a lofty and elevated mind formed by the constancy and magistery of divine virtues do we, when placed in harsh circumstances, scorn death and pains, if the praise of fame and the insignia of a most powerful dignity are bestowed on us by a good configuration of the Sun and Jupiter, and not by our own efforts?

7. Therefore, in vain do we repress the defects of a straying soul with counsel and reason. In vain do we regulate the illicit desires of our passions. In vain do we seek modesty and justice with an instinct of dignity and moderation! If it is Mercury, tempered with good aspects of the

---

[1]Reading *luxuriosis...voluptatibus* with MS **N** rather than *luxuriosi...<et> voluptatibus* with the printed text.

[2]The planet Saturn does not ever appear as bright as Jupiter or Venus and so is "dull" in comparison to them.

Moon and Jupiter, that inflames us with desire and longing for that virtue.

8. They also address individuals with this piece of disputation. In vain, O good man, do you have a choice of good things and bad things and the desire to flee from the bad ones. Why do you defend yourself with honorable precautions and with decisions of carefulness, if it is not your own knowledge, but either Saturn or Jupiter that provides all of this to you? We contemn the Gods, so it seems, and we make public the sanctified and venerable ceremonies of religions with a desperate ardor of sacrilege.[1]

9. Plowman, why do you invoke the Gods? Without the care of your divinity the furrow of the field has been evened by your own skill. You who arrange the grape vines[2] throughout the open field in a row with distinct orders, in vain do you dedicate the branches of the vines to your Liber with religious trepidation, if without the assistance of any divinity whatever they are either denied or bestowed by the course of the stars.[3]

10. You who promulgate laws and hand down judgments, take away your laws, take down the tables of the laws, and set us free from those most harsh punishments of yours. Mercury—as the astrologers will have it—performed that sacrilege. Venus perforned that adultery. The planet Mars armed this one for manslaughter, and drove that one to change the faith of the records,[4] or to mix poison. Mercury causes him to disturb the calm purified minds resting in the oblivion of the river Lethe with nefarious songs.

11. Behold this one inflamed with incestuous desires! You see him clinging to the embraces of boys—we attribute this very great evil to Mars and Venus. That one by your decree has been struck down by the

[1]This is an exact description of what Firmicus did in his book *De errore profanarum religionum* 'The Error of Pagan Religions', which is generally supposed from internal evidence to have been written about 346. Do we have here an expression of regret that he wrote that book? If so, this might imply a dating of c. 346 for this portion of Book I, but compare the note to *Mathesis* I. 10.14 below.

[2]Reading *per aperta *iugera *<vites> *uvarum in aciem* instead of *per aperta iuga olivarum in aciem*. The subject is the arrangement of grape vines in the field, not olive trees in an orchard.

[3]Remember that Firmicus was a lawyer by profession. From this point on, he adresses his readers as if they were members of a jury—presenting evidence to them, asking them questions, and challenging them to consider the facts that he lays before them.

[4]That is, to alter the contents of written documents by forgery—a severe crime among the Romans.

hand of the executioner; the sentence against him is decreed by the government. If not by his own desire, but by the evil aspects of the stars, he was driven to commit a crime, you, Judge, do not have a just basis for punishment, because you know that we are always incited to these faults by the malign fomentings of the stars.

12. These and other things they bring together in a similar fashion—inquiring whether we say the stars are animate or inanimate—so that, confused by the conclusion of this question, we may with difficulty bring forth our own judgment and opinion. For they turn to the contrary whatever will have been said about these matters, by the barbs of their syllogisms, so that the narrowed discourse is agreeable to the decision of their replies.

Chapter 3.

1. We certainly praise their talent in these matters and disputations, but we shun their proposition and institution. Because for us astrology has confimed its own truth by the divine and most manifest authorities of its responses and predictions.

2. Some of them also add that they agree with us to some extent. So that, harmony having been obtained by flattery, they may thrust aside this whole science with the hopelessness of doubt. [They say] that this doctrine does in fact have the greatest force, but they assert that due to the brevity of degrees and minutes, and to the very swift course of the stars,[1] and the headlong fall of the whirling rotation[2] of the sky, no one can attain to clarity. So that, by that very same definition of theirs the substance of the statement of the whole science may be overthrown.

3. We however, although we have but slight talent and an almost inefficacious manner of plain speech,[3] and since we ought to refute what they

[1]Firmicus perhaps had in mind the statement of Sextus Empiricus (c. 200 A.D.) in his *Pros astrologos* (*Against the Astrologers*), Sect. 70, that astrologers cannot make an accurate horoscope because of *tês toû kosmou kinêseôs alêptô tachei peripheromenês* 'the incomprehensible speed of the revolving motion of the universe'.

[2]*pronum rotatae vertiginis lapsum* in the Latin. Bram renders these words as 'inclination of the heavens'. Prof. Monat renders it as *du mouvement de révolution circulaire qui entraine le ciel* 'of the movement of circular revolution that draws along the sky'.

[3]An understatement inserted for modesty's sake, since Firmicus evidently tried

say with the verity of the thing itself and to confirm the precepts of this divine science of ours by the accuracy of its responses and predictions, nevertheless we shall reply to you, my friend Lollianus. I should begin by postulating that the faith of *verity* is required in all refutations, not splendor of oratory and substance.

4. And first of all, I would like for that vehement accuser of astrologers, who persecutes this art with such lofty oratory, to state whether he has undertaken any experiment in this science. To state whether no one has given true replies to his enquiry, or whether in fact he has simply refused to listen (expecting his ears to be defiled by those replies). And being severe and harsh, and in a manner disturbing the laws of all divinity, he has sharpened the barbs of his arguments [merely] with the license of polished speech.

5. If true responses were made to his enquiry, and the trustworthiness of verity followed after the statement of the one who responds, why then stigmatize what should be admired? Why should the perfidious accuser impugn the divine science with the spirit of a traitor?

6. But if by erratic responses, he who professes to know astrology, was unable to fulfill those things that he had said. And if they stain his responses with the mendacity of their promise, then that one's inexperience and rashness ought to be driven out, and his fallacious promise branded with infamy. For he is deserving of every evil, because it has come about through him that the study of this distinguished art has been cast ito the shade by the false mendacities of his responses.

7. But whoever does not truly wish to find out or hear anything and has not made true things from the respondents available to the judgment of his own ears—since he no doubt feared that the faith of verity might infringe his own rigid ideas—that man acts unjustly if he thinks to censure something that he would not[1] or could not perceive because of an obtuse intention of mind. For those judges are always unjust, even as we reiterate, who declare themselves on unknown matters. And he does not have any right to render a judgment, who is led to decree anything by the unskilled license of rashness, and who is not brought to the completion of his opinion by having examined the allegations of the parties.

---

to write elegantly.

[1]Accepting Skutsch's tentative emendation *noluit* 'he would not' rather than *potuit* 'he could'.

8. Therefore, if the one attacking is one who has both heard something from a most prudent astrologer and believed and proved it, then it is only from a malicious instinct of mind and a desire for discord that he has made vows to contradict noteworthy things. But if an unskilled professor replies false things to his questioning, then it is not astrology, but the fallacious and rash ignorance of that [individual] man that should be noted. But any person who has wished neither to hear nor to judge—in vain does he lay claim to the privilege of declaring himself, for he is not fit to be able to note the substance of that thing which he has not wished to put to trial.

Chapter 4.

1. But we freely understand that certain people discourage us in this study due to the contrary difficulty of this science. For truly there are arduous and difficult things that the mind (impeded by the earthly snares of sordid things, even though it is formed with the fiery immortality of divinity) cannot perceive with an easy method of inquiry.

2. For its divinity—which is sustained by an eternal agitation—when it is shut up in an earthly body, suffers some temporary loss of its own divinity, since its force and substance is inhibited both by its association with the earthly body and by the assiduous dissolution of mortality. Whence it comes about that all things that pertain to the investigation of the divine arts are always bequeathed to us only by difficult thought.

3. On which account, because we have freely and easily agreed in this part—showing why divine things are discerned through difficult inquiry—it may also be confessed that it is needful that the mind, which is immortal, if it has been separated from the defects and passions of its earthly body, and if, retaining the recognition of its own origin and seed, it has acknowledged the force of its own majesty, can easily attains all things that are difficult and arduous through the divine investigation of the mind.

4. Tell me! Who saw the course at sea in the sky? Who struck the spark of hidden fire from the rubbing of stones? Who recognized the powers of herbs? To whom does the whole nature of divinity both show and produce itself if not to the *mind*, which, having come forth from the celestial fire, has directed itself toward the ruling and direction of earthly fragility?

5. This one handed down the plan of this science. This one devised the computations. This one demonstrated the courses, regressions, stations, associations, augments, risings, and settings of the Sun and the Moon and the other stars—which by us are called 'wandering'—but by the Greeks are called *planets*.[1] And constituted in the fragility of an earthly body, he did not forget, but remembered to hand down all these things with the awareness of his own brief majesty.

6. Thus, it is apprehended and discovered in what sign the star of Saturn rejoices, and when his coldness is warmed by the action of alien heat. Thus, we collect his motions and courses through individual days and hours. Also, we predict when he is retrograde. At what time he returns to his first station. When the nearby light of the Sun rouses up the slow courses of his tardity by the regal authority of its own majesty. When, having departed from him, the ardor of the Sun bestows [again] the quiet power of slow motion. And after how long a time he will come again with slow motion to the same degree of a sign from which he had previously departed.

7. These same things are also observed in the case of the star of Jupiter and in like fashion. For even though in a briefer space of times, yet with a similar movement, it also runs through the twelve signs. Mars too, whom you see blood-red with kindled flashings of brillance, and terrifying with menacing coruscation of light. Lo, when he has come to Saturn, also when he has come to Saturn's domicile, his fires are tempered by the nature of the alien coldness. And even though the courses of this star are more swift, yet the same things [of motion] are also observed in the same fashion.

8. Likewise, the daily compliance of Venus and of Mercury are shown to us. For these stars go along together in the brief intervening space around the orb of the Sun. Either they both follow, or one star following behind concedes obedience to the other one going ahead. We know when they appear to us in their vespertine or matutine rising. When they are concealed—hidden by the orb of the Sun. And when freed from the splendor of his rays, they shine forth [again] with their own bright splendor.

9. What do we see in the course of the Moon, as we say when she feeds the ills of a worn-away orb with customary supplements—when, de-

[1]From the Greek *planêtês* 'wanderers'.

prived of light—she acknowledges the loss of her own proper majesty. For these conditions [occur] when she is near the Sun, either waxing or waning, and, having venerated the Sun as it were, she lowers the rays of her light. So that [later], adorned again by his fraternal rays when she has made the longer courses and measures of her own, reborn with shining splendor and renewed, she carries around the ornaments of [full] light.

10. Here is another thing we know more about, which, when it happens, always strikes the uninformed with a monstruous timidity. When the Sun at midday, destroyed by the rays of the Moon as if by some obstacle,[1] denies the brilliant light of his own splendor to all mortals (which, in the consulate of Optatus and Paulinus—as I may speak of more recent occurrences[2]—the wise intent of the astrologers had predicted to all men that it was going to happen). Or when again the Moon, shadowed by regions of terrestrial heights, is eclipsed in similar fashion, which we have frequently observed to occur in the serenity of a bright night.[3]

11. The genius of the astrologers collects all these things, and by skillful computation it has learned all about the secrets of the divine disposition. And so I should want you, whoever you are, to reply to my question about these things! Which do you think is the more difficult? To find the courses of the stars, which now found I have expounded. Which move now through the high, now through the wide, now through the deep. Who join themselves now to the regions and breezes of the south, now to those

[1]As Prof. Monat points out in his Note 25, Firmicus evidently did not understand the astronomical mechanism of a solar eclipse, or else was merely speaking poetically. It is not the Moon's *rays* that "destroy" the Sun, but rather its *globe* interposed between the earth and the Sun.

[2]This was the annular eclipse of 17 July 334, whose central path passed just to the west of the Italian peninsula. It seems to have been supposed by Theodor Mommsen (1817-1903) and the later scholars who followed him that the word *recentioribus* "more recent" means "in the last year or two," but this is not so! It merely means that eclipses have happened in the past, but this was one of the *more recent* ones. (The "most recent" one before that was the annular eclipse of 27 July 306.) For Firmicus's usage of the word, cf. *Mathesis* I. 7.14, where Plotinus, who died in 270, is cited as one of the *recentium exemplorum* 'recent examples'! All that is certain from Firmicus's statement is that he wrote *after* 17 July 334. In fact, if he had been writing as late as the beginning of 355, he could still have said that a "more recent" eclipse was that of 334. For there was no subsequent eclipse whose path of visibility came close to any part of Italy until more than twenty years later on 28 May 355. Mommsen's argument is therefore invalid!

[3]This appears to mean that the Moon appears to be momentarily eclipsed when it "passes behind" an elevated piece of ground, such as a hill or mountain.

of the north. Now they set, now they are hidden, now they are in direct course, now retrograde; now they stand in a static tardity. And they confound the intention of the investigators by that variety of their courses—or, once the courses of the stars have been found—to define afterward what their mixtures and their aspects accomplish through the whole extent of the lands.

12. For you, who are brought to agreement by this verity of reason, [namely] that we have found these courses of the stars with assiduous observation of computation—you must agree it is necessary that, having found the course of the stars, we should then easily see their functions and their power. For there are always difficult and arduous things, which we, unlearned and ignorant, approach with the inconstancy of fear, nor is it in easy fashion that we are able to learn anything that preceding instructions have not handed down to us.

13. So, just as we learn to recognize the first symbols of the letters with a certain spurning of aversion; so, as placed on an unknown path, we almost give up in the first steps. You see how those learning their first countings bend their fingers with a slow movement. The one whom you see giving up swimming from a frequent fear of drowning—yet after a little while, strengthened by the continual movement of his arms, having slipped through the highest spumes of the waves, he supports himself with an easy lightness of mobility. For all these things, i.e. letters, arithmetic, music, and the other things that we learn, we later run through in easy fashion, after the established discipline of genius has perceived the pathway from the first origin.

14. Therefore, because it is evident that it was more difficult to find the courses of the stars than to define what they bring about. For about the finding of their courses there is no doubt—which to those wishing to learn, we show first by calculation, then by the very sight of their eyes. Why then do you attack this science, [when by] agreeing to the principles and a part of it, you confirm the entire substance of it?

Chapter 5.

1. It follows [next] that we discuss the colors and customs [of men], and that we refute that whole topic of calumnious questioning with true forces of arguments. So that, having discussed and cleared up everything, we may come secure to the venerable secrets of this science.

2. "Why," he says, "are all those in Ethiopia black, and those in Germany white, if the course of the stars bestows figures and colors on mankind by the diverse mixture of their radiation?"

3. Indeed, we should [already] have fought back in this part of the questioning with a copious reply, so that the sly and calumnious comments of a false dissertation might be conquered by force. But [instead] we have compressed all the task of speaking into the sole powers of truth,[1] lest by the charms of copious language, and by abundance of speech, and by the license of argumentation, we should transfer the captive ears of our audience to the absurdities of false opinions.

4. And first indeed, I should like him to reply to my question, whether in this same populace in which we are now placed there is [only] one form and likeness for all men, even though there is one nature for all of us?

5. I think he will say this: that all our citizens are formed with a dissimilar variety of countenance, and that there is not the same form and likeness for everyone. And, if he is in doubt—which I think not—let him look when a multitude of the whole populace has collected itself together in one place (which customarily happens in theaters or in assemblies), and let him transfer the keenness and judgment of his own eyes to the form of the whole throng. And let him show me, if he can, any two of them among so many thousands of men who seem to be formed with the same and similar lineaments of [their bodily] members. Let fathers, children, and brothers come forth together; and, although there is a connection of all them joined by blood, yet they are still discerned with a diverse distinction of forms; and not one of them is found so like another that his countenance does not differ in some way from the countenance of the other.

6. Whence, it is indeed evident that the substance of our own kind, and the very form of the bare and lonely body, is formed from a commixture of the four elements by the artifice of a provident divinity. But colors and forms, and likewise character and habits, are distributed to us by nothing other than the perennial movement of the course of the stars.

7. For the stars have their own sense and divine prudence, because, animated by the pure concept of divinity, they conform with unceasing agreement to [the will of] that highest and master God, who arranged all

[1]Kroll would add a word to make the passage read *solis veritatis viribus <freti>* '<relying> on the sole powers of truth'.

things with a perpetual disposition of law, in order to preserve the order of his creation everlastingly.

8. For there is no man whom a sacrilegous desperation so arouses with rashness that on earth, where he sees all things are mortal, he says prudence exists, but in that place where all things are adorned with the immortality of perpetuity, he asserts with obstinate animosity of mind that there is no prudence, no reason, nor the order arising from foresight.

9. Who doubts that through these stars that divine mind has been infused into terrene bodies by the necessity of some kind of law, for which the descent is imparted by the orb of the Sun, but its ascent is prepared by the orb of the Moon?

10. For that divine mind and heavenly soul located throughout the body of the world in the manner of a circle, and placed now inside, now outside, rules and arranges all things, and, is conceived by the generation of its own origin for the management and preservation of all things with fiery and perpetual motion. And it does not set aside this task because of any fatigue, so that it sustains itself and the world, and all the things that are in the world, with its own perpetual and tireless mobility.

11. From this soul, these eternal fires of the stars, which, formed with a kind of globose rotundity, perform their circles and orbits with a swift hurrying, animated by the majesty of that divine mind, they transfer a part of the mind to terrene bodies, and they borrow the spirit from those perpetual fuels of the soul.

12. In this fashion, the immortal soul within us decks out the perishable fragility of the terrene body with the confidence of its own majesty, so that even it itself resembles to some extent its own author and origin, which, diffused through all living creatures that are begotten by terrene conception, brings about that they (animated by divine foment) flourish with the perpetual propagation of generation. Wherefore, since now we are conjoined with the stars through a certain kinship, we ought not to deprive those by whose daily courses we are both formed and likewise created, of their own proper powers by means of sacrilegous disputations.

Chapter 6.

1. Whence, that which you define us as doing, [namely] that we may recall men from the worship of the Gods and of religions with profane fu-

ror of mind—we who say that all our acts are brought about by the divine courses of the stars. You are mistaken, and you think contrary [to the truth], and you dissent from true reason. For we cause the Gods to be feared, we cause them to be worshipped, we show their divinity and majesty, when we say that all our acts are governed by their divine actions.

2. Let us therefore worship the Gods, whose origin has conjoined itself to us through the perennial movement of the stars, and let the human race always acknowledge their majesty with suppliant veneration. Let us invoke the Gods suppliantly, and let us offer promised vows religiously to the divinities, so that we may by means of the confirmed divinity of our mind resist to some extent the violent decree of the stars and their powers.

3. Socrates,[1] a man of divine wisdom, taught that we should do this, for when a certain person spoke to him about his customs and desires, which he had collected in easy fashion. "They are," he replies, "as you say; I acknowledge, I confess." And that most learned man disclosed the hidden things with ready confession. "But all these things," he adds, "have been overcome by me through the authority of prudence and virtue, and whatever defect the body had from its depraved matter, the conscious divinity of the mind has regulated itself well."

4. This is given to be understood—that that which we suffer and those things which stimulate us with certain provoking fires are surely of the stars, but that which we shun is of the divinity of the mind. But as for that which pertains to the laws, by which mens' sins are punished with severe chastisement, they were rightly established by a most prudent antiquity, for support was lent through these to a suffering mind, so that through them the force of the divine mind might purge the pernicious faults of the body.

Chapter 7.

1. But now because[2] <the order> of investigation has led us to the necessity—with a delayed response—which was being prepared on [the subject of] customs and colors, the fundamentals of which have been mentioned in part, let us also show that laws serve the power and neces-

---

[1]Socrates (c.470-c.399 B.C.), famous Greek philosopher.

[2]Accepting Kroll & Skutch's emendation *quia* 'because' for the *qui* 'who' of the MSS, and also accepting the editors' suggested addition of *ordo* 'the order'.

sity of the Fates, and that they always accomplish that which the authority of the Fates has decreed.[1]

2. And, so that we may prove it, we ought to recall longer examples. Behold this youth, whole in his strength, wealthy, innocent, and modest, incited by no impulse of domestic crime, compelled by no consternation of fear, has hung himself by a noose and destroyed himself. A friend broke the noose of another [person] already writhing, and one who had given himself over to death by his own punishment because of the shame of his life. The noose having been loosened, he is freed from the sentence of his own judging.[2] Who else did this, unless it was the force and necessity of Fate as the ministers of slaughter, who, appointed to produce a criminal, a man oppressed by his own evils and condemmed by the punishment of his own conscience, in the midst of peril of imminent death, would free him from danger?

3. This one on the other hand, for whom everyone affords testimony of innocence, having drawn his sword, fell upon it just as though he had been compelled [to do so], and thrust the menacing edge of the point into his innocent sides. This man of integrity, sober and chaste, at whose life and customs we have always marvelled—behold, having thrown [himself] down from a precipice, scattered [the members] of his body with lamentable laceration. This just person endures his life in wretched poverty; but that person, whom the infamy of a notorious crime has stained, is lifted up by happy increases [of fortune] and is loaded down with the greatest insignia of honors. Behold the pirate! After slaughters of innocents beyond number, he holds up his own happy children in his gory bosom. This innocent person and from all . . . of crimes is separated by envy.[3] To whom do you attribute this? Who permits these things to be done? To whom was so much [power] granted over us? Lend a hand and

[1]In the Roman religon, the Parcae or 'Fates' were three female divinities, whose decrees were immutable, even by the gods. For each individual, one of the Fates spun a thread, the second one measured it, and the third one cut it off.

[2]I take this to mean that the man felt that he was released from the necessity to kill himself. Bram has 'for the sentence of the judges', which does not seem to be correct, and Prof. Monat has 'by the sentence of the judge', which also seems to miss the mark, since the Latin word is *iudicantis* 'of the one judging' not *iudicis* 'of the judge'.

[3]Here the Teubner editors indicate a lacuna. Sittl notes that edition **a**, fills up the lacuna thus: *scelerum <contagione semotus, ab omni foelicitatis munere scelestorum hominum> separatur invidia* 'withdrawn <from the contagion> of evil deeds, is separated <from every gift of happiness> by the envy <of wicked men>. MS **D**[2] changes *separatur* 'is separated' to *separatus* 'separated' and adds

set us free hereafter from these struggles of conflict, so that all these things which frail and fallen mortality is accustomed to endure, you may also confirm by your own confession to be decreed by the fortuitous courses of the stars.

5. What shall we say about the glory and[1] honors of evil men and the flight and exiles of good men? You see this person tainted with servile stains protecting the squalors and disgrace of his own birth with the nobility of the consular fasces. This [other] person bearing the ornaments of freeborn blood is deprived of his deserved insignia of honors. This person, while yet in the first part of life, giving evidence of no ornaments of virtue, continues [advancing to] all the honors with headlong swiftness And this [other] person, already worn out with the feebleness of declining age, and [long since possessed][2] of the testimony of an outstanding life, now [finally] begins the first round of the entrance into honors.[3]

6. What scheme of things held that old man back? Certainly the merit of his life was promising all the ornaments of honors to him. What with sudden good fortune drove that youth to such a heap of honors, the like of which we had been unable to hope for hitherto, if that very force which we say [is that of] Fate, which is accomplished by the movement of the stars, had not acted to spur on this one [and] to retard that other one?

---

in the margin <*in exilium datur*>, so that the clause then reads 'this innocent person and one separated from every kind of evil deeds, by envy <is sent into exile>'. Both of these additions to the text seem to be efforts to supply a suitable contrast to the happy domestic situation of the pirate. The phrase *te… ab omni scelerum liberavit invidia* 'has freed you from all odium of evil deeds' occurs at the end at *Mathesis*, I. 30.15.

[1]MSS **ΩΨ** have *Quid de errore honoribus* 'What about error, honors'. But MS **N** omits *errore*, which seems to be either a false reading or a word followed by missing words. Skutsch suggests replacing *errore* with *gloria et*, so that the sentence would begin with 'What about glory and honors'. I have followed that suggestion.

[2]A few words are missing in the Latin text. I have supplied something that is perhaps appropriate.

[3]These sound like actual case histories known to Firmicus, but, as Prof. Monat notes, no one has suggested who they might be. A careful search of the historians of the fourth century might find suitable candidates. It is perhaps worth noting that Constantine I's eldest son Crispus (c.300-326) was given the title of Caesar in 317 and was consul in 318 and again in 321 and 324 only to be executed in 326. His younger half-brother Constantine II (c.317-340) was made Caesar as an infant in 317 and consul in the years 320, 321, and 324, when he was age 3, 4, and 7 respectively!

7. What should I declare now on the subject of the punishments with good reason of evil doings or crimes? You were saying a little while ago, "Frequently we have seen injuries of this sort imposed upon innocent persons with the consenting judgment of everyone."

8. The tally of an infamous vote brought to an end that most prudent Athenian and man of singular justice, who had received the cognomen "The Wise" because of the merit of his life and virtues.[1] But Socrates,[2] whose knowledge is decorated with the testimony of divinity, having formed the customs of men and arranged them by divine instruction, having been overwhelmed by false accusations, overburdened by the envy of bitter accusation, undefended and abandoned, succumbed to the harsh power of those judging him. How many times did Fortune make Alcibiades[3] a general, how many times an exile?

9. What should we say about this variety of lot? Alcibiades, instructed in the civil way of ruling by the divine precepts of Socrates, was enduring these things, and, although he had always and everywhere led the army with success, he could not avoid the envy of Fortune raging against himself. But perchance the desires of depraved passions seized him—as some will have it (for it is unecessary that we should confirm this in our own discussion)—and the unforseen force of an incautious rashness deceived him. Therefore let us bring forth another example, so that even thus you may be compelled to [acknowledge] the details of the avowal.

10. Fate betrayed Plato[4] with those virtues [of his] mind, with that doctrine of wisdom, and handed over that divine discipline of mind to the tyrannical cruelties and ridiculous powers of Dionysius.[5] If these things do not suffice, we may turn our attention to the shipwrecks of Pythagoras.[6] What sort of man he was is known to everyone; a man whose virtue, wis-

---

[1]As Bram points out, this is a reference to the Athenian statesman and admiral, Aristides (c.550-c.467). He was actually called 'The Just' rather than 'The Wise'. He was ostracized in 483.

[2]Socrates (c.470-399), famous Athenian soldier and philosopher. Having been tried and convicted on the specious charge of corrupting the youth, neglecting the city gods, and indulging in strange religious observances, he was condemned to death. His actual crime had simply been to be an independent thinker.

[3]Alcibiades (c.450-404 B.C.), Athenian statesman and general. Here we must translate *imperatorem* as 'general'.

[4]Plato (427-347 B.C.), famous Athenian philosopher and writer.

[5]Dionysius the Younger (d.c.345 B.C.), Tyrant of Syracuse. Plato had been sent to educate him, but the young man was willful and headstrong.

[6]Pythagoras (c.582-c.507 B.C.), Greek philosopher and mathematician.

dom, and prudence, both the divine thoughts of his mind and the judgments of men and Gods have proved.

11. Lo, he learned all things to the uttermost; and, lest anything should have been lacking to his divine genius, steeped also in foreign mysteries, he penetrated all the secrets of wisdom, and—to speak more truthfully—by the penetration of his divine mind, which was the first—nay indeed, the only one—placed in that earthly fragility, he discovered the nature and origin of the foreseeing divinity and the divine majesty. He pursued that beneficial—as some will have it—and foreseeing divinity day after day, by whose warnings and precepts, the foulness of his mind had been purged, and it had been disposed to all the ornaments of virtue; [yet] the most severe decrees of his own fellow citizens made [him to be] banished and an exile.

12. Fleeing his native land and the whole of Greece, he first went across to alien kingdoms—as an exile, he dwelt in Sybaris and Croton. But Fortune did not long detain him there; for as a fugitive he wandered, now among the Locri, now through Tarentum, and through almost all the regions of Italy. Lo, at last he was surrounded by raging flame, and together with him there perished a throng of unfortunates in a roaring inferno.[1]

13. What do you do now? Do you even now detract from Fate and disparage the force of the stars with obstinate animosity when you see the bad exits of good men, the fortunate deeds of bad men, the <dangers> of innocent persons, the secure states <of harmful ones>?[2] To whom do you attribute this? By whose decrees do you think these things are done? We are unjust, if, when the commands of the Fates denote all these things to us, we still oppose [them] with the animosities of rigid contradiction. In sum, it must be replied to you—because the present examples impel us to do this—that he who is harmful has sinned through the causation of Fate; and he who is condemned though innocent has suffered the severe sentence of punishment compelled by fatal necessity.

---

[1]This does not seem to be correct. Pythagoras had founded a philosophical society that came into disrepute after his death. But it was later in the middle of the fifth century B.C, that the society was suppressed, and a number of its meeting-houses were burned. One of these was the meeting-house at Croton (the modern Crotone, Italy), where 40 or 50 Pythagoreans were said to have been burned to death. Firmicus probably had that incident in mind.

[2]Some words are missing between *innocentium* 'of innocents' and *securitates* 'secure states'; Némethy's conjectures <*pericula et nocentium*> are shown in angle brackets.

14. We will come now to you, Plotinus,[1] singular man, so that we may strengthen our allegations by the pleading of more recent examples. What parts of philosophy did he not touch upon, since his teaching followed the insignia of his own life, when he displayed that which he used to teach, not by someone else's, but by his own example of virtue. A man from whose mouth, as if from some shrine, divine opinions issued forth. For that man was composed of all the ornaments of virtue, and strengthened by every study of divine arrangements, he was just, brave, circumspect, moderate, and one who believed himself able to overcome the assaults of Fortune through the reason of circumspection.

15. And so, first of all he chose a place as a quiet seat for himself, so that, separated from all the bustle of human society, he might free himself from the envy of Fortune. He was going to devote himself to just the fine points of divine instruction, so that he might arm himself against all the threats of Fortune by means of a whole and uncorrupted guard of virtue.

16. And so, resolute in that confidence of mind, he undertook the care and fostering of his own body as well, so that he might leave nothing vacant and bare where the license of savage Fortune might exert itself. He settled himself in a salubrious and pure part of the country; for he is reported to have chosen the pleasant soil of the Province of Campania to establish a seat for himself, where the quiet moderation of the air sustains all the inhabitants with a salubrious vegetation, where neither the force of winter nor the approach of the blazing sun, but a composed temperature is regulated from both. A place where health, acquired from the heat of the surging[2] springs and the salutary foment of the seething hot waters, is infused into men suffering from any sickness.

17. Settled there, he first spurned the insignia of honors, thinking those to be the true honors that the divine magistery of wisdom had bestowed on him. No desire for riches seized him, but he used to think those things were riches, by means of which a furbished soul could find the author of its own origin.

---

[1]Plotinus (c.205-270), famous Greek philosopher, the founder of Neo-Platonism. His lectures were collected and issued under the title *Enneads* by his pupil, the philosopher Porphyry (c.233-304), who also wrote a *Life* of his master. Plotinus's philosophy was adopted in part by the early Christians. He did not believe in Fate or in astrology.

[2]The published text has *ingentium fontium calore* 'the heat of the huge springs'. The Teubner editors rated *ingentium* as suspect; Skutsch suggested *ingenti fontium calore* 'the huge heat of the springs', but Ziegler suggested *surgentium*, which I have adopted.

18. Lo, in a certain part of his own declaration—improvident and incautious, as it seems to me—he attacks the force of fatal necessity, and with a severe rebuke of speech takes to task men who fear the decrees of fortune—attributing nothing to the power of the stars, reserving nothing for the necessities of the Fates, but saying that all things are placed within our own powers.

19. It is tedious to enumerate how he felt about different matters—by what [course of] reasoning he withdrew himself from the lot of Fate, by what argument of opinions he disturbed that force, i.e. of the stars and of Fate. But he narrated these things hitherto, [while then] whole and in good condition. He never turned his eyes or his mind to the end of Socrates or the death of Plato, in any case—as one suspects—ascribing many things to their minds [and] many things to their faults.

20. Lo, the whole power of the Fates imposed itself on him. Secure in that boldness of confidence [of his], first his members grew stiff with a frigid sluggishness of blood, and the keenness of his eyes lost the splendor of gradually weakened light. Later a deadly disease nourished by malign humours broke out all over his skin, so that his putrefying body, with wasting members, rotted away with the death of his corrupted blood. Day by day, and hour by hour, with the creeping advance of the disease, minute parts of his vitals flowed away, and whatever you had seen whole a little before, an ulceration of his weakened body forthwith disfigured.[1]

21. Thus, when all his form had been corrupted and dissipated, the figure of his body receded from him, and in the dead (as I may say) body his mind was retained as the sole survivor. So that, worn out by that continuation of grave disease, and compelled by his own torments, and convinced by the authority of true reason, he felt [at last] the force and power of Fate. And, as he was shaken violently by the laceration of his worn out body, he received the sentence of pronouncing Fortune.

22. What do we say now about the famous death of his man? Why were his virtues—i.e. wisdom, temperance, fortitude, and justice—unable to free him from those punishments of Fortune? And so, he too felt the force of Fate, and received an end which the vehement judgments of the stars had decreed for him. Exhausted by the harshness of illness, he taught all men by his own example—not by the license of his speech—that the power of the Fates can no way be defied.

---

[1]Firmicus alone gives this detailed account of Plotinus's terrible degenerative illness and death, which was perhaps a description of the final stages of leprosy.

23. You know also, as we return again to more ancient examples, what things Miltiades[1] endured after his victory, what things Themistocles[2] sustained after his triumphs—in what calamities of hardships they were involved by those very persons for whom it was seen [that] both liberty and their native land had been restored through their efforts.

24. Who aroused the madness of a raging populace against them? Who kindled the hatred? Who brought about an odium so bitter, that, unmindful of benefactions and the restoration of liberty, both from a grave instinct of furor and from the errors of unbridled fickleness, they struck down innocent men and men of action with the popular harshness of punishment,[3] unless it was the force and necessity of tireless Fate, which always dominates by [its] power?

25. If it is pleasing, let us now revert to Roman examples. Lo, that dastardly man and [one] polluted with every stain of infamy—Sulla,[4] I say—who from the first steps of his youthful age grew up in the laps of dandies through the misfortunes of sold shame. So many times he led the army fortunately, and—so that he might be called "The Fortunate"[5]—brought about innumerable shipwrecks to the republic.

---

[1]Miltiades (d.c. 488 B.C.), an Athenian general who fought first as a mercenary for the Persian King Darius I (521-485); but, having learned that Darius intended to invade Greece, he returned to Athens and was appointed one of ten generals to combat the expected Persian invasion. He was generally credited with being instrumental in the defeat of the Persians at Marathon in 490. But following that success he was appointed admiral of the Athenian fleet, attacked Paros, was wounded, returned to Athens, was fined for a political offense, imprisoned, and died in prison.

[2]Themistocles (C.514-449), Athenian soldier and statesman. He was responsible for the defeat of the Persian fleet at Salamis in 480. But he had made powerful political enemies at Athens, and about 471 he was ostracized and forced to flee to Asia Minor, where he eventually found favor with the Persian King Artaxerxes (reigned 464-424). He never returned to Greece but died in Magnesia, where he was greatly revered by the locals, who erected a massive memorial in his honor.

[3]Miltiades was assessed a heavy fine for military misconduct, and when he was unable to pay it, he was thrown into prison where he later died. Themistocles was exiled from Athens, but, as mentioned in the preceding note, he came to a happier fate than Miltiades.

[4]Lucius Cornelius Sulla (138-78 B.C.), Roman statesman and Dictator from 82 to 79. He was rejected for the praetorship in 98 B.C., but he later achieved it, and eventually became Dictator of the Roman Empire. It seems to be generally thought by scholars that Firmicus drew the details of Sulla's life from Sallust's *Histories*, of which only fragments have come down to us.

[5]Sulla was so generally fortunate that he began to be called *Felix* 'The Fortunate

26. Look how many times he was stained with the civil blood—the vitals of the nation having been lacerated. Lo, he imposed tables of proscriptions without number, and he was enriched by the parricidal collection of gory money. But now, even though to enumerate all his crimes would be difficult, still we shall enumerate a few of them, so that you may recognize from them the force of Fatal Necessity.

27. Seven thousand of our citizens were slain in the middle Forum at Rome by Sulla's order. Believe me, no other force—no blame for crimes, no will of the Gods—but rather the Necessity of the Fates, struck down that multitude with Sulla's hands.

28. Now what do you think the judgment is, what order of reason there is, that he who was never mindful of his own sex, who [long] past the excellence of a pleasing boyish age, [but as an] old[er] mature man kept up the disgraceful acts of the body in an inappropriate age, [and] full of faults he governed the Roman Empire? We know that he was disappointed in his first candidacy for the *praetorship*,[1] this man on whom the most grave Censorinus[2] with true and firm accusations cast the crime of the spoliation of his province [Cappadocia]. Who, as a legate[3] in the Cymbrian[4] War, prostrated by the fear in his degenerate mind, abandoned the Commander-in-Chief Marius[5] and the Roman Army. Although he was dishonored by these very great infamies, and afterward decorated with the authority of regal majesty, he yet turned our own army to our loss.

29. Permit me to unfold the crises of Sulla's rascalities in a still longer oration, for all these things are applicable to the importance of my disputation, if completely and most truthfully the Necessity of the Fates has been made clear by many kinds of misfortunes.

---

ate', a title which Prof. Monat notes that Pliny the Elder remarked on in his *Natural History* 7.137 "Lucius Sulla is the sole human being hitherto who has assumed the surname 'Fortunate', in fact achieving the title by civil bloodshed and by making war upon his country" (H. Rackham's translation).

[1]A *praetor* was a Roman magistrate of the next to the highest rank. He was elected for one year. Having held the praetorship was usually a necessary qualification to stand subsequently for election as consul.

[2]Gaius Marcius Censorinus (fl. 82 B.C.), Roman politician opposed to Sulla.

[3]A man of senatorial rank, commander of a legion, a rank approximating to the modern colonel.

[4]Here **A'DH** have Cimbrico, thus indicating that that reading was in their parent **Ψ**, where **Ω** (and **N** ?) have *in illyrico* 'in the Illyrian (war)'.

[5]Gaius Marius (155-86 B.C.), Roman general and politician, seven times a consul.

30. By a Sullan order, Sulpicius,[1] Tribune of the People,[2] was struck down by the heinous sentence of a murderous command, in which [Sulla's] tyrannical shame and his rascally desire was steeped. [For] without any hesitation he exercised at once all kinds of cruelty, so that he satiated the unbridled desires of his own mind with a daily outpouring of civil blood.

31. A man of Pretorian rank, viz. Marius the Younger,[3] who seemed to deserve well of the Republic in the judgment of all—[was treated thus] by a Sullan decree, First his legs were broken; then, detached from their position on the body, his forearms were detached from his shoulders and fell down; third, his tongue having been cut out, it left his voice [only] in his throat. At the last, when every part of his body had been mutilated, his eyes, which were spectators and witnesses, were gouged out. And, in so narrowed a body, so many torments were invented by the nefarious executioner of the nation, and scarcely was his mind destroyed by such great wounds, that then from the bleeding injuries his vital spirit was plucked out piece by piece.

32. But perhaps Sulla raged about with the atrocity of such savageness against men only? No! He also entered the names of women and married women on his tables of proscriptions,[4] so that he exercised the bloody power of his sword on the whole human race. His bloody desire had no limit, nor was it satiated by the limitless slaughter of the citizenry.

33. That Roman Nation, which had subdued all other nations, and afterwards, having traversed and taken possession of the whole world, and also having found the farthest shore of the ocean, was compelled to serve the nefarious command of Sullan power—the minds of everyone having been weakened by fear, and seized by the wretched trepidation of dread. In spite of the laws of Porcias and the laws of Sempronias,[5] and with a

[1]Publius Sulpicius Rufus (c.121-88 B.C.), Roman orator and statesman.

[2]The Tribune of the People was elected for one year, and after 149 B.C. automatically becme a senator. He had veto power over all laws and decrees except those of a Dictator.

[3]Gaius Marius Junior (109-82 B.C.), succeeded his father as head of the Marian Party, and was consul in 82, but was unable to withstand his political opponents. He retired to Praeneste, where he was cruelly tortured and murdered as Firmicus reports.

[4]Public proclamations that the listed persons were outlaws and enemies of the state, and that their personal property was subject to seizure by the state.

[5]Roman laws promulgated in the second century B.C. that granted certain rights of appeal.

groan from all the citizenry, he put out a third list of proscription, and, not content with this evil, lest any period of his own age be preserved empty of crimes, [Sulla], now a private citizen, slew Lucretius, and [although] he had laid aside the royal power, the pernicious cruelty of his mind persevered in him.

34. Do you want something else for your [contemplation] because we are dwelling on Sullan times? I shall mention the Servilian Lake, where the heads of many senators cut off at the neck hung as a demonstration of this most frightful crime. Situated among the very couches of the Gods, placed among sacred ceremonies, Sulla, ever secure and haughty, looked at the wounds of the Republic. What can be done more cruelly [than this]?[1] He heaped wretched miseries on children and wives on the pretext of public calamity—no pity no faith, no courage, no providence could [prevail] against Sulla!

35. Where now are those who believe our sins can be punished by human and divine law? Lo, Sulla is fed by nefarious slaughter. Lo, he runs wild with tyrannical military command, nor does any divine power oppose his desires. What do you think? What do you judge? Refute what we say! Show us the order of things! Where are the laws, where are the judgments? We are always forsaken by human and divine justice, because Sulla committed all these things which we have mentioned with impunity. Then, do no whips of the avenging Gods punish his crimes, although they were fed on such slaughters? <Among>[2] the authorities is there not one who brings forth his own sorrow with words and tears? Through him also the final fire[3] is snatched away from the dead. And was Justice unable to see this?

36. You say the sins of men are reported to the avenging Gods day by day: [Yet] all these things, just as you see, were done with impunity, and Fortune made of them all that it wished, and whatever the Fates had decreed for individuals, they were accomplished by the punishment of Sullan harshness.And so that you may also know that we have spoken this with true reason, a favorable event followed Sulla after these evils. He is loaded with the insignia of a perpetual dictatorship,[4] and he [later] gives up that

[1]Here and in what follows we see the lawyer Firmicus addressing his reader as he would a member of a jury.

[2]Usener signaled a lacuna before the words *imperia nec est* 'authorities, is there not'. I have conjectured the word *inter* 'among' to fill the gap.

[3]The formal rite of cremation.

[4]Something that had never been done before.

rulership by his own choice. The lacerated joints of the Republic and bloody money are conferred by his order on the fortunes of ignoble men. After these evils, he enjoys a quiet security. And, fattened on an abundance of crimes, by a decree of the entire Senate and the Roman People he is decorated with the name[1] of prosperous and perpetual Good Fortune.[2]

37. Where are those now who deny that our acts are governed by the fortuitous courses of the stars? This cruel, most perfidious person, whom we know to have raged with security through every kind of cruelty, attains all the ornaments of dignity. But Marius after his triumph over Jugurtha[3] and over the other nations which he conquered, after he freed the city of Rome from both foreign and domestic dangers, after purple triumphs,[4] after decorated and gilded palms, is then bound with the iron fetters of chains. Lo, an exile, he hides in the Minturnan[5] swamps; Lo, he is cast into the squalors of a prison. Do you see how he, a fugitive, comes to the mound of ruined Carthage!

38. What God had made either Marius an exile or Sulla Fortunate? The general Paullus promised high military commands to the soldier Marius; the legate Sulla deserted the Roman army. And yet afterwards, by the decree of Fortune, the former was made an exile, the latter was made Fortunate. <Discussing>[6] in too long an oration the force and necessity of Fate, and also the powers of the stars, we have deplored the cruelties done under Sullan rule in this sad account.[7]

39. Scipio,[8] after so many triumphs; after the destruction of Carthage and the prostration of Numantia; after traveling through Greece, Asia,

---

[1]Reading *Romani nomine* 'Roman, by the name' with the Teubner editors, rather than just *Romani* with **Ω** or *nomine* with **Ψ**. *Romani* seems to be required with *populi*, and *nomine* is required with *ornatur*.

[2]A reference to his surname Felix, the Happy or Fortunate one.

[3]Jugurtha (d. 104 B.C.), King of Numidia. Defeated by Marius, he was taken to Rome where he starved to death.

[4]Successful generals were sometimes honored with wearing purple in trimphal parades that included gilded palm branches.

[5]Usener's conjecture *Minturnensibus* 'Minturnan' is found in MS **N** where most of the others have the corruption *mittitur nec ibi* or something similar.

[6]Usener indicated a lacuna and suggested filling it with *tractantes* 'discussing'. Prof. Monat does not recognize a lacuna.

[7]Accepting Ziegler's emendation *tristi sermone* 'sad account' instead of *ad istum sermonem* 'to that account'.

[8]Scipio Africanus Minor (c.185-129), Roman soldier and statesman. He was murdered in his own home.

Bithynia, and traversing Syria; after the blameless acts of his dictatorship, was slain by a sort of private punishment within his private walls by the plots of domestics in a bitter agony of death, overwhelmed by the nefarious hands of those strangling his throat.

40. What good did faith do for Regulus,[1] that the force of Fate prostrated him after the wretched disgrace of captivity among hostile hands by the ceaseless atrocity of cruelty? What force other than Fate handed over the captive Crassus[2] and the Roman standards to the dissolute Kings of Persia? And certainly he had been a man of action, but the Roman army had protected his wealth,[3] which shone with its own ostentation.

41. After Pompey's fifth consulate, and after so many and such distinguished triumphs, on the bank of the River Nile, the sword of a eunuch had fallen with a heinous death on his unconquered and royal neck, which so many times had been encircled by a triumphal purple.[4] Who armed the hands of Cato[5] for his own [self-] slaughter? Who handed over the venerable blood of Cicero[6] to the effeminate desires of

---

[1]Marcus Atilius Regulus (d. 250 B.C.), Roman general and consul. He was defeated and captured by the Carthaginians and sent to Rome under parole to plead for a peace treaty, but he advised the Romans against it, and when to fulfill his promise he returned to Carthage, he was brutally put to death.

[2]Marcus Licinius Crassus (c.115-53 B.C.), Roman financier, triumvir (with Caesar and Pompey), and general. Successful as a politician, he sought military glory and embarked on an expedition in the Middle East, but after initial successes, the Parthians lured him and his army into an ambush, in which he was captured and killed on 8 June 53 B.C.

[3]The Latin has *virtutes* 'virtues', but Crassus was famous for being extremely rich, not for having outstanding virtues. I have therefore conjectured **divitias* 'wealth' to replace *virtutes*.

[4]Gnaeus Pompeius Magnus (106-48), Roman General and Statesman. Having arrived by sea at Pelusium in September 48 B.C., Pompey got onto a small boat to go ashore, and according to one account he was murdered in the boat by the eunuch Photinus, either at the order of or at least with the acquiescence of the juvenile King Ptolemy XII (c.61-47), who was watching from the shore. The king's intent was to curry favor with Julius Caesar, who was expected soon after. But it didn't work—despite their personal rivalry, Caesar resented the cold-blooded murder of his former friend.

[5]Marcus Porcius Cato (95-46 B.C.), Roman statesman, a political rival of Julius Caesar. When his military forces were defeated by Caesar's forces at Thapsus, he committed suicide.

[6]Marcus Tullius Cicero (106-43 B.C.), Roman orator and writer. After Caesar's assassination, Cicero allied himself with the forces opposed to Marc Antony. An order for his death was issued, and on 7 December 43 B.C. his carriage was stopped by armed soldiers, and he was beheaded.

Antony[1] amid the lugubrious and wretched lamentation of all? Caesar,[2] armed to the destruction of his own safety those whom he had [previously] freed from all fear by his own indulgence.

42. Do you see that always and everywhere Fortune is dominant! Do you see that the affairs of men are always varied and mutable![3] The brave man is overcome by the cowardly man. The inferior man has prostrated the good man. Justice does not profit just men. Providence often deceives the cautious. The unchaste and dissolute man is preferred in the seeking of honors to those who are chaste and sober. Men of action are despised; the shameless are praised; and whatever has profited this one, has deceived that one, [acting] with careless imitation.

Chapter 8.

1. All these things are conferred upon us by the courses of the stars. Fortune destroys us in these diverse ways. Whence, warned and formed by so many examples and so many reasons, we may thus prove the law of fatal necessity—not by license of arguments, nor by an abundance of words—but rather by the credible and right judgment of truth.

2. But indeed, those same ones who were contradicting this allegation of ours do agree to some extent, saying that there is certainly some force of Fortune and Fate, which they call *Himarmene.*[4] But they attribute certain things to this necessity by the license of their own disputation, which same things the law and the necessity of the Fates contradicts, and [so] it seems that it both can and cannot do anything.

3. For that which they call *Himarmene* they wish to be conjoined to the

[1]Marcus Antonius (c.83-30 B.C.), Roman soldier. Having been incorrectly informed that Queen Cleopatra had committed suicide, Antony fell upon his sword.

[2]Gaius Julius Caesar (100-45 B.C.), Roman general and dictator. He was stabbed to death by a group of former friends and associates on 15 March 44 B.C.

[3]As Prof. Monat points out, the Latin *varii...mutabilesque eventus semper* 'varied and mutable [are] the events always' is a modification of Virgil's famous quotation from the *Aeneid* IV.569-570 *varium et mutabile semper femina* 'fickle and inconstant is woman always'. Firmicus probably had in mind *Fortuna* 'Fate' and the *Parcae*, the three goddesses of Fate.

[4]From the Greek *heimarmenê* 'has been allotted' from the verb *meiomai* 'to receive one's portion or due'. This Greek word is also mentioned in Cicero's *On the Nature of the Gods,* I. 55.

nature of man and the other living creatures by some kind of association. And because we are made and begotten in such a way that, living for a certain time, [and] having completed the course of life, we are borne back from that unyoked fragility of body to that divine spirit who sustains us, we are obliged to complete that end by Fate and likewise by lot. So that, one and the same terminus of dissolution might bring to an end both us and all living things by that fatal law. But they want all things which pertain to the course of life to be placed within our own power, so that the life we live is ours, but the only [rulership] of Fate and lot seems to be that we die.

4. I know not what this diversity of conclusion accomplishes. I know not who can be persuaded [by] what is said. Some one grants that Fate exists and says the end of all things is brought about by fatal necessities; and with his own disputations, arising from that confession as it were, he prejudges, he lessens its power in the smaller parts, [while] he increases it in the larger—conceding many and more powerful things—so that he says that our acts are certainly placed within our own power, but he refers the end of living to the license of fatal lot! And in so inept a disputation, he exalts himself by the license of argumentation, so that although he attributes the license of punishing in some measure to Fate, and he concedes [to it also] the high command of all power, that which is less, he denies to it—namely, the powers of ruling man.

5. If Fate brings us creatures forth into the light, and opens the gates of life to earthly affairs to men coming [to birth]. If it is [through the rulership] of this, just as they confess, that whatever is exacted from us in the complete course of life by the necessity of death. If it fixes for us the beginning and end of living by the necessity of fatal law, what is left that is not placed in its power, when both the beginning of life are conferred by Fate on those being born; and the day of death and the end of living is terminated by its decrees and judgments?

6. Behold, this one, with his body not yet completely formed in his mother's vitals, he dies prematurely. That one, with his body completely formed and freed from the confines of his mother's vitals, is not quickened by the breath of the vital spirit. The life of the fleeing soul deserts that one, stationed in the earliest infancy of life among the beginnings of his infantile crying. This boy, cheated by frailty, but now of youthful age and trained by the whole instruction of schooling for all the acts of life (which a little before our opponent was saying were placed within our own power), is taken away by sudden death. But this one with a great extension of life, while lacking almost every sense and a will [of his own],

and already of declining age and a sickly old-age [at that], yet against his will he endures a long and tedious burden of life.

7. Who is it who brings to death either this one unborn, or this one on the day of birth, or this one after a little while, or this one in youth, or this one in old age? Let the critic find anything that we may follow; let him find that which can instruct us—that which shows the reason of truth to us who are suffering. By all means he is going to say [that it is] Fate and the necessity of human death, which distributes to all living creatures that are begotten in earthly matter the time of living by its own distribution of judgment, so that it denies to some a longer substance of living, [but] bestows it on others.

8. It is absurd that he, first confesses to [the existence of] fatal necessity, and thereafter denies Fate. And it is very unjust that that he should refute in the latter parts of [his] declaration, what he had asserted so strongly in the preceding part.[1]

Chapter 9.

1. What should we say about the diverse exits of death? This one by the urging of Fate is hung from a noose. But this one is pierced through by a sword. This one is drowned in the sea or in rivers. This one, handed over to savage flames and fire, is converted into ashes and glowing cinders. This one is cast down from precipices. This one is crushed by the ruin of falling roofs. The deadly virus of poison excludes the spirit of this one. This one is cooked little by little by the slow heat of fever; while this one, glowing from a swift conflagration of burning veins, is scorched by the violence of sudden heat. The unexpected madness of savage beasts feeds on this one.This one suffers destruction [by being] dashed to pieces. And the stroke of the venemous serpent draws the veins of this one together in death.

2. The Fates will describe this[2] variety of deaths to us. These are those decrees of the stars which we set forth a little way back. Hence, the wretched exits of illustrious men, and the happy exits of bad and harmful men. Hence, the life of men passes through diverse courses

[1]Bram omits the number of this paragraph and appends its text to Paragraph 7.
[2]Accepting the Teubner editors' emendation *hanc* 'this' for the *hinc* 'hence' of the MSS.

with Fate always decreeing [the circumstances]. Hence, it is evident that the beginning and end of life, as well as the totality of our actions, inclinations, and desires, and whatever that is that pertains to the application of human reason,[1] rests upon the unavoidable sentence of fatal necessity.

3. And so, convinced by the assurance of verity, let us yield. And let us confess (having followed the judgments of true reason) that nothing is placed in our own power, but everything is placed in the power of Fate. So that, whatever we either do or suffer, the whole of it is conferred on us by the judgment of Fortune.

Chapter 10.

1. We have thus explained and treated all these matters which have demonstrated the force of Fate and the laws of the denoting stars in a statement of true reason. So let us now revert to that question which we laid aside in the first part of this discussion—namely, the one concerning the colors and customs of men. So that, having cleared away that question, and secure and strengthened in every way by the confidence of firmness, we may explain all that which we promised to you, Lollianus, about this study.

2. Who asks why in certain regions the bodies of men are always dirty with a black color, but why elsewhere they shine with a pure splendor of whiteness? To him who asks about these matters, I shall reply with a brief statement of the argument, especially since the easily taught opinions of many learned men are extended to this subject.

3. In the heaven as a whole, which has a rotund shape, which embraces the lands, the seas, and all those things that are within them with the circular diffusion of a fiery spirit,[2] <there are five separate zones, nor>[3] is

---

[1]Rejecting Kroll's emendation *nationis* 'of race' and reading *rationis* 'of reason' with the MSS.

[2]Cf. Marcus Tullius Cicero, *On the Nature of the Gods*, I. xiv, Section 38, *Cleanthes ... ultimum et altissimum atque undique circumfusum et extremum omnia cingentem atque conplexum ardorem, qui aether nominetur, certissimum deum iudicat*. 'Cleanthes ... then judges that the most certain god is that remote and highest and diffused on all sides and all-surrounding and embracing fire, which is called the aether'.

[3]The Teubner editors indicate a lacuna, for which I propose the words in angle brackets.

there one and the same substance in [each of] these five zones, for some of them are of a single form and do not have any alien admixture, but others are of a mixed temperament composed with moderation.

4. The one of these five zones that is in the middle—kindled by the lights of the glittering Sun and parched by the scorching of its eternal heat—is tinted by the glowing color of perpetual redness. But the two that encompass the extreme parts of the world (hanging on the right and left sides), distinguished by a dark blue color, are ever flooded by dark rain storms,[1] and—stiffened by ice and eternal frost—are besieged by snow hardened by cold.[2]

5. Between these two frigid parts and that fiery one, which goes about the middle of the world, two remaining ones are placed, which the mixed temperament of cold and heat has formed with a mild moderation. These are the two zones which engender every kind of living creature within the limits of the land from that tranquil moderation of commixture. Through which [zones] for all, that are begotten, rising and setting throughout the whole age, the oblique order of the signs is wheeled around; in which the Sun and Moon and likewise the five wandering stars (which are called *planets*[3] by the Greeks) run about with an always precise and defined motion, so that, in consequence of the courses of these stars, every kind of living creature continues itself with perpetual propagation of its kind.

6. The force and nature of these five zones beget men of whatever race with uniform color, but yet, in such a fashion that in that very condition of unity, men's [individual] bodies are varied by every sort of radiation from the stars.

7. Hence, whatever race of men is adjacent to that zone that is kindled by eternal scorching of fire, even though it is placed under the parts of its zone, which is formed from a composite moderation, it nevertheless borrows fire for itself from its conjunctions with neighboring society in order to fashion the colors of men, so that it darkens men with an always black form of color in imitation of things that are burnt to a crisp.

---

[1]Accepting Bentley's conjecture (based on similar passages in Horace and Vergil) *imbribus* 'rain-storms' in place of the *nivibus* of **Ω**. But Prof. Monat prefers to read *nivibus* 'snows' with the MSS.

[2]Sections 3 and 4 are reminiscent of Vergil's words in his *Georgics* I. 233-236, where he speaks of the five zones, one red from the heat of the glittering Sun, and two others with ice and dark thunderstorms (or 'snows' **Ω**)

[3]That is *planêtai* 'planets' from the verb *planaô* 'to wander about'. Unlike the "fixed" stars, the planets are "wanderers" in the zodiac.

8. Those parts, however, which adjoin the zones of ice, and which—bereft of and deserted by the warmings of the Sun—are oppressed by the perpetual snows of wintertime, make those races of men (which the neighboring zone generated), to be adorned with the glow of splendid whiteness. But also in those regions that engender white men, and in those too that engender blacks, the power of many stars operates to vary the [individual] forms of men; and to each man, although there is [only] one [general] substance of color, it nevertheless assigns a diverse kind of formation.

9. For by what means do they severally recognize themselves by the proper lineament of the body? By what means do they know sons, brothers, relatives—by what means, citizens, strangers, neighbors, friends, guests—if the power of the stars does not ascribe various and diverse features to individuals?

10. And so let us consider the whole of the human race, and we will find on reconsidering how nefarious and impious crimes could have been committed if a single face of all [persons] had confounded the people with a formation of equal likeness. So that, deceived by the likeness, a brother might go in to his sister as if he were her husband. And someone else might with an unchaste grasp drag away a wife legally belonging to another man. Some might struggle with a conflict of erratic contention over a son. Others would not know who those were who had served them a little while earlier. Still another, born of free parents, might, because of a confused likeness, be dragged away as a slave by the obstinate error of the one leading him, if the greatest dissimilarity of features did not vary that uniform likeness of color. All of which things are tempered by the composite mixtures and aspects of the stars.

11. Lo, the whiteness of this one is dirtied to some extent by the over-shadowing of a thin black color, and the splendor of a small [bit of] whiteness illumines the black face of another. What should I say now about the locks of hair into which a various color secretly creeps? What should I say about the pupils of the eyes, which are always colored with different lights? Lo, the very bodies also in these particular races and in all the others are now long, now short, now slim with a slender slightness, now broad with an obese thickness. Whence, by manifest reasons it is proved that it is certainly due to the zones themselves that there are blacks and whites, but it is due to the stars that in this unity of color individuals are embodied in varieties of dissimilar forms.

12. But a disputation on the subject of the customs of the races is superfluous. For indeed we see many Asians—indeed the greater majority of them—displaying the insignia of sobriety. And the levity of the Greeks frequently receives the weight of a modest gravity. And the unbridled madness of the Scythians is mitigated by a certain clemency of humanity. And within the borders of the Gallic nation the populace grows strong in the prudence of wisdom. And the ornaments of honest faith decorate the subtle minds of the Africans. While the faults of braggarty are abandoned by very many Spaniards. And a sudden generosity has altered the avarice of the Syrians. It is not difficult to find stupid [persons] among those sharp Sicilians. And frequently the imperial rulership is transferred away from the Italians.

13. And we shall not offer you examples of this matter at length from ancient books. Our lord and Augustus and Emperor of the Whole World—the pious, happy, provident Prince Constantius II namely the geatest son of the divine Constantine I,[1] a Prince of august and venerable memory,[2] who was chosen to free the world from the controls of tyranny and to curb the domestic evils by the favor of his own majesty, so that, having been cleansed of the squalor of servitude by him, the gifts of secure liberty were restored to us, and so that we might put off the yokes of captivity from our long fatigued and oppressed necks. Whom, always fighting for our liberty, the most uncertain thing among human chances, the fortune of war never deceived; born at Naissus,[3] holding the helms of empire from the first age of life[4] (which he had obtained with fortunate auspices), he sustained[5] the Roman World to augments of perennial happiness by the salubrious moderation of his rulership.

---

[1]The Latin text reads *Constantinus scilicet maximus divi Constantini filius* lit. 'Constantine namely the greatest son of the divine Constantine'. Boll and Ziegler would emend the text to read: *Constantinus scilicet maximus divi Constantii filius* and render it 'Constantine, namely the Greatest, son of the divine*Constantius', for Constantine I the Great was the son of Constantius I Chlorus. This is based on the assumption that Firmicus was writing in 335 or 336. But if he was writing after 337 and before 340, then the Latin would be correct as it stands and could refer to Constantine II and Constantine I, However, if I am correct in dating this text to some time between 346 and 354, then it should read *Constantius II and Constantine I.

[2]This indicates that Constantine I the Great was already dead when it was written; hence, it was written sometime after 337. He was deified after his death.

[3]Constantine I the Great was in fact born at Naissus (the modern Nish, Serbia).

[4]He became joint Emperor in 306 at age 21and sole Emperor in 323.

[5]The text has *sustentat* 'he sustains', but I have emended it to *sustentavit* 'he sustained'.

14. O Sun, greatest and best, who possesses the mid part of heaven, Moderator and Mind of the universe,[1] Leader and Prince of all, who perpetuate the fires of the other flame-bearing stars by the moderation of your own light. And you Luna, who, placed in the lowest regions of heaven for the perpetuity of the genital seed, always <augmented or diminished,> with monthly light, you shine with the august radiation of the Sun. And you Saturn, who, placed in the highest point of heaven advance the dullness of your star,[2] with a slow course and with tardy motions. And you Jupiter, dweller of the Tarpeian Rock, who gladden the world and the lands with your ever salutary and benign majesty, and you possess the rulership of the second sphere. But you Mars Gradivus,[3] fearful always with red terror, who are contained in the third region of heaven. You too, faithful companions of the Sun, Mercury and Venus, Constantine I the greatest Prince and his unconquered children,[4] our lords and Caesars, by the consent of your moderation and complying with the judgment of the highest God, denoting perpetual rulership of the empire to them, make [them] also to rule over our posterity and the posterity of our posterity through the unlimited continuation of the centuries, so that, with every harshness of evils repulsed, the human race may attain the gifts of peaceful and perpetual happiness.[5]

---

[1]The Latin has *mens mundi atque temperies*; Bram's translation, which I have adopted, is apt.

[2]Accepting Kroll's emendation of *livedinem* 'dullness' for *libidinem* 'lust' of most of the MSS of the **ΩΨ** families (*ibidem* 'in that place' **N**). Another possibility is *hebetudinem* 'sloth' or 'dullness'.

[3]In the early Roman religion the god Mars acquired the surname 'Gradivus', whose meaning is uncertain (perhaps 'Marcher').

[4]Constantine I the Great (c.285-337) and his sons: Constantine II (317-340), Emperor of Britain, Gaul, and Spain (337-340); Constans I (c.320-350), Emperor of The West (340-350); and Constantius II (317-361), joint Emperor (337-350) and sole Emperor (350-361). If the phrase "his unconquered children" is taken literally, then these words of Book I could have been written at any time before the death of Constans I in 350 (after which Constantius II was the sole surviving son). But even so, this would only date the writing of Chapter 10 of Book I to some time prior to 350 (after which only one son was still living) not the *Mathesis* as a whole, for Firmicus probably wrote Book I first. And he plainly states in the Preface to Book I that the completion of the entire work was long delayed and not finished until his friend Mavortius was designated consul (355). And dating this part of Book I to sometime prior to 350 would be consistent with the possible reference to his other book, the *De errore*, which appears to have been composed around 346 (see the note to *Mathesis* I. 2.8 above).

[5]This pious hope later lapsed with the death of Constantius II in 361, when the Constantianian dynasty came to an end, since none of the three brothers had any male heirs.

15. But inpire us with a thin substance of talent, so that strengthened by your support, we may readily complete those things that we have promised to Lollianus, and, whatever we have conceived of the divine magistery of wisdom, we may explain with true definitions of statements.[1]

All these things[2] that are said, [are] discussed with a rigid judgment of authority; for, just as you know, every nativity, if it was a nice one, will produce fruit that is precooked as it were, but milder soon in the space of adult times.[3]

---

[1]Note that Firmicus hopes that he will be able to complete the *Mathesis*. This statement indicates that he wrote Book I first and then began work on the remaining seven books.

[2]Reading *Haec omnia* 'All these things' with MS **N** and the Monte Cassino library catalogue rather than *Nec omnia* 'And not all these things' **Ω**.

[3]The Teubner editors think that the words in this paragraph are an interpolation and not part of the original text. However, if so, it is an old interpolation, for the Monte Cassino library catalogue of 1532 states that the MS **Casinensis 361** contains "Scholia of the Mathesis on astrology that begin *Hec omnia que* [All these things]"; and this is actually the way this passage begins in some of the MSS rather than with *Nec omnia quae* 'And not all these things…', as it is found in some of the other MSS (and in the Teubner text). Also, in some of the MSS it begins Book II rather than coming at the end of Book I. And this is consistent with the library catalogue and with Poggio's statement that the **Casinensis 361** lacked Book I of the *Mathesis*.

BOOK II.

Preface.

1. We ought first to institute these books of astrology which we are going to write, so that those who wish to learn it, formed by proper beginnings, may more readily attain the knowledge of delivering [a reading], for one cannot obtain a true knowledge of it unless he has been instructed in the first principles.

2. For our own Fronto,[1] who had followed the *antiscions* of Hipparchus, brought forth opinions of astrological significations[2] [written] just as if he were speaking with those already perfected and skilled—but offering nothing on first principles, and nothing on instruction. And hardly any of the Latin [writers] have written works on the first principles of this art, except Julius Caesar who wrote a few verses.[3] and even those were taken from the works of another. But Marcus Tullius,

---

[1]An otherwise unknown Roman writer on astrology. But Bram (Index of Ancient Writers on astrology) suggests that the name Fronto might be a corruption of Fonteius Capito of the first century B.C., who is said to have written on astrology. However, Firmicus calls him "our Fronto," which might mean that he knew the man personally; but could perhaps also simply mean that he wrote in Latin.

[2]Firmicus uses a Latin form of the Greek word *apotelesmatika* 'apotelesmatics' or 'things brought to a completion', a derivative of the verb *apoteleô*, which means to bring to an end', 'to complete', or 'to fulfill'. I suppose 'astrological significations' is reasonably close to the meaning, although there is an implication that it is a signification that will necessarily be fulfilled.

[3]But there was also a tract *De astris* 'On the Stars' attributed to Caesar, dealing with the fixed stars appearing on various dates in the new calendar. It has perished except for fragments cited by later writers. Prof. Monat thinks Firmicus was referring to Germanicus Caesar's translation of Aratus's *Phenomena*, and he notes that Firmicus does not mention Manilius. However, as we shall see in Book VIII, Firmicus evidently had at least a portion of Book V of Manilius's *Astronomica*, but without the author's name.

prince and ornament[1] of Roman eloquence, lest he should leave anything untried that that divine genius of his had attained, also gave forth a few heroic verses on first principles.[2]

3. Therefore, we shall convey all those things that the Egyptians and Babylonians have said concerning this art, with the instruction in easy language, so that those who are being shaped for explaining the fates of men, imbued step by step, may attain all the knowledge of divinity.

4. But because we have made mention of *antiscions*, we ought not to pass over this place with concealment. Fronto followed the *antiscions* of Hipparchus,[3] which have no force and no substance. And yet there are true opinions of judgment and of astrological significations in Fronto, but an ineffective study of *antiscions*, for he followed someone who had not arrived at true reason. For those *antiscions* are true, just as our own Navigius[4] also proves, and which Ptolemy demonstrated[5] with a true definition from investigation. And we shall show in the latter parts of this book what sort they are,[6] by demonstrating what degree sends its ray into what degree; for Fronto wrote very true astrological significations, and they are contained very abundantly in the books and records of the Greeks. And so, having set aside that disputation for the time being, let us revert to the commencement of the instruction.

---

[1]Reading *decus* 'ornament' with **AK** instead of *deus* 'god' with the other MSS.

[2]Cicero translated the *Phenomena* of Aratus, but only an excerpt of his translation has come down to ua.

[3]This statement is surprising because it was Hipparchus who decided to adopt the vernal equinox as the beginning of the zodiac. This then would imply that if he had ever said anything about *antiscions* they would have been symmetrical to the beginning of Cancer (and Capricorn), not to the sign as a whole, and would thus agree with Firmicus's own exposition of the *antiscions*. Perhaps there was some old writing that was wrongly attributed to Hipparchus, and it is that to which Firmicus refers.

[4]Another unknown Roman astrologer, unless his name is a corruption of Nigidius, a Roman senator of the 1st century B.C. who was an amateur astrologer.

[5]This is not true of Ptolemy's only known astrological work. In *Tetrabiblos* I. 15 (Robbins's edition in the Loeb Classical Library), Ptolemy explains the "seeing" signs as being "equally removed from the same tropical sign." This is perhaps carefully stated so as not to disagree with the original definition. But the word *antiscion* is never used anywhere in the *Tetrabiblos.* It is obvious that Firmicus did not have any of Ptolemy's books, so he has taken his information either from secondary sources or from some spurious tracts attributed to Ptolemy. However, If Ptolemy had said anything about antiscions, he would presumably have measured them from the beginnings of the tropical signs.

[6]See Chapter 30 below.

Chapter 1. The Twelve Signs.

1. The zodiacal circle, in which twelve signs are fixed, and through which the five planets, the Sun too and the Moon direct their courses, is continually whirled about with an oblique motion.

2. These same twelve signs moreover are called by these names: Aries, Taurus, Gemini, Cancer, Leo, Virgo, Libra, Scorpio, Sagittarius, Capricorn, Aquarius, and Pisces.

3. There are different genders of these signs, for some of them are masculine and others feminine; and so, Aries, Gemini, Leo, Libra, Sagittarius, and Aquarius are masculine, but Taurus, Cancer, Virgo, Scorpio, Capricorn, and Pisces are feminine.

Chapter 2. The Domiciles of the Stars.[1]

1. The Sun and the Moon are allotted only one sign each of these twelve signs, but the other five planets, i.e. Saturn, Jupiter, Mars, Venus, and Mercury, are allotted two each, in which they severally have rulership and their established domiciles.

2. But the Egyptians do not call these stars by the same names by which we and the Greeks call them, for the one that is termed Saturn by us is called *Phainon* by the Egyptians; the one we call Jupiter, the Egyptians call *Phaethon*; the one that is termed Mars by us is termed *Pyroeis* by them; the one that is called Venus by us is called *Phosphoros* by them; the one we term Mercury, they call *Stilbon*.[2]

3. And so Leo [is the sign] of the Sun, and he has his domicile and power in that sign; and Cancer [is the sign] of the Moon. See how aptly, <how recondite, how secret,>[3] how in accordance with <Nature>[4] [it is]

---

[1]The title given in the Index. The MSS have the title 'Which [stars] have these signs or domiciles'. Here and in what follows I have translated the Latin word *domus* 'house' as 'domicile' to distinguish it from the modern term 'house', which is now only said of the *celestial* houses.

[2]By "Egyptians" Firmicus means the Alexandrian astrologers who wrote in Greek. The meaning of these Greek names is as follows: Phainon = 'shining'; Phaethon = 'radiant'; Pyroeis = 'fiery'; Phosphoros = 'light-bringer'; and Stilbon = 'shining'.

[3]The words in angle brackets are added by **N**.

[4]This word was conjectured by Sittl and later found in **N**.

that the Sun is the ruler of a masculine sign and the Moon of a feminine one, so that in accordance with their own gender they lay claim to domiciles similar to themselves as regards their own sex.

4. The other five planets, however, just as we said above, have two signs [each] in which they exert the power of their rulership, but of the two signs which they severally possess, one is masculine, and the other is feminine. But, so that it can be more clearly understood, we shall explain the whole [scheme] in detail.

5. Saturn has his domicile in Aquarius and Capricorn, of which Aquarius is masculine, Capricorn feminine. Jupiter has his domicile in Sagittarius and Pisces; but Sagittarius is the masculine one of these, and Pisces the feminine. Mars located his domicile in Aries and in Scorpio, of which Aries is masculine, Scorpio feminine. Venus's domiciles are Taurus and Libra, of which Libra is the masculine sign and Taurus the feminine. Mercury has his domicile in Gemini and Virgo, of which Gemini is of course the masculine sign and Virgo the feminine.

Chapters 3 & 4. The Exaltations and Falls.[1] *[II.3]*

1. We should also know about the *exaltation* and the *fall*. That is, what the exaltations of the several planets are, in which they are elevated by a certain natural sublimity of magnitude, and what their falls are, placed in which they are weakened by the diminished power of their authority.

2. And so, they rejoice when posited in their own exaltations, and they then denote the insignia of the greatest good fortune, whenever the majority of the stars in the genitures of men possess partilely the signs of their own exaltations. But then men are oppressed with the misfortunes of bad fortune, whenever the majority of the stars are posited in those [signs] in which they lose much of their own power by humble dejection.

3. Exaltations, moreover, are [so] called because when the stars are in those very degrees in which they are exalted, namely in the favorable houses of a nativity. they make <happy, illustrious, powerful, fortunate,

[1]In the Index, this chapter is split into Chapter 3 "The Exaltations" and Chapter 4 "The Falls." The MSS have "The Exaltations and Falls of the Stars" as a single chapter. In order to preserve the chapter numbers of the Index hereafter, I have assigned a double number to this chapter.

and wealthy persons. But in their falls they make>[1] wretched, poverty-stricken, low-born persons, and those on whom bad fortune is conferred in an incessant series [of mishaps].

4. For this reason, the Babylonians would have it that those signs in which the stars are exalted are their *domiciles*; moreover, we ought to understand—guided by this instruction—that all the stars are better <posited>[2] in their own exaltations than in their own domiciles.

5. The Sun is exalted in the 19th degree of Aries but is in his fall in the 19th degree of Libra.[3] The Moon is exalted in the 3rd degree of Taurus, and is in her fall in the 3rd of Scorpio. Saturn is exalted in the 19th degree of Libra; his fall is in the 19th degree of Aries.[4] Jupiter is exalted in the 15th degree of Cancer, but is in his fall in the 15th degree of Capricorn.[5] Mars is exalted in the 28th degree of Capricorn but is in his fall in the 28th degree[6] of Cancer. Venus is exalted in the 27th degree of Pisces and is in her fall in the 27th degree of Virgo. Mercury is exalted in the 15th degree of Virgo but is in his fall in the 15th degree of Pisces.[7]

6. On this account, the Babylonians will have it that these signs in which they are individually exalted are their domiciles, [thus] declaring that Saturn's domicile is in fact Libra, Jupiter's Cancer, Mars's Capricorn, the Sun's Aries the Moon's Taurus, Venus's Pisces,[8] and Mercury's Virgo.

---

[1]The words in angle brackets are supplied by MS **N**. They are omitted by the **Ω** and **Ψ** families of MSS due to homoeoteleuton (... *faciunt* | ... *faciunt*).

[2]**N** adds *esse collocatas* 'are posited'.

[3]The earliest preserved degree numbers for the exaltations are contained in the Greek verses of Dorotheus of Sidon (first century) cited by the early fifth century astrologer Hephaestio of Thebes; see *Dorothevs Sidonivs Carmen Astrologicvm* ed. By David Pingree (Leipzig: B.G. Teubner, 1976), Appendix II, pp. 323-324. The transmittal of these numbers expressed in Roman numerals in the Latin MSS has suffered some corruption.

[4]Reading with MS **N** 19 degrees for both the exaltation and the fall, which is confirmed by the same reading for the fall at 52,19. But while this must have been the reading of the archetype, it is wrong—Dorotheus has 21 degrees!

[5]The degree numbers shown are from Dorotheus. Most of the MSS have *XXI* and *XVIII* or *XIX* (**N** has *XVI* and *XVI*).

[6]The 28th degree according to Dorotheus and the **Ψ** family of MSS; the **Ω** family had variations *XXVI* **P** and *XXV* **RV**.

[7]The exaltation *signs* are due to the Babylonians, but the exact *degrees* of exaltation were supplied by the Alexandrians; their rationale is not known.

[8]The Babylonians actually designated both Pisces and Leo as the "exaltation" signs of Venus, but evidently the Alexandrian astrologers were content with just Pisces.

Chapter 5. The Decans. [II.4]

1. Each sign is divided into three parts, and each of these parts has a *decan*,[1] so that there are three decans in each sign, each of which possesses ten of the thirty degrees [of the sign] and exerts its rulership and power throughout the ten degrees. Furthermore, they are of unlimited power and license, in that[2] they denote the fates of men through the authority of their own power.

2. But these decans are also assigned to the individual stars, and if a star was in that very decan, even though it is in the domicile of another [star], it must be considered the same as if it were posited in its own domicile; for, when posited in its own decan, it performs the same things as it denotes when posited in its own sign.

3. In Aries, the first decan is [that] of Mars, the second of the Sun, and the third of Venus; Taurus's first decan is of Mercury, the second of the Moon, and the third of Saturn; Gemini's first decan is of Jupiter, the second of Mars, and the third of the Sun; Cancer's first decan is of Venus, the second of Mercury, the third of the Moon; Leo's first decan is of Saturn, the second of Jupiter, and the third of Mars; in Virgo, the first decan is of the Sun, the second of Venus, and the third of Mercury; Libra's first decan is of the Moon, the second of Saturn, the third of Jupiter; Scorpio's first decan is of Mars, the second of the Sun, the third of Venus; Sagittarius's first decan is of Mercury, the second of the Moon, the third of Saturn; Capricorn's first decan is of Jupiter, the second of Mars, and the third of the Sun; Aquarius's first decan is of Venus, the second of Mercury, the third of the Moon; in Pisces, the first decan is of Saturn, the second of Jupiter, the third of Mars.[3]

4. Some persons, wishing to explain this matter more subtly, attach three divinities to each decan, which they wish to have termed duty offi-

---

[1]The decans were originally 36 asterisms recognized by the ancient Egyptians and used to tell time at night. The fixed stars that appeared in them have not been identified. They were adopted by the Alexandrian inventors of horoscopic astrology in the second century B.C., distributed three to a sign, and assigned planetary rulers.

[2]Reading *eo quod* 'in that' with the MSS; the Teubner editors substitute *et qui* 'and who'.

[3]Note that the planetary rulers of the decans are assigned in the Alexandrian *heptazone* order (Saturn, Jupiter, Mars, Sun, Venus, Mercury, and Moon), beginning naturally with Mars, ruler of Aries.

cers,[1] i.e.*liturgos*, so that nine duty-officers can be found in each sign, so that each decan displays three duty-officers.

5. Furthermore, the nine duty-officers, which they say are posited in each sign, divide the powers of the divinities in an unlimited [number of ways], for they say sudden accidents, pains, illnesses, colds, and fevers are denoted by them, and what ever there is that is wont to occur without our wish or knowledge.[2] They will [also] have it that monstruous births are born to humans through them.

6. But out of necessity we pass over this part [of astrology] in this Book of Instruction, for even the Greeks, when in the first steps, have abandoned that subject with a certain disdain of concealment.[3] But now let the order of instruction return to the point from which it digressed.

Chapter 6. The Degrees of the Signs. [II.5]

1. Each sign has 30 degrees. A degree of a sign is as large a space as is comprised by the circle of the orb of the Sun or the Moon.[4] Each degree is divided into 60 minutes.

---

[1]The Latin word *munifices* 'duty-officers' is the equivalent of the Greek word *leitourgoi* 'civil servants'. Both words designate civil functionaries who carry out the orders of their governmenal superiors. These servants of the decans are mentioned in the Hermetic literature. See the "Discourses of Hermes to Tat" in *Hermetica* ed. & trans. by Walter Scott (Oxford: Clarendon Press, 1924. 4 vols.), vol. 1, pp. 414 ff. Note also that this nine-fold division of a sign is the ultimate origin of the *navâmśas* or 'ninths' so prevalent in Hindu horoscopic astrology, which was originally derived from Greek astrological treatises in the second century A.D.

[2]Cf. *Hermetica*, loc. cit. "Discourses of Hermes to Tat." These specific human ailments are not mentioned, but Hermes says: "The force which works in all events that befall men collectively comes from the Decans; for instance, overthrows of kingdoms, revolts of cities, famines, pestilences, overflowings of the sea, earthquakes—none of these things, my son, take place without the working of the Decans." (Scott's translation.)

[3]I think that Firmicus simply means that the Greek treatises that he had did not say much about the decans, and that is certainly true of the ones that have come down to us. Prof. Monat renders the Latin as "the Greeks have abandoned this chapter from the first steps, disgusted, to some degree, at being unable to explain it." Bram has: "The Greeks … stopped at the first stage and left the subject with a certain reluctance." But I prefer my own rendering.

[4]He means that the diameters of the Sun and the Moon are 1 degree, but actually, their mean diameters are only half a degree, namely 0°32′ and 0°31′ respectively.

Chapter 7. The Terms.[1] *[II.6]*

1. Even though the sign itself may be [subject] to the power of another [star] and contain the domicile of that other one, yet its degrees are divided amongst the several planets as if they were their own—which degrees are called the *terms* of the stars. The Greeks call these terms *horia.*[2] And we should consider this with a careful inquiry, for, when a star is found in its own terms, it is as though it were posited in its own domicile; all of which, so that it can be more clearly understood, we should explain in detail, so that from these terms the secrets of nativities may be known.[3]

2. Aries's ruler is Mars, as we have said, but its terms are divided among the several stars thus: from the 1st up to the 6th degree, Jupiter possesses the terms; from the 7th up to the 12th, Venus; from the 13th up to 20th, Mercury; from the 21st up to the 25th, Mars; from the 26th up to the 30th, Saturn. In this fashion the degrees of Aries are divided.

3. Taurus's ruler is Venus, of which sign the terms are divided thus: from the 1st degree up to the 8th, Venus possesses them; from the 9th degree up to the 14th, Mercury; from the 15th up to the 22nd, Jupiter; from the 23rd up to the 27th, Saturn; from the 28th up to the 30th, Mars. The stars possess these terms in Taurus.

4. Gemini's ruler is Mercury; the terms of this sign are divided thus: from the 1st degree up to the 6th, Mercury possesses [them]; from the 7th up to the 12th, Jupiter; from the 13th up to the 18th, Venus; from the 19th up to the 24th, Mars; from the 25th up to the 30th, Saturn.[4]

5. Cancer's ruler is the Moon; in fact, the terms of this sign are divided thus: from the first degree up to the 7th, Mars possesses [them]; from the 8th up to the 13th, Venus; from the 14th up to the 20th, Mercury; from the

---

[1]The Index has simply *De finibus* 'The Terms'. Most of the MSS have *De finibus in singulis signis* 'The Terms in the Individual Signs'. These are the Egyptian Terms originally prescribed by the Alexandrian astrologers. The rationale behind the assignment of the numbers is unknown.

[2]The Latin word *termini* 'terms' means 'boundaries' or 'limits', which is an exact translation of the Greek word *horia.*

[3]Since there are 60 sets of numbers defining the boundaries of the terms, the MSS obviously contain several errors. The earliest set of numbers that has come down to us for the Egyptian terms is contained in the Greek verses of Dorotheus of Sidon (first century) cited by the early fifth century astrologer Hephaestio of Thebes (op.cit., pp. 323-324). I shall note any discrepancies between these and those in Firmicus's text.

[4]Dorotheus has 13-17 Venus and 18-24 Mars.

21st up to the 27th, Jupiter; from the 28th up to the 30th, Saturn.[1] The stars possess these terms in this sign.

6. Leo's ruler is the Sun, but its terms are divided thus: from the first degree up to the 6th, Jupiter possesses the terms; from the 7th up to the 11th, Venus; from the 12th up to the 18th, Saturn; from the 19th up to the 24th, Mercury; from the 25th up to the 30th, Mars. Thus the terms of this sign are divided among the individual stars.

7. Virgo's ruler is Mercury; in fact, its terms are divided thus: from the first degree up to the 7th, Mercury possesses the terms; from the 8th up to the 17th, Venus; from the 18th up to the 21st, Jupiter; from the 22nd up to the 28th, Mars; from the 29th up to the 30th, Saturn.

8. Libra's ruler is Venus, but the terms of this sign are divided thus: from the first degree up to the 6th, Saturn possesses the terms; from the 7th up to the 14th, Mercury; from the 15th up to the 21st, Jupiter; from the 22nd up to the 28th, Venus; from the 29th up to the 30th, Mars.

9. Scorpio's ruler is Mars, but its terms are divided thus: from the first degree up to the 7th, Mars possesses the terms; from the 8th up to the 11th, Venus; from the 12th up to the 19th, Mercury; from the 20th up to the 24th, Jupiter; from the 25th up to the 30th, Saturn.

10. Sagittarius's ruler is Jupiter; the terms of this sign are divided thus: from the first degree up to the 12th, Jupiter possesses the terms; from the 13th up to the 17th, Venus; from the 18th up to the 23rd, Mercury; from the 24th up to the 27th, Saturn; from the 28th up to the 30th, Mars.[2]

11. The ruler of Capricorn is Saturn, but the terms of this sign are divided thus: from the first degree up to the 7th, Mercury possesses the terms; from the 8th up to the 14th, Jupiter; from the 15th up to the 22nd, Venus; from the 23rd up to the 26th, Saturn; from the 27th up to the 30th, Mars.

12. The ruler of Aquarius is Saturn, but the terms of this sign are divided thus: from the first degree up to the 7th, Mercury possesses the terms; from the 8th up to the 13th, Venus; from the 14th up to the 20th, Jupiter; from the 21st up to the 25th, Mars; from the 26th up to the 30th, Saturn.

---

[1]Dorotheus has 14-19 Mercury, 20-26 Jupiter, and 27-30 Saturn.

[2]Dorotheus has 18- 21 Mercury, 22-26 Saturn and 27-30 Mars.

13. Pisces's ruler is Jupiter, but the terms of this sign are divided thus: from the first degree up to the 12th, Venus possesses the terms; from the 13th up to the 16th, Jupiter; from the 17th up to the 19th, Mercury; from the 20th up to the 28th, Mars; from the 29th up to the 30th, Saturn.

Chapter 8. The Stars that Rejoice by Day or by Night.[1] *[II.7, first part]*

1. Having expounded and displayed the terms, we ought to explain which stars rejoice by day and whose *sect* they follow, and likewise which rejoice by night and whose sect they follow.

2. The Sun, Jupiter, and Saturn rejoice by day, and so Jupiter and Saturn follow the sect of the Sun. Therefore, when not posited in opportune houses in diurnal nativities,[2] they denote <dam>ages[3] and evils.....[4]

---

[1]The Chapter title given in the Index. In the text, the title of the Chapter is *De Stellarum Conditione* 'The Condition of the Stars', where *conditio* 'condition' or 'mode' is Firmicus's rendering of the Greek word *hairesis* 'sect'. Obviously, as noted previously, the Chapter titles in the Index were not written by the same person who wrote those in the received text. The sect of the planets was very important in classical Greek astrology, but it is ignored by modern astrologers.

[2]Bram accepts the Teubner editors' deletion of *non* 'not' and their postulating a lacuna after 'diurnal nativities'.

She then adds four more lines of her own to speak of the stars of the nocturnal sect. The addition is appropriate to the Chapter but not where it is placed.

[3]Reading **<dam>na malaque* 'damages and evils' with MS **H**; the other MSS have simply *malaque* 'and evils'.

[4]The Teubner editors have wrongly placed the words *malaque decernunt* 'and they denote evils' after the lacuna and followed by the words *Nam si deficientem Lunam deficiens Venus exceperit* 'For if Venus receives the waning Moon'. But the Latin text they publish at 49,14-50,7 as a continuation of Chapter 8 (their Chapter 7) does not belong here; it is actually the latter part of Chapter 11 (a Chapter they say is missing) as I have shown it. Bram did not notice this, but Prof. Monat did, although he takes no note here of the missing Chapters 9 & 10. Also, at this point (49,13), the older MSS descended from the lost MS **Ω** leave off and do not resume until Chapter 16.5 ("Pisces is a feminine sign. . . ."), at Teubner 53,16 (their Chapter 10). The intermediate text is from the later MSS descended from the lost 15th century MS Ψ and its exemplar the lost part of **Casinensis 361.**

Chapter 9. The Natures of the Stars.[1]

[This entire chapter is lost. It was probably similar to Teucer of Babylon's *The Nature and Force of the Seven Planets*, the Greek text of which is edited in *Catalogus Codicum Astrologorum Graecorum*. Vol. VII (Brussels: Henri Lamertin, 1908), pp. 213-224. For a translation, see the appendix to my translation of Rhetorius's *Astrological Compendium*.]

Chapter 10. The Rising of the Stars.

[This entire chapter is lost. It apparently dealt with the phase relationships between the several planets and the Sun and was probably similar to Paul of Alexandria's *Introduction*, Chapter 14 "The Phases that the Five Stars Make with the Sun," although some of this is dealt with in Chapter 12 below.]

Chapter 11. What the Moon Signifies when Joining to a Star.[2] *[II.7, second part]*

...For if Venus receives the waning Moon, or if Mars does so in a nocturnal nativity, it then denotes all kinds of prosperity and fortunate circumstances. But if the Moon, full of light or waxing, conjoins herself by any aspect to Venus or Mars, it makes the greatest calamities and the greatest misfortunes to be instigated. But this is why Venus is unfriendly to the waxing Moon—because they disagree between themselves with a certain natural dissonance of envy. Let it suffice that we have mentioned these things briefly in this Book of Instruction. For we shall explain everything about the Moon and about the other stars very fully in the rest of the books.

---

[1]Hereinafter I have numbered the chapters according to the Index; consequently the chapter numbers do not agree with those in the Teubner text, where only the *surviving* chapters are numbered. It would appear that at least one folio had fallen out of the archetype before any subsequent copies were made. Consequently, four (or more) pages of text were lost, comprising the latter part of Chapter 8, all of Chapters 9-10, and the first part of Chapter 11.

[2]The title of this chapter in the text is "The Applications of the Moon." As mentioned above, the first part of this chapter is lost.

Chapter 12. When the Stars are Matutine or when they are Vespertine. [II.8.1]

1. The five stars, i.e. Saturn, Jupiter, Mars, Venus, and Mercury are either *matutine*, or *vespertine*, or *setting*, or *hidden*[1] (which are called *aphaneis* and *synodikai* by the Greeks), or *acronychal*.[2] Moreover, we shall explain in what way they become such, or for what reason they receive these names. Those are *matutine* in their rising that arise preceding the orb of the Sun. But they are *vespertine* in their rising that follow the rising Sun. But *hidden* are those which the orb of the Sun hides.[3] *Acronychal* are those which rise when the Sun sets.

Chapter 13. The Configurations of the Stars.[4] [II.8.2]

1. We shall explain in the later books when these figures of the stars help and when they harm.[5] For we have not said this without cause. Moreover, in particular, it ought to be stated that the vicinity of the Sun is harmful to all the stars. But some will have it that Mars becomes fortunate when he is oppressed by the Sun's aspects, for, having venerated the Sun, he loses his natural malice.

---

[1]Since all these terms are now obsolescent in astrology, I will explain them. *Matutine* means "morning star," i.e. one that is visible in the east before the Sun rises; *vespertine* means "evening star," i.e. one that is visible in the west after sunset; *setting* means a star that sets as the Sun rises, i.e. one that is in opposition to the Sun.; and *hidden* means a star that is too close to the Sun to be visible.

[2]The Greek terms mean 'unseen', 'in conjunction', and 'at the point of night' (hence, 'at sunset'); the first two of these explain 'hidden', and the latter term, which I have rendered 'acronychal', means 'when the planet is in opposition to the Sun', so that it rises as the Sun sets. Astronomers call this phase 'in opposition'.

[3]Planets within 8 to 10 degrees of the Sun are not visible to the naked eye; hence, they are "hidden." They are also described by other writers as being *under the Sun beams* or *combust*. Modern astrologers favor *combust*.

[4]I have divided the latter two thirds of the Teubner Editors' Chapter VIII (their paragraphs 2 to 4) into two separate chapters to make the sequence of topics agree with the Index.

[5]The Teubner editors note that this promise was not fulfilled in the extant text of the *Mathesis*.

Chapter 14. The Customs of the Stars and at what Time they have their Strengths. [II.8.3-4]

1. We also ought to know this: with which one the matutine stars rejoice, and with which one the vespertine ones rejoice; for then they are protected, whenever they advance with a fortunate aspect. The other stars rejoice, posited with the Sun in their matutine rising. Then, the divine power of the Sun is protected by the best [sort of] aspect, whenever it is adorned with the matutine rising of the stars. But the stars become ineffective whenever they follow the orb of the Sun closely in a vespertine rising. Posited in the light of the Moon, they are protected by her strongest rays, when they go before her orb with any aspect.

2. Moreover, what the mixture of stars rising in the nativity effects, when the stars are made matutine, when vespertine. . . .[1] We ought also to show by how many degrees receding from the Sun the stars are made matutine.

Chapter 15. When the Stars are Matutine, When Vespertine.[2] [II.9]

1. For we shall explain[3] how the stars become vespertine and how matutine. The star of Saturn is matutine when it has receded 15 degrees from the Sun, i.e. when it has risen in advance [of it], it is matutine.

2. In a similar manner too [the star] of Jupiter is matutine when it rises ahead and is separated by 12 degrees, [but] Venus by 8 [degrees].

3. Mars too preceding and posited in the 8th degrees is made matutine. Mercury going ahead and in the 18th degree is matutine. But they are vespertine when the follow the Sun by the same number of degrees.[4]

---

[1]Kroll indicated a lacuna here, since the sentence is obviously incomplete.

[2]This title is from the Index. MS **N** has *Qua ratione stellae fiant matutinae aut vespertinae* 'By what Scheme the Stars are Made Matutine or Vespertine"; the other MSS have *Quibus partibus matutinae stellae vel vespertinae fiant* 'With which Degrees the Stars are Made Matutine or Vespertine'.

[3]MSS **DN** have *explicavimus* 'we have explained', rather than *explicabimus* 'we shall explain', but this seems to be incorrect.

[4]There is actually a difference in the number of degrees that each planet must be distant from the Sun to be visible in early morning or evening due to the brightness of the planet. But the numbers given here seem to be more influenced by the numbers usually assigned to the planets than to their differences in brightness.

Chapter 16. The Customs, Natures, and Risings of the Signs, and the Winds that are Subject to them. [II.10,1-5]

1. Now we ought to explain about the nature, forms, quality, substances, and risings of the 12 signs, so that we may impart the whole knowledge of this art very fully with clear expositions.

2. Aries is a sign in the sky [that is] masculine, equinoctial, solstitial, regal, fiery, <suited to> change,[1] quadrupedal, corporal, erratic,[2] with languid eyes, which by the Greeks . . .,[3] voiced, untamed, vile, and lustful. The domicile of Mars. The exaltation of the Sun around the 19th degree. The fall of Saturn around the 19th degree.[4] Triplicity by day of the Sun, by night of Jupiter.[5]

3. It is called *equinoctial* or *solstitial*[6] because in this sign the hours of the night and day are arranged with an equaled moderation,[7] which is called *tropicon isêmerinon*[8] by the Greeks. For, when the Sun is in Aries, it arranges the diurnal and nocturnal hours equally, so that the day has 12 hours, the night also 12. On this account, moreover, this sign is called

---

For example, 15 is half of Saturn's number 30, 12 is Jupiter's number, 8 is Venus's number and it is roughly half of Mars's number 15. Mercury is only visible near its maximum elongation from the Sun, which varies from 18° to 28°.

[1]Reading *ignitum, <aptum> ad *mutandum* (with *<aptum>* **N**) 'fiery, apt to change' instead of *ignitum, ad laniandum* 'fiery for being butchered'. The emended Latin is a rendering of the Greek word *eumetábolon* 'chngeable', which appears as an epithet of Aries in both Teucer and Vettius Valens. Bram translates the phrase *ad lanaiandum* as 'aggressive'. Prof. Monat accepts the Teubner editors' suggestion *lanatum* 'wooly'. But neither of those renderings is acceptable.

[2]The word *erraticum* 'erratic' could also be a translation of *eumetábolon*, but this is uncertain.

[3]Some words are missing in the Latin text.

[4]Again, the wrong degree number (19) is given for the fall of Saturn. Dorotheus has the 21st degree. Cf. the note to Chapters 3 & 4 above. Possibly, both here and above the scribe of the archetype or its exemplar wrote XIX by mistake for XXI.

[5]He means that the Sun is the ruler of the triplicity by day, and Jupiter is the ruler by night.

[6]Aries is equinoctial but not solstitial. Cancer and Capricorn are solstitial. See the note below.

[7]Reading **horae . . . componuntur* 'hours . . . are composed' (*componuntur* **DN**).

[8]Literally, 'tropical' and 'equinoctial'. Among the Classical astrologers, the term 'tropical' includes both the equinoctial signs Aries and Libra and the solstitial signs Cancer and Capricorn. Nowadays only the equinoctial signs are called 'tropical'.

Crios by the Greeks because when the Sun is in it, it *judges* as it were between day and night (which is called *crinein*), and because in this sign, it is *judged* again to be placed between winter and summer.

4. Moreover, it is called *tropical* for this reason—because the Sun placed in this sign makes the spring time, for spring begins when the Sun has entered the first degree of this sign. It is called fiery for this reason—because whoever in his nativity rulership ...

[The remainder of the significations of Aries, and all of those of Taurus through Aquarius are lost. The characterizations of Aries and Pisces were enlarged, and characterizations were supplied for the signs Taurus through Aquarius by the editor of edition **a**. These are translated in Appendix I.]

5. Pisces is a feminine, duplex, humid, watery, biform, scaly, spotted, crooked, mute, mobile sign; but one fish moves to the south, the other to the north. It is, moreover, the domicile of Jupiter. The triplicity by day of Venus, by night of Mars,[1] the exaltation of Venus around the 27th degree, the fall of Mercury around the 15th degree. Moreover, this sign is placed in the South Wind.[2]

[II.11.1-9]

6. Having explained the kinds and forms of the signs, and having described their nature in a diligent fashion, just as it has been handed down to us by the most learned teachings of the Greeks, we ought to show in the following section in how many years each sign arises in the nativity.[3] Moreover, we show how this is useful.

7. All the stars receive then their maximum power of denoting, and they then exert their own powers when the signs in which they are posited have risen. Moreover, they rise at various times and days and according

---

[1]Again, he means that the rulers of the triplicity are Venus and Mars.

[2]Following this, **A′** inserts a chapter heading *De Anaforis Signorum* 'The Risings of the Signs'. But the index does not countenance this, nor do all the MSS, so I have omitted the break. (I have also continued the paragraph numbers rather than starting them over again as the Teubner editors did.)

[3]Firmicus has in mind the application of the rising times of the signs to the timing of primary zodiacal directions, in which a degree is equal to a year. The numbers he gives are sometimes called "equatorial times," which are equivalent to 4 minutes of sidereal time.

to the climes;[1] whence we show which signs rise in which climes and at what time in this fashion.[2]

8. In the first clime, i.e. that of Alexandria, and in the second clime, which is that of Babylon,[3] and in all the rest of the regions that lie under these climes, the signs rise in this course of time: Aries rises in the 20th year, Taurus in the 24th, Gemini in the 28th, Cancer in the 32nd, Leo in the 36th, Virgo in the 40th, Libra likewise in the 40th, Scorpio in the 36th, Sagittarius in the 32nd, Capricorn in the 28th, Aquarius in the 24th, Pisces in the 20th.

9. In the clime that extends through Rhodes,[4] and in the other regions that lie under this clime, Aries rises in the 19th year, Taurus in the 23rd, Gemini in the 27th, Cancer In the 32nd, Leo in the 36th, Virgo in the 40th, Libra likewise in the 40th, Scorpio in the 36th, Sagittarius in the 32nd, Capricorn in the 27th, Aquarius in the 23rd, Pisces in the 19th.

10. But in the clime of the Hellespont[5] and the other regions that are under this clime, Aries rises in the 17th year, Taurus in the 22nd, Gemini in the 27th, Cancer in the 32nd, Leo in the 37th Virgo in the 42nd, Libra likewise in the 42nd, Scorpio in the 37th, Sagittarius in the 32nd, Capricorn in the 27th, Aquarius in the 22nd, Pisces in the 17th.

11. In the clime of Athens[6] and in the other regions that lie under this clime, Aries rises in the 18th year, Taurus in the 23rd, Gemini in the 28th, Cancer in the 32nd, Leo in the 36th, Virgo in the 41st, Libra likewise in

---

[1] *Climes* were bands of geographical latitude, which the ancients used instead of the precise degree of latitude.

[2] The rising times given by Firmicus are based upon arithmetical rising times devised by the Babylonians (before the invention of trigonometry by the Greeks). They were adopted by the Alexandrian astrologers in the early second century B.C. and were used by all the classical Greek astrologers until Ptolemy's tables became available in the fourth century. Vettius Valens, *Anthology* I. 6 & 7, gives handy rules for constructing tables of the rising times. They can be put in modern notation thus: $D = 2 \arccos(-\tan \varepsilon \tan \varphi)$; Aries rising time $= 80 - 5D/18$; interval $= D/9 - 20$. Where D is the length of the longest day (in degrees of sidereal time); ε is the Obliquity of the Ecliptic and φ is the geographic latitude of the place.

[3] The latitude of Alexandria is 31N12 and that of Babylon is 32N15; the rising times given are actually for Babylon according to what modern scholars call System "A."

[4] The latitude of the island of Rhodes is 36N00.

[5] The latitude of the "Hellespont" is about 41N03.

[6] The latitude of Athens is 38N00.

the 41st, Scorpio in the 36th, Sagittarius in the 32nd, Capricorn in the 28th, Aquarius in the 23rd, Pisces in the 18th.

12. In the clime of Ancona[1] and in the other regions that lie under this clime, Aries rises in the 15th year, Taurus in the 21st, Gemini in the 27th, Cancer in the 32nd, Leo in the 39th, Virgo in the 41st, Libra likewise in the 41st, Scorpio In the 37th, Sagittarius in the 33rd, Capricorn in the 27th, Aquarius in the 21st, Pisces in the 15th.

13. In the clime of the City[2] and in the other regions that are under this clime, Aries rises in the 17th year, Taurus in the 22nd, Gemini in the 27th, Cancer in the 32nd, Leo in the 37th, Virgo in the 42nd, Libra likewise in the 42nd, Scorpio in the 37th, Sagittarius in the 32nd, Capricorn in the 27th, Aquarius in the 22nd, Pisces in the 17th.

14. These are the risings of the signs, by which the individual stars are brought up to their [point of] efficacy.

Chapter 16a. Which Signs are Subject to which Winds. [II.12]

1. It is also proper that we know which signs are subject to which winds, for this knowledge is very necessary for us in astrological significations. The signs Aries, Leo, and Sagittarius are subject to the *North Wind*; Taurus, Virgo, and Capricorn to the *South Wind*; Gemini, Libra, and Aquarius to *Apheliotes*, which we call the *East Wind*; Cancer, Scorpio, and Pisces to the *Southwest Wind*, which is called *Lips* by the Greeks.

Chapter 17. The Dodecatemories. [II.13]

1. Now I shall show briefly how you may inquire about the *dodecatemories*, for some think that they can find the entire substance of the nativity from them, and they intimate that whatever is concealed in the delineation can be discovered from the dodecatemories.

2. Moreover, what the dodecatemories are is taught by this example. Whatever star you want to find the dodecatemory of, multiply its degree

[1]The latitude of Ancona is 43N37. The rising times are slightly off. A better set of numbers would be Aries 16, Taurus 22, Gemini 27, Cancer 33, Leo 38, Virgo 44, and the others in reverse order.
[2]That is, Rome, whose latitude is 41N52.

[of longitude] by twelve, and however many degrees there are, you will divide them among the signs, giving 30 degrees to each sign, beginning with the sign in which the star is whose dodecatemory is sought; and in whatever sign the last number comes to, that shows you the degree of the dodecatemory. But so that you may more clearly understand, we also give an example of this matter.

3. Put the Sun in Aries in the fifth degree and five minutes; twelve times five makes sixty degrees, twelve times five [minutes] makes sixty minutes, sixty minutes makes one degree, and by this the sum is 61. You give Aries, where we say the Sun is, 30, Taurus 30, [then] the dedecatemory is found in the first degree of Gemini.

4. Look also [to see] whether the Moon, full [of light] by day, throws her dodecatemory into the terms of Mars, or whether of little light, i.e. waning, throwws it into [the terms] of Saturn, or whether Mars in the DSC … or Venus into [those] of Mars, and Mars [into thoseof Venus … and they take their power from the terms and decans and the sects that may help or that may harm.[1]

5. The beneficence of Jupiter lapses when his beneficence is afflicted by the weakness of the sign, or the degrees, or the decan, or the exchanging of sect. But also the malevolence of Saturn increases more strongly when, provoked by the quality of the house, or by the terms, or by the decan, or by the sign, or by the [exchanging of] sect, he receives the power to do harm. In a similar fashion too [you may judge] the other stars.

6. Yet one thing should be known—that even though the planet Jupiter is a benefic, he cannot resist alone against the assault of Mars and Saturn if they constrain him with violent aspects. For else men would be immortal—if the benevolence of Jupiter were never overcome in the nativities of men. But because God the Artificer made man so that his substance, having passed through a certain space of life, is dissolved, it was necessary that when Jupiter, through whom the salutary guardianship of life is bestowed upon men, has been held back, the malicious or pernicious power of the malefic stars to extinguish man might persist with an augment of malice, so that, assailed by malevolent aspects, the composition of the body might be dissolved.

[1]The Latin text has two lacunae as indicated by the dots.

Chapter 18. The Eight Houses and the Angles[1] *[II.14]*

1. Now let us turn our attention to the exposition of the angles and of all the houses. For when all of these things have been diligently discovered by us, we ought to explain the several <houses of the nativity>,[2] through which the entire substance of the life of men is divided, but for the moment, [only] generally. For a little later, when we have come to the books of the astrological significations, we shall show in detail the method by which the several houses can be considered by secret inquiries. For he who is being instructed ought first to be instructed generally, so that, composed and shaped, he may more confidently learn the more secret parts of the nativity.

2. For when a house had been found by degree, it must be considered what sort [of a house] it is, in what sign, and in whose terms, and to what extent those stars bear testimony to it. Another matter that must be especially considered is the ruler of that house, i.e. of the sign—in which house it is placed, or in what sort of sign, or in what sort of terms—which matter must be inquired into with the greatest diligence. Also, whether it is adorned with the testimonies of the benefic stars, or whether on the contrary it is stricken with the onslaught of the malefics. Let us now revert back to the general definition of the houses, so that we may thus explain the order of the angles and of the other houses.

To be read carefully![3]

3. Generally the House of Life is in that sign where the ASC is located, the House of Hope or Money in the second sign from the ASC, that of Brothers in the third, that of Parents in the fourth, that of Children in the fifth, that of Illness in the sixth, that of the Spouse in the seventh, [and] that of Death in the eighth. All of which, making their beginning from the ASC, we have signified with the following definition of names: Life,

---

[1]The Index has the single chapter title "The Eight Houses and the Angles," but the received text has divided this into three chapters, which I have numbered 18, 18a, and 18b.

[2]The text has *singula †hominis* 'the individual ones of man', but some word or words should follow 'individual'. Némethy suggests *<loca> singula* 'individual houses'. I have accepted this and replaced the following *†hominis* 'of man' with **geniturae* 'of the nativity'.

[3]Sittl deleted these words. They may have been a marginal note in the archetype or its ancestor. But in their place, MS **N** has a title, 'On the Signification of the Houses'.

Hope, Brothers, Fathers or Parents, Children, Sickness, Spouse, and Death.

4. But, just as we said above, it suffices to have stated these things generally to form the beginnings for the learner. But later we shall take care to explain to what extent these houses are shown by the subtle definition of degrees. And of course you ought to know that those things which we say in the nativities of men—those same things are also effective in the nativities of women—being aware that [the star] of Venus shows the wife, the star of Mars the husband.

Chapter 18a. The Angles of the Nativity. [II.15]

1. In nativities, there are four angles—the rising,[1] the DSC, the MC, and the IMC, which houses are accustomed to be called by the Greeks by these names: *anatole*, *dysis*, *mesuranima*, *ypogeon*.[2]

2. The *rising* is the degree of the ASC . . . placed,[3] which is called *diametron dyticon*[4] by the Greeks.

3. But so that you may more readily understand, measure from the degree of the ASC through the other signs 180 degrees, and in whatever sign the 181st degree is found, in that very sign, <namely the seventh, it is found by degree. Which, so that you may understand it more clearly, in that very sign>[5] or degree of the nativity the DSC is located.

4. The MC is in fact the tenth sign from the ASC, but now and then the MC is also found *by degree* in the eleventh sign from the ASC.[6] But so

[1]Rather than the usual term *horoscopus* 'ASC', Firmicus puts here the less familiar *ortus* 'rising' and also in the next paragraph.

[2]Literally, 'rising', 'setting', 'midheaven', and 'under-earth'.

[3]The missing words were something like this: '<and the DSC is the degree> placed <to the opposite>'.

[4]The Greek words mean 'opposite setting'.

[5]Again, MS **N** supplies one or two lines omitted by **ΩΨ** due to homoeoteleuton (... *in ipso signo* | ... *in ipso signo*).

[6]Cf. Paul of Alexandria, *Introduction*, Chapter 30, "But it must be known that the culminating degree does not always fall in the 10th [house] from the ASC due to the inequality of the rising times of the signs, but sometimes in the ninth and sometimes in the eleventh." Possibly the Latin text should read *<in IX aut> in XI ab horoscopo signo*. As Paul says, the (astronomical) MC degree in moderate latitudes can fall in either the 9th, the 10th, or the 11th house of the Sign-House systems. Prof. Monat adds an inappropriate note.

that you may more readily understand, measure 270 degrees from the degree of the ASC through the other signs that follow, and in whatever sign the 271st degree is found, that is allotted the MC, which is called the *mesuranima* by the Greeks.

5. But the IMC, which is called *ypogeon* by the Greeks, is located in the fourth house from the ASC, but so that you may more readily understand, measure from the degree of the ASC, through a sequence <of three signs>,[1] 90 degrees, and where the 91st degree falls, there the house of the IMC, <i.e. the angle of earth,>[2] is placed.

6. These are the four cardinal points of nativities and of decrees (which we should always determine with a diligent system so that we may explain the entire substance of fate with the most accurate pronouncements.

Chapter 18b. The Favorable Houses. [II.16]

1. After these four angles, i.e. after the ASC, DSC, MC, and IMC, there are four more houses in nativities which have a favorable power,[3] i.e. *Goddess*, *God*, *Good Fortune* and *Good Daemon*, which are termed by the Greeks: *Thea*, *Theos*, *Agathe Tyche* and *Agathos Daemon*.[4]

2. *Goddess* is the third house, i.e. the third sign from the ASC; that house is called *Thea* by the Greeks as we just mentioned. But the sign is called *God* that is located in opposition across from that [previous] sign—that is to say the ninth sign from the ASC. That house is called *Theos* by the Greeks.

3. The *Good Fortune* is located in the fifth house from the ASC, which house is called *Agathe Tyche* by the Greeks. But the *Good Daemon* is located in opposition to that last sign, that is to say in the llth house from the ASC. That house is called *Agathos Daemon* by the Greeks.

---

[1]MS **N** adds *ordinem <trium signorum>* 'sequence <of three signs>'.

[2]MS **N** adds *<idest angulus terrae>* 'i.e. the angle of earth'.

[3]Deleting with Sittl *sequentem et* 'a following and'. But perhaps we should retain it and translate it as 'a secondary and'.

[4]Since these are omitted by MS **N**, they were probably written in Greek capitals in the archetype, i.e. ΘΕΑ, ΘΕΟC, ΑΓΑΘΗ ΤΥΧΗ, ΑΓΑΘΟC ΔΑΙΜΩΝ, but elsewhere in **N** they are usually transliterated. They mean of course 'Goddess', 'God', 'Good Fortune', and 'Good Daemon' (i.e. 'Good Spirit').

Chapter 19. Dejected Houses. [II.17]

1. The remaining four houses are said to be *inactive* and *dejected* on account of the fact that they are joined in no association with the ASC. Moreover, the first of these four remaining houses is that which is located in the second sign from the ASC, which house is called the *Gates of Hades* or *anafora*.[1] The house that is in opposition to this sign, i.e. in the eighth sign from the ASC, is called *epicataphora*.[2] But the last <houses>[3] are those of the *Bad Fortune* and the *Bad Daemon.* And the Bad Fortune is located in the sixth <sign>[4] from the ASC, but the Bad Daemon is placed in the twelfth sign from the ASC. But the Greeks call the Bad Fortune *Kake Tyche*.[5] The Bad Daemon, which is the twelfth sign from the ASC, the Greeks call *Kakodaemon*.[6]

Chapter 20. The Order of the Houses. [II.18]

1. Now we ought to know which of these twelve houses precede and which follow, i.e. which houses are first [and] which second, so that we can bring everything together in an accurate system.

2. The ASC precedes the DSC; the MC is put before the IMC; the eleventh house, i.e. the Good Daemon, is preferred to the Good Fortune, i.e. the fifth house; the ninth house, i.e. God, is put before Goddess; *anafora*, i.e. <the second house, is put before the *epicataphora*, i.e.>[7] the eighth house; the Bad Fortune, i.e. the sixth house from the ASC, is set ahead of the Bad Daemon, i.e. the twelfth house from the ASC.

3. Moreover, all these things must be known, so that when we have

---

[1]The Greek word means 'rising'. This is the only house that Firmicus specifically identifies as an *anafora*, but he may have intended it to designate both of the *anaforas* on the eastern side of the chart, namely the 2nd and 11th houses.

[2]The Greek word means 'falling down'. This is the only house that Firmicus specifically identifies as an *epicataphora*, but he may have intended it to designate both of the *anaforas* on the western side of the chart, namely the 8th and the 5th houses.

[3]The word *loca* 'houses' is omitted by **Ω**, but is present in **Ψ**.

[4]The word *signo* 'sign' is added by **A'**; **N** adds *loco* 'house', perhaps correctly.

[5]Again MS **N** omits the Greek words KAKHN TYXHN, which mean 'Bad Fortune', but MS **D** has KAKH TYXH.

[6]The Greek word means 'Bad Daemon' (i.e. 'Bad Spirit').

[7]This addition is conjectured by Kroll.

come to the astrological significations, mixing and blending everything together, we may strengthen our opinions with the faithful reason of truth.

Chapter 21. The Powers of the Twelve Houses. [II.19]

1. We ought now to explain in particular the significations of the twelve houses beginning with the ASC, so that, having expounded everything in sequence, the darkness of confusion may be illuminated.[1]

2. The first house is that part [of the chart] in which the ASC is placed. The life and spirit of men is contained in this house. The fundamental facts of the whole nativity are learned from this house. This house begins with that degree in which the ASC [was placed] and extends its powers through the remaining 30 degrees. It is, moreover, the principal angle as well as the framework and substance of the whole nativity.

3. The second house from the ASC is located in the second sign[2] and takes its beginning from the 30th degree from the ASC degree and extends its powers through thirty remaining degrees. The increases of hope and possessions are learned from this house. Moreover, it is an inactive house, unrelated to the ASC; for this reason, it is also called the *Gates of Hades*, because it is not conjoined to the ASC by any aspect.[3]

4. The third house is that which is placed in the third sign from the ASC, which takes its beginning from the 60th degree from the ASC degree and leaves off at the 90th degree. We may learn everything about brothers and friends from this house. The name of this house is *Goddess*. Moreover, it is the house of travel.[4] It also has a slight relationship with the ASC, since it is sextile the ASC.

---

[1]In this chapter, Firmicus will explain what is now called the Equal House system of house division, in which the houses are laid off at 30-degree intervals from the ASC degree. This was the second system devised by the classical Greek astrologers (the first being the Sign-House system), but it was seldom used.

[2]He means that the *beginning* of the house is located in the second sign from the ASC sign, and similarly for the rest of the houses.

[3]The classical Greek astrologers did not recognize the 30-degree aspect that modern astrologers call the semi-sextile, so there was no aspect between the 2nd house and the 1st house.

[4]Reading *peregrinationis* 'of travel' with MS **N** rather than *peregrinantis* 'of the traveling person'.

5. The fourth house from the ASC, i.e. the IMC, is placed in the fourth sign from the ASC, whose beginning, having started from the 90th degree, comes up to the 120th degree. This house shows us the parents, inheritance, assets, foundations, movables, and whatever pertains to hidden and remote sources of wealth. Moreover, this is an *angle* of the nativity, moreover it is called the *Imum Caelum*[1] for the reason that it is placed in opposition to the MC. But this house is conjoined with the ASC by maximum strength, because it aspects the ASC by square, and the ASC is square to it.

6. The fifth house from the ASC is located in the fifth sign from the ASC; taking its beginning from the 121st degree from the ASC, it extends up to the 150th degree. The number and kind of sex of the children are discovered from this house. Moreover, it is called the *Good Fortune*, because it is the house of Venus.[2] But this house is also conjoined with the ASC in the strongest association, and sometimes the degree of the MC is found opposite this sign.[3] For this reason, moreover, it is associated with the ASC by a very strong connection, because <it trines>[4] the ASC and is trined by the ASC.

7. The sixth house is located in the sixth sign from the ASC, which, taking its beginning from the 150th degree of the ASC, extends up to the 180th degree. In this sign we may discover the cause of a bodily defect and illness. This house is called the *Bad Fortune* on account of this—because it is the house of Mars. Moreover, this house is also an inactive house because it is conjoined in no association with the ASC, but sometimes the malice of this house is alleviated—if, when a star is posited in this house, another star in the tenth house from the ASC is in a fortunate aspect to it.

8. The seventh house is located in the seventh sign from the ASC, which, having started from the 180th degree, extends up to the 210th and there leaves off. Its beginning, moreover, is in the 180th degree. Another *angle* of the nativity is in this house; it is called the DSC by us, but by the

[1]'Bottom of Heaven'.

[2]Certain houses were said to be "the house," or "the joy" of a particular planet. These assignments were made by the Alexandrians because of a similarity between the nature of the planet and the nature of the house.

[3]Here Firmicus refers to the *astronomical* MC degree, which can sometimes fall in the 11th house of a chart drawn in the Equal-House system. See the note to the 11th house below.

[4]Skutsch adds <*de trigono respicit et*> 'it trines and'.

Greeks, just as we said above, *dysis*, which angle is placed opposite the ASC. From this house we seek the quality and quantity of marriages. But this house is also conjoined in a violent association with the ASC, for it is seen by opposition by the ASC.

9. The eighth house is located in the eighth sign from the ASC; which, having started from the 210th degree from the ASC, extends up to the 240th degree and there leaves off. This house is called the *epicataphora*. Moreover, it is an inactive house because it is not conjoined in any association with the ASC. From this house, the quality of death is discovered. Moreover, we should know that no star rejoices in this house save only the Moon, but even then only in nocturnal nativities. For if the waxing Moon is found in this house in a nocturnal nativity and Jupiter aspects her by sextile or trine, she being placed thus without any association or aspect of the malefics, in her own domicile, or in a domicile of Venus, or in a domicile of Mercury, or in a domicile of Jupiter, or in the terms of those stars which we have mentioned, it denotes the greatest good fortune, and riches without measure, and magnificent glories of power, and the evident ornaments of nobility.

10. The ninth house is located in the ninth sign from the ASC, whose measure, begun from the 240th degree, and extends up to the 270th degree. Moreover, it is the house of the *Sun God*. In this house we find the sects of men; moreover, it is about religions and of travels. And this house is conjoined by a very powerful aspect to the ASC, for it is seen by trine by the ASC.

11. The tenth house is located in the tenth sign from the ASC, which, taking its beginning from the 270th degree, extends up to the 300th degree and there leaves off. But this house is the principal one and more elevated in power than all the [other] houses. This house is called *Medium Caelum* by us, and *mesuranima* by the Greeks,[1] for it is located in the middle part of the whole World. In this house we find the life and spirit, also all the actions, the native land, the home, and all association, arts too,[2] and whatever is conferred on us by the approbation of [these] arts. From this house we readily discern the defects of the mind. The power of this house is conjoined to the ASC by the strongest association, for it is seen by the ASC by square.

[1]Both the Latin and Greek names mean 'Midheaven'.
[2]That is, 'professions'.

12. The eleventh house is located in the eleventh sign from the ASC, which house, having started from the 300th degree, is located up to the 330th degree. Moreover, this house is called by us the *Good Daemon* or *Good Spirit*, by the Greeks *agathos daemon.*[1] The MC is frequently located by degree in this house.[2] Moreover, it is the house of Jupiter, and it is conjoined with the ASC with no small relationship, for it sees the ASC by sextile, and it is seen by the ASC by sextile.

13. The twelfth house is located in the twelfth sign from the ASC, which house, having started from the 330th degree is located up to the 360th degree. This house is called by the Greeks *kakos daemon*,[3] by us the *Bad Daemon*. From this house the quality of enemies and the substance of slaves is shown to us with easy signification. We also find bodily defects and illnesses in this house. But this is also an inactive house because it is conjoined in no society with the ASC. Moreover, it is the house of Saturn.

Certainly too, in the nativity of both a man and a woman, the Sun shows the father, the Moon the mother, Venus the wife, Mars the husband.[4]

Chapter 22. The Names of the Twelve Houses and What they are Allotted and their Astrological Significations. [II.20]

1. Now because we have stated the qualities, names, and substance of the twelve houses, we ought to set forth these same houses with a brief signification. And so let us take the ASC as the beginning, whose primacy the rest of the houses support.

2. Therefore, it is fitting that these houses be called by the following names: Life, Hope, Goddess or Brothers, Parents, Children, Illness,

---

[1]Here again, MS **N** saw ΑΓΑΘΟΣ ΔΑΙΜΩΝ and left a blank space.

[2]This statement is not true of the Equal House system that Firmicus is explaining, since it can only happen in latitudes higher than 46° or so—say from Milan north—and even then only rarely except in northern Europe. Probably Firmicus had noticed this with charts drawn in the original Sign-House system, in which it can occur in lower latitudes. Despite his explanation of the Equal House system, he probably didn't use it. Most Greek astrologers used Sign-House, and the significations given in the *Mathesis* are all based on Sign-House.

[3]Again, MS **N** saw ΚΑΚΟΣ ΔΑΙΜΩΝ and left a blank space.

[4]These are the so-called *universal* rulerships, which have generally been used by astrologers, rather than *accidental* rulerships, which depend upon house placement and especially upon house rulership.

Spouse, Death, God, MC, Good Daemon, and Bad Daemon. Through these names and through these houses the substance of the entire nativity is sought; which, when you have diligently inspected them, and perceived them in your mind, and conjoined everything with mixed association, consider what stars possess these same houses.

3. You will also diligently inspect the *sects* of the diurnal and nocturnal stars, but also what sort of testimony the benefic stars afford in the several houses, and with what aspects the malefic stars strike these houses.

4. For, whatever house the benefic stars aspect, either by being placed in that same house or [aspecting it] by trine or sextile, they bring forth with good fortune everything that we have said was to be sought [from it].

5. But if, without the testimony of the benefic stars, the malefic stars alone—either being placed therein, or by square or by opposition—afflict these same houses; [then] according to the quality of each individual house, everything that we have said ought to be looked out in the individual houses they heap up with numerous disasters of misfortunes.

6. But if both benevolent and malevolent stars regard [them] with equal aspects, both the good fortune is lessened and the misfortune is mitigated, and the entire substance of the house is arranged with a moderate scheme of equality, so that, through the salutary guardianship of the benefic stars, they are freed from the hurtful malefics.

7. Also, look to see which star posited in which house, possesses the domicile or terms of which [other] star, and, if it is posited in the domicile of another, look at its ruler. What house of the nativity does it possess? And is it in the principal angles of the nativity, or in fortunate houses, or in inactive ones. And is it in its own exaltation, or else in its own fall. And see whether it is in those signs in which it rejoices, or is it in those signs in which it is made sad by a certain natural sorrow.

8. For, if the ruler of the sign is well placed, that star about which we are inquiring also borrows a part of its good fortune from the joy of its host. But if the ruler of its sign is afflicted in any manner, likewise that star about which we are inquiring, even though it is placed in opportune houses of the nativity and is strenghtened in a ready manner to perform something, [yet] from the affliction of the star that is the ruler of its sign, it is hindered by the afflictions of its partner.

9. And you can readily infer this from our own actions. If you have entered someone's house for the sake of hospitality, and the master of that house is in good spirits because of fortunate gains, then you too are a partner in his good fortune, for you borrow the delight of happiness from the good fortune of your host. But if your host is bent out of shape by wretched squalor and is involved in disheartening plights of misfortunes, then the shared torments of pain and misfortune also weaken you as well.

10. So also the stars—when the rulers of their signs are well placed … .[1] they disappoint, and to the condition of his own status, they adjust [both] the dweller in and the host of his own domicile with an equated kind of association. And they shape the power of the host according to their own license.

11. Take note also, if it is a diurnal nativity, where those stars are placed that rejoice in diurnal genitures, and where those are that rejoice in nocturnal ones. For if the stars that rejoice by day hold the principal places in a diurnal nativity and are found in the first angles, they denote the greatest increases in good fortune. But if the stars that we have said rejoice by night hold the principle places in a diurnal nativity or possess the first angles of the nativity, they indicate unlimited misfortunes with continual disasters.

12. We ought to observe this also in nocturnal genitures, but with a changed order of power, for if in a nocturnal geniture the stars which we have said rejoice by night possess the principal houses or the first angles of the nativity, in a similar fashion they denote the greatest increases of good fortune. But if in nocturnal nativities those that we have said rejoice in diurnal association possess the principal houses or the first angles of the nativity, they make the whole adornment of good fortune to be entangled with woeful occurrences of misfortunes.

13. If all of these things have been collected in a diligent manner, and if you have associated the mixtures of the benefic amd malefic stars, the strength of the houses, and the powers of the signs and degrees, with a balanced comparison of their connection, you can then delineate with a ready explanation of definition the whole man from his first day to his last day, and all of his life and hope, his brothers too, and his parents and children, illness, his marriage partner, death, religion, actions, honors,

[1]Some words are missing here—something like <*adiuvant sed cum male collocati*> 'they help, but when badly placed'. Bram renders the whole paragraph as "10. This is also true of the planets that are rulers of the signs."

travels, home, foundations, the substance of his friends [and] enemies, accusations, [and] dangers.

14. We have for the moment made sufficient mention of these things in this Book of Instruction. But when we have come to the astrological significations, we shall first say everything generally, and then with a subtle interpretation, showing everything with easy demonstration, lest any confusion arising from doubt should hinder your skill in delivering [an interpretation].

Chapter 23. The Qualitiy of Nativities. [II.21]

1. It is also fitting that we should know that it is a nativity of medium quality that has one star posited in its own domicile in the principal houses of the nativity. He who has two stars in their own domiciles in opportune houses of the nativity is elevated with moderate good fortune. He will be lucky beyond measure and powerful who has three. He who has four planets posited in their own domiciles attains a felicity nigh unto that of the Gods.[1] The substance of human kind can not endure beyond this number. But whoever has no planet posited in its own domicile will be unknown, of low degree, and always involved in wretched activities.

Chapter 24. Oppositions, Trines, Squares, Sextiles, and Disjuncts. [II.22]

1. In order to instruct an astrologer, we ought also to teach him in the beginning what an opposition, a trine, a square, a sextile, and an unaspected position is; also, what a right trine and a left trine, a right sextile or a left sextile is.

2. Aries's opposition is Libra, and Libra's is Aries; Taurus's opposition is Scorpio, and Scorpio's is Taurus; and all the rest of the signs in like manner. But in order that you may find this not only with your eyes but also by computation, we shall teach it with a brief example. From one

[1]The Roman Emperor Lucius Septimius Severus (145-211) had only one planet in its own domicile (Jupiter in Sagittarius), but he had three planets in their own exaltations (Sun in Aries, Moon in Taurus, and Venus in Pisces), which Firmicus would have pronounced equally remarkable. The Emperor had a successful career and was deified after his death. Unfortunately he kept his birth time secret, and it has not come down to us.

sign to another sign, which is the seventh [from it],[1] is an opposition; and this is always a malign and threatening aspect.

3. The trine is the fifth sign from the sign whence we begin, which is taught by this example: from Aries up to Leo is a trine; from Taurus up to Virgo [likewise]. Thus through all the signs whatever sign is the fifth, that is a trine.

4. We ought also to know what a *dexter* trine is, and what a *sinister* trine is. A dexter trine is the one that is behind the sign from which we start, and a sinister trine is the one ahead[2]; as, for instance, Aries's dexter trine is Sagittarius, but its sinister trine is Leo; and in similar fashion, Leo's dexter trine is Aries, and its sinister trine is Sagittarius; Sagittarius's dexter trine is Leo, and its sinister trine is Aries. So also you look for the trines in all the rest of the signs; this is a favorable and fortunate aspect.

5. The square is the fourth sign from the one from which we begin, which is taught by this example: Aries's square is the sign Cancer, and Cancer's is Libra, and Libra's is Capricorn, and Capricorn's is Aries.

6. But what a dexter square is, what a sinister square is, you will find in a similar manner, just as we said with the trines, for whatever is backward is a dexter square. Aries's sinister square is Cancer, its dexter square is Capricorn; just as in all the rest of the squares, that which is backward is dexter, that which is forward is sinister. And this is a menacing aspect and one composed of malicious power.

7. Sextiles are the same as trines, except that they are of lesser power; therefore, the sextile is the 3rd from that sign from which we start; for instance, Gemini is the sextile of Aries.

8. But what a dexter sextile is [and] what a sinister is, you will discover just as with the others; but, lest there be any controversy, we also give ex-

[1]The Romans counted both ends of an interval, so the opposite sign is the seventh from the first sign. We of course would say that it is the sixth. And similarly in counting the signs of the other aspects.

[2]*Behind* means 'before in the order of signs' and *ahead* means 'after in the order of signs'. For example, if a Planet is in Leo, then a Planet in Aries is 'behind' it in the zodiac, while a Planet in Sagittarius is ahead of it in the zodiac. And if you look at a sign from the center of the zodiac, then the right or *dexter* trine is the one to the right of it, and the left or *sinister* trine is the one to the left of it. The dexter aspects were considered to be more powerful, because by the clockwise rotation of the heavens, the planet at the dexter position rose (and culminated) before the aspected planet, while the planet at the sinister position rose and culminated after it.

amples of this thing: the dexter sextile of Aries is Aquarius, but Gemini is the sinister, thus too in the rest of the signs—that which is backward is dexter, and the sinister is that which is forward.

9. But those sextiles are more powerful which have a tropical or duplex sign in the middle, but those are inefficacious that are divided by solid signs.[1]

Chapter 24a. With what Aspects the Trine, Square, Opposition, and Sextile are Connected to the ASC. [II.23]

1. Now it must briefly be explained why we have said that some houses are connected with the ASC by the society of aspect, but some others are *averse* to the ASC and *alien* to it in a fashion, which terms we have not undeservedly termed *inactive*. For we ought to explain everything, so that this Book of Instruction may be fortified with the full substance of astrology.

2. All the signs are connected, linked to each other in turn. [Now] learn briefly why we say this. We have said that all the signs have 30 degrees. If, therefore, you make 12 times these degrees into one number, you get 360 degrees, which are divided through all the bodies of the 12 signs. Whence, the nearness of connection associates all the signs to each other in turn;. And so, whichever [of them] taken together a whole number [of times] makes 360 degrees; these same [signs] are connected to each other by an equated scheme of association.

3. We have said that the sextile is joined by the society of aspect with the ASC and with the others. Moreover, what a sextile is, we have both said previously and will now make known by degrees. Whatever degree is the 60th from the degree of the ASC, that very one shows the side[2] of the sextile. Therefore, if you combine 6 times 60, so that the whole number of 360 degrees is filled out, it is connected with equal society.

4. The trine, i.e. the fifth house from the ASC, and the others, whether it is a dexter trine or a sinister one, we have said to be connected with the

---

[1]A distinction unknown to modern astrologers.

[2]The aspects were viewed by the classical astrologers as multi-sided figures drawn within a circle; hence, they sometimes speak of the 'side' of an aspect, by which they simply mean the distance in degrees between the points of intersection of the corners of that side with the zodiac.

greatest association with the ASC or with the others. But let us also explain in what fashion this is done. Having started from the first degree of the ASC, we establish this house in the 120th degree. If, therefore, we triple 120 degrees, we complete the whole number of 360 degrees. This house is joined to the ASC by this [kind of] connection, but all the trines are joined together by this kind of association.

5. We have also said that the square is conjoined to the ASC by a most powerful association of aspect, but I shall also show briefly this scheme of connection. Having started from the degree of the ASC, we establish this house in the 90th degree; and so, quadrupling 90 degrees, we complete the whole number of 360 degrees. See how appropriately the square is the side of a sign! It is because the number of 90 degrees quadrupled completes all the substance of 360 degrees. Hence, for this reason it receives the name of square. This is the scheme in all the squares.

6. We have also said that the opposition is connected with the ASC in an association of aspect; but I shall also explain the scheme of this connection. <Having set out>[1] from the first degree of the ASC, we establish this house in the 180th degree; if, therefore, we double 180 degrees, we make the whole number of 360 degrees. Whence, because two whole numbers, i.e. joined together twice, yield the whole substance of 360 degrees, these houses are joined to each other with the greatest scheme of society. This is the scheme in all oppositions.

7. But those houses that are so placed that their degrees, by no doubling, tripling, or quadrupling, can make the whole number of 360 degrees, are not joined by any scheme of society with the ASC or with any other sign. And for this [reason], whatever sign is found outside this number is called *inactive* and *disjunct*.

Chapter 25. Which Signs are attributed to which Parts of the Body. [II.24]

1. We ought to explain which parts of the human body the twelve signs hold; for this also leads [us] most strongly to astrological influences, especially when you want to find the House of Illness or of Defect. Man's head is in the sign Aries, the neck in Taurus, the shoulders in Gemini, the heart in Cancer, the chest and stomach in Leo, the abdomen in Virgo, the

---

[1]Adds **A′**.

kidneys <and> the vertebrae in Libra, the nature in Scorpio, the thighs in Sagittarius, the knees, in Capricorn, the shins in Aquarius, the feet in Pisces. Thus, all man's members are distributed through these signs.

Chapter 26. Which God denotes how many Years of Life. [II.25]

1. Now we ought to explain this [matter]—which star denotes how many hours, days, months, [and] years—[and when] well placed, more, but badly placed, fewer.[1]

2. When you have diligently inspected the Ruler of Life, i.e. the Ruler of the Nativity, and you have seen in what house it is posited, and in what sort of sign, and in what sort of <degrees>,[2] but also [in the case of] the ruler of that sign in which the Giver of Life is posited, you have inspected in a similar manner in which house, and in which sign, and in which degrees, it is posited; and also, to what extent the Giver of Life and the benefic stars aspect the <Sun>[3] and the Moon, you will easily be able to define the substance of the whole life. For if the Giver of Life is itself also posited in a good house <and in a good sign>,[4] and in good degrees, the whole number of years is denoted, especially if Jupiter in a diurnal <nativity>[5] [or] Venus in a nocturnal one sustains the Giver of Life with a fortunate aspect.

3. If Saturn is the Giver of Life and decrees the whole number of years, he denotes 57 years; but if he decrees badly, he denotes 30 years, or 30 months, and 12 hours[6].

4. If Jupiter is the Giver of Life and decrees well, he denotes 79 years; if badly, 12 years, or 12 months, and 12 days, [and] 12 hours.

---

[1]This chapter gives what are called the 'great years' and the 'least years' of each planet. The great years are the sums of the degrees allotted to each of the planets in the table of The Terms According to the Egyptians. The least years are the minor recurrence cycles, in which number of years the planet returns approximately to the same longitude in the zodiac. O. Neugebauer, op. cit., vol. 2, p. 958, explains the Sun and Moon figures of 120 and 108 like this: their sum is 228, which is the number of solar months in the 19-year lunar cycle (12 X 19 = 228). But the reason for the 120/108 division is not known.

[2]Adds **Ψv**.

[3]Adds Kroll, having compared the text in iv 19.31.

[4]Adds **Ψv**.

[5]Adds **A′**.

[6]It should read 30 hours.

5. If Mars is the Giver of Life, [and] if he decrees well, he denotes 63 <years>[1]; if badly, 15 years, or 15 months, 15 days, 15 hours.

6. If the Sun decrees well, he denotes 120 years; if badly, 18 years; if moderately, 45.[2]

7. If Venus decrees well, she denotes 84 years[3]; if badly, 8 years, 8 days, 8 hours.

8. If Mercury decrees well, he denotes 108 years; if moderately, 79; if badly, 20 years or 20 months, 20 days, 20 hours.[4]

9. The Moon, if she decrees well, denotes 84 years; if badly, 25.[5]

10. If, therefore, the Ruler of Life or the Giver of Life, i.e. the Ruler of the Nativity, is in his own sign, or in his own exaltation, or his own terms, and if stars of his own sect afford good testimony to him, i.e. they aspect him with good aspects, and those stars that afford testimony are well placed, the greater number of years is denoted. But then they denote a midding age, if the Giver of Life is at least in his own terms, or in his own domicile, or in his own rising, but [with] the ASC in Libra.[6]

Chapter 27. The Ruler of the Times. [II.26]

1. The Greeks have termed the Ruler of the Times the *Chronocrator*; but the Sun receives the beginning of the times in diurnal nativities and divides [it] with the others; in nocturnal [nativities], the Moon receives it; and you should not admit any other scheme, because this is approved by everyone.

---

[1]Add **Nv**. And note that 63 years is probably a mistake for 66, which is the number given by Vettius Valens, *Anthology*, IV.30, and Paul of Alexandria, *Introduction*, Chapter 36. Probably the scribe of the archtype saw LXVI and miscopied it as LXIII—an easy mistake to make.

[2]Valens and Paul have 19 for the least years, and 69½ for the medium years. And probably we should add <and, 19 months, 19 days, and 19 hours>.

[3]Valens and Paul have 82, which is correct.

[4]Valens and Paul have 76 for the great years and 48 for the medium years.

[5]This line should read: 'The Moon, if she decrees well, denotes 108 years; if badly, 25 years, 25 months, 25 days, and 25 hours.' This means "25 years" or "25 months" or "25 days" etc. 25 years is a recurrence period of the Moon in the Egyptian calendar, for 25 X 365 = 9125 days, and in that number of days the Moon makes nearly 334 complete revolutions of the Zodiac, so that it returns to nearly the same degree.

[6]Perhaps because Libra is the sign of the balance, which would suggest a medium between the greatest and the least years.

2. When, therefore, the Sun is the Ruler of the Times, he holds the dominion for 10 years and 9 months. In similar fashion, also the Moon, when she is Ruler of the Times, will hold [it] 10 years [and] 9 months. Therefore, in a diurnal nativity, the Sun receives the first decade; the second [star], the one in the nativity who was found in the course of the signs in the second place; the third [star], the one who is after the second; and in similar fashion, the others. But, so that you may understand [it] more clearly, we teach [it] with this example.

3. If in a diurnal nativity the Sun was found in Aries, he will be the ruler of the [first] decade, but also in whatever other sign he was [found]. And whoever, therefore, was in Taurus, that one will be in the second place; and who was after Taurus, for that one is third; and so on with the others. We shall also proceed in this same way in nocturnal nativities, but beginning with the Moon.

4. But whoever is allotted the decade, even though he is the ruler of the whole time, still he divides the whole substance of the decade with all the stars, beginning with himself, and afterward handing over [the rulership] to those who are placed in order; first handing over to that one of them that is placed in order, whichever is found second in the map.

Chapter 28. The Division of Times. [II.27]

1. Furthermore, we shall briefly show how much the distribution of times is. The Sun receives 19 months, the Moon 25 months, Saturn 30 months, Jupiter 12 months, Mars 15 months, Venus 8 months, Mercury 20 months.

2. Moreover, we shall say what is done by this distribution of times in the Books of Astrological Influences,[1] and we shall show what each star denotes when it is taking the time from another star, because all those things that happen to us—good or evil—we gather from this scheme of times. The limits of life are also found thus, and the whole substance of the nativity, and everything that the order of the stars decrees.

3. Moreover, we find the year with very easy methods; for it always takes its beginning from the ASC, and the first year will be [the sign] in which the ASC is placed, the second in the second sign, the third in the third, and thus the others in order.

---

[1]At the end of Book VI.

4. Others do this same thing in diurnal nativities [beginning] from the Sun, in nocturnal nativities from the Moon; and [that] is [also] right.

Chapter 29. The Division of the Year. [II.28]

1. The days of the whole year are also divided by the individual stars. M oreover, how far they are divided, or from whence they receive their beginning, I shall also take care[1] to show ...[2]

2. when illnesses, when debilities, when gains, when losses happen, when joys, when sorrows. For when the benefic stars receive the days, we are freed from all evil; when malefics, the sudden blows of misfortune strike us.

3. And so, in whatever sign the beginning of the year is, the ruler of that sign receives the first days, and after him the others, according as they are severally placed. And so, which star is allotted how many days—this I shall also tell: the Sun 53 days, the Moon 71, Saturn 85, Jupiter 30,[3] Mars 42, Venus 23, [and] Mercury 57.

4. In this space of days, we can find all the things that happen to us, but first having looked carefully at the quality of the signs and houses. For well placed, if either the time or the months or the day was allotted, and it is benefic, it denotes all good things. But if a malefic star receives the time or the months or the days and is badly placed, it denotes misfortunes according to the quality of the places. Therefore, studying everything with prudent investigation, you will be able to explain most accurately the entire substance of the nativity.

---

[1]Reading *curabo* 'I shall take care' with Ziegler's emendation (Teubner ed. vol. II, p. 548) rather than *curae habebo*. . .'I shall have a care' followed by a lacuna and a new paragraph. (Bram follows the paragraphing of the printed text.)

[2]The Teubner editors indicate a lacuna here, and Prof. Monat agrees. But Bram ignores it, and it seems to me that the sentence is reasonably completed by the words in Paragraph 2.

[3]Jupiter should have 34 days. Vettius Valens, *Anthology*, 4. 3.12-20 explains how these numbers are calculated. To the number of months given for each planet in Chapter 28 above, double the number and add ½ and ⅓ of it. For Jupiter, this would give 2 X 12 = 24 + 12/2 + 12/3 = 34. The calculation for the Sun and the Moon gives 53 1/2 1/3 and 70 1/2 1/3 respectively. Firmicus or his source has rounded the Sun figure down and the Moon figure up. Mars is calculated at 42½, and it has been rounded down. The sum of all the numbers is 365 days (1 year).

Chapter 30. The Numbers of the Antiscions and their Astrological Signification. [II.29]

1. After all these instructions, and because a little earlier we put off the discussion of the *antiscions*, we ought now to explain that topic, lest anything may seem to have been passed over by us in this instruction. The antiscions were handed down to us by the teaching of the Greeks; for I do not want anyone to suspect that this [subject] is not treated of among the Greeks. For both Ptolemy,[1] who follows no other scheme than antiscions, and Antiochus,[2] when he says that Libra does not see Aries as if indeed in a mirror on account of the earth, which is in the middle, he indeed touched upon the scheme of antiscions; Dorotheus Sidonius,[3] in fact, a most learned man, and one who wrote astrological influences in most accurate and elegant verse, explained the theory of antiscions in clear statements, namely in his fourth book.

3. Now I shall briefly explain by what method antiscions are reckoned. The beginning of the antiscions is either from Gemini and Cancer or from Sagittarius and Capricorn. And so we begin, commencing from Gemini and Cancer. Gemini sends its antiscion into Cancer, and Cancer into Gemini, Leo into Taurus and Taurus into Leo, Virgo into Aries and Aries into Virgo, Pisces into Libra and Libra into Pisces, Aquarius into Scorpio and Scorpio into Aquarius, Sagittarius into Capricorn and Capricorn into

---

[1]This is wrong! Ptolemy never mentions the term *antiscion* anywhere in the *Tetrabiblos*. He does, however, mention 'the signs that behold each other' in *Tetrabiblos*, I. 15 "Again they say that the parts [of the zodiac] which are equally removed from the same tropical sign, whichever it may be, are of equal power … These are also said to 'behold' one another …" (Robbins's translation). But these are plainly the old pairs of signs, e.g. Gemini-Leo, Taurus-Virgo, etc., which are symmetrical to the whole sign Cancer, not to the solstice at the beginning of Cancer.

[2]Antiochus of Athens, who lived at the end of the 2nd century, was the author of two books on astrology, both of which are unfortunately lost except for excerpts and citations (such as this) preserved in the works of later authors, especially Porphyry and Rhetorius, both of whom copied whole chapters from Antiochus's book *Treasury*.

[3]Dorotheus of Sidon lived in the last half of the first century A.D. The book to which Firmicus refers is Dorotheus's *Pentateuch*, which has unfortunately not come down to us intact in Greek, although a few excerpts are preserved in the books of later authors. David Pingree has published an edition and English translation of the fragmentary and interpolated Arabic version of the *Pentateuch* as *Carmen astrologicum* (Leipzig: B.G. Teubner, 1976), but unfortunately the fourth book of the Arabic version is incomplete and contains nothing about antiscions.

Sagittarius. If, on the other hand, we begin from Sagittarius and Capricorn, they leave off in similar manner in Gemini and Cancer. And so, we ought always to investigate all these things with sagacious investigation, lest so honest a profession should on any occasion be overshadowed by false statements of astrological influences.

4. But that which we have just said about antiscions does not suffice unless the degrees shall also have been explained in particular—which [degree] sends into which [other] degree; and, on the other hand, whose antiscion it receives. And, among other things, it ought to be known that no degree sends into the 30th degree of a sign, and that the 30th degree sends an antiscion into no [other] degree.[1]

5. And so, this example that we have made from Gemini and Cancer will pertain to the antiscions of all the signs. The 1st degree of Gemini sends its antiscion into the 29th degree of Cancer; and again, the 29th degree of Cancer sends its antiscion into the 1st degree of Gemini, 2 into 28 and 28 into 2, 3 into 27 and 27 into 3, 4 into 26 and 26 into 4, 5 into 25 and 25 into 5, 6 into 24 and 24 into 6, 7 into 23 and 23 into 7, 8 into 22 and 22 into 8, 9 into 21 and 21 into 9, 10 into 20 and 20 into 10, 11 into 19 and 19 into 11, 12 into 18 and 18 into 12, 13 into 17 and 17 into 13, 14 into 16 and 16 into 14, 15 into 15 and 15 into 15, 16 into 14 and 14 into 16, 17 into 13 and 13 into 17, 18 into 12 and 12 into 18, 19 into 11 and 11 into 19, 20 into 10 and 10 into 20, 21 into 9 and 9 into 21, 22 into 8 and 8 into 22, 23 into 7 and 7 into 23, 24 into 6 and 6 into 24, 25 into 5 and 5 into 25, 26 into 4 and 4 into 26, 27 into 3 and 3 into 27, 28 into 2 and 2 into 28, 1 into 29 and 29 into 1.[2]

6. Thus, Gemini and Cancer send their antiscions into each other; for the degree from which it received an antiscion sends an antiscion to it from itself. And so, Taurus and Leo send into each other, so Virgo and Aries, so Libra and Pisces, so Scorpio and Aquarius, so Sagittarius and Capricorn.

---

[1]This is not strictly true. The 30th degree of Leo would cast its antiscion into the 30th degree of Aries, because the "30th degree" of Leo, as the ancients reckoned it, was what some modern astrologers would call "the 0th degree of Virgo," and the 30th degree of Aries was what they would call "the 0th degree of Taurus." But Firmicus had in mind the pairing of the signs Taurus and Leo, and to have said that the 30th degree of Leo cast its antiscion into the 30th degree of Aries would have seemed incorrect to him.

[2]The typical Roman was not good at arithmetic, so Firmicus is trying to make this as explicit as possible. But actually his statement and the table that follows are only strictly true for the degrees mentioned with zero minutes. For if we under-

7. Therefore, so that this may be more plainly understood, namely which sign sends its antiscion into which sign, I have written these degrees in detail, so that all obscurity may be resolved. And so, into whatever degree the first degree sends its antiscion, from that one it receives back an antiscion, so the second [degree], and so the other [degrees]. And so, we have written the degrees of Gemini and Cancer, which are suitable to serve as an example for the degrees of the rest of the signs, namely of those signs which we say send their antiscions into each other.[1]

1	29	15	15
2	28	16	14
3	27	17	13
4	26	18	12
5	25	19	11
6	24	20	10
7	23	21	9
8	22	22	8
9	21	23	7
10	20	24	6
11	19	25	5
12	18	26	4
13	17	27	3
14	16	28	2
		29	1

8. So Taurus into Leo, so Leo back into Taurus, so Aries into Virgo, so Virgo back into Aries, so Pisces into Libra, so Libra back into Pisces, so Scorpio into Aquarius, so Aquarius back into Scorpio, so Sagittarius into Capricorn, so Capricorn back into Sagittarius.

9. And so, if any stars do not aspect each other in the orderly arrangement of the nativity, it must be inquired whether they are connected to

stand "the 5th degree" to be any longitude from 4°00′ to 4°59′, then its antiscion will be in the range 25°01′ to 26°00′, which would be "the 26th degree." Or, if we adopt the procedure of the Babylonians and some modern astrologers and understand "the 5th degree" to be any longitude from 5°00′ to 5°59′, then its antiscion would be in the range 24°01′ to 25°00′, (most of) which would be "the 24th degree." But in this case we would have the pairing of the 5th and the 24th degrees, and in the previous case the pairing of the 5th and the 26th degrees. To persons accustomed to working with whole degrees without any consideration of the minutes, the pairings given by Firmicus would have seemed to be correct.

[1]A table of the antiscion degrees similar to the one that follows is found in all the MSS.

each other by the associated aspect of antiscions. For when they have sent their antiscions thus, they are connected with each other through their antiscions just as [much as] by a trine or square or opposition or sextile aspect. Thus, they denote [whatever they would] as if they were placed thus in the simple arrangement; and thus everything is completed by that kind of mixture. Because, when you have done this, you will be able to discover very easily everything that is sought in the fates of men. Moreover, there is this less obvious theory of antiscions that is proved by natural consensus, which theory I shall take care to explain at another time.[1]

10. Moreover, you will be able to discern how strong the force of antiscions is, and how much the scheme of antiscions is effective, from this nativity that we shall take care to submit. He,[2] in whose nativity the Sun was in Pisces, the Moon in Cancer, Saturn in Virgo, Jupiter in Pisces in the same degree as the Sun, Mars in Aquarius, Venus in Taurus, Mercury in Aquarius in the same degree as Mars, [and] the ASC in Scorpio[3]—the father[4] of this nativity, after twin ordinary consulships, was sent into exile. But [the Native] himself was also sent into exile because of the crime of adultery, and, snatched back from exile, was assigned the administration of the province of Campania, then the proconsulate of Achaia, but after that the proconsulate of Asia, and the prefecture of the City of Rome.

11. Any man, not knowing the scheme of antiscions, if he saw the Sun with Jupiter in the same degree in the 5th house from the ASC, i.e. in the

[1]As the the Teubner editors note, Firmicus neglected to provide this explana - tion—that is, it does not appear anywhere in that portion of the *Mathesis* that has come down to us.

[2]Theodor Mommsen identified this person as Ceionius Rufius Albinus, who was consul in 335 and Prefect of Rome in 336. Jerome Cardan, *De exemplis centum geniturarum* (Lyons: Hugetan & Ravaud, 1663, omnibus ed., vol. 5), p. 501, col. 2, mistakenly identified the nativity as being that of Firmicus's friend Mavortius Lollianus.

[3]These planetary positions correspond to the dates 13 to 15 March 303 around 10:30 PM LAT, at which times the tropical longitude of the Moon was in the beginning, the middle, and the end of Cancer respectively. But the tables from which Firmicus derived these positions probably contained a small positive error in the tropical longitudes, so the most likely dates are 13 and 14 March 303. At 10:30 PM on 14 March the the Sun was actually a degree and a half from Jupiter, and Mercury was 15 degrees past Mars. But the old astronomical tables had sizable errors in the position of Mercury, so the latter discrepancy is not surprising. Modern astrologers will note with interest that Uranus was rising in Scorpio in this chart.

[4]Gaius Ceionius Rufius Volusianus, who was consul in 311 and 314.

house of Good Fortune, [there also in the domicile of Jupiter],[1] would pronounce the father to be prosperous, fortunate, powerful, and other things of that same sort, but he would be unable to pronounce anything about his exile and the frequent plots against him unless he transferred his attention to the scheme of antiscions.

12. You will recall that we have said that Pisces sends an antiscion into Libra and Libra back into Pisces. Therefore, the Sun and Jupiter posited together in Pisces, sending an antiscion into Libra, into that sign in which it is humiliated and dejected, and also into the 12th house of the nativity, i.e. in the Bad Daemon, shows the paternal family to be of low degree, and it denotes a famous exile for the father himself. But Jupiter, whose force and power the aspect of the antiscion transferred from the sign Pisces to the sign Libra, in the 12th house, i.e. posited in the Bad Daemon by antiscion, aroused very many enemies both against him and against his father, and made those [enemies] superior.

13. There is also another thing that decreed the father's exile: for Saturn posited in Virgo was opposed to the Sun, and his antiscion looked back with an opposition aspect, for posited in Virgo, [Saturn] sent his antiscion into Aries; and so, his antiscion posited in Aries, and the Sun's antiscion, which had been sent into Libra, made contrary to each other by the opposition, by a decree of the highest order, made [him] to be sent into exile because of the fact that the antiscions of Saturn and the Sun were themselves in opposition.

14. But the scheme that made him an exile or the scheme that made him an adulterer (for he was accused of that crime) is shown by this scheme. We have said that Cancer sends its antiscion into Gemini, and so the Moon posited in Cancer sent her antiscion into Gemini, which antiscion Mars posited in Aquarius aspected from the right side[2]; and [Mars] is pernicious when he receives the light of the waxing Moon from either side. For a greater effect with many bodily faults at last made this same person an exile.

15. But Mars himself, posited in Aquarius, sent his antiscion into Scorpio, in which sign the ASC degree was posited. And first, indeed, posited in the IMC, he struck the degree of life, i.e. the ASC, with a violent aspect; then he aspected the Moon's antiscion in Gemini with a full trine;

---

[1]I have inserted this conjectural phrase in place of the meaningless words † *inde etiam Iovis Iovem cui dederit* †.

[2]That is, the antiscion in Gemini was in dexter trine to Mars in Aquarius.

third, his own antiscion sat upon the degree of the ASC; fourth, Mars's antiscion, which he had sent into the ASC, was in trine aspect to the Moon posited in Cancer.

16. And so, from all sides, the waxing Moon, struck by the aspects of Mars, made [him] first, burdened down with many illnesses, and finally an exile. And if Jupiter posited in Pisces had not aspected the ASC by trine, he would never have been freed from exile; and if [Jupiter] had not aspected the Moon in his own exaltation (for Cancer is Jupiter's exaltation) by trine, he would have perished by a violent death. But, we have also said in previous places[1] that the benefits of Jupiter of this sort leave off because of this—that on the third day,[2] the Moon posited in Leo [and] full of light, thrusts herself into the rays of Mars by opposition. For this day also, i.e. the third, works in many ways in the nativities of men.

17. But I shall also take care to explain what scheme made him an adulterer. Mars posited in Aquarius sent his antiscion into Scorpio; and therefore Mars's antiscion found <the opposition of>[3] Venus posited in the DSC of the nativity. For it is a wretched Venus, and one involved in many calamities, if, posited in the DSC, she is struck by a violent aspect of Mars. And again, Venus's antiscion sent into Leo saw Mars posited in Aquarius in the IMC by opposition; but from the IMC, Mars, without any scheme of antiscions, squares Venus. And so, by all these schemes, both through themselves and through antiscions, Venus and Mars in the principal angles of the nativity, assail each other either by square or opposition with an inimical sort of association. This scheme made him guilty of adultery.

18. But Mercury, posited in Aquarius, without the testimony of Jupiter, i.e. in a domicile of Saturn, and with Saturn in a domicile of Mercury, [the two stars] having exchanged their domiciles in turn,[1] makes him knowledgeable about secret writings. But because Venus sent her antiscion from Taurus into Leo, i.e. into the domicile of the Sun, and into the MC, it made the Emperor pronounce a sentence against him for these crimes.

[1]The Teubner editors note that Firmicus had not mentioned this earlier—at least in the received text.

[2]What we would call the *second* day after birth.

[3]I have added these words, since it is plainly the *opposition* of Mars's antiscion to Venus that Firmicus is talking about. Evidently some words have fallen out of the Latin text.

19. The Moon posited in her own domicile in the 9th, full of light, decreed the greatest honors for him, especially because in a nocturnal nativity, having followed the power of her own sect,[2] she had the prime place for denoting honors. Also, Saturn and Mercury having exchanged domiciles, decreed learning and such great knowledge of letters, that his speech and style are compared to [that of] the ancient authors.

20. Whose nativity this is, Mavortius my friend, you know very well. And so, having treated these things as a whole, you will find how much force there is in antiscions; which, if anyone shall have acquired it by diligent training, the effort of conjecture will never fail him when he is expounding the fates of men.

Chapter 31. What Sort of Life and What Sort of Practices Astrologers Ought to Have.[3] [II.30]

1. Now you, whoever you are, who is venturing to read these books, when you have received all the knowledge of divinity and when, steeped and initiated in the secrets of nature, <you have come to know>[4] the system of this sacred work, shape yourself in the image and likeness of divinity, so that you may always be adorned with the commendation of goodness. For it behooves him who daily speaks of the Gods or with the Gods to shape and instruct his own mind, so that he may always approach the imitation of divinity.

2. Wherefore, both learn and pursue all the ornaments of virtue. And, when you have instructed yourself therein, be easy of access, so that if anyone wishes to learn about something, he may approach you with no terror of trepidation. Be chaste, righteous, prudent, content with a small living and with small means, lest the ignoble greed for money defame the glory of this divine science. Take pains to surpass in your practices and your way of life the practices of good men and the way of life of priests. For the high priest of the Sun and the Moon and the other Gods, by whom

[1]In modern astrological terminology, they were in *mutual reception*.

[2]The Moon, a nocturnal planet, is "in sect" in a nocturnal nativity, such as this one; and here she is favorably placed in her own sign in an elevated house.

[3]This chapter is not listed in the Index. It is, however, a remarkable and unique code of ethics for an astrologer.

[4]I have inserted these conjectural words to fill the lacuna indicated by Sittl and the Teubner editors.

all earthly things are governed, ought always to instruct his mind in such a manner that he may be adjudged by the testimonies of all men to be worthy to be involved in such great ceremonies.

3. You will of course give your responses publicly, and advise the questioners of this beforehand. Namely, that in fact you are going to say to them in a clear voice everything about which they ask, lest by chance anything be sought from you about which it is not permissible to ask or to reply.

4. Take care that you make no reply to anyone who is asking anything about the state of the nation or about the Roman Emperor's life, for it is neither proper nor permissible for us to say[1] anything about the state of the nation because of nefarious curiosity. But he is both a miscreant and one deserving of every reproof if, having been asked, he does speak about the fate of the Emperor, because he will neither be able to say nor to discover anything. For you should know that even the *haruspices*,[2] however often they have been asked about the Emperor's situation by private citizens and have wished to reply to the questioner, always the entrails which had been destined for this [question] are [found to be] disarranged with an intricate confusion of the [normal] order of the blood vessels.

5. But neither was any astrologer able to expound anything true about the Emperor's destiny. For the Emperor alone is not subject to the courses of the stars, and he is the only one whose destiny the stars have no power of decreeing. For since he is the ruler of the whole world, his destiny is governed by the judgment of the highest God; and because the earthly expanse of the whole world is subject to the Emperor's powers, he himself is also constituted in the number of the Gods whom the Principal Divinity appointed to make and preserve all things.

6. This fact also confounds the *haruspices*, for whatever divinity has been invoked by them, because he is of lesser power, he will be unable to explain the substance of the greater power which is inherent in the Emperor.[3] For all free men, all ranks of society, all of the rich, all of the nobles, all honors, and all powers serve him. Having been allotted the power of license of a divine and immortal deity, he is established in the principal ranks of the Gods.

---

[1]Reading *dicamus* 'say' with Sittl, Ziegler and **PQR[b]VN** rather than *discamus* 'learn' with **MR[a]** and Kroll and Skutsch.

[2]Diviners who inspected the entrails of sacrificial victims.

[3]Deleting *enim* 'for' with **N** after *quae* 'which'.

7. Wherefore, whoever inquires anything about the Emperor, I do not wish you to embarrass him with a harsh and severe response, but persuade him with gentle speech that no one can discover anything about the life of the chief of state, so that, warned by your persuasions, he may—the error of his mind having been corrected—lay aside that furor of rashness. But I do not wish you to give any reply if anyone asks about anything evil; lest, when he has received a capital sentence for his illicit mental desires, you may seem to have been the cause of his death, which is alien to the priestly way of life.

8. You should have a wife, a home, and an abundance of honorable friends. Be constantly accessible to the public. Remain apart from all contention. You should not undertake any harmful business, nor should you let augments of money tempt you at any time. Keep separate from all eagerness for cruelty. You should never rejoice in the disputes of others or in perilous and pernicious enmities; but let a quiet moderation be pleasing to you in all association. Shun seditions; always shun boisterous contentions.

9. Bind the faith of friendship with strong ties. Take pains that your faith remains uncorrupted in all your actions. You should never pollute your conscience with false testimonies. You should never make use of the interest from money, lest a wretched augment of money be conferred upon you from the [financial] necessities of others. You should neither promise nor demand the faith of an oath, especially if it is demanded because of money, lest the divine assistance of the deities may seem to be implored because of a wretched gift of money.

10. To erring men, especially those to whom the ties of friendship have joined [you], show the right way of living, so that, shaped by your instruction, they may be freed from their former errors of life, so that you can educate the corrupt desires of men not only by responses but also by counsels. You should never be present at nocturnal sacrifices, either those that are held in public or in private. Nor should you join in conversation[1] secretly with anyone, but openly, just as I said above, under the gaze of all, you should reveal the learning of this divine art.

11. In delineating nativities, I do not wish you to explain very clearly the faults of men, but, as often as you come to that place, suspend your response with some hesitation of modesty, lest you should seem not [sim-

[1]Accepting Ziegler's emendation of *conseras* 'join in' for the *conferas* 'talk over' of the MSS.

ply] to *expound*, but rather to *reproach* that evil which the courses of the stars have decreed for the man.

12. Always keep yourself aloof from the enticements of spectacles, lest anyone should think that you are a fan of any part [of them]. For the high priest of the Gods ought to be separated and removed from the depraved enticements of pleasures.

13. When you have adorned your mind with these ornaments and defenses of virtue, undertake this work and with secure courage of mind go through the later books that we have written about the astrological significations. But if you have changed your own mind to any degree from those principles which we have spoken of concerning morals, see that you do not come to the secrets of this learning with an instinct of perverted desire or with a sacrilegious ardor of rashness.

14. Neither should you intrust the arcana of this religion to the errant desires of mind, for the perverted minds of men ought not to be initiated into divine cerimonies. But neither can the learning of this venerable science be at any time firmly fixed in a mind that is busied and polluted with corrupt desire; and the science always suffers the greatest loss when the immoral will of its professors stains it.

15. Therefore, be pure and chaste. And if you have separated yourself from all nefarious actions which are wont to destroy the mind; and if a right vow of living has freed you from all envy of evil deeds; and if you keep yourself purged [of evil] and mindful of the divine seed, [then] enter upon this work and commit to memory the following books. So that divinity may bequeath the whole science to you and may enter your mind with a hidden prophetic majesty. So that, having attained the true knowledge of divinity, in defining the fates of men and in explaing the course of life, you may be instructed not only by those things you have read, but [also] by your own mental judgments. So that more may be conferred upon you by your divinity of mind than by your mastery of what you have read.

BOOK III

Chapter 1. Man as an Image of the World. [III.Preface]

1. The whole discussion of astrology that pertains to the precise statement of astrological significations is now being transferred into statements. So that, having disclosed and demonstrated all those things that the divine ancients gave out, the complete system of this knowledge may be imparted by us to those men who are students of this art.

2. Therefore, Lollianus, my friend, we ought to know in the first place that God, the fabricator of man, with Nature pointing out the way, made man's form and state and his entire substance in the image and likeness of the World. For He composed man's body, like that of the World, out of a mixture of the four elements—fire, namely, and water, air, and earth—so that a moderate combination of all these might embellish a living creature to [resemble] a form like unto the divine. And so He composed man by the artifice of divine fabrication in such a way that, with Nature impelling, He brought together in a small body all the force and subtance of the elements. So that for the divine spirit, which descends from the celestial mind for the sustentation of the mortal body, He prepared a lodging—a frail one indeed—but still like unto the World.

3. On this account, the five stars, the Sun also and the Moon, with ignited and perpetual motion, sustain man as a sort of lesser world,[1] so that the living creature, which was made in imitation of the world, may be governed by a similar substance of divinity.

4. Wherefore, those divine men and worthy of all admiration, Petosiris and Nechepso,[2] whose knowledge approached the very secrets of divin-

[1]A *microcosm*, to use the Greek word.

[2]Two fundamental treatises of Horoscopic Astrology were written at Alexandria

ity with a divine mastery of science, have also handed down to us the nativity of the World, so that they might show and demonstrate that man, shaped in the nature and likeness of the World by those same principles by which the World itself is ruled and continued, is perennially sustained by fuels of perpetuity.

Chapter 2. The Chart of the World.[1] *[III.1]*

1. And so, those who followed Aesculapius and Hanubius,[2] to whom the most powerful divinity Mercury[3] entrusted the secrets of this science, have wanted this to be the Nativity of the World. They put the Sun in the 15th degree of Leo, the Moon in the 15th degree of Cancer, Saturn in the 15th degree of Capricorn, <Jupiter in the 15th degree of Sagittarius>,[4] Mars in the 15th degree of Scorpio, Venus in the 15th degree of Libra, Mercury in the 15th degree of Virgo, [and] the ASC in the 15th degree of Cancer.

2. And so, according to this nativity, and according to these conditions of the stars, and according to the testimony that they bear to this nativity, and according to those schemes, they also wish the fates of men to be arranged, just as it is contained in that book of Aesculapius that is called the *Myriogenesis*[5]. In short, so that nothing in the individual nativities of men may seem to be alien to that Nativity of the World. Let us, therefore, see which star accommodates its testimony to the luminaries, to what extent, and by what scheme of its own aspects.

---

in the early second century B.C. by unknown persons who wrote under the assumed Egyptian names of Nechepso and Petosiris. Those treatises are unfortunately lost except for a few citations by later writers.

[1]Since I have changed the title and numbered the previous chapter as the first, this chapter becomes the second chapter, thus differing from the numbering of the Teubner edition. I have shown the Teubner chapter numbers in brackets here and hereafter.

[2]Two early Alexandrian writers on astrology, whose books have not come down to us intact. Their names are those of the Greco-Roman God of Medicine and the Egyptian god Anubis, which names were chosen to give an impression of the divine origin of the books.

[3]That is, Hermes Trismegistus.

[4]Omitted by **Ω**, but present in **Ψv**, probably due to what Housman calls homeomeson (…parte XV… | …parte XV…)

[5]The Greek title means 'Ten Thousand Nativities'. This book was already mentioned in Book II and will be mentioned further in Books V, VI, and VIII. It is unfortunately lost.

3. Saturn first joins himself to the Moon, for he has followed the sect of the Moon; moreover, he follows the sect of the Moon for this reason—because, posited in a feminine sign, he received the opposition aspect of the Moon posited in a feminine sign. But in fact, when this same Saturn has made a transit to the sign Aquarius—namely in this nativity—he has on the contrary conjoined himself to the Sun with a similar aspect, and on the contrary to that sect to which the Sun belongs. For, posited in a masculine sign, he associates himself with an equable testimony of aspect, since he looks with aspect at the Sun by opposition, just as he did the Moon.

4. With this scheme too Jupiter is posited in Sagittarius, so that posited in a masculine sign and bearing testimony to the Sun by trine, he might first join himself to the Sun. On this account, posited in a masculine sign associated with the Sun and posited in a sign of the same gender, he follows the power of his transit first. But when he has made his transit into Pisces, he conjoins himself in equal condition in turn to the Moon; for in similar manner, posited in a feminine sign, he sees by trine the Moon posited in a femine sign with an equated scheme of sect.

5. In like manner also, the star of Mars, posited in Scorpio, because he is in a feminine sign, bears testimony by trine to the Moon; but when he comes to Aries, he passes to the testimony of the Sun; for, posited in a masculine sign, he conjoins himself to the Sun by trine aspect.

6. But, in the case of Venus, this scheme is changed; for, posited in Libra, since it is a masculine sign, she still bears testimony by square to the Moon. But when she makes a transit to Taurus, posited in a feminine sign and seeing the Sun by square, on the other hand, she offers testimony to him.

7. But in this nativity they wanted the star of Mercury to be common, because neither to the Sun nor to the Moon should it bear testimony by square or by trine or by opposition, nor should it conjoin itself with the Sun or with the Moon by that aspect, but rather it should be assigned by day to the Sun, if it is matutine, and by night to the Moon, if it is vespertine. All these things that we have stated they want also to be observed in the nativities of men, and they think that the fate of men cannot be found unless these aspects shall have been collected with sagacious inquiry.

8. But, lest the fabulous comments of men deceive anyone, and lest anyone think that this nativity was composed by most prudent men with-

out [any] cause, we should explain everything in detail, so that the most prudent scheme of this secret may be made known to all men by means of the most painstaking expositions.

9. [Actually], this was not the Nativity of the World,[1] for the World did not have any certain day for its origin, nor was anyone present at the time in which the World was formed by the plan of the divine mind and the provident divinity, nor could the exertion of human frailty extend itself all the way to the point that it could conceive or explain the origin of the World in ready fashion. Especially since the greater *apocatastasis*, i.e. restoration, will have been accustomed to be accomplished in 300,000 years through *pyrosis* or through *cataclysmus*;[2] for by these two ways, *apocatastasis*, i.e. restoration, is accustomed to be accomplished. Then, therefore, the flood follows the burning, i.e. the *cataclysmus* follows the *pyrosis*; for in no other way can the burnt up things be reborn, nor by any other way could they be recalled to their pristine shape and form, unless, by the admixture of water, the congealed dust of the embers could conceive the collected fecundity of all the genital seeds.

10. But, so that it might be that astrologers could follow this example in the nativities of men, the divine men fashioned this quasi-nativity of the World with prudent reasoning. And so it is pleasing to unfold the comments of this divine composition, so that the scheme of this admirable conjecture may be disclosed for the study of instruction.

11. They wanted to put the Moon in such a place so that first she would conjoin herself to Saturn and hand over to him the rulership of the times—not undeservedly—for because the primal origin of the World was uncultivated and rough and excessively savage with boorish behavior; and because the scheme of polite manners was lacking to rude men entering into the first (and to them unknown) vestiges of light, they wanted this boorish and rough time to be that of Saturn. So that, in imitation of that star, mortality established in the beginning of life might inure itself with boorish association and the inhuman provocation of savagery.

12. After Saturn, Jupiter received the power of the times (for the Moon was conjoined to him secondly), so that having abandoned the roughness of the pristine squalor, and with the savagery of boorish association laid

[1]MS **D** alone indicates a new chapter beginning with this paragraph with the heading *De prescripta figura non fuit genitura mundi* 'The Previous Figure was not the Nativity of the World'.

[2]These words of Greek origin mean: 'fire' and 'flood'.

aside, a more cultivated life of mankind might be delivered to purified customs. But in the third place, the Moon conjoining herself to Mars handed over to him the power of times, so that mortality, entered upon the right path of life and already established in a certain regularity of humanity, could conceive all the ornaments of arts and fabrications.

13. After Mars, Venus received the time of ruling; and, because man's knowledge, increasing step by step, also conceived the ornaments of judgment, this time, in which learned discourse refined the customs of men, and in which men were shaped by the natural science of the several disciplines, they wanted to belong to Venus. So that, advanced by the majesty of her delightful and beneficial divinity, they might govern their errant actions under the tutorship of foresight.

14. But they thought that the last time should be given to Mercury, to whom the Moon finally conjoins herself. What can be found that is more subtle than this arrangement? With all boorish acts having been cleared away, the arts having been invented, and training having been established through various actions, the exertion of human kind sharpened itself. And because a changeable streak in man cannot keep to a single course of life, confused by various principles and customs, the impropriety of malice arose, and the human race during that time both found and committed offences of crimes of life with criminal machinations. For this reason, they thought that the last time ought to be handed over to Mercury, so that, intent upon emulation of that star, the human race might conceive the full power of malice.

15. From these things, therefore, that were done in order, and by those men whoever they were who made the mutation of successive times, the nativity of the World was composed with the divine interpretation of conjecture; and to us thus far both the origin and the course of human kind is handed down, so that this would be that which we might follow as an example in the nativities of men. Moreover, lest anything might seem to have been passed over by us, everything must be explained that proves that man was formed in the imitation and likeness of the World.

16. We have stated that restoration is accomplished through fire and flood and this is approved by everyone. Also, the substance of the human body, when the course of life is completed, is dissolved in similar fashion. And however often the body of man by the natural ardor of heat, is too much relaxed, it disperses in vapor by the inundations of humors, so that it is always either boiled down by the ignited heat, or else it is dis-

solved by excessive sweating. Nor can the most prudent interpreters of the art of medicine declare that the substance of human kind is dissolved by a natural end, unless either moisture dissolves the fire; or else, with heat again predominating, the extinguished inner fire[1] will have dried up. Thus, in general, the Artificer Nature made man in imitation of the World, so that whatever thing either dissolves or forms the substance of the World, that thing also both shapes Man and decomposes him.

17. Now, why did they want the beginning of the twelve signs to be from Aries?[2] This also must now be explained because this question could not be explained in the Book of Instruction,[3] unless the Nativity of the World had also been shown, which I should not explain in the Book of Instruction, lest that exposition disturb the uninformed minds of the learners[4] with an obscure explanation.

18. Therefore, considering again the Nativity of the World, which we have said was composed most prudently by the wisest men, I have found that the MC of the nativity is placed in Aries. And so, on this account, because frequently—indeed *always*—the MC possesses the principal place in all nativities, and because that house is [located] above the prime vertex, and because [it is] from that house that we collect the foundations of the whole nativity—appropriately [then], the beginning of all the signs is given from that sign, especially since the greater part of the stars, and also both luminaries, i.e. the Sun and the Moon, have sent their aspects into that sign. From all of those considerations of the stars, it is fitting that the beginning [of the signs] be initiated from that sign.

19. Now, because these things have been stated and demonstrated, it ought to be defined what the individual stars denote in the individual houses of the nativity. And although some may think that this discussion is a generality, nevertheless it builds the talent of the learner by the easy tutorship of instruction, lest the astrologer—as if he were placed in darkness—should be disturbed by the vain confusion of error. But even though these things are thought by some to be defined only generally, many things should also be stated in detail in this book. For the stars will then have their own efficacy, if they are also located precisely in their own individual houses.

---

[1]Kroll would emend 'fire' to 'blood', perhaps correctly.

[2]MS **D** alone inserts a chapter heading before this paragraph *Quare Aries est primum signum* 'Why Aries is the First Sign'.

[3]Book II.

[4]Reading *discentium* 'learners', as the Teubner editors suggest, rather than *discentis* 'a learner'.

Chapter 3. What the Stars do when Posited in Each of the Houses.[1] *[III.2-14]*

Chapter 3a. The Star of Saturn.> [III.2]

1. Saturn partilely posited in the ASC by day, i.e. if he is in that very degree in which the ASC is, will make the birth to occur with a very loud outcry.[2] Moreover, the Native will be older than all his brothers; or, if one of them was born before him, that one will be separated from his parents. For always when this God is [posited] by day in any of the four angles, he will make [the Native] to be the first to be born or the first to be reared, or those brothers who were born before him <to be killed>.[3] He makes lofty individuals and those lifted up by a spirit of arrogance.

2. But if, with Saturn posited by day in the ASC, Mars possesses any other angle of the nativity or is in [a house] *anafora* to the angles, this signifies the occurrence of many evils. For it will make the greatest dangers and the loss of his inheritance. But frequently, if no benefic posited in a good house of the nativity has conjoined itself to those [stars] by a strong aspect, and if Mars has received any aspect of the waxing Moon, it makes those who die violently.

3. But if Saturn is posited in the ASC degree by night, whoever has him thus, is hampered by the greatest weaknesses, and he is always oppressed by much toil. And to some it will give activities around water, but in such a way that [the Natives] are always worn out by tedious work.

4. When Saturn holds the 2nd house from the ASC, it makes grave illnesses and the greatest losses. It is also the killer of the wife[3] and the chil-

[1]This is the title given in the Index. The Teubner editors numbered each following chapter separately, but I have distinguished them by an alphabetical suffix, since they are all considered to be parts of Chapter 3 in the Index.

[2]Cf. Rhetorius, *Astrological Compendium*, Chapter 57, "When the [star] of Saturn chances to be in the rising sign by day, it will produce a loud outcry and those things that are done for the Native through sound. And it also makes those who are first born or first reared or a lack of brothers before him; and always this god being present in the angles makes those who are first born or first reared or it destroys the brothers before him." Plainly, both Firmicus and Rhetorius derived these statements from the same source.

[3]Both Bram and Prof. Monat say the Native is the killer, but this is wrong. It is Saturn that is the killer because it is in the 8th house from the 7th, which is the house of death of the wife. Rhetorius merely says "it will make the loss of children and sizable disturbances."

dren, and the instigator of the greatest and most frequent disturbances; and it also dissipates both the paternal and maternal estates. But it makes the native more sluggish in all his actions, and it indicates continual bodily weaknesses.

5. But if, with Saturn placed thus, Mars was in any angle of the nativity and aspected the Sun by square or opposition, or if it aspected the waxing Moon in a similar fashion, it will make wretched and destitute paupers and those who injure their bodies with their daily work.

6. But if Saturn was in the 2nd house by day, slowly and gradually it will give increases to the paternal inheritance, but it makes the Natives themselves to be concealed, unnoticed, and poor in spirit, and always denying themselves something. But the means of livelihood are bestowed upon them by some acquatic occupations or by some business involving dampness.

7. Saturn posited in the 3rd sign from the ASC makes lazy, sluggish persons and those looking in vain for any wealth from inheritance. But if it is in this house with Mercury and the Moon, it will make wicked and stupid persons hurling sacrilegious words against divinity, always losing their own inheritance, [and also] thieves, but those for whom a favorable outcome never results from their theft. But if Mars conjoins itself in any fashion to these [stars] placed thus, it will make accusers,[1] sycophants, evil, malevolent, envious, malicious persons, and those always perishing by a bad death.

8. Saturn partilely posited in the 4th house, i.e. the IMC, will, if it holds this house by day, make those greedy for money, and custodians of gold and silver. But if it was in this sign by night, it dissipates the paternal inheritance, and it will cause the quick death of the father. It will also cause grave illnesses and cold bodily shakes. And it will always cause infamy in the first age [of life].

9. But if it aspects the Moon by square or by opposition, or if the Moon was posited in the same degree in which it was, it will make him to be barren of children. It causes the Native to adopt for himself the children of others, or it makes guardians of wards; and it disfigures [the Native] with some defect of illness from hidden pains. But it quickly makes the Native's mother to be a widow, and [a person suffering] from feminine [ailments]. And it imposes serious illnesses upon the Native, and it makes him to be worn out by chronic stomach pains.

[1]That is, the plaintiffs in a legal action.

10. Saturn posited in the 5th house from the ASC, if he was in this house by day, will make kings and military commanders, and he bestows the greatest insignia of power. But if, with Saturn thus placed, the Sun is found in the ASC degree, and Saturn receives the conjunction of the waxing Moon, it allots perpetual good fortune, and it denotes the trappings of superior power. But if, with Saturn thus placed, not the Sun but Jupiter was in the ASC, it will make [the Native to possess] the magistracies of minor places, [and to be] one to whom the governorship of individual cities is entrusted. Moreover, it will make them to be lords of the greatest inheritance, so that from their own abundant wealth they are also supporting others. But if neither the Sun nor Jupiter was in the ASC, and Saturn receives the conjunction of the waxing Moon, it will give assets and inheritances; but nevertheless, the Natives will frequently be without a wife, or they are joined in marriage to unworthy women.

11. But if Saturn holds that house of the nativity by night, with the passage of time some small portion of good fortune is allotted to the Native,[1] but it makes his strength inconstant, and it also shows him to be a man sluggish and lazy in all his actions. Moreover, if the waning Moon conjoins herself to Saturn, it makes some of them lose their inheritance, and it destroys whatever they had acquired previously with a wretched tearing away [of their assets].

12. Saturn posited in the 6th house from the ASC dissipates all the personal property, for it is always badly placed in this house. It also makes illnesses, especially if the waning Moon is conjoined to it; or if while declining she aspects it by opposition; or if while declining she aspects it by a square. It will make unfortunate, disreputable, erratic persons, who can never remain in one place.

13. Moreover, if Mars aspects Saturn posited thus by square or by opposition, or if he was with Saturn in the same sign, it will make hidden pains in the body, or consumption, or dysentery. And, if no aspect from a benefic star mitigates them placed thus, it will make the Natives to perish from these illnesses.

14. Saturn partilely posited in the 7th house from the ASC, i.e. in the DSC, if it is matutine—namely, in a diurnal nativity—will be good, and it decrees very great assets; but [only] then, when they have entered upon the threshold of old age; for thus placed it bestows the greatest [length] of

[1] Accepting Némethy's conjecture *homini*, 'to the man' instead of the *domino* 'to the ruler' of the MSS.

time to his old age. And it will make the Native to be a custodian of moneys. But it indicates hidden pains of body, for it makes those persons who have bloody discharges or those who are drawn up by muscular pains.

15. But if Saturn was vespertine in this house, it makes fistulas around the anus, and in like manner those who have bloody discharges, especially if Mars aspects it so placed in any manner. For it makes rheumatics and those who frequently have abscesses, and those whom the misfortunes of their wives always wear out with the heavy bitterness of sorrow.

16. Saturn posited in the 8th house, if it was located there by day, bestows increases in the Native's fortune as his age increases. But for some, when it is posited in this house in similar fashion, if it was in a sign of Mars or in the terms of Mars, it denotes money from the deaths of non-relatives.

17. But if it was posited in this house by night, it will make the loss of inheritance; if the Moon aspected it by square or opposite aspect, evil . . . .[1] if, with Saturn thus posited, the Moon posited in a domicile of Saturn aspects it with the preceding aspects. But if Mars aspects the Moon thus placed with Saturn from any place [in the chart] by any aspect, it makes those dying a violent death. But if not Mars but Jupiter aspects the Moon and Saturn posited just as we have said, it will make good men of good life and reputation, but always unstable in their relations with their wives. Moreover, a good aspect is a trine or a sextile.

18. Saturn posited in the 9th house from the ASC will make famous mages or renowned philosophers, or priests of temples, always famous in their reputation for magic. According to the quality of the sign, it also makes *haruspices*, prophets, [and] mathematicians[2] always illustrious for their true interpretation, and whose responses are such as if they were brought forth by a kind of divine authority. Moreover, it will always make some of them to persevere in worship in temples, or to be those who are put in charge of religions. Sometimes, it produces divine interpreters of dreams, but it also frequently makes long-haired philosophers.

19. But if Saturn is posited in this house by night, it will make [the Native to suffer from] the wrath of the Gods, and the displeasure of Emperors, especially if the Moon, with little light, applies to it in any fashion. Moreover, greater evils from the Gods or from the Emperor are denoted

---

[1]Some words have dropped out of the Latin text at this point.
[2]That is, astrologers.

for him who was born thus, if from any part [of the chart] Mars aspects Saturn posited thus with the Moon. But these evils are mitigated if from a fortunate house an aspect of Jupiter is made to Saturn, and if Saturn is in its own terms or in the Sun's domicile, or in its own exaltation, and if it has conjoined itself to Jupiter by a trine aspect.

20. Saturn posited in the tenth house from the ASC, partilely in the MC, will make Emperors, military commanders, prefects of the *praetorium*[1]. If, with Saturn posited thus in those places in which it is exalted, the Sun is posited in the ASC degree, [and] Saturn, moreover, just as we said before, was found in the MC by day, it will make honest farmers with honest customs, but wealthy ones, and those whose possessions are always adjacent to the sea or to rivers or to swamps. It will also give the greatest assets, great glory, and inheritances from greater persons, especially if Mars does not conjoin it placed thus with any aspect. But if Mars does aspect it placed thus with a very strong conjunction,[2] it will provide those things that we have said to a lesser degree.

21. But if it was found by night in the MC, it denotes misfortunes. It will cause the loss of his inheritance, it will deny marriage, it will deny children, especially if it is found in either the sign, the house, or the terms of a malefic star. But if a benefic star, i.e. Jupiter or Venus, aspects Saturn placed thus by night with a good aspect, those things in particular that we said a little earlier would be denied, are bestowed in some part. But in particular, the star of Saturn posited by night in any angle denotes the greatest evils for the nativity, for it kills the wives, ruins the children, and always indicates the bitter pains of bereavement.

22. But if placed thus it receives the conjunction of the waning Moon, he who has Saturn thus will be oppressed by the burden of poverty, so that he also has scarcely the necessities of daily life, especially if the Moon, posited in a feminine sign, and waning in light, conjoins herself to Saturn. But if Saturn posited thus receives the aspects of the waxing Moon, it denotes an unevenness of life, so that there is not in him, who has Saturn thus, one and the same course of life, but it is always changing itself with a mutable diversity.

23. But if, with Saturn placed thus, the star of Mercury was associated with it, it will give the greatest ingenuity of mind and long substance of

[1]Commanders of the Imperial Bodyguard.

[2]That is, with a very strong *aspect*, not necessarily a conjunction.

life, especially if it is the Ruler of the Nativity or the Giver of Life. But if that one is the one who is the Giver of Life and it is harmful, it subtracts thirty years from those years that were decreed. But it also denotes stronger[1] evils, however often it is placed thus against the Ruler of the Nativity, which the Greeks call the *oecodespoten*, or if it is posited against the Giver of Life, especially if Mars aspects it by a square or opposition aspect. For if it is posited thus, it denotes paralytics, deformed persons, hunchbacks, dwarves, stooped men, hermaphrodites, and whatever [sorts of men] are similar to these. Moreover, it denotes these things in accordance with the bodies and substance of the signs.

24. But if, with Saturn placed thus, the Moon receding from it conjoins herself to Mars, sc. in nocturnal nativities, it will make insane persons, lunatics, melancholics, or listless persons.[2] But if Saturn posited thus in a nocturnal nativity clings to the extreme [end of] the horn of the waning Moon,[3] it makes those suffering from tuberculosis.

25. Saturn posited in the eleventh house from the ASC denotes moderate goods; and when anything great is bestowed, it will establish the Native in that place and in that rank in which his father was established before him, but [only] after the thirtieth year of his life; for before the thirtieth year he loses whatever he has [already] acquired, and he is not able to attain any dignity or inheritance, unless he has passed through the space of thirty years.

26. Saturn posited in the 12th house from the ASC denotes crises from slave rebellions or dangers because of slaves, and whoever has it posited thus in his nativity is thrust into slavery. It will also make the greatest sicknesses, but also illnesses of more than the common severity, especially if, with Saturn thus placed, the Moon conjoins it in any fashion, and if no benefic star was posited in the angles of the nativity. For if, with Saturn thus placed, a benefic star was found in any angle of the nativity, those evils that we have mentioned are mitigated to some extent. All of which will be milder and less grave if Saturn was found thus by day, but stronger and more violent if it possesses this house in a nocturnal nativity.

---

[1]Accepting Kroll's conjecture *fortiora* 'stronger' instead of the reading *potiora* 'more acceptable' of the MSS.

[2]In the Latin, *melancholicos, languidos* 'melancholics <or> listless persons'. Probably, both terms refer to persons suffering from mental depression, and who are consequently inactive.

[3]That is, if Saturn is close to a tip of the Moon when it is crescent-shaped; hence, in close conjunction with it.

27. But with Saturn placed in all these houses,[1] inquire into its degree, so that you may find in what house and in what terms its dodecatemory[2] is posited, so that from the dodecatemory and from the terms of the dodecatemory you may find all the power of Saturn.

<Chapter 3b. Jupiter.> [III.3]

1. If Jupiter is posited partilely in the first angle. i.e. in the degree of the ASC, especially in those signs in which it rejoices—either in its own domiciles, or in its own terms, or in its exaltation—it will make nobles, renowned persons, always in charge of city-states, sometimes [members of] the First Ten of great city-states,[3] according to the measure of the nativity. He will be a good person, charming, benevolent, cheerful, [and] rich, especially if Jupiter is found by day in the degrees of the ASC, and if no malefic star from any degree opposes it posited thus. For if a malefic star aspects it posited thus with a contrary aspect, everything that Jupiter decreed is diminished in the greatest degree.

2. But if it is found in the degree of the ASC by night, it will make [him] to be the first-born among his brothers, or, the one who was born before him dies, or it will separate him <from his parents> and settle him in remote regions and places,[4] so that he himself has the first place in his father's house. In addition, it makes him to be well-nourished and it establishes his parents in the greatest good fortune. But if with Jupiter so disposed by night a malefic star resists, it will dissipate all the paternal and maternal property.

3. Moreover, Jupiter posited in the angles of a nativity will either make those who are the first to be born or it kills their elder brothers, so that he himself alone, just as I said above, has the first place in his father's house.

---

[1]That is, in any of the twelve houses.

[2]The "dodecatemory" of a planet is actually the calculated *position* of a planet in one of the dodecatemories, which are the 2½ degree subdivisions of the signs. For example, if Saturn were in 17 Leo, its "dodecatemory" would be in 24 Aquarius, which happens to be in the terms of Mars—not a favorable location! Firmicus evidently attached considerable importance to this consideration, since he repeats this injunction at the end of the chapter for each planet.

[3]A group of ten leading citizens with special municipal authority, such as the Council of Ten in Venice in later times, and our modern City Councilmen.

[4]Accepting Némethy's emendation *vel <a parentibus> eum separabit et in longinquis constituet regionibus ac locis*.

But if, with Jupiter in the ASC by night or day, the waxing Moon shall have joined herself to him by any aspect, it will make the greatest administrators, governors of cities, and those who are often put in charge of the greatest business affairs.

4. Jupiter posited in the 2nd house from the ASC denotes inheritances from non-relatives, and it will make the Native to be adopted by non-relatives. Moreover, it will give ownership of great amounts of moveable property and the greatest possessions if Mercury is well placed and makes a good aspect to it. But if, with Jupiter thus placed, and thus configured with Mercury, and Mars or Saturn aspects it from any part [of the chart], it will frequently change his status, and it will make it to be transferred from good actions to bad actions. And he who has Jupiter posited thus will always be changeable, beset by varied diversity throughout his whole life—so that now he is abounding in wealth, and now he is oppressed by the burden of poverty.

5. Jupiter posited in the 3rd house is neither good nor evil but is always arranged in an equable manner, so that now their inheritance is dissipated, but again unexpected wealth is heaped upon them.

6. Jupiter partilely posited in the 4th house from the ASC, i.e. in the IMC, makes men to be the greatest judges, or the givers of laws, or the interpreters of laws, and judicial experts. It also makes fanciers and breeders of pack-horses, [and], according to the quality of the signs, messengers of kings or generals or judges, and those to whom the care and anxiety of the first postal service is entrusted, and those who in connection with [their work in] the postal service are dispatched hither and thither[1] in frequent travel by order of princes or generals or judges. It will make those known to princes, put in charge of public affairs, and those who entrust themselves to the guardianship of the Gods. And those who demand remedies from the Gods and whom the Gods show the right way by a frequent sign. Many, moreover, when they have Jupiter thus, predict the future and frequently have the greatest honors in temples. Others, moreover, find treaures according to the quality of the signs. Moreover, Jupiter thus placed denotes a happy old age up to [the time of] death.

7. But if <with Jupiter located thus, the Sun was placed in opposition>,[2] it makes a noble and glorious father, but he will dissipate his as-

[1]Reading *huc atque illuc* with **Nα**.
[2]These words are added by **ΨNα**.

sets around middle age, but afterwards he recovers it again. Moreover, he will be later in his relations with women and separated from the affections of his sons. But if Jupiter was found [here] by night, it will make persons of moderate wealth and [those who become] more fortunate with the passage of time.

8. Jupiter posited in the fifth house from the ASC denotes great increases of good fortune, for it makes him[1] who was born thus to be honored in the greatest nations,[2] especially if it is found in its domiciles or its terms or its own exaltation or in the domicile of the Sun. But if, with Jupiter thus placed, Mars conjoins it with a good aspect, it will make military commanders, having[3] also the power of life and death. But if, with Jupiter thus placed without Mars, Mercury and the Moon conjoin themselves to it from any part [of the chart], it will make royal *procurators* or treasury officials.[4] But if, without all of those [stars], Venus alone conjoins herself to it from any part [of the chart], it will make him[5] to be decorated with an abundance of good fortune. For, just as we said above, if it is posited thus with Mars, he who has it thus will always be a famous person with royal power, and his judgments will be just as if divine documents are being revealed by him to all mankind. Moreover, he who has it thus will be strong in body with sturdy bones.

9. And if Jupiter receives a conjunction with the wind[6] of a waxing Moon, it will beget men of divine and almost immortal substance. More-

---

[1]Reading *enim <eum>,* combining the *enim* of most of the MSS with the *eum* of **A'α**.

[2]For *maximis publicis* 'the greatest public things' MS **N** has *actionibus publicis* 'public actions', but Ziegler first suggests *actibus publicis* 'public activities', which occurs in Paragraph 6 above and in several other similar places, but he later accepted Wikström's emendation *maximis *populis* 'the greatest nations', which occurs in v.3.33 and vi.23.1. Bram accepts *maximis publics* and renders it as 'important public affairs', but Prof. Monat accepts Wikström's emendation and has 'les plus grandes peuples'.

[3]Accepting Ziegler's emendation *habentes* 'having' for the *habebit* of the MSS or Kroll's emendation *dabit.*

[4]Procurators were departmental chiefs reporting to the Emperor. The word *rationales* denotes literally 'accountants', but it was used to designate imperial treasurers or important officials of the treasury.

[5]Reading *affluentis felicitatis ornatum* with Ziegler and **N** rather than *affluentia felicitatis ornatos*.

[6]By 'wind' Firmicus means 'direction', i.e. north or south latitude. And by a 'conjunction with the wind' he means that the planet and the Moon are conjoined in both longitude and latitude.

over, if Jupiter is posited thus, one should always observe[1] by which wind the moving Moon bears towards it, for that fact is acquired with difficulty.[2] For if, with Jupiter posited in the north, the Moon receding from the south, waxing or full of light, joins itself to Jupiter, namely with Jupiter posited in the fifth house from the ASC and in those signs in which it rejoices, or at least in its own domiciles or in its exaltation by day, it will make invincible Emperors, and those who hold the rulership of the whole world, especially if with Jupiter thus, the Sun, posited in those signs in which it rejoices or in which it is exalted, conjoins itself to it with a trine aspect. Moreover, it rejoices by day when it is adorned with the aspects of the Sun and Saturn, especially if it was placed in its morning rising.

10. But if Jupiter posited thus, just as we have said, receives the waning Moon, it will make men with honest habits and elevated with the grace of a moderate dignity, and those on whom the burden of poverty is never imposed. But if the waxing Moon conjoins itself in simple fashion to Jupiter placed thus without that conjunction of winds which we have mentioned, it will make consular administrators, frequently also ordinary consuls, especially if it was a diurnal nativity. But if Mercury has conjoined itself with association and aspect, it denotes long years and the greatest length of life. It will also give children of both sexes or twins, especially if it was the Ruler of the Nativity or the ruler of the degrees of the ASC or the ruler of the sign in which the Ruler of the Nativity is posited. But if it was posited in a nocturnal nativity against the Giver of Life (for Jupiter does not rejoice in a nocturnal nativity), it will take away twelve years from whatever age was decreed [for him].

11. But also if in a nocturnal nativity Mars or Venus or the Moon had shown itself to be in contrary course to it, it will make him who was born thus to be entangled in the greatest vices—namely, according to the nature and substance of the signs. For placed thus in human signs, it will make lustful persons and always those perverted with mad desire in love affairs, doing those things that women customarily do. But posited thus in quadrupedal signs, it will make hunters, and those fond of wild beasts, and those who are delighted by the deserted places of forests, and those involved in constant toil. But in earth signs it will make herbalists,[3] and

[1]Accepting the Teubner editors' suggestion of *observare* 'observe' for the meaningless *eum* 'him' or 'it' of the MSS.

[2]Presumably he means that the astrologer may only have the Moon's longitude at hand but not its latitude.

[3]*Herbarios* 'herbalists' were those skilled in the use of herbs for medical purposes.

those wanting to know more than the substance of human nature allows. But in water [signs], it will make fishermen, and those whose subsistence is around a river or sea or marshlands—hardworking of course, and often making a living from these arts.

12. But if, with Jupiter posited thus in a nocturnal nativity with those [stars] which we have said opposing it, and the Moon separates from it, it will make an uneven life, and it indicates more frequent troubles. But this evil is moderated to some degree if the Moon separating from it conjoins itself to Venus with an opportune aspect. But if with Jupiter posited thus, the Moon separating from it has no conjunction with any star, it denotes the greatest misfortunes, labors, and troubles. But if with Jupiter posited thus, the Moon is receding from it—and in a way, fleeing from it—and it casts itself onto the aspects of Mars by square or by opposition, it will make those dying a violent death according to the natural form and substance of the sign. For if Mars by opposition thus aspects the Moon receding from Jupiter in a nocturnal nativity—by that fashion which we have said—it will make quarrels, dangers, and always great struggles with an inferior. Wherefore, Jupiter in this sign by night frequently denotes evil disasters.

13. Jupiter posited in the 6th house from the ASC denotes the greatest evils, for it will frequently make the Natives to be exposed, more particularly if, while posited in the 6th house, it was the ruler of the sign in which the ASC or the MC is placed, especially if it was in a nocturnal nativity, and if it aspected the Sun, or Saturn, or Mars by opposition, and if while thus placed it aspected the waning Moon by a square, or if the waning Moon was with it in the same sign.

14. But if, thus placed without the malefic aspect of any star, it receives the light of the waxing Moon, those things that we have said will be mitigated to some extent; and it makes goldsmiths or those who decorate clothing with gold thread; and sometimes it makes silversmiths. But nevertheless, even if it has bestowed these arts, it will wear[1] out these same persons with frequent losses. For this house, i.e. the 6th, has its own prime signification of evil, and whatever star was in this house, i.e. in the 6th, will borrow the greatest powers of denoting evils from the fault of the house.

15. Jupiter posited in the 7th house from the ASC, that is in particular in the DSC—namely in a diurnal nativity—will make wealthy rich per-

[1]Reading *desudabit* 'wear away' with MS **N**, rather than †*desubitat* (no such word).

sons, and it denotes the span of a lengthy and happy old age. But in the DSC[1] it greatly disturbs the place of children and the spouse; for it is necessary that he lose a very dear and obliging[2] wife, and he will see the wretched death of a beloved son or daughter.[3] But if it was found by night in this house of the nativity, with advancing age he obtains increases in his fortune, but he will be of moderate wealth and with such assets that nothing is lacking to him.

16. Jupiter posited in the 8th house from the ASC frequently destroys the [Native's] fortune and makes the greatest enemies, and frequently insurrections by the people, and it makes [persons who are] always occupied in wicked acts. It also makes low-born persons and those displaying a foolish anger, preposterous persons and those whose madness proceeds to insanity—especially if, with Jupiter thus placed, a malefic star possesses any angle of the nativity. But if posited in this house it either has Mercury with it or aspects it with a trine aspect, and the waxing Moon conjoins itself to it with a good aspect, it will make either royal administrators or accountants, or those to whom the power of prosecuting[4] is granted; and they always die in the first age of life.

17. Jupiter posited in the 9th house from the ASC, if it is a diurnal nativity, will make him who is born thus to predict future things, and it always produces interpreters of the [will of the] Gods. Moreover, some of them also attain the priesthood, [and] it makes something of value from temples to be bestowed on others. But sometimes it makes both damages and mental agitation. But if it is posited in this house by night, it always makes those who dream false dreams and who frequently say something falsely about the Gods. And it also makes those who promise themselves some hope from the prophecies of the Gods, and who because of this always believe themselves to be inspired.

[1]Accepting Némethy's conjecture of *in occasu* 'in the DSC' in place of *nocturnus* 'nocturnal'.

[2]Reading *morigeram* 'obliging' with MS **N** rather than *moratam* 'mannered'.

[3]Apparently the position of the benefic Jupiter in the 7th, after which it disappears into the 6th house, implied the imminent demise of good things in the Native's life, such as the death of the wife or children. Paul of Alexandria, *Introduction*, Chapter 25, suggests the same thing somewhat less explicitly: "But it will also make a good marriage, except that it denotes few children and those who are saddened because of their wives and children."

[4]The 'power of prosecuting' can refer either to a public prosecutor or to some other official with the authority to draw up an official list of persons to be prosecuted.

18. Jupiter posited in the 10th house, i.e. in the MC partilely by day, will make principal managers of public affairs. And it will make one of the First Ten of the greatest nations,[1] and those on whom the greatest honors are conferred by the people, distinguished persons and those who would always like to avail themselves of the grace of ostentation, but it renders them extravagant in their life. It also makes some of them handle the business affairs of great men or [even] Emperors, and it will make others to be crowned throughout their whole life.[2]

19. But thus posited, if no malefic star posited in the IMC resists it, it denotes the greatest good fortune. But if a malefic star does resist Jupiter posited thus in the MC, then whatever in the way of honors or riches was conferred upon him in the first age [of life], all of that is diminished and dissipated in his later life and utterly destroyed, unless the DSC, i.e. the 7th house, was fortified by the light of another benevolent star. But if it was posited in the 10th house by night, it makes persons honest in their morals, but who are soon deceived, and whose personal wealth is destroyed by frequent and rapid expenditures.

20. Jupiter posited in the 11th house from the ASC denotes the greatest good fortune, and it bestows great fame. It also gives famous powers, even consulship[3], and it denotes proconsular rulership,[4] if the Sun and Venus are conjoined to it in good aspect, and if the Moon, receding from the south, conjoins herself full of light to Jupiter posited in the north, i.e. if she bears towards him in such a course as we have described in the 5th house.[5]

21. However, all these things are diminished, and they lose their efficacy, if Jupiter is posited thus in a nocturnal nativity. But if Mars placed in the 8th house of the nativity was contrary to Jupiter posited thus, [having once been] established in great and powerful fortunate circumstances and honored with the greatest wealth, everything that was bestowed upon

---

[1]Accepting Wikström's emendation *maximorum *populorum*. The First Ten are the leading officials of a city or state. See the note to III.3b.1 above.

[2]This refers to high priests who wore golden crowns as part of their insignia of office.

[3]Under the Republic, the consuls (two were elected each year) were the chief officers of the state, rather like joint presidents. But under the Empire they were of course subordinate to the Emperor and were something like joint Vice-Presidents.

[4]Once a consul's year of office was completed, he was styled 'proconsul' and was often put in charge of a province.

[5]Book III. 3. 9 above.

him by way of honors or dignity is changed by an incursion of miseries and misfortune.

22. Jupiter posited in the 12th house from the ASC denotes the greatest misfotunes. It always makes powerful enemies and those who hinder him with frequent [applications of] power, especially if a malefic star holds the ASC partilely, or if, with Jupiter posited thus, Mars was found in the 7th house from the ASC.[1] For if, with Jupiter posited thus, i.e. in the 12th house from the ASC, Mars was posited in the DSC of the nativity, i.e. in the 7th house from the ASC, it will without any doubt make those who die violently.

23. Moreover, these evils will be greater and particulary powerful due to a stronger disaster if the Sun and Saturn aspect Jupiter posited in the 12th house by opposition. Moreover, they will be wretched paupers, if, with Jupiter thus posited in a nocturnal nativity, the waning Moon opposes it by opposition. But if neither the Sun nor Saturn was in opposition to it, and they possess good houses of the nativity, and if the Moon with declining light does not conjoin Jupiter [with any aspect], it will make those who have Jupiter thus to be strong in some delicate art, or to be goldsmiths, or those embroidering garments with gold, or gilders, or workers in mosaic, or those making certain works of silver. Moreover, he is sought out and praised, whatever his art was, if the star of Venus conjoins Jupiter with a good aspect when it is posited thus.

24. In the case of Jupiter too, look into its dodecatemory carefully, so that you may ascertain its strengths from the dodecatemory in a careful manner.

Chapter 3c. Mars.> [III.4]

1. Mars posited partilely in the degrees of the ASC in a nocturnal nativity and in masculine signs will make military men; moreover, if it was matutine posited partilely in the ASC without any aspect of Jupiter, it will make †men more generous to others†,[2] wanting to give more than

---

[1]Here, *in VII. parte horoscopi* 'in the 7th part of the ASC' must mean 'in the 7th house from the ASC', rather than 'in the 7th degree of the ASC'.

[2]Most MSS have *nigrastros alteros longiores* 'dark complexioned, others taller', which is obviously corrupt. The word *nigrastros* is otherwise unattested; MSS **NV** have *nigrastos*, again 'dark complexioned', but both of these seem inappropriate for Mars. Ptolemy, *Tetrabiblos* iii. 11, has 'red and white complexioned, tall and robust, grey-eyed, with thick hair, somewhat curly'. Rhetorius

the substance of their wealth allows, so that they seem to be lavish [in their expenditures], but whose actions are always made public in every way.

2. But if the ASC is placed by night in a domicile of Mars, namely in a masculine sign, and Mars was found in that same sign, i.e. in the ASC, and Jupiter was with him partilely in that same sign or has aspected him with a solid[1] aspect, it will make generals, but those to whom the whole army is committed, lords of life and death, and at whose approach cities and the greatest provinces shake with fear; [they are] fortunate, strong, severe and those whose angers are always expressed with great indignations. But thus placed, it does not permit [him] to take delight with dear affection in either his spouse or his children.

3. But if it is found partilely by day in the ASC, it makes hot-tempered, bold, furious, foreigners, and always unsteady, and those who whatever they dare to try, they cannot complete in any way; but always whatever they have obtained flows out of their hands; moreover, the personal assets of those who have Mars thus are destroyed. But they lose the entire substance of life, wives too and children, and nothing from their paternal inheritance is saved, but they also lose this in their first age.

4. But if Jupiter itself, posited in its own domicile or in its own exaltation or in its own terms, aspects Mars posited thus by day with a trine aspect, or if it is partilely with him, his evils are in some part lessened. But I also know—just as I have found it in many nativities—that many with Mars posited in the ASC [and] sent into exile, administer public affairs well and vigorously.

5. Mars posited in the 2nd house from the ASC, if it is found in this house by day, denotes the greatest evils and great misfortunes, especially if it is matutine; for it will make him to be alienated from his parents and from his own home and always wandering about in foreign lands. But if, with Mars thus placed, the waxing Moon is with it or is placed in opposition or square aspect to it, it will make sluggish, weak persons, who fre-

---

has "hot-headed, reckless, daring, and foolhardy." MS **R** has *ingrasis* and MS **P**^{1} has *ingratos* 'disagreeable, ungrateful', which is perhaps more likely. And **αN**^{2} (in the margin) have *<homines> aliis largiores* 'men more generous to others'. I have adopted that conjecture, but it seems to me that more words are missing before it.

[1]The text has *solida* 'solid', which does not occur elsewhere with *radiatione* 'aspect'. It could mean 'strong', and Kroll conjectures *valida* 'strong', which may be right. Bram translates it as 'favorable', and Prof. Monat as 'powerful'.

quently receive wounds from iron. Moreover, it will debilitate him from cold or from wounds received from quadrupeds. Moreover, it will make some of the Natives to be exposed.[1] It often makes others to be captives or persons who are drawn from freedom into servitude; moreover, they will always be mentally agitated and placed in the most difficult situations. But if, with Mars thus placed, Jupiter makes a good aspect to it, and Jupiter is in its own domicile or its own terms, they will escape from all the dangers, or they are liberated from captivity, or they are released, and from servitude they are transferred again to freedom; but sometimes they will not have those things that are necessary to life.

6. But if it was found thus by night, it makes soldiers or athletes, but it is accustomed to ensnare them readily in a continuation of dangers. Moreover, dangers approach in a similar manner [even] if Jupiter and Venus as we have said above are conjoined to it with a good aspect.

7. Mars posited in the 3rd house from the ASC denotes some glory, but with the greatest effort. He who has Mars thus will desire the possessions of others and he will envy everone, and he will have evil knowledge of some very serious crime. But if with Mars thus posited, Jupiter is found in the 11th house or in the 7th, i.e. the DSC, it makes that when [the Native] has attained a position in public administration with great effort, he acquires the greatest resources of personal wealth.

8. Moreover, placed thus in the 3rd house from the ASC, if it conjoins itself to Jupiter, as we have said before, it bestows command and rulership of the greatest power and honor, so that all those who are joined to him by relation are surpassed by the nobility of his honor. For if it is posited in this house in its own domicile[2] or in its own degrees or in its own domiciles or in its own exaltation, and if Jupiter is conjoined to it just as we have said, it will make governors of rivers, generals, military officers, pretorian prefects, and those to whom supreme command is frequently entrusted.

9. Mars partilely posited in the 4th house from the ASC, i.e. in the IMC, if it was by night, will make military men, experiencing hardships and those who always are stationed in desert regions, or those who are in

[1]This refers to the ancient practice of taking unwanted newborns to some public place usually outside the city and leaving them there "exposed" to the elements. They were sometimes taken up by persons who wanted a child, but they were sometimes eaten by wild dogs.

[2]This position is mentioned twice.

charge of, or are trainers of, wild animals; sometimes it will make those who overthrow Emperors or judges according to the quality of the signs; but it will destroy the life and the assets of the parents. It will give wounds, bereavement, ruin; but it will give one son or none; for the one who has it thus is always hampered in all his actions.

10. But if it is found thus by day, it will weaken the whole body—it will make languid persons, epileptics, and those who frequently receive wounds from iron. It produces invalids, and those whom women always attack, and who are always worn down by the greatest annoyances from women. It will also make those who provide without [receiving] thanks for what they have given; for whoever has received anything from them is always ungrateful to them.

11. But if the Sun aspects Mars posited thus by square or by opposition or was with him, it denotes that all these evils are stronger and more frequent; for it frequently puts [the Native] in the greatest dangers. It will also make insane persons [and] lunatics if, with Mars posited thus, the ASC was found in a domicile of Mars, or if the House of Fortune was found in the place or domicile of Mars, or if the House of Desire or the House of the Daemon was located in a domicile of Mars.

12. Mars posited in the 5th house from the ASC, if it was in this house by night, and if it was posited in its own domicile, or in a domicile of Jupiter, or in its own terms, or in the terms of Jupiter, or in its own exaltation, and if Jupiter was with it, or if that [star] posited in its own domicile aspected it by trine, it will make the greatest fame, and it denotes great increases in his personal wealth and every kind of good fortune. It also causes honors by the people to be denoted, conjoined[1] with the regard of faithful friendship with powerful men or with the greatest administrators.

13. But if, with Mars and Jupiter posited thus, the waning Moon conjoins herself to the star of Mars with a fortunate aspect, it will make very powerful terrifying generals, and those to whom the greatest armies are assigned, so that they are given[2] the power of life and death; and in great administrations it denotes the power of *ius gladii*.[3] But if the Moon had receded from it, but Venus was with it or aspected it by trine, it will make

[1]Reading *coniunctos* 'conjoined' with the MSS rather than Kroll & Skutsch's emendation *coniungit* 'it conjoins'.

[2]Reading **dentur* 'they are given' rather than *dent* 'they give'.

[3]Literally, 'the right of the sword', i.e. the authority to punish criminals, including the authority to sentence them to death.

fortunate wealthy persons, and those who attain fame through their own efforts, and who are always pleasing because of their bodily charm.

14. But if Mars was posited by day in the 5th house from the ASC, it will destroy his personal assets, and he frequently changes his residence; and because of the misfortunes that happen to him, he always remains in foreign regions; moreover, he will be placed in no small dangers. But if, with Mars thus posited by day denoting these evils, Jupiter or Venus were posited either together with him or if they aspected him by trine or sextile, he will acquire great wealth from the inconvenience of travel, and he will be quickly recalled from his travel to his homeland.

15. Moreover, it must be feared that whenever posited thus by day it has an opposition to the crescent Moon; for that indicates the greatest labors and occupations such as those that are proper to an imitation of slavery. For even if he seems to be fortunate, his fortune will be such that he is always subject to the power of another person; for it makes legal advisors to the greatest judges. It will make accusations, revolts, riots, and losses and sudden dangers, and weakness in some part of the body, sometimes it makes such persons [to have] spells of insanity and listlessness, so that, burned up by the heat of too great fever, they are transported into insanity. It will also make chains, incarceration, and confinement, unless Jupiter aspecting the Moon posited in opposition to Mars or aspecting Mars himself may mitigate the miseries of those calamities. For whenever Jupiter aspects Mars and the Moon posited thus, it places those who were born thus in the greatest dangers, but having despaired of the assistance of everyone,[1] Jupiter makes them to be liberated with sudden assistance. Posited in this house by day, without the testimony of Jupiter, it also denies children.

16. Mars posited in the 6th house from the ASC denotes many evils, for it will harm the [Native's] children, and it will make unevenness in his life; and it denotes illnesses, namely in accordance with the nature of the signs—for in curved signs[2] it makes [the Natives] to die early, sometimes [as] cripples and hunchbacks. In this house the defects of all illnesses are discerned; if, however, that house was found partilely...,[3] and if Mars was partilely posited in that sign.

---

[1]Or, reading *periculorum* with MS **N** instead of *praesidio* 'assistance', "hopeless because of all the dangers."

[2]This is the only place in the *Mathesis* where "curved signs" are mentioned. In the other early writers, Vettius Valens applies that epithet to Capricorn, and Hephaestio of Thebes gives it to Scorpio (because of its shape?).

[3]Something is missing in this clause.

17. Mars partilely posited in the 7th house from the ASC, i.e. in the DSC, denotes the greatest evils and immense dangers. For it will make harassed persons, murderers and scoundrels, criminals, inventors of crimes, or torturers, or executioners, or traitors. But if, while posited in the DSC, it sees its own domicile by opposition, it will not make a person dying a violent death (for Mars never overturns his own domicile); but then it [merely] makes a short lifespan if the ASC and the Moon were protected by the guardianship of Jupiter. But if the ASC was not in a domicile of Mars, it produces short-lived persons, especially if it aspects the Moon full of light by square or opposition, i.e. posited in the ASC or the MC.

18. But generally, Mars posited in the 7th house from the ASC, i.e. in the DSC, by day and by night makes those dying violently according to the quality of the signs. Nevertheless, it denotes this evil more strongly and plainly in the signs of others; for if it was found in this house, then it makes pains and lacerations of the body, and it either makes him fall, or it destroys him, or it crushes down with perpetual and deadly calamities those placed in chains in prison.

19. In nocturnal nativities it will make pains and fevers[1] [resulting] from all his actions, but it frequently inflicts wounds from iron, and it makes those wounds to be cured by the fiery burning of cauteries. It makes hidden and unending pains in the body, especially when Mars was Ruler of the Times, or when from the full Moon he possessed for himself the distributed spaces of the Times.

20. But if, with Mars posited in the 7th house, Saturn is partilely posited either in the ASC or in the MC, or if the full Moon moves towards Mars or with little light towards Saturn, they denote the misfortunes of great evils—of deadly disaster. Then accusations, next chains, next imprisonment, next condemnations, and finally capital sentences are levied on him. For either he is thrown to wild beasts,[2] or he is cast down from a precipice, or he is crushed by a [building] collapse, or he is torn to pieces in a domestic uprising, or he is killed by armed robbers, or he perishes in a ship. But these things are denoted in accordance with the kind and quality of the signs. For in earth signs, it will make him to be thrown to wild

[1]Reading *dolores <et> aestus* as conjectured by Cumont and confirmed by MS **N**.

[2]Criminals given a capital sentence were sometimes executed by putting them in the arena with lions or other wild beasts.

beasts; but in fixed signs, it makes him to be crushed by a [building] collapse, or to be thrown down from a precipice; and posited in water signs, he is drowned in a shipwreck; but posited in human signs, it makes him to die by the sword.

21. But if the Sun was in opposition [to Mars] or was with him or was in another angle of the nativity, it makes those who are burned alive, so that, when posited in this house in any way, it ruins a man with wretched disaster and a lamentable murder [committed] with atrocity. But before the time of the end of his life, he who has Mars in the 7th house of his nativity will have occupations involving either fire or iron, or some sort of violence, or tortures, or homicides. But also Mars posited in the 7th house acts very strongly against the house of the wife and children.

22. Mars posited in the 8th house from the ASC, if it was in this house by day, either denies wealth or it makes those who have it to be stripped bare by proscription. But if [the Native] has the Sun and the Moon in opposition, it denotes blindness from his eyes having been put out. Moreover, posited alone in this sign, it will make penury, want, anxieties, disturbances, revolts, [and] dangers.

23. But if, with Mars posited thus, the Moon was in the *anafora* of the ASC, i.e. in the 2nd house from the ASC, or with that same Mars namely,[1] and Jupiter makes no aspect to them, and is unrelated to them, and does not aspect the ASC, it makes those dying a violent death, but one in accordance with the nature and the substance of the signs. For, if it was posited, just as we have said, in human signs, he will be killed by men with a sword But he who has Mars thus is killed by pirates or by armed robbers or by members of his own household. Whoever has Mars thus is slain, or, convicted of a varied diversity of crimes, he is killed by a sword in accordance with a sentence of judgment. Frequently, however, posited thus with Jupiter, just as we have said, without the testimony of Venus or Jupiter, it makes gladiators, but those who perish from the cruel brutality of slaughter with the public watching. But in terrestrial signs, it will make [the Natives] to be killed in deserted places, having previously been troubled by a manifold continuation of dangers. But in quadrupedal signs, it will make those who are seized by wild beasts to be torn to pieces with a pitiful laceration. But posited in water signs with the Moon configured in the manner that we have said, it makes them to be drowned either in pools of water or in the sea, or slain by pirates; and it makes them to be

[1]That is, 'or if the Moon is with Mars in the 8th house'.

destroyed in waves and floods. But posited in fixed signs, it kills them by their having perished from falling. But posited in fire signs, it will make them to be burned up.

24. But posited in this sign by night, i.e. posited in the 8th house from the ASC, it will make eager persons, involved in dangers, but sharp. However, it establishes those who have Mars thus to be in public or prominent actions, but nevertheless it denotes a violent or sudden death, such as people with apoplexy are accustomed to die. But if Jupiter aspects Mars thus placed with any aspect or if it was with it, those evil things that we have mentioned are mitigated for the most part.

25. But if Jupiter was found partilely in the ASC, and the ASC itself is in a domicile of Jupiter, and the star of Venus conjoins itself to Jupiter with a fortunate aspect, and it obstructs Mars in that hostile aspect that we have mentioned, all those ruins of calamities are changed for the most part. For the lamentable accidents and the always wretched inconveniences of misfortunes decreed by Mars, both in this and in the other houses, are changed and made mild if the attacks of Mars are mitigated by the good testimony of Venus and Jupiter.

26. Mars posited in the 9th house from the ASC will be good for life and fame; and if Jupiter was posited in the ASC with Mars posited in the 9th house, it makes fortunate persons and those who easily accomplish everything. But if, with Mars posited in the 9th house by night, Jupiter was found in the ASC degree, it denotes the greatest power of administration and the *ius gladii*,[1] and it makes him who was born thus to lead an army. And yet frequently it denotes inconveniences in travel when posited thus.

27. But if it was posited in the 9th house in a domicile of Mercury or of Venus, it makes learned and famous orators. But if it was either in its own domicile or in a domicile of Jupiter or in its own exaltation, and Jupiter was not posited in the ASC, it will make those who are terrifying to the Gods, and those who despise all kinds of perjury.

28. Mars posited in the 10th house from the ASC, i.e. partilely in the MC, namely in a nocturnal nativity, if it was found in a masculine sign in its own domicile or in Jupiter's, but of the gender that we have said, or in its own exaltation, will certainly make those exposed to many dangers and often deceived in various ways. But nevertheless, it will make pro-

[1] 'Law of the sword'. The power to exact death as a punishment.

vincial governors, generals, lords of life and death, [and] tribunes frightening to provinces and cities.

29. But if it is posited in the MC by night, in one of the signs that we have mentioned, [and] it receives the conjunction of the approaching Moon, but Jupiter possesses another angle of the nativity, and Mars is nevertheless posited either in its own domicile, or in its own exaltation, or in its own terms, it will produce powerful generals and lords of the whole Earth. But if the star of Jupiter abandons Mars posited thus and does not conjoin itself to it with any aspect, and if it was not found in the other angles of the nativity, it will nevertheless make armed soldiers, or prefects, or tribunes, or generals of a small place or of great provinces, and, even though they are established in a place of minor dignity, yet having the power of *ius gladii* and of life and death.[1]

30. But if, with Mars posited just as we have said, and Jupiter also posited just as we have said [earlier] in other angles of the nativity in those signs which we have mentioned and in those degrees, Saturn was found in another angle of the nativity, they will certainly be kings [or] Emperors, very terrifying potentates, exposed to many dangers, destroyers or founders of cities, but of only medium [life-span], i.e. short-lived. Moreover, some of them also come to a bad end; located in foreign places—they lose their lives and also their kingdoms, or they die under the power of others.

31. But if Mars was found in the MC in a feminine sign in . . .[2] of any star, either its own or Jupiter's, namely by night, it will nevertheless make persons of outstanding honesty; and yet, posited in the MC in a masculine sign by night or[3] in a feminine one, it denies children.

---

[1]The Latin text *armatos vel praepositos vel tribunos vel minoris loci duces aut magnarum provinciarum et licet in minoris dignitatis loco constitutos*... is corrupt. The word *armatos* is surely wrong. It appears only here in the *Mathesis* and is rare elsewhere. It makes no sense to say that this configuration of Mars makes common soldiers or important civic authorities or generals. Sittl conjectured **armatis [vel] praepositos* 'those in charge of armaments'. Mommsen would alter the text to read **maioris loci* 'of a major place' and **aut licet in minoris dignitatis loco constitutos* 'or even established in a place of minor dignity'. And Kroll suggested *provinciarum <praesides>* 'rulers of provinces' and *in *minori dignitatis loco* 'in a minor place of dignity'. I am uncertain how to rectify the text. The idea is, that without the reinforcement of Jupiter, Mars in the MC denotes lesser dignities but still powerful ones.

[2]The Teubner editors indicate a lacuna, probably containing these or similar words, 'in the domicile or terms'.

[3]Reading *<*aut*> 'or' rather than the <*et*> 'and' supplied by edition **a**.

32. But if it was found in this house, i.e. the MC, by day, it will make ineffectual men, whom it causes to be hindered in various ways in all their actions; it also denotes the greatest damages and the loss of their personal wealth; it will also make proscriptions[1] and legal judgments. For some it indicates the burden of travel; on others it imposes the greatest exigencies; it compels others to flee; it denotes exile for others; it makes some to perish abroad or in exile.

33. Mars posited in the 11th house from the ASC denotes many good things, and it bestows increases in the personal wealth and approval[2] by the people; it frequently gives the trappings of the greatest dignity if Jupiter makes a good aspect to it posited thus with the waning Moon ,or if it was with it, or if it conjoined itself to it by trine; for then it makes judges having the *ius gladii* with the greatest trappings of dignity.

34. Mars posited in the 12th house from the ASC, if it is found in this house by day, denotes the greatest sicknesses, and involves [the Natives] in bad bodily defects, and stirs up frequent plots by slaves, and makes the Natives to be such persons as the slaves always desire to harm; and they scatter manifold disgraces upon all of them through the agency of slaves.[3] Frequently too, on account of some who are incarcerated or put in custody, it denotes condemned persons, fevers, torments, anxieties, damages, and dangers. But all these things are mitigated if Mars was found posited thus in a nocturnal nativity.

35. Moreover, we should hope that in all nativities and in all houses Venus and Jupiter are always conjoined[4] to Mars by whatever aspect and from whatever house; for then his attacks grow faint to some degree, since by the testimony of those stars he is weakened. But we should also hope for that when[5] Mars possesses any angle of the nativity by day; for if he was found partilely by day in any angle of the nativity, he attacks

---

[1]Proscription was the publication of a person's name on a list of people declared to be outlaws or those whose property was to be seized and sold at public auction.

[2]MSS **NW** have *a populo honores* 'honors from the people' instead of *a populo amores* literally, 'loves from the people'. The Teubner editors say the reading *honores* may be right, and in fact it occurs at III.5.18 (p. 133, 15).

[3]Reading with MS **N**, *tales quibus . . . . omnibus eis*, 'such persons as . . . . all of them'.

[4]Reading **coniungant* 'conjoin' rather than *opponant* 'oppose' or <*sint*> *semper opportuni* 'are always fortunate' with **Nα**.

[5]Reading (with **Ψv**) ...*optare quando*... 'hope that when...' instead of ... *optare, ne quando*... '...hope that, lest when...'

against whoever was born [thus] with various kinds <of misfortunes>.[1] For, with Mars posited in an angle, if Jupiter conjoins itself to him by day,[2] and Saturn possesses another angle of the nativity, it will make those dying a violent death or those who bring about their own death.

36. Truly, if with Mars posited in an angle by day, Venus was found in another angle, it will make them to be worn out by the incessant attractions of love-affairs, or to be killers of their wives, or those who bring about their own death. But if Mars possesses any angle of the nativity by day, and Mercury is posited in another angle of the nativity, it will make dyspeptics and those who are condemned in some way. But if Mars was found in any angle of the nativity by day, and the Sun is posited in another angle of the nativity, it will always make them to be burned up in some way.

37. But if the Moon conjoins herself to Mars with a similar aspect,[3] and if the Moon is increasing in her light, it will make those dying violently, and it destroys their mothers with the violent death of murder. But if the Moon was unrelated to him, and without the conjunction of any star, he was found in any angle of the nativity by day, it denotes the greatest illnesses, bodily defects, sicknesses, and debilities. Moreover, he always rejoices when he conjoins himself to the waning Moon and to Venus; for, just as you recall, we have shown in the Book of Fundamentals that these three stars, i.e. Mars and the Moon, and Venus, are of the same sect.

38. If in fact Mars was posited by day in any angle of the nativity, and Mercury has received another angle of the nativity, it denotes great and unending dangers without any limit; for whatever amount of evil there is in human things, all of that is denoted by this conjunction of the stars. And we ought to remember this: that posited by day in the angles Mars also always denies offspring. If the House of Children is found in his sign, he himself being posited in an angle, then because he himself is ruler of this house, he will deny children. But also if the House of Children is found in the domicile of another [star], and the ruler of that sign is with Mars, or if Mars aspects him by opposition or square, it will deny children.

---

[1]Reading *vario…<infortuniorum> genere* 'with various kinds <of misfortunes>'with MS **N**.

[2]Omitting the words *in alio cardine per diem Mars fuerit inventus* '(if) Mars was found in another angle by day', which appear to be unnecessary.

[3]This means 'with a similar configuration' rather than 'with a similar aspect'.

39. But if Mars was the Giver of Life by night, he bestows the greatest span of age. If he was the Giver of Life in a diurnal nativity, he will make them to die when they are in the first stage of life. But if another [star] was the Giver of Life, and Mars resisted it by square or by opposition, it will subtract 15 years from that age that was decreed for him. But if he has the Moon placed in the middle between him and Saturn, it weakens and cuts off a part of the body according to the quality of the sign in which the Moon was found. But if he aspects the waxing Moon by opposition or square, he immediately destroys those who were born thus, or he will make them to be exposed.

40. But so that you may collect the power of Mars more exactly, inquire diligently into its dodecatemory and the terms of its dodecatemory.

Chapter 3d. The Sun.> [III.5]

1. The Sun posited in the degree of the ASC will give brothers with difficulty; moreover, posited in its own domicile or in its own exaltation, and conjoined by aspect to a benefic star, or protected by benefics, it bestows the insignia of a great nobility. But if the aspect of a malefic star approaches closely with the Sun posited in the ASC, it debilitates[1] the keenness of the eyes to a great extent. But because we have said that it denotes the greatest good fortune, we should explain everything in detail.

2. Partilely posited with Saturn in the ASC in those degrees in which we have said, by day, it will make Emperors and kings; but if its forces are lightly afflicted, it will make consuls and proconsuls, and it gives ordinary consulates. But if Mars aspects the Sun posited just as we have said, or if it is posited with him, it denotes the command and powers of generalship with the greatest envy and with great dangers and hindrances, great battles or difficulties.

3. But if with the Sun partilely posited in the ASC by day in those signs in which we have said, Jupiter possesses some other angle of the nativity, but Mars is partilely found in the MC, namely in a masculine sign, and the Moon is also in another angle of the nativity, full of light, or in the *anaforas* to the angles, it will make him who is born to rule throughout the whole earth,[2] so that established in such administration of power, his

---

[1]Accepting Kroll's emendation *debilitat* 'debilitates' instead of the *desiderat* 'desires' of the MSS.

[2]Reading with MS **N** *<per> totum orbem faciet imperare* 'it will make (him) to

power, even though he is neither a lord nor a king, is nevertheless directed through the spaces of the whole earth.

4. But if Mars was in the MC or in the DSC, with the Sun and Jupiter posited thus as we have said, but the Moon was found with Mars or is in the MC, namely full of light, or in the 8th house of the nativity, it makes those who were born thus to be generals or kings or administrators dying violently; or, made captive in some manner. It will make them to be laid low by a bad death—namely, according to the nature and substance of the signs. Moreover, it will sometimes make him, shorn of all his honors, to be deprived of all power.

5. But also if Mars was not conjoined with the Moon thus as we have said, and was found alone in the angles of the nativity, or in their *cataforas* or *anaforas*,[1] with the Sun posited in the ASC, just as we said before; nevertheless, it will make those who were born generals, or kings, or administrators to be captives or to die violently, or those who are deprived of their own power with the greatest dishonor. But also, if the Sun was found in the degree of the ASC, if Saturn possessed the MC partilely, it makes kings, generals, and the most powerful administrators in a similar fashion.

6. If with the Sun and Saturn thus posited, Mars was found in the 2nd house from the ASC or in the 8th, and the Moon full of light was found in the other angles, or in the 2nd house from the ASC or in the 8th with Mars, it makes those who were born, generals, or kings, or administrators, to die violently and to be exiles and captives. But if the Sun was found alone in the degree of the ASC, in those signs which we have said (for it is proper to have remembered this), and Mars was found in an *anafora* to the Moon, with the Moon posited in the other angles or in the *anaforas* of the angles, it makes those who were born to be kings, or generals, or administrators, similarly dying violently, or it causes them to be deprived of their honor.

7. But if the Sun was found in the degree of the ASC, and the Moon <was found> in the other angles of the nativity or in the *anaforas* or the *cataforas* of the angles, <and if Mars did not conjoin itself to them with any aspect, but the star of Jupiter is posited either with the Sun in the ASC

rule throughout the whole earth', rather than †*totum orbem faciet imperia* 'it will make commands the whole earth'.

[1]That is, the *succedent* houses. The *anaforas* are the 11th and the 2nd houses; the *cataforas* are the 8th and the 5th houses.

degree, or it is found in other angles or in the *anaforas* or *cataforas* of the angles, those who were born will be kings who possess the governorship of the whole world, overturning some states and supporting others. But if Mars posited thus aspects the Sun, the Moon, and Jupiter, or is posited with them, or is found in the angles, or in the *anaforas* or the *cataforas* of the angles>,[1] it will make bad deaths for those whom we have said, but it also denotes bodily defects and illnesses. But according to the nature of the signs and according to those parts of the body that we have said to be assigned to the signs, illnesses and bodily faults are denoted and the causes of death.

8. But if, with all of these placed just as we have said, Saturn was found in the *anaforas* or *cataforas* of the angles, they will indeed not have as much command as we have said; and yet it will nevertheless make men of very great power and famous judges, or those in charge of large legions, or tribunes, but capable and terrifying persons. But they will not continue in those dignities and powers, for it will make them to be either captives or to be sent into exile, or it makes them to die a violent death.

9. But in general, the Sun posited in the ASC sign will make free-born, noble persons. But in general, with the Sun posited in the ASC, if Jupiter, Venus, and Mercury were posited in other angles of the nativity,[2] it will make great men, and those for whom the greatest good fortune of property is provided by their parents, and those who increase in good and prosperous things from their first age, so that they are always isolated from the oncourse of poverty.

10. But if Saturn aspects all of these posited thus by trine or by sextile, or also it it was posited with them, it denotes perpetual good fortune for those persons [with that configuration]. But if to all of those thus placed, i.e. the Sun in the ASC sign, Jupiter, Venus, and Mercury in the other angles, and Saturn posited in trine or in sextile or in the same place with them, Mars makes any aspect or is posited with them, or if he aspects them all by square, or if he conjoins himself to this configuration of stars

---

[1]The words in angle brackets are found in **Ψαν**, but not in the MSS of the older **Ω** family because of **Ω**'s accidental omission of 12 or more lines (Teubner 129,19 *fuerit*—129,28 *cardinum*) of the archetype due to homoeoteleuton (...*in cataforis cardinum* | ...*in cataforis cardinum*).

[2]The Teubner editors point out that Firmicus seems to have been unaware that Mercury and Venus cannot be posited in "other angles" if the Sun is posited in the ASC.

by opposition, it will make the most important judges, [and] potentates, having the power of life and death, but also rapacious thieves and those who seize the possessions of others with an avaricious instinct of greed. But nevertheless, it makes these same persons, after the greatest depredation, or after the greatest robberies, or after thefts on a grand scale, to become exiles or those who die violently.

11. But if the Sun was found in the ASC sign by night, it makes [the Native] to be born of a poorer class. But if Saturn or Mars aspects the Sun posited in the ASC by night by square or by opposition or was together with it, and if the Sun had conjoined himself to them by any aspect, it certainly destroys the elder brothers, but it also destroys his own life and all the substance of his personal assets; and it also overturns[1] and destroys all his actions. But always the Sun posited in any angles of the nativity weakens all the older brothers, or it makes whoever has it thus to be born first among all his brothers.

12. The Sun posited in the 2nd house from the ASC will make those who seek [to acquire] personal property through their own efforts, and in their whole life they are pleasant and good. But it makes these same persons listless and short-lived, and it will make them to be entangled in various misfortunes, and those who are always distressed in their own lives by various consternations of terror.

13. But if, with the Sun posited in this house, Venus and Jupiter make a good aspect to it, either by trine or sextile, or if they are placed together with it, it will give some sudden benefit and some substantial increase in happiness; for it will make low-lying and abandoned men to be brought into the public[2] with an increase in dignity. But this is denoted for them along with great labor and with the greatest hindrance, and with the voluntary sacrifice of their personal property. Therefore, whoever has the Sun posited thus should not strive after anything, should not dare to do anything, since he should know that with the Sun placed thus he is hindered in all things.

14. The Sun posited in the 3rd house from the ASC denotes a bad death for the father; and it will make those who have it thus to be weak, but good and serious in counsel. Moreover, it will make city managers, or

[1]Reading *pervertit* 'overturns' with MS **N** rather than *pro versione* ' for †changing'

[2]Accepting Sittl's conjecture *ad publicum* (found later in **Nα**) for the *ad publicam* of the MSS and Kroll's conjecture *ad <rem> publicam*.

those handling public affairs, or those in charge of the treasury, or treasury counsels if Jupiter and Mercury have conjoined themselves to it with a good aspect; but they get a wife and children slowly.

15. But if it is posited in the 3rd house of the nativity in its own domicile or in a domicile of Jupiter, or in a domicile of Venus, or in a domicile of Mercury, or in its own exaltation, or in the exaltation of Jupiter or Venus or Mercury, it will make religious persons or worshippers of the Gods,[1] who dedicate the images of the Gods that[2] they have made, and who by order of princes or judges are in charge of the fabrication of temples. But in other signs posited as we have said, it makes low-level offices in temples or[3] some servile function.

16. But if, with the Sun posited in the 3rd house from the ASC, Saturn or Mars conjoins itself to him with any aspect, or if they were with him, it will make perjurers, treacherous persons, and those who are wretched because of frequent stigmatizing because of these actions—gluttons, and those who always frequent dirty and hidden places, and who utter irreligious words against divinity, but are seething with continuous agitations[4] of mind.

17. The Sun partilely posited in the 4th house from the ASC, if it was struck in this place by any aspect from Mars and Saturn, it first denotes the death of the father and the destruction of all his kindred or the ruin of all his personal wealth. But for those who have it thus, it denotes interruptions and many annoyances and contrarieties and to a large extent hindrances. But it will make a good old age, so that when he is established in that age, the greatest financial gains are bestowed on him; but he will be inconstant in his affection for his wife.

18. The Sun posited in the 5th house from the ASC will make likeable, respectable persons, and those who accomplish everything easily, and those on whom everything is conferred by the assistance of friends. But if with the Sun placed thus, Venus has associated herself with him in the same sign or by sextile,[5] it bestows the honors of crowns, and it will deco-

---

[1]Reading *vel deorum cultores* with MSS **NV**.

[2]Reading *quae 'that' instead of *qui* 'who' (deleted by the Teubner editors).

[3]Reading *aut* 'or' with MSS of the **Ψ** family (omitted by those of the **Ω** family).

[4]Accepting Skutsch's conjecture of *agitationibus* 'agitations' in place of *fatigationibus* ' wearinesses'.

[5]Since the old astrologers reckoned aspects by signs rather than by degrees, Venus could be in a sign that was sextile the sign that the Sun was in and could thus be considered to be sextile the Sun.

rate [the native] with magisterial robes; but also the greatest honors by the people are conferred upon him who has the Sun thus. But if malefic stars were with the Sun in this same house, they can denote nothing of evil nor perpetrate [anything] because of the natural goodness of the house, but it will only harm the children. But if it was found in this house alone, those good things that we have said will only be minor ones, and so it will harm the children—so that it indicates perpetual bereavements, or so that he experiences the greatest torments of sorrow from the death of children.

19. The Sun posited in the 6th house from the ASC denotes many evils, for it will always kill, and it will make serious and chronic illnesses. But if, with the Sun posited thus, Mars was found in the ASC, it will surely make public actions; and it frequently inflicts wounds on him by iron. And it will make his father to die a bad death, or to die early, or to be condemned for some reason. But it also makes all his assets to be lost in various ways if, with the Sun posited in the 6th house, no star was found in the 10th from the ASC, i.e. in the MC. For if, with the Sun posited in the 6th, any star possesses the 10th house, i.e. the MC, it will make opulent, wealthy, affluent persons, and those on whom the greatest good fortune is conferred by succession to their fathers. But if, with the Sun posited in the 6th house, no star was placed in the MC, but Jupiter and Venus were found with that same Sun in the 6th house, whatever evils were decreed are mitigated, and all the badness of ill fortune is prevented.

20. The Sun posited in the 7th house from the ASC denotes the greatest bodily defects and illnesses, especially if Mars and Saturn make any aspect to the Sun posited thus, or if they were located with him. For according to the nature of the malefic star, it indicates bodily faults and illnesses...[1] if [it was] Mars, hot and fiery ones. But if the Moon was with it or was found in the 7th house, or with the Sun posited in the 7th house the Moon was located partilely in the ASC or in the MC, it will make great men, powerful, noble, and those to whom the greatest powers are entrusted, especially if it was posited in its own domicile,or in its own exaltation, or in a domicile of Jupiter, and if the Part of Fortune,[2] partilely found by diligent computation, was posited in any angle.

21. But if with the Sun and the Moon posited thus, and with the Part of Fortune located thus, Jupiter holds any angle of the nativity, it will make

[1]Probably the influence of Saturn is missing here. Bram conjectures "Saturn, chills and vicious humors."

[2]Latin *locus Fortunae* 'the place of Fortune' or 'the house of Fortune'. But I think he is referring to the Part of Fortune.

Emperors [and] kings but good and benevolent ones. It will also make powerful generals and strong, moderate, and efficient administrators subjugating provinces and cities. But if with all of these – namely the Sun and the Moon and Jupiter and the Part of Fortune—posited just as we have said, Mars and Saturn were posited in the 2nd or in the 8th house from the ASC, they lose their rulerships, and they are deprived of honors or their own administrative positions along with the loss of their dignity; and they are overthrown either by enemy races or by adversaries and rivals. It will also cause them to bring death upon themselves by their own hands, but it will also make these same persons to be captives or exiles.

22. But if with the Sun posited in the 7th house of the nativity or in any other angle, Mercury posited in the same house, [and] either matutine or vespertine, joins itself to it, it will make learned persons who attain a great and varied knowledge of literature. But if Saturn conjoins itself to the Sun and Mercury posited thus, it makes malicious persons, malevolent and harmful, and those who would like to have a reputation [for handling] difficult literature, or those who make that same difficult literature.

23. But if the Sun, Mercury, and Saturn were found [thus] by night, it will make quarrymen, undertakers, or funeral directors, or those to whom the care or custody of tombs is entrusted. It will also make cowboys, stock-handlers, shepherds, tamers of horses and mares, shepherds,[1] swineherds, and [occupations] similar to these according to the nature and power of the signs. And if in a nocturnal nativity, with the Sun and Saturn posited in the 7th house but also along with Mercury, Venus was found in that same house or in the 6th house or in the 12th, †and Saturn posited Venus were with them†,[2] it will make eunuchs and man-like women, and those women who never join themselves in intercourse with men, or if they ever join themselves to a man, they will never conceive nor give birth.

24. But if Mars conjoins those posited thus with any aspect, or if it was found with them, it will make hermaphrodites, in whom a dual nature joins itself together. But if the Moon conjoins herself with any aspect to

---

[1]The occupation 'shepherds' is repeated again here.

[2]The Latin text is corrupt or some words are missing. Sittl would delete 'Saturn. . . with them'; Bram ignores them. The Teubner editors obelize them and suggest 'with Saturn posited, Venus was with them' or 'with <Mercury> and Saturn posited, Venus was with them'. We could also delete 'Venus' and read 'and Saturn was posited with them'.

all these posited thus, or if she were found with them, they will make chief priests of Cybele, and those who cut off their male organs with their own hands. They will also make pimps, and those who want to rent out whores under their own management.

25. But posited in the 6th house with the Sun, they will make these same things, if no star posited in the MC dissolves the brutality of this evil; for if any star was found in the MC, with all of these found thus, i.e. posited in the 6th house, everything that we have said is mitigated. But if Mercury was found with Saturn in the 2nd house of the nativity or in the 5th or in the 7th, with the Sun posited with them in the same house, it will make persons who are malicious in all their actions, or attorneys, or professional jurists, or law-clerks, or court-reporters, or those in charge of parks, or distributors of waters.[1]

26. But if Mars has conjoined himself in any association with those [stars] placed thus, in those houses which we have mentioned, or if he was found with them, they will be in charge [of judging) public murderers, and also reporters of those sentences, that are handed down on the heads of men, or [they will be] adjutants or registrars,[2] but those to whom the implementation <of punishments>[3] is entrusted, or jailers, or prison wardens and those to whom the public[4] bonds of chains are entrusted, or those in charge of executions, or executioners, and those who are accustomed to lacerate condemned men with whips, and other [occupations] similar to those.

27. But if <Jupiter>[5] and Venus conjoin themselves to all of these, posited in those houses just as we have said, or if they were found with them, they will indeed do nothing of those things that we have mentioned before, for they alone decree against those things. But with Jupiter and Venus, they will make priests, sacrificial assistants, and those who are in charge of sacrifices; or those who tend the sacred cattle intended for sacrifices or religious rites; or those who perform some official duty in temples; or those who get very great gifts from temples.

---

[1]Probably officials or engineers of the city waterworks.

[2]*Commentarienses*, lit. 'those keeping records'. One of their functions was to see that judicial sentences (including executions) were actually carried out.

[3]Accepting the word <*damnatorum*> 'of punishements' supplied by edition **a**.

[4]Reading **publica catenarum vincula* with Ziegler rather than *publicarum catenarum vincula*. *Cf.* v.6.10 (II 64.2).

[5]Supplied by **A′**, rightly as it seems.

28. But all of these stars that we have mentioned, posited together in the 12th house, also denote these same things in similar fashion, but those men will have both later fame and rulership from all those [occupations] in which they are established. But also [with] all of these in the 6th house, if any star, just as we have said before, is found in the MC, they denote those same things in similar fashion. But if the Sun was found alone with Mars in the 7th house of the nativity or in any other angle, or in the 2nd house of the nativity, or in the 5th, or in the 8th, or in the 11th, it will gives arts from fire and iron, and those who make things from some hard material. But the Sun and Mars posited together in the angles always denote these crafts.

29. The Sun posited in the 8th house from the ASC will make the father to die soon. But if Mars or Saturn was found with it, or was opposed to it by a diametric [aspect], or was conjoined to it by square, they will make insane, crazy persons, or those suffering from dypepsia or inflammation of the brain, but these defects of health are denoted in accordance with the nature of the signs.

30. But if, with the Sun posited in the 8th house, the Moon was placed in opposition, not yet weakened[1] by the conjunction but full of light; or,[2] if it was found in conjunction with the Sun in the 8th house, and Saturn and Mars were in opposition or were posited together [with them in the 8th house], or if they were conjoined with them by a square aspect, they will make the greatest illnesses and bodily weaknesses. For they oppress the [Native's] head with bad humors,[3] and from fixed and chronic humors that are accumulated about the head, they will make blind persons and lunatics, or those who decline steadily with chronic spells of unconsciousness. They will also make them to utter unintelligible words. They cripple the upper arms of others with serious injuries. On some they inflict leprous spots, impetigo, consumption, or dropsy. They make others to suffer from elephantiasis, others crippled, and others paralyzed. They [cause] the greater parts of the bodies of others to be amputated. But all these things are denoted in accordance with the differences and natures

---

[1]Reading *soluta* 'weakened' with the MSS, rather than Kroll's emendation *involuta* 'involved with'.

[2]The Latin text has *sed* 'but', but either it should read *aut* 'or' or else there are some words missing prior to that.

[3]This may perhaps be a description of what are now called "cluster" headaches, which are often accompanied by vasodilation, and which the ancients may have ascribed to the accumulation of "humors" in the head.

of the signs. For, posited in the 2nd house from the ASC and in the 6th and in the 12th and in the 8th, they make similar things, just as we have said.

31. But if, with all of them placed thus, as we have said, Jupiter and Venus are conjoined with any aspect, or if they are posited together, or if they are in trine aspect, or if they are cojoined to the Moon, all these illnesses that we have mentioned will be such that they can be treated and cured. But if, with the benefic stars, namely Jupiter and Venus, placed thus, a malefic star receives the conjunction of the applying Moon, there will be some bodily defect and continual sickness, but also by the providence of some divinity the severity of the illness is mitigated.

32. But if the star of Mercury is conjoined with all of these, posited as we have said—either posited with them or placed in sextile—it suppresses or mitigates those illnesses that we have mentioned, either by some remedy or by incantations, so that in every case by means of these remedies they are freed from the attack of illnesses—especially if the waxing Moon conjoins herself with Jupiter, or if the Moon with little light conjoins herself with Venus. But if, in that arrangement of the stars which we have set forth, the Moon always conjoins herself to the star of Mercury, and, placed with it, was aspected by benefic stars, either by trine or by sextile aspect, the Natives will flee to the Gods, and they will remain there, demanding remedies from them.[1] But if the Moon is conjoined with the star of Mercury, with the Sun and Saturn and Mars posited just as we have said, and if Jupiter and Venus were found in disjunct and dejected houses, they will make insane persons, lunatics, and those afflicted by a daemon, and who are entangled in perpetual calamities from those bodily defects, so that they also perish by a violent death.

33. The Sun posited in the 9th house from the ASC will make fabricators of [images of] the Gods, or maintainers[2] of divine images, or decorators [of the images] of the Gods, or builders of temples, or hymn-singers,

---

[1]In other words, they will go to the temples of the Gods, take up residence in the temples, and demand that the Gods heal them.

[2]*Cultores divinorum simulacrorum*. The word *cultor* can mean 'someone who takes care of something' or 'someone who worships it'. But here it plainly means 'conserver' or 'maintainer'. Cf. Rhetorius, *Compendium*, Chapter 57, Ninth House, which has for the Sun there the phrase *theôn kosmêtas* 'cleaners or polishers [of the images] of the Gods'. The images of the Gods in the temples obviously got dirty as time went by and needed to be periodically cleaned and restored to their original appearance.

and those who recite the praises of the Gods with a diplay of ostentation, from which things they will have fame and honors. And the Sun placed thus also makes a fortunate father, but it also denotes various and numerous changes in life for the Narive and for his father. And if, with the Sun posited thus, a benefic star was found in the *anafora* of the MC, then when established in foreign places, they attain the greatest augments of good fortune. But if a malefic star was found in this house, he will experience many misfortunes in foreign travel, and he will die in pain abroad.

34. The Sun partilely posited in the 10th house from the ASC in a diurnal nativity, i.e. in the MC, in its own domicile or in a domicile of Jupiter, or in that degree in which it is exalted, will make kings, to whom rulership is handed down from their father, or it will make generals, on whom this [mark] of honor is conferred in similar fashion—handed down from paternal honors—or it will make administrators and consuls and proconsuls, but those on whom this [honor] is conferred because of the paternal merit of dignity.

35. But if, with the Sun posited thus, Mars possesses any angle of the nativity, [it will give] the kingdoms, generalships, administrations, consulships, [or] proconsulships through dangers and through battles and through ill-will. But if the Sun was found partilely in the MC, in those signs that we have mentioned, but Mars was posited in the DSC, i.e. in the 7th house of the nativity, and the Moon full of light in another angle of the nativity aspected Mars, i.e. she was posited in either the ASC[1] or in the MC, it makes him who was born thus—whether a king, a general, or a consul, or a proconsul, or an administrator—to be an exile [or] a captive.

36. But also, if the Sun was posited in the MC just as we have said, but Mars was posited in the 2nd house of the nativity or in the 8th house, and the Moon received the aspect of Mars by opposition or by square, or if full of light she was with him, in similar fashion it makes those same persons that we have mentioned to be exiles [or] captives dying a violent death. But if, with the Sun posited just as we have said, Mars was not in those houses that we have mentioned, but Jupiter was found in the angles or in the *cataforas*, and the Moon possessed some angle of the nativity, and full of light she was in aspect to Jupiter, it will make those same kings and generals to extend their power throughout the space of the whole Earth.

---

[1]Here Firmicus uses the old word *hora* for ASC instead of *horoscopo*, which he does only 10 times in the entire *Mathesis*.

37. But ordinarily, the Sun posited in that sign in which the MC is, will make noble parents, honorable ones, especially if any benefic star makes any aspect to the Sun posited thus; but also these things are diminished if a malefic star impedites the Sun posited thus. But generally, the Sun posited partilely with Mercury in all the angles will make literati, fluent in speech and distinguished in various literary occupations, of which varied activities and some very great learning are denoted. Moreover, those who have the Sun and Mercury thus, if the star of Jupiter has conjoined it self to them, will be established with kings because of literary matters or their teaching; but Mercury will also make these things if it was found to be far away from the rays of the Sun, and if Jupiter and Venus make a good aspect to them posited thus without the ill influence of Mars and Saturn.

38. The Sun posited in the 11th house from the ASC will make fortunate and noble persons, and those whose fathers are decorated with the greatest splendor of honor, but with the passage of time they will receive increases of good fortune and dignity. Moreover, all these things will be greater if Jupiter was either posited together with the Sun posited thus or if it aspected the Sun by trine, or if the matutine Venus was found with it or aspected it by sextile; for all of these dignities are conferred on them by the kindness of friends. But if the Sun was found in the 11th house of the nativity and malefic stars were either with it or conjoined with it by some aspect, they will cause no impediment to their action or honors, but they alone harm the House of Children with the persistence of a harsh decree.

39. The Sun posited in the 12th house from the ASC will make persons of low degree and frequently slaves and captives, and it denotes the swift death of the father and the loss of all of his estate, also bodily defects and grave illnesses. And if a benefic star was found with the Sun in this house, it will still make [the Native to have] the very lowest status. But if a malefic star was found in this house with the Sun, it denotes perpetual illnesses and the severest bodily defects and perpetual servitudes.

40. But inquire diligently into the dodecatemory and the terms of the dodecatemory, lest the teaching of that work escape your notice in anything.

Chapter 3e. Venus [III.6]

1. Venus posited partilely in the ASC degree, if it was found in this house by night, will make men with divine talents. It produces friends of

Emperors or powerful men, and those to whom the business affairs of Emperors and great men are entrusted. It will also make the greatest orators and good men in accordance with the nature and quality of the signs. For if it was found partilely in the ASC in human signs, it will make chief priests, and those who in their priestly duties wear purple and golden robes, and who predict the future. Moreover, it will make pleasing, handsome, rich persons, if no malefic star with a powerful aspect goes up against Venus posited thus.

2. But if, with Venus posited partilely in the ASC in those signs which we have mentioned, the star of Mercury conjoins itself [to her] and was posited with her partilely in the same sign and in the same degrees, it will make [the Natives] to be crowned with crowns and fillets; it will also make [skilled] musicians, such that they are praised with the admiration of everyone.

3. But posited in sounding[1] signs and those of half voice,[2] namely in a nocturnal nativity, it will make hunters of various sorts,[3] friends of Emperors, making and finding something such as pertains to royal pleasures; it will also make those who are in charge of pleasures—but those which are prepared for royal delight—receiving very great salaries from Emperors,[4] so that the greatest wealth is conferred on them from the payment of [those] salaries. But posited in earth signs or in water signs, it will make men such as those who make perfumes and cosmetics, or who make splendid clothes,[5] or it will produce the greatest dyers [of cloth]. But posited just as we have said in quadrupedal signs, it will make noble, famous, good persons, fond of cattle, and those in charge of the royal animals.

4. But if it was found partilely in the ASC in a diurnal nativity, it will make disreputable, lustful, indecent persons; they will also be

---

[1]Accepting Kroll's conjecture *consonantibus* 'sounding' rather than *constantibus* 'standing firm", i.e. 'fixed'. Firmicus applies the term *consonans* 'sounding' to Aries. The voiced signs by most writers are said to be Gemini, Virgo, Libra, the first part of Sagittarius, and Aquarius. However, Teucer of Babylon also says that Leo is voiced.

[2]According to Teucer, the half-voiced signs are Aries, Taurus, Sagittarius, and Capricorn

[3]Reading *venatores* 'hunters' with edition **α** rather than *veneratores* 'those who reverence'. Rhetorius, *Compendium*, Chapter 57, First House, has for Venus there *thêreutas* 'hunters', and Cumont had noted that the word *veneratores* 'reverencers' in Firmicus should be changed to *venatores* 'hunters'.

[4]MS **N** has *imperatoribus* 'Emperors' rather than *imperatore* 'Emperor'.

[5]That is, 'couturiers'.to use the modern term.

linen-weavers, or embroiderers, or inventors of colors and dyers, or inn-keepers or tavern-keepers. But if Venus, posited thus by day, aspects Saturn in any other part [of the nativity], it will make effeminates, sodomites, or those who devote themselves to disgraceful[1] acts. But if Venus [is] posited in the ASC, it will give a wife in his early age. Moreover, if Saturn aspects Venus posited thus with a strong aspect, it will make dyers of chestnut-colored cloth,[2] or weavers, or inventors of pigments. But if Jupiter makes a good aspect to Venus posited thus, will make those in charge of the royal textile factories.

5. Venus posited in the 2nd house from the ASC, if it was found thus in a nocturnal nativity, makes discoverers of great arts and persons abounding in wealth, but who are frequently accused of infamous acts, and those on whom good fortune is gradually conferred. And those who are pleasing and delightful in [gratifying] their amorous desires.

6. But if it was found in this house by day, it denotes the greatest difficulties and a late marriage; it also stirs up lawsuits with some woman. Some are also made widowers by the early death of their wives. But if, with Venus thus placed, either the Sun or Saturn aspects it by square or opposition or is placed with it, they will make sterile persons and those who are inadequate in the performance of sexual acts, and who never marry a wife, and who are always involved in love affairs with boys. But these evils are denoted more strongly, if Venus is found thus in a diurnal nativity in a domicile of Saturn or Mars or Mercury or in their terms.

7. Venus posited in the 3rd house from the ASC will be good if Jupiter aspects her with any aspect, for the Native will receive a wife from a temple, or [she will be] a priestess, or the daughter of a priest. But if the star of Mercury or the Moon was found with Venus, these Natives will also be prophets, temple-keepers, or those in charge of temples and religions.

8. Venus posited in the 4th house from the ASC by day, i.e. in the IMC, will make a very great loss of inheritance and continual bereavements,[3] and it makes such persons as can only get things with difficulty. But

[1]Reading **turpibus* 'disgraceful' rather than *dulcibus* 'sweet' or 'pleasant'. Cf. *Mathesis* iv. 9. 7 "The Moon separating from Saturn and applying to Venus," where *turpes actus* 'disgraceful acts' are mentioned.

[2]The Latin word *spadastros* according to Souter, *A Glossary of Late Latin*, in the *Mathesis* means 'dyers in chestnut-brown'; it is otherwise unattested. Bram has mistakenly equated it with *spadones* 'eunuchs' and translated it as 'castrates'. But Prof. Monat translates it as 'dyers'.

[3]In particular, from the deaths of their wives.

when Mercury was conjoined to her in a partile aspect, it will frequently make adulterers [who are] also[1] proscribed on account of bad administrations either public or private.

9. But if it was found in this house by night, with the passage of time it will make praises, friends of great men, and those full of charm and handsome. But in their youth, i.e. in the first age [of life], respectable indeed and those for whom nothing is lacking, but implicated in some fault according to the proper nature and substance of the sign. For posited in tropical or bicorporeal signs it denotes the deaths of wives, and losses, and court suits on account of women or stirred up by women, Posited in fixed signs, it denotes obedient wives and those who are greatly loved by them, and those on whom fame and wealth are conferred by women, except for the sign Aquarius, for if Venus was found in that sign, namely in the 4th from the ASC, and the Moon aspected her either by square or by opposition, or if it was placed with her, it will make sterile persons and those who are unable to beget children, and those who never want to join themselves in conjugal affections, and who always rejoice in intercourse with boys.

10. Venus posited in the 5th house from the ASC will make good, kindly persons, and those who easily get whatever they want. It will also make [them] to be crowned with crowns and headbands[2]; if Jupiter makes any aspect to her, it will make renowned persons, <outstanding> because of some honor of nobility.[3] But if Mercury was posited with them, it bestows increases in life and promotions, but with the greatest infamy. Moreover, in every meeting it will make [them] victors, and those on whom the pleasing rewards of victories are bestowed. It makes them powerful in all things, and those who always predict the future; acquaintances of powerful men, and those on whom the greatest wealth is conferred by women or by their wives. Or those who arrive at the greatest degrees of dignity through the guardianship or the patronage of women or of their wives. But with the passage of time everything completed and perfect is allotted to them.

---

[1]Reading Némethy's conjecture (confirmed by **N)** *etiam* 'also' rather than the meaningless †*stoemen*.

[2]High priests of the pagan religions wore crowns and headbands made of red & white wool as emblems of their religious status. Cf. the equally elaborate headgear of the high Christian clergy.

[3]Reading *honore nobilitatis <praefulgidos>* with **N** rather than *honore nobilitatos* 'ennobled with honor'

11. But if it receives the light of the waxing Moon or if the waxing Moon conjoins itself to it, they attain administrative positions and fame with great envy. But it makes reliable persons and those who are separated from all falsehood, and who do not want to give or to receive the necessity of an oath about true things. But, when Venus is posited thus, it will make [them] quarrel with their wives with contentious conflict of quarrels on account of some suspicions.

12. Venus posited in the 6th house from the ASC by day and by night will give wives of low social status, or widows, or crippled women, and those never obedient to their husbands, if no star was found in the MC. But if a woman has the star of Venus in the 6th house of her own nativity, she will experience great difficulties and great dangers from childbirth; for either she will frequently abort or she will give birth with difficulty, so that from within her womb a cut-up fetus[1] will be brought forth by the physicians.[2]

13. But if with Venus in the 6th house, and in a nocturnal nativity, any star was found in the MC, it will make pleasing, becoming persons who are humored by their wives, and those whose wives bring them good fortune. And they obtain everything that they want. But if Venus was posited with no relation to the angles, and malefic stars that were posited in the angles make a strong aspect to the Moon, it will make those who were born to be exposed by their parents, and they will immediately perish.[3]

14. Venus posited in the 7th house from the ASC, if it was found in its own sign by night, makes a fortunate old age; moreover, it will give a wife slowly, and it denotes children with difficulty for those who have Venus posited thus. Moreover, it will make those who are troubled with the greatestest scandals from venereal matters according to the nature and quality of the sign. For if it holds this house [while] posited in tropical signs or scaly or wandering ones, and Mars was with her or was conjoining itself to her in strong aspect by opposition or by square, it makes unchaste, lustful, and disreputable persons.

---

[1]Reading **fetus* 'fetus' rather than *pecus* 'animal' as given in the Latin text.

[2]This refers to an embryotomy performed by the attendant physicians when the woman was unable to deliver the fetus.

[3]Reading *malivolae stellae quae in cardinibus fuerint constituti Lunam forti radiatione possederint,<eos qui nati fuerint> expositos a parentibus faciet* with MS **N** (which omits *et statim faciunt*); but in *Mathesis* vii. 2. 6 the phrase *aut statim peribunt* 'or they will immediately perish' occurs, which is also appropriate here as *et statim peribunt*.

15. But if Saturn makes any aspect, i.e. by square or by oposition or by being with her, to Venus posited thus with Mars in those signs that we have mentioned, women who have Venus [posited] thus with that configuration of stars will have sexual relations with other women unchastely and immodestly because of lust. But these faults will be stronger if that combination of stars was conjoined in Capricorn or Aries.

16. If Venus was posited in the 8th house in a diurnal nativity, it will give a wife slowly, and when it has given one, it will give either a low-class one or a widow or one disfigured with severe ugliness. But if Mercury was with it and some malefic star aspected Venus posited in this house together with Mercury either by square or by opposition, or if it was found with them in this house, all of the Native's estate is dissipated, or he is stripped bare of it by some proscription. And his death is caused by *gonorrhea*, i.e. by a flux of semen,[1] or by [bodily] contraction, or by spasm, or by apoplexy. But if Venus was found by night in this house, it will make wealthy men, and those on whom good fortune is conferred by the death of great women; but a quick death is denoted for the Natives and one without pain or torment.

17. If Venus was posited in the 9th house from the ASC in a diurnal nativity, it will make him who has Venus thus to be battered by the constant disturbance of some demon. Moreover, it will make those who dwell in temples—dirty persons and those who always go about thus, and who never cut their hair, and those who want to announce something to men as if it was said by the Gods—the sort of persons who are usually [seen] to be in temples, who are accustomed to prophesy. Venus posited thus also frequently makes interpreters of dreams. But these things will be stronger if Saturn makes any aspect to Venus posited thus.

18. But if it was found in this house in a nocturnal nativity, it will make divines, worshippers of the Gods, and those who are steeped in sacred things and in religions; but those on whom [religious] offices or gifts are bestowed from the temples. But if, with Venus posited thus by night, Mars and Saturn conjoin themselves to her by opposition or by square or were together with her, it will make those who are harassed by women, or on whom a serious misfortune is heaped by women, and those to whom women are always ungrateful—especially if she was found in tropical signs with this configuration of stars.

[1]A literal translation of the Greek word, but that disease is characterized by a purulent rather than a spermatic discharge. Certainly a potentially fatal venereal disease is meant, but not necessarily the one that we call gonorrhea.

19. But if the star of Jupiter aspected Venus posited thus by trine or by sextile, or if it was found with her, it will make those with whom women fall in love. It will make charming, pleasing persons, and those who attain everything easily, and those who are dominant over their wives. Others take charge of the care of women, or they are business managers of women. Others having Venus thus, stay in the palaces of kings or in the homes of powerful men on account of the production of those things which are necessary for the care of women. They are always pleasing and necessary because of these, and they are furnished some promotions on account of these things. And they acquire the greatest increases of wealth from these things.

20. But if Mars posited in opposition or in square aspects Venus posited thus, especially if he is posited in the angles, they will have enemies; they will also see the grave deaths of children; they will also be enemies of their children either because of adultery or debauchery. But if Mercury with the star of Jupiter aspects Venus thus placed by square, or Saturn alone was found in opposition, with Mercury in square or posited with her, or if Saturn and Venus together were posited with Mercury—namely in the house that we have mentioned—it will make sterile men without semen, lovers of boys, lustful men, and those involved in murders or dangers or criminal acts on account of these faults. But if a woman has Venus thus, just as we have said—namely with that configuration of stars—she will always imitate the acts of men.

21. If Venus was found in the 10th house from the ASC, i.e. in the MC, it will make famous and crowned persons and those on whom great fame and the greatest good fortune are conferred. But if she was found in this house with Mercury, it will make those who are skilled in chords and instruments,[1] authors of training courses in music,[2] and those who easily acquire whatever they want. If Saturn and Mars are in no aspect to her, and she herself is matutine, it makes musicians who perform in public and who are honored by the people. But if Saturn conjoins itself to her with any aspect, it will make persons of ill repute, and of second place in those arts from which they profit, and who never claim first place for themselves; and those who entrust their own property to the management of others.

---

[1]Reading <*chordarum et instrumentorum*> *cordatos* with edition **α** and **N**[2] rather than just *cordatos* 'wise' or 'skilled' with the others. This seems appropriate for Mercury conjunct Venus in the 10th.

[2]Accepting Kroll's addition <*musicae*> *disciplinae* 'of musical training'.

22. But if a woman has Venus posited thus, she will be indecent, lustful and displayed for the pleasure of all, and always involved in the acts of prostitutes, which she adopts for herself to earn money for the necessities of life; or she hires herself out to the keeper of a house of prostitution; but these acts are performed in accordance with the quality and substance of the signs. For <posited> in erratic or in tropical signs, or in the domiciles of Saturn, or in scaly [signs], <just as we have said, it makes a woman of that sort. But if in those signs>,[1] just as we have said, a man has Venus posited as we have said, he will be totally disreputable, and one who commits indecent acts of many sorts. But Venus posited thus as we have said in those signs and in that configuration of stars, so that it was found in a feminine sign; and with the Moon, increasing in light, and also in a feminine sign, aspected Mars by square or by opposition, it will make eunuchs or self-castrated high priests of Cybele or hermaphrodites. And it will make those who, aroused by the perverted passions of lust, always do and submit to those things that women submit to.

23. Venus posited in the 11th house from the ASC, if it was vespertine, and if it was posited thus and Mars and Saturn aspected it from some other part [of the nativity], it will make sterile persons and those who cannot beget [offspring], and who get married with difficulty. And it frequently makes lovers of boys or of actresses, or those who are in charge of commerce, especially if she was posited in tropical signs, but gradually increasing their personal assests. And it makes those on whom increases in honors or also of wealth are conferred by the support of friends. Still, it will make good-natured and charming persons. And if Venus thus posited receives the conjunction of the applying Moon, it will make opulent, rich persons, of the greatest power and fame,[2] and those to whom the guardianship of the greatest powers is entrusted; sometimes it will make [members of] the First Ten of noble cities.[3]

---

[1]These words (omitted by Bram) are supplied by MS **N**. Evidently two lines were omitted in both **Ω** and **Ψ** due to homoeoarchon (*sicut diximus.../sicut diximus...*). This raises a possible question about the source of **N's** supplement; for if my *stemma codicum* is correct, then the copyist of **Ω** must have omitted the line when copying from the archetype, and the copyist of **Ψ** also omitted the same line when copying from **Casinensis 361**. A similar instance is found in Book IV, Chapter 13, below. This is discussed in the Preface.

[2]Accepting the Teubner editors' emendation *maximae potentiae et gloriae*, or we could accept Némethy's emendation *maximae appetentes etiam gloriae* 'also trying to get the greatest glory'.

[3]Members of a select Committee of Ten of the leading officials of a city. This same signification is given for Jupiter in the 10th. However, the word 'noble'

24. But if she was found matutine in this house and has received in a similar manner the conjunction of the applying Moon, it will make those who are powerful from their first age and like those to whom some power is granted from their first age, so that the faithful merit of friendship joins <them> to great men or to Emperors,[1] and who down to the last day of their lives are adorned with the grace of charm. And these things will be stronger if Mercury conjoins itself with any aspect to Venus and the Moon posited in this house, or if it was posited with them in this same house.

25. Venus posited in the 12th house from the ASC, if it was found thus in a nocturnal nativity, will make [the Native] to be tormented with the constant pain of sadness because of women. If Mars and Mercury aspect [Venus] thus placed with a strong aspect, it will frequently make treacheries from slave-girls involving him because of lust. It makes a turbulent mind, and it denotes the fires of shameful love from an instinct of lust. But some join themselves in wedlock with servant-girls; others unite in intercourse in the marriage bed with public prostitutes, because of which the offspring of children is always denied.

26. But posited in this house by day, it denotes murder because of women, or the atrocity of a bad death according to the nature and quality of the signs, for this star has various powers of denoting [things], but they can be difficult to discover. For, just as in paintings the artist records the liniaments of the limbs from a varied diversity of mixtures and makes a certain form of the body from blended colors by an imitation of the likeness of the body, so also the conjunction aspect of the stars by the concord of their association when blended together borrows a certain force for itself in turn from the conjoined powers. And it borrows its substance for itself from the various color of fires that depict the combined fates of men in the manner of a picture with the combined government of their association.

27. For, that which we are saying is so is proved by these reasons. When Venus is posited just as we have said, if Saturn conjoins [her] with any aspect, it makes minds that are entangled with perverse faults and that are turned to no useful actions, especially if this conjunction of Ve-

---

does not seem appropriate for 'cities'; perhaps we should read **magnarum civitatum* 'great cities'.

[1]Reading with Ziegler (and partly with MS **N**) *fidelis amicitiae merita <eos> coniungant.*

nus and Saturn was found in a nocturnal nativity. But if while placed thus she was conjoined to Jupiter, she is freed from the assault of the preceding maliciousness; for [then] the greatest advantages are bestowed. For they will acquire increases in their assets by their own actions, and they will be removed from every defect of faults; that is, if the Moon had no aspect by opposition to Venus placed thus with Jupiter.

28. But if the Moon was found in opposition, it will make persons of bad reputation, lustful, or lovers of boys. And it will make those sweating from their intercourse with women to be struck with the heavy disgrace of a bad reputation, for heavy disgraces from incests and debauches are denoted by this combination; for they are caused to have intercourse with their sisters, or nieces, or daughters, or the wives of their brothers; but nevertheless, from that incest the greatest financial rewards will accrue to them, and [also] some reward of dignity.

29. But always Venus posited together with the Moon or conjoined [with her] by square denotes the attractions of [sexual] love, or the defect of a bad reputation and a propensity to foulness,[1] or it will entangle [the Native] in troublesome defects of mind, or it makes those who are perverted by impure or lustful desire, or it strikes them with a very bad reputation from their incestuous love affairs. For, just as we have said, they either have intercourse with their sisters, or if it is with non-relatives, they will join together in debauchery with two sisters that are known to them; or they will have intercourse with their daughters or with their mothers, or with their daughters-in law, or with the wives of their step-children; or they will burn with the fault of lustful desire around their brothers' wives, or they will have intercourse with their nieces, or with their in-laws, or with the sons of their sisters.

30. But if a woman has Venus posited thus, it will make her lustful and one who is involved in the promiscuous pleasures of [sexual] love, and always caught up in the disgrace of a bad reputation and burning for incestuous love affairs; for she will either have intercourse with her brothers or with her sons, or with her parents, or with the sons of her paternal uncles, or with her daughters' husbands, or with her paternal uncles, or with the paternal uncles of her own sons,[2] or with her sons-in-law, or

---

[1]Reading *foeditate* 'foulness' with **W** (see the Preface to the Tebner edition, p. XXIV) rather than *felicitate* 'good fortune' **ΩΨ** *falsitate* 'falsity' **N** or Kroll's conjecture *infelicitate* 'misfortune'.

[2]That is, with her brothers-in-law.

in-laws; or she will call two brothers to one pleasure of the bed; but it makes some women desire the acts of men.

31. But then it makes these things stronger if, conjoined with the Moon in that aspect in tropical signs[1] or in erratic[2] or scaly[3] or bicorporeal[4] ones, [and] it was in that combination of aspects that we have mentioned. Which things will be stronger and more forceful if Mars or Saturn is in opposition or in square to both of them, i.e. the Moon and Venus, posited as we have said, or [even] to one of the two, or if one of the former two was posited together with one of the latter; or if the Moon joined together with Venus in that relationship or jointly posited in that relationship, were located in a domicile of Mars or Saturn, or if they were together in the signs of Mercury, or if one of the two posited in a sign of Mercury aspected the other by that relationship that we have mentioned.

32. Venus posited in her vespertine rising, but posited in a good sign in a nocturnal nativity, if she was in a favorable aspect to Mars, denotes good increases of good fortune; for it makes powerful persons and glorious powers, and it bestows the greatest insignia of honors, and it bestows riches of opulent abundance. But if by day she conjoins herself by any aspect to Mars, it denotes misfortunes of many and great evils. For she rejoices by night if she conjoins herself to the Moon, Mars, and Mercury, and then she makes men famous for their very great good fortune, whenever she was conjoined with these in a nocturnal nativity by a good aspect.

33. But if Venus was with the Sun in this house of which we are speaking, by the statement of all prudent persons it is certain that she will be most unjust. For Venus is badly placed, if she is posited with it; for she does not rejoice in association with the rays of the Sun[5]; and whatever seems to be evil and wretched in human affairs, she denotes all of that when posited with the Sun. But she rejoices when she is posited *behind* the Sun, i.e. when she is matutine; then, whatever amount of good she has decreed will increase with a stronger augment of good fortune.

[1]What are called today "cardinal signs"—Aries, Cancer, Libra, and Capricorn.
[2]It is uncertain which signs Firmicus called 'erratic'; the only one that is called 'erratic' in the preserved text is Aries, and as mentioned in the note to Book II, Chapter 3, that may be a mistake.
[3]Pisces is the only sign that Firmicus specifically identifies as 'scaly'.
[4]Gemini, Virgo, Sagittarius, and Pisces.
[5]That is, when she is 'under the Sun beams' or combust.

34. But if she was found to be the ruler of the ASC, and she was also the Ruler of the whole Nativity, or if she decreed [the Native's] life when posited in good signs and in favorable houses of the nativity, she bestows the greatest length of life. But if the Giver of Life was unfavorable to the Ruler of the Nativity or to the Ruler of the ASC in a diurnal nativity, it subtracts eight years from that [length of] time of life that was decreed. And thus placed, she denotes defects, but such as do not stain [the Native] with a severely bad reputation.

35. But also inquire into the dodecatemory and the terms of the dodecatemory of Venus, so that you may discover the secrets of the things decreed by all the methods.

<Chapter 3f. Mercury.> [III.7]

1. Mercury partilely posited in the degree of the ASC in those signs in which it rejoices in a diurnal nativity makes philosophers, masters of the grammatical art, or geometers, either often dealing with celestial things or those who are interested in them, so that they can recognize the presence of the Gods, or persons skilled in sacred literature. It also frequently makes orators and lawyers, especially if it is found in this house, either in its own signs or in other signs of voice.

2. But if the Sun or Saturn or Jupiter aspects Mercury [posited] thus in a diurnal nativity, it will make great men, who are crowned with sacred and glorious wreaths; it also makes such persons as are entrusted with the greatest business affairs of Emperors. But if Mars aspects Mercury thus placed by square or by opposition or was found with him partilely in the ASC, it ruins him who was born thus with a manifold succession of evils; for the evils that arise from this configuration of Mercury and Mars cannot be defined or identified. But if Mars aspects Mercury thus posited by trine, it makes a man occupied with good and successful actions.

3. But if Mercury was found thus partilely in the ASC in a nocturnal nativity, it makes those who are divine in their judgments, and who attain everything that they desire always with very easy procedures; it also makes persons who are honorable in their behavior and serious in their reasoning. It also makes those in charge of hiring, or of equipment, or of honoraria, or of business transactions, or of banks, and those handling negotiations for loans. Placed thus by night it also frequently makes interpreters for Emperors or the most powerful judges; but it de-

notes all these things according to the difference and quality of the signs.

4. Mercury posited in the 2nd house from the ASC, if it was found to be matutine, will make obscure men with wicked minds, unsuited to the knowledge of letters, and a person who is deprived of every means of life. But if it was vespertine in this house, and it is a nocturnal nativity, it will make money-lenders, businessmen, or those who maintain the care and management of other people's things. But if it was found thus in a diurnal nativity, it makes philologists or those skilled in laborious letters,[1] and those who do not want their nature to be compared with that of the rest of men; for they will aspire to [learn] everything that training derived from formal education has not handed down to them. Nevertheless, it makes those whose lives are miserable and who always wear themselves out [dealing] with various kinds of deficiencies.

5. But if Jupiter makes any kind of aspect to Mercury thus placed, or if Jupiter was found with it, and the Moon was associated with them in a good configuration, it makes those who are in charge of great and famous places, but who do not have supreme authority, and in their actions[2] they are subordinate to the power of another person. Moreover, it makes those who are in charge of great affairs; [that is], it makes those who control royal resources by means of their own direction, and who have all the royal revenues and treasuries entrusted to their own good faith and direction. But this happy situation of theirs will be terminated in a short space of time.

6. Mercury posited in the 3rd house from the ASC will make priests, mages, chief physicians, mathematicians, and those who discover and learn through their own efforts whatever was not handed down to them by the tradition of others. Moreover, it makes wise, fortunate persons and those who engage in all [types of] actions in a ready fashion. But if Jupiter aspects Mercury posited thus by trine or by sextile, or if it was found with him, it will make men of great mental ability—those of great and divine counsel. But if Mars unites with Mercury and Jupiter posited thus with any aspect, it will make royal procurators, famous generals, powerful administrators, and those to whom the assets of royal wealth are entrusted. And it makes persons of such mind and strength that they are able to conquer all things by the virtue and good attitude of their mind.

[1]Probably those who are skilled in foreign languages.

[2]Reading *ipsis actibus* 'those acts' with MS **N** and edition **α** rather than *ipso actu* 'that act'.

7. Mercury posited in the 4th house from the ASC, [i.e.] in the IMC, will make sharp persons and those in charge of public affairs, and they are strong in various kinds of learning. But if it was found in this house in its matutine rising, it makes masters of certain secret arts. But if, with Mercury thus posited, Mars and Saturn possess other angles of the nativity and aspect Mercury either by square or by opposition, they will make accusations, confinements, imprisonments, and frequently condemnations. But if it was found vespertine in the 4th house from the ASC, i.e. in the IMC, it will make goldsmiths, or diggers of gold, or masters of some hidden arts, or those who are seen to be instructed in computation and calculation, or it will make chiefs[1] of wrestlers and those in charge of wrestlers.

8. Mercury posited in the 5th house from the ASC, if it was found in its morning rising, will make hoarders of gold and riches, and those who acquire the greatest abundance of personal wealth by means of their own foresight, but it makes those in charge of great sums of money belonging to others, and those who seem to have divine customs. Moreover, it denotes the greatest abundance of life for those with Mercury posited thus; and they will have a fruitful offspring of children.

9. But if it was found vespertine in this house, the Native will not be able to handle money in any fashion, but it will make the total amount of money, or of gold and silver, and of other movable assets that was deposited [with him] to be dissipated by lavish expenditures. It will surely make businessmen and those in charge of public affairs with some sort of administration. According to the quality of the signs, it sometimes makes school-teachers, or geometers,[2] or astrologers, and those who find the course of the stars by skilled computation.[3] It also makes those in charge of wrestling schools and their directors.[4]

10. But if Mercury posited in this house receives the conjunction of the waxing Moon, it makes the whole body of a man to be spotted with white blemishes, or it will implicate [him] in severe illnesses according to the nature and quality of the signs. But if the waning Moon conjoins herself to Mercury posited thus, it will involve the man in dishonorable illnesses,

[1]Probably coaches in wrestling schools are meant.

[2]This would include those who were experts in geometry like Euclid, but probably land-surveyors are meant (a meaning that is still retained in the Italian word *geometra* and the Modern Greek *geométrês* with the same meaning).

[3]That is, astronomers.

[4]Probably 'coaches'.

and it will frequently make him stray from the right manner of living because of perverse cases of insanity.

11. Mercury posited in the 6th house from the ASC will make [the Native] acquire the greatest fortune for himself, either from the learned fluency of his own speech, or from the practice of law, or from business, or from gifts of the Gods—especially if, with Mercury placed thus, another star was found in the 10th sign from the ASC.

12. But if it was found to be matutine in the 6th house in a nocturnal nativity, it makes interpreters, fishermen, fowlers, [and] sculptors, if, with Mercury placed thus, any star was found in the 10th house of the nativity. But if it was posited matutine in the 6th house in a nocturnal nativity, and the 10th house from the ASC had no star, it makes ill-natured, malicious persons, authors of evil counsel, thieves, and those who desire other peoples' things with an envious ardor of mind; and those who rejoice in the misfortunes of other people, and accusers.[1] And those who persecute their in-laws and their own relations with bitter hatreds. It makes slow-witted and mentally blind persons, and those on whom all kinds of malice is conferred.

13. But if it was found vespertine in this house, it will make wise, serious, secretive persons, who are in charge of accounts, or measures, or granaries, or storehouses, or equipment, or business transactions—from which activities they derive great profit. But if thus placed it receives the conjunction of the applying Moon, it will make secretaries, either of judges, or of governmental authorities, or of the Senate, or those who hold a position with Emperors and have some power of instruction, or who are appointed to manage the affairs of their own principal according to their own devices, especially if, with Mercury posited thus, the Moon or some other star possesses the 10th house of the nativity.

14. Mercury posited in the 7th house from the ASC, i.e. in the DSC, if it was found in a diurnal nativity, will make those who have Mercury thus to be involved in serious offenses and to burn with desires for miserable passions. Moreover, they will be very much either lovers of boys or of virgins, but these Natives are allotted debauched women for wives;. And frequently, they undertake the care and defense of disreputable men. But this is also denoted according to the quality of the signs; for if it was found in this house in those signs in which it does not re-

[1]Accusers are persons who institute legal charges against others.

joice, i.e. in a domicile of Mars or in a domicile of Saturn, or in other places in which it is debilitated, it will make those in charge of whores, and pimps, and those who are sordid from the squalors of that kind of infamy. But if Mars was found in opposition, or in the MC, or in the DSC, i.e. in the 7th house, posited with Mercury, it will make a life of little time: it makes consumptives, fugitives, exiles, and condemned persons.

15. But if it was found by night in the 7th house of the nativity, i.e in the DSC, it will make business managers of rich women and those on whom the greatest good fortune is conferred from sexual activities. And it makes those who discover [methods] of calculation, or music, or documents, or difficult writings. I know that Mercury in this house has often made pebble-jugglers.

16. Mercury posited in the 8th house from the ASC, if it was found to be vespertine by day in this house, will make those who are sluggish, and who dare to do nothing and want to do nothing, always stuck in laborious activities, foolishly malicious [and engaged] in no usful activities. But if when posited in this house it was in a domicile of Saturn or in the degrees of Saturn, it will make deaf and dumb persons, especially if, when it is placed thus, Saturn aspects it with any aspect.

17. But if it was found to be vespertine by night in this house, it will make those who inherit from non-relatives and who find hidden wealth by chance. They will also be lucky and at the same time happy, but they are depraved and easily fatigued by continual spells of weakness. But posited in this house matutine, it will make those who are born thus to increase their money without limit and to desire great acts Moreover, it will make others <who share> †responsibilities, trusts, or managing, or faithful and steadfast <guardians> of legal documents†, and frequently heirs of inheritances from unrelated persons.[1]

---

[1]A word, such as *participentes* 'those who share' seems to be missing, and *actuum* 'performances' is suspicious. Also, the following *instrumentorum fidos stabilesque <custodes>* may not be correct; the phrase *instrumentorum fides* is a legal term that means 'the credibility of documents' and MS **R**[a] actually has *fides*; Sittl indicates a lacuna after *stabilesque*, where Kroll conjectured *custodes* 'guardians', but more and different words than that may be missing. However, the orginal signification can be obtained from Rhetorius, who has *poieî tinâs de kai phrontidôn* ê *pisteôn* ê *oikonomiôn* ê *grammateiôn methêsontas* ê *kai allotriôn klêronomous* 'it also makes some who share in responsibilities, or fiduciary relationships, or managing, or legal documents, or even those inheriting from unrelated persons'.

18. Mercury posited in the 9th house from the ASC, if it was found in this house wihout the aspect of any star, will make contentious, contradictory, argumentative persons, claiming that they know things that were not imparted to them by any formal instruction; malicious persons, but those who cannot complete anything by effective thought.

19. But if it was found matutine in this house, it will make priests, divines, diviners from entrails, augurs,[1] mathematicians, astrologers, [and] physicians, and those who derive their life support from these arts and professions. But these things will be stronger if it was protected by the aspect of a benefic star; for [then] it will make fortunate, prosperous, great, powerful persons, and those on whom all the insignia of good fortune are bestowed. But if malefic stars aspect Mercury posited thus, or if they were found in opposition or in square, it will make irreligious, sacrilegious person, despoilers of temples, condemned persons, or those who should be condemned, and those who always wander about in foreign places as fugitives, or who are crushed down by being condemned to exile.

20. But Mercury posited vespertine in this house will make priests, mages, physicians, artisans, and those for whom their life support is derived from these arts, and persons of such talent that they can learn through their own effort whatever was not handed down to them by formal education.

21. Mercury posited in the 10th house from the ASC, i.e. in the MC, if it was matutine in this house, makes remarkable persons and great in their actions. For if Jupiter from any part [of the nativity] aspects Mercury thus posited by trine or by sextile in a diurnal nativity, they will be great, powerful persons, handling the business affairs of the greatest cities, or those of Emperors or of powerful men, faithful, benevolent, wise, [and] serious persons. But in a nocturnal nativity,[2] if Venus aspects Mercury posited thus with any aspect, it will make those things that we have shown that it would make with Jupiter in a diurnal nativity. But if Mars aspects Mercury thus posited from another part [of the nativty], i.e. by square or by opposition, coming advancements are held back because of various kinds of offenses; and on account of this, they will frequently be

[1]Civic or religious functionaries who were charged with taking and interpreting the omens on important occasions.

[2]MSS **ΩN** have *nocturnis genituris* 'nocturnal nativities', possibly correctly, although the singular is more common.

exiles or those suffering the onus of some kind of condemnation. But also, if the Moon conjoins herself to Mars by any aspect, it will also make those dying violently.

22. But posited in the 10th house vespertine, it will make travels and continual changes of place; it also makes [the Natives] to be public in their actions. But if Saturn aspects Mercury posited thus from another part [of the nativity], either by opposition or by square, it will always make [them] to be occupied in watery activities, and it makes their duties to be either near the sea or near a river or near swamps. But it also denotes bodily defects and illnesses resulting from an abundance of humors.

23. Mercury posited in the 11th house from the ASC will make talented persons, indispensable for all activities, and those to whom the conduct of great business affairs is entrusted; but then it denotes greater duties if it was conjoined to Jupiter by a favorable aspect.

24. Mercury posited in the 12th house from the ASC will make talented persons. If it was matutine, it will make those established in great business matters, or it makes contractors handling public business,[1] so that some of them are in danger in some business transactions, [but] in these same they have favorable results. But when it is vespertine and posited in this house, it will make those initiating business matters and inventors of many business matters.[2] For not without cause did the wisest men take note of this house, and not without cause did they put birth and the time of a woman's labor in this house; for the mother giving birth to offspring is assigned to this house.

25. For the 6th house also affects the 12th, so that when all the other stars are posited in these houses they have sluggish actions; but Mercury found in this house will make learned persons, grammarians,[3] orators, geometers,[4] school teachers, selling their own speeches and legal defenses by the constant marketing [of them]. Or it will make those who come to the aid of men in difficulty with the defense of their own

[1]The reference is probably to private agents who collected state taxes for a percentage of the take. As Firmicus notes, this could sometimes be a risky business, although a profitable one.

[2]Probably what we would call 'deal makers' and 'entrepreneurs'.

[3]Those skilled in language, such as literary scholars or philologists, or high-level handlers of written documents.

[4]Those skilled in geometry (and probably in mathematics). This would include teachers of geometry or more likely those who made practical application of skill in that subject, e.g. surveyors and engineers.

speeches, defending them and liberating them from dangers; for they will be such as are seen by all to be very wise, and persons on whom increases in all kinds of learning are bestowed. But then it makes this, either when it was conjunct Jupiter or when it was not afflicted by any aspect from the malefic stars.

26. But if Mars aspected it by opposition or by square or if it was together with it, it will make accusers, concealers, deceivers, malicious persons, [and] evildoers. It will also make evildoers, poisoners, or those who make forgeries by some malicious artifice, so that they incur severe penalties on account of the malice of these crimes; for they will be condemned either as evildoers or forgers. Moreover, it will make them falsify either documents, or records, or public records; or, having been condemned for this, it will make them die a bad death. It will also make the greatest condemnations and dangers either from slaves or on account of slaves.

27. But if the Moon, with her light increasing, conjoins Mercury and Mars placed thus, it will make those dying violently, but who are punished by judicial censure. But if the Sun was also found with them without any testimony of Jupiter, it will make them to be burned in flames. But all these things are denoted in accordance with the quality of the signs.

28. But because we have said that Mercury conjoins itself with all [the planets] in an easy fashion, and is good with the good [planets] and evil with the evil ones, we ought to explain what it denotes when it is associated with each of them in nativities. Posited by day with Jupiter and the Sun in fortuante houses of the nativity, it denotes the greates good fortune; but if it was found by day with Mars, it will make calamities of the greatest bad fortune. And by night it is altered in similar fashion, for it is good with Venus and the Moon and Mars, but with the Sun it denotes the greatest evils and bad fortune. And, so that we may teach this more clearly, we ought to explain all of it in detail. But first [you should] inquire diligently into Mercury's dodecatemory, so that you can arrive at all the secrets of the nativity.

Chapter 4. Mercury with the Sun. [III.8]

1. Mercury, partilely posited with the Sun in the ASC by day, will make kings, generals, and powerful men; but if they were found partilely in this house by night, they will make the father to be low-class and ob-

scure. Moreover, [the Natives] will always be [involved] in public occupations, but obscure and wretched ones according to the nature and quality of the signs.

2. The Sun and Mercury partilely[1] posited in the 2nd house from the ASC denote an increase in personal property and a position of command over the acts of others.

3. The Sun and Mercury posited in the 3rd house from the ASC will make diviners from entrails, interpreters of dreams, physicians, divines, augurs, astrologers, mathematicians, and those who always predict the future, but whose art and training is brought to the notice of all.

4. Mercury posited partilely with the Sun in the 4th house, i.e. in the IMC, will make obscure persons and those skilled in secret or illicit arts, but honorable and serious ones. But if they were posited thus in the 4th house of the nativity, it must be very specially considered in what sign they are posited, and who is the ruler of that sign; for it is very dangerous if Mercury was found to be posited in a domicile of Saturn in this house.

5. The Sun partilely posited with Mercury in the 5th house from the ASC will make well-born persons and those who accomplish everything easily, but those who are exposed to many dangers and who do not have lasting good fortune, and those who deceive many [persons] in an easy manner.

6. Mercury partilely posited with the Sun in the 6th house from the ASC will make ignoble persons, slaves, toilers, [and] sluggish persons, and those whose fathers are unknown, and who are made orphans by [the death of] their parents; those who are slow in their actions, and those who can accomplish nothing if no star was found in the 10th house from the ASC. <But if any star was found in the 10th house from the ASC>[2], [it indicates] the distinctions of riches, noble birth, and glory [for them], especially if a benefic star was found in the 10th house.

[1]The Latin text has *partiliter* 'partilely', i.e. 'conjoined in the same degree'. But this word seems to be often confused with *pariter* 'together', which is probably what is meant here and in the other sections that give the significations of Mercury with another planet in one of the houses.

[2]This supplement is found in **A′** and edition **α**; hence it was probably present in **Γ** (but not in **Δ** or in **N**; it is found in the margin of **D**, copied either from **Γ** itself or one of its scions). Its omission was apparently due to homeoteleuton (.. . .*fuerit inventa* | . . . *fuerit inventa*), but its absence from **ΩΔ N** is puzzling.

7. Mercury with the Sun partilely posited in the 7th house, i.e. in the DSC, if it was found by day in this house, will make the greatest things and powers to be entrusted to him who is born thus, but it will make him to die by a violent death. But if it was posited partilely in this house by night, it will make him to endure many evils, toiling and getting his living from daily work, and always occupied in bad and dirty jobs; for they will be occupations that are either dirty or squalid or bad-smelling, and those occupations that demand constant vigilance from the workers, which are those of hide-finishers, fullers,[1] wool-workers, bakers, cooks, and jobs similar to those. And it will also make persons with stomach disorders or those having bodily defects in early life.

8. Mercury partilely posited with the Sun in the 8th house from the ASC will make weak, depraved persons and those who are easily deceived; but . . . .[2] posited in this house, they will make a violent death, and frequently they denote insanity.

9. Mercury partilely posited with the Sun in the 9th house from the ASC will make exorcists and those who free men suffering from the incursion of demons by means of their remedies, so that the greatest sustenance of life is furnished to them from [the exercise of] these arts.

10. Mercury partilely posited with the Sun by day in the 10th house from the ASC, i.e. in the MC, in those signs in which it rejoices or in which it is exalted, will make rulers of the whole world or those with the reward of power who are placed in charge of many and the very greatest provinces, especially if Jupiter lends his testimony to them.[3]

11. Mercury partilely posited with the Sun in the 11th house from the ASC denotes increases in good fortune with the passage of time.

12. Mercury partilely posited with the Sun in the 12th house from the ASC in a diurnal nativity will make paupers, unfortunates, [and] slaves, who always perish while traveling.

---

[1]Clemens Herschel in his edition of Frontinus's *De aquaeductibus* (p. 267) says this of fullers: "To some extent, the Roman fuller took the place of the modern laundryman; at all events he was a much more important member of the community, and much more numerously represented in it, than the modern fuller. One of the finest blocks in Pompeii belonged to the guild or *collegium* of fullers."

[2]Something may be missing in the Latin text.

[3]Benito Mussolini had this position (in the Sign-House system), but he did not have the favorable Jupiter aspect.

Chapter 5. Saturn and Mercury. [III.9]

1. Mercury and Saturn partilely posited in the degree of the ASC in a diurnal nativity make those who hide away money, attorneys, or legal experts, or law-clerks, but listless and who soon fail. But if they were posited in this house by night, they will make slaves or free men made captive, and they are handed over to powerful men to serve them because of their having been captured. But if Saturn and Mercury were found in a feminine sign in a nocturnal nativity partilely in the ASC—namely in the ascendant—they will make eunuchs, or men without any semen, and who cannot copulate—shameful, disgraceful, vile, indecent sodomites.

2. Mercury posited together with Saturn in the 2nd house in a diurnal nativity will make herbalists,[1] physicians, and those through whom health is restored to men, but they are also rich and famous in their actions. Moeover, according to the quality of the signs, they will be orators, or business managers of powerful men. But if they were found in this house by night, they will make beggars, destitute persons, lunatics, or temple servants; frequently too, they will be charged with crimes and placed in custody; nevertheless, they are always mourning and childless, and weak in some part of the body, or suffering from some bodily defects.

3. Mercury partilely posited with Saturn in the 3rd house from the ASC will make workmen who raise water from deep wells, gardeners, managers of moderately-sized country estates, or undertakers and funeral directors, or custodians of the cadavers of the dead, or door-keepers of sepulchres.

4. Mercury partilely posited with Saturn in the 4th house from the ASC, i.e. in the IMC, will make masters of illicit or secret arts, or those knowing about them, but evil persons and those who get their daily living from evil arts. But some of those having Mercury with Saturn thus will either be in custody or they are condemned in some manner; but all their actions are varied according to the nature and quality of the signs, and according to the arrangement of the other stars.

5. Saturn and Mercury posited together in the 5th house from the ASC will make those who were born thus to change their living quarters frequently, and those in charge of grain or crops[2] or of certain places, <mer-

[1]Probably a herb doctor is meant.

[2]Reading *frumentorum* 'of crops' with **αA'**; MSS **ΩΔ** have *fugitivorum* 'of fugitives'. But the whole sentence looks suspicious; perhaps some words have

chants>[1] of gems or pearls or perfumes, or persons in charge of metals. It will also make sculptors of images.[2]

6. Mercury and Saturn posited partilely in the 6th and in the 12th house from the ASC denote the same things in similar fashion. For if they were found by day in these houses, they will make those who are knowledgeable about many subjects, strong in the knowledge of secret arts, and who want to know everything having to do with humans, but malicious and envious, and those who are involved in vices and illnesses. But Saturn and Mercury posited by night in the 6th and in the 12th houses will make authors of false documents, wicked, malicious, malevolent poisoners, but who are always involved in the greatest evils and the greatest difficulties. But if Mars, by day or by night, makes any aspect, either square or opposition, to Mercury and Saturn thus posited, it will make men involved in unavoidable evil who are punished by the reproach of a public death.

7. Mercury and Saturn posited together in the 7th house from the ASC, i.e. in the DSC, will make[3] those who inherit from women and are burning with desires for great wealth and lovers of women. But if they were found by night in this house, they will make those who are wretched in all relationships of life, who are burdened down with the greatest debts, and are also physically defective and weak. Moreover, they will be ill-natured and wicked—some of them indeed are accused and put in public custody.

8. Mercury posited together with Saturn in the 8th house from the ASC denotes increases in [the Native's] personal property and honor with the passage of time; but some acquire property because of the death of a non-relative; however, they will incur illness either from bladder stones or from stomach trouble. But posited together in this house by night, they will make paupers, those who are proscribed, feeble or wrinkled persons, and those for whom humors . . . .[4] they will make [those] perishing from

---

dropped out.

[1]Accepting Némethy's addition.

[2]Reading with MS **N** *etiam simulacrorum sculptores* 'also sculptors of images' rather than *etiam et sacrorum <simulacrorum> sculptores* 'also and sculptors of sacred images'. MS **D** has *etiam et symulacrorum sacrorum sculptores.* These were of course 'images of the Gods'.

[3]Reading *facient atque* 'will make and' with **A′** rather than *forte vero et* 'but strongly and' with **ΩΔ**.

[4]Something is missing in the Latin text.

damage, if the Moon with little light is moving towards Saturn or when full of light towards Mars.

9. Mercury posited together with Saturn in the 9th house from the ASC will make prophets, or clothers of divine images, or bearers [of religious objects] in ceremonies.

10. Mercury posited with Saturn in the 10th house from the ASC, i.e. in the MC, will make those who are the heirs of unrelated persons or discoverers of the greatest things. Sometimes they will be secretaries, or agents, or business managers of the greatest men. But if a <benefic> star aspects them posited thus, it will make orators of divine talent, or teachers of the arts of oratory, or grammarians,[1] or those put in charge of all of these with an authority of some power, or school-masters, or masters of revenue clerks . . .[2] to scrutinize celestial things. Some practice computation, others will be discoverers or masters of difficult writings.

11. Saturn and Mercury posited together in the 11th house from the ASC denotes those things that we have said they denote in the 5th house.

12. Mercury and Saturn partilely placed in the 12th house from the ASC denote that which we have set forth more clearly for the 6th house.

Chapter 6. Mercury and Jupiter. [III.10]

1. Mercury posited partilely with Jupiter in the ASC in a diurnal nativity will make famous and glorious persons, in charge of cities, or [members of] the First Ten of the greatest cities, those who administer justice and who restore laws to provinces or cities, but who always take pleasure in just causes. But if they were found thus by night, it makes business managers or agents or those in charge of business affairs. But sometimes it makes secretaries of great or powerful men, those in charge of negotiations, banks, storehouses, and banking business, but sharp, talented persons, and those on whom the greatest good fortune is conferred because of the good quality of their talent.

2. Mercury and Jupiter partilely posited in the 2nd house from the ASC in a diurnal nativity will make heirs of the property of non-relatives,

---

[1]Those skilled in language; but probably the reference here is to what we call civil 'secretaries', such as 'secretary of state', i.e. high level government officials working with documents and issuing written instructions.

[2]Some words are missing here—probably "or it will make them."

those who are adopted by strangers, those who are masters of many farms and of stored produce, and those on whom, with the passage of time, the greatest increases in good fortune are bestowed. But if they were found partilely by night in this house, they will make sculptors[1] who do not have perpetual good fortune and whom the course of life very frequently disappoints.

3. Jupiter and Mercury partilely posited in the 3rd house from the ASC will make mages, but always powerful in outstanding goodness, hymn-singers, or bearers [of the images] of the Gods, or those who initiate men into religions and consecrate them, and those who predict the future by means of warning from the Gods; or it will make them to be in charge of the sacred games. Jupiter and Mercury posited together denote these same things in the 9th house from the ASC.[2]

4. Mercury and Jupiter posited together in the 4th house from the ASC will make inventors of calculating devices and organs, or guardians and protectors of minors, but who [also] undertake the guardianship and defense of women. But some of them discover things by chance, [while] others know the ways of hidden treasures, from which the greatest good fortune accrues to them.

5. Jupiter and Mercury partilely posited in the 5th house from the ASC denote the same things in similar fashion both by day and by night; for they confer many powers and nobility with the passage of time; moreover, they will be more adept in all actions and those who easily get what they want. Posited together in the 11th house of the nativity, they denote these same things.

6. Mercury and Jupiter partilely posited in the 6th house by night and by day denote the same things in similar fashion if they are found to be matutine. For they will make those who, in all business matters, are capable and sensible, [and] who are in charge of either all sorts of legal cases, or contests, and revision of the public accounts, or governmental accounts, or financial transactions, or some religious matters, so that they will have the greatest riches from the gifts of the Gods, especially if, with

[1]Reading *sculptores* 'sculptors' with **DN** (MS **D** has *sculptores* in the text, but in the margin *aliter stultiores* from **Γ** or one of its scions), rather than *stultores* 'stupid persons' with **Ω,** or *stultiores* 'rather stupid persons' with **A′**.) Cf. Mercury with Jupiter in the 6th house below (Par. 8).

[2]We recall that the 3rd house is named Goddess and the 9th house is named God, so both have to do with religious functionaries and ceremonies.

these placed thus, there was any star posited in the 10th house from the ASC.

7. But if the Moon is placed thus, so that it conjoins itself to them by aspect when it is posited in the 10th house from the ASC, they will be rich, affluent persons, lords of much money or much gold, and those who attain the greatest fruits of possessions; fortunate, prosperous persons, and those who arrange the actions of kings by their own intercession, superintendents of the royal grain stores or of treasury monies, and those in charge of provinces and cities.

8. But if it was a diurnal nativity and, with Jupiter posited with Mercury in the 6th house from the ASC, it will make those who are mediocre both in their life and personal property and actions. But if they were found thus by night, they produce interpreters of business transactions, and fishermen, or fowlers,[1] or sculptors, or those who are always burdened with laborious tasks, or those performing servile duties, or those who are engaged in such occupations as those involving offensive odors and squalid with heavy dirt, i.e. either fullers, or tanners of hides, or boot-makers,[2] or bakers, or woolen-workers, or occupations similar to these.

9. Mercury posited together with Jupiter in the 7th house from the ASC, i.e. in the DSC, denotes the same things in similar fashion both by night and by day. For it will make the greatest good fortune to be conferred by women, and it will make those in charge of public services, and the leading men of the people or of cities or [members of] the First Ten, of longer life and good old age, and with good counsels and personal morals, and who always desire good things. But these things are lessened in nocturnal nativities if Saturn aspected Mercury posited thus with Jupiter by opposition or by square, or if he was found with them.

10. Mercury and Jupiter partilely posited in the 8th house from the ASC, if they were found thus in a diurnal nativity, will make those of moderate status in life and who get the means of life for themselves from some inventions. For they disgrace the youth of some, but with the passage of time they denote moderate increases in assets. But if they were found by night in this house, either they will discover something from

---

[1]Accepting Cumont's emendation *aucupes* 'fowlers' for the *augures* 'augurs' of the MSS. *Cf.* iii. 3f.12.

[2]Accepting Sittl's reading (= edition **v**) *caligarios* 'boot-makers' instead of Skutsch's emendation *gallicarios* 'makers of Gallic boots'. *Cf.* iv. 3f.13.

which they can have the greatest support of life, or a sizable inheritance passes to them, and with the passage of time they are elevated to the greatest good fortune; but yet it will make them defective in body and sluggish.

11. Mercury and Jupiter posited in the 9th house denote those things that they decreed when posited in the 3rd house of the nativity.

12. Mercury and Jupiter in the 10th house from the ASC denote great acts and great administrations and great powers according to the measure of the nativity.

13. Mercury and Jupiter posited partilely in the 11th house from the ASC denote those things that we have said they denote in the 5th house.

14. Mercury and Jupiter posited together in the 12th house from the ASC, if Mercury was matutine, will make secretaries of the king or of the senate, or short-hand recorders of princes, or those who administer the greatest states, but who greatly and frequently offend, and who are weighed down by the burden of misfortune in the last part of life; or else they perish by a violent death if they are posited thus in a nocturnal nativity. For in a diurnal nativity they persist in these actions and these duties even to a small extent, and they seldom offend. But when vespertine and posited in this house with Jupiter, it will give more deliberate actions and an unfavorable fate; but some will be involved in public or laborious occupations.

Chapter 7. Mercury and Mars. [III.11]

1. If Mercury and Mars are posited partilely in the degree of the ASC, namely in a diurnal nativity, they will make those who spit up blood, and those suffering from heart-burn, and short-lived persons and unfortunates; for it will make them to be condemned either on account of women, or because of illicit love affairs, or secret writings, or because of misdeeds ,or because of falsity; and they will make them to die a violent death.

2. But if they were found partilely in the ASC by night they will make great persons, in charge of great regions, generals, or emissaries, or protectors, or attendants of Emperors, or the greatest administrators, on whom the greatest good fortune is conferred by the occurrence of battles. But if Saturn aspects Mercury and Mars by square or by opposition when

they are posited thus by night, it will make them to suffer many dangers, and they are very often deceived; for they are hindered in all their actions; for Saturn posited thus will make indolent and artless men,and those who are weighed down by every burden of misfortune.

3. Mercury posited together with Mars in the 2nd house from the ASC make the Natives to be exposed; and if they are reared, they will make them fugitives for some reason. They frequently make exiles, sometimes also captives; generally, they will make them to be stripped bare by proscription.[1] Some of them are afflicted with grave illnesses or serious bodily defects. They will make others die violently if they aspect the Moon when she is full of light. If they were found thus by night, they will make those of bad mind—evil-doers, obscure and rash persons—and those who are deceived in all their actions. But it will make those who have many kinds of occupations, for they will be either tax administrators, or tax-collectors,[2] or spies. It makes some of unsound mind or madmen.

4. Mercury and Mars posited together in the 3rd house from the ASC will make those obtaining the support of life from occupations involving fire or iron. Moreover, they will be the sort who predict the future and who always dwell in temples; but they are terrifying to all those who have any dealings with them even if they know nothing or if they do nothing; but they will have increases in good fortune with the passage of time.

5. Mercury posited with Mars in the 4th house from the ASC, i.e. in the IMC, will make sluggish persons, poor in all their actions and in all their circumstances; and they will be constantly at odds with their parents and relatives, so that through them the greatest plots are always heaped upon their parents or relatives. They will also be bail bondsmen, and on account of this they are shaken up by the greatest dangers. And they fall into humility and poverty; because with these [posited thus] it will happen that they will be instigators or practitioners of some illicit arts. Or they are implicated in the greatest snares of dangers as accessories caught in some of these [crimes], so that they are punished by a sentence of condemnation. Others involved in these disasters are crushed by attacks of severe and lengthy illnesses, especially if when placed thus they aspect

[1]That is, they are declared to be enemies of the state, and their belongings are confiscated.

[2]Lat. *publicani aut vectigaliarii* 'tax administrators or tax collectors'. Tax administrators had the responsibility of seeing that taxes were collected, but they employed field collectors to bring the taxes in.

the Moon by opposition or by square. If Mercury and Mars and the Moon were found in the 4th house of the nativity by night, it will make directors, tribunes, generals, powerful men, and administrators, but who perish by a violent death.

6. Mercury partilely posited with Mars in the 5th house from the ASC make strong persons, virile, undefeated athletes in all contests, but those who are assigned to various places for their dwelling, and those who are granted their livelihood by the public or by the treasury for the greatest wages. But in every contest they make them superior and frightening to their own adversaries.

7. Mercury and Mars partilely posited in the 6th house and in the 12th from the ASC denote the same things in similar fashion. For if they were posited in these houses by day, they denote illnesses and the greatest bodily defects. Moreover, they will make the Natives both to be put in custody and also to have some acquaintance with prison, and to be condemned because of some accusation. For either they are arrested, or indicted, or made liable to lawsuits from some false deceptions of accusations; for they are arrested or indicted because of slaves and something to do with slaves or men of low degree, or they are those who are already placed in custody because of some crime. And they perish with the greatest torments and the greatest violence and atrocity, especially if, when posited in these houses, Mercury and Mars aspect the full Moon from another part [of the nativity].

8. But if Mercury was posited with Mars in the 6th or in the 12th house from the ASC, it makes those entangled in many debts and in money loaned out at interest. But they will also cause mental disturbance and [spells of] unconsciousness. They also produce persons who are sluggish in all their actions. And they denote the greatest accusations and serious envies, but which arise either from slaves or on account of slaves. Others will be tormentors of slaves, so that they wear them out either with hunger, or traps, or tortures, or incessant demands for work. But those who have Mercury with Mars in these houses will never persevere in their occupations, because they will transfer [their efforts] from one occupation to another.

9. Mercury partilely posited with Mars in the 7th house from the ASC, i.e. in the DSC, if they were found partilely in this house by day, they compel those who have them thus to kill a woman or their own wife with their own hand. Or they will kill themselves or others, either on account

of a woman, or on account of a wife, or on account of perverted desires or some sort of love affair. Or, having committed some sort of crime because of something like that, they are put in public custody or in prison and condemned because of the accusation of that offense.

10. But in general, those who have Mercury and Mars thus commit homicides and [bring about] their own deaths according to the quality of the signs; for they will be either prowlers, or armed robbers, or murderers, or pirates, or [criminals] like those. And, having been apprehended in these crimes, they are punished by a severe sentence of judgment.

11. But posited thus in a nocturnal nativity, it will make them to be defrauded by the unjust actions of women, or they will be married to shrews and beget children by them, and they will always be entangled in the greatest offenses.

12. Mercury partilely posited with Mars in the 8th house from the ASC, if it was found thus by day, will make the sort of persons who can get nothing of those things that they desire, but they are persons beset by dangers, who lose every bit of their personal property. But some of them will be insane and raging madmen, others are thrown into custody; or they will be condemned, and frequently they will end by dying a violent death.

13. But if they were found by night in this house, they will acquire some resources from evil arts or from evil occupations, and they are those who day by day increase [their participation] in evil and nefarious actions. They will be thieves or house-breakers, or those who are accustomed to refuse [to return] things that are entrusted to them or credited to their own resolute trustworthiness. Or they are those who invent and carry out criminal acts. For they will make torturers, or executioners, or traitors to their own people, and those who acquire the greatest amounts of good fortune and wealth from these arts. But death will come to them with violence or with some severe torments, or they will die while suffering from the defect of serious insanity.

14. Mercury posited together with Mars in the 9th house from the ASC will make unjust, irreligious persons, [and] perjurers; but, despite that error of mind, ministers of the Gods. But they also despoil and strip bare those very Gods whom they serve. That is, they are those who make the temple offerings[1] to be their own booty. But they do these things exces-

[1]Accepting Kroll's emendation *donaria* 'offerings' rather than the meaningless *dominari* 'to be dominated'.

sively if the [stars] were found distant from the aspects of the Sun, or in each other's degrees,[1] or in the domicile of the Sun. And these things will especially[2] occur if the Moon full of light conjoins herself by square or by opposition to them posited thus.

15. Mars and Mercury posited together in the 10th house from the ASC make wretched and ineffectual men. They will be delighted by constant sea-voyages. And they will be lovers of wrestling halls. And they sell their own life to powerful men or kings because of some bodily defect. Moreover, they will always have some stain or bodily defect according to the quality and substance of the signs.

16. But Mercury posited together with Mars establishes [them] in public activities. or in administrations, or in business affairs; but in the course of time they never persevere in those occupations. For, either having been attacked or accused, they are banished; and they are frequently sentenced, and sometimes they are oppressed by false accusations. By which misfortunes their personal wealth is thus destroyed, so that they are harassed by a heavy [payment] of interest. But they are also oppressed with grave kinds of damages or condemnations, on account of [having given] a guarantee or some kind of surety.

17. But if Jupiter has conjoined itself with some association of testimony to Mercury and Mars posited together, or if it was found together with them, it will make persons great in all their activities and in business, and those to whom many business affairs are entrusted, and those who in a similar manner both lose and gain personal wealth equally. But if Venus has conjoined herelf to them with any aspect, or if she were found together with them, it will make imperial tax-collectors, who exact the annual payments to the treasury, auditors of accounts and those who are accustomed to handle major business affairs.

18. But Mercury with Mars denotes diverse and manifold kinds of activities or administrations; for this variety comes forth according to the quality and substance of the signs. For posited in a domicile of Mercury or in its degrees, they make lovers of wrestling or athletes destined for the public contests. But posited in the signs or in the degrees of Mars, they make fights, lovers of weapons, soldiers, hunters willingly taking care of wild beasts, and those in charge of wild animals, messengers or couriers

---

[1]That is, in each other's terms—a sort of mutual reception by terms.

[2]Reading *praesertim* 'especially' with MSS **DN** rather than *arte* 'by art' with the other MSS.

of kings. But posited in a domicile of Venus or in her degrees, they make linen-weavers, clothes makers, embroiderers, dyers, and those handling perfumes or gems or pearls in some fashion. But posited in a domicile or in the degrees of Jupiter, <they will make tribunes possessing regions or some cities. And posited in a domicile of Saturn or in its degrees>[1] those having official positions dealing with wicked and crminal persons; for they will make torturers, executioners, murderers, accusers, and traitors to their own people. But in the domicile of the Sun or the Moon, they will make bronze-workers, makers of iron tools, statue makers, furriers of hides,[2] murderers, and those getting the necessities of life from fire or iron. For the exchange of signs denotes the activities of different kinds of businesses.

19. Mercury posited together with Mars in the 11th house will make those who perish in a battle and some are lovers of wrestling, others of weapons; but persons strong in their counsels, and who always receive favorable results from all of their actions.

20. Mercury and Mars posited in the 12th house from the ASC, the sixth house shows especially what they may do.[3] <denote the greatest kinds of misfortunes and disaster. For those who have Mars and Mercury thus commit the crime of falsification,[4] or they are led by the association of bad conscience to all criminal acts. Or constantly burdened down by the heavy interest of debts with the [resulting] loss of honor, they are forcibly dragged to public judgment, so that by a depraved ardor of greed, dishonoring sacred trade agreements, they try to refuse things entrusted [to them], so that from that perfidy or from preceding criminal acts a change of opinion of the public rises up against them.>[5]

---

[1]Two or three lines of text omitted by **Ω** due to homoeoteleuton (. . .*in partibus constituti* | . . . *in partibus constituti*), but preserved in **A'DNα** and hence in their common source **Ψ**.

[2]The Latin *pelliones coriorum* 'furriers of hides' perhaps indicates workers who scraped the fur or hair from hides to make smooth leather—a dirty and smelly occupation.

[3]Bram & Prof. Monat render the last phrase, which is given by **ΩΨ**, as "has the same meaning as the sixth."

[4]In Latin *falsi crimen*. In Roman law this was a serious offense that included the crimes of forgery, counterfeiting, bribery, impersonating an official, etc.

[5]This lengthy supplement is found in MS **N**, where it has replaced the erased clause ... *quid faciant, sextus locus specialiter ostendit* 'the sixth house shows especially what they may do' and has been partly written in the margin. There does not seem to be any obvious palaeographic reason for the omission. Kroll

Chapter 8. Mercury and Venus. [III.12]

1. Mercury and Venus partilely posited in the ASC in a dirunal nativity make guards or protectors of Emperors or those who by their own watchfulness preserve the safety of the prince, or those who are ordered to control the funds or the royal treasury by their own arrangements, and to whom the duties of this sort of administration are entrusted. For they will make musicians, choristers,[1] and those who devise musical modes,[2] or certainly public magistrates, or orators, or grammarians,[3] or inventors of laws, or those who excel in [the use of] numbers.[4]

2. But if they were found in the degrees of the ASC by night, they will make sharp, talented persons, and those who easily accomplish whatever they want to do. Moreover, they will be either crowned [high-priests] or those who are in charge of priests, or bearers of religious images, and those who with the passage of time receive increases of dignity. Moreover, they will make those who are skilled in [making] some sort of harmony, or who are in charge of the royal documents, but whose speeches and conversation are full of charm and grace.

3. Mercury and Venus posited together in the 2nd house from the ASC in a diurnal nativity will make those transacting much business and those who are employed in noble actions but persevering for a longer time in these, they are delightful and pleasing person both in their lives and in their habits, but drunkards and lustful. But if it was found to be matutine in this house, it will make those seeking personal property through their own efforts, fortunate individuals, literate, and displaying some education in music, cheerful and honest, and famous for the splendor of their charm.

4. But if it was found to be vespertine in a nocturnal nativity in this house with Venus, it denotes great wealth, and with the passage of time it

---

and Ziegler point out that the same supplement is found in the partial edition **α** and suggest that **N** copied it from there, but that seems unlikely for the reasons stated in the Preface to the present translation. However, they also note that the words of the supplement are found in a somewhat fuller form in *Mathesis* vi.17.3-4, where they are given as a signification of Mercury opposite Mars; and in the Addenda to the Addenda, Ziegler suggests that that was their source.

[1]The Latin word *choricus* means a member of the chorus. They both danced and sang. I think here it means 'singers'.

[2]That is, composers.

[3]Possibly 'language teachers', but more likely middle or upper level persons working with official documents.

[4]Possibly 'accountants'.

bestows increases of the greatest good fortune, for they will be princes of states, they will be in charge of laws, and those to whom the management of the largest provinces is entrusted. Others find something from which they receive the beginning of good fortune; [and] heredities of the greatest size are bestowed on others.

5. Mercury and Venus posited together in the 3rd house from the ASC will make [those who have them thus] to be victors in the sacred games, or priests, or prophets or those who clothe [the images] of the Gods, or those exercising the greatest duties in temples, or those in charge of the priests, or masters of the sacred games, or ambassadors imbued moreover with good morals,[1] and those to whom a city entrusts its own petitions with trust.

6. Mercury and Venus posited together in the 4th house from the ASC will make those skilled in obscure writings,[2] mages, philosophers and often those dealing with celestial things, or those who cure suffering men, and who are accustomed to be helpful to men of whatever class. But posited matutine with Venus in this house, it will make the Natives to go from slavery to freedom, and it brings them up from an ignoble state to splendor and nobility. But they take on the protection and defense of wretched or servile women, or old women, or virgins, and on account of these they seek out acts of various kinds.[3] But they will make those persons involved with acts, habits, negotiations, and business affairs in accordance with the the substance and quality of the signs.

7. Mercury posited together with Venus in the 5th house from the ASC denotes the greatest personal assets with the passage of time, and in a similar manner it bestows the visible signs of good fortune. And it denotes those who acquire the greatest gifts and rewards from women or from their wives, and those who are joined by acquaintance with powerful men.

8. Mercury found together with Venus in the 6th house from the ASC in a diurnal nativity denotes abundance of assets from accounts, or busi-

---

[1]Reading with **N** *bonis aut instructos moribus* 'with good or imbued morals' and altering *aut* 'or' to *autem* 'moreover' to read as shown above. MS **D** has *bonis instructis moribus* 'imbued with good morals'. The Teubner editors suggest reading *bonis moribus et institutis* 'with good morals and principles', which amounts to the same thing.

[2]The reference is to mystical or esoteric writings, which were afloat in the ancient world even as they are today.

[3]Reading *actus varii generis* 'acts of various kinds' with **αA'**.

ness dealings, or from calculation, or from education, or from a gift of the Gods, especially if, with these posited thus in the 6th house, any star was found in the 10th house of the nativity. But they obtain a wife with difficulty, for they will be lustful and disreputable in some manner because of that.

9. But if it was found matutine in this house with Venus in a nocturnal nativity, for the sake of matrimony, they will couple themselves with servant girls, or widows, or prostitutes. But they will have laborious and servile occupations and around water, if, with them placed thus, no star was found in the 10th from the ASC. But if there was one, it will make those who get many things by their own effort, for they will be travelers, businessmen, ship-captains, sailors, or fabricators of gold.

10. But if it was found to be vespertine in this house with Venus, it will make wise, talented persons, musicians or organists, or dyers of [various] colors, or sellers of spices, or gems, or pearls; it will make some of them to be perfumers or discoverers of medicinal cosmetics. Posited thus it will also frequently make those who are in charge of metals, so that from these activities the greatest foundations of wealth are acquired.

11. Mercury and Venus found together in the 7th house from the ASC denote bodily defects resulting from obscure illnesses; for they make persons with liver trouble, frenzied persons, those suffering from melancholy,[1] and illnesses similar to those; but always estranged from the affection of their wife, and infamous down to the last day of their life.

12. But if it was found in this house by night with Venus, the greatest amount of riches will be conferred upon them by their wives, and, with the passage of time, they gradually acquire grand honors and the visible evidence of the greatest good fortune, especially if Mars and Saturn do not aspect them posited thus from any part [of the nativity]—but especially if Saturn does not. For if Mars and Saturn were conjoined by any aspect to them posited thus, those things that we have said are turned to the contrary.

13. Mercury and Venus posited together in the 8th house from the ASC when vespertine in a diurnal nativity produce ineffective persons making no progress in life, and who cannot do anything. They will also

[1]A condition that the ancients ascribed to an excess of *black bile*—probably characterized by weakness and listlessness, and possibly what we would call 'mental depression'.

make persons who are always involved in laborious jobs. Moreover, they will be defective in mind and body and persons who marry with difficulty And they will be sterile and those who cannot generate offspring. Moreover, they will die, either as spastics or infected with gonorrhoea, or from apoplexy or inflammation of the brain.

14. But found together by night in this house, they will make those who are heirs to the estate of a non-relative, or those who have the responsibility of managing the estates of non-relatives. But they will be good, benign individuals, fathers of families, and those on whom very much is conferred by women or by their wives. Some of them will invent something that will be sufficient for the sole support of their lives. But they will have an early death without pain or torment.

15. But when matutine and posited in this house with Venus, it will make those who learn many things and who know everything, also discoverers, and those who accomplish with ease whatever they want to accomplish, but who obtain increases in personal property as they grow older.

16. Mercury and Venus <posited> together in the 9th house from the ASC will give <prophesying>[1] women as wives, but [these stars] will make those men to be raised higher[2] or made greater, and those for whom the support of their life is sought from temple duties. Moreover, they will make either priests or those who, stationed in temples, predict the future, or *haruspices*,[3] or astrologers, or augurs, or mages, or those who are accustomed to explain everything.

17. Mercury posited with Venus in the 10th house from the ASC will make public actions and those who are honored by the people or by cities, but who incur infamy from the actions of their wife. But posited matutine with Venus in this house, it will make inventors of musical modes,[4] but [also] actors and those destined for public spectacles. But they will be unfortunate in their marriages, for they will have either public whores,[5] or

---

[1]The words in angle brackets are supplied by MSS of the **Ψ** family, but MSS of the **Δ** family and edition **α** have *vaticinantes* 'prophesying' while those of the **Γ** family and edition **v** have the corruption *vaginantes*.

[2]Accepting Kroll's emendation *altius* 'higher', but **N** has *actus* 'actions' and **Ω** has *artus* 'strength', either one of which might be the correct reading.

[3]Diviners (from the inspection of entrails).

[4]That is, composers.

[5]Reading *meretrices publicas* with **A** instead of *meretrices et publicas* 'whores and public women'.

actresses, or wives of ill repute. Some of them will also be lovers of boys and involved in the depraved pleasures of many lustful passions.

18. Mercury posited with Venus in the 11th house from the ASC will make those handling the business affairs of women and those to whom the assets of women are entrusted, so that from that action the greatest basis of wealth is conferred upon them, but afterwards they are placed in contrary situations or in the greatest losses.

19. Mercury posited with Venus in the 12th house from the ASC, if it was found thus by day, will make lovers and those laboring under some fault of love affairs, but open and known for all these faults; and yet it will make them to be reported because of this,[1] and compelled to be condemned as a result of that report. It will [also] make them die a violent death on account of those faults of mind that we have mentioned.

20. But if they were found by night in this house, it will make many prosecutions by women of low degree, or it will make those who are driven by the impulse of love to couple themselves with a whore. But it will [also] make mechanics[2] and those who seem to be occupied in many different ways[3] in those occupations; but who frequently depart from tradition. And those who in their actions and business dealings, or by their own abilities, are usually deceived in frequent fashion.

Chapter 9. The Moon. [III.13]

1. The Moon partilely posited in the ASC in a nocturnal nativity, if it was full and was found in those signs in which it rejoices, denotes great increases of good fortune, It makes the Native to be put first among his brothers, both by age always and by merit. But if it was found partilely in this house by day, it will make pilots of major ships.

2. But if with the Moon posited thus by day, Mars and Saturn possess any angle of the nativity, that is if they were in square or in opposition or if they were found with her, they will make pirates who are famous because of the cruel atrocity of their savageness, or judges placed in charge

[1]Reading with **N** *et tamen propter hoc deferri faciet* 'and yet it will make [them] to be reported'.

[2]Designers, makers, or maintainers of any kind of mechanical device.

[3]Reading *institutiis* 'ways' with Buechler and Cumont rather than †*iustitiis* 'legal conclusions'.

of out-of-the-way places.[1] But if no benefic star aspects the Moon thus placed with a malefic star, it will make those who were born thus to be exposed,[2] or it denotes no duration of life, and it will make them to die immediately, or it denotes a bad end of life and a violent death.

3. The Moon posited in the 2nd house from the ASC in a nocturnal nativity will make famous persons [involved] in notable actions, but luxurious and devoted to the delightful joys of pleasure, and those on whom, with the passage of time, a greater amount of wealth will be conferred.

4. But if it was found in this house by day, it either kills his parents immediately, or it separates him from his parents, or it makes his parents to be separated by a divorce, and it diminishes the value of his personal property by various kinds of losses. Others who have the Moon thus are occupied in continual travels, and they divide their own occupations among many places; but it makes their lives to be such that they are subject to some [person in] power. But if it was in this house with little light and Saturn was posited in the degree or in the sign of the ASC, it causes blindness from sudden wounds to the eyes. But if, with the Moon posited thus, Mars was found in the degree or in the sign of the ASC, it will make pains in the joints, or dislocations, or fractures. It debilitates others with the continuous pain of hemorrhoids.

5. The Moon posited in the 3rd house from the ASC will make the mother of low degree or one dishonored with the stain of some disgrace. But if the Moon was found in this house with Jupiter, those who have it thus will be supplied sustenance from the treasury funds or from public provisions.[3] But if, with Jupiter and the Moon posited in this house, Mercury has conjoined itself to them with any aspect, it makes high priests of one of the greatest Goddesses, or priests of a most powerful religion, or dispensers of public <funds>,[4] or financial managers.[5] But if Venus was

[1]The word 'judges' here indicates governmental officials in charge of a remote district with the power of life and death. An interesting modern example is the Texas Judge Roy Bean (1825-1903) "The Law West of the Pecos."

[2]Unwanted infants were sometimes simply carried outside of town and abandoned.

[3]Probably, from a government stipend or from public welfare distributions.

[4]Reading *publicarum <pecuniarum> *dispensatores* (< > KSZ | *my conjecture). These were probably imperial treasury officials with authority to authorize payments.

[5]The Latin word *correctores* 'financial managers' in the late empire meant officials who managed municipal funds. It could be translated roughly as 'city managers'.

found with the Moon in this house, they will have occupations involving paints and dyes and perfumes, or wine, or flowers.

6. But if in a nocturnal nativity the Moon was found in this house with Saturn alone, it will make sluggish individuals, who attain nothing of those things that they desire, and those who utter sacrilegious words about all religions, and those on whom the greatest misfortunes are inflicted by the wrath of the Gods. But if by day the Moon was found in this house with Mercury and Mars, they will produce sacrilegious individuals, despoilers of temples, men who are unjust, impious, irrelgious, and murderers.

7. The Moon posited in the fourth house from the ASC, i.e. in the IMC, if it was found there by day, denotes the mother to be of low class, and one who leaves behind a surviving husband. But if Saturn was found in another angle of the nativity, and Venus was in the DSC, the mother is transferred from freedom to slavery, and sometimes she is made a captive. But if by night the Moon was found in this house full of light, it will make a mother who is noble <and> rich, and it will make the Natives to be elevated greatly with continual increases of wealth.

8. But if with the Sun partilely posited in the ASC, the Moon was found in the fourth house, i.e. in the IMC, . . .[1]

[The remainder of the significations of the Moon in the fourth house, and the significations of the Moon in the 5th through the 8th houses are missing in the Latin text. Apparently, as Mommsen supposed, a leaf had fallen out of the *archetype*, (or alternatively the copyist of the *archetype* accidentally turned a leaf of his exemplar without copying it). The surviving Latin text continues with the latter part of the significations of the Moon in the ninth house.][2]

. . .[3] they will receive the <greatest> increases of good fortune; it calls some to practise the greatest religions; it makes others to be entrusted

[1]Rhetorius has 'they are thought worthy of praise and presidency and sovereignty or a kingdom…'

[2]Rhetorius gives two sets of interpretations for the significations of the Planets in the houses. The second set is similar to what Firmicus has, so I have listed them for the Moon in houses 4 to 9 in Appendix 2.

[3]Rhetorius begins the significations of the Moon in the 9th house with 'The Moon in the 9th by night [makes] notable persons who live abroad; some of them benefit [in some way] from the temples of the Gods, some others are entrusted with the business affairs of women…'. (See Appendix 2 for Rhetorius's complete signification.)

with the business affairs of women. But if it was found thus by day, it will make foreigners of low degree and their lives are shattered by errors and dangers, For some it denotes low offices in temples; and it makes others to carry out servile duties in temples, especially if a malefic star aspects the Moon placed thus.

9. The Moon posited in the 10th house from the ASC, i.e. the MC, if it was found partilely in this house in a nocturnal nativity in those signs in which it is exalted or in which it rejoices—namely, increasing in light, and with Jupiter protecting it with fortunate aspects—it will make the greatest Emperors or powerful administrators, to whom the power of life and death is entrusted in ready fashion. When posited thus, it also gives ordinary consulates. But if it either precedes or follows the MC degree in the next house and is placed in nearby degrees, it will produce generals, tribunes, and administrators; but if it is platically posited in the same sign, it yields those who are great in all their actions and adorned with various kinds of good fortune. But if, with the Moon thus posited, Saturn possesses any angle of the nativity, it denotes envies and misfortunes in frequent fashion.

10. But the Moon posited by day in the MC will make those who are middling in life and in all their actions and who are usually deceived in frequent fashion. But if by day, with the Moon posited thus, the Sun was found partilely in the ASC in his own domicile, or in his own exaltation, or in a domicile of Jupiter, it will make great administrators of the largest provinces or of the largest city-states, and proconsuls, but terrifying in their administration. But if, with the Moon and Sun posited thus—namely with the Sun in the ASC in those signs which we have mentioned, and the Moon in the MC—and if Jupiter protects both of them or one of the two with a fortunate aspect, it will make Emperors, very powerful in good fortune and justice, and whom all regard with the trepidation of terror.

11. The Moon posited in the 11th house from the ASC denotes those things which from the preceding explanation we have shown it doing in the 5th house.[1]

12. The Moon posited in the 12th house from the ASC in a nocturnal nativity denotes a short time and space of life; but if Jupiter or Venus or

[1]But unfortunately the Latin text of the signification of the Moon in the fifth through the eighth houses is missing. See Appendix 2 for the significations that Rhetorius has.

one of the two were found partilely in the ASC and the Moon was posited just as we have mentioned, and it is a nocturnal nativity, it denotes the possession of some authority along with good fortune. But if, with Mars and Saturn partilely posited in the ASC, or one of the two, the Moon, <in a nocturnal nativity>,[1] possesses the 12th house of the nativity, it will make many and evil misfortunes and serious accidents and illnesses et bodily defects, both for the Native and for his mother.

13. But if, with no [star] in the ASC, the Moon was found alone by day in the 12th house from the ASC, it denotes the loss of personal property, miserable acccidents, and travel. But if it was found in similar fashion in this house by night, it will make wretched impoverished persons of either poor or servile origins to be born, and toilers and those who are always occupied in inglorious actions, and whose body or mouth is dirty with the foulness of a bad odor. And those who are accustomed to be frequently cheated and endangered, and who contract some bodily defect from the inconveniences of travel.

14. But also inquire diligently into the Moon's dodecatemory and into the terms in which the dodecatemory [is posited]; for whatever is concealed in the nativity from the general arrangement of the stars, all of that is made public and shown explicitly by the dodecatemories and their terms. For, if you want to explain the entire substance of the astrological significations from the efficacy of the dodecatemories and from the terms in which they are found, you will not be mistaken; for the Babylonians attribute the supreme power of [astrological] decrees to the dodecatemories, but Ptolemy to the antiscions,[2] [and] we to both.

---

[1]MS **N** adds these words.

[2]This is one of the three places where Firmicus mentions Ptolemy. In all three, he says that Ptolemy favored the use of *antiscions*, which is false (Ptolemy does not even mention the word). Evidently, Firmicus did not have a copy of Ptolemy's *Tetrabiblos* and had taken that false statement from someone else's book.

Chapter 9a. <The Moon in the House of Fortune.>[1] *[III.14]*

1. If the Moon was found in the House of Fortune,[2] and so posited that she applies to Jupiter <or>[3] is with him, it denotes positions of leadership, management positions, glory, and good fortune. <But>[4] if she was located in this house with Venus or if she applies to Venus, she bestows the honors[5] that we have mentioned with the elegance of grace.

2. But if posited in this house while increasing in light she moves towards Mercury or is with him, she makes [the Natives] happy, powerful, and very wise, and those who attain honors, glory, dignity, and the basis of their personal wealth by means of the felicity of their talent, or the grace of their instruction. But if posited in this house while waning she moves towards Mercury or was with him, it denotes illnesses, bodily defects, malice and stinginess.

3. But if, posited in this house in a diurnal nativity, she moves towards Mars or is with him, it denotes military service, glory, power, and positions of high command in these activities; it also makes athletes according to the quality of the signs, but those who surpass others by virtue of their ability.

4. If, posited in this house in a nocturnal nativity and waxing, she moves towards Saturn or is with him, it decreases the Native's paternal and maternal inheritance; it makes his mother to be either a widow, or to have an illness, or a bodily defect, or to perish by a bad death. But it makes the Natives themselves to be wretched and overworked in their first age, but becoming fortunate with the passage of time.

5. But if by day [and] waxing she moves towards Saturn or is with him, it will make him who is born [thus] to be quickly bereaved of his parents, and it causes his personal wealth to be destroyed by wretched

---

[1]This chapter is not listed separately in the Index and may have been considered to be a continuation of the preceding Chapter 9. The title is added by edition **v**.

[2]The House of Fortune is the house of the Sign-House system in which the 'Part of Fortune' calculated by degrees (and perhaps originally calculated simply by counting signs) falls. In this, the original system of houses devised by the Alexandrian inventors of horoscopic astrology, the rising sign is the 1st house, the next sign is the 2nd house, the one after that the 3rd house, etc. In particular, the 10th sign was the 10th house or 'the midheaven'.

[3]Add **Nva.**

[4]Adds **N**.

[5]Reading *honores* 'honors' with **v** and Ziegler.

squanderings. But also, both good fortune and increases in their personal wealth are conferred upon them with the passage of time. But when waning by night, it also denotes these same things in similar fashion. But if, posited in this house by day with little light, she moves towards Saturn or is with him, it denotes illnesses from bodily faults and the misfortunes of a bad death and proscription.

6. But if the House of Fortune was found in the 10th house from the ASC, i.e. in the MC, or in the 11th, in which house the degree of the MC is found in very frequent calculations,[1] and if the waxing Moon was there and so moves towards Saturn or is with him, and the Sun is partilely <posited>[2] in the ASC, it makes fortunate, wealthy, glorious, noble persons, and it denotes the visible signs of the greatest power. But it makes those same person to be involved with bodily defects and illnesses.

7. But if the Sun was not posited in the ASC, and she is moving towards Saturn, or is with him, we have shown in a previous explanation what that denotes. But if, posited in this house in a diurnal nativity and waxing, she moves towards the Sun or is with it, she will produce powerful, factious administrators and judges; and if Jupiter conjoins himself to them by any aspect, it will produce positions of command.

8. But if, posited in this house [and] waning in a diurnal nativity, she moves towards the Sun, with the passage of time it bestows power, glory, and administrative positions. But if by night, waning in the House of Fortune, she moves towards the Sun or is with it, it will make persons humble in their first age, and those who are always deceived. But with the passage of time they acquire personal wealth and glory and honors, and the greatest positions of authority.

9. But always, if the Moon was found in the same degree with the Sun, both in this house and in other houses of the nativity and in other signs, and she had not [yet] freed herself from the whole society of the Sun, it will involve those who were born thus in dangerous and humble actions in their first age; but with the passage of time, after grave losses, it bestows an abundance of personal assets.

---

[1]Here Firmicus speaks of 'the degree' of the MC, which is the astronomical MC degree. It can occasionally fall in the 11th house of the Sign-House system (but not *frequently* as Firmicus says), but usually it falls in the 9th or the 10th. As mentioned in a previous note, Paul of Alexandria, *Introduction*, Chapter 30, says that it can fall in the 9th, the 10th, or the 11th house.

[2]*<constitutus>* 'posited' add **A Nα**.

10. Moreover, in all nativities it will be proper for you to observe the course of the Moon, not only on that same day on which a man enters the first vestiges of light, but we should also investigate with careful consideration to which star the Moon conjoins [herself] on the third day,[1] or by what aspect, or, separating from which [star], she moves toward which [other], for on that day nourishing food is first given to the man that is born. And so it must be sought on the third day whether she has little light or is full, and to what extent the benefic or malefic stars aspect her. For also on the third day, just as on the first, she denotes all things in similar fashion, which, if they were collected by a diligent investigation, we will never be disturbed with erratic confusion in explaining the fates of men. Which consideration, lest anything should seem to have been omitted by us, we shall explain[2] in the Fourth Book.

---

[1]Since the Romans counted both ends of an interval, Firmicus actually means what we would call 'the second day'. And usually the Moon will then be in the next sign after its sign at the time of the nativity.

[2]Reading *explicabimus* 'we shall explain' with **VΔ**, rather than *explicamus* 'may explain'.

Book IV.

<*Preface.*>[1]

1. Conflicts of legal cases, and quarrelsome contests of—as I may say—snarling contention, have attended those providing legal assistance. From which activity, nothing else was conferred upon me day after day but a heap of dangers, and a heavy burden of ill-will. For, with the upright confidence of steadfastness, I was always opposing factious men, and those whom the depravity of violence delighted; or those who were clinging to[2] others' [property] with an instinct of avaricious desire; or those who seemed terrifying to wretched men because of the fear of legal judgments. Hence, for me, the malign malice of envy and storms of dangers were contrived by the depraved desires of dishonest men.

2. And so I abandoned that activity, lest, by the legal agreement of uninformed men and accusers,[3] while I was watching out for the interests of others, I might involve myself in the greatest trickery and the greatest crises of dangers, with those [who were] always and unceasingly raging against me and fighting me with a bitter continuation of hatreds, [so that] with no other means of restoral, but to be set free[4] by a mind with con-

---

[1]This title is added by the Aldine edition **a**, and is not mentioned in the Index.

[2]Reading *inhaerebant* 'clinging to' with the MSS rather than *inhiabant* 'coveting' conjectured by Haupt and initially accepted by the Teubner editors but corrected in the Addenda et Corrigenda.

[3]MSS **MPR** have *imperitorum ac debitor* 'of uninformed persons and a debtor', which is ungrammatical. MSS **DN**'s have *imperitorum ac debitorum* 'of uninformed and indebted persons'. Haupt conjectured *imperitorum ac delirorum* 'of uninformed and crazy persons'. MSS **FIOZ** have only *imperitorum* 'of uninformed persons'. Bram, not knowing what to make of the first part of this clause, omits it from the translation. But Prof. Monat adopts Beaujeu's conjecture *imperitorum ac *delatorum* 'uninformed men and accusers', which I have also adopted.

[4]Reading with most of the MSS, *nulla alia ratione restitutionis quod liberari*

tempt for forensic gains, I displayed a pure and faithful legal action of defense for struggling men and for those alarmed by the various diversity of things.

3. And so, [now] established in retirement, and freed from the fights of legal contests, and having also removed myself in a way from the wicked snares of envy, and from perfidious men, from gross envy, and from thieving—rather indeed, from outright robbing by permitted power—[and] freed from all care of anxiety, I have written these books for you, Lollianus, so that removed in a way from earthly association from whatever source, and clearing away the faults of mind, which I had contracted from dealing with depraved men, I might apply myself to celestial and divine discussions.[1]

4. And so, in this book there will be explained what we promised in the latter parts of the Third Book, i.e. all the kinds and forms of the Moon, also the conjunctions, the separations, and everything that pertains to the power of its divinity; also, the House of Fortune and [the House] of the Daemon,[2] the Ruler of the Nativity, which the Greeks call the *oecodespotes*,[3] which will be treated in a thorough manner, and I shall also explain the efficacies of the one that denotes actions. But I shall also demonstrate the full and empty degrees and their decrees. Also I shall show the masculine and feminine degrees together. And the Moon will again receive the last parts [of the book].

5. For, having read carefully and compared in the contrary diversities of their opinions, all the things that Mercury and Chnubis[4] handed down to Aesculapius, the things that Petosiris explained and Nechepso, and the

---

animo 'with no other means of restoral but to be set free by a mind' rather than with the emended text, *nulla alia ratione restiti, nisi quo liberali animo* 'by no other means I resisted, except by a liberal mind'.

[1]The Latin text of the first three paragraphs as found in the MSS is obviously corrupt, and the editors have attempted to emend it, but their efforts have not been entirely successful. There seem to be three main points: (1) Firmicus wearied of court battles; (2) he aroused enmities and incurred dangers by defending some of his clients; and (3) he gave it all up and retired, so that he might devote himself to celestial and divine things.

[2]The original version of what are now called 'the Part of Fortune' and 'the Part of the Daemon' or 'the Part of Spirit'.

[3]The Greek *oikodespotês*, literally 'house-ruler', but the term was also used for the Ruler of the Nativity.

[4]Accepting Reitzenstein's conjecture *et Chnubis* for the meaningless *einhnus vix* of the archetype. This is presumably the same author mentioned earlier as Hanubius. Also called Anubion.

things that Abram, Orfeus, and Critodemus[1] set forth, and all the other masters[2] of this art, we have written these books making the divine science known to all Romans, so that that which seemed to some to be most difficult for some persons on account of the narrowness of the Latin language, [yet] with the demonstrated freedom of the Roman language, I could explain with true and clear interpretations.

Chapter 1. The Moon has the Greatest Substance of the Life of Man.[3]

1. We promised in the introduction to this book that we would explain all the courses of the Moon and what they signify; for all the substance of the human body is ruled by the power of this divinity. For after the breath of life has become established in the completed human being, and after the spirit of the divine mind has infused itself into his body, the Moon sustains the form of the composed body according to the quality of her courses. Whence, we ought to consider her courses with a careful examination, so that we may be able to explain all the substance of the human body.

2. For otherwise, the nature of man will be unable to endure, unless his body shall have been built upon a a firm foundation for the support of his life. And they err, who think that only the plan of the life and the spirit should be drawn in nativities, which is to say the ASC and the MC; for from these places the substance of the life and the spirit is found. But along with the ASC degree and the MC we ought also to find the courses of the Moon with sagacious and skillful enquiry.

3. For God, the fabricator of man, composed this creature with a divine and singular plan of knowledge. He bound together the divinity of an immortal spirit with the shackles of a mortal and earthly body, so that the spirit, diffused both externally and internally, and obliged by some great necessity of serving the frail fragility of the body, might govern itself by

---

[1]Three early astrologers, perhaps of the 1st century B.C. or A.D., whose books have not come down to us except in excerpts cited by later writers. Critodemus was the author of *Horasis* 'Vision' and *Pinax* 'Table', of which excerpts are preserved by Vettius Valens and Hephaestio of Thebes.

[2]Reading *antistes* 'masters' with MSS **LW** rather than Sittl's conjecture *scii* 'those knowledgeable', or *antiscia* 'antiscions' **NV**, or the †*antisci* of the other MSS. But maybe Sittl was right.

[3]This title is from the Index.

the license of divine power.

4. Therefore, the spirit does not have an untouched hiding-place, [and consequently] it can neither, surrounded [as it is], fasten onto nor explain the substance of its own divinity, unless the body shall have provided a whole and undefiled framework for the support of the spirit, so that the spirit and the body are conjoined by a plan of equal necessity, and each in turn, sustaining itself by the forces and powers of its own nature, may explain the man, made by the divine and terrene society of conjunction, with an untouched likeness and form of the completed work.

5. Wherefore, we ought to know that the Moon undertakes the body of man and what is reckoned of its powers; because we feel in our bodies both the augments of the waxing Moon and the hurts of the waning Moon. For the marrow of the human body increases when the Moon is waxing; but when it shall have begun to be empty and it leaves off from its light, the human grows faint with an attentuated weariness of body; but also, when the Moon is waning, the human body decreases, and again, with the regular complements of the waxing Moon, it is inundated.

6. Thus, all the substance of the earthly body is governed by the foresight of this divinity. For, placed in the lower parts of the sky, and because of her nearness. she is allotted the rulership of the Earth, and sustaining all the bodies that are animated by the inspiration of the divine mind, by the multiplex variety of her own course while running through all the signs with quick rapidity, and associating herself with all the stars by incessant conjunctions. And having borrowed from contrary combinations and disparate elements, the whole substance of that composite work, she both procreates all the bodies of living creatures that have been conceived, and destroys those that have been generated.

7. Therefore, it must be worked out, and in every nativity that substance in which the Moon is posited must be sought out with great diligence; for by how much the Moon transports herself with swift movements, and by how much she conjoins herself to all the stars with swift rapidity, by just that much we should consider her courses with diligent contemplation. For both the first day and the third day denote the same things in similar fashion, also the seventh and the fortieth[1] show the substance of the whole life through the Moon.

[1]The MSS have 'eleventh' by mistake. Cumont notes (CCAG 8.4, 206 note 1) that Rhetorius, *Astrological Compendium*, Chapter 81, has 'the third and the seventh and the fortieth'; see my translation p. 132 and note 2.

8. But the Ruler of the Nativity and the Giver of Life are also found from the conjunctions of the Moon; and the last day of life is also learned from calculations of the Moon. But also the Ruler of the Times, which the Greeks call the *chronocrator*, the Moon along with the Sun shows us; for in nocturnal nativities, she takes on the beginning and the rulership, but in diurnal nativities, the Sun [does this]; which—what sort it is or where it is used—we explain in the later Books.

9. We have stated that the Moon's many appearances and forms are in the Book of Instruction, but now we may also explain these same things briefly; for we should mention everything that is more difficult more frequently, so that we may grasp those difficult things more easily from frequent explanation.

10. And so, the Moon is either synodic or full, or at the quarter, or crescent, or gibbous; and having changed through these forms she completes her course of monthly light. Therefore, we ought to look carefully at the increases or decreases of her light, and the changeable kinds of her diverse forms, considering the nativity on both the first day of birth and again on the third day, and with which [stars] she conjoins, and from which she separates and departs; And to what extent she associates herself with second conjunctions after the first conjunction, also with which star she conjoins by latitude; when she moves by high [latitude] or when by low; which stars she aspects by trine, which by square, [and] which by opposition. Also, when she moves towards which stars when she is full of light or with little light. To what extent she is joined to stars of her own sect, when, posited in the same degree, she is conjoined with synodic union[1]; and when, placed in the same degrees, the Sun seizes upon her and hides her with his own disc. So that, when we have thus investigated and considered all these things in the nativities of men, we may attain the full knowledge of delineation.

[1]Partile conjunction.

Chapter 2. What the Moon Denotes when Moving towards a Star.

<Chapter 2a. The Moon to Saturn.> [IV.2]

1. If the Moon applies to the star of Saturn, and increasing in light conjoins herself to Saturn with that association or thus moves toward Saturn, it denotes widowhood for the mother and constant pains in feminine parts [of the body]; it makes the [Natives] to be occupied in temple activities, and it dissipates their personal assets with various losses; but again, with the passing course of time, it makes them to acquire another amount of assets through their own efforts.

2. But if it is joined to Saturn when it is waning and with little light, it will make the parents to be either of low class, or slaves, or immersed in the squalor of miserable misfortune. And it destroys the mothers of these persons, either through illness, or else it certainly makes them to die violently when they[1] are in their younger years;. But it also makes them either to have bodily defects, to be crippled, or short-lived, or to perish by some bad end, especially if [the Moon] was found to be in this conjunction in appropriate houses of the nativity, i.e. if it is conjoined partilely in the ASC.

<Chapter 2b. The Moon to Jupiter.> [IV.3]

1. If the Moon applies to the star of Jupiter and is conjoined in that relationship while she is increasing in light, or if she is moving toward Jupiter, it will make fortunate, glorious, wealthy persons, lords of many and large buildings and the most extensive possessions. But those having the Moon thus also predict the future, either through their own divinity of spirit, or through a warning of the Gods, or from oracles, or from the learning of some venerable art. And yet if the star of Mars sees the Moon placed in this conjunction by square or by opposition, all these things are diminished and there is the greatest danger to life.

2. But if she was in this conjunction with little light, it will make [the Natives] to be adopted, or first exposed and then returned to their parents, acquiring personal assets for themselves through their own efforts. And it

[1]That is, the Natives.

renders them such as those who rise in the world gradually and with the passage of time, and who have the power of some certain fame. But these things are completed then if Mars does not aspect the Moon placed thus—either waxing or with little light—by opposition or square.

3. But if Mars does make that aspect to Moon placed thus, it will make exposed persons weighted down with a life-long burden of slavery.[1] Or it will make them to be born of a mother who is a slave-girl, or who is crippled. Or they themselves are certainly made to be cripples in some part of their body, and they are weighed down with the wretched burden of misfortune, especially if Mars aspects this conjunction in a diurnal nativity or Saturn in a nocturnal one; but Saturn does it then when the Moon has little light.

<Chapter 2c. The Moon to Mars.> [IV.4]

1. If the Moon applies to the star of Mars and while increasing in light joins herself in association with Mars, or if she moves toward Mars, and if it is a nocturnal nativity, it makes hot-tempered, prone to dangers, violent persons, but those who are wont to be deceived in numerous ways, and whose life is subjected to the greatest dangers. And yet they are capable persons bringing all things to completion—either dedicated to arms or placed in charge of athletic contests—especially if they were posited in the principal angles of the nativity. And yet these persons will have bodily defects or be in distress. And either illness kills their mothers before their time, or it makes them to die violently.

2. But if it is a diurnal nativity, and the Moon is conjoined thus to Mars, it will make them weak in every part of their body, or a part of their body will be amputated. It harms the eyes of some; it debilitates the stomach of others with a continuation of hidden defects. It makes some to be short-lived or to die a violent death. But it makes and denotes all these things according to the inherent nature of the individual signs. And a diverse variety of decrees is found according to the diverse situation of the angles, and according to the cadent houses of the angles, and according to those signs that we have said to be disjunct from association with the ASC.

---

[1]Exposed infants were sometimes taken up by slave dealers, thus entering slavery from birth.

3. For in those signs that we have said to be disjunct from any association with the ASC, i.e. in the sixth from the ASC or in the twelfth house, if the Moon increasing in light joins together with Mars, it diminishes the Native's inheritance; it separates his parents; or, his parents having been slain, it will make [the Native] to be worn down with the miseries of sadness. The body of some will be cut to pieces by the slicing of iron. Others suffer such wounds, that they can be healed in no other way than by cautery. Moreover, it bestows professions that always work with either fire or iron. It will make others to be soldiers, but those who are worn down by the constant burden of military life. But in the fifth house or in the eleventh from the ASC, or in the second, or in the eighth, or posited in the ASC itself, if the Moon moves toward Mars by day, it denotes bodily defects in the sides and a short time of life; and it makes those dying violently.

4. But if it is a nocturnal nativity and it moves toward Mars with little light—namely, in those houses that we have mentioned—it will make great men, powerful, terrifying, and effectual, who subjugate the greatest cities by the exercise of some power, especially if it was found [posited] thus in the most important angles of the nativity.

5. But if it was found thus by day in the principal angles of the nativity, it dissipates the father's assets. But it also weakens the parents themselves, or it kills them with a violent death. Nevertheless, it will make public artisans or soldiers, but those who are involved with illnesses or bodily defects, or it frequently denotes the greatest dangers, and demise by a violent death.

<Chapter 2d. The Moon to the Sun.> [IV.5]

1. If the Moon moves towards the Sun and joins herself to him by a partile aspect in whatever kind of aspect, it will make persons who experience frequent dangers—miserable downcast persons, and those who are laid low in wretched circumstances and by the degredation of humble association in their whole life. Occasionally it makes spastics and those who are hampered by constant bouts of illnesses. It makes some of them to be epileptic; for some it denotes the inconveniences of estrangement, and for others it generally denotes periods of unhealthiness.

<Chapter 2e. The Moon to Venus.> [IV.6]

1. If the Moon moves towards Venus, and Venus receives the aspect of the approaching Moon partilely; and if the crescent Moon has applied to Venus, it will make the parents to be noble and elevated by the force of the greatest power. But for those who were born thus, it indicates the burden of a wretched orphanhood after having been separated quickly from the affections of their parents,. They will of course always be well-known and noble, and those who always succeed in every action; and those who easily get everything that they desire, and who are illustrious with the greatest honors of power—full of charm and grace—but who get all of these increments in the course of time.

2. But if the waning Moon bears to Venus thus, it denotes great actions, the greatest honors and the insignia of great power, and those on whom the greatest augments of happiness are conferred by their parents and from their first age. But it makes them to be brought into disrepute by constant rumors[1]. . .it is sought.

3. But if the Moon, in whatever configuration of her own orb, bears to Venus, it will always make those who are involved in perverted faulty acts of love, and who because of this are battered by constant scandals—unchaste, lustful persons and always burning with excessive desire for love affairs with women; and those whom incestuous desire always inflames to illegal couplings. For either they always debauch their own sisters, or the wives of their sons, or the wives of their step-sons, or they have intercourse with their own step-mothers, or they seduce the concubines of their fathers with secret desire; or a similar injury is imposed upon their uncles through them, especially if Mars aspects this conjunction by opposition. For if it is a diurnal nativity,and the Moon posited in the angles of the nativity bears thus to Venus, but Mars is found in the DSC or in the MC, it will make them to die by the sword on account of these crimes.

4. But if in the nativity of a woman the Moon bears thus to Venus, she will always be restless with an envious passion, and one who is excited to promiscuous lusts by depraved desires. And one who conceives longings for incestuous and illicit desires and is always burning with impure desires for libidinous pleasures. For she has intercourse either with her

[1]Perhaps a whole line of text is lost beginning here. But **Nα** omit …*adpetatur* '…it is sought', perhaps rightly.

brothers, or with her sons, or with the sons of her brothers, or with her own uncles—or, with a perverted ardor of desire—she brings to her marriage bed step-sons captivated by her own attractions,. Or she joins her own known relatives to herself in debauchery. It makes others to be viragos, especially if, with Venus posited in tropical or erratic signs, or in bicorporeal, or scaly ones, the Moon moves to her, [and] the Moon too is posited in similar signs.

5. But these things are always roused up with stronger ardor if Mars or Saturn aspects the course of the Moon with a square or opposition aspect, especially if it has begun to aspect the Moon with these same aspects. Moreover, these evils will be stronger, if Mars or Saturn aspects Venus and the Moon—posited as we have said – in a domicile of Saturn or Mars without any fortunate testimony of Jupiter.

<Chapter 2f. The Moon to Mercury.> [IV.7]

1. If the Moon moves towards Mercury and conjoins herself to him by an aspect from her own course and is full of light, it will make wise, talented persons, and orators shining with the greatest nobility of eloquence, especially if Mercury was found posited in fortunate houses of the nativity in its own signs or in its own degrees, and if Jupiter aspected it by trine. For then, from the merit of their writings and the splendor of their eloquence, the greatest visible [rewards] will be conferred upon them. For these persons, by the power of their own eloquence, suppress the fickle minds of the people, and those aroused to turbulent sedition, and frenzied minds. And by the authority of their own oratory they can calm those aroused by the indignations of a desperate frenzy. [Also], they will know [methods of] computation; they will know music; they will always engage in wrestling; and they understand the secrets of celestial and divine discussion. From which opportunities the foundation of glory and the greatest leading position is decreed for them.

2. But if the Moon moves towards Mercury posited thus with that kind of testimony from Jupiter, it will make [the Native] to be put in charge of the accounts of the treasury or of the people, or it will certainly make persons such as those to whom even the deposits of foreign nations are entrusted. It will also make transactions of money to be entrusted to them in continuing associations.

3. But if the waning Moon moves towards Mercury, it will make malign, malicious, wicked persons, unstable in their desires, wavering in error,[1] and those who always leave all their counsels hanging because of manifold, erratic doubt. And who reverse their own actions with constant changes, and who deny things that have been credited to them, or who desire to make secret [writings] public. And those who give out counsels entrusted to themselves with public denunciations, impostors, always deceiving because of a malicious desire, or those who unite their conscience with house-breakers or with thieves. They will of course be weak in body, listless, deformed, and those whom an acquired illness disables with malicious humors.

Chapter 3. The Moon when she Moves Towards None [of the Stars], and Which one she first Touches after an Empty Course, or from Which one she Departs, and to Which one she Runs, and what she does in each House, and from which Star she Runs in empty [Course] and is not moved to any [Star], to which she Applies, or from Which [Star] to Which, and in what Configuration. [IV.8]

1. But if the Moon is so posited that she moves towards none [of the stars], and she does not conjoin herself to any star by her own aspect, and if a benefic star does not sit upon [any of] the angles, it will make disheartened, poor persons, and those who are lacking all the necessities, and those to whom the supports of daily life are denied, and who always desire the support of strangers for sustaining their life, and who support the want of poverty with a wretched beggary. Moreover, they will be entirely inferior to their parents; and in fact their bodies will be weak, listless, and worn out with a persistent leanness. They will be attacked by malign humors, and they are worn down by the continual swelling of wounds; but a malignant humor always renders [them] liable to stony joints under the skin, especially if, while running through emptiness, which the Greeks call *cenodromon*,[2] the Moon is struck by a square or

---

[1]So the Teubner text, which has *instabiles cupiditatibus, errore dubios*; but **Δ** has *instabiles cupiditatibus <erroneos vel cupiditatis> errore dubios* 'unstable [persons], vacillating in their desires or from the error of their desire, wavering', perhaps rightly (although the word *erroneos* does not occur elswhere in the *Mathesis*).

[2]This is a transliteration of the Greek *kenodromon*, literally 'empty course', but

opposition aspect of Saturn or Mars, or, if running through emptiness on the third day of the nativity, she was struck by those same aspects that we have mentioned, or if malefics were posited in the angles.

2. But truly if while running thus, i.e. through emptiness, she met with an aspect of the benefic stars, it will always make the Natives to be empty and bare in their first age; but it also makes them to be worn out with constant labors; and it harasses them with continual attacks[1] of miserable [circumstances]—seeking their support from the greatest sweaty jobs and the greatest labors. And although it has made them close to fortunate conditions, it makes them to sink down again from their highest step [of success] into downfallen dejection. And sometimes, when they are brought up to the very top, it does not permit them to seize complete good fortune. For, directing her own courses through empty signs, it makes their first age to be involved with wretched and various instances of misfortunes. But although it has harrassed the mind and body with a serious continuation of misfortunes, and it has shattered their youth with many dangers, and has dragged them along in this and that wretched travel [experience], then [finally] it denotes increases of many good things and the greatest good fortune, so that, however much of their first age was taken away by misfortunes, that same amount of good fortune is conferred upon their later age.

3. But if, running through emptiness, she afterwards conjoins herself to Saturn or to Mars, it will make unlucky persons, lunatics, epileptics, and those who from their first age down to their very last are weighed down with various kinds of misfortune. It will make paupers, wretched, destitute individuals, and those whose body is bare [except for] rags hanging down, guardians of tombs, or those who are enclosed in prison with perpetual punishment.[2]

<Chapter 3a. The Moon Separating from Saturn and Applying to Another Star> [IV.9]

1. Having explained and demonstrated the conjunctions of the Moon with diligent signification, the discourse is transferred to another inter-

---

which astrologers have called *void of course* since the Middle Ages.

[1]Accepting Ziegler's suggestion of *incursionibus* 'attacks' in place of *rationibus* 'reasons'.

[2]That is, those who are serving a life sentence.

pretation—namely, of the Moon itself—lest anything in such subtle disputations may seem to have been passed over by us, especially since the entire substance of life may be collected from the courses of this divinity.

2. <The Moon from Saturn to Jupiter.>[1] The Moon separating from Saturn, if she conjoins herself to the star of Jupiter or moves towards Jupiter, and if she was conjoined in that association while waxing, will make opulent, rich, famous, noble persons, in charge of great peoples or great cities. On some it bestows the greatest inheritances, on others treasures, on others the greatest gifts.

3. But if it had little light, it denotes nothing of the sort. But it makes business administrators, managers, or those to whom the defense of private things is entrusted, and who waste away in foreign business affairs, or it makes pilots, or skippers, or managers of taxes, and those whose occupations around water include the right of hiring so that from these acts some small means accrue to them.

4. The Moon from Saturn to Mars. If the Moon, separating from Saturn, joins herself to Mars [while] full of light, she denotes illnesses and bodily defects, and she will make the Native to die in his first age. But if [she has] little light, it denotes the torments of a long and very severe illness for the mother, and it makes her to be affected by some bodily defects, and it brings the danger of a bad death for that same mother, so that she perishes while continually vomiting blood. And it makes those who were born [thus] to be worn out with the wearinesses of a wretched orphanhood, or it makes their parents to be estranged by a perpetual disagreement.

5. But it demolishes both the father's and the mother's estate by various kinds of losses, and it inflicts frequent wounds [made by] iron upon them, and it denotes illnesses of such a sort, that in order to effect a cure, a remedy is applied to them by burning them with branding irons. It also makes chronic pains in the hidden parts [of the body], or it makes them to fill out the gift of life depressed by the suffering of a lengthy illness, or it makes them to die violently in various ways—for they perish either drowned in rivers, or burnt up [in a fire], or they hang themselves with a noose, or they kill hemselves with a sword.

6. The Moon from Saturn to the Sun. If the Moon separating from Saturn moves towards the Sun, it denotes the greatest misfortunes and the

---

[1] Adds MS **V**.

greatest disasters; for it will make insane persons, lunatics, epileptics, those afflicted with dropsy, and lepers. But it perpetuates these misfortunes with a persistent frequency, so that down to the last day of life they are caught in the snares of disaster.[1]

7. The Moon from Saturn to Venus. If the Moon separating from Saturn conjoins herself to the star of Venus, if she was waxing, it will make great, noble, and powerful persons, fortunate, wealthy, and rich, and certainly[2] with some great power, savage, lustful, and those who are battered with severe infamy from these [faults]. But if she was of little light, it denotes the depraved enticements of love affairs, or it makes [them] to be involved in impure and indecent passions, or it denotes disgraceful actions in continual succession. But neverthelesss it makes these same persons to be seeking and possessing the greatest abundance of wealth, and for whom both good fortune and the greatest power are provided by the assistance of money.

8. If the Moon separating from Saturn conjoins herself to the star of Mercury, and is waxing or full of light, it makes obscure, secretive, reserved persons, knowledgeable about secret and illicit writings, or occupied with celestial religions or skilled computations, interpreting the courses of the stars. It also makes those in charge of business affairs and public teachers of the liberal arts. It makes orators sparkling with the splendor of their eloquence, or teachers adorned by the testimonies of everyone.

9. But if the Moon had little light, then either it impedes the sound of the voice or it deafens the ears. But it also debilitates the bodies of those who have it thus with wretched weariness; it makes persons suffering from melancholy, jaundiced, splenetic, consumptives, those suffering from dropsy, [or] lung disease, and with a restricted opening along with the harsh inconvenience of pain it cuts off the collected fluid of the bladder.[3]

---

[1]King Charles VI of France (1368-1422) had this configuration.

[2]Reading *quidem* 'certainly' with **PR^{b}VN** and **α** rather than Kroll's conjecture *cuiusdam* 'a certain'.

[3]As Skutsch noted, this is apparently a reference to strangury.

<Chapter 3b. The Moon Separating from Jupiter and Applying to Another Star.> [IV.10]

1. If the Moon separating from Jupiter moves towards Mars, and it is a nocturnal nativity, and the waxing Moon joins in association thus with Mars, it makes great powerful persons, holding cities or the largest regions with their own powers, but it denotes that the power of that supremacy is accompanied by anxieties and dangers. Nevertheless, these persons will not be without bodily defect or illness, but they are such as those who easily endure everything, especially if Mars was found in the principal houses of the nativity. But if, with Mars so posited in the dejected houses, the Moon moves towards him, it denotes arts involving fire, but it makes those person humble and downcast, and it denotes illnesses and bodily defects, and in frequent instances the danger of a bad death.

2. But if by day the waxing Moon separates from Jupiter and joins herself to the star of Mars, it will make those who are exposed, slaves, those weighed down with the wretched burden of beggary, beset by bodily faults and illnesses; and those whose servitude is like captivity, and who lose their life by a violent death.

3. But if the waning Moon in a nocturnal nativity is departing from Jupiter and moving towards Mars, it will make those who are foremost[1] and famous; and if Mars was found in the principal houses of the nativity, and the Moon with little light is separating from Jupiter and moving towards Mars, it will make judges, generals, and those to whom the greatest command of power is entrusted. But if Mars was found in dejected houses of the nativity and thus, just as we have said, the Moon is moving towards it, it will make soldiers, athletes, or those who seek their life support from fire and iron, or it will make physicians and surgeons.

4. But if by day the Moon, waning and separating from Jupiter, moves towards Mars, it destroys the paternal and maternal inheritances and kills the parents in [the Native's] first time of life, and it imposes the burden of extreme beggary [upon him]. On others, it inflicts a bodily defect of bitter pain. Sometimes it makes slaves, sometimes captives, but generally those

---

[1]The Latin text has *primos* 'foremost'; Kroll suggests changing it to *mimos* 'mimes', but Némethy suggests *<civitatum decem> primos* 'First Ten [men] of cities', which phrase occurs several times elsewhere in the *Mathesis*, and is equivalent to 'city councilmen'.

dying a violent death, especially if—with the Moon running thus—Mars was found in the angles of the nativity or if it was in the *anaforas* or the *cataforas*; for then, those things that we have said . . .[1] when the Moon has conjoined herself to Mars posited in those houses with that association.

5. If the Moon separating from Jupiter moves towards the Sun, it destroys the paternal and maternal inheritance with various kinds of tearing away, and it alienates the Natives from their parents, or it puts them on some lengthy journey. Some others it makes exiles, still others fugitives, on others it imposes the slavery of a dishonest captivity, especially if the Sun or the Moon was found in a domicile of Saturn or Mars.

6. If the Moon separating from Jupiter moves towards Venus, but if it is waxing or full of light, it will make the parents to be very brilliant with the authority of noble power, and who may have attained the greatest power. But it causes him who was born [thus] to be alienated from his own [people], and it makes him to be quickly bereaved of his parents. But nevertheless it also denotes power, glory, and nobility for him, but it bestows all these things with the passage of time. And it denotes the greatest augments[2] of good fortune from his wives. It will also make them to be charming, pleasant, and attractive, and those for whom the greatest power is procured by their pleasantness and charm.

7. But if separating from Jupiter it moves toward Venus diminished in its light, and it is in the princpal or necessary houses of the nativity, it denotes never-ending increases in good fortune; and he will be exceedingly fortunate, in whosever nativity it is found thus, for it denotes honors, powers, *fasces* in youth,[3] and the insignia of magnificent power, and those on whom this benefice is conferred by their parents. And it denotes

---

[1]Some words are missing in the Latin text; the Teubner editors suggest adding <will all be stronger>.

[2]Reading *maxima...augmenta* with **NP[a]V** rather than *maximae...augmentum* with **A** and the Teubner editors.

[3]So I have rendered *fasces praetextas*, lit. *fasces* [a symbol of great authority] and 'togas with purple borders' [worn by youths of prominent families, and high public officials]. I take this to mean great power bestowed upon a young man. Three examples that occurred in Firmicus's lifetime were the sons of Constantine I the Great: Constantine II, who was raised to the rank of Caesar in 317, when he was still an infant; Constantius II, who was raised to the rank of Caesar at age 7; and Constans I who was proclaimed Caesar at age 13. A medieval Christian example is Theophylact of Tusculum, who was made Pope in 1032 as Benedict IX at age 12.

the insignia of the most powerful dignity for them placed in the first steps of their maturity. And it makes increases of wealth and good fortune to be conferred [on them] by their wives and by women.

8. If separating from Jupiter, the Moon moves toward Mercury full of light, it makes critics, i.e. persons of good judgment, good, benign, glorious persons; for they will either be tax superintendents of the treasury, or those in charge of religions, or interpreters of law. From which occupations the greatest <increases> of good fortune[1] and the greatest wealth is bestowed on them, in such a way that that good fortune will last during their whole lifetime.

9. But if separating from Jupiter with little light it moves toward Mercury, it will make those seeking the substance of life or their life's support from letters, or from education or from storehouses,[2] and from business dealings. Some will find <hidden things>[3]; others will deny [that they have] things entrusted to them, so that from that treachery they get the foundations of wealth for themselves.

10. If the Moon is separating from Jupiter and moves toward Saturn when it is waxing or full of light, it will make those who are adopted by non-relatives or those who [act as] fathers of non-related offspring, or guardians, or business managers of minors. Others are caused to find exposed or discarded children after a lengthy space of time. They will always be involved in watery or humid activities, or in wandering about in constant travels or in sailing for the sake of commerce, so that their life's support is sought from that [sort of] occupation.

11. But if separating from Jupiter with little light, the Moon moves toward Saturn, it will either make the Natives to be exposed; or it will impose the burden of servitude [on them]; or it indicates the misfortune of a miserable captivity; or it makes other bodily defects or illnesses, so that their entire life, worn out by the severe bitterness of pain, quickly incurs a termination by a miserable death. But if it was a nocturnal nativity, and the Moon with little light was separating from Jupiter and moving toward Saturn, it makes them to die a violent death of some sort.

---

[1]MS **N** has *maxima felicitatis <incrementa>* 'the greatest increases in good fortune'.

[2]Probably the grain silos or storehouses maintained by the government.

[3]*<absconsas res>* 'hidden things' supplies Némethy.

<Chapter 3c. The Moon Separating from Mars and Applying to Another Star.> [IV.11]

1. The Moon from Mars to the Sun. If the Moon separating from Mars moves toward the Sun, it denotes the greatest bodily defects and illnesses, and it bestows a short time of life, and it makes the Natives to die violently, and in general it denotes the greatest inconveniences of misfortune. But [with it] placed thus it makes some of them [to dwell] abroad and to die in foreign territories.

2. The Moon from Mars to Venus. If the Moon separating from Mars moves toward Venus and is waxing or full of light, it makes adulterers, lustful individuals, lovers, and those who are always devoted to amorous desires, and involved in frequent instances of danger. Moreover, they will practice the arts either of pigments and perfumes, or of [precious] stones and pearls; and dyers are frequently made by this configuration of the Moon. They will also engage in commerce involving some metal; and they are made innkeepers according to the signs or the houses, so that they prepare those things that are necessary for eating and drinking as a famous and public business.

3. But if separating from Mars with little light the Moon moves toward Venus, it will make successful, happy, fortunate persons, but [also] rich ones. These will of course molest women and abduct rich ones, but as legal wives, from whom they will obtain the greatest signs of good fortune; for through these women they are dignified with the greatest embellishment of dignity, especially if it is a nocturnal nativity. <But if it is a diurnal nativity>,[1] it will make hard-working persons persisting in various kinds of jobs, and who are struck with frequent disgrace because of sexual affairs, and those who are always aroused by wishes for promiscuous lust.

4. The Moon from Mars to Mercury. If the Moon separating from Mars moves toward Mercury, full of light in a nocturnal nativity, it will make soldiers and athletes—sometimes famous ones. It will make others who are in charge of public and famous activities; but they will be malign, malicious persons, and those whose desire for every kind of criminal offense increases day by day; for they will be either executioners or headsmen, and those to whom public authority grants the license to de-

[1]Supplied by Kroll. One line was omitted in the archetype due to homoeoteleuton (*...genitura* | *...genitura*).

nounce [illegal activities]. But if the Moon has this configuration by day and is full of light, it denotes the inconveniences of a miserable judicial sentence, so that they are caused to be deported by the sentence of a judge, and as a result of this sentence to die violently.

5. But if separating from Mars with little light the Moon moves towards Mercury in a diurnal nativity, it denotes desires for endless crimes[1]; for it makes marauders [and] highway robbers, but those who, apprehended in this crime, are punished by a severe judgment of the presiding judge. Others are crushed to death by the collapse of falling dwellings. Insanity changes others from a correct course of life. But if it was <with little light in>[2] a nocturnal nativity, it will make those in charge of prisons and prison guards, and those who get their living from this duty. They will surely be lovers of ships and athletics, and those who pursue quadrupedal animals as a constant duty. They will surely have bodily defects, and they are worn out by the constant inconveniences of dangers.

6. The Moon from Mars to Saturn. If the Moon separating from Mars when full [of light] or waxing moves toward Saturn, it makes slow, sluggish persons, and those who cannot profit from any of their activities, and who get none of those things that they want. But it makes the mother to be a widow or encumbered by bodily defects and illnesses; but it destroys her with a demise by a bad death. It [also] dissipates their finances from continual losses; and it makes them to be afflicted by various bodily defects.

7. But if the Moon waning in light separates from Mars and moves toward Saturn, it denotes hunger, sicknesses, illnesses; it makes lunatics, bleeders, cripples, paralytics, hunch-backs, short-lived persons; or, if it was none of these, it makes those dying violently. But the mothers or fathers of some of them are oppressed by bodily defects according to the quality of the signs And this configuration either kills them before [their time], or it makes them to die violently.

8. The Moon from Mars to Jupiter. If the Moon separating from Mars moves toward Jupiter in fortunate houses of the nativity, it makes generals leading an army, powerful, imperious, and terrifying in every way, and those who hold provinces and cities by the power of their own power. They will certainly be rich, wealthy, with much money, and those who

---

[1]Accepting Kroll's emendation of †*inmensum* and reading **infinitorum criminum decernit cupiditates*.

[2]Adds MS **N**.

get everything that they want in the easiest way, and who are the victors in the conflict of all battles.

9. But if it has little light, and separating thus from Mars, it moves toward Jupiter, it will make those destined for some public battles, but who are always honored with the commendation of goodness Or it makes famous soldiers, and it denotes continual additions of good fortune for them, and it decorates[1] those same extensively with frequent promotions of honors, and it makes famous persons of various sorts. Nevertheless, it inflicts hidden bodily defects [on them], and it will make them to be involved in frequent illnesses.

<Chapter 3d. The Moon Separating from the Sun and Applying to Another Star.>[2] *[IV.12]*

1. The Moon from the Sun to Venus. If the Moon separating from the Sun moves toward Venus and it is a diurnal nativity, it will make sterile persons and those who cannot generate offspring, and those who are joined in conjugal affection with difficulty; for they marry wives who are sterile, or aged, or maid-servants—and the latter nevertheless sterile—or they pursue disgraceful and wretched intercourse with boys, for which reason offspring of chidren is perpetually denied to them. They will of course be involved in perverted offences of amorous activities, either given over to indecent or wretched desires, and always occupied in servile work and servile occupations, getting insufficient recompense, and seeking the greatest support of life for themselves through their own efforts, and who get increases in good fortune with the passage of time.

2. But if separating from the Sun the Moon moves toward Venus by night, it denotes many wives; it makes affable, pleasant, well-accepted persons, and it denotes great actions and great wealth; they will be nobles, shining with the brightness of fame. Moreover, it makes imperial, powerful, rich persons, and those on whom the greatest good fortune is bestowed, especially if Saturn has afflicted neither of them by a square or opposite aspect. Moreover then, this good fortune and these honors are

---

[1]Reading *decorat* 'decorates' rather than *patet* 'it is plain'.

[2]From this point on, the *Liber Hermetis*, Chapter XXVII, offers a description of the effects of the Moon's separations from the Sun, Venus, and Mercury. It appears that the LH was translated from a Greek source that was similar to the one translated by Firmicus. The two translations are sometimes very similar, but at other times they are different.

[only] denoted if this conjunction was in the necessary houses of the nativity.

3. The Moon from the Sun to Mercury. If the Moon separating from the Sun moves toward Mercury and it is a diurnal nativity, it makes those who experience dangers in their life and actions, and those who are perverted with bad morals and always with sacrilegious error and denying [the existence of] divinity; but these at the same time also refuse [to give up] things that have been entrusted to them.

4. But if the Moon separating from the Sun by night moves toward Mercury, it makes public scribes, from which letters they seek their life's support; nevertheless they will be honored[1] for this occupation in their own cities, and those who are preferred in the judgment of all to all men of the same business. Frequently, nevertheless, if Jupiter aspects them with a trine aspect, they undertake the administration and protection of cities.[2] Moreover, they will be inventors of difficult literary documents, or of some kind of wisdom, or of celestial religions. And they will be those to whom the secrets of divinity are entrusted, or they will be involved in actions dealing with secret or illicit documents.[3] Some will find hidden things; an inheritance is bestowed on others, if indeed Mars and Saturn together were not configured with them.

5. The Moon from the Sun to Saturn. <If the Moon separating from the Sun> moves toward <Saturn>[4] and it is a diurnal nativity, it destroys the inheritance, divides the parents and indicates the inconveniences of a wretched orphanhood for the [Natives]. But with the passage of time it denotes the greatest abundance of wealth for them, and it allots increases of great good fortune, and it bestows the ownership of many buildings.

6. But if the Moon separating <from the Sun>[5] by night moves toward Saturn, <it denotes> orphanhood <and>[6] it diminishes the inheritance,

[1]Accepting Cumont's emendation *honorati* 'honored' instead of *ornati* 'decorated'.

[2]Probably some important official, such as a city manager is meant.

[3]Cf. *Liber Hermetis* (ed. Gundel), p. 80,19 *perversarum litterarum intelligibiles* 'those knowledgeable about perverse documents'.

[4]Adds edition **v**. Presumably a conjectural addition, but the words could easily have been omitted in the archetype due to homoeoteleuton (...*Luna ad Saturnum* | ...*Luna ad Saturnum*).

[5]Adds edition **v**.

[6]<*decernit et*> 'and it denotes' adds MS **N**. The Teubner editors conjecture <*indicit et*> 'and it indicates'.

and it denotes the inconveniences of bad travels. It also makes severe bodily defects and severe illnesses, or it makes [the Natives] to be involved in accidents of severe and violent dangers.

7. The Moon from the Sun to Jupiter. If the Moon separating from the Sun moves toward Jupiter, and it is a diurnal nativity, it bestows the signs of luck and good fortune from the parents. Some of them will obtain the greatest regions of cities; and they will indeed be provided with the benefit of unlimited good fortune.

8. But if the Moon separating from the Sun by night moves toward Jupiter, it will make those procuring the substance of means for themselves through their own [efforts], and those who are devoted to constant travels. But it disappoints them in their early youth, and when they are older,[1] it <bestows> famous commendations, kindnesses,[2] and a suitable abundance of wealth.

9. The Moon from the Sun to Mars. If the Moon departing from the Sun moves toward Mars and it is a diurnal nativity, it destroys his parents by a quick death, so that he himself is thus weighed down by the burden of orphanhood. Moreover, the parents frequently die violently due to that configuration. And for the Natives themselves, it denotes the defective blindness of sight; or it makes them weak from the amputation of some part of their body; or it kills them in their early age; or, if it has done none of these things, it makes them die a violent death.

10. But if the Moon separating from the Sun by night moves toward Mars, it makes violent, cruel persons, and those who always commit dangerous crimes, or it makes those suffering from bodily defects and illnesses. Nevertheless, it denotes public activities and military service,[3] or it makes famous athletes, and especially if both Mars and the Moon were found in the important houses of the nativity. But if this configuration was in dejected houses <without> the testimony <of any good star>,[4] it diminishes their wealth, it makes them to be deprived of their parents, it makes their life humble, it denotes bodily defects and illnesses, or it certainly makes them to die violently. And it makes their occupations to be

[1]The Latin has *fuerint †eorum provectu temporis aetatis*, which is corrupt, but which plainly means 'with the passage of time in their life'.

[2]Reading *bonitates* with MS **N**.

[3]Reading *militiamque* 'and military service' with **Ψα** rather than *malitiamque* 'and malice' with **Ω**. *Cf. Liber Hermetis*, which has *militiis* 'in military service'.

[4]Adds edition **α**, omits MS **N**, but similar words A′.

either from fire, or from iron, or from metal, or it surely makes persons of the sort that are always weighed down with an unbroken succession of labors.

<Chapter 3e. The Moon Separating from Venus and Applying to Another Star.> [IV.13]

1. The Moon from Venus to Mercury. The Moon separating from Venus and moving toward Mercury, if it is waxing or full of light, makes defenders[1] or business managers of noble women, and those who by the assistance of women receive some rank of promotion. Nevertheless, they will be dyers or pearl-sellers or inventors of perfumes, frequently musicians, and physicians, or managers and coaches of athletes, but lustful and aroused by constant desires for sexual relations, but pleasant persons and delightful in sexual intercourse.

2. But if the Moon separating from Venus with little light moves toward Mercury, it denotes bodily defects, indecencies, and illnesses; but it will make their occupations to be various and numerous – for it will make either orators, or turners, or modellers, or sculptors, or dealers in paints, or inventors of colors, or vendors of medicine, or restaurant keepers, and those who maintain the management and provision of exotic pleasures and delights.

3. The Moon from Venus to Saturn. If the Moon separating from Venus moves toward Saturn, if it is waxing or full of light and it is a nocturnal nativity, will give a wife of either an advanced age, or it brings a public woman[2] to the sharing of the marriage bed, or he is allotted a wife from among his relatives. So that nevertheless from the support of his spouse he attains a principal place of honor and increases in his rank and the distinctions of promotion.

4. But if the Moon separating from Venus with little light moves toward Saturn in a diurnal nativity, it makes those notorious for passive desires for pleasure and given over to depraved pleasures, and who are battered by frequent infamy because of their lustful acts. They will surely be disgraceful persons, unstable, wretched in their servile dejection, whoremongers or pimps. But if this is the nativity of a woman, she will be

[1]Legal representatives.

[2]That is, a whore.

a public whore, and one who seeks her life's support from her body stationed in a public place with the loss of honor.

5. But if the Moon separating from Venus with little light in a nocturnal nativity moves toward Saturn, it will either make sterile persons, or eunuchs, or high priests of Cybele, or hermaphrodites, or certainly persons of the sort that are driven to endure womanly acts by the passion of wretched lust. They will surely be short-lived or dying a violent death.

6. But if [the Moon] departing from Venus with little light moves toward Saturn by day, it will make those suffering from bodily defects, feeble persons, and those whom some malignant humor always attacks, but who are exhausted by a wretched continuation of hard work. For they are either made to raise water every day from deep pits, or they are ordered to clean out pits and sewers continually, or they will be gardeners—but wretched ones—or sailors, or water-carriers, or fishermen, or divers.

7. But the quality of the signs frequently changes these jobs, for it will make ploughmen, cowboys, stable boys, shepherds, and those who are ordered to clean out or tidy up the stables of pack-horses; it also makes many who are guardians of tombs; or certainly undertakers, who by the decree and consent of all take on the task of burying men. But it denotes these things in accordance with the variety of the houses or signs, concerning which variety we have also spoken of very fully in connection with other astrological judgments.

8. The Moon from Venus to Jupiter. If the Moon separating from Venus moves toward Jupiter, it will make great, powerful, and noble persons, in charge of cities, and persons whom it makes to be elevated by the support of women. They will surely be pleasant and charming; and yet they will be lovers of women, and persons who, thanks to their charm, get everything that they desire.

9. But if separating from Venus with little light it moves toward Jupiter, it will give the foundations of wealth from feminine persons,[1] and it will make persons of the sort on whom the favor of good fortune and fame is conferred in their early years by their parents. It will give inheritances to some; it causes others to find the greatest profits; or it denotes honored offices in temples.

[1]Accepting Sittl's conjecture *muliebribus* 'feminine persons' (confirmed by MS **Q** and accepted by the Teubner editors) rather than *mulieribus* 'women'.

10. The Moon from Venus to Mars. If the Moon separating from Venus moves toward Mars in a diurnal nativity, and if the Moon is waxing or full of light, it denotes destruction by a wretched calamity from the passion of some love affair, and on account of this it indicates the serious threat[1] of dangers, so that they come to both incarceration in prison and the threat of condemnation; and those who perish by a violent death because of this. It will make some to be exposed,[2] others to be subjugated. It makes still others to be sold into the wretched burden of captivity—namely, in accordance with the power of the houses <and the signs>.[3]

11. But if the Moon separating from Venus by night moves toward Mars and is waxing or full of light, it makes artisans who are always violent, and hasty,[4] and who suffer from bodily defects and illnesses. But if the Moon departing from Venus moves toward Mars in a nocturnal nativity, it will make men who are terrifying and powerful, and who subjugate the greatest regions with their own abilities and powers—especially if either Mars or the Moon was in the ASC or the 5th sign from the ASC. If this configuration was in the rest of the houses, it either makes artisans or athletes or soldiers, but those who are involved in continual occurrences of dangers.

12. But if separating from Venus with little light in a diurnal nativity it moves toward Mars, it demolishes their personal wealth with wretched losses, and it makes them to be wretched, cast down into low position, and it denotes bodily defects and illnesses. It makes some of them exiles; it puts others to flight; it imposes the burden of servitude on others; and it kills still others in the first part of their life. It generally makes those who die violently because of women, or because of the lures of some love affair; for on account of that, it denotes ambushes, dangers, and judicial sentences.[5]

13. The Moon from Venus to the Sun. If the Moon separating from Venus moves toward the Sun, it separates the parents with bitter dissension;

---

[1]Accepting Skutsch's emendation of *discrimen* 'threat' instead of the *crimen* 'crime' of the MSS.

[2]Accepting Wikström's conjecture *exponi* 'exposed' (noted by Ziegler in the Addenda Addendis) for the *expoliari* of **A α**, the *expelli* of **N**, or the *expoli* of the other MSS.

[3]Adds edition **a**.

[4]Accepting Wikström's conjecture *calidos* 'hasty' (noted by Ziegler in the Addenda Addendis) for the *callidos* 'crafty' of the MSS.

[5]Bram adds "or a violent death," but this is not in the Latin text.

or it indicates the burden of a bitter orphanhood on the Natives; and it denotes restrictions in their personal wealth and life. It makes indecent persons, and those who are involved in wretched entanglements of love affairs,[1] but when they have gone out of the early time of youth, with the passage of time [it gives] increases in personal wealth, and whatever they desire they easily get.[2]

<Chapter 3f. The Moon Separating from Mercury and Applying to Another Star.> [IV.14]

1. The Moon from Mercury to Saturn. If the Moon separating from Mercury full of light moves toward Saturn and it is a diurnal nativity, it always makes either stammerers, or deaf persons,[3] or their words are impeded by the slow sound of their voice. Moreover, they will have jobs from reckoning, or from teaching, or from business affairs, or from travels, or from the interpretation of words; and they always penetrate into celestial secrets. Others undertake the care and management of waters,[4] or the custody of prisons; so that from these jobs their life's support is acquired.

2. But if the Moon separating from Mercury by night full of light moves toward Saturn, it will always make [the Natives] to be worn out by constant labor around water—workmen devoted to endless labors—and those who are accustomed to hire out their bodies for some task—porters seeking their [life's] support from their shoulders and their back. It places some in custody, it thrusts others into prison.[5] It will make others to die oppressed by the squalor of prison and public custody—contaminated[6]

---

[1]Reading *amorum amplexibus implicentur* with MS **N** rather than *amorum <vitiis> obligentur* 'embarassed by the faults of love affairs' with the Teubner editors.

[2]Reading *et quicquid desideraverint, facile consequantur* with MS **N** and edition **α.**

[3]Because without special training, deaf persons cannot speak or can only make meaningless noises.

[4]Accepting Sittl's conjecture *aquarum* 'waters' (confirmed by MS **N**) for the *aliquarum* 'of others' of the other MSS. Perhaps workers on aqueducts or on city water distribution systems.

[5]Reading *intrudit in carcerem* 'thrusts into prison' with **Ψ**, instead of *instruit in carcere* 'teaches in prison' **Ω**.

[6]Reading *coinquinatos* 'contaminated' with MS **N** rather than the *comatos* 'long-haired' of the Teubner editors.

and disfigured by filth; especially if this configuration is made in the signs of the malefic stars.

3. But if the Moon separating from Mercury with little light moves toward Saturn, it will make beggars, paupers clothed in rags, and sunk in the calamity of wretched poverty.[1] It makes some to serve in temples; it impels others to prophesy. It generally makes lunatics, or it denotes the faults of sacred illnesses; it makes epileptics and madmen with wretched agitated movements.

4. But if the Moon separating from Mercury by night with little light moves toward Saturn, it either makes them to be exposed; or it indicates the squalor of wretched servitude; or it imposes[2] the burden of a bitter captivity. It also denotes the most severe illnesses or bodily defects, or it kills the Native in the first time of life; or it makes them to be condemned in some fashion. But if there is none of these, it makes them to die violently.

5. The Moon from Mercury to Jupiter. If the Moon separating from Mercury moves toward Jupiter, it will make great, powerful persons, to whom the secrets of the Emperor's letters are entrusted; or those who guard royal wealth and the treasuries of kings with faithful defense; and those who have the power of giving commands and making arrangements in the royal household. It generally makes teachers or royal messengers; but it also makes temple-keepers, prophets, or high priests. So that, from these honors or from these opportunities, the greatest insignia of good fortune are bestowed on them; and so that from these occupations they collect increases of powerful wealth.

6. But if the Moon separating from Mercury with little light moves toward Jupiter, they are put in charge of accounts; or it makes them to be put in charge of business affairs involving interest; or it makes agents and the sort to whom public and treasury funds are entrusted; or it makes those put over public weights or revenues; or it makes judges of private lawsuits. And it denotes the greatest increases of wealth from these occupations, but it also bestows the honors of good fortune. It denotes inheritances for some; it causes others to find things deposited and hidden. Things that are entrusted remain [safe] with them, and they persist in keeping them without any default of fraud; so that, from these things fame and wealth and great good fortune are provided for them.

---

[1]Reading *egestatis* 'poverty' with **Ψ** rather than *gestis* 'things done' with **Ω**.

[2]Reading with MS **N** *indicit . . . imponit* 'indicates . . . imposes' rather than the other way around.

7. The Moon from Mercury to Mars. If the Moon separating from Mercury moves toward Mars in a diurnal nativity, and the Moon is waxing or full of light, it will make irreligious persons, perjurers, deceitful persons, and those whose malice increases day by day for every crime. They will be burglars, thieves, and those who plunder temples always with a sacrilegious furor; they will be highway robbers, murderers, and always armed for the slaughter of men. But apprehended in these crimes, they are handed over to the chains of custody and prison; and by the severe sentence of a judge they are punished by the sword; or they perish in some way or other by a violent death because of these crimes.

8. But if it is a nocturnal <nativity> and the Moon full or waxing is departing from Mercury and moving toward Mars, it makes generals and military tribunes, but terrifying ones and those elevated to tyrannical powers. Or it makes defenders or protectors of cities, but those who never persevere in the license of their powers, and who always fail in some way. Some of them are put to flight; others are sent into exile; still others die a violent death—especially if Mars and the Moon were found in the principal houses of the nativity.

9. But if the Moon separating from Mercury in nocturnal nativities full of light is moving toward Mars in dejected houses of the nativity, it denotes the perpetration of the crime of parricide. For [driven] by the parricidal madness of rage, they kill their own children; or the rage of perverted greed drives the latter to fraternal slaughter. Or it causes a parricidal demise for the parents through them; or they murder their own relatives. Or adverse conjugal affections stain the marriage bed with the blood of a mangled spouse. So that, everywhere, with a various instinct of furor they attack with murderous madness. But these things are denoted in accordance with the variety of the houses and signs. But their death will always be violent or public; for the serious crisis of dangers is caused for them because of slaves, or because of persons brought into custody, or because of condemned men. And having been condemned because of this, they die a public death.

10. But if with little light in a diurnal nativity the Moon separatimg from Mercury moves toward Mars, it will make forgers,[1] criminals, and

[1]The Latin word *falsarios* 'falsifiers' designates a person who commits the crime of *falsum* 'falsifying'. This broad term covers forgers, counterfeiters, giving false testimony at a trial, or even bribing judges or other officials to get them to issue a decree based on false premises. It was a capital offense under Roman law.

burglars, thieves or accessories of highway robbers, and fences,[1] From which crimes they are either placed in custody or they are condemned with a severe sentence. Others are made public executioners, and those to whom [the carrying out of] public sentences is entrusted; or they are made court reporters of civil lawsuits; or <those who> carry out the duties of <torturers>[2]; or they are made assistants of men of that kind. And from this configuration, they are made custodians of condemned criminals, or wardens of a public prison.

11. But if the Moon separating from Mercury with little light moves toward Mars in a nocturnal nativity, it either makes soldiers, or armorers, or athletes. Or it will destine for certain battles [men who are] effective, terrifying, famous, and whose duty comes to the notice of everyone.[3]

12. But if this configuration was located with Mars or the Moon in the ASC or in the 5th house from the ASC, it makes those who are killed by some violent kind of death. For in the other houses of the nativity it denotes bodily defects, illnesses, dangers, and laborious occupations, and constant watches, or some violent business. But all these things, just as we have often said, are varied in accordance with the diversity of the signs.

13. For with Mars posited in <erratic>[4] or in tropical signs, if the Moon separating from the Sun or from Mercury, posited in the signs of the malefic stars, moves toward Mars by opposition or square; or if she conjoins herself to him with close or partile association, it will make furriers, tanners, boot-makers, cooks, or coppersmiths, fulfilling their own crafts or duties from fire or from iron. But if this configuration was in a sign of Venus, it will make linen-weavers, dyers, modellers, or shop-keepers. But if this configuration was in a domicile of Mercury or of Mars, it makes those fond of arms or of wrestling, and those carrying out the duties of public business affairs. But if this configuration was in a domicile of Ju-

[1]The Latin *latronum conscios et receptores* designates those with personal knowledge of criminal acts and those who receive stolen goods. The former offense was not serious unless a major crime had been committed, but receiving stolen goods was considered to be as serious as robbery itself.

[2]There is a lacuna in the Latin text. The words in angle brackets are conjectures of Némethy, probably correct, since executioners and torturers are often mentioned together in connection with Martian influences.

[3]The Latin text is corrupt. I have cut it down to this: *et quorum officium ad omnium notitiam perveniat*, which preserves some of the words but not all.

[4]Added by Kroll.

piter, it makes tribunes, generals, and those in charge of great legions, or rulers of cities and provinces.

14. But if this configuration was in a domicile of Saturn, it denotes offensive, wretched, and infamous duties; for it will make either torturers or executioners or accusers, or sellers of wild beasts, and Marsians[1]—persons of the sort who are accustomed to hunt snakes. It will [also] make masters of wild cattle or beasts. Some will be fishermen, others fowlers. It compels some to raise water from the deepest pits with continual labor. It will make others to be workers in rural places or truck-gardens. It makes others to be skippers, sailors, or steersmen; others builders; others workers in quarries; others undertakers, or those always taking care of burials. <But if this> configuration <is in a domicile>[2] of Mars, the decrees are varied in a variety of ways.

15. The Moon from Mercury to the Sun. If the Moon separating from Mercury moves toward the Sun, it produces those who are either retarded in mind or hindered in their speech or deaf-mutes, or paupers and those crushed down in the wretched squalor of poverty, foreigners always wandering, and those who never have a settled place and home. But these misfortunes are moderated with the passage of time, and, having passed the time of youth, they earn small means of life by various jobs.

16. The Moon from Mercury to Venus. If the Moon separating from Mercury full of light in a nocturnal nativity moves toward Venus, it will make them <having leadership in public activities>,[3] and they will find the first place in all their activities. It also denotes fame and increases of great good fortune. It makes some of them orators, but <those excelling>[4] in abundant speech. It makes others poets, and it ennobles them with the authority of their divine verse, or it establishes them in a constant continuation of honors in the services of the Gods, or in the services of Emperors. Or it brings them good fortune and power from the persons and recommendations of women, or from some womanly acts [done] with the grace of charm.

[1]The Marsii were an ancient Italian people who were reputed to be wizards and snake-charmers.

[2]Added by MS **N.**

[3]Reading *publicis actibus providentiam habere* with MS **N**, rather than *publicis protegi ab aere.*

[4]I have added these words, since Sittl indicates a lacuna here.

17. But if the Moon separating from Mercury full of light moves toward Venus, it will make devisers of either perfumes, or paints, or colors, or medicines, or precious stones, or those making expensive tunics by their own skill, or organists, or pantomimists, or those who practice all sorts of leaping, or those who delight others with their sweet voice. But it makes those who are moderate in life, and who have neither an abundance of wealth, nor are deprived of the necessities. But increases in wealth are bestowed on these persons with the passage of time. It also makes persons lustful in sexual intercourse, and always involved in some defects [of character], and those who are struck with constant bad reports because of this.

18. But if the Moon separating from Mercury with little light in a nocturnal nativity moves toward Venus, it makes rich, powerful, imperious, great persons and those to whom the defense of regions or of the greatest cities is entrusted, especially if the Moon, freed from any aspects of the Sun, is found in the ascending sign; but also if Venus, in a similar manner freed from the Sun's aspects, is found in those houses that we have mentioned and receives the course of the approaching Moon. But if this configuration was in other houses of the nativity, it will make honest persons transacting much business; and they look for the foundation of wealth for themselves from their own efforts.

19. But if [the Moon] with little light moves toward Venus by day, and this configuration is in the MC or in the 10th house from the ASC, it bestows the prizes and crowns of the sacred games; or it makes them to be in charge of the sacred games, or builders of temples, or dedicators of images, or certainly temple-keepers, or high priests, or those carrying out great duties in temples.

20. But if this configuration is in other houses of the nativity, it makes persons of middle means, and those who are accustomed to practice metallic trades. And it generally makes tanners, and those who are accustomed to trade in perfumes. It also makes those who are polishers of precious gems, or who paint gems another kind of color with various kinds of coloration. Or it makes decorators,[1] or sculptors of images, or it will make artificers, or those who sing[2] sacred songs in temples, or it will

[1]Reading with the Teubner editors *ornatores* 'decorators' with **Ω** rather than *tornatores* 'turners' **Ψ**.

[2]Reading *sacra carmina *cantantes* 'singing sacred songs' rather than *sacra carmina precantes* 'foretelling sacred songs' **Ω** or *sacra carmina praecantantes* also 'foretelling sacred songs' **Ψ**, although, as is noted in the Teubner edition Addenda, the latter reading makes a proper clausula.

make flute-players in temples. And it makes those who have ideas about celestial things, or those who know celestial secrets, or who learn by heart concealed and hidden things in an easy fashion, so that their life's support is sought for them from these trades.

<Chapter 3g. Special Significations of the Moon's Motion.>[1] *[IV.15]*

1. The Moon separating from Saturn. If the Moon separating from Saturn moves towards nothing, but directs her own course through emptiness, and is waxing or full of light, it demolishes the Natives' inheritance with wretched losses, and it makes the Natives to be alienated from their parents, or it makes them orphans from the death of their parents in their early life. It generally makes sluggish persons, or it keeps them occupied with lengthy travels.

2. But if she has little light, it will make a constant cold feeling around the belly,[2] which the Greeks call *psychrocoelios*,[3] and those suffering from endless faults of phlegm, skinny persons, splenetics, those suffering from dropsy, lung disease, dysentery, or strangury, and those who are tormented by the hidden pains of bodily defects. But it denotes these things according to the quality of the signs.

3. If the Moon separating from Jupiter moves towards nothing but directs her own course through emptiness and is full of light, it will make travelers constantly departing, paupers, and those who with the passage of time lose all the distinctions of good fortune. But if she has little light, it will make those who are exposed, captives, and those whose life is crushed down by the burden of servitude. Some of them will be afflicted with bodily defects [and] illnesses; and it makes others to be short-lived.

4. The Moon separating from Mars. If the Moon separating from Mars moves towards nothing but directs her own course through emptiness and is full of light, it dissipates the inheritance and kills the parents in the first step of [the Natives'] life; or it imposes some bodily defect on them; or

[1]This chapter gives the Moon's significations when it is *void of course*.

[2]See iv.7.5 below.

[3]This rare Greek word is also found in Ptolemy, *Tetrabiblos*, iii. 12, and in Hephaestio, *Apotelesmatics*, ii. 13.18. The *Liber Hermetis*, XXXIII, has the Latin translation *ventres frigidos* 'cold bellies'.

the danger of a bad death. Indeed it either casts them down from high places, or from quadrupeds. It denotes for them dangers, or the greatest bodily defects, or illnesses. It makes others to die violently in a public death.

5. If the Moon with little light separating from Mars moves toward nothing, it either makes them to be alienated and separated from their own family, and it dissipates their inheritance with various losses; or it gives [them] laborious crafts, so that they are always involved with fire or iron; or it makes them to be wretched soldiers.

6. The Moon separating from the Sun. If the Moon separating from the Sun moves towards nothing but directs her own course through emptiness, it will make paupers, unlucky persons, wandering travelers, and those who waste away in servile tasks, and afflicting others with various [unpleasant] tasks that they take up. It makes them give up because of various kinds of despair; but with the passage of time, the dangers of this kind of misfortune are reduced; and the wretched ruination of present calamities is changed to some degree, Once they have gotten rid of the burden of poverty, a small life's support is provided for them; and they are impelled to aspire to some other tasks.

7. The Moon separating from Venus. If the Moon separating from Venus while waxing moves toward nothing, but directs her own course through emptiness, it will make those who are passive in sexual relations, and who never retain the love of their wives, but who always[1] delight in incestuous embraces. But it makes these same persons to be destitute paupers, and those who, by subjecting their own shoulders to labors, seek the support of their daily life. But if the Moon has little light, it makes depraved, disgraceful paupers, and those weighed down with the constant burden of miseries; or it always directs them toward dishonorable and wretched crafts and tasks.

8. The Moon separating from Mercury. If the Moon separating from Mercury moves toward nothing, but directs her own course through emptiness and is full of light, it will make grammarians, orators, physicians, musicians, and those who know the courses of the celestial stars by their skill in computation; or those handling the duties of making loans and business affairs, and from which occupations they attain fame and wealth, but with the passage of time.

[1]Reading *sed qui semper* 'but who always' with Sittl and MS **N**, rather than Kroll's conjecture *et qui* 'and who' or the *et quicquam* of the other MSS.

9. But if [the Moon] has little light, it denotes bodily defects from humors; or it indicates the serious hazard of dangers from waters. It harms the minds of some; it ties the tongue of others; it harms the ears of others; but it will make all of these persons strangers to letters. It will make others to prophesy, but in temples; it awards some the eternal guardianship of temples; it makes others attendants or servants of temples.

<Chapter 3h. The General Significations of the Moon.> [IV.16]

1. Now all the different kinds of things that the Moon accomplishes in her swift course should be explained, so that we may seem to have explained everything both in particular and in general.

2. If the Moon applies to Saturn, it makes the parents wretched; but if she conjoins with Mars, it makes both parents humble, but it also[1] indicates miseries for the father. If she moves from Mars to Saturn, i.e. if Mars and Saturn possess both sides of her, it denotes <the fault of> a sacred <illness>.[2] But if she moves from Saturn to Mars, it makes these same things more moderately; but then it denotes bodily defects for women when Saturn attacks her with his aspects. But then it makes lunatics if the figure of the Moon is coupled together with Saturn and Mars, either by aspect or by being together,[3] and with Jupiter and Venus in unrelated signs. For if Jupiter and Venus aspect with a good aspect all these conjunctions or separations, through which wretched destruction is denoted for men, the destruction of the bad decrees and wretched calamity are lessened.

3. He will be fortunate and indeed very fortunate; and with all his good fortune, it also denotes the embellishment of modesty, if she is conjoined to Jupiter and Venus, or to one of them, in those houses in which she rejoices without an inimical aspect of Mars or Saturn. For then it denotes

[1]Sittl has *ambos parentes faciet. . . humilitatem patri* 'it will make both parents . . . humility for the father'; but **Nα** have am*bos parentes facit humiles item patri* 'it makes both parents humble, and also for the father', which I have adopted.

[2]There is a lacuna after *sacrae* 'sacred' (so indicated in **Ω**). The Teubner editors propose *sacrae <valitudinis vitium decernit>*, which is very similar to the phrase *sacrarum valitudinum vitia decernit* in III. 3f. 3 above.

[3]The passage *si figura Lunae vel scema vel similtudinem Saturni comparetur ac Martis* is corrupt. **Ψ** has *...vel scema vel similitudine Saturno comparetur ac Marti*; whence, I conecture **simul* 'together' for †*similitudine* 'by likeness', and the passage will read as above.

good fortune, then honors, then all the distinctions of life. Moreover, she rejoices in either the ASC or in the 5th house from the ASC or in the 11th house from the ASC adorned with the conjunctions of Jupiter and Venus. But also in the 8th house of the nativity in a nocturnal nativity and in those signs in which she rejoices, having attained the testimony of Jupiter and Venus she denotes the greatest good fortune.

4. And so, whatever house of the nativity you wish to consider—either for [the Native's] nature, or rearing, or his race, or parents, or brothers, or marriages, or his offspring, or the last day of his life—you should diligently inspect the course, the conjunctions, and the separations of the Moon, her †longitudes and altitudes†,[1] and who receives her conjunctions.

5. We ought also to fear[2] in every nativity that the Sun does not receive the conjunction of the Moon coming to it; for afterwards, receding from the opposition of the Sun, hastening to the conjunction, she begins to feel losses of her light; in whatever configuration of her own light [she is], it denotes destruction of everyone according to the measure. For if her aspect is strong, it denotes strong evils and the destruction resulting from great misfortunes; if her aspect is middling, the destruction resulting from evils is lessened.

6. But if while waning she comes to those rays of the Sun[3] and is glued[4] in a way to that orb of his, and, taken from the sight of men, [so that] she is not visible, then it denotes more powerful evils; then it denotes the destruction resulting from all calamities, in accordance with those astrological significations that we have noted in the preceding part of this book.

---

[1]It is not clear what Firmicus is talking about. Bram thinks that *longitudines altitudines* should be translated as 'elongation [sc. from the Sun] and exaltation', but *altitudines* is plural and the Moon has only one *altitudo* 'exaltation'. And the word *longitudo* does not appear anywhere else in the *Mathesis*. I think the whole phrase is corrupt. You would expect some mention of waxing and waning or of the Moon's being 'full of light' or 'with little light'. (The word *latitudo*, which could be miscopied as *altitudo* only appears elsewhere in iv. 6, 2, where Kroll has emended it to *altitudo*, but neither word makes sense there.) Prof. Monat renders the phrase as '[her variations] in width and in height'—perhaps referring to the size of the Moon's disk—but I don't think the old astrologers paid any attention to the physical size of the Moon.

[2]Reading with Sittl *Exspectare* 'to fear' rather than Kroll's emendation **Spectare* 'to look'

[3]That is, she comes *sub radiis Solis* 'under the Sun beams'.

[4]This refers to a close conjunction (within 3°), which is called *kollêsis* 'gluing' in Greek.

7. But if freed from the conjunctions of the Sun by day, the Moon conjoins herself to Saturn while adding to her numbers,[1] <it denotes increases> of very good things <and of great good fortune—good fortune beyond measure>, <and> the insignia <of all good things beyond measure> are conferred[2]; for he will be fortunate and very fortunate indeed, in whose nativity the Moon was found thus with Jupiter.

8. But if she was found thus with Mars, just as we have said, it denotes destruction resulting from great evils; <for they will be>[3] according to the nature of the signs, those dying a violent death; but these evils are somewhat mitigated if Mars was found in a feminine sign. But if she was conjoined in that aspect with Venus in the MC or the IMC, it denotes a good marriage, especially if she was unrelated to the configurations of Mars. But if this configuration was located in other houses of the nativity, it certainly denotes a good life, but they will marry with their own relatives.

9. But if Mars aspects that conjunction, it denotes illicit intercourse with wretched desire. But if that conjunction was with Mercury, it denotes infinite bodily defects and unheard of evils in a continuous manner. Whence, we ought to pray and request with the best prayers that the Moon does not conjoin herself to Mercury with that aspect.

10. But if the Moon conjoins herself by night with little light to Saturn when it is retrograde or static, it denotes <the inconveniences>[4] of the greatest misfortunes. Some of them die violently according to the nature <of the signs>,[5] or according to the power of the houses. But these misfortunes are to some degree lessened if Saturn was found in a feminine sign.

11. But if she conjoins herself to Jupiter by night with this aspect, the Native will abound in all good things. But also, if she was conjoined to Mars with a similar aspect, it denotes the insignia of great good fortune; but these are made even greater if Mars is adding to his numbers. But if

---

[1]'Adding to her numbers' means 'while moving faster than her average motion'; i.e. when she is 'swift' according to the older astrological terminology.

[2]The words in angle brackets (*et magnae … bonorum*) are omitted by **Ω**, three or four lines having been omitted due to homoeoteleuton (*…bonorum* | *…bonorum*) but preserved by **Ψ** and editions **αv**.

[3]Adds **Ψ** and editions **αv**, in place of *enim aut* 'for either' **Ω**.

[4]Adds Kroll.

[5]Adds Sittl.

she conjoins herself to Venus with that aspect, either in the MC or in the 5th or in the 11th house from the ASC, or in the ASC itself, it will be good for marriage, if Saturn does not afflict them with any aspect. Moreover, they will be even more fortunate if Venus, retrograde from the principal houses . . .[1] it will harm, and it will generally make those with tuberculosis.[2] But then it denotes the good things more strongly when this configuration was by night. Moreover, the good things are of course diminished; and all the bad things [that are decreed] by these stars increase in a diurnal nativity.

12. Having explained the course of the Moon and shown it in a detailed manner, let the subject of the discussion be transferred to the definition of the promised work—namely to the explanation [of the House] of Fortune;. For we cannot explain the entire substance of fate unless this house has been determined in a most careful manner. For just as we seek to find in the ASC which [star] is in that same house; which one is setting; which one is in the IMC; which one is in the other houses—as well as where the ruler of that sign is posited in which the ASC is placed. So <we should>[3] also determine the House of Fortune in a similar manner. I shall show in an easy way which house is the House of Fortune And, when you have found it, by inspecting the relationships and aspects of all the stars, you will be able to explain [the signification of] this whole House with a true and faithful judgment.

Chapter 4. Finding the House of Fortune and what that Finding Denotes. [IV.17]

1. In every nocturnal nativity, compute from the Moon up to the Sun; in a diurnal nativity, compute from the Sun up to the Moon; and whatever the number of signs was, count that many signs beginning from [the sign of] the ASC; and whatever sign has the last number, that sign shows [you] the House of Fortune.[4]

---

[1]Sittl indicates a lacuna here. Probably one or more lines were missing in the archetype. The word 'retrograde' here means 'removed'.

[2]Bram renders the latter part of this sentence as 'Then she will not be harnful but may make many consumptive.'; but Prof. Monat gets it right, *elle sera nuisible et donne bien souvent des phthisiques* 'it will be harmful, and very often it gives those with tuberculosis'.

[3]Adds **A**.

[4]This was probably the original way to determine the House of Fortune (i.e. by counting whole signs).

2. But this is an approximate computation, which we have put [here] for this reason—lest anything may seem to have been overlooked by us. But the House of Fortune is found by degrees in this way, which you ought to follow in every instance. For then a true definition is brought forth in astrological significations, whenever the individual houses have been found by the degree method. So Life, so Hope, so Brothers, so Parents, so Children, so Illnesses, so the Spouse, so Death, <so Journeys or Religion>,[1] so Actions, so Friends, so Enemies, so everything else that is searched for in the makeup of a human being, you will explain with true definitions. All of which we shall therefore explain when we have come to the interpretation of the Barbaric Sphere; for the divine Abram and the very wise Achilles have tried to find these things with the truest methods.[2] But the House of Fortune, about which we are beginning to speak, is determined by this method.

3. If you are dealing with a diurnal nativity, you will begin to search for the House of Fortune by having tracked it down with this method—beginning from the degree of the Sun, [count] the degrees of all the signs down to that sign in which the Moon is, and to the degrees of the Moon, and whatever sum all the degrees have made, [then] having added to the degrees of the ASC those you have collected; beginning from the ASC,[3] divide the whole amount among the rest of the signs, giving thirty degrees to each sign; and in whatever sign the last degree of the number falls, that place shows you the sign and substance of Fortune.[4]

4. But in a nocturnal nativity, beginning from the degree of the Moon, and going through the following signs in a similar fashion, up to the degree of the Sun, you collect all the degrees of the signs, and, having added the degrees of the ASC, through all the signs which are after the ASC,

[1]Adds **N**.

[2]See Book VI, Chapter 32.

[3]The Latin is corrupt; in particular, the phrase *in dextram partem*, which both Bram ("numbering on the right side") and Prof. Monat ("going...towards the right.") accept. But the measurement must be made to the *left* of the ASC not the *right*! The Latin (238.25-239.1) should therefore read *...additis horoscopi <partibus> [inchoans] computationem is collegeris, ab horoscopo incipiens *integram partem [ab horoscopo] signis ceteris divide...*

[4]Or perhaps we should emend the text to read 'that shows you the sign of the House of Fortune (omitting the word *substantiam* 'substance'). Note carefully that it is not the *degree* of Fortune (sc. the *Part* of Fortune) that is determined, but rather the House of Fortune (i.e. the *sign* in which the degree falls). However, in Paragraph 6 below, he tells us to notice the ruler of the terms in which the degree of Fortune (i.e., the Part of Fortune) falls.

you make a single sum of the numbers, which, beginning from the degree of the ASC, you divide allotting thirty degrees to each sign just as we said before; and in whichever sign the last degree of the number falls, that degree will show you the House of Fortune.

5. From this House the quality of life and the amount of the personal wealth, and the course of good fortune and misfortune is shown.[1] Love also, and what sort of affection there is of men for women, is learned from this House.[2] And the effects of rearing, and all desires is sought from the substance of this House. This House shows the fatherland in an easy way. Moreover, it is called, just as Abraham designated it, the "House of the Moon."

6. See, therefore, who the ruler of the whole sign is, and the ruler of that degree—that is, in the degrees[3] of what star that degree is—and in which house is both the ruler of the sign and also the ruler of the degree, namely of that degree in which the House of Fortune was found, and in which houses of the nativity they are posited—whether in principal houses, i.e. in the angles or in the *anafora* houses, or in the dejected [houses]—whether in their own exaltations or in their domiciles or in [signs in which they are] dejected.[4] And whether the ruler of that sign, from the domicile in which it is [located], aspects its sign—that is the House of Fortune—with a fortunate aspect. And if the ruler of its degree—i.e. if the ruler of the terms, in which the House of Fortune is found—aspects that very degree from the house in which it is [located] with a fortunate aspect; and if they are both in turn joined to each other in cardinal houses.

7. And when you have gathered together all these things in a careful manner, and it is a nocturnal nativity, again take note of the degrees of the

[1]Reading *ostenditur* with the MSS rather than Kroll's emendation **ostendi datur*. And changing the preceding accusatives to nominatives.

[2]The Latin text is wrongly punctuated.

[3]That is, the *terms*.

[4]Here MS **D** of the **Δ** family leaves off with *deiectionibus* (p. 239,29) three lines from the bottom of f. 76^{v}; it resumes at *Mathesis* iv 8. 36 (p. 256,1 *geniturae*). There is no break in the text of MS **D**, but there is a mark between the two words where the lacuna occurs and a marginal note *Hic desunt 4 vel 5 folia*? 'here 4 or 5 leaves are missing'. This would seem to indicate either that the lacuna was in **D's** exemplar or that the copyist carelessly failed to copy several leaves, and the defect was not noted until **D** was later collated with a MS of the **Γ** family. Note that this large lacuna is approximately the same size as those of 18 and 16 Teubner pages in Books VI and VII.

Moon; but if it is a diurnal [nativity, the degrees] of the Sun, and see who is the ruler of the degrees—namely in a diurnal [nativity, the degrees] of the Sun, but in a nocturnal one [the degrees] of the Moon—and whether it aspects the House of Fortune with a cardinal aspect. But if one of these was found to be the ruler of all the degrees, and it is posited well in the nativity, and in those signs in which it rejoices, or in which it is exalted, or in which it is the ruler, it denotes a fortunate nativity. But if that [star] is posited with the Sun or the Moon and it aspects the House of Fortune, greater good fortune is denoted by the multiple aspects. But if it happens that the Moon and the House of Fortune is located in the angles, good fortune is also denoted thus by the multiple aspect.

8. But if there is not just one ruler of the sign in which the House of Fortune is and of the degrees, nor of the degrees of the Sun nor those of the Moon. The one will obtain the first place in denoting who has the greatest power; and if it is a benefic and found in benefic signs, or in its own exaltation, or in its own domicile, and, posited in the principal angles of the nativity, it aspects the House of Fortune cardinally, it denotes a great and noble nativity.

9. But it makes these things then if it is partilely posited in the angles. For if it was [only] platically found in those houses in which we said, it denotes a middling nativity, so that he is not exceedingly fortunate, nor is he crushed down by the restrictions of poverty. But if both of them fell well—the ruler of that sign in which the House of Fortune is and the ruler of that degree in which the last degree[1] was found—and they are posited in good signs, that is in those in which they rejoice, or in those in which they are exalted, or in their own domiciles, and if they are posited in the angles partilely, it denotes such great good fortune, that he who was born thus is associated in every way with Emperors. But if they were not found partilely in the signs of the angles, but [only] platically, it denotes increases of a middling good fortune.

10. But if the ruler of that sign in which the House of Fortune is found, and also the ruler of the degree itself, i.e. the ruler of the terms, and the ruler of those degrees in which the Moon is found in that same nativity, are well placed, either in those [signs] in which they are exalted, or in their own domiciles, and they possess the principal places of the nativity, or they are located in those houses in which they rejoice, it will make Emperors. But those whose empire is extended through the space of the

[1]The degree of the Part of Fortune.

whole earth, and those whose power is so great that they approach the divinity of the Gods.

11. But if no one of those stars of which we have made mention falls well, he who is born thus will be crushed down to the last day of his life with the burden of misfortune. Which, when it occurs, look partilely at the MC and that sign that is in the *anafora* of the ASC; and if no one of those stars of which we have made mention is well located, see whether in the MC or in the *anafora* of the ASC a benefic star is found that is following the power of its own sect; for if it is found, the misfortune of the preceding evil is improved with the passage ot time.

12. But if, with the three that we have mentioned badly posited [and] the MC and the *anafora* of the ASC bereft of all protection[1] of the benefic stars, this nativity will be unfortunate and wretched, crushed down with a continuation of all evils.[2] But also inquire into the *dodecatemorion* [of the degree] of Fortune, lest the meaning of the astrological significations escape your notice.

Chapter 5. The House of the Daemon. [IV.18]

1. We find the House of the Daemon by this method, which we have put in this book for this reason—because Abraham showed it to be the House of the Sun in a similar manner and had entered upon it, so that the House of the Sun might be separated from the House of the Moon. Which house is found in this way: in a diurnal nativity, you find the degrees of all the signs from the degree of the Sun up to the degree of the Moon, and you distribute this whole sum through the following signs beginning from [the degree of] the ASC, and in whatever sign the last degree falls, that shows you the degree of the Daemon. But in a nocturnal nativity, you find the degrees of all the signs from the Moon up to the Sun, and you distribute that whole sum among all the signs beginning from [the degree of] the ASC, and in whatever sign <the last degree falls, that> degree of the nativity shows <you>[3] the [House of] the Daemon.[4]

[1]Accepting Ziegler's emendation *nudus omni benivolarum stellarum praesidio* 'bereft of all protection of the benefic stars' instead of Kroll's *omnium benivolarum stellarum praesidio* 'the protection of all the benefic stars'. *Cf.* vi. 32. 44 (II 186,21) where the same exact phrase occurs.

[2]Reading with MS **N** *omnium malorum* 'of all evils' instead of *omni malorum*.

[3]Added by Kroll & Skutsch, one line of the original text having been omitted by **ΩΨ** (hence by the archetype) due to homoeoarchon (*pars* . . . | *pars*. . .).

[4]Alas! As the Teubner editors noted, this method of calculation is wrong! In-

2. This house is also called *the substance of the mind*. From this house we seek actions and the increases of all assets; and it shows what sort of affection a woman has for a man. But this house also and [the houses] in square and opposition to it show us the native land in a manifest fashion. See, therefore, which malefic [and] which benefic stars aspect this house, and thus [you can] explain the astrological significations in accordance with the testimonies of the individual stars.

Chapter 6. Finding the Ruler of the Nativity. [IV.19]

1. . . . .[1] the ruler of <the nativity>,[2] which the Greeks call *oecodespoten*, by what method you ought to determine it. For it possesses the sum of the whole nativity, and the decrees of the individual stars are allotted by it; which, if it is well posited in those signs in which it rejoices or in which it is exalted, or in its own domiciles, and the nativity was of its own sect, and it was not struck by a harmful aspect of the malefics, nor was it devoid of the protection of the benefic stars, it denotes all good things in accordance with the quality of its own nature, and a whole number of years [of life]. But if it is impedited by the malefics or deserted by the benefics, all of its efficacy languishes in a debilitated [state].

2. To what extent you can find [this], I shall explain from all the statements given out by the ancients. Some have wanted to determine the Ruler of the Nativity in this manner—saying that that one is the Ruler of the Nativity which was found posited in the principal houses of the nativity in its own signs or in its own terms. But others were taking the Ruler of the Nativity from the Sun and the Moon, saying that the Ruler of the Nativity is that one in whose terms the Sun or the Moon was found—that is, the Sun in a diurnal nativity, and the Moon in a nocturnal one—and that is logical. Others have said that one to be the Ruler that was the Ruler of the Moon's †exaltation.[3] But others have said that that one is the Ruler of the sign in which the Moon will be, when the Moon has left that sign in

---

deed, it is backwards—since it is in fact merely a repetition of the method for finding the House of Fortune. The instructions given here for diurnal and nocturnal nativities should be interchanged to find the House of the Daemon.

[1]The beginning of this paragraph is lost.

[2]Adds **A**.

[3]Skutsch has conjectured *altitudinis* 'exaltation' rather than the *latitudinis* 'latitude' of the MSS, but neither of these makes any sense! The Latin text obviously

which it is after the birth of the man, and has entered into the second place.

3. And we also follow that logic; for that is the truest [method and the one] approved by everyone. But you <should> also discuss all these things that we have said in a careful way[1] <and> you will find that the Ruler of the Nativity <can>[2] be found posited thus, because your attention follows this logic. We shall also teach it by means of an example.

4. If any first natal hour has the Moon in Aries, [then] because the Moon makes her transit to Taurus in the second place, Venus will possess the rulership of the nativity, because Taurus is a sign of Venus; and thus in the rest of the signs. Yet we ought to know this—that neither the Sun nor the Moon can be made rulers in any nativity. For, being rulers of the whole [world?], they reject being allotted the rulerships of <individual charts>.[3] If, therefore, the Moon was found in Gemini on the day on which a man was born, neither in Cancer, i.e. in her own domicile, nor in <Leo, i.e. in>[4] the domicile of the Sun, does she point out the Ruler of the Nativity. But when she has passed these signs, i.e. Cancer and Leo, and comes to the sign <Virgo>,[5] then she makes known the Ruler of the Nativity. Therefore, because Virgo is a domicile of Mercury, that [star] is made the Ruler of the Nativity.

<Chapter 7. What the Star does that is found to be the Ruler of the Nativity.>[6] [IV.19.5]

5. **Saturn**. If Saturn is made the Ruler of the Nativity and is favorably posited in the nativity and a waxing Moon decrees the rulership to it, it

has a false reading of *latitudinis* in the MSS, and some words may have dropped out of the sentence; or, we could simply read *signi* 'sign' instead of *latitudinis*.

[1]Reading *<*debes*> *diligenti ratione discutere* rather than accepting Kroll's emendation of *discutere* to *discute*. *Cf.* iv.9.2 below (p. 258.8 in the Teubner text), where this exact phrase occurs.

[2]Reading with MS **N** <*et*> *invenies* 'and you will find' and *sic positus* <*potest*> *inveniri* 'can be found posited thus'.

[3]The Latin text is defective. I have adopted the Teubner editors' suggested addition.

[4]Adds **A**.

[5]Adds MS **N**.

[6]This title is from the Index; it does not appear in the text. I have inserted it, but I have kept the Teubner numbering of the succeeding paragaphs for convenient

will make men who are conceited, high-spirited, honored, good, serious, of good counsel, and those whose good faith is always approved by proper judgment, and who fulfill all business affairs with procedures of proper judgment. But they will always be estranged in their affection for their wives and children. They will surely be withdrawn and self-centered,[1] consuming a moderate amount of food, and rejoicing in much drink. They will be of middling [size] in their body, pale-faced, and sluggish with a cold belly,[2] and who are accustomed to throw up <food>[3] constantly. And those whom a malignant humor will always attack, and whom a contracted internal pain[4] will torture in some constant way. But the life of these people will be malicious, laborious, troubled, and afflicted by constant mental pains, always having their life's support around water or in a watery place.

6. But if when being made made Ruler of the Nativity it is in its own domicile, or in its own terms, or in a domicile of Jupiter, or in its terms, or in the domicile of the Sun, and if it is a diurnal nativity, it will make persons who are famous and noble in their life; and it denotes entire good fortune according to the power of the houses. But if it is found in the terms of Mars or in a domicile of Mars, or in the domicile of the Moon, it will make sad, hard-working, dirty, humble, obscure persons, and those who by the continual mourning of sadness . . .[5] are defiled.

7. But these evils will be stronger if it is a nocturnal nativity, and if the Moon with little light decrees the rulership to it. For then it denudes the head with a scarcity of hair, or it shamefully makes them bald with falling hair, and those whose eyes are accustomed to be hampered by sudden [bouts of] blindness; or whose eyes lose their keenness from repeated cataracts.[6] It also makes those with lung disease, persons suffering from dropsy, gout, epsilepsy, or those who are spastic; especially if it is made

---

reference to the Latin text.

[1]I take *sibi vacantes* to mean 'self-centered' (Prof. Monat agrees). But Bram translates it conversely as 'not much occupied with self'.

[2]See iv.3g.2 above.

[3]Adds MS **N**.

[4]The reference is to colic.

[5]Some words seem to be missing.

[6]The Latin has *adsidua suffusione* 'continual flowing or running', but *suffusione* by itself usually refers to cataract (so-called since it looks like something pouring down in the eye). And this is probably what Firmicus meant, since he was most likely translating the Greek word *hypochysis*, which means 'cataract' (cf. Ptolemy, *Tetrabiblos*, III. 12 (ed. Robbins, p. 322,13).

Ruler of the Nativity, and, posited in a dejected [position] of signs or degrees, it receives an aspect from the waning Moon.

8. But if benefic stars join in good aspect with it posited [as] having the rulership—just as we have said—the guardianship of some God or effective medicine will cure those illnesses. But if a malevolent star worked against Saturn posited thus—just as we have said—those evils that we have mentioned are increased with the greatest increment of calamity. Moreover, it will make deaths from a long and serious illness, which sickness is caused by a bad overflowing of humors. Moreover, they will die in places [that are] wet, or in watery, hidden, and unknown places. If it is in a domicile of Mercury or in its terms, it makes evil-doers, poisoners, bad people, perjurers, enemies of both their brothers and their parents.

9. **Jupiter**. If Jupiter is Ruler of the Nativity, it will make magnanimous men trying to achieve great things, and those who are always trusted, and who are always inspired [to do] great acts. And those who give themselves more than their resources of wealth and power call for. Imperious persons, and those who are noble, famous, and honorable in all their actions, lovers of elegance, cheerful, and those who want to be amused in every way, taking much food, loving their friends, and capable, affable, straightforward—and those who are always accustomed to do well.

10. But their body is constructed in a moderate manner, and the form of their body will be elegant, shapely, and white; they will have beautiful eyes and a head adorned with thick locks of hair, making footsteps with a steady pace. But their life will be famous, noteworthy, full of good fortune from their trustworthiness; and they will surely get everything that they desire. But they are also always ready for good associations, and they are protected by the testimony of great men. They always love their wives and children with tender <affection>,[1] and their children attain the greatest increases of dignity, so that great merit of dignity comes to them from the honors of their children. It will make illnesses involving the heart[2] from wine or from in-

[1]Adds Kroll.

[2]Most of the MSS have *valitudine carcaicorum*, which Sittl, Kroll, and Skutsch correct to *valitudines cardiacorum* 'illnesses involving the heart', which is probably correct, since Ptolemy, *Tetrabiblos*, IV. 9 (Robbins's ed. p. 428,22) mentions *kardiakôn diatheseôn* 'heart conditions'. Sittl conjectured *valitudinem *carcinosam* 'a cancerous illness', but the word *carcinosam* does not appear anywhere else in the *Mathesis*. MS **N** and edition **α** have *valitudines circa iecur*, 'illnesses of the liver' (adopted by Prof. Monat), but the word *iecur* does not ap-

digestion, but death will come from hilarity and †rectal prolapse[1] and sexual intercourse.

11. But you ought to consider Jupiter, when it is the Ruler of the Nativity, in the same way as [you did] Saturn, and also the other stars. For what was said about one as an example, that should also instruct you for the rest. For if Jupiter is made the Ruler of the Nativity and holds the first angles of the nativity [posited] in his own domicile, or in his exaltation, or in his terms, or in the domicile of the Sun, or in the exaltation of the Sun, and if it is a diurnal nativity and it is adorned with the testimonies of the benefic stars, and the Moon is moving toward it full of light, and Mars is not possessing any angle of the nativity or resisting it, or attacking the light of the waxing Moon, it denotes all the indications of good fortune.

12. But if it is in those signs in which it is humiliated, or in the terms of other [stars], or in dejected and inactive houses of the nativity, and if both itself and the Moon are struck by bad aspects of the malefics, [then] declining in strength and deprived of all freedom of power, it denotes nothing great in the nativity, nor a complete number of years [of life]—for if the malefic stars aspect it by square or by opposition, they subtract a number from the decreed time of years according to their own strength.

13. **Mars**. If Mars is made the Ruler of the Nativity, it will make rugged, invincible persons, and those who cannot be subjugated by any means, excitable, contentious persons, daring, prone to dangers, violent persons, who are accustomed to be deceived in frequent ways, gluttonous persons who digest much food in the easiest way, strong, equable, vehement. And persons with red hair, bloodshot eyes, imperious, and always claiming the principal insignia of power for themselves. They are always practicing arts involving fire and hot iron, but they are preposterous in their hot temper. And they do not have good affection for their wife, or their children, or their friends. They are daring, and those who crave other people's possessions with an envious desire. But it will make

---

pear anywhere else in the *Mathesis*. Jupiter rules exuberance, and the cause here is excessive excitement leading to a heart attack or stroke.

[1]The Teubner text has *deiectione ani*, literally 'casting down of the anus'. Bram translates the phrase as 'hemorrhoids'. But most of the MSS have *uni deiectione* 'casting down of one', which makes no sense; edition **a** has *deiectione alvi* 'casting down of the belly' (adopted by Sittl). And MS **N** and edition **α** have *deiectione victus erit* (om. **N**) *et debitus* 'he will be defeated and indebted by being cast down'. The text is obviously corrupt, and what Firmicus wrote is uncertain—possibly some sort of rupture.

bodily defects from fire and iron, i.e. from cuts and burning; and he frequently falls down from the highest places or breaks his extremities; but it will make his death to be either sudden or violent.

14. If Mars receives the full Moon, it either kills those seized by armed robbers, or it hands over accused persons to public powers and accusations; and it makes the oppressed to be struck down by public sentences. But also, if its malice was inflamed by a solar aspect, it denotes fires and death by public burning. But it denotes these more strongly if, when made ruler in a diurnal nativity, it possesses the principal angles; or if it was found in the MC or the DSC, and the full Moon posited in another angle is in aspect to Mars, and if while full she grants the rulership to Mars.

15. But if it is a nocturnal nativity, and Mars is found in a <domicile>[1] of Saturn or in a domicile of Jupiter or in their terms, or in its own domicile, or in its own terms, and it is located in the 5th or in the 11th house from the ASC, or in the MC, or in the ASC, and it aspects the waning Moon, or if the waning Moon has decreed the rulership to Mars, and the star of Jupiter conjoins itself by trine aspect in the angles, it will then make generals and tribunes who are terrifying and powerful, and who obtain the greatest regions and many cities, and those to whom the judgments over the whole world are entrusted.

16. But if Mars is posited in the DSC, i.e. in the 7th house from the ASC, along with that configuration which we have mentioned—after all those things, it makes them to die a violent death. For Mars posited in the DSC always indicates the danger of a violent death, but that death, just as we have often said, is accomplished in accordance with the quality of the signs, all kinds of which in their special significations we have shown in Book III. But always, if it is posited in Jupiter's terms mitigated by the testimonies of Jupiter or Venus, it lays aside the ardor of its own malice.

17. **Venus**. If Venus is made the Ruler of the Nativity, it makes men who are enoyable, cheerful, talkative, constantly playing games, lovable, pleasing, charming, ardent lovers, pious, just, and those in whom the virtuous and uncorrupted ties of friendship endure to the end. But their body will be tall and fair; they will have eyes sparkling with the pleasing brightness of charm. They will have thick hair, either softly waving or arranged with the pleasing charm of beauty, or tightly curled hair; it

[1]Adds **A** and edition **α**, but omitted by **ΩN**.

makes the same sort of persons with long, curly hair, enjoying much drink, eating a moderate amount of food, and those who long for sexual intercourse with a constant ardor of desire, and who digest all foods very easily. They will certainly be noble and cleanly in their whole life, and in their life their mind and habits always cling fast to the delights of music.

18. But Venus denotes all these things according to the quality of the signs and houses. For placed in dejected houses and allotted the rulership of the nativity, it makes organists and painters, but those who paint the entire likenesses of the body.[1] Moreover, posited in the principal houses of the nativity, it will make famous persons and those crowned with diadems or with golden headbands of crowns, and devisers of sacred teachings. And it binds men to women and women to men with good affections.

19. But [being] vespertine helps women, and [being] matutine helps men. For this reason, the divinity of Venus is said to be two-fold. For it will make fertile persons and those rejoicing in many offspring, and those on whom the greatest delight is conferred by their daughters. But it [also] makes bodily faults affecting the sexual and privy parts. But it denotes famous and noteworthy deaths. But we ought also to determine with careful inquiry the configurations of this star when it has the rulership, and also the power of its sect.

20. For if it is found in a nocturnal nativity in the 5th house from the ASC or in the 11th or in the ASC or in the MC, or in its own domicile, or in its own exaltation, or in its own terms, and it receives the rulership from a waning Moon, and a well-placed Jupiter aspects it by trine; or if the Moon moves to it with little light without any testimony from Saturn, it denotes golden robes and the insignia of consular *fasces*.[2]

21. But if Mars aspects that configuration by trine, it also bestows the distinguished authority of power and proconsular rule along with those honors, especially if Mars is found in his own domicile, or in a domicile of Jupiter, or in his own terms, or in the terms of Jupiter, or in his own exaltation; and if Venus is free from the rays of the Sun.[3]

---

[1]That is, full-length portrait painters.

[2]*Fasces* were a ceremonial bundle of rods that were carried before a consul or other high Roman magistrate to indicate his authority.

[3]That is, if Venus is not under the Sun beams or combust.

22. But if, with Venus located thus, Mercury is either found in his own domicile, or in his own terms, or in his own exaltation, or in a domicile of Venus, or in the terms of Venus, and he is posited in fortunate houses of the nativity, it will make poets, but those whose poetry is ennobled with the sparkling splendor of grace. But if it is a diurnal nativity, it denotes the same things none the less, but it weakens all of that to some degree. But if it is a nocturnal nativity, and Saturn, posited in the angles of the nativity or in fortunate houses, strikes that configuration with a malign aspect and aspects the waning Moon, everything that we promised before is hindered.

23. But if Venus, having obtained the rulership, is found in dejected or in inactive houses, in the house, or the domicile of Saturn, or indeed in the terms of Saturn, <and with the Moon>[1] posited in the angles of the nativity with little light and moving towards Saturn—but by day full of light and moving toward Mars—it will make vile, shameless, lustful persons, and those who are involved in continual occurrences of calamities; and those who are struck by public infamy because of those desires for love affairs; and those who because of their illicit desires or the crime of adultery are involved in the dangers of public charges, and because of this they are made to die violently with a famous death—especially if with these posited thus, Mars in the DSC of the nativity aspects Venus with a menacing aspect.

24. **Mercury**. If Mercury is the Ruler of the Nativity, it will make wise, talented persons, learning everything, unassuming, desiring to learn the secrets of all arts; and if indeed it is found in its own domicile when it is allotted the rulership of the nativity, or in its own terms, or in its own exaltation, or in a domicile of Venus, and if it is in trine aspect, it will make poets and orators equipped with an abundance of pleasing speech.

25. But if it is found in the domicile of the Moon, it will make eloquent persons, but those whose speech is brought forth without grace. But if it is found in a domicile of Saturn or in its terms, and Jupiter and Venus are in good aspect to it, and either it is in the angles of the nativity or else Jupiter possesses some angle of the nativity or is in the 3rd house from the ASC, it will make those dedicated to some particular religions and knowledgeable about secret and magical arts—mathematicians, astrologers, *haruspices*[2]—and those seeking the secrets of all religions and of

[1]Adds edition **v**.

[2]*Haruspices* (singular, *haruspex*) were diviners employed by the Romans to practice *hepatoscopy* or the inspection of the livers of sacrified animals. This

the sky itself, and those to whom ambassadorial duties are entrusted. They are fond of their brothers, and those who want to protect their own relations with the faithful assistance of friendship, and who are bound by the deepest bonds of friendship. They are just, religious persons, and removed from all the fault of extravagance, and who carry out everything with the firm reason of judgment.

26. But if Mars applies to Mercury in any way, or if it aspects it by square, and if Mercury is in the 3rd house of the nativity in human or vocal signs provided with the testimony of Jupiter, and with Jupiter partilely posited in the ASC or in the MC, it will makes lawyers, orators whose talent shines with the unconquered license of power, and it makes him gain everything through his own powers.

27. But if Saturn, posited in fortunate houses of the nativity, aspects this configuration in a nocturnal nativity, it will make, plots, dangers, accusations, and crises; and it adds the danger of unpopularity with the people. But if, with Saturn[1] aspecting thus, Mars is found in the DSC, and it receives the full light of the waxing Moon, it will make those to die by the sword who are publicly accused because of misdeeds, or because of illicit sacred [ceremonies], or because of counterfeiting.

28. But when Mercury is Ruler of the Nativity, it will always make the body medium and graceful, and whose face is rendered pale by a thin pallor; but it adorns his eyes with the loveliness of beauty. They will certainly be consuming a modest amount of food and drink, and wealth is bestowed on all of them because of the merit of their literary skill. And on account of letters, or on account of the honor of their learned speech, they are often accustomed to be made ambassadors. And they are those who are delighted by the arcana of secret and religious literature.

29. For Mercury will also make teachers of either the grammatical arts, or oratory; or they will be interpreters, and teachers of philosophical literature. And those who handle all the duties of business in an easy fashion—both receiving and displaying commerce faithfully. They will certainly be sought out as useful persons in all business negotiations. And they acquire an abundance of wealth through their own efforts. They are fathers of families removed from all enjoyment of luxuries; just persons, minding their own business, and withdrawn from the din of public

was a favorite divinatory practice of the Etruscans.

[1]Here unfortunately MS **N** leaves off (at p. 252,30), having lost 2 leaves between ff. 85 & 86; it resumes at (p. 260,1) *Mathesis* iv. 10. 7.

association, and those who respect all religions and Gods with some trepidation.

30. But if it possesses the House of Bodily Defects and Illnesses and is restricted by the meanacing aspect of the malefic stars, it denotes bodily defects caused by humors. And if the Moon is badly located, it makes spastics, or lunatics, or epileptics. And death is always brought to them either from waters or from humors.

<*Chapter 8. What the Ruler of the Nativity does when Joined to Another Star.*[1]> *[IV.19.31]*

31. And so we ought to know, just as we stated above, that[2] the Sun and Moon never receive the rulership of the nativity. But placed with the rulers of the nativity or conjoined with them by a good aspect, or placed in the terms of the Ruler of the Nativity, or located in their domiciles, and making fortunate aspects to its place, they denote much that is communicated from their own nature. For even though there is another Ruler of the Nativity, much is conferred on it by the Sun and the Moon from their fortunate aspect. Therefore, I shall briefly explain what the Sun along with the Ruler of the Nativity denotes from the equated power of their association. For we have [already] stated in detail in the Book of Instruction what space of time they denoted individually.

32. **The Sun with the Ruler of the Nativity.** If the Sun is conjoined with the Ruler of the Nativity by the aspect that we have mentioned, along with the other things that the Ruler of the Nativity gives, these things are also conferred by the Sun in accordance with the powers of its own nature. And so it makes men who are full of faith but conceited,[3] raised up by a spirit of haughtiness, wise, and[4] composed with the moderation of equity, humane, religious, and those who always have complete affection for their own fathers.[5] It also makes those who are tall and hand-

---

[1]I have inserted this chapter title here as given in the Index, although it does not appear in the text.

[2]Reading *quod* 'that' rather than *quia* 'because'.

[3]Accepting Wikström's emendation (approved by Ziegler) *inflatos* 'puffed up or conceited' for the *inflato (spiritu)* 'inflated (spirit)' of the text. *Cf.* iii. 2. 1.

[4]Omitting *omnia* †*spiritu* in the text.

[5]Reading *integro semper* *<*adfectu diligent*>. **A α** have *integro semper* <*amore colant*>, which means about the same thing, but my conjecture is more metrical.

some, but whose head shines with yellow tresses of hair. It also makes farmers of fields seeking wealth by their own efforts, effective, wise persons, and those who always rejoice in their delight of moist[1] regions.

33. It also makes persons of the sort who complete all their actions with the greatest honesty. But these persons will be separated from the affections of their wife and their children. But it denotes bodily defects, and illnesses affecting the eyes, and the other parts of the body. And frequently it will make them to be burned up in a fire. But it denotes that their demise in death is violent and public in foreign lands. The Sun increases the time of life if it is well located and holds the terms of the Ruler of the Nativity,[2] and if some aspect of the malefic stars does not impedite it.

34. **The Moon with the Ruler of the Nativity.** If the Moon is conjoined with the Ruler of the Nativity in the same aspect that we have mentioned, along with the other things that the Ruler of the Nativity gives, these things are also conferred by the Moon in accordance with the powers of its own nature. And so it makes men who are steadfast, *honorati*, *ordinarii*,[3] honorable, and large in their body, but it denotes [the characteristics of] the body in accordance with the quality of the sign—corpulent, but for whom the handsome beauty of the body enhances [their appearance]—those eating much food, [and] enjoying little drink. But their life is also changed in an unequal fashion, so that their personal wealth is both continually increased, and yet again continually diminished by losses. It also makes them to dwell continually in watery places.

35. But if always makes them favorably disposed toward their wives, and children, and mothers; and [yet] it will make them to be separated from their fathers' affections. But if a malefic star aspects the Moon, it will always make bodily defects affecting the eyes. For it either harms the appearance of the eyes by a wound, or it damages the keenness of the eyes by an obscuring cloud of cataract. But it makes their body to be marked by a variety of white spots—for it always inflicts the malignant wounds of leprosy. Or it deforms the body with continual contraction, or it debilitates those same persons with a trembling weakness of the body;

[1]Accepting Sittl's emendation *aquosarum*.

[2]Since the Sun does not rule any of the terms, this presumably means 'if the Sun and the Ruler of the Nativity are both in the terms of the same planet'.

[3]Both of the Latin terms in italics refer to public magistrates. The *honorati* 'honorary ones' had an imposing title but did not take an active part in managing public affairs. The *ordinarii* 'ordinary ones' were those who were actually active.

or a disease compounded of malign humors indicates a bad demise of death.[1] But the testimony of the benefic stars mitigates[2] these things.

36. When, therefore, the Ruler of the Nativity is found from the course of the Moon, we should not view it in only one way, but we ought to shape it from all the mutual configurations of the stars. For when one is with another, or when it offers its own testimony in accordance to its own nature, it either enhances or diminishes. And the Ruler of the Nativity—provided with the aspects of the others, and from the individual stars that offer their testimony to it, and the influence of the decree having been changed by the power of the house and the sign—combines its own efficacy with the aspects of the others.

37. If, therefore, the ruler is a malefic, it is alleviated by the fortunate aspects of the benefic stars, and the whole malevolence of its evil is changed. And, even though it is [still] ready to do harm, a certain amount of grace is added from the testimony of the benefic stars, especially if it coincides with the aspects of all the benefic stars. But [the influence of] a malefic star is also alleviated by the house and the sign.

38. If, therefore, there are many [indications], in which there is a beneficial assistance, it also receives the appearance of a beneficial intent, and it assumes a vow of denoting more favorably, if, from its association with the benefic stars, it changes its intention of doing harm. Then, misfortunes and serious accidents are corrected into fortunate actions. Then, those who are accused and placed in grave dangers are freed, either by judicial sentences or by imperial amnesty. Then, God cures illnesses, and all evils of misfortunes attempted against them are suppressed.

39. But if a sole malefic star receives the authority of ruling, it works against the man in a harsh unbroken series [of hardships], and it exercises the strength of its own authority with the power of great necessity. Thus again, the benefic stars, if they are not impedited by the menacing aspects of the malefic stars, denote everything of good fortune and the decora-

---

[1]The words *malignis humoribus* 'malign humors' are followed by the phrase *concreta peste* 'with compounded disease', whose meaning is uncertain. It occurs again at vi.15.6 *maligno humore concreta pestis*, where it appears to be the subject of the phrase, but its meaning is still uncertain. Prof. Monat transxlates it as 'to contract the plague' at the first instance, but he ignores it at the second. Bram ignores it in both places.

[2]Accepting Kroll's conjecture **mitigat* for the *publicat* of the MSS. With this word (*publicat*) edition **α** leaves off.

tions of all dignities. But if an inimical aspect of the malefic stars attacks, they cannot denote any part of their promised good fortune.

40. Thus, we should always inspect all the combinations and aspects diligently, for otherwise the substance of fate as a whole cannot be explained, unless all these things have been noted by diligent investigation. We ought also to collect [all] that in a diligent manner, and when a malefic has attained the rulership of the nativity, whether it is posited in fortunate houses of the nativity, or in fact, in ineffective and dejected ones, and whether it is located in its own domicile or in its own exaltation. For from all of these [observations], when everything was put together, and when from the nature of the stars and the signs, and when from the powers of the houses and the angles you have collected everything, and also from the influence of the diurnal <and nocturnal> sects, you will be able to explain this whole subject with very true and certain statements; and this subject contains the sum of the whole nativity, showing the end of life and all the substance of what is decreed.

Chapter 9. How the Climacteric Years are Found. [IV.20]

1. When, therefore, you begin to consider a nativity, and when you examine the whole course of the stars in a diligent manner, and you see the power of the houses and the angles, and you collect everything in a particular way, placed in the beginnings of [interpreting] the astrological influences, you should collect in a diligent manner nothing else at first but the time of life and the power of the Ruler of the Nativity. For frequently, although with some stars well arranged, the Ruler of the Nativity denotes a restricted span of living; hence, everything that the well posited stars decreed, is changed by the immature advent of death.

2. Therefore, you ought to discuss the time of life in a diligent manner [as indicated] by the Sun and the Moon and by the ASC degree, and, what is most important—also by the Ruler of the Nativity. All of which things, even though they are sparsely stated in this work, are both contained in detail and explained in the single book *On the Ruler of the Nativity and the Chronocrator* that we have written for our friend Murinus.[1] And so it must be worked out, and the Ruler of the Nativity must be determined

[1]That book has unfortunately not come down to us, and Murinus is otherwise unknown. As Bram notes in Endnote 68, the name Murinus "is not a Roman one, but a descriptive one signifying 'mousy'."

with all the exertion of care. So that, having found the space of life from it, and from the chronocrator distributed to the individual stars, we can explain everything that was decreed.

<Chapter 10. When the Climacteric Years Occur.>[1] *[IV.20.3]*

3. Of course, in addition to the other climacteric [years], also the seven and the nine years, running through all the time of life with their multiplied system, by some natural and hidden reason they always afflict men with various crises of dangers. Whence the 63rd year, because it receives the sum of both numbers together, is called *androclas*,[2] for 9 times 7 makes 63, and again 7 times 9 makes 63 years in similar fashion. And so, because the course of both numbers in that year occurrs in an equal manner, it always imposes the peril of a great danger. For if the seven and nine year [periods], which the Greeks call *ebdomadici* and *enneadici*,[3] always indicate serious dangers for men, what will the 63rd year do, which completes the sum of both numbers multiplied together and bound to each other in turn? For this reason it is said by the Egyptians to be the *androclas* [year], because it breaks and weakens all the substance of man.

4. Therefore, among the other dangers that are denoted by the malefic stars in accordance with the anaforas of the signs and the menacing aspects, we ought also to collect these dangers in a diligent fashion. And therefore, we ought to look into these dangers and into those that we collect from the seven and nine year periods, [to find] in those times the one in which the peril of danger threatens, and how the benefic stars aspect the Moon and the Ruler of the Nativity. For if Jupiter and Venus are found in fortunate houses of the nativity—<for example>[4] in the ASC—and they aspect the Moon partilely, and they also aspect the Ruler

---

[1]I have inserted this chapter title here as given in the Index, although it does not appear in the text. But I have continued the numbering of the paragraphs from the preceding chapter for convenience of reference to the Latin text.

[2]This rare word is the Greek *andróklas*, which means 'man-breaking'. It does not occur in Ptolemy's *Tetrabiblos*, nor in Paul of Alexandria's *Introduction*, nor in Hephaestio's *Apotelesmatics*, but it does appear in the form *androklástês* in Vettius Valens's *Anthology* V. 8. "according to Critodemus" (ed. Pingree, p. 226,18), where Valens says the year 63 is 'a man-killer, dangerous, and death-bringing'.

[3]Greek words meaning "sevens" and "nines."

[4]Something is missing before 'in the ASC', so I have supplied this phrase.

of the Times and the Ruler of the Nativity, the threatening onset of dangers is alleviated by the salutary protection of the benefic stars, and men are freed from imminent dangers.

6. Moreover, there is not just one substance of dangers—for either from plots, or from voyages, or from journeys, or from damages and the loss of personal assets, or from illnesses, or from sexual desires, or from debility of the body, or from wild beasts, or from the collapse of buildings, or from mire and precipices, all the peril of dangers is brought forward.

7. Therefore, when you see what sort of peril is in a place, consider, just as we have said before, how the benefic stars aspect the ASC or the Moon, or from what house, and to what extent they aspect the Ruler of the Nativity and the Ruler of the Times, so that when you are comfortable with the substance of the Natives' life, then you can see by what means they can avoid the perils of imminent <death>[1] or threatening danger.

8. Also, you ought to consider that star which has occasioned the danger, i.e. the one that is the Ruler of the Times, and see in which house, and in which sign, and in which degrees of the nativity it is placed; then, when does it denote the danger, and to what extent do the benefic stars aspect it. For if the star that makes the danger is found in good houses, or in those signs and terms in which it rejoices, and if it is aspected by benefics, and it is well posited in the nativity, it lessens the peril of imminent danger. But if it is otherwise, and with the power entrusted to it, it receives the ability to harm, it makes the man to be entwined in the snares of unending miseries, so that imminent death or danger can in no way be avoided.

Chapter 11. Actions. [IV.21]

1. Now we ought to know which [star] denotes [actions] for individual men and what actions it denotes.[2] Moreover, there are three who denote actions for men—Mars, Venus, and Mercury. Therefore, that one of

[1]Adds Kroll; cf. the same phrase at the end of paragraph 8.

[2]This must be originally from one of the early astrological texbooks, since it is also found in Ptolemy, *Tetrabiblos* IV 4 (where the planets are listed in reverse order: Mercury, Venus, and Mars); Paul of Alexandria, *Introduction*, Chapter 26 (in which the selection rules are given but no details); Hephaestio, *Apotlesmatics* II. 19; and Rhetorius, *Astrological Compendium*, Chapter 82, which like the present chapter of the *Mathesis* is extensive.

these three [stars] denotes actions which was either in the MC or in dexter trine to the MC, or in sinister trine, or which was found in [one of] the other angles.

2. <**Mars**>. If, therefore, Mars decrees actions and is well posited and conjoined in a fortunate aspect with the benefic stars, and if it is a nocturnal nativity, it gives [the profession of] arms, military command, and glory, and the free use of the sword. And it denotes the insignia of the greatest powers, insofar as the power of the whole decree permits.[1] Or it certainly makes [those practicing] famous and noble crafts involving fire and iron, and which are brought to everyone's attention by the well-known judgment[2] of nobility. Moreover, posited in ineffective or dejected houses, and in those signs in which it does not rejoice, it denotes some respectable crafts, but one with obscurity.

3. But if with Mars thus posited, the benefic stars give good aspects, from some act of his, or from his work, he gets some fame and an abundance of wealth. But if Mars was deserted by the benefics, while [still] having the power of denoting actions, and if malefic stars aspect it, it will make persons who are subordinates, hard-working, and who spend more than they gain from their crafts.

4. **Venus**. But if Venus decrees actions and is in either her own domicile, or in her own degrees, and is partilely posited in the ASC, or in the MC, or in the 11th house from the ASC, or in the 5th, for posited in these houses it denotes [actions]. And if it is also a nocturnal nativity, it will give great actions, and it denotes the insignia of great fame, especially if Jupiter aspects it with a trine aspect, or if the Moon is moving towards it with little light. For it establishes [the Native] in such great authority of power, that the one who has Venus thus is comparable to kings or Emperors.

5. Then it denotes golden crowns and golden robes embroidered with palm branches,[3] <and> it ennobles [them] with the power of consular or proconsular *fasces*[4]; according to the clime and the measure of the nativ-

[1]MSS **DN** have *prout potius se decreti potestas extulerit* 'insofar rather as the power of the decree exerts itself'; the Teubner editors have *prout se decreti *totius potestas extulerit* 'insofar as the power of the *whole* decree exerts itself'. Perhaps we should read *prout *poterit se decreti potestas extulerit* 'insofar as *it is able,* the power of the decree exerts itself'.

[2]Reading *iudicio* 'judgment' with the MSS, rather than Kroll & Skutsch's emendation **indicio* 'indication'.

[3]It was customary for generals to wear such robes in a triumphal procession.

[4]Accepting Kroll's addition and emendation.

ity. It will make superintendents of athletic training, and governors of Asia, high priests of the provinces, always famous and noble, and whose insignia of honor are conveyed throughout the whole space of the world, pleasant, likeable, charming, just persons, and those for whom everything they want is of benefit. But the total insignia of good fortune is conferred on them by women or by their wives.

6. But if it was not in those houses, or in those signs, or in those terms, and [instead] it was found in other signs or in other terms, it will always give honorable and cleanly crafts; for it makes goldsmiths, gilders, gold-platers, silversmiths, musicians, organists, and portrait-painters. But if it is found in dejected and in ineffective houses, it makes inn-keepers, restaurant-keepers, shop-keepers, perfumers, and those who are accustomed to sell crowns made from a variety of flowers on holidays and sacred days, and all those things that are necessary for joy or delight.

7. But in general, if there is a benefic star with the one that denotes actions, or if it makes a trine aspect to it, it denotes glory , fame, and nobility for that action; and it bestows the greatest increments of wealth And however many benefic stars aspect and conjoin the one denoting actions, immense increases in good fortune are bestowed in like amount. And from that same action he receives a name of great fame, especially if the benefic stars that offer their testimony, proceeding in a right course,[1] are found in their morning rising.

8. But if malefic stars alone, without the testimony of the benefics, aspect the one that denotes actions, they denote low position in life and subordinate and laborious actions; and they make the sort of persons who are always battered by continual scandals in their actions. But if malefic and benefic stars act jointly in an equal manner on the one determining actions, they all do everything for the one determing [actions] in accordance with their own [individual] natures—but those who make the major aspects will be the stronger.

9. **Mercury**. If Mercury decrees action and was posited in the principal houses, just as we have said before about Mars and Venus, and is in his own exaltation or in his own terms or in his own domicile, it denotes everything in accordance with its own nature, for it makes either kings, or those in charge of judges, or those entrusted with royal accounts, or instructors of Emperors, or it denotes actions similar to these according to

[1]That is, they are 'direct'.

the nature of the signs and the power of those [stars] that give their testimony to it. It also makes orators, chief physicians, mathematicians, astrologers, and *haruspices*; but it denotes these [occupations] according to the quality of the signs.

10. For posited in solid signs, it denotes [those proposng] the greatest [legal] judgments and reasons.[1] But if it is found in tropical signs, it denotes occupations involving exchange[2] or interpretation. Posited in equinoctial signs, he is in charge of the public weights. But found in duplex signs, it denotes wise, talented individuals, inventors, astrologers, and all [occupations] that seem similar to those arts and disciplines.[3]

11. Generally, therefore, we ought to know this: that whenever Mercury decrees actions, if he is adorned with the testimonies of the benefic stars, it denotes fame, and the progression of honors, and the insignia of the greatest authority. But on the contrary, the malefic stars denote humilities and wretched infamies. But there is no small difference in those things decreed by the nature of the stars.

12. For Mars asserting its testimony will make leaders, daring persons, experiencing many dangers, quickly mobile, and who are mistaken in every way, and who are never subjugated by the exercise of any power. But Saturn will make gentle, profound, reserved, proud persons, and those who [do] everything with dissimulation. You will also need to do this with the other two stars; all of which, when it has been collected by you in a diligent fashion, you will be able to explain the whole substance of the decree, And so the characters of men are sketched out by you, in such a way that in the manner of a picture all the liniaments of their bodies may be discerned from your responses. And the hidden effects of their character may be found.

[1]Bram translates *iudicia maxima...rationesque* as 'important judges and record-keepers'; Prof. Monat renders the words as 'responsibilities and very important duties'. But I think the words refer to the actions of a lawyer in court.

[2]The word *mutatione*, literally 'changing' was applied to various kinds of transactions, but not usually to money-changing as Bram has translated it. I have translated it simply as 'exchange'.

[3]Omitting †*ac ratione* (Teubner, p. 263,27).

Chapter 12. Empty and Full Places and their Significations. [IV.22]

1. Now it is proper for me to set forth the revered divine secrets of this doctrine, which the ancients[1] delivered with the greatest trepidation, and which they bequeathed entangled with enigmas of obscurity for this reason—lest the divine secrets made public might come to the notice of profane men—so that with an intent and calm mind, and one not occupied with any [other] considerations, whatever I may have said in this treatise may be imparted by the easiest methods.

2. We stated in the Book of Instruction that the individual signs have three decans each. Moreover, these decans themselves are of great divinity and power, and through them all fortunate things, and all unfortunate ones, are denoted. So also, Nechepso,[2] a most just Emperor of Egypt and a very good astrologer, inferred all the bodily defects and illnesses through these very decans, showing which decan would produce which health problem. And because one nature is conquered by another nature, and because frequently one God conquers another God, from their contrary natures and from their contrary powers, he found the cures for all illnesses from the instructions of divine reason.

3. And so, 36 decans possess the whole zodiacal circle, and that number of Gods, i.e. of decans, is distributed through the 12 signs. But even though there are three decans in each sign, the divinity of their power does not extend through all 30 degrees, but in each sign the three decans possess some degrees and forsake others. And so, there are *full* degrees, in which the decans were found, but [also] *empty* ones, to which degrees the divinity of the decans never comes.[3]

---

[1]Reading with MS **N** *<divina> secreta, quae veteres.*

[2]One of the fundamental treatises of Horoscopic Astrology was attributed to Nechepso, who was often called "the king" by later astrologers. The book was probably written in the early 2nd century B.C. The Twenty-sixth Dynasty of Egyptian kings were rulers of Saïs. The second one of these was Nechepso, who ruled for 6 years around 615 B.C. But there is no reason to suppose that he had anything to do with astrology.

[3]It seems reasonably certain that the Alexandrian astrologers had a catalogue that contained the longitudes of the stars of the Egyptian decanal asterisms. By noting the positions of those stars in the Alexandrian fixed zodiac, it would have been possible to construct a table showing the extent of the areas where there were asterisms and also the extent of the areas in between them. This is how they arrived at the numbers that Firmicus is going to show us. Since he mentions Nechepso, the table of full and empty degrees may have been present in Nech-

4. Therefore, whoever has in his nativity the Sun and the Moon and the five planets in full degrees, will be a G*od*, elevated to the support of the greatest majesty. But it can never come to pass in the nativity of a *man* that the ASC, the Sun, and the Moon, and the five planets are all posited in full degrees. For those who have [only] one star in full degrees will be middling, but those who have two will accede to all kinds of good fortune. Those who have three will gather in the manifold distinctions of good fortune immeasurably. Those who have four will accede to the power of royal good fortune. Beyond this number, the stars cannot possess the full degrees in any nativity. But those who have neither the ASC nor any star in full degrees will be wretched, always deprived, and poor, caught up in every [sort of] crisis of misfortune with a succession of miseries.

5. Certainly, therefore, you ought to consider this matter diligently for all the houses and for all the stars; for if the ASC is in full degrees, the [Natives] will be very well provided for in the necessities of life, in the virtue of mind, in the condition of the body, and in the power of authority. But those who have the ASC in empty degrees, will be small in body, dejected in mind, weak in strength, always subservient to more powerful persons and subordinate in every common task, and those who lose the authority of freedom in all [their] undertakings.

6. In similar fashion too, the MC degree, if it is found in empty degrees, offers an empty efficacy of its own signification; but if [it is] in full degrees, it offers everything complete and unspoiled that the house itself is accustomed to offer. In similar fashion, the Part of Fortune, similar too the Ruler of the Nativity. And in similar fashion also, the [star] that we have designated to offer [an indication of] actions. For all of these, even though they may be posited in fortunate houses, will lose their power of acting freely if they are not in full degrees; but if they do possess full degrees, all those things that we have promised that they would decree, they denote with unspoiled power.

---

epso's book, which is unfortunately lost. As explained in my paper "The Classical Zodiac," *A.F.A. Journal of Research*, vol. 7, no. 2 (Summer, 1995): 9-16, the Alexandrian fixed zodiac had its zero point at about 352° of tropical longitude in the mid-2nd century B.C. Therefore, since the full and empty degrees were actually fixed star positions, the mid-20th century location of those degrees would be shifted by about 21.2° from the longitudes in Firmicus's table. Hence, to use the table today, either subtract 21.2° from the mid-20th century tropical positions, and enter the table as it stands, or add 21.2° to the longitudes shown in the table, and then enter the modified table with tropical positions for 1950.

7. I shall, therefore, explain the full and empty degrees, so that no blotch of envy shall stain the secrets of this branch of learning; I shall also set forth the names of the decans,[1] so that everything that we have promised may be made known to you, making a beginning with Aries. For those are the *full* degrees, in which you find the names of the decans, but the *empty* ones [are] those which the decans have left bare.[2]

8. I. Aries. In this sign, i.e.in Aries, we shall show which are the full degrees [and] which are the empty ones in a special way. And so, in Aries [there are] 12 full degrees [and] 18 empty degrees.[3]

1st	place	degrees	3	empty
2nd	place	degrees	5	Senator
3rd	place	degrees	9	empty
4th	place	degrees	4	Senacher
5th	place	degrees	5	empty
6th	place	degrees	4	Sentacher

9. II. Taurus. In the sign of Taurus, which are the full degrees [and] which are the empty ones, is shown in this example. Moreover, in Taurus there are 20 full degrees [and] 10 empty degrees.

1st	place	degrees	3	empty
2nd	place	degrees	7	Suo
3rd	place	degrees	2	empty
4th	place	degrees	8	Aryo

[1]The decan names were originally Egyptian, but they have been corrupted several times, so that they hardly resemble the original Egyptian names. First, they were transliterated into Greek, then from Greek into Latin, and then they were miscopied by the medieval scribes. Hephaestio, *Apotelesmatics*, i. 1, gives the names in Greek, some of which resemble the names in Firmicus's list, but others are entirely different. For the original names, see O. Neugebauer and Richard A. Parker, *Egyptian Astronomical Texts* (Providence: Brown University Press, 1960-1969. 3 vols.), vol. 3, pp. 170-171, but even the Egyptian lists of the decans are in some disagreement.

[2]The following table, or rather, a similar table in some Greek astrological text, is the origin of the "light and dark" degrees that are found in the works of the Arabian astrologers. Cf. al-Bîrûnî, *The Book of Instruction in the Elements of the Art of Astrology*, trans. by R. Ramsay Wright (London: Luzac & Co., 1934), Section 457. Most of the "light and dark" degrees are also found embedded in the *Liber Hermetis*, a medieval Latin translation of one or more Greek astrological texts. They sometimes agree closely with Firmicus's list, but at other times disagree.

[3]The sums should be 13 and 17, or else some of the numbers in the table are wrong. There are similar errors in the sums and/or the numbers in the tables of the rest of the signs below.

5th	place	degrees	5	empty
6th	place	degrees	5	Romanae

10. III. Gemini. In the sign of Gemini, which are the full degrees [and] which are the empty ones, is shown in this example. Moreover, in Gemini there are 18 full degrees [and] 12 empty ones.

1st	place	degrees	7	Thesogar
2nd	place	degrees	2	empty
3rd	place	degrees	5	Ver
4th	place	degrees	3	empty
5th	place	degrees	6	Tepis
6th	place	degrees	7	empty

11. IIII. Cancer. In the sign of Cancer, which are the full degrees [and] which are the empty ones, is shown in this example. Moreover, there are 19 full degrees [and] 11 empty degrees.

1st	place	degrees	7	empty
2nd	place	degrees	6	Sothis[1]
3rd	place	degrees	2	empty
4th	place	degrees	4	Sith
5th	place	degrees	2	empty
6th	place	degrees	9	Thiumis
7th	place	degrees	1	empty[2]

12. V. Leo. In the sign of Leo, which are the full degrees [and] which are the empty ones, is shown in this example. Moreover, there are 21 full degrees [and] 9 empty ones.

1st	place	degrees	7	Craumonis
2nd	place	degrees	4	empty
3rd	place	degrees	3	Sic
4th	place	degrees	6	empty
5th	place	degrees	10	Futile

---

[1]One would suppose that this might be the decanal asterism that contained the fixed star Sirius. But Sirius's longitude in the Alexandrian zodiac would have been about 23 ♊, which seems too far away, although if Sirius was at the beginning of the asterism, it might extend into Cancer. Hephaestio, *loc. cit.*, names the first decan of Cancer "Sothis." Unfortunately, it has not been possible so far to identify the stars that made up the Egyptian decanal asterisms.

[2]This line should probably be deleted (to make the total = 30 degrees).

13. VI. Virgo. In the sign of Virgo, which are the full degrees [and] which are the empty ones, we show in this example. Moreover, there are 14 full degrees [and] 16 empty degrees.

1st	place	degrees	5	empty
2nd	place	degrees	4	Thumis
3rd	place	degrees	2	empty
4th	place	degrees	6	Tophicus
5th	place	degrees	6	empty
6th	place	degrees	4	Afut
7th	place	degrees	3	empty

14. VII. Libra. In the sign of Libra, which are the full degrees [and] which are the empty ones, is shown in this example. Moreover, there are 19 full degrees [and] 11 empty ones.[1]

1st	place	degrees	5	Seuichut
2nd	place	degrees	5	empty[2]
3rd	place	degrees	8	Sepisent
4th	place	degrees	3	empty
5th	place	degrees	6	Senta
6th	place	degrees	3	empty

15. VIII. Scorpio. In the sign of Scorpio, which are the full degrees [and] which are the empty ones, we show in this example. Moreover, there are 16 full degrees [and] 14 empty degrees.

1st	place	degrees	3	empty
2nd	place	degrees	5	Sentacer
3rd	place	degrees	6	empty
4th	place	degrees	6	Tepisen
5th	place	degrees	2	empty
6th	place	degrees	5	Sentineu
7th	place	degrees	3	empty[3]

16. IX. Sagittarius. In the sign of Sagittarius, which are the full degrees [and] which are the empty ones, is shown in this example. Moreover, there are 23 full degrees [and] 7 empty ones.

---

[1]Reading '11' with MS **N** rather than '12' with the other MSS.

[2]Reading '5' with MS **N** rather than '6' with the other MSS, thus making the total 30 rather than 31. This agrees with the Arabic tradition. Cf. al-**Bîrûnî**, *op. cit.*, Section 458, p. 270.

[3]Here MSS **PR** of the **Ω** family leave off, and the remainder of Book IV and

1st	place	degrees	9	Eregbuo
2nd	place	degrees	3	empty
3rd	place	degrees	7	Sagon
4th	place	degrees	4	empty
5th	place	degrees	7	Chenene

17. X. Capricorn. In the sign of Capricorn, which are the full degrees [and] which are the empty ones, is shown in this example. Moreover, there are 13 full degrees [and] 17 empty ones.

1st	place	degrees	7	empty
2nd	place	degrees	3	Themeso
3rd	place	degrees	5	empty
4th	place	degrees	4	Epiemu
5th	place	degrees	5	empty
6th	place	degrees	6	Omot

18. XI. Aquarius. In the sign of Aquarius, which are the full degrees [and] which are the empty ones, is shown in this example. Moreover, there are 19 full degrees [and] 11 empty ones.

1st	place	degrees	4	empty
2nd	place	degrees	5	Oro
3rd	place	degrees	4	empty
4th	place	degrees	6	Cratero
5th	place	degrees	3	empty
6th	place	degrees	8	Tepis

19. XII. Pisces. In the sign of Pisces, which are the full degrees [and] which are the empty ones, is shown in this example. Moreover, there are 13 full degrees [and] 17 empty ones.

1st	place	degrees	6	empty
2nd	place	degrees	6	Acha
3rd	place	degrees	3	empty

Books V-VIII survive only in the MSS of the Ψ family.

4th	place	degrees	5	Tepibui
5th	place	degrees	6	empty
6th	place	degrees	2	Uiu
7th	place	degrees	2	empty

20. The ancients left this doctrine enwrapped in various obscurities, lest this very true and immutable system should come to the notice of everyone. But even the great Petosiris touched upon this part [of astrology] lightly, not because he did not know about it (for he had entered upon all the secrets of divinity), but he did not want to teach [it], lest he abandon the immortal instruction of his work. And so, when you have gathered together the <force> of all the stars, and that of the ASC, and of all the houses, you will look finally to find the number of the degrees in the individual stars, and the individual houses that are resident in the individual [full] degrees, and in the empty ones. For then, in accordance with what we have said previously, you will be able to explain the substance of the entire decree [of the nativity].

Chapter 13. Which Degrees[1] are Masculine and Which are Feminine. [IV.23]

1. Now I shall set forth the masculine and feminine degrees. We should know that in all the signs, both of the masculine and the feminine gender, there are both masculine and feminine degrees. For from these degrees it is found which nativity is masculine or feminine. There are, therefore, 197 masculine degrees, and 163 feminine ones; moreover, which [degrees] are masculine in the individual signs, and which are feminine, I shall explain in detail.[2]

2. Of Aries, from the 1st to the 7th are masculine degrees; from the 8th to the 12th, feminine; again, from the 13th to the 16th, masculine; from the 17th to the 22nd, feminine; from the 23rd to the 30th, masculine.

[1]The Index has *signa* 'signs', but the text explains which *partes* 'degrees' are masculine and feminine, so I have changed it.

[2]The origin of this table is unknown as is the rationale behind it. But presumably it referred to the Alexandrian fixed zodiac. It passed to the later astrologers and ultimately to the Arabs, for we find a very similar table in al-Bîrûnî', *op. cit.*, Section 457, p. 269. Al-Bîrûnî begins the section by saying, "Many controversies exist as to the sex of the various degrees of the signs…." And in fact, the degree numbers in his table occasionally agree almost exactly with Firmicus's table but more often disagree in part or even totally.

3. Of Taurus, from the 1st up to the 7th are masculine degrees; from the 8th to the 17th, feminine; from the 18th to the 30th, masculine.

4. Of Gemini, from the 1st degree up to the 17th, masculine; from the 18th up to the 23rd, feminine; from the 24th up to the 30th, masculine.

5. Of Cancer, from the 1st degree up to the 2nd are masculine degrees; from the 3rd to the 7th, feminine; from the 8th up to the 10th, masculine; from the 11th up to the 12th, feminine; from the 13th up to the 18th, masculine; from the 19th up to the 20th, feminine; from the 21st up to the 27th, masculine; from the 28th up to the 30th, feminine.

6. Of Leo, from the 1st degree up to the 5th are masculine; from the 6th up to the 7th, feminine; from the 8th up to the 15th, masculine; from the 16th up to the 26th, feminine; from the 27th up to the 30th masculine.

7. Of Virgo, from the 1st up to the 7th are feminine degrees; from the 8th up to the 12th, masculine; <from the 13th up to the 20th, feminine; from the 21st up to the 30th, masculine>.[1]

8. Of Libra, from the 1st up to the 5th the degrees are masculine; from the 6th up to the 10th, feminine; from the 11th up to the 21st, masculine; from the 22nd up to the 28th, feminine; from the 29th up to the 30th, masculine.

9. Of Scorpio, from the 1st up to the 4th the degrees are masculine; from the 5th up to the 10th, feminine; from the 11th again up to the 16th, masculine; from the 17th up to the 19th, feminine; from the 20th up to the 27th, masculine; from the 28th up to the 30th, feminine.

10. Of Sagittarius, from the 1st up to the 2nd are masculine degrees; from the 3rd up to the 5th, feminine; from the 6th up to the 12th, masculine; from the 13th up to the 24th, feminine; from the 25th up to the 27th, masculine; from the 28th up to the 30th, feminine.

11. Of Capricorn, from the 1st degree up to the 8th the degrees are masculine; from the 9th up to the 12th, feminine; from the 13th up to the 19th, masculine; from the 20th again up to the 30th, feminine.

12. Of Aquarius, from the 1st up to the 9th are masculine degrees; from the 10th again up to the 12th, feminine; from the 13th up to the 19th, masculine; from the 20th again up to the 30th, feminine.

---

[1] Adds MS **N**; omitted by **ΩΨ** due to homoeoteleuton (*...masculinae* | *...masculinae*). Bram omits it, but Prof. Monat has it.

13. Of Pisces, from the 1st degree up to the 10th are masculine degrees; from the 11th up to the 20th, feminine; from the 21st up to the 23rd, masculine; from the 24th up to the 30th, feminine.

14. Having explained all these things and having shown them in a diligent manner, the discussion hastens to the end of this book. But because in the beginning of this book we have said many things about the courses of the Moon; the latter parts of it may also be closed in a similar end, so that the most potent divinity of the Moon may seem to have given to this book both its beginning and its end. Therefore, what the Moon denotes, posited with the other stars in the angles, I shall explain in general with very true and manifest statements, so that in the Fifth Book we may open up the secrets of astrology without any envy.

Chapter 14. What the Moon Denotes when Found in which House and with which Stars, and her Separation [from which Star]. [IV.24]

1. If the Moon is [posited] together with the Sun in the ASC, in those signs in which it rejoices or in which it is exalted, or in its own domicile, already freed from the rays of the Sun, it makes the parents to be adorned with a famous splendor of wealth. It signifies this same thing similarly when the Sun is similarly posited in the MC degree. But in the DSC, i.e. in the 7th house from the ASC, and [also] in the IMC, if it was posited together with the Sun, it makes the parents to be either slaves, or wretched persons, or of low degree, or proscribed, or beggars; but it denotes these things in accordance with the quality of the signs or the degrees.

2. But if Mars aspects the Moon thus placed with a menancing aspect, and if it is contrary to both of them, i.e. the Sun and the Moon with a particular aspect, it debilitates the body with some serious defect, and it frequently indicates blindness of the eyes. But if they were in these same degrees, the Sun and the Moon together and Mars, it throws down both the parents and the Natives themselves with the wretched humility of degredation; and it denotes violent kinds of death.

3. If the Moon is found together with Saturn in the ASC, it will make those who are the first to be born or the first to be reared, but it imposes the wretched burden of widowhood on their mothers, or it makes them to be kept occupied in temple activities, or it indicates a severe crisis of ill-

ness in the female parts [of the body]. It also denotes this same thing in the MC, if it is found together with Saturn in that house.

4. But in the DSC, i.e. in the seventh house from the ASC, and in the IMC, it makes the mother to be oppressed by the squalor of servitude; but it makes those who were born thus to be either captives or separated from their parents; but it denotes these things in accordance with the quality of the signs and degrees.

5. If the Moon is found together with Jupiter in the ASC, it makes the mother to be adorned with a splendid kind of nobility, but it makes [the Natives] themselves to be religious and some sort of diviners of future things. They will certainly be famous, noble, and powerful. It denotes this same thing too when Jupiter is posited in the MC degree.

6. But posited together with Jupiter in the DSC, i.e. in the seventh house from the ASC, and in the IMC, it will ruin the father's finances. But afterwards they will acquire the greatest financial assets, either through the guardianship of friends or through inheritances from relatives. But in all nativities you should look at the power of the degrees and houses, just as we have often said.

7. If the Moon is found together with Mars in the ASC, it shows the mother to be a foreigner or a cripple. But either their own eyes or their stomach are crippled. But if it is a durnal nativity, he will be crippled in his whole body, or it cuts off a part of his body. And <it denotes>[1] this same thing in the MC degree. But if it is found with Mars in the DSC, i.e. in the seventh house from the ASC, or in the IMC, having abandoned their fatherland, they dwell in foreign regions.

8. But if Mercury is found with them, it will make armed robbers, pirates, murderers, despoilers of temples, sacrilegious persons, and those who always commit the crime of falsification, and who, on account of all these crimes, are punished by a public punishment;[2] but all things, as we have frequently said, are denoted in accordance with the quality of the signs.

9. But also if Saturn makes any aspect to them, they are placed in public custody, in a public prison, and in public bonds of chains, so that the unshorn dirtiness of their hair always disfigures them. And it places them in such necessity that they demand food from enemies. Others come to

[1]Adds **C**.

[2]A public execution, since falsification was a capital offence.

the end of their life remaining in custody and in chains. But if Jupiter aspects all these from any part [of the chart], it makes them to be assigned to servile duties in temples.

10. If the Moon is found together with Venus in the ASC or in the MC, it will make well-known nobles and those on whom the greatest insignia of power is conferrred. But in the DSC, i.e. in the 7th house from the ASC, and in the IMC, it shows the humble birth of the mother.But those persons never lack anything for the complete support of life; but they are always struck with some kind of infamy in the first age of their life. Indeed, in all signs and houses, if the Moon is found with Venus, it makes husbands of two sisters or wives of two brothers, or it joins relatives with the marriage bond.

11. If the Moon is found together with Mercury in the ASC or in the MC, it will make those who are famous for the grace of their writings, and nobles, and those who are suited to every sort of business activity. But if it is found in the DSC, i.e. in the 7th house from the ASC, or in the IMC, it denotes activities involving matters of credit, [and] duties involving interest and accounting. It is sufficient that we have said these things in the last parts of the book; for this last discussion was occupied with this—that it might effect the recall of all the preceding statements. . . to your memory. [1]

<Chapter 14a. The Moon's Separations.> [IV.25]

1. Now we ought to make known to you in what manner the Moon separates and also in what manner she is joined, which the Greeks call its *synafae* [and] *aporroicae.*[2] For in all the signs, she both departs from many [planets] and is joined by an aspect to many. For in whatever sign and in the terms of whatever star she is found, departing from this one, she bears toward that one; and in the same sign she has entered the terms of some other star in the second place.

[1]Sittl indicates a lacuna here following the words *et omnium* 'and of all the'. But MSS **AB** and Wikström delete *et omnium* 'and of all the. . ., which I have adopted (showing only the ellipsis). Némethy and Brakman would keep *et omnium* and add <*tractatuum*> 'treatments', so that the phrase would read 'and of all the <subject treatments>', which might be correct.

[2]These Latin neologisms are derived from the Greek words *synaphai* 'applications' and *aporroiai* 'separations'.

2. Look, therefore, to what degree the Ruler of the Terms aspects her or is posited in the same house [with her]. And, having grasped the preceding astrological influences, you will be able to explain the whole fate of a man with true statements. Look also, in the third place, at the degrees of which star she enters—for from that one[1] she receives the power of denoting [something]—and proceed thus down to the last degrees of that sign, so that you can find everything in particular that pertains to the efficacy of the Moon.

3. For it must be known that in all the signs, whenever the Moon possesses the last degrees, she bears to none, for she is prevented from doing so by the obstacle of the next sign.[2] But also again, when she is posited in the first degrees of a sign, she departs from none, but then only the efficacy of the [next] conjunction is investigated. For all the power of the preceding degrees is forfeited from her having passed over the dividing line, which is between both the signs, and she is allotted another efficacy from the first degree of the sign.

4. This is the partile conjunction and separation of the Moon; for we make platic [aspects] from whole signs. But in every partile consideration, we ought to treat everything with reason. Whence again, we have spoken to you with these same admonitions, so that, whenever you cast a chart, you inspect the entire body of the decrees equally, and you combine everything from the aspects of the individual stars, and you also carefully inspect the power of the houses and the degrees. But you also compare the nature of the signs with the qualities of the houses. And you should also inspect the sects of the stars, and likewise their forms, and the separations and applications, and the conjunctions of the Moon. For thus, whatever [chart] you have dealt with, you will be able to explain with the truest opinions, if you have gathered together all of these things with the sagacious investigation of diligence.

5. Now, the rest of the treatise is transferred to the beginnings of the Fifth Book, so that, having explained and demonstrated everything relating to the individual astrological influences, the whole discourse may be transferred to the Barbaric Sphere.

---

[1]Reading *ex* 'from' with the MSS rather than the Teubner editors emendation of *et* 'and'.

[2]Since the classical astrologers viewed the signs as households divided by walls, they did not recognize aspects from the end of one sign to the beginning of another as the moderns do. In effect, it was the signs that were in aspect, rather than the individual degree positions of the planets within the signs.

THE MATHESIS
BOOKS V-VIII INDEX

Here begin the chapters of Books V-VIII.

Book V has this:

<i. 1-35> Also the bare Angles and what they denote, and what the ASC and the other three Angles denote in the signs in which they are placed.

<i. 36-38> The ASC found in Individual Minutes shows the Substance of the whole Life.

<ii.> What the ASC found in the Terms of the Stars, and from which the Ruler of the Terms is seen, or what the ASC itself denotes.

<iii.-vi.> What the stars denote when placed in which Terms or in which Decans or Domiciles.

Book VI has this:

<i.> The Powers of the Twelve Houses.

<ii.> The bright and regal Stars of four Signs.

<iii.-viii.> The Trine Aspect of the Stars.

<ix.-xiv.> The Square Aspect of the Stars.

<xv.-xx.> The Opposition Aspect of the Stars.

<xxi.> The Sextile Aspect, and when it is a true Sextile.

<xxii.-xxvii.> The stars placed together, with the hindering or helping Aspects of the others.

<xxviii.-xxxi.> Various Aspects of the Moon and the Sun; what the Stars do when posited in various Houses or Terms; and what they do when they are affected by the Aspects of others.

Book VII has this:

<i.-viii.> The State of Life and the Quality of Death and the Bodily Defects of Men.

<ix.> Which one of the Parents may die first.

<x.-xxi.> About all the things that happen in life.

<xxii.> Royal Nativities.

Book VIII has this:

<ii.> The ninetieth degree from the ASC and the Moon.

<iii.> Seeing and hearing signs.

<iv.> Which degrees are placed in which members of the signs.

<v.-xxx.> What the ASC found in which degrees of the signs may do or may denote.

<xxxi.> What degrees of the signs are bright and what they denote with the ASC or with the Moon posited in them.

<xxxii.> The Truth cannot be found unless all things and all configurations have been considered.

<xxxiii.> The Divine Mysteries ought not to be readily taught or given out.

Note. I have edited the Latin text of the Index from MSS **E** and **O**. The Index is also found in MSS **DUG**. However, in this part of the translation, I have shown the Teubner chapter numbers. It appears that this Index was present in the lost MS **Ψ** or in its exemplar, presumably **Casinensis 361**. But if it was present in the latter, the fact that there are two separate indices (for Books I-IV and Books V-VIII) and that each of them begins with the words *incipiunt capitula librorum* 'here begin the chapters of the books' would seem to indicate that the archetypal MS from which **Casinensis 361** was copied consisted of two volumes as I suggested in the Preface. That would account for the fact that the MSS of the **Ω** family contain only the first four books of the *Mathesis*. Either volume two of the *archetype* was not at hand when MS **Ω** was copied in the 11th century or else the copyist did not realize that there were two volumes and simply failed to ask for volume two.

In fact Peter the Deacon, the 12th century scribe of MS **Casinensis 361**, says specifically that *astronomiam ex veteribus libris collegit* 'he copied astrology from old books'. Notice the plural 'books'. And, as stated in the Preface to the present translation, it seems likely that the

15th century MS **Ψ** was copied directly from Peter's MS and that MS **N** was later collated with Peter's MS of the *Mathesis*, which is unfortunately now lost.

Book V.

Preface.

1. We have discussed the greatest fundamentals of our promise, Mavortius; and our adult prose has made progress, increasing step-by-step. For we have set forth in an easy explanation of discourse all those things that seemed to some to be difficult to explain and to be involved in the enigmas of obscurity. If, therefore, a capable intellect and one motivated by the desire of a burning mind shall have devoured those books, and if it is understood by [the aid of] an opportune aspect of the stars, he will attain to the divine secrets of this science. And, having been initiated into all the learning of this science, he will receive the entire body of divine interpretation, so that he can both discover and explain the fates of men.

2. But the student may expect something more of us. For the principles of the preceding books have been fashioned, so that from those things that we have written thus far, the substance of the greater work may be looked for. Therefore, I would not deceive the desire of an inquiring mind with a false promise. All the malice of envy having been set aside, and all the torpor of idleness having been banished,[1] I shall [now] come to the complete secrets of astrology, so that your attention to these principles may not be abandoned because of the fault of envy and malicious silence. Therefore, we shall deliver fully that which we have promised—explaining all things to your prudence in detail.

3. But, lest our bare speech be devoid of divine guardianship, and lest the ill-will of some malevolent man opposing these very efforts attack them, You[2] God, whoever You are, who day by day continue the course of

---

[1]Another indication that the *Mathesis* was not written all at once but intermittently over a period of years.

[2]Reading *tu* 'you' with edition **a** (*et tu* 'and you' **DU**), rather than nothing with

the *Caelum* with rapid speed, who perpetuate the waves of the restless sea, who have strengthened the solidity of the earth with the immovable strength of its foundations, who have restored the exertion of earthly bodies by nocturnal slumbers, who return again the grace of the sweetest light to restored powers, who sustain the fragility of the body with the divine inspiration of mind, who enliven all the substance of your own work with the salutary breezes of the winds, who bring forth the waves of springs and rivers with tireless necessity, who make the variety of the seasons with the certain course of days. You, who are the sole Governor and Prince of all things, the sole Emperor and Lord, whom all the power of the divinities serves, whose will is the substance of perfected work, whose nature combined with incorruptible laws has decorated the whole substance of eternity, You, the Father of all things and also the Mother, You, Father to yourself, and also Son—tied with one bond of necessity. To You we stretch out our suppliant hands, You we venerate with fearful supplication.[1]

4. Pardon us for trying to explain the courses of Your stars and their effects. It is[2] Your [doing] that some divine inspiration has incited us to give this interpretation. With a pure mind, and withdrawn from all earthly association, and purged of the stigma of all offenses, we have written these books for Your Romans, lest, when every [other] branch of learning has been translated, this subject may seem to have been the only one to which Roman genius had not aspired.

5. And You, Courses of the Perennial Stars, the Moon too, the Mother of human bodies, and You, O Prince of all the Stars, who take away and likewise return the light in the monthly courses of the Moon—the Sun, namely, the Best and Greatest—who arrange everything[3] day by day with the moderation of Your Majesty, by whom the immortal spirit is distributed by a divine disposition to all living things, You who alone open

---

the Teubner editors.

[1]This prayer to God is translated elegantly by Lynn Thorndike, HMES I, 530-531 (1923), and also by Bram, *op. cit.*, pp. 155-156. Note the phrase 'Father of all things and also the Mother'. Bram says in Endnote 70 "...the notion of a bisexual god...belongs to the Sol Invictus of Elagabulus..." Note also the phrase "Father to yourself and Son." This would not have been displeasing to Christians, although they would not have liked the Father/Mother God mentioned earlier.

[2]Accepting Ziegler's emendation of *est* 'it is' for the *sit* 'let it be' of the MSS.

[3]I have ignored the words *super omnia* 'above all things', that the Teubner editors also mistrusted, and that seem to be unnecessary.

the doors of the celestial realm, to whose judgment of fates the order is arranged.

6. Pardon [us] that a pleasing speech arrives at the secrets of Your Divinity. Neither a sacrilegious desire nor the ardor of a profane mind has driven us to this task, but a mind shaped by divine inspiration has tried to explain everything that it has learned, so that whatever the divine ancients have brought forth from the Egyptian sanctuaries might be passed on to the temples on the Tarpeian cliff.[1] And so, give me the protection of Your Decree, and strengthen my trepidation by Your Majesty of mind, lest, devoid of the protection of Your Divinity, I may be unable to find the order of the promised work.

I. The Ascendant.[2]

1. The signs too, my dear Mavortius, have from their own nature the greatest power of denoting without the presence of any star. And in many nativities, that bare substance of the signs is effective. But this efficacy is only found in the angles. For the angles, even if they are left bare of the testimonies of the stars, also receive the power of denoting.[3] What [they denote], so that you may more clearly understand, I shall show with the authority of that reasoning.

2. **The ASC in Aries.** If the ASC is found in Aries, the MC will be in Capricorn, the DSC in Libra, and the IMC is found in Cancer.[4] And so, what the ASC posited in Aries, and what the three angles of the rest of this [chart] denote, I shall explain for the moment in general terms. When the ASC is in Aries, it denotes many things in youth, it denies brothers, or it [only] preserves one out of many brothers. But it debilitates that one with the bitterness of some bodily defect. It always pursues his name with hatred. His father's wealth does not continue in the same state, but now

[1]The Tarpeian Cliff was on the east side of the Capitoline Hill, which constituted the religious center of Rome and contained among others the Temple of Jupiter Optimus Maximus, the most important temple in the City.

[2]This title is omitted by **N** and **v**. Hereafter, the section and chapter titles in Books V-VIII are not given by all the MSS, and consequently the Teubner editors have bracketed most of them. However, since they are useful to the reader, I have retained them with the admonition to the reader that they were probably not in the text of the archetype.

[3]The ASC, MC, DSC, and IMC angles each have their own signification.

[4]Here and in what follows Firmicus uses the Sign-House or the Equal House system of house division, in which all the angular houses are at 90-degree intervals.

demolished it is dispersed, and having been dispersed it is reacquired. He will certainly seem to be more lavish[1] to some from his excessive liberality, [but] the constancy[2] of his liberality will be displeasing to others. And he will bestow his beneficence on ingrates, so that equal favors are never returned to him. He will surely be inconstant; and his head will always be tormented by various kinds of pains.

3. If the MC is partilely in Capricorn, it denotes the ornaments of some persisting fame, and it will make many to flatter him with some shallowness. He will be in charge of some business affairs and letters, furnishing support for their daily life to many, sustaining the wealth of other persons by his personal management. [He is] talented in many necessary things, and one to whom the secrets of concealed religions are entrusted. And he will penetrate into celestial secrets if the star of Mercury aspects this house from any location,[3] or if Mercury is found in this very house.

4. But the third angle, i.e. the DSC, [also] lays claim to the ability to denote. It, if it is found in Libra, denotes a life in constant association with a royal house, or it establishes him in public affairs. He will, moreover, be inconstant due to some unevenness in his life, so that all periods of good fortune are always followed by bad luck—periods of prosperity by misfortune—so that from the highest degree of dignity, he is recalled to the lowest with fallen humility. For the malice of envy impugns all his renown, especially if Jupiter does not aspect the ASC by trine, or if it is not in it; for then these ills will grow stronger.

5. The fourth angle will be the IMC. With Aries rising, it will always be in Cancer. It will make famous persons, and those adorned with the fillets of crowns, and statues along with portraits of them are denoted if Jupiter, posited in the ASC, aspects this house, or if it is found in this house. Some of his relatives will be opposed to him, either because of themselves or because of someone necessary to them. He will be squalid with unshorn shabbiness of hair, and he will always be well-supplied with an abundance of necessary things, especially if Jupiter is found in any angle of the nativity.

---

[1]Accepting Némethy's conjecture *profusior 'more lavish' rather than †*tutior* 'safer'

[2]Edition **v** and Némethy have **inconstantia* 'inconstancy', rightly?

[3]Note that an aspect from a planet to an empty house is said to be effective. This was also taught by the 17th century French astrologer Jean Baptiste Morin (1583-1656), who had read the *Mathesis* and may have found that precept here.

6. **The ASC in Taurus.** If the ASC is found in Taurus, he will be worn out with many successive periods of hard work, and whatever he has attained in his first age, he always loses. But afterwards, what he has lost is amassed with an increase of joy, and he will have the ornament of good fortune, and he will see his enemies laid low with a continuation of miserable humility. If the MC is in Aquarius, he will be associated with more powerful persons, always with the grace of friendship. And he will always have his life from public actions, and he will always be involved in watery affairs.[1] And he will; be one who is never struck by the ill will of accusation. He will certainly have both additions to his personal wealth, and also losses.

7. If the DSC is found in the sign Scorpio, he will be wise in every association in his life, rearing the children of others by the duties of management,[2] He loses his first wife by the intervention of death. But if it is [the nativity of] a woman, she loses both her husband and also her son. If the IMC is found in Leo, it will make those seeking the basis of personal wealth through their own efforts, and those who may attain the greatest abundance of wealth through various plots of their own, but which [plots] would preserve them in a condition of perpetual good fortune. But these things are denoted in accordance with the measure of the nativity.

8. **The ASC in Gemini.** If the ASC is found in Gemini, when placed in the first beginnings of life he will work hard, and comfort will always be afforded to him by his parents. He will certainly always be steeped in celestial religions[3] and bound to the faithful friendships of greater men. And he is one who loses his inheritance. If the MC angle is in Pisces, it establishes his life in a watery place, and he will possess his personal wealth from a wet substance. And a living will be conferred upon him from the assets of others, or his power or his personal wealth will be divided between two cities.

9. If the DSC is found in Sagittarius, some demise of either his own brothers or his relatives is caused by him, and his mind will be tormented through various periods of time by the greatest concerns of anxieties.[4] He

---

[1]Note that Aquarius, although an air sign by definition, is always associated with water by the classical astrologers because of its name.

[2]Accepting Wikström's emendation, *alienos <filios> nutriens* 'rearing the children of others'.

[3]Accepting Wikström's emendation *religionibus* 'religions' instead of Skutsch's emendation *secretis* 'secrets'.

[4]Reading with MS **N** and edition **a** *maximis sollicitudinum curis cruciabitur*

will have enemies, and, having left his fatherland, he will waste away in foreign nations; but having returned afterwards to the paternal *Lares*,[1] he will think that he has been restored by the protection of the Gods. If the IMC angle is in Virgo, he will be hampered from his first age by a varied series of labors, but with the passage of time he will attain increases of the greatest good fortune. But these things will come about for individuals in accordance with the measure of the nativity, which we have frequently said that you must observe in all things.

10. **The ASC in Cancer.** If the ASC is found in Cancer, it will always make persons sharp in their mental ability, but who accomplish everything with a moderation of tardiness. It will make serious, learned persons, and those who are accustomed to become greatly angered, and who pursue all evil persons with severe indignation; [they are] strong, [and] moderate, but those whose indignation may be very easily pacified. They will certainly have their life's support from public or from royal positions, by which the means of life are conferred upon them; and they will always be occupied in public necessities, but many people, compelled by various needs, will flatter them. But if, with the ASC posited in Cancer, Saturn is in it or aspects it, it will either make a violent death or they will fall into a great defect of illness, or their own brothers will die before them by various kinds of deaths.[2]

11. If the MC angle is in Aries, he will be involved in continual association with more powerful men, or his daily provisions are provided for him by the means of unrelated persons, and he will always be trying to get and desiring good things. But his personal wealth is changed with continual diversity, and however often it is lost, just as often it is recovered again. If the DSC is in Capricorn, he will always be attacked by a hidden enmity; but afterwards he is reconciled with a quiet moderation after [suffering] many inconveniences of instability. He will certainly be talented, equipped with sharp investigative abilities of mind, and suffering from the torments of some hidden pain; or he will be worn down by endless mental pains.

---

rather than *maximis sollicitudinibus cruciabit.*

[1]The *Lares* were the images of the particular household gods that were kept in each home. Here the phrase *paternal Lares* seems to refer to his homeland.

[2]Reading *propriores fratres. . .variis mortibus* 'own brothers. . .various (kinds of) deaths with the MSS rather than **priores fratres. . . vicariis mortibus* 'elder brothers. . . substituted deaths' with the Teubner text. The word *vicariis* does not occur elsewhere in the *Mathesis*.

12. If the IMC angle is in Libra, he will be worn down by many labors, and attached to public services, or given over to popular associations, it will dissipate the bulk of his previous wealth. He will certainly be fortunate in all his powers, and he will be a person necessary to others. He will have his means of subsistence from literary activities, and he will be one to whom hidden secrets are entrusted by others. He will survive to the extreme times of old age, and he will be given tribute by a good honor of burial, and if Mercury is found in the following sign, he will be the first among all the male children. But if Venus is found in the 2nd house, extended times of life will be given to a daughter—if the Ruler of the Nativity is well posited as we have said before and aspected by the benefic stars.

13. **The ASC in Leo.** If the ASC is found in Leo, he who has the ASC thus will be involved in many labors and many dangers. But he will be known to all throughout the whole time of his life; he will also be free-born, having free power, and one who exercises the poison of malice in all [his actions]. He will conceive intentions of ordering and commanding, acquiring an abundance of wealth through his own efforts. But if Mars is found partilely in this same house, or if the Sun with Saturn[1] aspects it by square or opposition, it altogether denies children. But if Jupiter is found in a similar manner, it will give one daughter.

14. If the MC is found in Taurus, he will have his life in a public place or in a temple. But he will contract marriage with a widow woman, or with one debauched by another person, or with one of subject and servile condition, or with an old woman, or [with one] who is struck by public scandal. And the greatest honor will be conferred upon him by a very powerful man. Moreover, he will be knowledgeable about all things, and he will be made happy by increases in his prosperous good fortune.

15. If the DSC is in Aquarius, his life will have both additions and losses. He will be pleasant. . .[2] but he will be approved of in some things. If the IMC is found in Scorpio, he will have the leading place in some business affairs. But if Mars makes any aspect to this house, he will sometimes be in custody, but in a free [one].[3] But if Mars is found posited

---

[1]Reading *cum Saturno ipsum* with **Δ** rather than *eum ipsum* 'it itself' with the Teubner editors.

[2]Ziegler thinks some words are missing here. I would estimate that two or three whole lines of text are missing, since this description of the effects of this DSC is that much shorter than those for the other signs.

[3]The Latin has *in custodia aliquando sed libera*. Presumably this means that he

thus in his morning rising, he will be a soldier, or he will be in charge of weapons; but he will die in outlying and foreign places, brought down by a sudden or violent death.

16. **The ASC in Virgo.** If the ASC is found in Virgo, he will be involved in many labors and many anxieties, he will be one to whom divinity predicts all things either through dreams or some prophecy, or certainly through [divinatory] responses and the casting of lots. But it also always perpetuates his own prayers to divinity in an unbroken series. . .[1] rushing into illicit <acts>[2] of love affairs through the passive desires of the eyes; and one who desires to have sexual intercourse with every woman with addicted desire. But he will labor under these faults only until the rising of this sign is completed. He will certainly be cheerful, humane, and one in whom the pure need for friendship endures, and to whom the anxiety of some loss applies. He will be knowing many things and inquiring into the secrets of all studies, keeping everything in the confines of his breast. [But] always going[3] decorated with the commendation of honesty, and one upon whom some great good fortune and a great abundance of wealth is conferred, either because of the grace of his pleasing speech, or because of his handling of business affairs, or because of succession, or because of sacred things.

17. If the MC is found in Gemini, it will give personal wealth from public <places> or from sacred things,[4] but this will be when he has entered the threshold of old age. He will be a worshipper of religions and of the Gods, a just person, and one whom the greater part of the citizenry may try[5] to obey. Also one looking into hidden things with incessant inquiry, knowing many arts and branches of learning. And in the last time of his life the duties of a virtuous and upright life are shown by him to many.

---

will be under legal custody, but he will not be incarcerated—a possible modern example would be 'house arrest'. Bram translates it as "he will be in some kind of custody, but a loose kind." A similar fate is mentioned for the Native with Saturn in Gemini (v.3.12 below).

[1]Some words are missing here. We could supply, <But he is often> to begin the last part of the sentence.

[2]I have added this word.

[3]So MS **N** (*se ire*) 'going', but *se ire se* 'going himself' **DU** and *se* 'himself **Γ**. But Kroll emends *se* and *se ire* to sed 'but'; Ziegler would emend *se ire* to *severae* 'serious'.

[4]Accepting Wikström's emendation *publicis <locis> aut ex sacris*.

[5]Ziegler suggests *cogatur* 'are made to' instead of *conentur* 'may try'.

18. If the DSC is in Pisces, he will go through many foreign places, be known to many men, and many of them will flatter him with an assiduous favor of allegiances. He will be pleasant, fortunate, cheerful, sharp, involved in many occupations, and always ready for every association, and noble. If the IMC is found in Sagittarius, personal wealth will be conferred on him by his own [people], and many will flatter him. He will be known to all, rendering thanks to the Gods for his good fortune; or public sacred things are entrusted to him. And he will be made happy by the good fortune of his children, and having again begotten fortunate offspring, it will mitigate the pain of lost children. He will be handy at everything; he will also be learned and outstanding for the speed[1] of his activity.

19. **The ASC in Libra.** If the ASC is found in Libra, he will have illnesses, and he will be involved in many snares of dangers; and a throng of adversaries will continually batter him; and he will have contentious struggles about true and precise things. He will certainly be religious and a worshipper of the Gods, but one whose life may always be changed by a variety of inconsistencies. But he will be unconquered in all things, and such a one that he will appear to be inferior in nothing—a famous person. But the matter of children will be changeable—for the whole number of children will never last for him. He will be a person who wants to have right judgment in all things, serving divine and celestial religions.

20. If the MC is found in Cancer, he will be occupied with some famous acts. He will be maintained in a religious position or in public ones, and in his old age the greatest insignia of fame are conferred on him, so that the last time of his life is adorned with the splendors of nobility. In his old age he will be prosperous, well-off, and rich; and with the passage of time every amount of good fortune gradually comes to him; he will get children slowly, or he will have [just] one son. But if Jupiter makes any aspect to that house, he will rejoice in many and fortunate offspring.

21. If the DSC is found in Aries, he will have profit from watery things or in watery places. He will be worried by some fear, and he incurs some danger to his life in uninhabited places, and he will be battered by a lengthy continuation of dangers. He will be distinguished by many and frequent travels. He will certainly have a hidden bodily defect; and, when he is placed in his old age, the greatest good fortune will be conferred on

[1]Accepting Ziegler's suggestion of *velocitate* 'speed' in place of the *felicitate* 'good fortune' of the MSS or Skutsch's suggestion of *facilitate* 'ease'.

him. But his wife will suffer from the dangers of insanity. If the IMC is found in Capricorn, his personal wealth will be altered in various ways, and whatever he has acquired is lost again, and [yet] again whatever has been lost is found. But all his personal property is gained through his own powers and strengths, so that when posited in the last stage of life, he will be adorned with the greatest increment of good fortune. He will, moreover, be caused to adopt for himself a child of someone else's offspring, or he will get children from a woman of low degree.

22. **The ASC in Scorpio.** If the ASC is found in Scorpio, it will make persons who are sharp, irascible, active in their first age, but they will be led through many kinds of misfortunes. But in fact they are actually raised up afterwards by some favorable authority, and they will be granted great happiness;[1] if Jupiter makes any aspect to it; they will be famous and they will always hope for protection by the Gods, and they will understand the sacraments of sacred or celestial religions. They will be in another place, or they are transferred into another city by their own effort. They will always be elevated by an upright spirit, displaying the ornaments of intelligent speech. They will be the sort of persons to whom variety is always pleasing. Because of their friends, they always become involved either in business affairs or in dangers, and after [suffering] many misfortunes from the loss of children, they will again rejoice in fortunate offspring.

23. If the MC is found in Leo, his life will be worn down by various kinds of toil and by various hard tasks; and he will be subjugated to some more powerful person either for the sake of honor or for sustenance. He will be strong, and one whom many will flatter with the passage of time, and who may transfer many things from his own personal assets to others. He will be placed in some [position of] power; it will increase the amount of the paternal assets.[2] If the DSC is in Taurus, he will have many adversaries, all of whom he will always see to be overcome in a variety of ways. He will be the sort of person who is driven to sexual intercourse by desire [aroused] by the eyes, and who suffers from some kind of scandal. He will both acquire and lose personal wealth, and however often he has lost it, he will get it again. If the IMC is in Aquarius, he will have his life's <support> near water or from water, <but from these same> there comes a danger <to his life>,[3] and whomever he benefits, that one is always ungrateful to him.

---

[1] I have changed the punctuation of the Latin text.

[2] Or "he will increase the amount..."

[3] There is a lacuna in the Latin text according to Skutsch, who suggests the addi-

24. **The ASC in Sagittarius.** If the ASC is found in Sagittarius, it will make many adversaries, and his personal wealth is obtained or collected from some unhoped for source. He will frequently be occupied in foreign places; [and] he will navigate some great river or great sea. He will always be put in public associations, And he will have his life and likewise his profit[1] in watery things or in watery places. He will acquire many arts and many skills; he will be wise, talented, and knowledgeable about all things. If the MC is found in Virgo, he will be placed in great advancements, and thanks to his power he will be preferred to many others. He will acquire the greatest power of authority; a crowd of those who hear them will obey his orders; and many people will have their life's support and living from him; and [yet] to whomever he supplies that sort of thing, that person will always be ungrateful to him.

25. If the DSC is found in Gemini, he will have both children and grandchildren, but at the time when he has entered the threshold of old age. And he will be the sort of person who endures all pains in very easy fashion, and who defies losses by the upright authority of his mind. Others read secret literature, or they demonstrate the arrangements of celestial and sacred things. They will be talented, just, wise, and those who always attack their adversaries with crafty tricks, learning[2] all [subjects], and those on whom good fortune is conferred with the slow passage [of time]. If the IMC is in Pisces, he will have his life's support in watery places. He will be the sort of person to whose faith all things are entrusted. He will be well-known and noble, but he will always be estranged from his wife or from her affections. But if Jupiter makes any aspect to this house, he marries readily, and he will have pleasing conjugal affection; but he marries a wife known for debauchery or adultery.

26. **The ASC in Capricorn.** If the ASC is found in Capricorn, he will always display friendship with pure affection towards his friends. He will be crafty and cheerful,[3] and nothing will be lacking to him for his life's support. He will travel <a lot>.[4] And those to whom he provides life's

tions shown in angle brackets. Again, this section seems to be rather short.

[1]Reading *lucrum* 'profit' with MS **N** rather than *fructum* 'income' with edition **v** or *factum* 'deed' with the **Γ** family of MSS.

[2]Accepting Ziegler's emendation of *discentes* 'learning' for the *docentes* 'teaching' of the MSS.

[3]The words *subdolus* 'crafty' and *laetus* 'cheerful' do not seem to go together. Possibly one or the other is wrong.

[4]The word *assidue* 'frequently' is added by Wikström, probably rightly.

support will always be ungrateful to him. He will be likeable, of pure[1] mind, and always irksome to the Gods because of his lengthy and protracted prayers! He will be the sort of person for whom the amount of wealth is abundant. He will be addicted to passions for women, and one who strives to disparage those same women after having satisfied his lusts; And persons learning by heart the secrets of some sacrament or of sacred things, or of some alien [way of] life, or of hidden religions.

27. If the MC is in Libra, he will be pious, endowed with an honorable grace of speech, and learned. He will renew his vows to the Gods, after being freed from some needs or from some dangers. He will have fortunate actions, but afterwards he will be oppressed by bad actions. Good fortune will be conferred on him by the misfortunes of others; and he will have profit from the deaths of others, or from some old thing; and he will find hidden opportunities of good fortune.

28. If the DSC is in Cancer, he will have the greatest annoyances from his own kinsmen, and he will be entangled in the greatest dangers.[2] If the IMC is in Aries, he will be involved in the greatest errors, and, after [their] inconveniences, he will receive repose in his life, but his life will be altered by a variety of action. For now he will be in the highest grade of dignity; and then he is called back to the very lowest grade with a loss of dignity. But this instability is produced for him by his friendships with the powerful. It takes away his wife and his first son, or certainly whatever child is born will be afflicted by a severe defect of health.

29. **The ASC in Aquarius.** If the ASC is found in Aquarius, whatever he has acquired is torn apart again by some sort of losses; and whatever he has or seeks, he loses again; but whatever is lost is generally recovered in an easy manner. He will take on [the task of] helping many persons, and he will furnish life's support to many; and those for whom he has strongly done anything will be ungrateful to him. And being placed in grave danger, and despaired of by all men, he is freed [from it] by the protection of the Gods. He is attacked by many persons with an envious screeching. Moreover, he will handle the duties of [dealing with] divine literature, or sacred things, or religions. And by his good acts he will be known to great men.

---

[1]Accepting Ziegler's suggestion of *puri* 'pure' for the *parvi* 'little' of the MSS, but perhaps the MSS are correct.

[2]This description of the signification of the DSC seems to be excessively short. Some words may have fallen out of the text.

30. If the MC is found in Scorpio, he will be strong, but he will be shaken up by a hard life and by hard relations with others. He will make his passage from place to place; and if he is talented, he will perform servile duties, but afterwards circumstances ensue prosperously for him in all things. But in the beginning he will suffer from miserable misfortunes affecting his wife and children, and afterwards good fortune is conferred on him by the notice of greater men. If the DSC is in Leo, he will fall out with his wife due to some kind of quarrel. For he couples himself in matrimony with an unworthy woman, or with an old woman, or one who is experienced in[1] or is captivated by various passions in love affairs. And he will suffer from plots [against him] by his own people, and enemies will rise up against him with sudden law suits. And by his own strength and his own courage, he takes away[2] a wife of alien law or an alien bride; or he certainly contracts marriage with a widow.

31. If the IMC is in Taurus, he will be a great man, and he will associate with many powerful persons, and he will have fame in all things. And he will control the assets of many people, so that many things are entrusted to him because of the integrity of his habits. And he will die after a great space of time, weighed down by the lengthy burden of old age if the Ruler of the Nativity, having agreed with the force of its own sect, and posited in the principal houses of the nativity, fortified both by sign and by degree, decrees the whole number of its times [of life].

32. **The Ascendant in Pisces.** If the ASC is found in Pisces, he will be talented, wise, a faithful and necessary friend, and he will be advanced by some business affairs, and yet so that another power is preferred to his power and honors. He will have enemies, but he will win out over them by very easy methods, and from some lengthy business affairs he will attain fame. But with the passage of time, he attains the ornaments of a greater dignity, and he will have an increase of great good fortune. And he will be constantly known for his travels with the notice of many.

33. If the MC is in Sagittarius, he will be involved in many errors, and he comes to various crises of dangers. He will be active in all asso-

[1]The Teubner editors, following edition **a**, delete the phrase *excipiatur vel* 'is caught up in', but the **Δ** Family of MSS has *experiatur vel* 'is experienced in', which, although that word does not occur elsewhere in the *Mathesis*, I am inclined to accept.

[2]Ziegler indicates a lacuna here since the topic of discussion changes abruptly from *enemies* to *marriage*, but I am uncertain about this, so I have let the text stand unbroken.

ciations, and he will have no small struggles with more powerful persons, and he will incur plots because of some person. And everything that he has at first he loses, and then he acquires rulership over other people's things, always displaying the faithful bonds of friendship. But desire collected through the eyes always impels this one to sexual intercourse.

34. If the DSC is in Virgo, he will be wise, and he will provide sustenance for other unrelated men. He will be the sort of person to whom faithful secrets are entrusted. He will lift up many friends with his own sustenance or his own guardianship, and a great heap of riches will come to him. And his friends are frequently ingrates. And he will be charming around his wife and tied [to her] with affections of love. But she will also frequently be ungrateful to him. He will suffer grave torments of pain from the misfortunes of his wife and children.

35. If the IMC is in Gemini, he will be worn out by many illnesses, and he will be applied to many labors. He will have some pain or hidden bodily defect. And, after the greatest inconveniences of misfortune, good fortune will be conferred on him, so that he will both get the necessities of life from others, and, all his earlier things having been lost, riches are conferred upon him by a sudden stroke [of good fortune]. He will possess and hold resources that provide everything to him, and when he is weighed down by the burden of old age, he will die by a sudden death in foreign places. But for this, the Ruler of the Nativity must be looked at.

36. Some will think that all these things are said generally, but there is a true substance in them. For if you read Aesculapius's *Myriogenesis*,[1] which he claims that the venerable star Mercury imparted to him, you will find the status of all nativities explained by the individual minutes without any additions from the stars. For by placing the ASC in the single minutes, it explains the whole status of life, likewise all the acts and forms, and the last day of life, also the kinds of dangers by very true and manifest reasons. For since there are 30 degrees in each individual sign

[1]The Greek name means 'the Ten-thousand Nativities'. It was a book, as Firmicus explains, that contained individual significations for each *individual minute* of each *degree* of the zodiac—21,600 significations! Marvelous detail! And obviously determined by some theoretical scheme, since a minute of the zodiac rises in 4 seconds of time, which would preclude any possibility of deriving the significations from actual cases. Unfortunately, that book has not come down to us.

and 1,800 minutes, by placing the ASC in one [particular] minute, it thus describes the complete fate of men.[1]

37. But that man, sprung from the divine race, and conceived by the propagation of the divine race, and steeped in the training of the venerable divinity, has left [us] the very famous instruction of this work. Because in us the substance is fragile and fallen, so we do not deserve to be instructed [personally] in such instructions. And so we may follow the footsteps of the divine men; and whatever is handed down by them, we may transfer with <clear>[2] interpretations.

38. But I don't want you, my dear Lollianus, to search for the *Myriogenesis* in these books. For when our mediocrity has completed this [present] work with the favor of the propitious divinity, then I shall pass on to you the secrets of that work in another 12 books.[3] But [for] now all things must be learned step-by-step, for otherwise we cannot come to the *Myriogenesis* unless our mind has recognized the secrets of the first principles.

II.

1. And so, because we have said in general terms {what the angles of the *Caelum* signify, now we shall explain more particularly what}[4] the ASC posited in the terms of the stars does. Receive[5] with an attentive mind those things that we are saying and by repeated reading commit them to memory. For otherwise you will not be able to explain the fates of men, unless your tenacious memory has held them fast by frequent exercise.

---

[1]This sort of thing has also been attempted by Hindu astrologers, who have produced individual significations (called *nadi*) for fractional parts of each degree. The usual procedure for using them is to start with a calculated part of a degree and then run up and down the list of readings until one seems to fit the Native, after which that entire reading is assumed to be his fate.

[2]Brakman would add *diligentissimis ac veris* 'the most painstaking and true' before 'interpretations', but Ziegler prefers *manifestis* 'clear', which is very common in the Mathesis, and I agree.

[3]Here Firmicus promises to translate the *Myriogenesis* into Latin for Mavortius. If he ever did this, it has unfortunately not come down to us.

[4]The words in braces are from the spurious (but seemingly appropriate) supplement inserted by the editor of edition **a** to fill the lacuna in the Latin text.

[5]Reading *accipe* 'receive' with **Δ**.

2. **The ASC in the terms of Saturn.**[1] If the ASC is found in the terms of Saturn, it will always make persons who are sluggish and slow, reserved with deep taciturnity of mind, bad, malicious persons, and those who are separated from all grace of goodness, and whose advice always has slow effects, and who attack everyone with various kinds of hatred, and whose anger continues with everlasting indignation. But if, with the ASC posited in the terms of Saturn, Saturn itself is found partilely in those same terms, it will deny brothers, or it throws down those who are born first with a miserable death, or it denotes the misfortune of perpetual childlessness, so that the offspring of children is always denied to them.

3. If Jupiter is found in the terms of Saturn, i.e. in those in which the ASC is placed, it will make tight, greedy, shabby persons, and those who avoid the grace of joy during their whole life, always involved in servile work and habits, and who transfer all of their own possessions to others by deed of gift. But if Mars is found in those very degrees, it will make villainous, cruel persons, and those possessed by the bitterness of total malice, and those who always hire themselves out in various ways for various acts or sell their services for them. But their malice and crime can never be concealed, but their crime and evil doing is detected because of their own ardor of rashness.

4. If the Sun is found in those degrees, it will make those who are even-tempered in their behavior, but prepared for every poison of malice, and who always abandon their own imperfect and incomplete counsel. If Venus is found in those same degrees, it will make those who are dirty in their sexual acts, and who long for the property of others with an envious desire. If Mercury is found in those same degrees, it will make those who are dirty in all their associations, and who are frequently handed over to prison or to public custody, and who are involved in miserable dangers because of crime. If the Moon is found waxing in those same degrees, or is full of light, it produces those who are <sluggish>[2] in mind and body. But if it has little light, it spoils the whole body with malign humors, and it either makes those suffering from dropsy, or disfigured by a bluish pallor; or it certainly denotes insanity.

---

[1]Here and in the rest of this chapter, the section titles are only found in the **Γ** family of MSS and may not have been present in its exemplar **Ψ** (or in **Cas 361** or in the archetype). But I have retained them for the convenience of the reader.

[2]Accepting Wikström's conjecture *<languidos> animo* 'sluggish in mind' cf. v.6.2; but *<vanos> animo* 'idle in mind' occurs in **B**^{2}**Nv**, yet the word *vanus* is rare in the *Mathesis*.

5. **The ASC in the terms of Jupiter.** If the ASC is found in the terms of Jupiter, <it denotes all the ornaments of virtue and wisdom. But if Jupiter was found in those terms,>[1] it will make magnanimous persons, but those armed with the ardor of severity. If Saturn or Mars was found in those same degrees, and if it is a diurnal nativity, it will make perfidious persons and those who never fulfill the faith of their own promises; those feigning wisdom and thinking themselves to be wise; those who are humble in life and depressed with the miserable squalor of sadness. But if it was found in these terms by day, all these things will be mitigated to some extent.

6. If Venus is found in these degrees, it will make those suited for all duties of goodness; but in their marriage events never follow them fortunately. They will be benign, seizing the fruit of all good things from continual good fortune. If Mercury is found in these terms, it will make persons always decorated with good habits, and withdrawn from every evil, and who understand everything simply; and those who are seen to deliberate about very many things. If the Moon is found in these terms, it denotes all the ornaments of good fortune; and it gives a good substance of body; and it bestows health with the defects of illness excluded. If the Sun is found in these degrees, it denotes the same things as the Moon in similar fashion.

7. **The ASC in the terms of Mars.** If the ASC is found in the terms of Mars, it will make those who are always adorned with a sharp spirit. If Saturn is in these terms, it will make sharp persons similarly, but those whose anger perseveres in perpetual indignation. If Jupiter is in those terms, it will make sharp persons similarly, but those who desire to excel in all things. If Mars is found in his own terms in the ASC, and it is a diurnal nativity, it makes [them] to enter into all the offenses of crimes from a depraved desire of rage. It makes rash persons but those involved in numerous accidents of misfortunes, and who are worn down by work[2] of incessant labor. But if it is a nocturnal nativity, it will make strong, cruel, irreligious, grasping persons, and those who disperse the things of others with various kinds of squandering.

[1]This supplement is found in MSS **GN** and in edition **a** (or **Nv** according to Prof. Monat), two lines of the archetype having been omitted in **Ψ** due to homoeoteleuton (*…fuerit inventus* | *…fuerit inventus*). Note the unusual combination of sources.

[2]Accepting the *opere* 'work' of the MSS with Wikström, rather than Kroll & Skutsch's conjecture *onere* 'burden'. Cf. *assidui …operis laboribus* 'labors of incessant work' in v.2.9 below.

8. If the Sun is found in those degrees, it will make crafty individuals who both get involved in trickery and are overwhelmed by it. If Venus is found in those degrees, it always indicates the desire for adulteries; and it causes those same adulteries to be carried out. And it makes such persons as those who work hard at every kind of beauty [enhancement], so that they are said to be beautiful; and those on whom all the fruit of the affections of men are bestowed. If Mercury is found in those degrees, it will make determined murderers, and those who from the nefarious desire of lust crave illicit sexual intercourse with boys. They are extravagant, profligate persons, and those in whom no judgment of truth is ever found, [but] clever, always dancing with frisky drunkenness. And those who without advice or who have assumed permission strive to pay their own [expenses].

9. If the Moon is found in those degrees, it will make persons such as those who confound their adversaries in various ways, and who in return are confounded by those same adversaries in very similar ways.[1] Also, they are weighed down by the labors of their constant work; and they are those for whom the pain of a serious wound is caused by fire or by iron. But if it is a diurnal nativity, and the Moon is full of light, it makes a strong bodily frame. But if it is a nocturnal nativity, and the Moon has little light, it will make strong individuals and those whose body is strengthened by appropriate strength. And those who are transferred [from place to place] by varied and continual departures and changes.[2] But a violent death is always denoted for these persons.

10. **The ASC in the terms of Venus.** If the ASC is found in the terms of Venus, it will make musicians or lovers of musical things, good, benign, benevolent, mild-tempered persons, and who desire to benefit everyone. But if it is a diurnal nativity, and Venus herself is found in those same degrees, it denotes the insignia of great dignities, and it conjoins [the Native] by the merit of friendship to powerful men or to Emperors. It also denotes increases in fortunate offspring.

11. If Saturn is found in those same degrees, and it is a diurnal nativity, it also makes haters of women and those who curse conjugal affections. But if it is a nocturnal nativity, it will make impure, indecent, dirty persons involved in the faults of miserable lust. And who cannot undertake natural intercourse, but who contrary to nature are seized by an outra-

---

[1]Reading **conficiant*. . .**conficiantur* rather than †*conspiciant*. . . †*conferantur*.
[2]Reading with Wikström *profectionibus <et> commutationibus*.

geous madness of lust. They will always err in their various advices and ficklenesses, and they will be the sort of persons who always curse all good persons with bitter hatred. If Jupiter is found in those terms, it will make erotic, lustful, voluptuous persons, but remote from all the ill-will of cruelty, and who aspire to every duty of moderation; famous artisans, and those who attain insignia of honors in temples.

12. If Mars is found in those same degrees, and it is a diurnal nativity, it denotes the inconveniences arising from sudden disturbances; and it disturbs the composed order of life; and he always gets engaged in popular sedition. Or it denotes various inconveniences of dangers on account of women. It will surely make musicians, always applied to sweet[-sounding] organs, or devoted to the poetic arts. Or it will certainly produce sculptors or decorators; or it denotes technicians [having] a fine talent for those arts. But if it is a nocturnal nativity, and Mars is found in those same degrees, it will give a marriage with a very powerful and noble woman, so that through her a magnificent abundance of wealth is conferred upon him. But he will be tormented with the pain of anxiety from excessive zeal.

13. If the Sun is found in those same degrees, it denotes fortunate actions in a constant manner. But it will give the inconveniences of miserable dissension in marriage. It will give profits, and join him to powerful men by the merit of friendship, so that he will glow with the fortunate recommendations of the most powerful men. If Mercury is found in those same degrees, it will make lustful persons; and those always adorned with the goodness of their manners, wise persons, and those who try to be useful to everyone, grammarians, astrologers, <divine poets>[1]; and those whose fables are adorned by the grace of their charm; pleasant, likeable persons,; and adorned with the splendors of all learning, and who produce many things by the power of their own talent; orators, but adorned with a noble fluency of speech, or poets shining with a divine splendor of poetry, whose orations or poems are entrusted to memory by the judgment of posterity.

14. If the Moon is found in those same degrees, it makes artisans and those who always work at clean arts; it makes sculptors, but those whom the grace of their own work commends. But it denotes these things then <if it is a diurnal nativity. But>[2] if it is a nocturnal nativity and it is found

---

[1]Add **Nv**.
[2]Adds Ziegler to fill an obvious lacuna.

thus, it will give the support of life from watery actions; or business dealings; or from fishing, but it makes them to be separated from all duty of association. It produces zealots, but adorned with goodness of mind, and who arrange everything with an evenhanded moderation.

15. **The ASC in the terms of Mercury.** If the ASC is found in the terms of Mercury, it will make literati, and those who with the most faithful duties carry out those actions entrusted to them; learned persons always adorned with right judgment; trustees or principal men of cities placed in charge of public affairs; reasonable persons and those who exact fiscal payments always with faithful duty. But if Mercury is found in those degrees, in which the ASC is, it will make astrologers, mathematicians, *haruspices*, but always decorated with every duty of virtue; And those who learn about all future things by some method, but they are always adorned by every duty of virtue, and those on whom honor is conferred from the notice of this by men.

16. If Saturn is found in those degrees, it will make unfortunate, sad, taciturn persons; and those who always restrain the order of their words with a certain moderation of speech; and who retain secrets with a faithful silence; but progressing slowly in everything, working very hard, and who always arrive at a bad reputation with the people. For they will be poisoners, and those whose malice makes use of every toxin of poison; maintaining their own angers with perpetual rage until they are vindicated either by chance or by their own merit; watching [everything] sufficiently with needful moderation; and those who are accustomed to prophesy everything that is going to be, so that both the status of the future and the present state of affairs are made known to them in manifest revelations through dreams; but who yield to every impulse in their counsels.

17. If Jupiter is found in those same degrees, it will make persons skilled in the law, physicians . . .[1] so that they arrange the affairs of powerful men by their own intercession.[2] They will surely be known to the people's party. But they are always concerned with adultery, so that they always both desire adultery and commit it. But by night, it will make those born to be pleaders, others notaries, but famous ones and always

[1]Some words seem to be missing here. Edition **a** inserts these words to fill the gap: 'counselors, lawyers, and those very skilled in forensic matters'.

[2]Accepting Ziegler's conjecture *disponant* 'arrange' instead of *dependant* 'depend upon'. In Roman law, 'intercession' is the act of assuming an obligation or surety of some sort.

adorned with good testimony, so that the grace of that testimony persists to the last day of their life.

18. But if Mars is found in those same degrees, and it is a diurnal nativity, it will make bad, malicious, malignant persons, and those who struggle with constant contentions, cruel, rash, and those who are not pacified by any considerations of humanity; noisy, shameless persons, perverted by an insane rage, and who reject everything with the defect of satiety; fickle persons, and those who are diverted from everything by the easiest persuasions; defrauders, scoundrels, and those who commit every crime with a nefarious ardor of mind. But if it is a nocturnal nativity, all these things are mitigated to some degree.

19. But if the Sun is found in these same terms, it will make famous persons, nobles, and those who are always adorned with popular fame; and whose nobility traverses through the extent of the whole state; and whom the people acknowledge by the defense of their own intervention. They will certainly be carrying out the duties of many activities. But if Mercury itself is found with the Sun in the terms of Mercury in the ASC, just as we have said, they will be the sort of persons who perform everything with the correct logic of counsel; and who are preferred by all because of their incorruptible wisdom.

20. If Venus is found in those same degrees, this makes those things that we have shown that Mercury does in the degrees of Venus. It will make great, fortunate, pleasing persons; and those who get everything easily; and who by public speaking convince the multitude [to give them] everything that they want; cheerful, learned, elegant persons, lovers of music; poets, but those whose poems are adorned with the splendor of nobility. And those on whom the means of good fortune are conferred from the accidents of others.

21. But if the Moon is found in the terms of Mercury, and it is a diurnal nativity, it will make artisans, but those who are preferred to [all other] artisans. But if it is a nocturnal nativity, it denotes the duties of all the arts, and those who are delighted by all their exertions; talented persons; and those who handle the business of foreign merchandise, knowing everything. And those who are transferred here and there for various reasons; and who despise all sorrows with a certain indifference.

III.

1. Because we have stated the decrees of the ASC in detail, we shall now explain what the stars posited in the individual signs <denote>. And I shall explain in detail <their significations>[1] in any place, lest when some malevolent reader has accepted our books, he might say with the hissing of envy that we have denied something to you.

2. **Saturn in Aries.**[2] In whosoever's nativity Saturn is found in Aries, it will make [him] to be involved in evils and unfortunate actions in the first time [of life]; and it will always hinder [him] in everything. But also, when Saturn has completed the first round of its course, i.e. the first 30 years, it diminishes his paternal and maternal estate, and whatever the Native has received from these assets, will always be either diminished or lost. And he will be worn out by continual losses and frequent damages; but after it has taken away the assets of his prior wealth, with the passage of time, it will make another amount of wealth to be conferred upon him.

3. They will certainly be listless and subject to dangers, incurring grave instances of dangers in the years divisible by seven, or in those divisible by nine; and they will be weighed down by these dangers if they are lacking any protection from a benefic star at that same time, and if Saturn is the Ruler of the Nativity. In their first age, there will be discord with their wife [and] they will disagree in quarrels.[3] They should surely avoid marriage with virgins. For it quickly separates his virgin wife from him either by sudden death or by divorce.[4] Saturn posited thus will give a wife slowly or one who is corrupt, or a widow, or one debauched by someone else, or one who has borne children by another husband, and whom the stain of some disgrace brings into disrepute. But then it denotes a wife, when the transiting Saturn (i.e. the one of that time) either aspects the Moon by square, or the Sun trines Saturn itself from Leo or

[1]There is a lacuna in the Latin text. I have shown my suggestion for the missing words in angle brackets.

[2]Here and below, the **Δ** Family of MSS omits the titles, and the Teubner editors think that they were not in the archetype, but I have retained them for the convenience of the reader.

[3]The Latin text is corrupt, but this seems to be the meaning.

[4]Accepting Skutsch's suggestion of *Virginem* 'virgin' for the *Num* 'whether' of the text, and Kroll & Skutsch's suggestion of *separat* 'it separates' for the *separatur* 'it is separated' of the printed text. But the Latin text of both this and the preceding sentence is corrupt.

Sagittarius. For with Saturn posited thus, whatever wife he is allotted will be obedient to him, and she will persevere in true affection for him down to the last day of his life.

4. But then he will also get children whenever Saturn is found in the same aspect that we have said. And he will then beget offspring fortunately, if, with Saturn posited in Aries, Jupiter is in any aspect to the Moon. But if it is not, he will either lose the offspring that is begotten, or it will certainly never denote any offspring for him. But if Saturn has returned to Aries from another place, it denotes serious ruin from dangers. And it provokes his brothers with bitter hatreds of enmities.

5. **Saturn in Taurus.** If Saturn is found in Taurus, those who have it thus prosper in all their acts because of their own abilities. But it diminishes whatever they receive in their first age; and through their very own efforts they acquire an abundance of personal wealth. But in their first youth they are weighed down by various circumstances; and they will be subjected to others; and out of necessity they will flatter more powerful men. They will have difficult times in their first age, and in those times they will be worn down by serious weaknesses; and from the want of necessities they will suffer restrictions in their life. For in their first age, they will be troubled by the aggravations of feverish wounds; and they are embarrassed by some very severe bodily defects; and overwhelmed by grave illnesses. And [yet] freed from the crises of inconveniences, they attain the extent of a long life.

6. All their paternal inheritance will be destroyed, and <they get> nothing from either their paternal or maternal estates, <but through their very own efforts> they will always receive <the resources of others and> the remainder <of the maternal assets>.[1] But Saturn posited thus makes his mother to be weighed down by the restrictions of poverty, due to the loss of her personal property; and it makes her to take on the dire straits of begging, unless the star of Venus—giving her testimony to Saturn with good aspects—alleviates the maternal inconveniences of misfortune. And the testimony of Venus alone does not suffice for this, unless the Moon also makes a fortunate aspect to Venus in the nativity. They surely attain the greatest insignia of good fortune by their own strengths and their own merit; but they are weighed down by the burden of misfortune, until Saturn has completed the first circle of his course.

[1]The words in angle brackets are supplied by MS **N**, two lines having been omitted by **Ψ** due to homoeoteleuton (...*materna substantia* | ...*maternae substantiae*).

7. Moreover, dangers are brought upon them either from accidents or from illnesses or from travels. They will, moreover, have a grave danger either in their 9th, or 14th, or 15th or 32nd year; but in the time of danger, if they are supported by the defense of benefic stars, they escape the danger of a threatening demise; and they receive [additional] time up to their 43rd or [even] up to their 53rd year.[1] For in those times they will be [involved] in plots and losses, and in accidents. But if the benefic stars hold [sway] at those times, at the time of the dangers they are freed from all those dangers.

8. But before 32 years [have passed], Saturn never allows them to marry wives, nor will virgins be given to them as wives. Which, if they are given, they will acknowledge children by them that are lost and unrelated to their own love affairs.[2] But they are frequently[3] allotted foreign wives or those debauched by others. But then they will give wives when, after 30 years, Saturn enters into Cancer, or it is posited in Virgo or in Capricorn.

9. **Saturn in Gemini.** If Saturn is found in Gemini, it will disturb his first age with dangers and illnesses, and it will make [him] to be freed from all crises with difficulty. Those crises will certainly be more dangerous that are imposed in years divisible by seven or nine. He will, moreover, have dangerous times in whosoever's nativity Saturn is found thus down to 23 years [of age]. He should, moreover, fear illnesses in those years, especially when Mars is in signs square to this sign. For they will have confusions, quarrels, <illnesses, oppositions>[4]; and he will often be engaged in great labors.

10. He will not get anything great from either his paternal or maternal inheritance, <but he will get all his increases in dignity and personal wealth through his own efforts>.[5] But he will be crushed down by the

[1]The numbers in Paragraphs 7 and 8 are probably not all correct. They seem to indicate when Saturn would form a square or opposition or conjunction by transit to its natal place. However, instead of 'up to their 43rd or [even] up to their 53rd year', MS **N** has only 'up to their 52nd year'.

[2]I believe that I have caught Firmicus's meaning, but Bram translates the sentence as "If they do marry virgins, their children die, or they themselves are estranged from the love of their wives."

[3]Edition **a** emends *feliciter* 'fortunately' to *frequenter* 'frequently', which I have accepted; but the Teubner editors defend *feliciter*. Bram has, "They will be more fortunate if they take foreign wives..." and Prof. Monat has, ...it will be their good fortune."

[4]Adds **N**.

[5]Adds **N**, two lines having been omitted by **Ψ** due to homoeoteleuton (*...consequetur* | *...consequetur*).

burdens of labor and misfortune whenever Saturn transits Cancer, Libra, Aries, and their squares. But he will then make progress in everything when Saturn departs from his first station in Leo or in Capricorn. Saturn posited in Gemini will also make bodily defects. And it denotes the greatest opponents in [court] cases <and in>[1] contests. It also makes both quick and frequent losses of personal wealth, so that he is frequently tossed about by various conflicts. And when he has come to the last dangers of life, it makes him to be appointed afterwards to [some] great affairs by the order of someone in authority; and he will be associated with famous and powerful men because of his official position. He will certainly be famous and noble in all his actions; and he will be constantly traveling; and he will be transferred to various regions.

11. But a virgin will not be given to him as a wife. But if the testimony of Jupiter has strongly given a virgin for a wife, he will be separated from her either by divorce or by the danger of [her] death. He will nevertheless be without children, or he will beget [only] one child. But when Saturn has come to the sign Scorpio, then he will be both fortunate and famous and wealthy. But then he will also be allotted a widow as a wife, with whom he will abide without any quarrel down to the last day of his life.

12. Many things will also be entrusted to him, and he will pay out many things, and he will have many quarrels with more powerful men, and he will be in danger from those same quarrels, unless the star of Jupiter, running well then in the nativity, mitigates the crises of those dangers. For those who have Saturn thus, will always be hostile to great and powerful men, always seeking the protection of inferior men for themselves; and they will frequently be placed in free custody.[2] They will let their hair grow long on account of the misfortune [engendered by] some friendship,[3] or on account of the misfortune of the death or the miserable torments of some condemned person. But when they have been shaken up by various instances of danger, they are then raised up by the augmentation of a prosperous good fortune, so that they acquire both praises and

---

[1]Adds **N**.

[2]I assume that *in libera custodia* means that they will be placed in the custody of some persons, but they will still be free men—i.e. not incarcerated, or perhaps "under house arrest." A similar fate is mentioned for the native with the DSC in Aquarius (v.1.15 above).

[3]Kroll suggests *amici* 'friend' instead of *amicitiae* 'friendship'; Skutsch suggests *tristitiae* 'sadness'.

personal assets, and so that a sudden inheritance comes to them. For then they acquire both wealth and the ownership of the largest landed properties.

13. **Saturn in Cancer.** If Saturn is found in Cancer, those who have it [posited] thus will be involved in insurrections, lawsuits, and in many controversies. And whatever came to them from their father or from their mother they always lose through a miserable loss; but they acquire the greatest wealth through their own efforts and their own ability. And their life will be such that they are always both acquiring and losing [property]. But they will have dangers from some disturbance or from illnesses—but in the years that are multiples of 7 and 9, until they have passed their 23rd year.

14. For up to that age they will be worn out by the greatest dangers. But if at the time of the dangers, benefic stars have the rulership of the times; or if they aspect Saturn or the Ruler of the Nativity with a fortunate aspect; or if a benefic star is the Ruler of the Nativity and is well posited, the instances of the dangers that come are decreased. But if at the time of the dangers, just as we have said, the nativity is aided by benefic stars, there will be losses of parents or of brothers, or losses from conflicts of lawsuits, but he himself will be freed from all dangers. But when Saturn is posited in its own domiciles, then it denotes losses, then storms, then illnesses, then lawsuits in an incessant manner. But if it is found in [the signs] opposite its own domiciles, it denotes those same things in a similar manner.

15. But when it is in Gemini, it will disturb these persons, and it will involve them in sudden anxieties and dangers. For then it indicates both misfortunes, and it will shake them up with a continuation of those evils until it transits the sign Cancer. For when Saturn comes into the tropical degrees of Cancer, then it will make the loss of his personal fortune, and it will put him in such straits that the kindness of some non-relative sustains them. Then there will be disturbances, then insurrections, then various dangers to his life. But when Saturn has transited the tropical degrees of Cancer, the preceding evils will be gently lulled, so that they are removed from anxieties and from dangers.

16. But also his first wife will never stay [with him], nor does a fortunate outcome ever follow them in their first [marriage] contracts. For in their first life they are joined with inferior women or with those who are degenerate in some way, but they afterwards expel those same women

because of a firm mental judgment.[1] But if Saturn posited in this sign either has the Moon with itself or makes a strong aspect to her, it will deny children; or[2] they will be deformed by some foulness of color,[3] colored with an abundance of black bile, and contracting constant inconveniences from black bile. They will be despaired of in their illnesses; and after [those] illnesses, they recover with difficulty.

17. They will be straightforward in mind, humane, sympathetic, supporting the financial difficulties of non-relatives, receiving inheritances from non-relatives, and having their life support from them. They will also be the fathers of un-related children; they will have concealed bodily defects; they will also be endowed with such dignity, that they also seem to be rulers of their own brothers. They will certainly be rich and well off; known to many and powerful men; deliberate in all their actions; and those who do not want to become swiftly involved in public occupations. [But] separated from all servitude, and adorned with the splendors of an honorable and divine mind, they always live their own life in favorable business activities.

18. **Saturn in Leo.** Those who have Saturn in Leo in their nativity will be attacked by constant envy. They will have their strength in the first years of their age. Occasionally destined for famous and glorious actions, they will acquire the greatest rewards from those same actions; and they get the ornaments of the greatest good fortune. Occasionally they will be separated from those actions, and will also[4] be free from all management. But from their parents they either receive nothing at all, or, if they have received anything, they lose it. But in their first age and in their first youth, they will be listless, subject to dangers, and involved in many activities. They will also suffer some bodily torments, and they will be worn down by pains in their bodily extremities.

19. But they are never able to marry virgin wives. If they have got

---

[1]Notice that they do not *divorce* the women. but merely drive them out of the house! An example of this was the Christian Saint Augustine (354-430), who expelled his common-law wife of ten years, and the mother of his two children, when he perceived "by a firm mental judgment" that her presence was an obstacle to his personal ambition for ecclesiastical advancement. He had Saturn in the 1st degree of Cancer.

[2]Reading **aut* 'or' rather than *et* 'and.

[3]This sounds like the children of a white father and a dark-complected mother who passes her dark skin on to the children.

[4]Reading *etiam et* 'and also' with the MSS of the **Δ** family rather than *qui* 'who' with **Γ** or **quin* conjectured by Kroll and Skutsch.

them by violence, they are separated from them in some way. But it will make wives to be allotted to them who at some time have already borne children. But until Saturn has completed the first circuit of its course, they will neither marry, nor acquire an inheritance, nor achieve fame. For whatever they have got before that time, they lose. And Saturn posited in this sign denotes marriages with two wives; for also [if there are any] beyond that number, those that they acknowledge by any kind of custom, they either always forsake or bury.

20. But they will have sorrows from the accidents of their children. And if the Moon is either with Saturn or applies to it, they get children with difficulty. But also whenever it has entered a tropical sign, it then denotes misfortunes. But also, when going around, it comes to Pisces and to Gemini, it denotes the same things as [when it is] in the tropics.[1] But in the rest of the signs it produces [effects] with the greatest advantages. For then it denotes the complete insignia of fame. Certainly in business affairs, and in actions, and in their entire life they are constantly changed. They will navigate great rivers and seas; and they will make their way through deserted places; and whatever their parents have never dared to do, they accomplish in the easiest ways.

21. They will also have many brothers, either from another father or from another mother, but they will be better than all their relatives,[2] elevated on account of a most powerful office. They will certainly be very wise; enemies of foreigners; irascible, good, benevolent, learned; and those who preserve an uncorrupted honesty in all transactions; persons of good counsel, upright and of uncorrupted mind; friends of many, and those who complete everything with the strongest efforts. They will surely have a scar on some part of their body. And they will continually experience losses of their dignities, so that they frequently fall down from a high degree of dignity with some humiliating degradation. <But this will happen when it> has entered <one of the tropical signs>,[3] in which we have said that it denotes dangers.

22. They will surely have personal wealth bestowed upon them by some gift from a non-relative, but so great that they will we able to allevi-

[1]The "tropics" for the classical astrologers were what are today called the "cardinal" signs—Aries, Cancer, Libra, and Capricorn.

[2]Reading *omnibus affinis meliores*, but I suspect *meliores*. Perhaps something is missing. Bram translates it as "superior to all relatives and attain high office."

[3]I have conjectured the words in angle brackets to fill the lacuna indicated by Ziegler in Line II 36,12.

ate the financial difficulties of others. They will be defenders of children,[1] always providing assistance to men who are suffering. But when they have accomplished all these things, they will die after a long life, and their spirit will pass into heaven close to the Gods. For Saturn posited in Leo recalls to heaven, and to the beginnings of their own origin, the spirits of those who find themselves thus on earth, freed from innumerable restrictions.

23. **Saturn in Virgo.** Those who have Saturn in Virgo in their nativity will suffer illnesses and inconveniences in life in their first age; but they are then involved in stronger evils when Saturn has made its transit to Capricorn or to Taurus, or when it has entered a duplex sign. For in those signs it indicates disturbances, losses, anxieties, sorrows, and the sudden advents of dangers. But passing through the other signs, it denotes good actions, good jobs, and the bestowal of very good fortune; so that from these actions they acquire fame and an increase of personal wealth, or they certainly acquire a state of repose, freed from inconveniences and toils and dangers. That time [of life] will have joy and fame.

24. But if in the nativity Saturn has come to the sign Virgo, it will not be able to denote any good fortune for them. They will surely have more from their own exertions than from the inheritance of their parents; and now they will be humble, and now elevated. They are constantly transferred from places and from business activities, and whatever is first acquired by them is destroyed with miserable and excessive losses. And when the entire amount of their wealth has been destroyed, they again acquire another abundance of wealth. But they even demolish that in equal fashion, and they can never possess their desired wealth.

25. They will always be unstable around women in their early life, but also women will be allotted to them in their early life by laws,[2] and they

---

[1]Instead of *liberorum defensores* 'defenders of children', Némethy would conjecture **libenter reorum defensores* 'willing defenders of those accused', which seems to harmonize better with the last clause of the sentence.

[2]Ziegler thinks there is a lacuna in this sentence, and he suggests adding … *in prima aetate <non perseverabunt et quascunque fu>erint legibus sortiti uxores*, which would make the sentence read 'but also women <will not stay with> them in their early life, <and whatever> wives are allotted to them by laws …'. Edition **a** emends the text to read *mulieres <illae quas> illis in prima aetate erunt legibus sortiti uxores* 'those women who will be allotted to them by laws in their early life as wives'. Bram renders this sentence and the two that follow it as 'Wives allotted in early life will not stay with them; the legal wives they take later will not agree with them and they will not have a happy life with them'.

will not agree with them, and they will not get any advantages of usefulness through them. In fact, they will not be allotted virgins as wives, but they either marry those debauched by others, or those who have already borne children. But if by any chance they are allotted virgins as wives, they are rapidly separated from their company. But they will not have the acquaintance of just one woman; [and] they are surely involved with low-born and contemptible women, but[1] they always cherish them with faithful affection.

26. They will surely be wise, amply-informed in learning and knowledge, involved in many occupations, seeking many things. And they will destroy whatever they have acquired from those occupations, as well as the substance of their own wealth. And they will sustain constant losses for others, and they will be deceiving about those same losses with deceptive falsity. They will also be ready for and addicted to dangers, when they are located in public places. They will be involved in popular activities, known to all and familiar to all. They will be saddened by the misfortunes of their children. And they will dissipate their personal wealth when Saturn is found in an angle of the nativity, or in the necessary houses. They will have bodily defects and constant pains in the necessary parts of the body. Some of them will also be allotted relatives for wives.

27. But if Saturn is the Ruler of the Times, dividing the times among himself and the other stars, they will be [involved] in anxieties, in injuries, and in travels, suffering the inconveniences of travel without cause. And they will be in such dangers, that they come to many crises. For some of them will have dangers from high places, or from precipices, or from wild beasts, or from a quadruped, or from water. And so, put before their own eyes they will see the dangers of death, so that then they would think themselves to be born again.

28. They will come into the sight of great and powerful men, and when they have been established among them, they are freed by their aid. And when they have been freed from all the dangers, they are raised up to the joys of good fortune. They will surely be contentious, and those who can never sustain the truth of modesty. They will be generous, long-lived; and those on whom good fortune is slowly conferred. But then it will be permitted if Saturn is not the Ruler of the Nativity.[2]

---

[1]Reading *sed* 'but' with **N** rather than *et* 'and'. Skutsch would emend the text to read 'and they are always cherished by them with faithful affection'.

[2]Accepting Kroll's emendation of *licebit* 'it will be permitted' for the *lucebit* 'it will

29. **Saturn in Libra.** Those who have Saturn in Libra in their nativity adorned with the testimonies of the benefic stars will have the greatest supports of wealth. But if Saturn is bare of the testimony of the benefic stars, they are not able to have any life support. But they will also lose in an easy manner whatever they have acquired—either from their parents or from others. But if a malefic star makes a bad aspect to Saturn placed thus, along with the preceding evils, serious crises are denoted. But then there will be more serious dangers, when the dangers are in years divisible by seven or nine, so that they will only be freed from these dangers with the greatest difficulty.

30. They will nevertheless be in such dire straits, that they seek the means of daily life from others; and then dishonor, then financial hardships, then every damage of misfortunes is inflicted [on them]. But if at the same time that dangers threaten, a benefic star possesses fortunate houses of the nativity, they are relieved of all the burden of misfortunes. But also, whatever they have acquired in the first stage of life is destroyed by miserable losses—especially when Saturn has entered the sign of Cancer. For then they will be in difficulties, in losses, in accusations, in illnesses, [and] in prison.

31. When Saturn is found in the dexter square, but also when Saturn has entered the principal houses of the nativity, it then denotes the inconveniences of all [kinds of] misfortunes on all sides. Then there will be proscriptions; then, losses of personal wealth; then, they are pressed down by the burden of beggary; then, Saturn will give sorrows to parents from the misfortunes of their children; then, their paternal wealth is destroyed; then, it denotes financial restrictions, then anxieties, then accusations and court cases. But also, when it has entered its own domicile again, it denotes these same things in similar fashion.

32.[1] Also, at that same time, he will mate with unworthy, or foreign, or servile women. But he will suffer these things until Saturn has completed the first circuit of its course, i.e. 30 years. But after that time, they will display unrestricted conjugal affections to whatever sort of wives they are allotted—captivated by their charms.

33. Saturn also denotes this same thing in the nativities of women.

---

be clear'. But Kroll would add *Sed tunc <eis substantiae facultatem acquirere> licebit* 'But then it will be permitted <to them to acquire an adequate amount of wealth>'.

[1]Bram omits this entire paragraph and misnumbers all the following paragraphs.

They will certainly be wise, reserved, of good counsel, knowledgeable, learned, great, wanting everything, imperious, well-known, famous, involved in great matters, and uniting themselves with greater men by the bond of friendship. And holding the insignia of honor in great cities or among great nations. They will certainly be the sort of persons who can never be cheated and deceived, [but] contentious, learning many things and knowing many things, and those who are quickly freed from dangers. But they are severely tormented by nerves and by pains in the nerves.

34. They will be put in charge of public places, assisting some persons, and from others having powers over men. They will be fortunate if . . .[1] is found in good houses of the nativity, they will hold the property of strangers, and they will be responsible for many things. They will be the sort of persons to whom the Gods predict the future, and who foresee the future by means of an instinct from their own mind. They acquire control over properties and possessions, handing down their own wealth to their children; and they acquire wives and children according to the decree of their own nativity. Moreover, they will certainly die [after] having divided their wealth among their children and being free from all dangers and anxieties—if, however, the full space of life has been decreed to them by the Ruler of the Nativity. Which condition you ought to take note of in all nativities, just as we have frequently said.

35. **Saturn in Scorpio.** Those who have Saturn in Scorpio are attacked by many disturbances in the first [part of their] youth and by many dangers; and they will never have authority over their paternal and maternal inheritances. But also if anything does accrue to them from their paternal or maternal properties, all of that is diminished by various dispersions. But the lives of their parents will be neither famous nor noble. But they themselves will be reared in their first age in the most delightful conditions, but afterwards they will be in straitened circumstances, and in periods of servitude,[2] and in hard work, and in illnesses. And they will get their daily life support with great difficulty and in the most straitened circumstances and with great labor.

36. Moreover, similar dangers are denoted in the years divisible by seven and nine up to the 43rd year of life. But if at the time of dangers

[1]Skutsch thinks that the name of a star is missing, but not necessarily, for the phrase could be translated '...if it (sc. Saturn) is found in good houses...'. Bram omits the phrase altogether.

[2]Accepting Ziegler's conjecture *servitiis* 'servitudes' for *exitu* 'death'

those dangers are alleviated by the support of the benefic stars, they escape the crisis of threatening dangers; nevertheless yet [those years] also disturb them with constant troubles. But when Saturn makes a trine aspect to his own place—especially however when he is in Cancer—it will make sadnesses, sorrows, travels, [and] straitened finances.

37. But when it comes to Leo and makes a station in that same sign, then it will give the beginnings of good fortune; and[1] he makes them to make progress in every way. Then the insignia of an honorable reputation are conferred, then they are honored by [being given] official positions[2] in famous businesses. For as soon as it has made its first station in Leo, the whole nativity is transferred to the beginnings of good fortune. For then pains, sadnesses, and anxieties are entirely put to sleep. But those who have Saturn in Scorpio do not persevere with their first wives. But thus placed it does not denotes the wives to be virgins, but either widows or those who have been joined to others. They will surely have relations with many women, but they are separated from some of them by death, and from others by divorce.

38. <Saturn>[3] posited in Scorpio will surely make illnesses and bodily defects in the extremities of the body, and chronic pains in the secret and hidden places. But if Jupiter, found in fortunate houses of the nativity, makes a fortunate aspect to Saturn in Scorpio, both the sorrows, and the illnesses, and the bodily defects are reduced. But Saturn posited in the House of Children will be harmful, and those children that are begotten first are destroyed in various ways. Afterwards, the Natives will rejoice in dear offspring.

39. But when Saturn has returned to this same sign, i.e. to Scorpio, they will be stronger, and they are made powerful and famous in places and among peoples, and many people are made kindly disposed towards them at that same time. It also denotes these same things in the nativities of women. For just as we have said in the Book of Instruction, those things that are said in [connection with] the nativities of men—those same things also are also effective in the nativities of women.

40. **Saturn in Sagittarius.** Those who have Saturn in Sagittarius will be involved in many dangers and many sicknesses. And they do not get

[1]Adds Wikström (instead of Kroll's addition of *tunc* 'then'.)

[2]Accepting Skutsch's suggestion of *officiis* 'offices' in place of the *initiis* 'beginnings' of the MSS.

[3]Accepting Ziegler's suggestion of *Saturnus* instead of †*si*.

anything from either their paternal <or maternal>[1] estates. But they will be involved in the greatest damages and anxieties; and, having obtained the greatest wealth through their own efforts, they again lose those same things through a miserable loss. But they are involved in sicknesses and various kinds of illnesses; and then they will have a series of dangers when they have come to years divisible by seven or by nine.

41. But they are freed from these dangers by very easy means. But also when Saturn has entered the square houses of the nativity, i.e. when it has entered onto either the MC or the IMC degree,[2] it will make some vanities in the mind;. And it will make disturbances and domestic disagreements, sadnesses, and inconveniences. It will [also] make damages, incarcerations, lawsuits, losses, inconveniences, and sadnesses. But when it is in Pisces, then it will give the beginnings of good fortune; and when it has made its station in that same sign, it denotes the insignia of life and fame; and it bestows an increase in personal wealth.

42. But when it has come to Gemini and Cancer, then it will be harmful to him in every way. When it has come to Sagittarius, and Capricorn, and Aquarius, it denotes disturbances and uprisings [against him]. When it has come to Pisces the second time, it will make them famous again, and everything that they have lost, they acquire with the greatest increase in their assets.

43.[3] But those having Saturn fortunately[4] [placed] thus are never allotted virgins for wives; and they are always allotted foreign[5] wives; and they will always have continual sorrows from the misfortunes of their children. But if Jupiter does not aspect Saturn posited in Sagittarius, it will neither give wives nor children. They will certainly have grave sorrows on account of a woman, or for the sake of women; and they will encounter serious dangers to life in water or near water.

44. **Saturn in Capricorn.** Those who have Saturn in Capricorn,

---

[1]Adds Skutsch.

[2]Accepting Wikström's emendation of *aut* 'either' instead of [*ad*] (deleted).

[3]In Bram's translation, Paragraph 43 is added to the bottom of Paragraph 42 and the combination is misnumbered Paragraph 41, so that the following Paragraph 44 is numbered Paragraph 42. And thereafter, down to Paragraph 48 the Paragraphs are numbered 2 too small.

[4]Reading *prospere* 'fortunately' with the MSS as Wikström recommends, rather than accepting Skutsch's emendation *in horoscopo* 'in the ASC'.

[5]Accepting Ziegler's emendation of *peregrinas* 'foreign' for the *ternas* 'three' of the MSS.

namely in tropical degrees,[1] all of their wealth and all their fate will be changed by continuous degradation. For as often as they attain the ultimate degree of good fortune, they are troubled by some deceptive consideration; and they are held by the inequality of misfortunes, until Saturn completes the first circuit of his own course and has expended the power of his own time.

45. Moreover, they will go through these life crises as long as Saturn transits Gemini and Cancer. They will certainly be the sort of persons who hope to have the greatest assets of personal wealth, but <they have> nothing great on deposit. But contrary to their expectation of riches, they are weakened by domestic restrictions; and their paternal and maternal inheritances are always destroyed. But also, they lose anything that they have received at that time in some manner or other, and they reduce their entire wealth.

46. They will also be involved in travels and in illnesses, and they will have life crises in the 5th and 7th and 9th years of their life, especially when that number of years is tripled. For then they will be [embroiled] in illnesses, in losses, in disturbances, in sorrows, and in injuries. They will also be overwhelmed by the greatest misfortunes, unless they were supported by the assistance of the benefic stars. For then there will be misfortune, then poverty, and all the other things that we have said, if the protection of the benefic stars does not weaken the impact of those evils. Moreover, they will be [embroiled] in those evils when Saturn, having entered his own places, has come to a dexter trine.[2]

47. But in general, being posited in Capricorn, when Saturn has come to Gemini and Cancer, it denotes the inconveniences of all kinds of difficulties. But when it will be in Leo in that same degree in which it was in Capricorn, then it denotes the greatest actions and increases in a prosperous good fortune. But posited in this sign, it does not give a virgin as a wife, but it also separates that same wife [from the Native] by divorce or by death. But also, whatever [women] were first engaged to them, it does not permit <to be married to them>,[3] or to stay married. But they will be allotted wives debauched by others. And these persons beget children by two women; nevertheless, they will have sorrows from the continual deaths of their children; or else children continue to be denied to them.

---

[1]The classical astrologers considered Capricorn and Cancer to be tropical signs (as well as solstitial).

[2]The meaning of this statement is not clear.

[3]Added by Ziegler to fill an obvious lacuna.

48. But they will have pains and illnesses either in their bodily extremities or in their hidden or genital parts. But they encounter the greatest storms of life and the greatest dangers when Saturn has entered Cancer. But when it has made its transit to Leo, freed from those storms, they experience a tranquil serenity with the greatest increase of good fortune. For then Saturn bestows repose; then increases in money; then wealth; then good health; then joy; then a proper order in life with all misfortunes set aside.

49. **Saturn in Aquarius.** Those who have Saturn in Aquarius will be downcast in their first time [of life], and whatever paternal [inheritance] they get, they lose. But also, whatever they have at first they demolish by loss; and then they make progress in great actions through their own efforts. Moreover, they will have the greatest storms of life from illnesses, but they are freed from all of those. There will, moreover, be a series of dangers in the years divisible by seven or nine down to the 43rd year of life.

50.[1] Moreover, there will be the greatest dangers at that time—there will be illnesses; there will be lawsuits; there will be frights; there will be travels; there will be such humiliations that they come to the harm of captivity and enslavement; there will be financial straits; there will be labors. But all of these will be such that they are like unto a miserable death. But after all of these dangers, if Jupiter and Venus are well posited in the nativity, they attain fame, profit, and the insignia of dignity. They will also have either a bodily defect or ill health, or a noticeable scar from fire or iron.

51. But whatever wives were allotted to them legally will be useless and such persons as live outside the letter of the law. But they will labor under these inconveniences whenever Saturn has come to the sign Leo. For before it has come to Leo, it diminishes his personal wealth. Then it denotes losses; then injuries; then things done in vain; then the deaths of domestics; then such great misfortunes that men, shattered by continuations of evils, eagerly attempt to bring about their own death.

52. But also, when it is in square [to its natal position], it denotes these same things in similar fashion, so that these inconveniences of evils increase day by day. Then sorrows [come] from the death of relatives; then a dull time; then there will be miserable inconveniences of poverty, espe-

[1]Again, Bram has combined two Paragraphs (49 and 50) and numbered the combination Paragraph 47, so that the remaining Paragraphs are numbered 3 too small.

cially if these come in the 7th or 9th year in addition to the squares. For then there will be imprisonment; ignominious beggary; and the dirtiness of unshorn hair, especially if Saturn posited in Aquarius is [also] Ruler of the Times.

53. It <will also so depress>[1] many of them that they will be involved in laborious actions in those times.[2] But from those actions they are afflicted with various kinds of dangers that they cannot easily evade; and [they will be] in such a condition that they will not find any path to good fortune, but everything will be destroyed . . . [3] moreover, strongly pleading public cases. But if, with Saturn posited thus, Jupiter is found in the necessary houses of the nativity, and in those times in which there are dangers, they are spared flight or lengthy travels.

54. But when Saturn has fulfilled all these things, and when the greatest time of life has run through these evils, then little by little—freed from misfortunes—they hold up their heads, and, cleansed from all the squalor of shabbiness, they are clothed in the honest vestments of dignity. [Then] they are counseling themselves, and raising their own life up step by step, and establishing themselves with the dignity of wealth, such that the rule and governance of men is entrusted to them. They will, moreover, be famous; holding the insignia of the greatest power; put in charge of regions and peoples with the authority of power; so that in public places and cities an everlasting memory of their dignity remains.

55. Then, they are conjoined by friendship with powerful men; then with kings, in accordance with the measure of the nativity. Then they get gifts; then places in temples; then priesthoods; then joys. Then they receive the fruits of wealth, then they will possess rulership over servants, then over buildings; then over men and women; then movable goods, then money is bestowed [on them]; and they will be opulent with such great riches that they also support others with their wealth. Then, all their relatives are supported by the assistance of their protection. But when they have experienced the conveniences of that good fortune, and when they are endowed with the magnificent affluence of riches, and they have captured the fruits of those same riches, they will die with a good reputation at a ripe old age.

---

[1] I have inserted these words to fill a lacuna in the Latin text.

[2] Reading *temporibus* 'times' with MS **N** rather than *templis* 'temples' with the other MSS.

[3] Ziegler indicates that some words are missing from this sentence.

56. **Saturn in Pisces.** Those who have Saturn in Pisces will possess neither their paternal nor their maternal inheritance; and they are left bare with everything lost. But also, whatever [possessions] of what ever kind they possess in their early age, they also lose with miserable loss. But by performing great actions by themselves, they acquire a supply of wealth. They will also have the greatest illnesses and the greatest dangers, especially when they have entered their seventh or ninth years, i.e. those divisible by seven or by nine; and a continuation of the dangers is extended up to the 33rd[1] year of their age.

57. But there will not only be illnesses among these dangers, but also lawsuits and accusations levied without cause and without any proper basis. There will be disturbances, and sudden uprisings, and constant mental torments, and unexpected dangers in waters, and quarrels with women. But those first wives they have been allotted do not benefit them. But Saturn posited in Pisces does not denote virgins as wives. And when it has been going around in all the angles of the nativity, it will make them to be involved in the greatest difficulties and the greatest contrarieties—especially when it is placed in the first circuit of its own course.

58. But when Saturn has completed the first 30 years and has entered the space of its second age, then Saturn denotes the inconveniences of evils. But when it has come to Cancer, then it denotes better times for them. But when it has entered the sign Leo, then it improves their affairs; then they get fame, then wealth, then the greatest honors; then the outcome of all their actions is favorable. Then trust; and then the affairs of great men are entrusted to them, from the administration of which they get increases in their personal wealth.

59. Moreover, in their extremities, or in the <hidden>[2] part of their body, <there will be defects>[3]; they will also have constant pains in those parts; and they will also have very large scars from iron. But they will have continual sorrows from the accidents [befalling their] children. But when Saturn has shattered them with a storm in their earlier times, then [later] it denotes joy for them both from children and from conjugal grace. According [of course] to the measure and substance of the nativity, which the other stars have decreed by their own authority.

[1]Kroll suggests the 43rd year instead of the 33rd. That year is mentioned above at v.3.7, v.3.36, and v.3.49.

[2]Add Kroll and Ziegler.

[3]I have added *vitia erunt* 'there will be defects' to fill the lacuna indicated by Kroll and Ziegler. They would add *laborabunt* 'they will suffer'.

IV.

1. But now, having explained the decrees of Saturn, let us come to the decrees of Jupiter.

2. **Jupiter in Aries.** Those who have Jupiter in Aries will be disturbed in every action in their first age, until the contrary [influences] of the nativity have completed [their action]. But when those times have been completed, then promotion, then fortunate actions, then good times, then a time of progress, then actions in the greatest affairs are denoted. Then they are joined in friendships with powerful and great men, or, established in great and royal houses, they are entrusted with the duties of firm administration. Then they acquire the greatest wealth; and they receive the power of ruling. And they are comforted by an increase of happiness from their wives and children. For then the insignia of power and honor are bestowed, then the rule and power over men are allotted [to them]. Then in all lawsuits, and in all contentions over actions and lawsuits, they emerge the victors; and whatever they have handled with quiet thought, all of that is brought to completion in the easiest way.

3. For Jupiter makes men adorned with the commendation of goodness. They will certainly have some sort of mark around their mouth. They will, moreover, be masters of the personal assets of strangers. They will be devout in the worship of the Gods, and they will faithfully preserve the secrets of all. And they are assigned to administrative duties by more powerful men or by kings—being imperious in all their actions and strong. But their first times will be difficult, but afterwards they will bring everything to completion, guided by the constant warning of the Gods, especially if, posited in the principal houses of the nativity and not in dejected ones. [and if] Saturn, or Mars, or the Sun, or Mercury, or Venus, or the Moon, aspects it by trine.

4. **Jupiter in Taurus.** Those who have Jupiter in Taurus will have the greatest fame and the greatest powers, but afterwards . . . [1] it has fulfilled the times. For in the first times, they are shaken up by a grave storm of dangers. For they will be involved in illnesses, and in servitudes, and in lawsuits. And then contentions with more powerful persons; then losses; then toils; then injuries are denoted. But after they have been oppressed, they will have prosperous outcomes in all transactions. Then they are al-

[1]Kroll indicates a lacuna here. Some remarks about Jupiter's cycles is perhaps lost.

lotted moments of fame; then friendships with powerful persons; then powerful men entrust the secrets of their own life to them.

5. Moreover, they will sail on the great sea or on rivers; they will also be involved with wicked or with disreputable men, serving in <secret>[1] religions. But their life's support is bestowed on them by women; and through them they acquire the insignia of some great dignity and of the greatest honors. Nevertheless, they will be just, strong, and displaying love for their friends. They will be frank in their speech; they will look out[2] vigorously for their friends. They will certainly be rash and strong in every dispute of rivalries, in which[3] they never desire to benefit themselves, but they always desire to benefit their friends.

6. But they have friends who are frequently ungrateful, and, having erred, they are frequently put right. They will be children of two fathers—of one, by nature, and of the other, by adoption—or else of two mothers. But in the beginning they will have both joy from their wives and afterwards sorrows—and similarly from their children. Having the greatest insignia of good fortune, they help many people. But it denotes all these things in accordance with the measure of the nativities.

7. **Jupiter in Gemini.** Those who have Jupiter in Gemini will be in the greatest fame and powers and in friendships, adorned with all wisdom[4]; and when they have acquired many things, they lose those same things again; and their life is varied with continual change. For in the first time of life, they will be involved in disagreements; and in many troubles; and in losses, and in financial straits; and in illnesses. And they will have continual sorrows from their wife and from their children, until they have completed 45 years of their life. For within that space of time of the nativity, those things about which the Ruler of the Nativity decreed,[5] whatever they may be, are destroyed.

---

[1]Kroll indicates a lacuna here and suggests inserting *<nefandis>* '<abominable>', but I have accepted Brakman's suggestion of *absconsis* 'secret'.

[2]Accepting Kroll's and Ziegler's emendation **excubabunt* 'they will look out', rather than *excusabunt* 'they will plead'.

[3]Reading *in quibus sibi* with **Δ**, rather than *qui sibi* with edition **a** and the Teubner editors.

[4]The Latin text is corrupt. I suggest emending it to read *<et> in amicitiis (Wikström); *omni *sapientia ornati.*

[5]The Latin text is uncertain here. The Teubner editors have †*de quo* 'concerning which' with **DGv**, but **N** has *cum quo* 'with which', **O** has *ergo* 'therefore', etc. But Kroll and Skutsch suggest emending the whole phrase to read *<quae> genituræ *dominus decreverit* 'which the Ruler of that Nativity decreed', which

8. But truly, when that time has been traversed, then they will have fame; and then the assistance of [abundant] resources. In the first time, they will also have disagreements with their wives. But afterwards they will have fortunate marriages; <and actions>[1] in public places; and from these they will receive the insignia of good fortune. But these things are denoted in accordance with the measure of the nativity, and in accordance with the mixtures and the aspects of the other stars, which it is proper for you to observe and remember in all cases.[2]

9. **Jupiter in Cancer.** Those who have Jupiter in Cancer will be friends with powerful persons and will have interactions with them, preserving their secrets with faithful silence. And when Jupiter has begun to possess their times, then inheritances; then honors; then the insignia of fame are bestowed on them. But good fortune and the faith of friendship will never last for them, but they will frequently be poor—especially[3] when Saturn has entered the principal houses of the nativity, or when it has come to Aquarius or to the sign Pisces. Then they are involved in difficulties arising from the greatest crises; then dangers; then turmoils; then damages; then illnesses occur. Then [there will be] quarrels with powerful men or with relatives. And then they will undergo false accusations and the ill fame of common public talk.

10. But these things are mitigated, however,[4] when Saturn and Jupiter are found in the squares of this sign. But when Saturn has come to this same sign, and has applied to the star of Jupiter, it will produce [good things] without limit, and even more when it has made its transit into the sign Leo. For when it has entered its second station[5] in the sign Leo, it de-

---

both Prof. Monat and I have adopted. Bram ignores the phrase altogether.

[1]Kroll indicates a lacuna here and suggests *habitabunt* 'they will live'. Wikström suggests <*vitam*> *habitabunt* 'they will live their life'. Possibly <*actus*> 'actions' might be better, since *actus publici* 'public actions' is a frequent phrase in the *Mathesis*. And the punctuation could be changed to *...matrimonia, possidebunt <et actus> in publicis locis…* ' marriages, and they will have actions in public places…'. Bram translates the phrase "They will hold high public office."

[2]Skutsch would read *in omnibus <genituris>* 'in all <nativities>', but Wikström and Ziegler think that addition is unnecessary.

[3]Reading **praesertim* 'especially' rather than *pecuilariter* with MS **A** and the Teubner editors, which means about the same thing, but does not occur elsewhere in the *Mathesis*. The other MSS have the meaningless words *peculia tergum* 'small savings back'.

[4]Reading *tamen* 'however' with **Δ** rather than *tunc* 'then' with **Γ** and the Teubner editors.

[5]That is, when it has turned *static direct.*

notes [spells of] good fortune, fame, and the insignia of some honor. Then they will rule over many men; then they will overcome the dishonesty of all their adversaries; then a favorable fame raises their reputation; and then they will also have the ability to be able to support others.

11. But when they are fortunate, they again lose their state of good fortune. But these things are denoted according to the diversity of the decree. They will have joy from a woman or a wife; they will also rejoice over the conception of offspring. And they acquire the ownership of buildings and movable property.

12. **Jupiter in Leo.** Those who have Jupiter in Leo will be [involved] in many labors and exhaustions until Saturn has left Pisces and has come to the sign Aries. For when Saturn aspects Jupiter posited in Leo by trine, then they attain power, then fame, then renown, then the support of powerful friends. And, established in instruction, they receive the greatest rewards; <then they come> to all actions, advanced by favorable <promotions. Then>, having <a pleasing time>,[1] they will handle the duties of management. But their first wives will not benefit them.

13. But they are not allotted virgins as wives, but women debauched by others. They will certainly be fortunate, having obtained the insignia of good fortune through their own efforts; but afterwards their paternal inheritance is lost. They will, nevertheless, be strong in mind, lavish, generous, and those who crave the things of others with a depraved desire.

14. **Jupiter in Virgo.** Those who have Jupiter in Virgo will be elegant, honorable, well brought up, and chaste, capable, faithful, always esteeming their friends with good affection, noble in their habits, contentious, powerful, and hard-working. But not having a single course in life, until Saturn transits opposite that sign in which it was posited in the nativity. But also, when it is in Pisces, they will be involved in storms, in damages, in illnesses, in sorrows, and in anxieties.

15. But when Saturn has passed out of Pisces, then [they will have] fame, and then power. Then they are allotted wives who are chaste and kindly, catering to the comfort of their husbands. They will have sorrows from their children until the times of Saturn have been completed. They will be [held] in great honor and [established] in great powers—powers that are denoted in accordance with the nature of the nativity.

[1]These additions are from **N**, a line having been omitted by **Ψ** due to homoeomeson (…*tunc ad omnes*…| …*Tunc gratum*…).

16. **Jupiter in Libra.** Those who have Jupiter in Libra will always have agitations and disturbances in their first age, especially if Saturn is found in opposition to Jupiter or in opposition to the Moon. For then losses, then domestic dissensions, then sadnesses, then disgraces, then lawsuits, then travels, then enmities, then the demolishing of personal wealth are denoted.

17. But when Saturn has gone past these oppositions, and Jupiter has begun to run through the fortunate houses of the nativity, then they will receive the beginnings of good fortune; then fame and joy are denoted. Then they get the proper foundations of personal wealth, whenever Jupiter, after the passage of Saturn, has come to the fortunate houses of the nativity. Then it joins them to powerful men, or to generals, or to kings. Then public notice, and then nobility is denoted, according to the substance of the nativity. Then the secrets of powerful men are entrusted to them. And then the property, then the personal wealth of powerful men are given to them in trust.

18. They will certainly be artisans, vineyard keepers, possessing the management of much movable property. They will have joy from their wife and children, but after[1] they have first been worn out by misfortunes. And in all court cases the decrees will be in their favor, but [only] if they are litigating without their wives. For then they will have fortunate outcomes in everything, if they are separated from all participation of joint effort. They will have some mark on their body. They will also be children of two fathers or of two mothers.[2] They will be possessing control of others' assets, religious worshippers of the Gods. But the first time of their life will have the greatest difficulties; but the last time will be honored by honorable actions.

19. **Jupiter in Scorpio.** Those who have Jupiter in Scorpio will be famous, powerful persons, especially when Saturn has come to the summer tropical signs. For posited in the other signs, and in the first square of the nativity,[3] they will be [involved] in illnesses, and in disturbances, and in accusations, and commotions, and lawsuits, and disagreements, and in low positions in business matters. But when Saturn has gone out of the first square, i.e. when it has made its transit into Pisces, <they will be>[4]

---

[1]Reading **post* 'after' instead of *cum* 'when'.

[2]That is, they will be reared in broken homes.

[3]That is, in the first square from its position in the nativity, namely in Aquarius

[4]Adds **D**.

[involved] with powerful men, with generals, with kings, preserving their secrets with faithful silence.

20. They will sail over great rivers and seas; and they will carry out the greatest business affairs through sterile and disreputable men or women. They will be favored by the crowd, having the insignia of power among the people. They will be equally strong both in mind and body, and they will acquire control over great wealth. They will have delight from the affections of their wife and children, but with an earlier dissension laid aside. They will also be put in line by more powerful men and by kings for the power of some administrative office, and once established <in that power>,[1] they will do many things.[2] These persons, who have been worn out in their first age, rejoice in a fortunate old age. But here what we have said in the sign Aries should also be noted.

21. **Jupiter in Sagittarius.** Those who have Jupiter in Sagittarius will be famous, powerful, noble, well-known, generals, powerful persons, or friends of generals or powerful persons, rich, affluent, [and] learned. But whatever they have acquired they will lose as long as the star of Saturn transits the primary houses of the nativity. For then they will be [involved] in disturbances, in pains, in uprisings. And whatever they desire to bring to completion will not have a fortunate outcome.

22. Moreover, in those times they will be in financial straits and in hard work, until Jupiter, having completed the second circuit of his own orbit, comes to his own place with fortunate aspects. For then, gradually, it denotes all fortunate things in accordance with the power of the places; then it bestows public acclaim; then fame, then power, then increases in personal wealth. Then it will give cheerfulness, then joy; and then it denotes marriage and children. But those who have Jupiter thus will possess inheritances from strangers. They will certainly be good persons, well-suited to every duty of human courtesy.

23. In the first time of their life, they will certainly be unstable; and they will disagree with their wife. But when they are in the middle course of life, they rejoice with favorable good fortune. But if in their nativity Saturn strikes Jupiter posited in Sagittarius either by square or opposition aspect, either they will not have wives, or they will not have children—especially if Jupiter is found in the terms of Saturn. They will cer-

[1]Accepting Skutsch's suggestion et <*in ea potestate*> for filling the lacuna before *constituti* 'established'.

[2]This entire sentence is omitted by Bram.

tainly be men of great good fortune, generous, likeable, friends of many, well-known to everyone, decent, honorable, adorned with every kind of goodness, especially if, posited in the primary houses of the nativity, and especially if it <aspects>[1] one of the other stars by trine.

24. **Jupiter in Capricorn.** Those who have Jupiter in Capricorn will be famous, friends of powerful persons, preserving the secrets of friends with faithful silence. They will be fortunate, but [only] when Jupiter has completed the space of his second circuit. For before that time, in whatever honor he was [established], he is cast down from the power of that honor, and they will be in financial straits, and serving in very difficult actions with stigmatizing low positions, serving the very lowest rank of men, until Saturn has transited the second trine of that same sign.

25. For before that time, they will be caught up in very many pains, and in losses; and in lawsuits, and in quarrels. And they will see the deaths of their own people; and they will be involved in many misfortunes; and, they will be situated in such misfortunes that they want to be freed by death from that continuation of evils. But when Saturn has transited those places that we have mentioned, all the evils having been excluded and lulled, they will attain the greatest advantages of good fortune. And supported by their associations with many persons, they will be put in charge of great financial resources, according to the strength and substance of the nativity.

[**Note:** the significations of Jupiter in Aquarius and Pisces, and the significations of Mars, the Sun, Venus, Mercury, and the Moon in the signs are all lost (62 chapters), as are the significations of Saturn, Jupiter, Mars, the Sun, and Venus in the terms of the other planets (27 chapters). But all of this was supplied by spurious text in edition **a**. The true text of the *Mathesis* resumes with the latter part of the signification of Mercury in the terms of Mars.]

V.

1. **Mercury in the Terms of Mars.** [The beginning is lost] ...If you join in association with such persons, you should never entrust the secrets of your faith to them; you should never entrust anything [to them] in a simple manner, <for they will refuse the subsequent surrender of

[1] Adds **N**.

them>[1], and they will add to their impudence by the irreligious defense of perjury. They will be armed for every crime of dishonesty, especially if with Mercury posited thus, Mars is also found in the terms of Mercury; or, if Mars, made superior, strikes Mercury posited in dejected houses with a square aspect.

2. Then also on account of these criminal deeds they are condemned either to long-term custody in prison or to perpetual exile. Or, possessed by the fear of their previous crimes,[2] but also fearing the severity of an imminent sentence, and having deserted their paternal Lares,[3] they are led in a fugitive wandering to remote and distant places. But if, with Mercury and Mars posited thus, the Moon full of light applies to Mars by square or opposition, and the benefic stars do not make a good aspect to them; nor, with the malice of Mars or of Mercury mitigated by the testimony of Jupiter or of Venus, they are punished with a severe sentence on account of these crimes.

3. **Mercury in the Domicile or the Decan of the Sun.** If Mercury is found in the domicile or decan of the Sun, and it is a diurnal nativity, it will make those who are middling in spirit and equally in mind, also middling in learning and reasoning, but it will also cause them to handle difficult and malicious documents, and it assigns [them] duties involving troublesome documents; or it will consign [them] to public duties. It will also make [them] wise with a certain curiosity [about them], involved in secret and illicit actions and unproductive duties.

4. But if it is a nocturnal nativity, it will make those who are either out of their senses, or it debilitates the ears or the tongue; it denotes mistakes and faults in their life, or it makes the sort of persons whom the judgments of a bad reputation always pursue, and whom a correct judgment of good report never recommends.

5. **Mercury in the terms of Venus.** If Mercury is found in the terms of Venus or in her decan, it denotes everything in similar fashion in a diurnal and nocturnal nativity. For then it will make the speech of men to be adorned with the graceful splendor of charm; and it conjoins them with powerful or royal persons by the love of friendship; and all of their actions have a fortunate outcome.

---

[1]I have supplied these words to fill the lacuna indicated by Ziegler.

[2]Accepting Wikström's emendation *criminum priorum<timore> possessi*.

[3]The household gods of his father's house. Here, it is simply a reference to the native's homeland.

6. They will be steeped in difficult[1] documents; they will comprehend all [kinds of] computation and all the techniques of mental ingenuity; or they will be put in charge of athletic men with the honor of some power; or they composes musical tunes with a sweet sound; or they certainly follow the system of poetry; or they will be dyers of colors; or the sweet odor of pleasant fragrances is provided by them, or offerings of precious gems; or they will handle the duties of foreign business, so that in every way personal wealth is granted to them from these actions. They will certainly be lustful in sexual intercourse, and those who corrupt the marriages of others with a depraved mental desire. They will be full of moral faults, and those who are always battered with constant scandal because of these faults.

7. What Mercury denotes in the Moon's domicile, was stated in the first parts of this book.[2]

VI.

1. **The Moon in her own domicile or in her own Decan.** If the Moon is found in her own domicile or in her own decan, and it is a nocturnal nativity, it denotes great wealth and the insignia of great fame; and it assigns a position of some power, especially if she is found in the principal houses of the nativity. She will make those acquiring suitable amounts of wealth through their own efforts, capable, popular persons, and craftsmen. But if it is a diurnal nativity, she will make hard-working persons, foreigners, and those whose life is shattered by a frequent continuation of dangers. Or it always indicates illnesses and bodily defects with the torture of sharp pains. Indeed, in a nocturnal nativity, if she holds the 9th house from the ASC while posited in her own domicile or decan, it denotes riches, fame, and rulership with the greatest power.

2. **The Moon in the terms of Saturn**. If the Moon is found in the terms of Saturn or in his[3] decan, and she is full of light, it makes sluggish

[1]Accepting Kroll's suggestion **difficilibus litteris* 'difficult documents'—a common phrase in the Mathesis—rather than *duplicibus litteris* 'twofold documents', which occurs nowhere else in the *Mathesis*. Bram, however, translates the latter phrase as 'two languages', but I disagree.

[2]The Teubner editors note that the passage that Firmicus refers to has not come down to us. It was in the great lacuna that gave the influences of the planets Mars, Sun, Venus, Mercury, and the Moon in the individual signs of the zodiac.

[3]Reading *decano* '[its] decan' with MS **N** rather than *suo decano* 'her own decan'

persons, cold both in mind and also in body, and those who are [totally] devoid of all boldness, and yet having a disposition possessed[1] by the ardor of rashness. And those whose intestines are attacked by the torments of a cold humor. But if she is of little light, it makes the sort of persons whose desires and actions never result in fortunate outcomes; and those who, having lost the resources of their personal wealth, are pressed down by the miserable burden of poverty. They are tardy in all of their actions and sluggish in mind and likewise in body. It will make some of them to be afflicted by tuberculosis or afflicted in their spleen; it tortures the kidneys of others with sharp pain[2]; it weakens others with a troublesome outpouring of blood.

3. **The Moon in the terms of Jupiter.** If the Moon is found in the terms or in the decan of Jupiter, and she is full of light, it will make men who are honorable, capable, and who always complete all their actions by favorable methods, acquiring personal wealth for themselves by their own capability. It takes some to foreign places to conduct business. But if she has little light, it denotes misfortunes and orphanhood from the death of their parents, and it diminishes their inheritance. It denotes a mediocre life with some low status; or it will produce pains in the muscles if she is found in the signs of the malefic stars.

4. **The Moon in the terms of Mars.** If the Moon is found full of light in the terms of Mars or in his own decan by day, it will make those who are exposed, or those of low degree; or it denotes some [bodily] defect or illnesses; or it will make them to be involved in violent or sudden instances of dangers. But if it is a nocturnal nativity, either it separates the parents by some fault of dissension; or it shows the mother to be of low degree. But it shakes up some of them by the inconveniences of travel, others by the inconveniences of sicknesses.

5. But if by day she has little light in those degrees or decans that we have mentioned, it dissipates the inheritance and denotes duties involving dangerous business transactions. And from those transactions it denotes vain crises or miserable illnesses or defects. But if it is a nocturnal nativity, and she has little light, it will make effective persons and those handling many duties, strong, glorious persons; and those to whom the duties of public business are entrusted; but those who waste away in for-

---

with the Teubner editors and the other MSS.

[1]Accepting Ziegler's suggestion *ardore <possessum>*.

[2]Probably a reference to the severe pain resulting from kidney stones.

eign regions. And those who always have a fortunate outcome in all their activities.

6. **The Moon in the domicile or decan of the Sun.** If the Moon is found full of light in the domicile or decan of the Sun, and it is a diurnal nativity, it will make ordinary citizens, but ones who are entrusted with public offices. It will make competent persons, and those who complete all kinds of official duties with a successful outcome.[1] But if she is found in opportune houses of the nativity, i.e. if she <possesses> the MC <or>[2] the ASC <with a partile aspect and when full> of light she is adorned with an aspect from Jupiter,[3] she will make powerful Emperors or kings; or the kind of administrators to whose power jurisdiction over the entire world is entrusted.

7. But if she has little light, [they will be] humble both in mind and also in their life, and those who never persevere in any occupation. It will make the mothers of some of them—debilitated and stricken by a lengthy continuation of illness—to suffer the dangers of an evil death.

8. **The Moon in the terms of Venus.** If the Moon is found in the terms or in the decan of Venus, and she is full of light, it will make those involved in scandalous love affairs, and devoted to incestuous desires of lust—indecent, lustful persons, and those who are always taking part in diverse love affairs. But if she has little light, it denotes good actions with the greatest increase of good fortune; and it denotes marriage with fortunate auspices [with someone] from the number of their relatives.

9. **The Moon in the terms of Mercury.** If the Moon is found in the terms or in the decan of Mercury, and she is full of light, it will make treacherous persons and those who refuse [to return] things entrusted [to them] with a stubborn fury of mind and due to their own greedy desires. It will also make house-breakers, thieves, evil-doers, and those who are accustomed to embellish their own falsehoods with some shadow of the truth They will certainly be hard-working workmen, but those who never receive the fruits of their labors, and those who are tormented by the laborious anxiety of constant labor.

10. But if she has little light, it will make either those suffering from tuberculosis, or insane persons; or those who are mentally disturbed; and

---

[1]This entire sentence is omitted by Bram.
[2]Adds Kroll.
[3]The other words in angle brackets are added by MS **N**.

evil, malicious persons; and those who freely take up every poison of evil-doing; and those who defend evil men or evil deeds with stubborn boldness, and whose dishonesty in every crime grows day-by-day. But these same persons are also accustomed to harm those similar to themselves. But if Mars is found in those same degrees with the Moon, it joins those same persons to armed robbers by the agreement of a bad conscience; or it makes them to be involved in various criminal accusations. And it puts [them] in prison, or it binds them with public bonds of chains. But if none of these things happens, it prostrates the wretches with a miserable death. It humbles both their personal wealth and their life. It denotes bodily defects, illnesses, and harsh dangers of death in a miserable disaster.

VII.

1. All these things have been especially imparted to you, my dear Mavortius; and we have omitted nothing that the divine ancients and the interpreters of this discipline have brought forth in their work of competent ingenuity and learned speech. But let us impart to your prudence that which we have frequently said with these same admonitions—that you should compare *all* the force of the stars, the *mixtures* of all the signs, also the *efficacies* of all the degrees for the *powers* of the houses.[1] And you should *not* try to explain the entire substance of a nativity from the course of one star!

2. But you should link the ASC with the powers of the 12 houses; and also compare some stars with the other stars. And look to see which stars are joined to the ASC with what aspects, and to what extent the stars either attack or enhance their own forces. See also what forms the natural characters of the signs and degrees attribute to the individual stars; and also what the authority of the individual houses and angles denotes. When you have collected all these things with a careful investigation, then, having inspected the substance of the nativity, bring forth your opinions on individual matters, but these same opinions [should be] formed by a previously [made] orderly comparison.

3. You should also inspect carefully the risings and *anaforas* of the signs. For when Jupiter has entered the house of Venus, it does not always denote wives, nor does its entrance into the House of Children be-

[1]Bram begins paragraph 2 here.

stow children. But it [only] produces these things for those for whom the substance of the whole nativity has decreed wives or children. And Mars going around does not always make a menacing aspect to the ASC from the DSC, nor does Saturn coming to the ASC degree always denote a grave series of dangers with a general harshness of malice. But [only] for those for whom dangers are decreed by the whole substance of the nativity. Then, the sequences of all the dangers brought forth by the *anaforas* of the signs,[1] and [the stars] made rulers of the times, are accomplished.

4. Whence, when you have combined the mixtures of the individual stars and the powers of the degrees in accordance with our very frequent admonition, you should prepare your mind with careful conjecture shaped by the divine instruction. For frequently the goodness of Jupiter is changed if it is lodged in an evil sign; and being lodged safely in a good degree weakens the malice of Saturn. And you ought not to expect danger from an evil house, when a beneficial star aspects that same house,. And the menacing aspects of the malefic stars are weakened by the good nature of the house. Thus, the mixture of houses, degrees, signs, and stars combines in the nativities of men. If you have collected all of those things with an even moderation, you will be able to explain the entire fate of a man with the truest opinions.

5. But since we have [now] explained this book, let our discussion be transferred to the principles of the Sixth Book. For in it I shall explain to you all the mixtures of the stars with very true interpretations, so that when we have explained that book, our interest may be transferred to the special interpretation of astrological decrees.

[1]Some words may be missing after these words.

Book VI.

I.

1. Frequently, my dear Mavortius, our speech has informed you about nothing other than the mixtures of the stars in all the [previous] statements. But it has said nothing about the substance of the decrees without bringing in the efficacy of their mixed composition. Especially when, in the nativities of men, the first angles do one thing and the second angles do something else.

2. For the first angles consist of the ASC and the MC; the second angles receive the IMC and the DSC; and from the always varied and contrary power of these four angles the substance <of every nativity is known>,[1] and all the stars denote something when established in the first angles in accordance with the powers of their own nature, but something else in the second angles.

3. But both the fifth and the eleventh houses from the ASC, i.e. the Good Fortune <and the Good Daemon>,[2] disagree with the inert humility of the lazy houses, nor are they <joined>[3] in any aspect with the lazy and dejected houses,[4] <but> they are associated <in a fortunate association of aspect with the ASC>[5]. But the ninth and the third houses from the ASC are allotted a third [and lesser degree of] efficacy, because a maximum fellowship of association also joins these houses to the ASC.

---

[1]The words in angle brackets are supplied by edition **α**.

[2]Added by the editors Kroll and Ziegler.

[3]This and the following words in angle brackets are added by MS **N**.

[4]This is not true. The 2nd and 8th houses are in square to the 5th and 11th houses. But perhaps we should read *aliqua <bona> radiatione* 'by any good aspect'.

[5]Added by **N**. One line having been omitted by **Ψ** due to homoeoteleuton (*…radiationis societate* | *…societate radiationis*).

4. But the second and the eight houses from the ASC are separated from any bond with the ASC by a dissolved fellowship of association . . .[1] all the scheme of association excludes the sixth and the twelfth houses from the ASC and impugns [them] with a fallen humility of dejection.[2]

5. From this variety of the houses, the power of the stars is either enhanced, or it is dejected—just as we have shown in the preceding explanation. For in the Third Book, we recount what the individual stars denote posited in each house.

6. But you should implore by every possible prayer that in no way should the sixth or the twelfth house from the ASC, and also the second or the eighth house, obtain the courses of either the benefic or the malefic stars in the decrees [affecting] men. For these houses produce inimical influences when occupied by all the stars.

7. For whichever one of the stars occupies these houses either loses the salutary guardianship of its goodness, or, if it was a malefic, it is reinforced more strongly in harming, [so that] it is strengthened in its power of malice. Malefic stars posited in these houses with the Moon generally denote all kinds of misfortunes without any remedy; but the benefics confined in the obscure—as it were—humilities of these houses, lose the salutary guardianship of their power.

8. But the diverse and changeable condition of the stars effects one thing in diurnal nativities and another thing in nocturnal nativities. And they have different powers of denoting when the individual stars are conjoined by trine or square or opposition aspect.

9. For by these combinations, every association of mixtures is tempered—by them, the entire power of the decrees is comprehended. For in turn, the stars, always opposed to each other because of their own natures or their own conditions, compose the fates of men with an equable moderation of variety.

10. Now I shall explain to you, my dear Mavortius, the substance of the mixtures, so that I may impart to you the complete instruction of this divine prudence. But before our discussion comes to an explanation of the mixtures, I shall tell you a few things about the royal powers of the bright stars, so that this book's principles may be adorned by explanations of these august stars.

[1]Ziegler notes a lacuna here, but perhaps only the word *nam* 'for' is missing.
[2]This is the reconstruction of the sentence by the Teubner editors.

II.

1. We have found bright stars and those shining with an august radiation of majesty in all the signs, but *royal stars* in [only] four signs—namely, in Leo, in Scorpio, in Aquarius, and in Taurus. But I shall show in a brief statement in which degrees you may find the august light of these same stars.[1]

2. The 5th degree of Leo has a star shining with lucid splendor.[2] If the Moon was found with this star while increasing in light, particularly while possessing the angle of the ASC or the MC, it denotes kingdoms and the greatest imperial [kinds] of power.

3. But the 20th degree of Aquarius is also decorated with a similar splendor of majesty.[3] For also if the Moon has arisen in this star, i.e. in the 20th degree of Aquarius, when she was full of light, and if she possesses the primary angles of the nativity, in a similar manner it denotes the insignia of royal power and imperial dignity. But also the 15th [degree] of Taurus[4] and the 27th,[5] and the 30th[6] <in the primary angles> of nativi-

[1]Firmicus is now going to report the positions of the stars as he found them in some earlier Greek text, in which they were probably referred to the Alexandrian fixed zodiac. And it is possible that the author had added about 5 degrees to the longitudes found in Hipparchus's Catalogue of Stars, which we do not have. But we can approximate those longitudes by adding about 2°20 to the longitudes in Ptolemy's Catalogue (which was 2°40 from Hipparchus's Catalogue). In the notes that follow I will for convenience show Ptolemy's positions incremented by 2°20 . If the unknown author of the Greek source determined the 5° increment by using the formula for the Trepidation of the Equinoxes given in the 4th century by Theon of Alexandria and attributed to "old astrologers," then his epoch would have been about –168 + 240 or about 72 A.D. See the list of stars in Appendix 3.

[2]This is Regulus or α Leonis, a star of the first magnitude. Ptolemy's Catalogue plus 2°20 would put it in 4°50′ Leo.

[3]This same statement is found in several of the classical astrological texts, but there is no bright star there, nor does one appear there in Ptolemy's Catalogue of Stars. However, it is possible that the star's longitude was reported in error in the Greek source. The brightest star (today) in that region of the sky is Fomalhaut or α Piscis Austrinus. Ptolemy's Catalogue +2°20 would put it in 9°20 Aquarius. Perhaps in the Greek source a *theta* was misread as a *kappa*, thus changing the longitude of the star from 9° to 20°.

[4]The first magnitude star Aldebaran or α Tauri. Ptolemy's Catalogue plus 2°20 would put it in 15°00′ of Taurus.

[5]El Nath or β Tauri, a second magnitude star, would have been in 28°00′ Taurus. But another possibility is Capella or α Aurigae, a first magnitude star, which would have been in 27°20′ Taurus.

[6]Probably Al-Hecka or ζ Tauri, a third magnitude star, which would have been

ties[1] are also decorated equally with the light of majesty. For if the Moon was found in the 15th degree of Taurus, it bestows <the authority> of the most powerful <administrative offices>,[2] and it denotes increases of an affluent wealth, if she has possessed the primary angles of the nativity.

4. But if the Moon was found in the 27th degree of Taurus, it denotes the insignia of a great dignity, and it makes the sort of men who sustain the life of the greatest peoples by their own power, donating to the public whatever was popular as determined by study, dedicating magnificent and outstanding offerings to the temples, so that because of these things they are honored by everlasting splendors of glory.

5. The 30th degree of Taurus also, just as we have said, sparkles with the divine light of majesty; for also if the Moon was found in this degree, it denotes the insignia and authority of great power. But if, when posited in that degree, it was found in the primary angles, it denotes those in command of leadership and a kingdom, especially if Jupiter with a fortunate aspect has seen her increasing in light.

6. For then, elevated by the freedom of action of their own power, possessing rulerships over both sea and land, they lead the army fortunately both through the sea and through lands. The 7th degree of Scorpio will also accomplish these same things. For the splendor of a similar majesty decorates that degree.[3]

7. But the Moon posited in that degree in the primary angles, along with the preceding insignia of dignity, denotes the horror of a harsh cruelty and excessive terror. For those who have the Moon thus, when established in the greatest freedom of action of power, rage against all men with the passion of unrestrained greed.

8. For the moment, we have assembled these little things for you from the books of the *Myriogenesis*, but when we have explained that work, we shall also deliver those things promised. Now we set forth all the mixtures of the stars, just as we promised, so that, with every constitution of

---

in 30°00′ Taurus.

[1]Reading *geniturarum* 'of nativities' with **ΔG** rather than *Geminorum* 'of Gemini' with **AB Patav.,** and adding the words in angle brackets.

[2]Ziegler suggests these words to fill an obvious lacuna in the Latin text.

[3]Probably we should read *XV* '15th' rather than *VII* 'seventh'. The star in question is undoubtedly Antares or α Scorpii, a first magnitude star, which would have been in 15°00′ Scorpio.

the mixtures laid out, we may explain everything that we have promised. For about the bright stars of all the signs, I shall tell you everything in particular in the last Book, i.e. in the Eighth,[1] and also about their decrees.

III.[2]

1. **Saturn and Jupiter in Trine.** All the stars, if they aspect each other by trine—whether they are benefic or malefic stars—are coupled together with fortunate blendings of mixtures; and indeed the badness of the malefics is mitigated by this aspect. But the salutary benefits of the benefics grow stronger.

2. Therefore, if Saturn is conjoined to Jupiter by a trine aspect, and that configuration avoids the inactive and dejected houses, and they are both in those signs in which they rejoice, or one of them posited in its own domicile aspects the other by trine, and they are associated with the ASC by a partile aspect, they denote unlimited prosperity with great good fortune[3]—especially if one of the two—i.e. either Saturn or Jupiter—receives the light of the waxing Moon.

3. For then Saturn bestows rulership over unlimited <riches>[4] and great possessions; then it denotes sowing fields,[5] then pastures … and

[1]Book VIII, Chapter 6.

[2]The Teubner editors note that the significations of the aspects given in Chapters III-XXVII agree in part with the similar significations given in the tract of the Anonymous (sc. Anubio), *On the Planets*, found in the Venetian MS **Marcianus 334** (14th century) and edited by Kroll in CCAG 2, 160-180. The original author is not named, although he is alluded to by an occasional *phêsi* 'he says', and the ultimate source may have been Dorotheus (1st century); the text also cites Vettius Valens (second century) from time to time. The Teubner editors give excerpts from the Greek text in footnotes to the Latin text. Bram and Prof. Monat omit them. However, I have translated most of the cited portions of the Greek text in footnotes. The numbers after the word 'Greek' are references to the page and line number in CCAG 2. The reader may also wish to compare David Pingree's translation of the Arabic version of Dorotheus's *Pentateuch, Carmen Astrologicum* (Leipzig: B.G. Teubner, 1976), Book II, Chapters 14-19, which gives the significations of the trines, squares, oppositions, and conjunctions of the seven planets.

[3]Greek (163,35 – 164,1): 'it makes great wealth'.

[4]*<divitiarum>* adds Ziegler, or *<copiarum>* or *<facultatum>*, all of which mean about the same thing.

[5]Greek (164,1-2): 'sowing and vineyards and foundations and houses, for Saturn rules these'.

plantations.[1] It also produces public builders of some sacred buildings, so that the greatest merit of dignity comes from their construction. It will also make commissioners of treasury exactions or those in charge of sacred funds[2]; and it confers the greatest dignity of authority over these activities.

4. It will also produce those who are infinitely superior to the dignity of their father. But according to the measure and substance of the nativity, it confers on some the duties of procuration[3]; on others the advantages arising from the greatest inheritances;[4] on others the profits acquired from foreign labor. Nevertheless, it recommends all these [persons] to powerful and very great men by the uncorrupted introduction of trust.[5]

5. But if, with Saturn and Jupiter joined by trine aspect just as we have said, Mercury is associated with an equal aspect,[6] it commits the secrets of sacred and inaccessible religions [to them], or it makes [them] handle the affairs of great cities or regions[7]; and it makes them to be such men as those to whom kings entrust all the affairs of their own action. Frequently too, they assign [them] the office of a distinguished commission.

6. But these [persons] are worn out by excessive misfortunes due to accidents [befalling] their children, and they are losing children; or they are caused to raise the offspring of others,[8] or they certainly get back their own children, [who have been] reared by others, after a considerable

---

[1]Reading *silvasque* 'and plantations (of trees)' with **Δ**.

[2]The Latin has *sacrae annonae*, lit. 'sacred harvest or grain supply. But the word *annonae* also seems to be used in a monetary sense, cf. iii. 3e.3, where I have translated it as 'salaries'. So here it perhaps simply means 'funds'.

[3]Administration of private or public funds and property.

[4]Greek (164,2): 'trusts and inheritances'.

[5]So the Latin text as emended by the Teubner editors, but I am suspicious of it. MS **N** has *Hos omnes tamen aut potentes et maximos viros incorrupta fides insinuatione conmendat* 'Nevertheless, all of these, or the powerful and greatest men, the uncorrupted trust recommends by insinuation', which doesn't seem quite right either. I think the Latin text is not quite sound.

[6]Greek (164,4): 'and Mercury being combined with these, they give public offices through communication, or it will make mystics, or they become tax-collectors for kings'.

[7]Accepting Ziegler's suggested emendation of *regum* 'kings' to *regionum* 'regions'. Cf. VI. 23. 2 below. The Greek (164,7) has: 'others are ambassadors and they are put in charge of their native country' [but the Greek text is uncertain].

[8]Greek (164,11): 'and many times too they rear the children of others'.

length of time. But these things are accomplished then if it is a diurnal nativity without the testimony of Mars.

7. For if Mars has struck this mingling [of influences] with a menacing aspect, or if it is a nocturnal nativity, all these things that we have mentioned are diminished. This <denotes>[1] more amply both the reprehension of ill-will and oppositions, and it strikes [him] with the hidden ill-will of bad insinuation,[2] or the inimical testimony of Mars opposes the whole of whatever good was decreed.

8. **Saturn and Mars in Trine.** If Saturn is joined to Mars by trine aspect, and that relationship is in opportune houses of the nativity, and they are both in those signs in which they rejoice, or in those degrees in which they rejoice, and the testimony of Jupiter or of Mercury is not lacking to them, they will make [those who get] the greatest financial rewards, and they denote increases in their daily money-making.[3]

9. They will also make men such that a fortunate outcome follows all their actions, and those who in every action are raised up by the authority of power, acquiring for themselves the greatest insignia of dignity through their own efforts. [They are] well-known, noble, powerful persons, and those governing the affairs of the greatest cities. But these persons see the deaths of their elder brothers in a frequent manner.[4]

10. **Saturn and the Sun in Trine.** If Saturn is joined in trine aspect to the Sun, and they are both posited in opportune houses of the nativity, and separated from all humilities, [and] if it is also a diurnal nativity, they amass the dignities of life by constant promotions of dignity[5]. And they denote the power of the greatest fame; and they confer public notice and nobility. They will also make the parents of those persons to be decorated with a similar increase in dignity,[6] especially if they had that aspect while posited in masculine signs. But if it is a nocturnal nativity, and after their paternal assets have been destroyed, they will make wealth to be bestowed on them by their own ability.[7]

---

[1]Ziegler suggests adding the word *decernit* to fill an obvious lacuna in the text.

[2]Greek (164,13-14): 'it arouses slanders and false accusations and losses'.

[3]Greek (165,3): 'prosperity and success and producing leadership'.

[4]Greek (165,6): 'however, they see the death of their older brothers'.

[5]Greek (165,31-33): 'they produce progress and fame in life and noted rulerships, and especially in masculine signs and by day'.

[6]Greek (165,34-35): 'and the father's life is renowned'.

[7]Greek (165,35-36): 'but by night, wealth; and thus he will be; however the pater-

11. **Saturn and Venus in Trine.** If Saturn is conjoined in trine aspect to Venus, and they are both posited in opportune houses of the nativity, and separated from all humilities of dejections, they will make the life of men to be famous with gentle moderation.[1] And they embellish men's behavior with the ornament of chaste and honorable association; and they make them to be <separated from all impurity of lewdness, but also pleasing in their chastity> and famous <for their purity>,[2] so that because of that fame [of theirs], envy[3] is aroused against them by inferiors.[4] But they make these same [persons] to be coupled in nuptial affections late [in life].

12. **Saturn and Mercury in Trine.** If Saturn is conjoined with Mercury in trine aspect, and they are both posited in opportune houses of the nativity, and separated from all humilities of the dejections, they will make persons who are wise, talented, and always devoted to all the duties of learning.[5] But they will make their character to be adorned early with the weight of seriousness; and they produce those whose advice is always valid with vigorous reasons. But they will give actions either from business,[6] or they certainly put them in charge of public and treasury accounts, or they will make royal secretaries, so that from these positions the greatest amounts of wealth are conferred upon them. But it is fitting that we remember that only the star of Mercury rejoices in the 12th house from the ASC.[7]

13. **Saturn and the Moon in Trine.** If Saturn is conjoined to the Moon in trine aspect, and they are both posited in opportune houses of

---

nal possessions are not preserved to the end'.

[1] Greek (166,17): 'it makes steadfast, and dignified, and circumspect persons'.

[2] Adds MS **N**, a line having been lost in **Ψ** due to homoeoteleuton (...*inpuritate* | ...*puritate*).

[3] The text has *invidia illis* †*a satis*, which is corrupt. Skutch would read **invidiae illis [a] satis* ' a goodly amount of envy towards them'. Other possible readings are suggested. I have chosen to read *invidia illis* [*a satis*], although one or more words may be missing.

[4] Greek (166,18-19): 'they are injured by weaker persons; however, they do not marry early'.

[5] Greek (166,30-31): 'it will make sensible persons, and intelligent ones, firm in their judgment, and indirect'.

[6] Greek (166,31-33): 'and their actions [will be] from business or documents or keeping accounts or from commerce, from which he will be independent and his life satisfactory'.

[7] But Mercury is usually said to have its joy in the 1st house, and Saturn has its joy in the 12th.

the nativity, and the Moon is full of light, those who have them thus always work their way [into the good graces of] kings, Emperors,[1] or powerful men by favorable or lucky recommendation. And the greatest insignia of fame is denoted by this configuration. But if the Moon had little light, the aforesaid increases in good fortune are diminished.[2]

14. But we ought also to remember this about the Moon—that she alone is found fortunately in the 8th house from the ASC in a nocturnal nativity—especially if in that house she is full of light in those signs or terms in which she rejoices. For then she denotes the insignia of good fortune and of dignity; then the greatest amounts of wealth; then dignities; and then rulership from the power of that house. But posited by day in that house, she denotes these same things similarly, if Jupiter is found in the 11th house from the ASC.[3]

IV.

1. **Jupiter and Mars in Trine.** If Jupiter is conjoined with Mars by trine, and they are both posited in fortunate houses of the nativity, and separated from all humilities of dejections, they denote the greatest commands of dignity,[4] and great power of free action. And they make persons of the sort who complete all their actions in the most fortunate manner. And they also denote offices of the greatest administration. And they make them such persons as those upon whom frequent honors are conferred by royal decrees.

2. **Jupiter and the Sun in Trine.** If Jupiter is conjoined with the Sun by trine aspect, and they are both posited in opportune houses of the nativity and separated from all the humilities of dejections, they denote the greatest increases in nobility, and the support of affluent wealth.[5] Also the insignia of great fame is bestowed, and they will make the greatest joy

---

[1]Greek (167,18): 'it makes familiars of kings and renowned persons, especially if the Moon is waxing'.

[2]Greek (167,20): 'but if she is waning, what was said will be more moderate'

[3]76,11 *Sed ...similiter ... decernit* 'But posited ... similarly ... she denotes' omits **Γ**, having omitted two lines from **Ψ** due to homoeoteleuton (... decernit | ... decernit); but **Δ** has it.

[4]Greek (171,2): 'they give rulerships and dignities from rulers; and it makes active persons'.

[5]Greek (171,17): 'a cause of wealth and fame and marriage and the begetting of children and a well-known life'.

from the good fortunes of children. And they always adorn the life with the bright splendor of dignity.

3. **Jupiter and Venus in Trine.** If Jupiter and Venus are conjoined by trine, and they are both posited in fortunate houses of the nativity, and separated from all humilities of dejections, they denote the greatest grace of charm,[1] and they associate these persons with all good things by amiable relationship. And they always indicate the faithful love of their wives for them. But increases of personal wealth and the insignia of dignity are bestowed on them by the protection of either their friends or their wives.

4. **Jupiter and Mercury in Trine.** If Jupiter and Mercury are conjoined by trine aspect, and they are both posited in opportune houses of the nativity, and separated from all humilities of dejections, they will make talented, wise persons,[2] strengthened by the very acute power of their talent; and who carry out all their business dealings with actions that are always fortunate.

5. They will also put them ahead of all men because of the merit of their magnificent and very powerful dignity; and they make them the sort of persons who are always both praised and [found] pleasing. They will also make secretaries[3] who are put in charge of public and fiscal funds, and who carry out public duties without any blame, taking care of royal requirements with their own arrangements. They will make some of them to understand the secrets of celestial bodies.[4]

6. **Jupiter and the Moon in Trine.** If Jupiter and the Moon are conjoined in trine aspect, and they are both posited in opportune houses of the nativity, and separated from all humilities of dejections, and the Moon is also full of light, they will make famous men decorated with the fame of nobility.[5] And they assert the testimony of good fame, but in accordance with the rest of the substance of the nativity.

7. On some they bestow the authority of most powerful administra-

---

[1]Greek (171,27): 'it makes charming, desired persons, those advancing by means of women and friends'

[2]Greek (172,5): 'it makes shrewd persons, certainly intelligent and efficacious and revered and well-known in the city, esteemed by many'.

[3]Greek (172,7-8): 'secretaries or civil administrators, entrusted by kings, and blameless in their actions'

[4]Greek: 'and others are acquainted with the celestial stars'

[5]Greek (172,22): 'famous and prudent persons'

tions.[1] They put others in charge of the army; and to still others they entrust the governorship of the greatest provinces. But they make these same persons well-known because of their honest and uncorrupted government, so that their trust is always adorned with the uncorrupted authority of power.

V.

1. **Mars and the Sun in Trine.** If Mars and the Sun are conjoined in trine aspect, and they are both posited in opportune houses of the nativity, and separated from all humilities of the dejections, they denote the insignia of the greatest power and the greatest dignity[2]—especially if in a nocturnal nativity the Sun is posited on the dexter side of Mars. For then the powers of glorious authority are denoted; and then the supreme authority of public offices is denoted.

2. But if, with these posited thus, Jupiter—posited in the principal houses of the nativity—makes a fortunate trine aspect to them from the other side, and if an aspect from the Moon in a good house is made to them, then they entrust the greatest administrations and military forces [to them], and they denote unlimited insignia of dignity—along with the power of the greatest authority. But these things will be stronger if Mars, and the Sun, and Jupiter are posited in masculine signs.

3. **Mars and Venus in Trine.** If Mars and Venus are conjoined in trine aspect, and they are both posited in opportune houses of the nativity, and separated from all humilities of the dejections, they denote daily profits from a constant succession of business enterprises; and with this configured relationship they make marriages of good fortune; and the Natives will be the sort of persons who always behave with pleasing modesty. And, encouraged by their haughty spirit of power, they pursue many marriages, and they accomplish these in the easiest manner.[3]

[1]Greek (172,22-25): ' they will be governors or judges when the aspect is in a domicile of Jupiter … or armed soldiers when it is in a domicile of Mars'.

[2]Greek (174,25): 'it makes rulers; but it will be rulership over the noblest, if indeed he is born by night, [and] the Sun has the dexter side and Mars the sinister one … then … it makes powerful rulers; and if Jupiter is also trine these and angular, with the Moon being in a good house, then they also become lords of life and death'.

[3]Greek (175,1): 'they give wealth and marriage with a beautiful bride. It makes a love of ornament and haughtiness, and those seeking marriage with many women'.

4. **Mars and Mercury in Trine.** If Mars and Mercury are conjoined in trine aspect, and they are both posited in opportune houses of the nativity, and separated from all humilities of the dejections, they make intelligent persons,[1] explaining themselves about all their actions by successful reasons of advice. And they make those for whom a fortunate outcome follows in every business association, and who can minimize the restrictions of all necessities with the authority of their own advice—sharp effective persons carrying on duties involving business matters, and computations, or documents.[2]

5. **Mars and the Moon in Trine.** If Mars and the Moon are conjoined in trine aspect, and they are both posited in opportune houses of the nativity, and separated from all humilities of the dejections, and if the Moon has little light, and it is also a nocturnal nativity, they denote all the ornaments of good fortune; and they bestow prosperous outcomes on all actions with constant good fortune.[3] They also cause all things that they want to be acquired in a very easy fashion.

6. But if Jupiter aspects this mixture of Mars and the Moon with his own testimony,[4] they denote the greatest honors and commands of the greatest dignity; and they bestow fame also and the authority of great power. But if the Moon is full of light, they debilitate the body with a constant continuation of illnesses.

VI.

1. **The Sun and the Moon in Trine.**[5] If the Sun and the Moon are conjoined in trine aspect, and they are both posited in opportune houses of the nativity, and separated from all humilities of the dejections, and

[1]Greek (175,14): 'efficacious and intelligent persons, successful in counsels, and sharp in their actions'.

[2]Greek: 'these too augment their livelihood by writings and teaching and keeping accounts'.

[3]Greek (175,26): 'active persons, easily prevailing in desired actions'.

[4]Greek(175,27-29): 'but if in addition Jupiter is in aspect, commanding, renowned, and certainly powerful; but by day, increasing her light, [it denotes] difficulties in the livelihood and in the body'.

[5]The Teubner editors add a note here to warn non-astrological readers that the Sun cannot make trines to Venus or Mercury; hence, those configurations are not given in the Latin text. But the scribe of MS **D** evidently did not know that, for he left a considerable blank space on the page for text that he supposed was missing in his exemplar.

†conjoined[1] it happens that they are conjoined thus with a fortunate aspect, but the insignia of good fortune are denoted by them, if they were adorned with the fortunate testimony of association with others,[2] or the light of the waning Moon … it receives …[3] of the waxing [Moon]†.

VII.

1. **The Moon and Venus in Trine.** If the Moon and Venus are conjoined in trine aspect, and they are both posited in opportune houses of the nativity, and separated from all humilities of the dejections, and the Moon has either little light or full light,[4] and it is also a nocturnal nativity, then by themselves they denotes the insignia of the highest good fortune.

2. Then actions, then fame are denoted by the configuration of this aspect. Then the maternal affection for children is increased; then the fidelity of chastity preserves marriages unbroken; then <the parents>[5] of children always ingratiate <themselves>[6] by the charm of lovable affection. Then brothers are esteemed with reliable affection, then the grace of charm is given; then the joy of good fortune, and then a famous quantity of power is given.[7]

VIII.

1. **The Moon and Mercury in Trine.** If the Moon and Mercury are conjoined in trine aspect, and they are both posited in opportune houses, and separated from all humilities of the dejections, they denote

---

[1]The Latin text between the daggers is defective. The Greek (176,28) has: 'the dexter configuration. Nevertheless, one must look at the testimonies of the stars'. That is not immediately helpful. I have translated the published Latin text, but as the Teubner editors note, the paragraph is so defective that it doesn't make much sense. It is a favorable configuration, but presumably the aspects of some planets were also mentioned in the original, and they have been lost.

[2]Greek (176,28-29): 'the configuration is fortunate, but it is necessary to look at the testimonies of the stars'.

[3]Ziegler indicates a lacuna here.

[4]The MSS have *minuta* 'little light' **Γ**; but *plena* 'full of light' **D;** and *vel minuta vel plena* 'either little light or full of light' **N**, which I have adopted.

[5]Skutsch suggests this addition.

[6]Reading <*se*> *insinuant.*

[7]The Latin text is shaky. Bram omits part of the paragraph and condenses the rest.

everything in accordance with the variety of the signs. For to some it denotes the embellishment of fluent speech; for others the insignia of outstanding arts are denoted by this configuration; and to others the sweet sound of music is given. They make others to be painters, but the sort of persons whose arts are always made well-known by an outstanding excellence.

2. They denote the powers of arms for some; others are given training in athletics. They assign others to be singers of sweet melodies for the public pleasure. But they always make all of these persons known with faithful approval by the judgment of the people. They often make some who handle business affairs. But they do all of these things in accordance with the testimonies of the rest of the stars, and in accordance with the forces of the houses and signs.

IX.

1. Now I shall explain to you the decrees of the square aspect, which relationship always consists of a strong and menacing aspect. For from this configuration the virtue of the malefic stars is increased, and the protection of the benefic ones is overcome by the menacing aspect, which, along with the opposition aspect always attacks with equal power in perpetrating evils.

2. **Saturn and Jupiter in Square.** If Jupiter and Saturn were conjoined in square aspect,[1] and Saturn is superior, possessing the superior part of a dexter square, but Jupiter, made to be in a sinister square, is seen to be inferior, they both denote dangers to the native's life, and they diminish the amount of his personal wealth.[2] And they make all of their plans to turn out bad; they hinder their actions; and they disturb their minds with various mental conflicts. And they attack their fathers with various kinds of calamities; they also dissipate the paternal wealth with various kinds of losses.

[1]Greek (164,17): 'And when Jupiter is in square with Saturn, and Saturn is superior, therefore it is dexter.'

[2]Greek (164,17-24): 'they decrease the possessions; for the malefic is found predominant because of its being superior; whence it is also a hindrance to actions,; and it makes contrary purposes; and it hurts the father, and it destroys the paternal wealth ... but if the [star] of Jupiter is superior to Saturn, the evils are weaker, for [they indicate] some renown for the father, and for the child with the passage of time they indicate some progress in his livelihood'.

3. But if Jupiter, made superior, and possessing the dexter side, aspects Saturn posited in the sinister square, the misfortunes of the preceding calamities are mitigated. And they make the parents famous with some splendor of fame and praise, and in accordance with the measure of the nativity, daily advantages of wealth are bestowed upon them.

4. **Saturn and Mars in Square.** If Saturn and Mars are conjoined in square aspect, and Saturn is made superior, and possessing the dexter [side of the] square, it aspects Mars posited in the sinister square with a menacing aspect,[1] they always obstruct all the Natives' actions because of an ineffective effort arising from this configuration. And they make them to be hostile to every duty of business because of a dull listlessness of mind.

5. They also always indicate illnesses of various kinds, so that cold mixed with heat shatters their body with a continual shivering. But this configuration also destroys the assets of the paternal wealth. And they always show the deaths of the Natives' brothers from a serious occurrence of misfortunes.

6. But if Mars, made superior and possessing the dexter side, aspects Saturn posited in the inferior place with a square aspect, the demise of death is quickly prepared for the Native's mother by this configuration. But effective work always leads them to all acts of a fortunate undertaking—all the disgrace of the previous ills having been put to rest.

7. But nevertheless, the paternal wealth is also dispersed by this configuration. But these same individuals are disturbed by a constant continuation of damages. And always the dishonesty of their domestics inflicts the malignant wound of infamy on them.[2]

8. **Saturn and the Sun in Square.** If Saturn and the Sun are conjoined in square aspect, and Saturn, possessing the superior right part of a dexter square, aspects the Sun posited in a sinister square with a menacing aspect, that configuration weakens the insignia of a preceding honor,[3] and

[1]Greek (165,11-16): 'it makes those shaking in their body,and feverish, and gravely ill, and inactive; and it destroys the paternal wealth; and they also bury their wives But with Mars prevailing over Saturn, the father dies before the mother. This kind of configuration is energetic in activities related to livelihood. Moreover, the paternal wealth is thus lost'.

[2]Greek (165,16): 'these same also suffer ill will from members of their household'.

[3]Greek (166,2-4): 'his father will suffer loss of his livelihood or convulsion, and

it indicates the loss of dignity with a bitter loss of honor, and it deforms their body with a continuous contraction of the sinews.

9. But it also afflicts their parents with that same disgrace of misfortunes; and it also makes those same fathers to die before the mothers. But it also makes them go wrong with various kinds of mistakes, and it denotes rather injurious consequences of <malicious>[1] association; and it always indicates grave illnesses from bitter cold of humors; it both cuts off and at the same time shatters the personal wealth and also all actions.[2]

10. But if the Sun, made superior and possessing the dexter side,[3] aspects Saturn posited in the lower place with a square aspect, that configuration disperses the paternal wealth; and it always indicates serious enmities among the male domestics; and it always opposes[4] every mental impulse and all actions with obscure thought. But it also never allows plans to have fortunate outcomes; and in the first age [of life] it indicates the bitter and frequent inconveniences of illnesses; and it debilitates the body, worn out by a manifold continuation of illnesses.

11. **Saturn and Venus in Square.** If Saturn and Venus are conjoined in square aspect, and Saturn, possessing the superior part of a dexter square, aspects Venus posited in a sinister square with a menacing aspect, that configuration indicates the grave burden of beggary due to a dilapidated inheritance;[5] and it also always indicates destruction by bitter calamities due to women; and it does not bestow any charm of beauty;[6] and it never allows their desires to have a fortunate outcome.

---

he will also die before the mother. Moreover, with regard to the Native, [there will be] difficulty engendered in his livelihood and outrages from many persons'.

[1]Adds Brakman.

[2]Greek (166,4-5): 'it causes illnesses in the body from shivering and fever because of the mixing with the Sun, and especially from shivering … they are cut off, but they are also attacked in these acts'.

[3]Greek (166,6-8): 'with the Sun prevailing over Saturn, the paternal wealth is dispersed, and there will be enemies against the members of the household'.

[4]Greek (166,8-11): 'and both the impulses of the mind and the actions are darkened, and plans are destroyed; and other illnesses at another time; they are also afflicted with bodily ailments in the first time of life, and the livelihood is not remarkable for the father'.

[5]Greek (166,20): 'losses of livelihood, damages and sorrows from female persons'.

[6]Greek (166,20-26): 'these persons are both devoid of loveliness and unfortunate in their actions; with Venus prevailing over Saturn, the women who will be taken will be blameless but austere and having a commanding temperament, but loving their husband and preserving their favor with him, but secretly they will be longing for each other'.

12. But if Venus, made superior and possessing the dexter side, aspects Saturn posited in the lower place with a square aspect, this configuration bestows wives with honorable and chaste habits, but who claim for themselves all the power in ruling the home, [while] loving their husbands with faithful and uncorrupted affection, so that the conjugal grace of both of them unites them jointly; but both of whom try to hide their own love with some dissimulation.

13. **Saturn and Mercury in Square.** If Saturn and Mercury are conjoined in square aspect, and Saturn, possessing the superior part of a dexter square, aspects Mercury posited in a sinister square with a menacing aspect, that configuration denotes exiles from the first natal day;[1] and he always pursues all his actions with a cold listlessness. It also makes him to be always subject to the powers of other people—in all their actions carrying out favorable services in business affairs; but it indicates the greatest storms of jealousy directed against them.

14. The tongue-tied condition of some will make a stammering sound of voice;[2] it will make others to be silent because of dulled ears[3]; and these defects will persist, unless the preceding evils are mitigated by the testimony of Mars.[4] But if Mercury, made superior and possessing the dexter side, aspects Saturn posited in the lower place[5] with a square aspect, nothing of good is denoted by the relationship of this configuration, but only a small amount of the badness of the preceding misfortunes is mitigated.

15. **Saturn and the Moon in Square.** If Saturn and the Moon are conjoined in square aspect, and Saturn, possessing the superior part of a <dexter>[6] square, aspects the Moon posited in a sinister square with a menacing aspect, this configuration will make the body to be worn down by malicious humors; and it will make those who are separated from all actions by a sluggish listlessness of mind; and it produces the sort of persons who can never dare to do anything. But this configuration also al-

[1]Greek (166.34): 'by preference opposing, it destroys plans, spirit, and it causes actions; but it makes them obedient to other persons, but it signifies slanderers'.

[2]Greek (167,1-3): 'and some will be stammering or stammerers and faltering in speech or babbling or mute'.

[3]In olden days, deaf people seldom learned to talk.

[4]Reading **praecedentia mala testimonio Martis fuerint mitigata*.

[5]Greek (167,3-4): 'but with Mercury prevailing over Saturn, the configuration is not good, and yet the evil is less'.

[6]Adds MS **N**.

ways dissipates the maternal wealth by miserable losses, or it makes children to undertake matricidal struggles because of enmities to their mothers.

16. But if the Moon, made superior and possessing the dexter side, aspects Saturn posited in the lower place with a square aspect, this configuration prostrates the mother with a miserable death, and it surrounds the Native with a bitter continuation of dangers; and it indicates grave incidents of illnesses from malignant humors. But also, if marriage was decreed by the help of other stars, this configuration hardens the wife's mind by a bitter conflict of displeasures. But it also makes the Natives to be deprived of all assistance from friends and children.

X.

1. **Jupiter and Mars in square.** If Jupiter and Mars are conjoined in square aspect, and Jupiter, possessing the superior part of a dexter square, makes a menacing aspect to Mars posited in a sinister square, that conjunction denotes the insignia of the greatest fame, and it always makes these same persons known by good recognition, and it denotes famous insignia of honor.

2. It will make some to be involved in military positions; it assigns others to royal households; and it denotes duties in noble and public activities. It makes [them] to be elevated by these official duties, so that they pursue these duties with the greatest increase of dignity. But these persons are never able to preserve the assets from their paternal inheritance well.[1] But this configuration always indicates continual sorrows from accidents to [the native's] children, or it will certainly make the children to be conceived late.

3. But if Mars, made superior and possessing the dexter side, aspects Jupiter posited in the lower place with a square aspect,[2] that configuration sharpens every mental impulse exceedingly,[3] and it will make [them]

[1]Greek (171,6-8): 'but he is not a good keeper of the paternal property and of his own livelihood; but he also grieves for his children, for it makes either childlessness or short-lived children'

[2]Greek (171,8-11): 'But Mars prevailing over Jupiter [makes] sharp-tongued persons [*οξυλάλους] in attacks; and those whose livelihood is ruined, and those who toil in vain in royal service and enterprises or in civil service, from which false accusations and reproaches are raised'.

[3]Accepting Wikström's emendation **immensum* at II,89, 7.

to go wrong in their whole life with various kinds of error; and without cause it always causes men to suffer the inconveniences of great toil. But that toil comes from either public or royal actions, and furtermore it denotes more fully the dangers of bad insinuations and bitter accusations from the aggressive zeal of his enemies.

4. **Jupiter and the Sun in Square.** If Jupiter and the Sun are conjoined in square aspect, and Jupiter, possessing the superior part of a dexter square, aspects the Sun posited in sinister square with a menacing aspect,[1] that configuration denotes the insignia of dignity through either his own merit or that of his father, but it also bestows increases and promotions to good and great honors, and it always grants recommendations with good testimony, and many of them will experience the merit of dignity.

5. But if the Sun, made superior and possessing the dexter side, aspects Jupiter posited in the lower place with a square aspect,[2] that configuration will make one decorated with a famous splendor of nobility, but it makes the father's wealth to be proscribed with a miserable confiscation; and it stirs up dangerous disturbances by strong and evil enemies.

6. **Jupiter and Venus in Square.** If Jupiter and Venus are conjoined in square aspect, and Jupiter, possessing the superior part of a dexter square, aspects Venus posited in a sinister square with a menacing aspect,[3] that configuration always associates [him] in friendships with many persons, and by the assistance of women, it will make both actions and profits to be conferred upon [him] in the same fashion; and it always adorns the whole substance of his life with an honorable dignity. And it will make these same persons to observe the religions of the Gods with a faithful ardor of veneration.

7. But if Venus, made superior and possessing the dexter side, aspects Jupiter posited in the lower place with a square aspect,[4] it both denotes from that configuration the attractions of love affairs, and it will cause [him] to spend time in the care of clothes and the body, so that from that

[1]Greek (171,19): 'it is the cause of the greatest advancement, and good association with the father and the child, and besides of the pre-eminence of many'.

[2]Greek (171,21-24): 'and if the Sun is superior to Jupiter, the father will be very famous, but his wealth is diminished; for if he is made public in the city or among the people, [then] sometimes too his enemies inherit his property'.

[3]Greek (171,29): 'friends of many, having sales and profits from feminine persons, cultured certainly, [and] religious'.

[4]Greek (171,31-34): 'but if Venus is superior to Jupiter, they will be exceedingly fond of love, having in the case of women a fondness of beauty and a fondness

configuration he will always be dressed nicely, and it always indicates luxurious desires for pleasures. But however often fortunate delights of joy are attained, the same number of times the altered decrees of fate change these same to the contrary.

8. **Jupiter and Mercury in Square.** If Jupiter and Mercury are conjoined by square, and Jupiter, possessing the superior part of a dexter square, aspects Mercury posited in a sinister square by a menacing aspect, from that configuration jobs in connection with documents, or letters, or arts are denoted,[1] and it makes them to be put in charge of book-keeping and computations; and personal wealth and activities are conferred upon them from some sort of public defense.

9. But if Mercury, made superior and possessing the dexter side, aspects Jupiter posited in the lower place with a square aspect,[2] that configuration will make adequate amounts of wealth; but these persons always hinder themselves in every action, avoiding all good things as if they were bad, from an unnatural mental fear; and they will be the sort of persons who whatever others want to get at the greatest price—all that which even if by chance it has fallen to them—they disdain with an obstinate judgment of mind. But they do not want benefits to be conferred upon them by others, and these same persons do not try to get anything good for themselves.

10. **Jupiter and the Moon in Square.** If Jupiter and the Moon are conjoined by square aspect, and Jupiter possessing the superior part of a dexter square, aspects the Moon posited in a sinister square with a menacing aspect, it denotes infinite riches for both the mother and for [the Native] himself,[3] and that configuration denotes riches without limit for the mother and for the Native himself, and it denotes the greatest jobs in business, and, due to their merit of the greatest dignity, it places them

---

of decoration; however not succeeding thus in attempted actions'.

[1]Greek (172,11): 'it signifies grammarians, accountants and auditors; and for these their livelihood will be from public administration'.

[2]Greek (172,13-17): 'but if Mercury prevails over Jupiter, their livelihood will not be without means, but by disorder they accomplish many contrary things, and they turn the good things into bad things; and although others want to receive [benefits], these are not wanting to receive [them], and they avoid the good things happening spontaneously to them, and they are ungrateful for kindnesses'.

[3]Greek (172,30-32): 'and it will give action and livelihood to his mother and to him, and he will be superior to his own kindred on account of his honored status, and established in precedence among the people, having a great name and much fame in the city'.

over all their relatives; and it always makes him posited <in the highest> degree <of dignity>,[1] known to the people by fame, and he will always be adorned with an outstanding testimony of fame.

11. But if the Moon, made superior and possessing the dexter side, aspects Jupiter posited in the lower place with a square aspect,[2] that configuration bestows many insignia of good fortune. But it also denotes recommendations and fame, and it always makes them known to powerful men and kings with a fortunate recommendation. But this same good fortune does not last through all <time>.[3] For at some time it denotes losses of personal wealth and impairments of honor, and it lessens the insignia of dignity, and it will make them, oppressed by a sluggish listlessness of mind, to be withdrawn from the administration of the preceding business affairs.

XI.

1. **Mars and the Sun in Square.** If Mars and the Sun are conjoined in square aspect, and Mars, possessing the superior part of a dexter square, makes a menacing aspect to the Sun posited to its left, this configuration omits no single occurrence of the misfortunes, and it always impugns all opportunities for advancement and the series of promotions with a malignant arrangement of decree.[4]

2. But if the Sun, made superior and possessing the dexter side, aspects Mars posited in the lower place by a square aspect, a miserable demise is prepared for both the father, and for him who was born with this configuration, a heap of misfortunes is [also] inflicted, and various inconveniences of calamities are denoted; it stirs up insurrections, it indicates fights, it arouses dangers to be feared of public punishment.

3. But it always disturbs[5] both the sound foundations of mind and

---

[1]Adds Ziegler to fill an evident lacuna.

[2]Greek (172,32-35): 'but if the Moon prevails over Jupiter, it signifies honor and association with leading persons; however, with the passage of time, some things are diminished, and it will bring inaction at some time'.

[3]Adds **N**.

[4]Greek (172,31-34): 'and if the Sun prevails over Mars, it is destructive for him and for his father, for it brings about very many accidents, and it snatches away property'.

[5]Reading **exagitat* 'disturbs' (suggested by Kroll and Ziegler) for the *ex*... of the MSS.

counsels;[1] ...of others[2]; and it indicates the miserable burden of blindness in the eyes. But this series of dangers is aroused more strongly in a diurnal nativity, especially if that configuration was conjoined to the ASC by a menacing aspect, or if Mars, posited in the DSC or possessing the MC degree, or posited in any other angle, receives the light of the waxing Moon.

4. Then with miserable dismemberments they destroy those prostrated by a public punishment; then, with the limbs torn apart, the honor of burial that is due is denied by public punishment, so that the greater calamity of the demise is increased after death by a continuing danger. But also in a nocturnal nativity these same things are carried out in a similar order of procedure.

5. **Mars and Venus in Square.** If Mars and Venus are conjoined in square aspect, and Mars, possessing the superior part of the dexter square, makes a menacing aspect to Venus posited in the sinister square, that configuration denotes all [kinds of] evils. Then it indicates quarrels and dangers to be feared from accusation; then dangers that have arisen because of women strike the man.[3] But if this configuration is in tropical signs,[4] then all the impurity of indecency grows stronger in the effeminate bodies of men; then men experience the ardors of feminine lusts; then they are dishonored with the wreck of disgrace and judgment by the stigmas of an unchaste indecency.

6. But they even compel their own wives to enter into adulteries, and they abandon them to the embraces of strangers with the submission of prostituted decency, and they cause matrimony coupled with bad auspices to serve the lusts of strangers with a miserable necessity of calamity, or, lying hid in the mind of a pimp, they freely allow the adultery of the wife. And if <this was in the nativity> of women,[5] they always toler-

---

[1]Greek (172,34-35): 'and it causes mental derangement for those, of whom it also has destroyed the eyes; and worse in a diurnal nativity'.

[2]I would put the comma after *aliorum* (Teubner II. 93,11) to make it the last word of the lacuna, rather than the first word in the following clause.

[3]Greek (175,4): 'it signifies disputes, fights, and losses because of women'.

[4]Greek (175,5-7): 'and if they are in tropical signs, a homosexual; he will be a passive sodomite, effeminate, experiencing unnatural lust ... they cooperate in the adulteries of their wives, or, knowing about it, they will tolerate it'.

[5]Adds Ziegler. Greek (175,7-9): 'and if it is the nativity of a woman, she similarly allows many sorrowful situations in which she has intercourse with strangers other than with her husband.

ate that perverse[1] compulsion of a prostituted body with a bitter mental pain.

7. But if Venus, made superior and possessing the dexter side, aspects Mars posited in the inferior place with a square aspect,[2] it denotes those same things in similar fashion. But those who have Venus thus exercise their own crime secretly, so that infamous dealings of prostituted decency are shielded by concealed impurities of lusts, so that with a bad conscience they hide whatever was demanded by the depraved desires of the mind, especially if Jupiter aspects any one of these by trine or is with them.

8. **Mars and Mercury in Square.** If Mars and Mercury are conjoined in square aspect, and Mars, possessing the superior part of the dexter square, aspects Mercury posited in the sinister square, that configuration denotes fearful outcomes of all evils;[3] it always weakens a man with an injurious succession of pains; and it always opposes all his actions with various contrarieties, and it will always make these same to be known by malign rumors; and it arouses fearful dangers of bitter accusations, so that from the calamities of these dangers they are either placed in custody or in prison. But these evils gather strength in a diurnal nativity, but in a nocturnal one they are somewhat mitigated.[4]

9. But if Mercury, made superior and possessing the dexter side, aspects Mars posited in the lower place with a square aspect, that configuration will produce evil, malign, and malicious persons, always equipped with a very bad and pestiferous mental desire, practicing all the functions of frauds, greedy persons, and those who feed upon the things of others with a fickle mental desire, and those who pass from one man to another, always seeking with a careful plan[5] someone on whom they inflict the wound of a pestiferous bite,[6] so that caught[7] in their nefarious contrivances and left in

---

[1]Accepting Ziegler's suggestion of *perversam* 'perverse' for *per virum* 'by a man'.

[2]Greek (175,9-10): 'but if Venus prevails over Mars, it makes the same things, but more stealthily and not visible'.

[3]Greek (175,17-18): 'the cause of many terrible things, causing anguish and the actions of hindrances, producing slanders and accusations'.

[4]Greek (175,18-19): 'and more by day, but less by night'.

[5]Accepting Ziegler's emendation *cogitatione* 'plan'.

[6]The word 'bite' is to be understood as in the English expression 'to put the bite on someone'.

[7]Accepting Ziegler's emendation of *captivi* 'captured' for *destituti* 'left in the lurch', which is repeated at the end of the clause.

the lurch by clever frauds, those whom an injurious dishonesty always arms for their advantage, stripped bare by malignant frauds, they allow the entire substance of their own personal wealth to pass away.

10. **Mars and the Moon in Square.** If Mars and the Moon are conjoined in square aspect, and Mars, possessing the superior part of the dexter square, aspects the Moon posited in the sinister square with a menacing aspects, that conjunction indicates the bitter burden of widowhood for the mother,[1] and it kills that same woman with the forces of infirmity, or with a flux of blood, or with the atrocities of a miserable death; but it will make those who are born thus to be involved with the bitter incursions of spirits, so that the mind, possessed by the power of a malignant spirit, bestows the power on a spirit ruling in the body,

11. Especially if Mars is found in the terms of Saturn, and the Moon is either in the terms of Mercury or in the terms of Mars—for frequently the badness of the preceding evil is mitigated by the terms of the benefic stars.[2] But when such persons are possessed by the calamities of misfortunes, seeking to escape from these perils of incursions, they flee to the beneficial aid of some deity, so that they may thus be freed from the peril of this danger.

12. But if the Moon, made superior and possessing the dexter side, aspects Mars posited in the lower place by a square aspect, that configuration makes the mother to be of an ignoble and lower-class family,[3] but it also always indicates straitened circumstances arising from miserable neediness. Fate also ruins the life, and personal property; and among these misfortunes, along with an increase of hard luck, it also denotes bad wives.

---

[1]Greek (175,30-35): 'it surrounds the mother with poverty ... and it kills the mothers of some with bloodshed or a miserable death; but those suffering from madness take refuge in temples, and more so when Mars is in the terms of Saturn, and the Moon in the terms of Mars or Mercury, for many times the power of the terms either intensifies or slackens (the indication)'.

[2]The Teubner editors think that either Firmicus was confused when he wrote this clause or else some words have dropped out of the text. However, Firmicus's thought may have been that while positions in the terms of Saturn, Mercury, or Mars would make the bad indication worse, positions in the terms of the benefic stars would mitigate the evil. This does not disagree with the Greek text.

[3]Greek (179,32-33): 'shame for the mother and neediness in livelihood, but in it there are errors and the destruction of good fortune.

XII.

1. **The Sun and the Moon in Square.** If the Sun and the Moon are conjoined in square aspect, possessing either the dexter or the sinister sides in angles, they are allotted power from the testimonies of the other stars in the decrees for men. For when an aspect of the benefic stars is made to this configuration,[1] <from the power>[2] of that association the greatest actions, a sufficient standard of life, and the insignia of a famous dignity are all conferred [upon them] by favorable recommendations.

2. But if the malefic stars make a malign aspect to that configuration of the Sun and the Moon without the protection of the benefics,[3] the greatest dangers to life and the greatest inconveniences from misfortunes are denoted. But if with the aspects of the malefic stars added thus,[4] the Moon full of light applies to Jupiter, and Jupiter receives the conjunction of the waxing Moon, it denotes the insignia of nobility along with the greatest envy. But if the protections of the preceding conjunction with Jupiter are denied, the injurious badness of the malefic stars is strongly increased.

XIII.

1. **Venus and Mercury in Square.** If Venus and Mercury are conjoined in square aspect, regardless of which one of them possesses the dexter square,[5] they denote everything in the same equal fashion. For this

---

[1]Greek (176,30): 'being aspected by Jupiter, they are they cause of actions, fame, and association'.

[2]Adds Brakman.

[3]Greek (176,31-32) : 'but aspected by the malefics, dangerous for both their livelihood and for their life itself.

[4]Greek (176,32-34): 'but if aspected by the malefics, and the Moon is applying to Jupiter, [they are] famous, but slandered'.

[5]Modern astrologers would consider that Venus and Mercury cannot ever be in square aspect because Venus can only be a maximum of 48° from the Sun, and Mercury can only be a maximum of 28° from the Sun, the total of which is 76° for their maximum mutual distance. However, the classical astrologers reckoned aspects by the signs inhabited by the planets, not by their distance in degrees; and it is possible for the two planets to be in signs that are in square aspect to each other. For example, suppose that Venus is in 21 Aries and Mercury is in 7 Cancer. Modern astrologers would say they are not in aspect, but the classical astrologers would say that they are in square.

configuration denotes distinguished occupations in some pleasing art,[1] or the teaching of some great doctrine is set forth by this configuration, so that from the performance of that instruction they acquire fame of distinguished association. Malignant talk spreads ill-fame about them because of their love affairs with women.

2. **Venus and the Moon in Square.** If Venus and the Moon are conjoined in square aspect, and the Moon, possessing the superior part of the dexter square, aspects Venus posited in the sinister square with a menacing aspect, that configuration denotes the greatest amounts of riches.[2] But it always afflicts men with various kinds of losses because of women, or it always imposes the harm of ill-fame.

3. But if Venus, made superior and possessing the dexter side, aspects the Moon posited in the lower location with a square aspect, it always increases the greatest good fortune with favorable increases,[3] and it denotes better things than the preceding advantages, and that configuration enhances both actions and life with honorable association, and it preserves intact the love of their wives for them, and it denotes pure and honest affections of the spouses; it also denotes full advantages of joy, and the insignia of famous art, and the order of honorable association, and the grace of pleasant speech with the greatest good fortune. But nevertheless, these same persons desire sexual relations with others [driven by] an impatient desire. It also bestows the honest reputation of chastity on their mothers. But these Natives are allotted obedient wives who were emancipated from slavery by others.

XIV.

1. **The Moon and Mercury in Square.** If the Moon and Mercury are conjoined in square aspect, and Mercury possessing the superior part of the dexter square, aspects the Moon posited in the sinister square with a menacing aspect, from this configuration there is denoted a person distinguished for his knowledge and for his learned abundance of utterance with honorable speech. But danger is frequently brought to these persons by an uprising of the people.

[1]Greek (177,30-32): 'refined, skilled in an art or in teaching, and being known because of these; however, being blamed in connection with sexual acts'.

[2]Greek (179,34-35): 'on the one hand it will give prosperity, but on the other it always brings harm to men from female persons, and it brings blame upon them'.

[3]Greek (178,1-2): 'it will give good things on top of good things, and action, and a good fashion of livelihood.

2. But if a malefic star, made superior, aspects Mercury posited thus with a square aspect, so that in fact it aspects the Moon by opposition, but it aspects Mercury by square, it inflicts the fearful crime of falsification,[1] and it makes those who are detected in this crime to be either placed in custody or to be thrown into prison, or else they suffer chains and exile by the censure of a public sentence.

3. But if the Moon, made superior and possessing the dexter side, aspects Mercury posited in the lower place by a square aspect, this configuration will make unstable, light-minded persons,[2] and it turns their plans crossways here and there with varied thoughts, and their mind is never changed by reason[3] of a single plan.

4. The square aspect denotes these things in the nativities of men, [and] the authority of the Fates produces these judgments from the square aspects every day. Which judgments you ought to inspect carefully in every examination [of a nativity], especially since these same, squared with an unchanged order of the stars, may also make the decrees of the determinations to be changed.

5. But, having explained these, I shall [next] explain the efficacies of the oppositions. Moreover, we have stated very clearly in the Book of Principles which are the *dexter* squares and which are the *sinister* ones.

XV.

1. **Saturn and Jupiter in Opposition.** The opposition aspect always attacks itself with contrary power, and it stands against itself with an inimical kind of relation; and it, therefore—just like the square—is a menacing aspect.

2. Whence, if Saturn and Jupiter aspect each other by opposition, and posited in opposite houses they strike each other in turn with the distant power of their own forces, that configuration denotes many unfortunate

---

[1]Falsification, which included forged documents, altered wills, and counterfeiting, was a capital crime under Roman law.

[2]Greek (180,1-3): 'light-minded in their plans, thinking of nothing steadfast, and therefore those who like something, [but] wherever they may be liking it, they whirl them around'.

[3]Accepting Ziegler's emendation *ratione mutatur* 'by reason it is changed' for the *rationem utatur* of the MSS.

outcomes in all their actions, and it always indicates bitter torments of sorrow from accidents to their children.

3. But if Saturn is angular, posited in the ASC degree,[1] and Jupiter posited in the DSC aspects it by opposition, after grave misfortunes in youth, in the last time of old age tardy advantages of good fortune are conferred [on them].

4. **Saturn and Mars in Opposition.** If Saturn and Mars aspect each other by opposition, and posited in opposite houses, they strike each other with the distant power of their own forces,[2] that aspect denotes the inconveniences of very serious dangers and many anxieties. For it will make them to be involved in many and evil contrarieties; but it will also make them to be struck by the bitter disgrace of scandal; and it indicates the miserable wants of neediness; and it will make the body to be worn out by a continual series of illnesses and a continual series of toils.

5. For it always imposes grave dangers to life, and it frequently shows the image of a fearful death; and it denotes attacks resulting from quarrels among members of the household, and it stirs up frequent storms of terrifying insurrections. It also denies the offspring of children; and it will make the father to be struck down quickly by death; and it perpetuates toils on top of toils.

6. But if Saturn and Mars posited in water signs aspect each other by opposition[3] just as we have said, then the raging disturbance of the waves exposes submerged shipwrecked persons to violent winds and severe storms,[4] or it will make them while submerged in the waves of rushing floods to be involved in [an even] graver series of dangers; or a disease compounded of malignant humors[5] indicates strong and perpetual calamities of illnesses.

---

[1]Greek (164,26-28): 'and if Saturn is in the ASC, and Jupiter is in the DSC, the first [times] of life are unlucky, but the last [times] are lucky'.

[2]*Cf.* Paragraphs 4 and 5 with the Greek (165,17-20): 'it opposes the acquisition of livelihood'. 'The configuration shows jealousies and want and bodily mistreatment and dangers to life and childlessness, enmity in the household, the swift death of the father, miseries on top of miseries, and certainly hardships on top of hardships'.

[3]If Saturn and Mars are in opposition, they cannot both be in water signs. Perhaps we should read 'If Saturn and Mars are in opposition and either of them is in a water sign…'

[4]Greek (175,20-21): 'and in water signs, shipwreck and dangers from rivers or from floods'.

[5]Cf. iv.8.35, where malignant humors are said to be the cause of death.

7. But if one of the two, either Mars or Saturn, posited in a feral sign aspects the other by opposition,[1] it brings the miserable likelihood of danger from quadrupeds, or from a wound by a wild animal, or by a beast. Or a poisonous potion ingested into the innards of others denotes a bitter demise of death from a lamentable calamity.

8. But if posited in quadrupedal signs,[2] or if one of them is found in a quadrupedal sign aspecting the other by opposition, along with those evils that we have stated to be produced by the preceding definitions, [then] crushed down by the heavy weight of ruins, and worn down by the injury of a damaged body, they either die or they are made to undergo dangers close to death.

9. But all these misfortunes are then increased by a strong heap of calamity, when Jupiter does not mitigate them posited thus with any aspect. For if possessing the angles of the nativity, the Moon posited in any angle aspects them with that same aspect or by square, then this configuration denotes more serious dangers—then fugitive wanderings, then exiles and public deaths;[3] then, robbed of the honor of freedom, they impose the yoke of slavery [on them].

10. But if posited in the 5th or in the 11th house from the ASC,[4] or in the 9th or in the 3rd, they aspect each other by opposition, they extinguish all hope of a favorable good fortune, and, having fallen into a low position, they denote an end[5] of miserable degradation. But these misfortunes grow stronger in the middle time of life.[6]

11. But if posited in dejected and sluggish houses[7] they aspect each other by opposition, they will certainly do less harm; but from that configuration they denote sorrows and the inconveniences of a miserable poverty. But all of these fearful dangers are mitigated by the fortunate

---

[1]Greek (165,21-22): 'and in feral [signs], damage and danger from wild animals or from drinking poison'.

[2]Greek (165,22-23): ' and in quadrupedal [signs], disasters from similar [creatures], and stronger when they are the Moon's rulers'.

[3]Greek (165,24): 'and in the angles they kill'.

[4]Greek (165,24-25): 'but in the *epanaphoras* they snatch away good hopes'.

[5]Reading *exitum* 'end' with **Ψ** rather than *exitium* 'destruction' with the Teubner editors.

[6]Greek (165,25-26): 'and in the middle times [of life] they bring destruction'.

[7]Greek (165,26-29): 'but in the cadents they harm less, and yet they cause sorrows and banishment; but they also make some to be living abroad, or [to be] freed slaves when they are angular in the opposition aspect; for they are the authors of great dangers when they are opposing each other'.

testimonies of Venus and Jupiter, and the malice of the malefic stars is blunted by the fortunate testimony of a beneficial God,[1] and the menacing ends of the preceding dangers are dissolved.

12. **Saturn and the Sun in Opposition.** If Saturn and the Sun aspect each other by opposition, and posited in opposite houses they strike each other in turn with the distant power of their own forces,[2] and if the beneficent star of Jupiter does not aspect them from any part [of the chart], they will either make the father to be entwined in difficult financial straits; or they certainly impose the burden of a difficult life on the Natives themselves; or they denote the restrictions of poverty along with some tenacity. On others they inflict the danger of a bitter illness.

13. But also if they have any reserves of wealth, either those perish with them while they are still surviving,[3] or their reserves are destroyed with miserable losses after the [Native's] death. But also ending by a bad death is denoted by this configuration, and the whole substance of the Native's life is shattered by a varied and evil series of labors.[4] But the badness of these evils is strongly increased if they make that aspect when they are posited in feminine signs.

14. **Saturn and Venus in Opposition.** If Saturn and Venus aspect each other by opposition, and posited in opposite houses, they strike each other in turn with the distant power of their own forces, they make men addicted to whorehouses and who regularly resort to whores, [driven] by indiscriminate lustful desires,[5] so that because of this they are battered with severe notorious disgrace.

15. They will also make them to be kept from the bonds of matrimony because of their lusts; but also, if matrimony is decreed for them from some other feature of the nativity,[6] it bestows a wife with a loss of her

---

[1]By 'God' Firmicus means 'star'.

[2]Greek (166,12-13): 'with Jupiter not being in aspect, the father is ill and stingy or injured.

[3]Greek (166,13-15): 'and he is also extravagant with his abundance and causing [it] to disappear, and they destroy the remaining property; or he will also die a bad death'.

[4]Greek (166,15-16): 'and for the Native, unending toil, and especially in a feminine sign'.

[5]Greek (166,27): 'those fond of whores and indecent persons, and those without wives'.

[6]Greek: (167,27-29)'those marrying common and wanton women or injured women or slaves'.

own sense of honor; or certainly a wife is denoted for them, whom it always stains with the miserable contamination of pestilential vice; or she will be a wife dishonored by the squalor of common slavery, or she always associates with slaves with the pleasure of prostituted decency. But also all enjoyment of sexual pleasure is denied to them.[1]

16. **Saturn and Mercury in Opposition.** If Saturn and Mercury aspect each other by opposition, and posited in opposite houses they strike each other by the distant power of their own forces, placed thus they impede the tongue with a slow sound of the voice,[2] so that in those jaws with slow efforts the impeded words fail; or the words are confused by a tongue-tied condition.

17. But these evils are more strongly strengthened if Saturn aspects Mercury posited in a mute sign,[3] or if Mercury hidden by the rays of the Sun[4] is struck by an opposition aspect from Saturn. But also, if Saturn makes an opposition aspect to the Moon conjoined in that same configuration with Mercury, those things that we have said are more strongly strengthened, unless the testimony of Mars—provided in any way—dissolves the disadvantage of the preceding evil.[5] For, with the other [stars] that we have mentioned being without the testimony of Mars, a deadly weight of distress is indicated.

18. But along with these evils, the learning of wisdom of the mind is denoted, and the skilled mastery of applications is conferred. But they are always intent upon the ineffectual study of their own art; and they always roughen up their countenance with the sadness of austerity; and they are supported by a lofty spirit of arrogance. But these same persons generate various concerns[6] of anxieties every day, and with the passage of time they are preferred to their own brothers.[7] For whichever older brothers

---

[1]Greek: (167,29)'and those free from pleasures'.

[2]Greek (167,5-6): 'those slow in speech and having difficulty [reading *dysekphoron*] in talking, or those who stammer'.

[3]The mute signs are Cancer, Scorpio, and Pisces.

[4]Greek (167,6-8): 'and especially with Mercury being under the Sun beams or in a mute sign; and especially worse if, in the presence of these, the Moon is also conjoined to Mercury or to Saturn'.

[5]Greek (167,12-15): 'nevertheless, with Mars aspecting [them], the distress is dissolved, and they will be miserable and intelligent and learned, but not being aided or winning anything because of that, but always hated and deceitful'.

[6]Reading **curas* 'concerns' rather than †*audias*, and keeping *generant* 'they generate'.

[7]Greek (167,15-16): 'as many times they are also superior to their brothers; and

there were, they are separated from them either by their departure by death or by long journeys. But it also kills their mothers at an early age.[1]

19. **Saturn and the Moon in Opposition.** If Saturn and the Moon are in aspect by opposition, and posited in opposite houses they strike each other in turn by the long power of their own aspects, they will first certainly destroy the substance of the maternal wealth,[2] but they also weaken the mother herself by a varied continuation of sorrows and hidden illnesses, or they also involve her in a perverse sadness of mind.[3]

20. But if the ray of benefic stars departs from these, and if they are devoid of all testimony of the benefic stars, then a dishonorable foulness of body disgraces the mother, and damages shatter her with constant attacks. But a varied series of dangers always rises up against them.[4] But Saturn and the Moon denote these in accordance with the variety of the signs.

21. For if one of them posited in quadrupedal signs aspects the other by opposition, the crisis of danger is brought about by animals of that sort.[5] But if posited in the signs of wild beasts they aspect each other, an incident of the greatest danger is brought about from wild animals, or from beasts, or from the venomous bites of serpents. But if the opposition that we have mentioned was in human signs, an incident of calamity will rise up from the plots of various men.

22. But if posited in watery signs they make their aspect with a sturdy opposition,[6] the miserable danger of pestilence either from inundations of water, or from malign humors is brought forward; and if help from the benefic stars has not broken the power of the menacing aspect, the whole form of the body is altered[7] by the calamity of a vicious illness; or the

---

if some are brought forth earlier, they will perish [or 'be killed']'.

[1]Greek (167,16-17): 'and the father dies before the mother'. Should we then read *patres* 'fathers' in the Latin rather than *matres* 'mothers'?

[2]Greek (167,28-31): 'it destroys the maternal property, and it gives secret pains to the mother herself, or she will be surly and distressed; but if a benefic does not aspect [it], the configuration is terrible for the bodily parts'.

[3]Accepting Ziegler's conjecture *perversa animi* for the *perversorum* of the MSS.

[4]Greek: (167,31)' for it signifies danger according to the nature of the zodiacal signs'.

[5]Greek (167,31-32): 'if in quadrupedal [signs], from quadrupeds; but if in feral [signs] from that kind [of creature]'.

[6]Greek (167,33-34): 'and if in water [signs], from waters or from bad humors; but if there is no help, he is also injured'.

[7]Greek (167,34-35): 'and their limbs are broken'.

clear light of their eyes is obscured by the shadows of a miserable blindness.[1] They compel others with [Saturn and the Moon] posited thus to forsake their native land because of some necessity.[2]

XVI.

1. **Jupiter and Mars in Opposition.** If Jupiter and Mars aspect each other by opposition, and posited in opposite houses they strike each other in turn by the long power of their own aspects, they denote an entire unevenness of life and repeated losses to the personal wealth.[3] But also from this aspect hatred is aroused against them with repeated offenses by all of their friends; and the greatest series of dangers is caused either by boisterous associations or by rash actions.

2. **Jupiter and the Sun in Opposition.** If Jupiter and the Sun aspect each other by opposition, and posited in opposite houses they strike each other in turn by the long power of their own aspects, they make the paternal wealth to be dissipated by miserable losses;[4] but also, all the life and assets and the status of past dignity are reduced by miserable reductions of honors, so that persons of inferior rank are always preferred to them[5] with the authority of power. But these things are diminished in a diurnal nativity, [while] in a nocturnal one they grow stronger.

3. **Jupiter and Venus in Opposition.** If Jupiter and Venus aspect each other by opposition, and posited in opposite houses they strike each other in turn by the long power of their own aspects, this configuration opposes all courses of advancement and every wish for promotion.[6]

4. But it does not ever denote faithful affections of friends,[7] but instead the friends act against them with crafty and treacherous plans, and they are not ever willing to speak to them with true talk, but they are always

---

[1]Greek (167,34): 'for their eyes are darkened'.

[2]Greek: (167,35) 'and some are driven out of their native land'.

[3]Greek: (171,12-13) 'it makes inequality and a scattering of personal assets; and it makes the friends into enemies… it signifies distress from rashness and also from confusion of thoughts.

[4]Greek (171,25): 'destructive of the father's personal wealth'.

[5]Greek (171,26)'and the Native will be subordinated to a lesser man'.

[6]Greek (171,36): 'not good for the advancements'.

[7]Greek: (171,37) 'but no friend is true to them'.

trying to deceive them with deceptive dissimulations[1]—doing something with malicious intent, and saying something else with feigned goodness of speech. But also the friends, incited by serious indignations from quarrels, rise up against them with various kinds of dissension; and on whomever they confer any kindness of favors, immediately those same persons rise up against them with serious dissensions of enmities; and on whomever they confer anything out of their own generosity, contrary favors are always repaid to them by those persons.[2]

5. They will, however, have the greatest increases of good fortune in those things. They will also possess a sufficient amount of wealth.[3] But if Jupiter is found in the terms of Venus, they will always have favorable results for their desires, but in fact they never persist in stable affections for marriage.[4]

6. **Jupiter and Mercury in Opposition.** If Jupiter and Mercury aspect each other by opposition, and posited in opposite houses they strike each other in turn by the long power of their own aspects, that configuration attacks those who have acquired training in learned speech. But it also incites fearful insurrections of the people; and it frequently indicates strife due to popular indignation;[5] and it will always make [them] to be made known badly to more powerful men or to kings by the partisanships of envious persons. But it also frequently shows the sharply-felt deaths of brothers, or it dissociates the Natives from fraternal affections by a severe quarrel, and when a connection of blood joins them together, they fight hard against each other in a parricidal quarrel arising from [personal] hatreds.[6]

7. **Jupiter and the Moon in Opposition.** If Jupiter and the Moon aspect each other by opposition, and posited in opposite houses they strike each other in turn by the long power of their own aspects, and the Moon is

[1]Greek (171,37-172,1): 'saying something, but contriving something else secretly, from which they will also have insurrection'.

[2]Greek (172,1): 'and they receive bad compensation from them'.

[3]Greek (172,2-3): 'but in other actions they will be fortunate, and they will have a sufficient income'.

[4]Greek (172,3-4): 'and they are unstable in legitimate marriages, but successful in sexual relationships with other persons'.

[5]Greek (172,18-19): 'bad for those studying speech, for it signifies uprisings and the wrath of the people.

[6]Greek (172,20-21): 'and the death of brothers and punishments and condemnations against kinsmen'

full of light,[1] and the Moon's number of degrees precedes Jupiter's degrees,[2] this aspect denotes the principal insignia of dignity and it ennobles their life with a famous power.[3]

8. But it also denotes all the ornaments of power, and it makes the sort of person who can never submit to the power of others, and who always resists the powers of others with the grace of virtue and firmness of mind. But if the Moon has little light, none of the preceding good things are denoted, but instead the greatest ruins of misfortunes. But these evils grow even stronger if it was a nocturnal nativity.

XVII.

1. **Mars and the Sun in Opposition.** If Mars and the Sun aspect each other by opposition, and posited in opposite houses they strike each other in turn by the long power of their own aspects, and it is a diurnal nativity, that aspect prostrates the father with a miserable atrocity of death, or it always blinds the lights of the eyes with some grave illness.[4] But it makes the Natives themselves to be cast down from high places with miserable injury; or it always brings on some serious danger unexpectedly; and it makes all their actions to be obstructed by serious oppositions.[5] But if it is a nocturnal nativity,[6] with weakened powers it debilitates all their assets with an exhausted weakness of body, and with their wealth tattered and dissipated it imposes the poverty of beggary.

2. **Mars and Venus in Opposition.** If Mars and Venus aspect each other by opposition, and posited in opposite houses they strike each other in turn by the long power of their own aspects, and it is a diurnal nativity, they will always make [the Natives] to be entangled in wavering moral failings,[7] but they also denote the inconveniences of illnesses in an inces-

---

[1]Greek(173,1) 'the Moon increasing in light'.

[2]Greek (173,3-4): 'and especially when the Moon prevails over Jupiter, being of more degrees' But this would seem to mean 'when the Moon is separating from Jupiter'.

[3]Greek(173,2-3) 'for he will be commanding and an imperious person in his manners and not like any other.'

[4]Greek (174,36): 'destructive of the father or it also injures the eyesight'.

[5]Greek (174,37): 'danger to him from high places, and many oppositions'.

[6]Greek (174,37-38): 'and these things [it signifies] by day, but by night weakness and decline in income'.

[7]Greek (175,11): 'unsettled and wandering about'.

sant manner. But Venus and Mars posited thus always oppose marriage and children with an envious clash.[1] But if they aspect each other by opposition when they are posited in tropical signs, they denote those things that we have said above that they denote by square,[2] especially if they strike each other with that aspect from Capricorn and from Cancer, and if Jupiter does not furnish any testimony to them.

3. **Mars and Mercury in Opposition.** If Mars and Mercury aspect each other by opposition, and posited in opposite houses they strike each other in turn by the long power of their own aspects, that configuration denotes the greatest of misfortunes and the greatest destructions of calamity.[3] Or, from having altered the faith of tables and documents, those who have Mars and Mercury thus, incur the crime of falsification. Or by the association of an evil conscience they are joined to all crimes;[4] or they join a group of criminal life with evildoers and poisoners. Or, always burdened down by the heavy interest of debts, with the loss of honor, they are forcibly brought to public justice.

4. Or possessed by a depraved ardor of greed, [and] polluting the religious dealings of trust, they try to refuse to hand over things deposited or entrusted [to them], so that from that perfidy or from the preceding crimes, the danger of a public sentence rises up against them,[5] and, subject to the judicial powers, they are disturbed by the threatening terror of cases [brought against them]. Others, excited by the terrors of the preceding crimes, and worn down by the burdens of an evil conscience, are separated <from their own native land by fugitive>[6] errors, especially if Mercury was

[1]Greek (175,11-12): 'and Venus [is] envious (or, malicious) both in marriage and in children'. The Latin has *invido stridore*, where the word *stridor* normally indicates some sort of annoying *noise* (cf. Matthew 8.12 *stridor dentium* 'gnashing of teeth'), but Firmicus seems to use *stridor* both here and elsewhere to mean simply a disturbance, disagreement, or clash. We should perhaps translate the sentence "But Venus and Mars, posited thus with a hostile clash, always oppose marriage and children."

[2]Greek (175,12-13): 'and if they are also in tropical signs, it makes the same things as the squares'.

[3]Here, and for several lines following a shorter form of the text is also found added to iii.7.20 by MS **N**.

[4]Greek (175,20-22): 'it makes forgers and those with group knowledge of poisoners, becoming involved in securities and debts, wherefore many times they say, they no longer care for the honesty of judicial proceedings'.

[5]Greek (175,22-23): 'and because of these they are brought to trial by judges, and they endure fears'.

[6]Adds Ziegler to fill a lacuna.

found in the terms of Saturn, or if it was in a domicile of Saturn in a diurnal nativity, and Jupiter does not aspect any one of them by trine.[1]

5. **Mars and the Moon in Opposition.** If Mars and the Moon aspect each other by opposition, and posited in opposite houses they strike each other in turn by the long power of their own aspects, they will either make short-lived persons, or persons pursued by an oppressive succession of dangers;[2] or they do not denote marriage, or if marriage is decreed by the support of other stars, they will destroy the wives that are given to them by miserable atrocities of death.[3] But they will also kill the Natives themselves with an evil demise of death, or they throw them down with a public punishment,[4] especially if the Moon is full of light.

XVIII.

1. **The Sun and the Moon in Opposition.** If the Sun and the Moon aspect each other by opposition, and posited in opposite houses they strike each other in turn by the long power of their own aspects, they make the life and status of the man, and the rank of his wealth, and all the insignia of his dignity to be altered in various ways. For then, having acquired riches, both the burden of poverty is brought [to him], and [then] the inconveniences of poverty are again relaxed by the consolations of other riches. They also make the blemishes of an unsightly illness on his face, but they also weaken his body with miserable contractions.[5]

XIX.

1. **Venus and the Moon in Opposition.** If Venus and the Moon aspect each other by opposition, and posited in opposite houses they strike each other in turn by the long power of their own aspects, unhappy marriages are denoted by this aspect;[6] but posited thus they do not experience being

---

[1]Greek (175,23-25): 'and these are also excluded from their own country, and especially if they are in the terms of Saturn or in their own terms, or in Mercury's own signs'.

[2]Greek (176,1): 'it makes short-lived persons, and they give frequent dangers'.

[3]Greek (176,2): 'for they are unmarried, and they bury the wives'.

[4]Greek (176,2-4): 'and there is a bad end for them, for it makes madness and the cutting off of bodily parts, or imprisonment'.

[5]The Greek text does not contain any significations for this aspect.

[6]Greek (178,5): 'not good for marriage'.

raised up by any class of good fortune—either they never give children, or they destroy any offspring that are born by a miserable death.[1] But they themselves experience frequent evils and many injuries from their wives.[2]

XX.

1. **Mercury and the Moon in Opposition.** If Mercury and the Moon are in opposition, and posited in contrary houses they strike each other mutually with the long power of their rays, they arouse the attack of a maddened multitude and of popular sedition [and] bloody crises, so that a malign voice of the people always pursues them in a public gathering.[3] But they also indicate a dejected consternation of fear in their mind and words.[4]

XXI.

1. **Sextiles.** When the stars are in sextile aspect, they denote those things that they are said to denote from a trine aspect. But the effect of their decrees is diminished to some degree, and, set apart with feeble powers, the aspect composes its own efficacy with lesser power in all nativities. But it is proper for you to remember this—that sextiles are sluggish in their powers if they are divided by tropical or duplex signs, but that they are [entirely] ineffective when a fixed sign intervenes[5]

XXII.

1. **Those that are in Conjunction.** In order that we may make known to you in general terms, my dear Mavortius, the whole efficacies of the mixtures, since we have cleared up the mixtures of the trines together

---

[1]Greek (178,7-8): 'and it signifies childlessness, for if children are born, they are killed'.

[2]Greek (178,8-9): 'and they are maltreated by [their] women, and they suffer dangers [from them]'.

[3]Greek (179,21-22): 'from uprisings of the people it stirs up both disorders and loud cries'.

[4]Greek (179,22): 'and he says that they are faint-hearted and discouraged'.

[5]In other words, a sextile from Pisces to Taurus or from Gemini to Leo or from Virgo to Scorpio or from Sagittarius to Aquarius is weakly effective (as compared to a trine aspect). But a sextile from Aries to Gemini or from Cancer to Virgo or from Libra to Sagittarius or from Capricorn to Pisces is ineffective.

with the squares, and since we have explained in particular all the aspects of the oppositions, we shall now designate the conjoined associations of the stars in a clear exposition of discussion, so that, having shown all the composition of the mixtures, we may come to the specific decrees of the astrological influences.

2. **Saturn and Jupiter in Conjunction.** If Saturn and Jupiter received a single lodging of degree, and posited together in one house they are joined together in equal power of association, [and] if they are in fortunate houses of the nativity and in those signs or degrees in which they rejoice, conjoined by that aspect of association, [then] by that association they denote the insignia of good fortune, increases in wealth, advantages of fame, uncorrupted supports of virtue,[1] and fortunate offspring of children—especially if it is a diurnal nativity.

3. For then they impose the greatest actions, the duties of procuration,[2] then wealth from the assets of another. But if from a higher house Mars strikes them posited thus with a menacing aspect, everything that we have said is altered by the hostile aspect of Mars.[3]

4. **Saturn and Mars in Conjunction.** If Saturn and Mars received a single lodging of degree, and posited together in the same house they are joined together in equal power of association, if this conjunction was in fortunate houses of the nativity, it composes the morals of men with an equal moderation of seriousness, and it moderates all the passions of mind with mild compromises.

5. For the ill-advised rashness and the unruliness of passion of Mars, and its impatient rashness of inflamed heat, is tempered by the cold of Saturn conjoined to itself, and the fires having been diminished which the nature of its own heat arouses, it borrows seriousness for molding the behavior of men from the association of cold joined to itself, so that the heat of Mars for molding behavior is always blunted by the sluggish cold of Saturn. And so, when the heat of Mars has warmed the chill of Saturn, and when the conjoined chill of Saturn has extinguished Mars's flames, from that moderation of composition the perfected ornaments of seriousness take hold of the behavior of men.

[1]Greek (161,32-34): ' And Saturn being with Jupiter, both of them being oriental and direct, it is useful in management and trust and the matters of others, and they entrust property'.

[2]That is, administration of actions and assets.

[3]Greek (161,34-35): 'but they will also be honorable if Mars is not in aspect'.

6. But nevertheless, action is impeded by the contrary dissensions of these stars, since in business affairs one of them calls back but the other urges on. But also those who have Mars and Saturn thus never attain what they want favorably; but always, with sadness of spirit, and ineffective desire, they abandon their unfulfilled wishes for the things they desired.[1] But they are also involved in various dangers of illnesses, and their bodies are worn down with a continual succession of spells of weakness; and the destruction of black bile is continually stirred up against them to their injurious bodily harm.[2]

7. But death also quickly overwhelms the father and at the same time the mother; the paternal property is also dissipated by various losses[3]; and it also prepares an evil destruction for the brothers through their own [actions]. But those who were born first are either thrown down by a miserable destructive death, or, deprived of all the protection of good fortune, they admire the power of fraternal fame with the greatest respect of humility. But on these they frequently impose the greatest difficulties and anxiety from grave errors.

8. But all of these things grow stronger if they possess any angle[5] of the nativity with that same association of degree. For then their spirit <is bent, but they bear up> strongly <under all labor and all instances of dangers with constant>[6] strengths of mind;[7] unless Jupiter, posited in the first angles and in those signs in which it is exalted, or is in its own domicile, or posited in fortunate houses of the nativity, will mitigate all the dangers of evils.[8]

9. **Saturn and the Sun in Conjunction.** If Saturn and the Sun received a single lodging of degree, and posited together in the same house

---

[1]Greek (162,5-7): 'and they are not good with contracts, for they are hindering and making failures in their actions'.

[2]Greek (162,3-5): 'Saturn being with Mars is dangerous for the body, and especially when one of them is making a conjunction with the Moon or it is the ruler of the sixth, for they excite the black bile and illnesses from fever along with shivering'.

[3]Greek (162,7-8): 'and they disperse the paternal assets because Saturn hinders the paternal person, as they also signify the father's early death'.

[4]Greek (162,9): 'and they either kill the elder brothers, or they make them sickly'.

[5]Greek (162,12): 'and the evils will be worse if they are posited in the angles'.

[6]This and the previous addition are from **N**.

[7]Greek (162,11): 'unalterable and revengeful in their resolutions'.

[8]Greek (162,13-14, from Dorotheus): 'if moreover the Aegis-bearer (Jupiter) does not overpower their destructive strength'.

they are joined together in equal power of association, this conjunction destroys all the paternal property, but it also denotes a miserable demise of death for the father himself, and these evils are strengthened more strongly in nocturnal nativities,[1] or if Saturn is found in either his matutine or vespertine rising. Then a heavy heap of misfortunes <attack>[2] the father; then a miserable series of dangers always occurs; then harsh occurrences of evil things are denoted for the brothers—if Saturn and the Sun are conjoined in this relationship in a nocturnal nativity.

10. But if posited in the same sign they were separated by such diversities of degrees, that in fact the Sun has few but Saturn has more degrees, then along with a miserable outcome of calamity the danger of an evil death is indicated; but all those things that we have said will occur, along with a strong continuation of evils;[3] but also, along with all these evils, his property is shattered or proscripted,[4] and with the entire substance of his fortune destroyed, the final burden of poverty is imposed upon him. But also spells of weakness are brought on by corrupt humors, and all his forces are overwhelmed by the worn-out weakness of the body. A miserable onset of blindness attacks the eyes of others.[5]

11. But this same conjunction will always make these same persons to be suitable farmers, so that after a lengthy space of time the foundations of wealth are conferred upon them from the suitable culture of their fields.[6] These same persons will certainly always be oppressed by sadness. But if the Sun and Saturn were posited together in the domicile of the Sun or in a domicile of Saturn, they do indeed make a famous father, but one devoid of all the support of riches.[7] But the Sun and Saturn posited together provoke these Natives themselves against their fathers with

---

[1]Greek (162,20-22): 'it brings an evil death to the father . . . and it destroys the paternal property, and is worse by night'.

[2]Adds **N**.

[3]Greek (162,22-24): 'and if the Sun is in fewer degrees, and Saturn in more, the indication for the father is worse—death and all the things mentioned are more terrible'.

[4]Seized by the state.

[5]Greek (162,28-29): 'and they are causing illnesses from distress due to humors and from the eyes'.

[6]Greek (162,29-30): 'and those having them thus are fond of the farming life, and they meet with success in that alone, being luckless [otherwise]'.

[7]Greek (162,30-32): 'but also if Saturn is in a feminine sign, or if the Sun is in a domicile of Saturn, and they are joined together thus, the father is famous but indeed not wealthy'.

parricidal hatreds of enmities. But these stars always attack these same Natives with the miserable decrees of the misfortunes which we have mentioned.

12. **Saturn and Venus in Conjunction.** If Saturn and Venus received a single lodging of degree, and posited together in the same house they are joined together in equal power of association, this conjunction denotes marriages with unworthy women, and it always produces miserable misfortunes in matrimony. For it denotes either sterile or weak wives, for whom some notable bodily defect disfigures the entire shape of their body, or a severe infamy strikes her,[1] or from these misfortunes the offspring of children is also denied to them.

13. Those persons having Saturn and Venus thus never have children, or they beget them slowly,[2] but these Natives themselves will always be frigid with regard to venereal desires, and their mind is always inconsistent with inconstant variety.[3]

14. Saturn and Venus posited together in the nativities of women also indicate these same things. But these things are stronger if Saturn and Venus are found together in Capricorn or in Aquarius. For these signs always badly corrupt Venus, especially if she is associated with Saturn. For then the malice of this conjunction cannot be mitigated either by the presence of Jupiter or by his testimony.

15. **Saturn and Mercury in Conjunction.** If Saturn and Mercury possess a house with the equal association of one degree, they always impede the sound of the voice with a stammering confusion of the tongue, or they make hampered words to be brought forth in slow speech, or they always attack the hearing with a serious illness; and Mercury and Saturn posited together never permit their desires to be fulfilled.[4]

16. They will also be devoid of faithful testimony in all of their actions.[5] Those having Saturn and Mercury thus will also be hardened by a

[1]Greek (163,5-6): ‘ they give unworthy marriages with women, since Venus with that star [indicates] a woman plainly unclean of marriage and one disgraced and injured’.

[2]Greek (163,8-9): ‘then too she will be childless and having few children or having them slowly on account of the combination with Saturn’.

[3]Greek (163,10): ‘the mentality of the wives is also unstable’ The Latin text is corrupt, but the meaning seems to be clear.

[4]Greek (163,17-18): ‘and these persons are ineffective’.

[5]Greek (163,15-16): ‘liars, culprits, ambushers, deceivers; such persons, he says, are not to be believed whenever they speak.

rigid authority of mind, and always composed with an obstinate and sad dissembling,[1] but these persons will conceal the counsels of their own mind with a deep silence of malice. But they steep their native talent with many studies of learned subjects.

17. **Saturn and the Moon in Conjunction.** If Saturn and the Moon have received a single lodging in a degree, and are posited together in the same house they are joined together in equal power of association, they always attack all impulses and all thoughts of mind with the weak agitation of fear.[2] But the maternal property is also destroyed with miserable losses by this configuration—also their mothers[3]—but these stars also disable the Natives themselves with a severe continuation of illnesses. But if it is a diurnal nativity, and the Moon is full of light, and there is a fortunate aspect from the benefic stars, the badness of all these evils is prevented.[4]

18. But if it is a nocturnal nativity, and the Moon has little light, this conjunction denotes all kinds of misfortunes and every destruction of evils. But even, if the testimonies of Venus and Jupiter together are added, yet with their salutary protection scorned, the destruction of disaster is strengthened.

XXIII.

1. **Jupiter and Mars in Conjunction.** If Jupiter and Mars are posited together, and located together in the same sign, they are joined with an equal power of association, they denote the greatest insignia of important positions,[5] and they confer the greatest power of authority. For they make men holding the governance of great cities, or great regions, and those having powers of famous authority over the greatest peoples.

2. They will also be of the sort who attain everything that they desire by a fortunate turn of events, especially if they are posited in fortunate

[1]Greek (163,19): 'they will be very sly and inquisitive'.
[2]Greek (163,25): 'their actions will be ineffective'.
[3]Greek (163,24-25): 'destructive of maternal persons and of the life of the mother'.
[4]Greek (163,29-31): 'and by day when she is increasing in light and with the benefics aspecting, there will be a prevention of evils'.
[5]Greek (169,31-32): 'Jupiter with Mars is the cause of advancement and property and of political dignities and of rulership over the people and of unceasing successes'.

houses of the nativity, or in the primary angles; or if. in the 5th or in the 11th house from the ASC, they are located together in a domicile of Jupiter or in a domicile of Mars.[1] For then the rods of authority, then arms, then the greatest armies are entrusted to them; then, established in great honors, they are allotted the authority of magnificent power.

3. **Jupiter and the Sun in Conjunction.** If Jupiter and the Sun are posited together in the same sign, and Jupiter is hidden by the rays of the Sun, it diminishes the whole order of good fortune by various degradations.[2] But if Jupiter, freed from the rays of the Sun, and posited in his matutine rising, is coupled with the Sun in the same sign, it denotes the whole substance of life,[3] and the fruits of these kinds of good fortune, also with the greatest power of honorable position.[4] And they will be seen to have been begotten for the good of their parents, so that from the day of their coming into the world all the insignia of good fortune are bestowed on their parents. But also they themselves who have Jupiter and the Sun thus will rejoice happily with the offspring they have begotten.[5]

4. **Jupiter and Venus in Conjunction.** If Jupiter and Venus are posited together in the same degree or in the same sign, they denote the insignia of honor with the greatest grace of charm[6]; they also always associate with good and great men in faithful friendships.[7] They also always make

[1]Greek (169,32-34): 'and if these (stars) being together are in a domicile of Jupiter or Mars, they signify mighty men and rulers'.

[2]Greek (170,1-2): 'if it is under the Sun beams, there will be a lack of all the good things (of life)'.

[3]The text has *fatum substantiam vitam* 'fate, substance, life', but this cannot be correct. Kroll suggests *totam substantiam vitae* 'the whole substance of life', but calls attention to vi.11.12 above, which has *Fatum quoque vitam substantiam ... prosternit* 'Fate also destroys substance, life' (but we should read with the MSS *vitae substantiam* 'the substance of life'). I have accepted Kroll's emendation, but perhaps some words have fallen out of the Latin text.

[4]Greek (170,2): 'but if it is not under the Sun beams, good fortune and the acquisition of livelihood and advantage'.

[5]Bram erroneously reverses the signification, saying: "...from the day of birth all their parents' good fortune will be bestowed on them." But the Greek (170,3-4) has 'and these are begotten for the sake of the good fortune of the parents, and the latter have these advantages from their newborn children'. And Dorotheus says (trans. by Pingree): "...good fortune and property and gain and luck to his parents.'

[6]Greek (170, 5-6): 'it shows a censor, and one who has been adorned with graces and the love of many'.

[7]At this point Ψ leaves off without any indication of a gap, evidently having failed to copy several leaves of its exemplar, and does not resume until vi.29.24.

those persons who are endowed with an honorable manner of morals, and who observe the commandments of all religions with an upright faith. Those who have Jupiter posited thus with Venus will also be outstanding with a clean honesty of beauty—joined always to judges and kings by a lovable bond of affection.[1] But the testimony of good repute always brings them to all kinds of fame, and, both the insignia of honorable position and the greatest supports of wealth are conferred upon them by the most powerful women.[2]

5. But those having Venus and Jupiter thus are also allotted a happy and fortunate married life. They will also have children[3] if an aspect of the malefic stars does not attack them. But these persons are led to sexual adventures by a desirous inclination of the mind,[4] very often expressing their own desire by various sexual relations.[5] Jupiter and Venus posited together in an equal manner denote these same things in the nativities of women.[6] But if Mars makes a menacing aspect to Jupiter and Venus posited together in the solid houses of the nativity and to the Moon aspecting them equally from any house, they will be battered with frequent rumor and severe blame of infamy on account of relatives.[7]

6. **Jupiter and Mercury in Conjunction.** If Jupiter and Mercury are posited together, they will make powerful men of good counsel, expressing <words>[8] shining forth with the splendor of magnificent eloquence,

---

MS **N** alone supplies the text of 18 Teubner pages, except that MS **W** also has the first page and the last 6 pages of **N**'s supplement.

[1]Greek (170, 6-8): 'and the well-disposed and pious and polite, and the desired by the side of leaders, and auspicious and famous'.

[2]Greek (170,8): 'these persons increase their livelihood from some notable women.

[3]Greek (170,10-11): 'and they also marry well and have good children if Saturn and Mars do not aspect them'.

[4]Probably a reference to the numerous sexual adventures of the god Zeus (Jupiter).

[5]Greek (170,9-10): 'but they are amorous persons par excellence, and they engage in intercourse with many women'.

[6]Greek (170,11): 'the same consideration also (applies) in the case of women'.

[7]Greek (170, 11-14): 'with Jupiter being with Venus in powerful houses, if the Moon aspects them and Mars bears witness from anywhere, with regard to related persons there will be blame arising from intercourse'. Dorotheus says (trans. by Pingree) "...a disgusting and shameful affair involving one of his relatives will be added." Judging from the Greek and from Dorotheus, one or more words may be missing in the Latin text.

[8]Adds Skutsch.

adorned with all wisdom, and steeped in the instruction of all fields of instruction; and they perfect them to such a degree, that everyone acknowledges them with a certain admiration.[1] For these persons, steeped in the training of the oratorical art, with the greatest facility of fluency, exercise the eloquence of learned and glorious speech. This conjunction will make others, endowed with the grace of their talent and with the power of learned speech, to handle the offices of the royal letters with the greatest honor.[2]

7. **Jupiter and the Moon in Conjunction.** If Jupiter and the Moon, posited together in the same sign, are joined with an equal power of association, they denote <abundance>[3] in life and financial assets and increases in the greatest good fortune, especially if the Moon conjoins herself to Jupiter partilely in the same sign. For then an unlimited heap of riches comes, and they denotes that sort of insignia of good fortune for him, so that without limit he is better in every way than his own parents.[4] But if it is a nocturnal nativity, and the Moon possesses more degrees, but Jupiter resides in a smaller number of degrees, it always debilitates and diminishes all the substance of his fortune with the greatest loss.[5]

XXIV.

1. **Mars and the Sun in Conjunction.** If Mars and the Sun, posited together in the same sign, are joined in an equal power of association, from this association they prepare for the swift—or certainly an evil—death of the father.[6] But if posited together they possess any angle of the nativity, or if they are in any *anafora* of an angle, then they denote ruin[7] with an unceasing continuation of paternal calamity; they also destroy the resources of the father's wealth with miserable losses.[8] They will injure the

[1]Greek (170, 23-24): 'it announces prudence, and fluency in words, and [persons] noble in mind, because of which they are also revered in the city'.

[2]Greek (170, 25-26): 'for they become grammarians or royal secretaries, orators, and also wise men'.

[3]Adds Ziegler.

[4]Greek (170,33-34): 'for it also makes them nobler than their parents'.

[5]Greek (170, 34-35): 'but if it is in a nocturnal nativity, and if the Moon has more degrees [the rest is missing]'.

[6]Greek (173, 34-35): 'it signifies that the father dies swiftly or dies an evil death'.

[7]Greek (173, 35): 'and if Mars is also angular or *anafora*, it is worse'.

[8]Greek (174, 4-5): 'and the paternal livelihood is dispersed'.

eyes of some, or they inflict wounds from iron or fire.[1] But they also disturb the right order of reasoning with an altered stability of mind.[2]

2. **Mars and Venus in Conjunction.** If Mars and Venus posited together in the same sign are joined in an equal power of association, that conjunction of Mars and Venus will produce debauched individuals and adulterers, so that possessed by a depraved ardor of desire, and incited by the stimuli of unrestrained lust, with misleading promises for the sake of performing debauchery they pursue the ties of another marriage.

3. But if Mercury is found with them, or if he aspects them by square, they denote declarations, accusations, lawsuits on account of these crimes, but from this conjunction they also denote insurrections and riots and unending disgraces. But if Jupiter, posited in fortunate houses and in his own signs or located in his own exaltation, makes a favorable aspect to them posited thus, they are freed from these crimes by the aid of some power.

4. But if Mars, with Venus and Mercury posited together, possesses any angle of the nativity without the testimony of Jupiter, or if in other houses of the nativity it receives the light of the waxing Moon; or if, with these posited thus, Saturn receives the light of the waning Moon, they are punished with public censure for the crime of adultery, or debauchery, or incest. But if Mars and Venus are posited together in tropical signs, those things that we have shown them to do in square in tropical signs, they do the same things when posited together in tropical signs.[3]

5. **Mars and Mercury in Conjunction.** If Mars and Mercury posited together in the same sign are joined in an equal power of association, this conjunction will surely make wise men and those educated in the studies of the greatest branches of learning,[4] but liars and those versed in every kind of malice, so that they exercise their ability in every kind of fraud, and so that in all disputes they always want to argue with deception.

6. But if Jupiter makes a fortunate aspect to this configuration, they de-

---

[1]Greek (174, 3-4): '(for) some they also hurt the eyes, or they injure the body from iron and fire'.

[2]Greek (170, 4-5): 'others suffer from madness or damage to their understanding'.

[3]Greek (174, 6): '(posited) together with Venus, they do the same things (as they do when) in square'.

[4]Greek (174, 7-8): 'liars, but intelligent and with knowledge of many things by choice; in disputes having trickeries for the most part'.

note [those involved in] famous contests of athletics.[1] But if Venus makes any aspect to them, it impels the Natives by a depraved mental desire to[have] love affairs with boys.[2] But if an aspect of Saturn is added to all these, those Natives whom we have mentioned will be struck with serious infamy.[3]

7. But if the Sun with his own orb overshadows Mars and Mercury posited together, and they are all in some angle of the nativity,[4] i.e. Mars and Mercury together and the Sun posited with them, and the Moon posited in any angle of the nativity aspects them,[5] they will make men equipped with a wicked mental desire, always applied to every kind of crime, and all of whose statements are always stained by false speech. They will also be the sort whose criminal falsehoods are comparable to the crimes of armed robbers.[6] These change the truth of documents for their own advantage by the false alteration of letters.[7]

8. But if Jupiter, posited in fortunate houses of the nativity, and in those signs in which he rejoices, or in which he is exalted, or in his own domicile, makes a fortunate aspect to them, it both covers up his misdeeds and denotes the greatest supports from wealth. But if, without the suitable testimony of Jupiter, Saturn makes a menacing aspect to them, his misdeeds and crimes having been made public, it denotes the evil and maximum ruin from punishments.[8]

9. **Mars and the Moon in Conjunction.** If Mars and the Moon posited together in the same sign are joined in an equal power of association, that conjunction will make men who are rash and those to whom success frequently comes fortunately in all things, especially if they are posited in any angle of the nativity. But for these persons, either a brief

---

[1]Greek (174, 8-10): 'some (will be) coaches, athletes, chariot-drivers, and becoming famous in all these [occupations], if indeed the benefic (stars) are in aspect'.

[2]Greek (174, 10): 'but they will be lovers of boys'.

[3]Greek (174, 10-11): 'and if Saturn is in aspect, it makes much blame'.

[4]Greek (174, 16-17): 'and if with Mars and Mercury together, they are found under the Sun beams and angular'.

[5]Accepting Ziegler's conjecture rather than Skutsch's emendation, and comparing the Greek (174,17-18): 'and also (if) the Moon aspects them, they will be givers of bad advice and liars'.

[6]Greek (174, 18-19): 'those having the way of life of armed robbers'.

[7]Greek (174, 18): 'and they are also forgers'.

[8]Greek (174,19-20): 'but if aspected by Saturn, they are reviled, and they suffer dangers'.

span of life is denoted or an untimely exit of death impugns the course of life.[1]

10. On some of them it imposes the defect of a constitutional illness, and it denotes that crises of all [sorts of] dangers must be feared, or if none of these [occurs], it denotes the lamentable and miserable exit of a bad death, or it exercises the power of iron or the sword against him.[2]

11. But also the miserable inconveniences of illnesses are denoted for the mother by this conjunction,[3] so that day-by-day her body is stricken by a miserable debility. But if Jupiter, posited in fortunate houses of the nativity or in the primary angles, located in his own domicile, or in his own exaltation, makes a fortunate aspect to these [stars], the dangers of all these misfortunes are mitigated.

XXV.

1. **The Sun and Venus in conjunction.** If the Sun and Venus posited in conjunction in the same sign are joined together with the power of equal association, they will certainly make famous men and those who attain all their desires in very easy fashion; but [only] if Venus is matutine in a diurnal nativity and vespertine in nocturnal ones.[4] But <if she is vespertine in a diurnal nativity and matutine in nocturnal ones>,[5] it joins these same persons in miserable unions of marriage, or it denotes a wife [obtained] with difficulty, or it brings maidservants to the society of the marriage bed, or it disfigures the face of the decreed wives with a dishonorable foulness. For some it denotes wives who are paupers, for others wives of advanced age; or such person as have Venus and the Sun thus are allotted wives who, sunk in some miserable misfortune, are dishonored by some disgraceful association.

[1]Greek (174,21-22) 'he is rash and not unsuccessful, and particularly [when they are] angular. Some are short-lived.

[2]Greek (174,22-24) 'others are injured, and they incur dangers; and still others die miserably, or they are cut off by swords.'

[3]Greek (174,24) 'and the mother will be sick.'

[4]The Greek (176,13-17) has: 'And the conjunction with Venus, in her vespertine rising at night and in her morning rising by day, [denotes] famous and effective persons; but if it is vespertine by day and matutine by night, middling. And the conjunction of these [stars] is munificent, and successful in undertakings, and especially in governing the common people'.

[5]These words are added conjecturally by Skutsch to fill an evident lacuna in the only MS **N**.

2. **The Sun and Mercury in Conjunction.** If the Sun and Mercury are posited together in the same sign, that conjunction . . . subordinate to the powers of others . . . they denote occupations . . .[1] They never shine in public[2] activities. They certainly make men who are wise in their advice, always concealing the secrets of their advice in a deep silence. It also makes those who are concerned about everything, and who always carry out all the duties of life with careful thought, concerned with a superstitious fear in all observances of sacred things, suspicious, and who are also always concerned in small things with various uncertainty.

3. But if Mercury is posited in its morning rising[3] and retains the direct order of its course, it denotes a principal position in all business dealings, making preparation for every duty of direction, and those who bear with them the ornaments of free speech, fortunate individuals and those who attain everything they want successfully. But these learn the course of future events with a divine incitement of mind. They will certainly be religious, just, worshippers of the Gods, frequently high-priests. But fortunate offspring of children are also denoted for these.

4. **The Sun and the Moon in Conjunction.** If the Sun and the Moon, posited together in the same sign are joined in an equal power of association, and it is a diurnal nativity, this conjunction will make those raised up with the lofty authority of power and who accomplish every duty of command with the greatest firmness and with the greatest strength. But if it is a nocturnal nativity, and still within the orb of the Sun the Moon is confined devoid of light, and, having abandoned the orb of the Sun, she shines with renewed light, it will make humble, disheartened persons and those subjected to all the power of authority, weak in strength, and devoid of all the protection of valor.

5. But if, having abandoned the orb of the Sun, and being freed from the preceding restriction, she carries around the free ornaments of her reborn light, and is (still) located in the same sign with the Sun, it makes effective persons and those carrying on all the duties of business transactions, and those persons easily obtain all the insignia of rank. But

---

[1]Ziegler and Kroll indicate lacunae, and unfortunately the Greek text omits this conjunction.

[2]Accepting Ziegler's emendation of *publicis* 'public' for *publicatis* 'made public'.

[3]Greek (176, 19-21): 'but with Mercury being in its morning rising, they have been educated, or grammarians from sagacity being rich and well off and governing others'.

if, with the Sun located in a masculine sign, the reborn Moon occupies a sign of the feminine gender, it will make important persons or first citizens of cities, shining with the bright splendor of nobility, adorned with wisdom and the commendation of goodness, and persons of the sort who always display the affections of pure and faithful friendship, coupled with the chaste and decent association of friendship.

6. But if the Sun and the Moon are adverse with the rays of their own light, then the life of the parents is separated,[1] and the association of the marriage bed is separated by various dissensions. But if the Sun and the Moon are conjoined with a fortunate aspect, that is by trine, just as we have said previously, down to the last day of life the parental partnership is preserved in a union of faithful love. But if with the Sun and the Moon together in adverse (relationship), Mars or Saturn possesses their middle place with a menacing aspect, a constant quarrel and the discord of perpetual dissension is prepared for the parents.

XXVI.

1. **Venus and Mercury in conjunction.** If Venus and Mercury, posited together in the same sign with equal power of association, they enhance men with a pleasing charm;[2] and they make the sort of persons who very easily get everything that they desire, but a desirous inclination of mind impels them to association with many women. Posited together they also denote the ornaments of learned speech, so that their speech shaped by learned education, always seduces the ears of their audience with the pleasing charm[3] of their speech, or they produce compositions of musical lyrics and distinguished instruction in poetics.

2. But they enhance these same [actions] with the ornament of respectable <arts>.[4] But if, posited at the same time in their own signs, they pos-

[1]Ziegler thinks something is missing here, but **N** has *separantur* 'are separated'. I have conjectured **separatur* 'is separated', which may be correct if nothing is missing.

[2]Greek (177, 24-29): 'The conjunction of Venus and Mercury is harmonious; it makes chatterers and sociable and amiable persons, loving their friends and loving beauty and having a mind to education and prudence … and all of these things are either heightened or incited by the tropical decree and the phases of the stars'.

[3]Accepting Wikström's emendation of *grato lepore* for *grata †tolleratore* **N**.

[4]Adds Ziegler.

sess the primary angles of the nativity, or if they are found placed in their own terms in fortunate houses of the nativity, then those <good things that we have mentioned before>[1] are fulfilled with a greater power of the decrees. But if at the same time they are placed in dejected houses, they will make musicians, but those devoted to popular pleasures.[2]

3. But if the malefic star Mars aspects Mercury and Venus located together, they denote easy marriages, but with some scandal and disgrace.[3] For then they are equally desirous of having sexual intercourse with boys and women, and with the greatest delight of mind they pursue debauches without limit.

4. But if Venus and Mercury are posited together in the same sign with the ASC, then a divine intellect is denoted for men; then their speech is adorned with a magnificent splendor of eloquence; then their poems are said to be have been written with divine inspiration. But all of these things are increased with a greater heap of good fortune, if Jupiter and the Moon, themselves posited in fortunate houses of the nativity, make a good aspect, that is a trine, to Venus and Mercury located together in the ASC.

5. **Venus and the Moon in Conjunction.** If Venus and the Moon, posited together in the same sign are joined in an equal power of association, they denote all the ornaments of virtue.[4] But they enhance these same persons with a pleasing honesty of beauty; and they make them to be adorned with the dignity of prominent position.[5] But they always denote unstable marriages with this configuration.[6] For no one having the Moon and Venus together perseveres in the affection of his wife with a firm and stable evidence[7] of love.

6. But it will also cause the feelings of the wife to be alienated due to his own fondness for the vice of his own desires, desiring sexual inter-

[1]Adds Ziegler.

[2]Probably a reference to "popular music" as distinguished from more elegant compositions.

[3]Greek (177, 29): 'and around women they are unstable and fickle'.

[4]Reading with Wikström and Ziegler *omnia virtutis ornamenta* instead of *nimia* †*viris ornamenta* **N**.

[5]Greek (177, 33-34): 'good for reputation and acquisition'.

[6]Greek (177, 34-36): 'they are unstable and adversarial and inimical in their marriage agreements; for it also brings about bad deeds and troubles from relatives or friends'.

[7]**N** has *amoris iudicio* 'judgment of love', but I think we should read *amoris* **indicio* 'evidence of love'.

course with other women from a headlong ardor of desire. Likewise too, he causes his own wife to be implicated in desires, so that whatever is polluted by those passive desires of their own longings, all of that also the sins of the straying husband recommend to the wife for a similar application, so that she also does whatever her husband learned how to do from depraved desire, so that an adulterous husband makes his wife an adulteress inspired by his own examples.

XXVII.

1. **The Moon and Mercury in Conjunction.** If the Moon and Mercury posited together are joined in an equal power of association, they teach all doctrines with the greatest power of <eloquence>.[1] For those who have the Moon and Mercury together grasp everything that they learn in the easiest fashion.

2. But also the Moon and Mercury posited together bestow an easily trained talent for wisdom. But if (while) posited together they are devoid of the testimony of Jupiter, they make liars and those persons, all of whose acts are always altered with an unstable and varied ease. But it also makes their mothers wise; but they always inflict scandal upon them from having sexual intercourse with low-class men. But in this conjunction, the Moon is better if it possesses the smaller number of degrees, and if Mercury is found in the greater number of degrees.

XXVIII.

1. Now that we have completed all of this, let our discussion be transferred to examples of decrees. We shall briefly remind your knowledge that in every nativity you should consider to which [star] the Moon first conjoins herself before the man is born.[2] For if a benefic star receives the rising of the Moon or is posited together [with her], or made a fortunate aspect to her, it will make that one, whom the imminent birth made a neighbor to her light, to allot a good rank to the nativity. But if the associated partnership was one of the malefic stars, the nativity is prepared for moderate and inglorious substance.

---

[1]Adds Skutsch, having compared iv. 2f.1 "The Moon to Mercury."
[2]The Latin is awkward, but this seems to be the meaning.

2. All the powers of the combinations we have explained to you, my dear Mavortius—what the individual stars joined in trine aspect accomplish, what they denote in square aspect, what they bestow when joined in equal union, what the sextiles accomplish with their authority of lowly power. But so that we may explain all these things more clearly for your knowledge, I shall introduce to you all the secrets of the decrees, confused [as they are] by every reason of the astrological significations, and with powers coupled together and conjoined in turn, so that whatever we have set forth in a general way, we may explain again in detail in the statements joined (hereto).

XXIX.[1]

1. **The Nativities of Slaves.** If the Moon and Jupiter are conjoined in partile aspect, and Saturn is posited partilely in dexter square to them located partilely together, and Mars strikes those same by square with a menacing aspect, but the Sun is in the 6th or the 12th house, the nativity of a slave is denoted by that configuration; and Jupiter, attacked from both sides, is not able to free [the Native] from inevitable slavery.

2. If the Moon is found in the MC, and Jupiter is placed in that same house, and Mars receives the conjunction of the waxing Moon, and Saturn makes a menacing aspect to the conjunction of Mars and the Moon, it will certainly make good slaves, but always weighed down by the burden of misfortune.

3. If Mars and Saturn together aspect the Moon by opposition, and no one of the benefic stars makes a fortunate aspect either to the Moon or to those that are joined in opposition, that configuration will either make slaves; or, deprived of the support of their parents, it will make [them] to be weighed down by the miserable burden of orphanhood.

4. If Saturn and Mars aspect Venus and the Moon posited in different houses by square or opposition, and the opportune testimony of Jupiter is denied to all of them, that configuration will make those born of slave parents, weighed down by the burden of slavery.

5. If Jupiter and Venus make a fortunate aspect to the ASC degree, and if the Sun and the Moon make any aspect to that same degree, i.e. the

[1]MS **W** begins here.

ASC, but Mars and Saturn separate their malign aspects from the ASC degree, a fortunate birth will be reared fortunately.

6. But if Saturn and Mars make a menacing aspect to the ASC degree without the protection or the testimony of the benefic stars, or, with one of the malefics posited in the ASC, [while] the other posited in the DSC strikes the ASC with an opposition aspect, they will either die when they are in the first part of life, or, having entered the first part of life, vital food is denied, or the offspring that is born is exposed by the stubborn will of the mother. But if with the malefics posited just as we have said, Venus or Jupiter offers its testimony to the ASC, the one exposed is collected and reared by the protection of a stranger's pity.

7. If Jupiter is partilely posited in the ASC, and Mars partilely opposed aspects the ASC and Jupiter partilely, with the other stars offering no testimony to them, this configuration denotes wealth of a moderate amount. But <it indicates> many .... of enemies <and that> protection is denied.[1]

8. But with Jupiter and Mars placed thus just as we have said, namely with Jupiter in the ASC and Mars posited in the DSC, if Saturn or Mercury makes any aspect to Mars, they will either make lunatics or epileptics oppressed by a mental frenzy.

9. But if with Jupiter posited in the ASC degree, Saturn posited in the DSC, i.e. in opposition, aspects Jupiter and the ASC, in a diurnal nativity, and the full Moon is moving toward Jupiter, they denote riches, good fortune, and increases of the greatest happiness. But if with Jupiter posited in the ASC, Venus is found in the DSC, i.e. in opposition, it denies brothers and likewise children. But nevertheless they denote an increase in riches and good fortune.

10. If Saturn is partilely posited in the ASC, and it has Mars partilely posited in the DSC, i.e. in opposition, or partilely in the IMC conjoined in aspect to itself and the ASC, and the Moon, is moving either toward Mars when full or toward Saturn with little [light], that configuration denotes a grave and miserable demise of death. For either, eaten by wild beasts, their bodies are dismembered by miserable lacerations, or it will make them to be thrown down a precipice, or their body is crushed by the collapse of a falling roof, or certainly the one who has Saturn and Mars thus, is destined for a bitter murder, and is handed over to the bloody hands of

[1]Some words have fallen out of the Latin text. The words in angle brackets are my suggestion for part of what is missing.

highway robbers. Or, drowned by bitter storms and tempests,[1] he is overwhelmed by an unheard of kind of death.

11. But the event of death will come according to the kind of signs. For, posited in animal and [especially] wild beast signs, they bring the bites of wild beasts to those prepared for death.[2] But posited in solid signs they are dashed against the roofs of tottering buildings. Posited in water signs they either make them die in battles or the savage blade of highway robbers wreaks its vengeance on their throat, or they are certainly punished by some judicial power.

12. For generally speaking, with Saturn posited in the ASC, if Mars is found in the DSC, it denotes the demise by a miserable death. But then they are punished by the sentence of a judicial authority, when Mercury afflicts all these by square.

13. If Mars is posited partilely in the ASC, and the star of Jupiter aspects it from the DSC, i.e. by opposition, that aspect denotes dangers and anxieties and sorrows in middle life; the dangers, moreover, [will be] from insurrections and riots; but it will also cause lawsuits and damages in a similar fashion. But for these persons, after many shipwrecks in life, fortunate times are denoted in their old age. But it will give wives who are either maid-servants, or [women] of advanced age, or public <whores>,[3] or those practicing some trade. But the whole number of brothers is not preserved in that same city, but all the brothers are separated from them either by travel or by death.

14. If with the Moon posited in any angle, Mars is posited in opposition, and to Saturn. . . ,[4] or is found in the same degree, or it aspects the ASC from any angle partilely, but Jupiter is found in the 6th house from the ASC, or in the 8th, or in the 12th, with the Moon, he who was born lives so long as the Moon is found with Jupiter. But as soon as the Moon has crossed over Jupiter's degree, then a speedy death is immediately denoted for him who is born thus.

15. If the Moon and the Sun are conjoined synodically, and Mars is found in the same sign in the middle between the Sun and the Moon, and

---

[1]Reading with *Ziegler <procellis> *tempestatibusque submersus* rather than *tempestatibus quasi submersus*. That phrase occurs above at vi. 15. 6.

[2]Probably a reference to the practice of executing criminals by exposing them to wild beasts in an arena.

[3]Adds Ziegler.

[4]Some words are missing.

Saturn aspects them partilely by square, the one who has the stars thus will die overwhelmed by corrupt humors, or they are seized by the furors of insanity, or they will have a miserable demise from inundations of the sea.[1]

16. But if with these <stars>, i.e. with the Sun and the Moon, <posited> just as we have said, Mars and Saturn are found in the 8th house from the ASC, but all the other stars are posited in the 6th or in the 7th house from the ASC,[2] it will make lunatics or epileptics, and those whose mind an angry or malignant divinity always disturbs, so that, with all their reason of mind disturbed, they blurt out words suddenly without any reason.

17. If the wife's Moon is found in the husband's nativity in the 12th house from the ASC, i.e. if that sign in which the wife's Moon is posited is found in the Bad Daemon of the husband,[3] it will make the wife to undergo all the injuries from her husband,[4] and it reconciles her with control of her mind, such that down to the last day of her life she patiently endures the injuries from her husband.

18. If on the other hand that sign in which the husband's Moon is posited is located in the Bad Daemon of the wife, you will pronounce the wife to be an adulteress from this, and such a person as will impudently attack her husband with all kinds of injuries,[5] so that all kinds of adultery may be charged against the wicked woman by her husband.[6] But also the husbands who are sustaining these injuries bear patiently everything that the wives have done.

19. But if the wife and the husband have the Moon posited in the same sign in their own nativities, or if Jupiter makes a fortunate aspect to the husband's Moon, or if again the husband's Jupiter makes a similar aspect

---

[1]Accepting Wikström's emendation *a maris [stellis] inundationibus* 'from inundations of the sea' for the *a mari stellis inundationibus* of MSS **NW**. Cf. 106,22 *ex aquarum <in>undationibus* 'from inundations of waters' **a**.

[2]Accepting Wikström's emendation *his <stellis> id est Sole Luna sic ut diximus <constitutis> Mars et Saturnus in VIII...*

[3]Accepting Kroll & Ziegler's conjecture **mariti* 'of the husband' for the *aut Mars* 'or Mars' of the MSS.

[4]The Latin has *omnibus mariti iniurias* 'all the husband's injuries' i.e. all the injuries (perpetrated by) the husband.

[5]Reading **omni iniuriarum genere* 'all kinds of injuries'.

[6]The Latin text of this clause is awkward and probably corrupt, but this seems to be its meaning.

to the woman's Moon, or if the Moons of both nativities are joined by a trine aspect, love coupled by an equal bond[1] of affection always sustains them by the desire for pleasures.[2]

20. If Venus is found in an earth sign, and posited in that sign she possesses the 7th house from the ASC, or the MC, or is located in the 12th house from the ASC, and she receives a partile opposition from Saturn, it denotes the misfortunes of a long and protracted widowhood from that aspect.

21. But if Venus is found posited thus in her morning rising, it indicates the misfortunes of widowhood for them when they are in their first age. But if she is found to be in her evening rising, the inconveniences of widowhood are denoted <in her old age>.[3] But <these configurations> compel some men, possessed by an incestuous ardor of desire, to enter into illicit sexual intercourse with their own daughters.

22. If the Moon and Venus, conjoined partilely in a nocturnal nativity and posited in feminine signs, possess the DSC or the MC, and Mars and Saturn aspect them by opposition, they will make fathers, from an incestuous ardor of furor and an instinct of nefarious desire, to be coupled with their own daughters in illicit bonds of matrimony.

23. If the ruler of the Sign of Marriage posited in a feminine sign possesses the DSC or the MC, it compels virgins to <do> unchaste things because of desire. But we find the kinds of things <that they do> by the varieties of the stars.[4] For if Saturn is found to be the ruler of the Sign of Marriage, the debauchery is prepared for the virgin either by her father or by her uncle or by her step-father, or by an old man, or by a slave. But if Mars is made the ruler of the Sign of Marriage, and it too is posited just as we have said, the flower of virginity is snatched away with some violence.

24. But if Venus is made the ruler of the Sign of Marriage,[5] and she is also <posited> just as we have said, <the voluntary crime of debauchery

---

[1]Accepting Lessing's emendation **vinculo* 'bond' for *vel cum loco* 'or with the house' of MSS **NW**.

[2]Accepting Ziegler's emendation **desiderio<rum> cupiditate* for the *desiderio cupiditatis* 'pleasure of desire' of the MSS.

[3]There is a lacuna in the text, and I have supplied the necessary words in angle brackets.

[4]Here too I have supplied some words that are missing in the Latin text.

[5]The supplement contained in MS **N** (and partly in MS **W**) ends with *domina* 'ruler' and Ψ resumes with *fuerit effecta* 'is made'.

is committed in the nocturnal watches of sacred ceremonies. But if Mercury is {made} ruler of the Sign of Marriage>[1] [and it is also] posited [just as we have said] before, [then] captivated by the persuasions of promises, they sacrifice their own virginity to the desire of a corruptor. But on occasion crimes are also aroused, and the disturbance of a seditious voice is raised. But the crises of dangers are also made greater if Mars is found with Mercury.

XXX.

1. If Jupiter and Venus posited together in a sign of Saturn possess the same degrees, and Saturn is in the next sign, i.e. it was found in the second sign, so that it first receives the conjunction of the applying Venus, and Mars aspecting the Moon is joined to Venus by any aspect, and Saturn also aspects the Moon partilely,[2] and the Sun is in the MC, with the Moon, and the ASC in Cancer, [then] aroused by the incestuous ardor of furor and the guardianship of some power, they are allotted marriage with their own mothers, or, possessed by a preposterous ardor of mind <and an incestuous> desire <of furor>,[3] they invite their own nieces to the society of the nuptial couch. But if this was the nativity of a woman, that same woman will be joined in matrimony with either her father or her stepfather. Old memories of readings say that Oedipus[4] had such a nativity. For the ASC was in Cancer, the Sun in Aries, Saturn in Pisces, Jupiter and Venus in Aquarius, Mars in Libra, the Moon in the nebula of Cancer, and Mercury was with the Sun.

2. If the Moon was found in the terms of Mercury, and if she received a star of the masculine gender, especially if she was found in Aquarius, and if Venus was not joined to Jupiter by trine aspect, he who has these stars thus are never allotted children.

---

[1]The words in angle brackets are supplied by MSS **NW**. The word 'made' and the words that follow in braces are suggested by the Teubner editors to fill an obvious gap in the Latin text.

[2]Reading **partiliter* 'partilely' rather than *pariter* 'together'.

[3]Adds Ziegler.

[4]Oedipus was a celebrated King of Thebes, who according to tradition unwittingly murdered his father and married his mother. Whether he was actually a historical person or merely a mythological figure is unknown. He is mentioned by Homer, so if he was a real person he must have lived before the 8th century B.C. and possibly as far back as the Trojan War (13th century) or even earlier. Obviously there could have been no record of his birthdate, so the horoscope is merely one designed to illustrate his character and life events.

3. If the Moon was found in the ASC in equinoctial <signs>, i.e. in Aries or Libra, but Jupiter and Mars conjoined partilely were posited in the MC or in the DSC, and Venus and Saturn partilely conjoined in Capricorn or Aquarius, and possessing the same number of degrees, aspect Mars and Jupiter by any aspect, they will make sterile persons, effeminates, and castrated Gallic worshippers.

4. If Saturn and Mars conjoined in a domicile of Venus with an equal association of degrees were posited together, possessing the DSC or the MC, and in opposition to them Venus posited in a domicile of Mars is in an opposite relationship to Saturn and Mars, this arrangement of the stars shows us the nativity of a eunuch.

5. If Mars and the Moon were opposed to each other by an opposition aspect, and both of them, posited in opposition, receive the same degrees, but Venus was located in dexter square to them, and Saturn aspecting Venus by opposition afflicts the Moon and Mars by a sinister square, so that in fact it aspects Venus by opposition but the Moon and Mars by square, and Mercury possesses the MC, either hermaphrodites or certainly eunuchs are generated by this mixture of stars.

6. If Saturn and Venus, located together in a sign or in the terms of Venus, possess the [same] degree, and Mars is made unrelated to them, this configuration either denotes a pauper or a wife of advanced age. But if Jupiter makes a trine aspect to Saturn and Venus placed thus, or if it is found with them, from that testimony of Jupiter a wife who is a widow is denoted, but one who is affluent and well-provided with riches.

7. If Venus is found in the MC together with Jupiter, that configuration denotes a wife known for her adultery. But if, with these placed thus, the star of Mercury approaches that same consortium of degrees, having abandoned that same husband whom she was allotted during the adultery, she passes again to the marriage of another husband. And she will either do this captivated by the love of a youth, or having pursued sexual intercourse with some pauper, or longing with an innate desire for the humility of sexual intercourse with low-born persons—so that by whichever situation, she is allotted the society of an inferior man by the lures of a depraved love.

8. If the Moon is found partilely in the MC, and the Sun is posited partilely in the ASC, but Jupiter partilely posited in the *anafora* of the ASC is joined to the Moon by a trine aspect, the famous insignia of nobility are denoted by that configuration.

9. If Jupiter aspects Venus posited in the MC by a trine, or if he is with her, and Venus is separated from all the aspects of the malefic stars, the greatest insignia of good fortune are conferred by this configuration through the support of women, or the Natives receive the beginning of good fortune from some feminine work. But it makes these same to play pieces of musical songs sweetly, or to pluck the lute and the lyre, or certainly to dance with graceful charm by the supple bending of the body.

10. Jupiter posited partilely in the MC always impels [the Native] by a miserable inclination to lust for having sexual intercourse with dirty women. But if Mars is found with it, and it is possessing the same degree, another person will seize his wife violently. But if the star of Venus is configured with these, a woman withdrawn from money-earning is joined in conjugal grace with famous men.[1] But if the Sun is configured with all of these by square, these Natives are joined by criminal desire to their father's concubines or to their own step-mothers, and they join in the association of matrimony with the discarded wives of their father. But when the marriage is completed because of depraved desire, the matrimony that was performed with all [circumstances] unlucky is dissolved by the intervening flight of the woman.

11. If Mars was found with the Moon in the MC, and Jupiter was partilely posited in the ASC, but the Sun was in the DSC aspecting Jupiter by opposition but Mars and the Moon by square aspect, that conjunction denotes a marriage with deadly conflict of combat. Then, the threatening swords of the contenders inflict serious wounds, then a serious battle is aroused with combats of a savage passion, then the contracted marriage is bloodied with the groans of the fallen and the clash of the warriors with a violent profusion of blood.

12. Such a decree Paris Alexander is said to have had, from whose marriage the famous combats of battles and the fabled destruction of his fatherland occurred. But the whole decree for PARIS ALEXANDER[2] was composed in this manner. The ASC was in Aquarius, the Sun in Leo,

---

[1]This sentence is not translated by Bram.

[2]This is the famous Paris, son of King Priam, and Prince of Troy, who according to Homer's *Iliad* abducted Helen and precipitated the Trojan War. He was a historical person born possibly thirty or forty years prior to 1200 B.C., which is now believed to be the approximate date of the Trojan War. But of course no birthdate could have been known for him a thousand years later, so this is simply a schematic chart that was postulated to exemplify his character.

Moon in Scorpio, Saturn in Leo, Jupiter in Aquarius, Mars in Scorpio, Venus and Mercury in Gemini.

13. If Saturn and Mars are partilely posited in the MC, or, posited in other angles, they aspect that same house by square or opposition, and the salutary protection of Jupiter and Venus does not mitigate their malice, this conjunction will make hard-working paupers oppressed by the miserable burden of poverty and shattered by the daily continuation of labor, so that they seek their miserable life's support by the daily labors of their body. But if Mars aspects that same house by opposition, with Saturn posited in the MC or in the IMC or certainly in the ASC, and they are all devoid of the divine testimony <of Jupiter>,[1] along with the preceding evils custody in a public prison and the iron bonds of chains are denoted. But if, with these posited thus, Jupiter makes a good aspect to the Moon full of light, they are set free after many labors and after many crises.

14. If Mars is found partilely in the MC, and the star of Saturn, posited in the neighborhood, possesses the second sign from it, that configuration will produce hardworking paupers and those seeking their life [support] by [the work of their] hands. But a sad countenance also always beclouds their face. But also if Mars posited in the MC aspects...[2] with equal degrees, and Saturn is posited in the second sign from the MC just as we have said before, greater burdens of unhappiness are denoted, and a heap of greater misfortunes is added. But also, those who have them thus never get what they want.

15. If the Moon is found in the lips of Aries or in Capricorn, or if it possesses the lips of Taurus[3] in similar fashion, it will make women who are certainly viragos; but it always impels men to all the faults of lusts, so that aroused by the miserable stimulus of lust they conceive vows of indecent and shameless sexual intercourse. But if the Moon is posited in those parts of the signs that we have mentioned, and Mercury and Mars, posited with the Moon in the same fashion, possess those degrees, and the Moon is separating from the star of Mars, in whatever degree of the

---

[1]Adds MS **N**.

[2]The name of the planet aspected is missing

[3]Ptolemy's (Hipparchus's) Catalogue of Stars does assign any stars to the lips of Aries, Taurus, or Capricorn. Bram translates the Latin words *labris* and *labra* 'lips' as 'cusps', but Prof. Monat renders them as 'lips'. However, all three of the signs have 'horns', so perhaps we should read **cornibus* and **cornua* 'horns', instead of 'lips'. Although in viii.4.10 both men and women with the Moon in the *ore* 'mouth' of Capricorn are said to be indecent.

sign the Moon is found, from that degree is found the fault of lust. <But if Jupiter aspects these posited thus by trine, or if it is found with them>,[1] the improbity of the aforesaid faults is covered up and mitigated.

16. But if Venus is found with them without the testimony of Jupiter, every [kind of] fault of shameless infamy is denoted—men both submit to womanly acts with a voluntary ardor of passion, and they carry out indecent actions from the ardor of depraved lust. But if this is the nativity of a woman, it will make [her] a whore who has lost her sense of honor, and who surrenders her own body to the depraved desires of lust, awarding her own sense of honor to the power of a pimp for the sake of daily wages; and she will be prostituted in public lodgings, even though she may seem to have been born of proper people.

17. But if the Sun and the Moon and the ASC are posited in the nativity in such a way that in no manner are they configured with each other, so that the Sun does not aspect the ASC, and again the Moon neither aspects the Sun nor similarly the ASC, and they are not conjoined by any association of their degrees, then they are worn out by so great a burden of poverty, that those who have them thus, weighed down by the diverse burden of misfortune, come to the final outcome of beggary.

18. If the Sun and the Moon possess signs of the feminine gender, and the ASC is found in a feminine sign, and if Mercury is posited partilely in the ASC, they are compelled to cut off their genitals with their own hands.

19. If the Sun and the Moon are partially posited in the ASC, or one of them precedes the ASC and the other follows it, so that this is done in the sign of the ASC, and Mars is posited in the *anafora* of the ASC, and Saturn is joined to Mars with some aspect of testimony, it imposes the miserable burden of blindness on the eyes.

20. If the Moon is found in the MC, and Venus posited in the IMC makes a partile aspect to the Moon, that configuration joins sisters to their brothers as wives with the ardor of incestuous desire.

21. If Venus is posited in dexter square to the Moon, it will make men ready for all the duties of business, and who acquire the support of many friendships for themselves, and whom their wives always love with faithful affection; and it makes them conjoined to all their friends by lovable

[1]Adds MS **N**, two lines having been lost in **Ψ** due to homoeoteleuton (*...invenitur* | *...inventus*).

esteem. But these things grow stronger if Jupiter makes a trine aspect to one of the two.

22. If the ASC was found in the sign Virgo, and in that same ASC Mars and Mercury and Venus were partilely posited, but Jupiter located in the DSC possesses the sign Pisces, and it is joined in partile aspect to those in the ASC, but the Sun is placed in the *anafora* of the ASC, i.e. in Libra, and the Moon placed in Capricorn possesses the 5th house from the ASC, but Saturn posited in the 9th house from the ASC holds the sign Taurus, the one who has all of these thus will be such an orator, that the sentences of his statements are offered in the manner of a thunder bolt, so that by his judgment either the minds of the multitude who are quiescent are aroused, or those who are [already] inflamed are easily pacified. His sayings will also be such that a posterity contentious in its boldness learns them by heart for the increase and nourishment of their talent. Such an orator persecuted [King] Philip [II] of Macedon [382-336] not by the force of arms but by the freedom of his speech, as we shall explain more clearly. This nativity inspired the divine talent of DEMOSTHENES.[1]

23. If Mars and Mercury and Venus were located together in Sagittarius in the terms of Venus, and the ASC possesses the terms of the same degree, but Jupiter posited in Gemini aspects all of them by opposition from the DSC, and is conjoined to them with a society of equal degrees,[2] but the Sun in the sign Capricorn, and the Moon in the 5th house from the ASC holds the sign Aries (for in these degrees it makes blind persons), but Saturn is posited in the 9th house from the ASC, i.e. placed in Leo, this nativity makes a divine poet [the author] of a certain heroic poem, so that he was writing about Martian conflicts and the fearsome struggles of battles in a famous nobility of verse. Such a nativity made the divine HOMER,[3] author of the poem *The Iliad*.

---

[1]The famous Athenian statesman and orator Demosthenes was born about 384 B.C., at which time Jupiter was in Taurus and Saturn was in Taurus or Gemini in the Alexandrian zodiac. So this is another schematic horoscope intended to exemplify the Native's character, rather than an attempt to create a speculative chart based on the actual date of his birth. He bitterly denounced King Philip in his speeches, some of which are still preserved under the title *Philippics*.

[2]An elegant way of saying that the opposition was partile.

[3]The ancients had no record of Homer's birth and in fact knew virtually nothing about him except that he was said to have been blind. Modern scholars suppose that he lived in the 8th or 9th century B.C. The horoscope is another schematic chart intended to exemplify his character.

24. If the ASC was found in Aquarius, and Mars and Mercury and Venus were partilely posited in the ASC degree, and the Sun posited in the *anafora* of the ASC holds the sign Pisces, but the Moon located in Gemini and posited in the 5th house of the nativity sees the ASC by a trine aspect, and Saturn holding the 9th house from the ASC is posited in the sign Libra, this nativity represents the interpreter of divine and celestial principles, who with pleasing speech, and composed by the power of his divine talent, and shaped by a certain celestial education, with a true license of discussion, comes to all the secrets of divinity. This nativity is said to have been [that] of PLATO.[1]

25. If the ASC was found in Libra, and Mars and Venus and Mercury were posited partilely in that same ASC, but Jupiter posited in the DSC, i.e. posited in the sign Aries, aspects Mars, Venus, and Mercury and the ASC by opposition, but the Sun posited in Scorpio is located in the *anaphora* to the ASC, also the Moon posited in Aquarius is holding the 5th house from the ASC, and Saturn placed in the 9th house from the ASC is located in Gemini; this nativity yields the divine poet of lyric song, who composed choruses in a free rhythm with serious moderation of religious verse. Such a nativity bestowed on PINDAR and ARCHILOCHUS the modes of the sweetest verse by the divine inspiration of their talent.[2]

26. If the ASC was found in Aries, namely in the terms of Jupiter, and Mars and Venus and Mercury were posited partilely in the ASC, and Jupiter posited in Libra, i.e. in the DSC, aspected the ASC by opposition, but the Sun posited in the *anafora* of the ASC possessed the sign Taurus, and the Moon posited in the 5th house from the ASC holds the sign Leo, but Saturn posited in the 9th house from the ASC holds the sign Sagittarius, this nativity

---

[1]Here again we have the same schematic horoscope with the triple conjunction of Mercury, Venus, and Mars with the Sun in the next sign, and the Moon in sinister trine, Jupiter in opposition, and Saturn in dexter trine. Plato is said to have been born in the spring of the year 427 B.C. If this is true, the positions of Jupiter in Leo and Saturn in Libra are wrong, for at that time Jupiter was in Virgo, Saturn was in Sagittarius, and Mars was in Gemini. But the framer of this horoscope was not concerned with trying to construct a speculative chart for the approximate date of Plato's birth, but rather with postulating a chart that he thought suited the character of Plato. Thus, this chart displays the same aspect pattern as those of Demosthenes, Homer, Pindar & Archilochus, and Archimedes.

[2]Pindar and Archilochus were famous early lyric poets. Archilochus seems to have invented elegiac verse; he was born somewhere around 675 B.C. Pindar was born between 522 and 518 B.C. No birthdates were available for either of them, so the horoscope is simply another schematic chart that was proposed to exemplify their character.

makes the divine inventor of the art of mechanics. This very one is ours, by whose talent a fabricated sphere shows the rotation of the sky and the courses of all the stars by an example of divine imitation.[1] This is the Syracusan ARCHIMEDES,[2] my fellow citizen,[3] who often overthrew the Roman troops with his mechanical arts. Marcellus[4] established in the triumph of his victory among the celebrating sound of the soldiers, and having donned the triumphal crown, bewailed that man with plaintive mourning.

XXXI.

But we have recounted to you, my dear Mavortius, at sufficient length the decrees of illustrious men. Now let us return to the order of work we have undertaken.

1. If Saturn is posited in Libra, namely in the terms of Jupiter and in its own exaltation, and the ASC is found in the same degree, but Venus posited in Aries sees the ASC from the DSC by an opposition aspect, and Mars and the Moon, conjoined in an equal society of degrees, are located in the MC, and the Sun and Mercury posited in Gemini are holding the ninth house from the ASC, and Jupiter posited in Aquarius and making his station possesses the fifth house of the nativity, this nativity denotes the most powerful command of a kingdom, or it denotes the insignia of a potent dignity.[5]

---

[1]This says that Archimedes built a mechanical device like the Antikythera Machine, but in the shape of a sphere.

[2]Like the others in this chapter, this is not a true horoscope but only another schematic chart postulated to suit the historical character of the subject. In fact the positions Sun in Taurus, Jupiter in Libra, and Saturn in Sagittarius do not occur within the limits usually given for Archimedes's birth, namely 290-280 B.C.

[3]Translating Skutsch's conjecture *civis meus* 'my citizen' for the *quis meus* 'who my' given by **Γ**, which is plainly wrong, or the *qui naves* **Δ** 'who the ships'. But the reading of **Δ** is entirely possible: 'Archimedes, who the ships, who the Roman troops, often overthrew with his mechanical arts'. History records that Archimedes focused giant mirrors on the Roman ships and set them ablaze. Firmicus undoubtedly knew that story, so the reading of **Δ** may be correct.

[4]Proconsul Marcus Claudius Marcellus (c.270-208 B.C.), Roman general, conquered the Sicilians at Syracuse in 212 B.C. He had ordered that if Archimedes was found, he was not to be harmed, but was to be brought safely to him. However, a soldier for some reason flouted the order and killed Archimedes, thus saddening the general.

[5]If correctly stated, these positions correspond to the date 15 June 79 B.C., except that Venus was in Cancer instead of Aries. The person is unidentified.

2. If the Moon is found in the twelfth house from the ASC, i.e. in the Bad Daemon, and it is in a sign that is said to be of the triplicity of Saturn, i.e. in Aquarius or in Gemini or in Libra, and the Sun posited in the sixth house from the ASC sees the Moon with an opposition aspect, and they are conjoined in like society of degrees, and Jupiter is posited in the eighth house of the nativity, from this nativity the inconveniences of a laborious poverty and a miserable beggary are denoted.

3. If the Moon and Mars are posited in the seventh house from the ASC, i.e. in the DSC, and they are posited in a sign in which the triplicity of Mars is found, i.e. either in Cancer or in Scorpio or in Pisces, and Jupiter is partilely located in the MC, and the Sun is joined to them by a trine aspect, this nativity will make an athlete, but one who as a victor in the sacred games[1] will win the famous insignia of crowns.

4. If Venus is found posited in a feminine sign in the DSC of a nativity, and Mars is found similarly in a feminine sign, and the Sun too and the Moon possessing feminine signs, this nativity shows you a homosexual man.

5. If Saturn and Mars are posited together in the degree of the ASC, and it is a sign of the feminine gender, and Venus and Mercury posited in the DSC hold a feminine sign; or if Mars and Saturn partilely posited in the MC have a sign of the feminine gender, <and Mercury and Venus posited in the IMC a sign of the feminine gender>,[2] this nativity will produce public homosexuals,[3] or certainly the self-castrated priests of Cybele. But if this nativity was that of a woman, it will make a public whore with her shame marketed.

6. If the Moon and Mars were located together in the eighth house from the ASC, and Mercury, posited in opposition, sees them with a partile aspect, this nativity will make armed robbers with an unrestrained passion for cruelty, but we discover their [particular variety of] crimes in accordance with the varieties of the stars. For if Mars and the Moon were

[1]Reading *<in> sacris certaminibus* 'in the sacred games' with edition **a**, rather than Kroll's conjecture *sacri certaminis* 'of the sacred game'. But Firmicus sometimes mentions the singular and sometimes the plural. These games were athletic contests associated with sacred ceremonies. Cf. Cumont, *L'Égypte des Astrologues*, p. 75 ff., and the winners were revered by the public, much like our present-day winners of the Olympic Games.

[2]Adds MS **N**, the line having been omitted in Ψ due to homoeoteleuton (*...generis signum* | *...generis signum*).

[3]Presumably, professional homosexuals.

located in earth signs, established as a robber in deserted places, he will stain his robbing hand with a profusion of blood. But if they are posited in water signs, they produce cattle rustlers, always opposing the men pursuing them with a menacing sword. But, posited in fixed signs, they produce famous housebreakers, but those who, armed with a sword, inflict on sleeping men both the loss of their personal property and danger to their life. But all of these, apprehended in these crimes, are punished by the severity of a public sentence. But if Mars and Mercury are posited together in the IMC or in the DSC, but the Moon is either opposed to them or in square, or is with them full of light, they denote those same things that we have mentioned.

7. If Saturn and Venus were posited in the DSC of a nativity, but Mars was posited in the 8th house from the ASC, but Mercury was either with Mars or with Saturn and Venus, and Jupiter does not combine with any one of these with a favorable aspect, this nativity will either make slaves or a priest of Cybele, but those who maintain all the faults of an immodest indecency.

8. If Mars was found in the degree of the ASC, and Venus partilely posited in the DSC, but the star of Saturn possessed the MC degree, and the Moon was posited in the IMC, this nativity will produce an indecent man.

9. If Mars was found in the MC, namely in a feminine sign, and Saturn and Venus were posited in the 11th house from the ASC, but the ASC was arranged with Jupiter and the Moon and Mercury in a sign of Venus, those who have these stars thus seduce either their own mothers, or their nieces, or the sisters of their mothers, because of an incestuous desire for sexual pleasure.

10. Venus posited with Saturn in the ASC, located in whatever sign in whatever degrees, by the license of its power, [this] nativity denotes public whores or wives of advanced age, especially if Jupiter does not aspect them.

11. Jupiter and Mars, if they were posited together in the MC, make men decorated with the commendation of goodness and those on whom the insignia of very good fortune are always conferred, especially if that conjunction was in a domicile of Jupiter or in the terms of Jupiter.

12. If Mars was in the MC or in the domicile of the Moon, and Jupiter is posited together with Venus and Mars in that house, and the Moon full

of light moves towards Jupiter, that association denotes the insignia of the greatest good fortune.

13. If Mercury, Saturn, Mars, and Venus, together with the Moon, stand together in the MC, conjoined with equal association of degrees, they indicate want and the burden of miserable poverty; and they make these same [persons] to be door-keepers, compelled to this compliance by the necessity of beggary, but they also show the deaths of their children by the repeated calamity of misfortunes.

14. If Mars and Venus were posited together in the 5th house from the ASC, and the Moon was partilely posited in the ASC, they denote the insignia of a famous nobility; and the faithful love of kings is denoted by this association. But these persons are allotted wives known by their adulteries. Also, togas with a purple border and golden clothes and the insignia of golden crowns are denoted for them as an embellishment of honor.

15. If the ASC was found in the sign of a malefic star, and that malefic star was posited in the 12th house from the ASC, it will make men to be torn apart by the bites of dogs. But if the 12th house from the ASC is located in the sign of a malefic star, and that malefic star (namely, the one whose domicile we have said to be the 12th house) is posited in the 7th house from the ASC, i.e. in the DSC, it indicates that same danger of death. [At least,] a weak exit of death and the dangers of serious misfortunes must be feared unless the good testimony of Jupiter and Venus together mitigate it with the salutary guardianship of their divinity.

16. If the Moon and the Sun were posited together in the triplicity of Mars, i.e. either in Cancer or in Scorpio or in Pisces, and Mars itself was found in the MC or in the DSC, they will denote continual inconveniences in travel, and those persons spend the very last day of their life located in strange regions or[1] in foreign <places>.[2]

17. If Mars was found together with the ASC in his own triplicity, i.e. either in Cancer or in Scorpio or in Pisces, and with Mars in the ASC, Venus and Mercury were posited in the DSC, and they are conjoined to Mars in an equal number of degrees, those who have these stars thus will be evil murderers of their own wives.

---

[1]Reading *aut* 'or' with MS **N** instead of *et* 'and'.

[2]Accepting Skutsch's addition of <*locis*> 'places'.

18. If the ASC was found in a sign of Venus, and Venus is partilely posited in that same ASC, but Mars and the Moon are posited together in the DSC in a sign of Mars, namely in the terms of Mars, the mother of this nativity will die from having been struck by a sword.

19. If the Moon was found in the MC, and in the IMC Saturn and Mars and Jupiter are posited together, he who has them thus will receive the serious yoke of captivity remote from his paternal *Lares*.[1]

20. If the Moon was found in the MC, and Mars and Saturn posited with her, joined in an equal association of degrees, they will make either procurers or ministers of foul passions, so that . . . sought, the sustenance of life might be acquired for them.[2]

21. If Saturn is found in the 6th house from the ASC, and Venus and Mercury are located in the 12th house from the ASC, and all of these afflicting each other with an opposition aspect are joined together in an equal number of degrees, then with an incestuous ardor of desire they bring their own daughters to the coupling of the marriage bed. But also if Venus and Mercury and Jupiter have exchanged their own domiciles they denote this same thing in similar fashion.

22. If Venus and Mercury and Jupiter and Saturn are all posited together partilely in the 11th house from the ASC, and they are all joined in an equal number of degrees, thus placed they denote the wives to be housemaids of the most powerful men.

23. If Saturn and Venus are partilely posited in the MC, and Jupiter does not aspect them, and this nativity is that of a woman, she will have sexual intercourse with eunuchs or with sterile men with an ineffective desire for pleasure.

24. If Venus and Jupiter are posited together in the 5th from the ASC or in the 11th, and no benefic star aspects them from any part [of the nativity], they denotes difficult marriages or animosities in marriage, so that, always involved in bitter dissensions, they engage in quarrels of spiteful hostility between themselves.

25. If Mars and the ASC are joined together in an equal number of de-

---

[1]Accepting Kroll's emendation of *laboribus* to *laribus*, translated as above. The Lares were the household divinities of a family. Hence the phrase is simply an elegant way of saying 'away from home'.

[2]Obviously, some words are missing from this sentence, and one or more of the words in the MSS may be faulty.

grees, and if they are posited in a domicile of Jupiter, and Saturn trines Mars and the ASC, and the Moon is posited in the last degrees of the ASC, those who have these stars thus will either have sexual intercourse with their mother or certainly with their step-mother. But if this is the nativity of a woman, she will either have sexual intercourse with her own father or with her own step-father because of an incestuous desire of lust; and nevertheless that woman will be impatient with regard to all lust from the fault of prostituted decency. But if Saturn is found in the 5th house from the ASC, and Mercury is with Venus in the 11th from the ASC, they denote marriages with their step-daughters with heinous desire.

26. If Saturn is found in any angle, and it makes a menacing aspect to Mercury posited in opposition [to it], the offspring of children is denied by this aspect.

27. If with the Sun posited in the ASC, Mars is found with Saturn in the *anafora* of the ASC, some defect is inflicted upon the right eye. But if the Moon is posited in the ASC, and Mars and Saturn are found in the *anafora* of the ASC, the left eye receives that same defect; but these things [occur] in a nocturnal nativity. But if the Moon is found in the MC, and the Sun is posited in the ASC, but Saturn holds the 9th house from the ASC, and Mars is posited in the 11th house from the ASC, namely <in the Good Daemon>[1]. . . .

28. . . . and it makes an opposition aspect to the Moon posited in the 6th house from the ASC, but Saturn and the Sun are partilely conjoined in the 8th house from the ASC, they inflict the ruin of blindness. But also if the Moon is found in the IMC, and Saturn and the Sun and Mars posited in the 8th house from the ASC aspect the Moon by trine, they denote blindness and bodily debility along with miserable beggary. But also if Saturn is found in the 12th house from the ASC, and the Sun and the Moon and Mars posited together make a trine to Saturn, they also denote blindness from this association.

29. But also if the Sun and Mars are posited in the 8th house from the ASC, and the Moon posited in opposition to them in a human sign is found with Saturn, this aspect also denotes blindness along with bodily infirmity. But also if Saturn is posited in the DSC and Mars in the ASC, but the Sun is in the *anafora* of the ASC, and the Moon is posited in the

[1]I added this where the Teubner editors indicate a lacuna that extends to the beginning of paragraph 28, but other words are also missing.

6th house from the ASC, with the passage of time blindness <is indicated>[1] from the illness of cataract . . . they bring blindness from the defect of <cataract>.[2] But also if the Moon is in the ASC, and the Sun is posited in the 7th house from the ASC, i.e. in the DSC, it brings the greatest defect to the eyes.

30. If Mars is found in the MC, and Saturn is posited in the 11th house from the ASC, but the Sun is in the *anafora* of the ASC, and it makes an opposition aspect to the Moon posited in the 8th house from the ASC, with one eye put out, the light of one eye is preserved.

31. If Mercury and the Moon are posited together and are conjoined in an equal number of degrees, and they have a sinister square to [where] Mars and Venus are posited, they either deform the body with a pointed head, or they spoil the keenness of the eyes with a wrong mixture of lights, or they will make the neck to be turned down on one side.

32. If the Sun is found in the ASC, and Saturn is posited in the IMC, and the Moon possesses a dexter trine to the ASC, this association of configurations inflicts the peril of blindness. But also, if Saturn and the Moon are posited together in a tropical sign, and Mars and the Sun are posited together in opposition to them, then from this configuration too a danger to the eyes is always afforded. But if, with them posited thus, Jupiter is found in the MC, it eases all the inconveniences of poverty.

33. But also, if Saturn and the Moon are found in the MC, and the Sun and Mars are posited in the 8th house from the ASC, the misery of blindness is also denoted thus. But also if the Sun is found in the ASC, and Saturn is posited in the *anafora* to the ASC, with the Moon also posited in the MC, and if Mars is found in the 11th house from the ASC, the misery of blindness is also denoted thus. But also if the Sun is found in the ASC, and Saturn is in the *anafora* to the ASC, with the Moon also posited in the MC, and Mars is found in the 11th house from the ASC, the misery of blindness is also denoted thus.[3]

34. If the Sun and the Moon are conjoined in conjunction in a tropical sign, and the Moon is deprived of all the splendor of its light, and Mer-

[1] I have added **indicatur* 'is indicated' where the Teubner editors show a lacuna in the text.

[2] Adds Ziegler, who notes that the last preserved words in this sentence repeat the last few words before the lacuna. Presumably several words are mising.

[3] Note that the last sentence of Paragraph 33 is an exact duplicate of the preceding one.

cury is [configured] with them, it denotes the greatest wisdom and an outstanding intellect, and knowledge of many things, along with blindness of the eyes, and with debility of the body.

35. If the Moon and Saturn and Mars are posited together in equinoctial signs, they stain the whole body with certain noticeable marks, or they disfigure it with white kinds of marks. Or certainly a gently creeping scabby eruption will possess the whole body, or the form of the roughened body is changed into one of little falling scales, or itching will bother the man every day, or they certainly denote leprosy with an ugly disfiguration.[1]

36. If Mercury and Saturn and the Sun are posited together in the 7th house from the ASC, i.e. in the DSC, and the Moon is conjoined with Mars in the 8th house from the ASC in the equal association of a degree, it either produces cripples, or weak persons with their hands cut off, or it certainly makes insane persons suffering from the defect of a fallen mind.

37. Now, my dear Mavortius, I shall show you an amusing decree, [so that] instructed by the example of it, you will also be able to define similar nativities. That misshapen and crippled Greek, whose form of a conflated body Homer told us about in his divine poems, who, with the laughter of all a wise man reproves with a severe reprimand—he had a decree composed in this fashion. If the ASC is posited in Aquarius, with the Sun and Saturn conjoined in the equal society of a degree in Capricorn, i.e. in the 12th house from the ASC, but Jupiter is in the ASC or posited in the *anafora* of the ASC, and Mars with the Moon in the 9th house from the ASC possesses the sign Libra, but Mercury and Venus are posited in the ASC, i.e. in Aquarius, this decree shows us the nativity of THERSITES,[2] for he was unwarlike, weak, silly, and always impatient with a babbling verbosity. The nativity shows all these things that have been written.

38. If Venus is posited in Capricorn and it strikes Saturn with an opposition aspect, it makes such persons as those whose wives curse them in all ways; and their bodies, having exuded heavy moisture, give off an offensive flood of a goat-like smell.[3] These same persons will also always

---

[1]Accepting Ziegler's emendation *<de>figuratione* '<dis>figuration'.

[2]Homer says in the *Iliad*, II. 212 ff., that Thersites was the ugliest soldier in the Greek army besieging Troy in the 12th Century. Like the other early charts, this "horoscope" is merely intended to exemplify his character.

[3]That is, when they sweat a lot, they really stink

be infamous for their errant[1] sexual intercourse and amorous lust, and the sort of persons who desire depraved sexual relations of promiscuous lust from an inclining[2] mental desire. But Jupiter mitigates these things somewhat if it aspects Venus by trine, or, with the rest remaining, it cleanses such an outpouring of odor.

39. If the Moon and Saturn and Venus are posited in the 7th house from the ASC, i.e. in the DSC, since they will make perverts with effeminate softness of body who imitate the exits of the old fables, always dancing on stage, especially if Mars posited in the MC makes a square aspect to those posited thus as we have said. Then it will make indecent persons and those devoted to every fault of lustful infamy, and who are always joined to their own wives in indecent or unchaste intercourse. But if Jupiter from the IMC aspects by square all these [stars] posited thus, i.e. in the DSC, then along with all these faults it will also make lovers of boys.

40. If Jupiter and Saturn and Venus are joined together partilely in the MC with an equal association of degrees, and Mars posited in the IMC aspects all of them by opposition, they make lovers of boys, but who make up for that lustful fault by the prostration of their own body.

41. If Jupiter and Venus and Saturn are posited together in the 7th house from the ASC, i.e. in the DSC, an inheritance is conferred by the death of the wife. But these will themselves be shattered by a grave continuation of illness, and the offspring of children is denoted for them [only] with difficulty. If Mercury is posited in the MC and Venus and Saturn and Jupiter are posited with it, it denotes foreign wives, but ones abounding in a great affluence of riches.

42. If Saturn is posited in the ASC, but Mercury and Jupiter are posited in the 7th house from the ASC, it denies children. But if that composition of order is changed, i.e. if Jupiter and Mercury are in the ASC, and Saturn posited in the 7th aspects them by opposition, it denotes that same thing in similar fashion.

43. If Mercury and Venus are posited together in the IMC, and Saturn possessing the degree of the MC strikes them with an opposition aspect, it denotes the wife to be a woman of advanced age. But also he mixes with his own wife in vile intercourse.

---

[1]Accepting Wikström's emendation **ex errati<co>* 'from (their) errant'.

[2]Accepting Skutsch's suggestion of **prona mentis cupiditate*; *cf.* vi.23.5 where that exact phrase occurs.

If Venus is posited in the MC, and Saturn is joined to it in the MC with an equal association of degrees, but the Moon posited in the IMC makes an opposition aspect to those same, it denotes either wives who are sterile, or certainly of an advanced age, so that children are perpetually denied to them from that matrimonial union.

44. If Mercury is posited in the 5th house from the ASC, and Mars is conjoined with it in an equal association of degrees, when posited thus they denote sisters as wives.

45. If Saturn is posited in the MC, and the association of Jupiter and Mars in the same house comes to it posited thus, it will make all kinds of sadness to be got from their wives, so that it never indicates the happiness of conjugal kindness for them.

46. If Venus located in her vespertine rising is in the DSC, i.e. in the 7th house from the ASC, and, with Venus posited thus, Saturn is located in the degree of the MC, it will make men sluggish in venereal acts, but it will also make women who are always frigid in intercourse—with their venereal desire put to sleep, and every bit of lust extinguished.

47. If Mars and the Moon are conjoined in equal association of degree in the MC, and with them Venus and . . .[1] Mercury posited together aspects by opposition, this decree in the nativity of a man will produce public worshippers of Cybele, but it makes women to be whores, devoid of all the guardianship of shame.

48. If Saturn and Jupiter are together in the IMC, or if they are in the DSC, i.e. posited in the 7th house from the ASC, it indicates the weight of great sadness from the misfortunes of their children. But if Mercury is found with them in the same houses, and Venus posited in the same house is joined to them with an equal association of degrees, it will make women who are sterile, and men—devoid of virile desires—will be separated from all intercourse. But if they are posited just as we have said in a tropical sign, it will make the natural body of the woman to be glued together with an uncorrupted entrance. But if Mars is also found with all of these, it will make castrated priests of Cybele carrying out the sacred ceremonies.

49. If Mars and the Moon are found posited in the ASC, and, with them posited thus Mercury possesses the MC degree, and Saturn posited in the

[1]Ziegler indicates that some words are missing here.

DSC aspects them by opposition, but Mercury aspects them by square, they will make children to die from early accidents of death[1] [while still] posited in a tender age and still crying in the bosom of their nurses.

50. If Mercury is posited in the IMC and Mars, Saturn, and Venus are conjoined to it in an equal society of degrees, posited thus it will make the children to die before their fathers' own gaze by miserable and harsh necessities of deaths.

51. If Mars is found in the IMC, but Saturn is posited in the DSC, and the Moon posited in the ASC is joined to Mars by square, but to Saturn by opposition, death is quickly prepared for the wife from that association.

52. If Jupiter is found in the DSC, i.e. in the 7th house from the ASC, but Mars and Mercury are both posited together in the ASC in an equal society of degree, it will deny children. But also if Mercury and Jupiter posited in the angles aspect each other by opposition, so that one is in the ASC and the other is in the DSC, or one is in the MC and the other is in the IMC, it makes the male children to die by miserable atrocities of deaths. But also, if Mercury posited in any angle makes an opposition aspect to Saturn posited in the opposite angle, the offspring of children is denied by this.

53. If the ASC is posited in tropical or in duplex signs, and Mars and Mercury are conjoined in the ASC in an equal society of degree, but Jupiter aspects the ASC and them by opposition, it either makes epileptics or it certainly always makes insane persons with a perturbed mind.

54. If Venus is partilely posited in the ASC, and Saturn posited in the IMC aspects Venus by square, it makes men assigned to services in temples, who, with their pattern of mind changed[2] by a secret inspiration of divinity, and, possessed by the inciting[3] power of religion, they predict the future to present-day men, so that from that activity they acquire their daily life's support.[4]

---

[1]Accepting Némethy's emendation of *mortis* 'death' instead of the *satis* 'enough' of the MSS.

[2]Bram translates *mutato mentis ordine* as 'their minds are deranged', but I disagree.

[3]Accepting Némethy's emendation *instigantis* 'inciting' for the †*instantis* 'urgent?' of the printed text.

[4]Accepting Ziegler's conjecture *alimenta* 'supports' for the *augmenta* 'increases' of the MSS.

55. If the ASC is in Virgo, and Jupiter, Mars, Mercury, and Venus are posited in that same ASC, but Saturn in Pisces, i.e. posited in the DSC, sees all of these that we have mentioned with an opposition aspect, and the Sun posited in the *anafora* to the ASC possesses the sign Libra, but the Moon is posited in Aquarius, and all of them are in their own terms, i.e. Jupiter, Saturn, Mars, Mercury, and Venus, from this nativity the destiny of a most powerful Emperor is shown.[1]

56. If Mars is posited in the ASC, and the Moon is either moving toward Mars or is separating from him, humility of life, serious defects of illness, and harsh occurrences of dangers, and assaults of miserable calamity are denoted[2] by that association of conjunction. But if Mars is also found in the DSC, and the Moon is separating from it, it causes these same things in a similar fashion.

57. If the Sun . . .[3] is posited, and the ASC is conjoined with it in an equal association of degrees, but Mars and Saturn and Jupiter posited in fortunate houses of the nativity aspect each other by trine, they will make tyrants who are cruel, terrible, and effective, and they make persons of the sort who, in the slaughter of men and in their cruel savagery in punishing wretches, always act with a cruel ferocity.

58. If the Moon is found in the ASC, and either Saturn or Jupiter posited in the DSC, i.e. in the 7th from the ASC, aspects her by opposition, the conscience of the one who has them thus, will be stained by a secret murder. But if in the DSC, i.e. in the 7th house from the ASC, namely in a tropical sign, the Sun and Mars and Mercury are conjoined in an equal association of degrees, that association of stars will produce a murderer, an armed robber, always drenched in human gore, and armed for every kind of cruelty. But if Saturn is found with them, it shows us the type of death. For, having been apprehended in those crimes, by a severe judgment of judicial sentence, nailed onto a "Y" framework, he is raised up on a cross.

---

[1]These positions (in the Alexandrian zodiac) correspond to the dates 27 and 28 September of 96 B.C., but only Mars was in its own terms (if the Egyptian terms are meant). The person is unidentified. Possibly Ptolemy XI Auletes, King of Egypt, who died in 51 B.C. supposedly aged 44 or 45.

[2]Accepting Ziegler's emendation of *iunguntur* 'are joined' to *decernuntur* 'are denoted'.

[3]The MSS leave a blank space here. Edition **a** suggests supplying <in Aries or in Scorpio>.

59. If Jupiter is <in those degrees of Pisces>[1] in which Andromeda is posited, and Saturn receives the conjunction of the coming Moon, the greatest inconveniences of misfortune are denoted by that configuration. But if Mars makes an opposition aspect to the Moon thus placed as we have said, it will make men apprehended in planning a crime to be raised up on a cross.

60. If <Venus> is posited <in Taurus>,[2] and she holds those degrees in which the Pleiades are posited, and the Moon is full of light, and Mercury and Mars are either conjoined with her in an equal society of degrees, or they aspect her by a menacing square aspect made from a superior position, whoever has them thus, having been captured by armed robbers, will perish—struck down by the blade of a threatening sword.

61. But also if Venus is found in Taurus with the ASC, and it strikes the Moon posited full of light in the MC with a square aspect, it will accomplish the same thing that we have mentioned in a similar fashion. But also if the ASC is found in Taurus, and Mars posited in Leo aspects the ASC with a menacing aspect from the IMC, it will make [him] to die by the sword. But also, if the ASC is found in Libra, and Mars in Capricorn, i.e. in the IMC, aspects the ASC by square with a menacing aspect, it will also make him to die struck down[3] by a sword.

62. Moreover, it must be known that if with the ASC posited in Aries or in Scorpio, Mars is found in the DSC or in the MC <or in the IMC>,[4] with [only] a light testimony of the benefics, it denotes nothing of evil, especially if it is a nocturnal nativity. For Mars always protects his own domicile, and never overthrows it when posited in the DSC.

63. If <in . . . the ASC>[5] is so posited that the domiciles of Saturn are posited in the DSC, and Saturn itself is posited in the MC, it will make men to die suffering from dropsy. But if those signs that we have mentioned possess the ASC, and Mercury is posited in the MC, it will make

---

[1]<in those degrees> adds edition **a**, and <of Pisces> adds Ziegler, having compared viii.17.1.

[2]The words in angle brackets are supplied by edition **a**.

[3]Reading *percussus* '(him) struck down' with the **Δ** Family of MSS rather than *percussos* '(them) struck down' with the **Γ** Family. The whole paragraph refers to one Native.

[4]Adds Ziegler.

[5]The words in angle brackets are suggested by Ziegler to fill an obvious lacuna, but other words are missing. Perhaps *Leone aut Cancro* 'Leo or Cancer' should be inserted, since they are the signs opposite Aquarius and Capricorn.

men to die by poison. But if, with those signs in the ASC, Jupiter is found in the MC, a sudden death from indigestion,[1] or from too much to drink, is denoted in the course of drinks and meals, and in the course of the happy noises of the guests. But if, with those signs that we have mentioned in the ASC, Mars and the Sun are posited in the MC, either they will perish by the sword, or they are burnt up by a conflagration of fire. But if, with those signs in the ASC, the Moon is found in the MC, it will make them to die struck down by the sacred illness.[2] But if, <with those signs in the ASC>,[3] Venus is found in the MC, it will make them to complete their gift of life either weighed down by bad humors, or drowned by rushing waves.

64. If Mars and Mercury are posited together in the 8th house from the ASC, it will make bad thieves who crave the things of others with a depraved desire of mind, and who, possessed by an excessive furor of mind and the fault of greed, always hotly pursue the wealth of others with the unjust desires of longing.

65. If the Sun is found in the ASC, and the Moon is posited in the DSC, but Saturn and Mars are either posited together with the Sun or with the Moon, or one of the malefic stars is posited either with the Sun or with the Moon, [and] the other malefic star holds one angle of the following angles, he who has them thus will be exposed.

66. If Mars is posited <in the DSC>,[4] and Mercury posited in the MC is joined to Mars by a square aspect, it will make public and malicious prosecutors. But also, if Mercury is found in the DSC, and Mars posited in the MC aspects Mercury by square, it will produce armed robbers, but those who are frequently stained by human blood.

67. If Mars is found in . . .,[5] and Saturn is posited in the *anafora* of any angle,[6] but the Moon and Jupiter are posited together in a dejected house, those who are born thus live until the Moon quickly transits Jupiter in her

[1]This seems to refer to death from a stroke or from a heart attack, both of which sometime appear initially to be acute indigestion.

[2]Namely, by epilepsy.

[3]Adds Ziegler.

[4]I have added this to fill the lacuna, since the next sentence plainly reverses the configuration. Bram and Prof. Monat mistakenly adopt the addition *in horoscopo* 'in the ascendant' offered by edition **a**.

[5]The location of Mars is missing. Edition **a** inserts *in horoscopo* 'in the ASC', and this is accepted by Bram and Prof. Monat.

[6]Bram mistakenly has 'and Saturn is on any angle'.

course. But if the Moon is conjoined to Jupiter by a faithful aspect, they live until Saturn transits the angle, making its first occurrence. But if the Moon's rays are unstable, they live as many days, just as we have said, as those days that the Moon is found with Jupiter. But if, with Mars and Saturn posited as we have said before, and Jupiter posited in a dejected house, and with the Moon posited in the principal angle, i.e. in the ASC degree, they will make short lived persons with a bad danger of death.

68. But if Saturn is found in the MC, and the Moon posited in the IMC is joined by an opposition aspect to Saturn, but Mars posited either in the DSC or in the MC, makes a menacing aspect to the Moon, possessing equal degrees to [those of] the Moon, <so that>[1] the fetus bursts forth all at once from the narrowness of the womb, [and] delivers itself to an oncoming death.[2] But also, if the Sun is found in the ASC, and the Moon posited in the DSC is joined to the Sun by an opposition aspect, and Mars or Saturn is posited with one of them, i.e. either with the Sun or with the Moon, or, with one of them being there, the other holds some other angle, the one who is born will be exposed.

69. If the Sun is found in the 6th house from the ASC, and Saturn posited in the 12th house from the ASC aspects the Sun by opposition, but also the Moon and Mars in the 12th house from the ASC with Saturn in equal society of degrees conjoined to the Sun, they also oppose themselves by opposition, they make weak persons, and paralytics, [so that] the network of their nerves having been dissolved, their whole body is deformed with weak and dispersed strengths.

70. If Saturn and Mars and the Moon posited together, and conjoined in an equal association of degrees, are posited in the 11th house from the ASC, and Jupiter aspects them by trine, or is posited namely in the DSC or in the 3rd house from the ASC, but the Sun holds the ASC partilely, this nativity shows us a tyrant.

71. If Mercury, Venus, Saturn, and Mars are posited together in the 11th house from the ASC in equal aspect, they make a luxurious person who is involved in lavish expenditures and lewd desires.

72. If Mars and Mercury are posited together in the 5th house from the ASC, and Saturn, placed in a superior position, aspects them by square, or if it was posited with them—conjoined in an equal association of de-

[1]Adds Ziegler.
[2]That is, by a miscarriage.

grees—they will make forgers, or those who copy public moneys by counterfeit artifices of coinage. But if the Moon gives the nod by any agreement to these posited thus, they will produce cruel[1] armed robbers and murderers. But if Mars and Mercury hold the 5th house from the ASC, and the Moon aspects either Saturn when she has little light, or certainly Mercury or Mars when she is full of light, it denotes demise by a public death, because of the crime of forgery,[2] so that those who are detected in that crime are punished by a severe judicial sentence.

73. But if with the Sun posited in the ASC, and with Mercury posited with that same [star], Saturn and Mars posited in the DSC aspect the Sun by opposition, they will make those apprehended in the crime of forgery to be raised up on the cross. And the good testimony of Jupiter cannot lessen this danger, but deprived of his salutary assistance, the threatening aspects of the malefic stars generally denote the demise of a public death.

74. If Saturn and Mars are partilely posited in the ASC, and the Sun and Mercury posited together in the DSC aspects them by opposition, from that association of aspects either a foot is amputated or a hand. But afterward, when they are wounded by that mangling of the body, they also meet with a miserable demise of death.

75. If in the same sign the ASC degree is found in the middle between Saturn and Mars, it shows a lamentable instance of disastrous misfortune. For within the viscera of the mother, mangled by a difficult birth, the fetus is destroyed by miserable lacerations, so that, with the parts of the viscera cut up, all the members are brought forth by the assistance of a cruel artifice.

76. If the Moon posited in a duplex sign possesses the MC degree, and Saturn is posited in the DSC and Mars in the IMC, it will make epileptics. But if the Moon is in conjunction with the Sun, and Mars is posited together with her, and the Moon along with the Sun and Mars holds the MC degree, and Mars is posited in his morning rising, and Saturn is either posited with them or is in the DSC, they will make epileptics in a similar fashion, who, changed by an insane furor of mind, lose the correct order of life. But if, with Mars and the Moon and the Sun posited just as we have said, Saturn is found in the IMC, and it aspects those in the MC by

---

[1]Accepting Ziegler's conjecture *inprobos* 'cruel' instead of the *in posteris* of the MSS. Némethy suggested *praeposteros* 'outrageous'. Bram accepts the reading of the MSS *in posteris*, and translates it 'later'.

[2]Under Roman law, forgery was a capital offense.

an opposition, then depressed by some mental defect, and thrown down from a precipice, they will receive the exit of a miserable death. But in general, if Mars and Saturn are posited together in duplex signs[1] and they are together in the DSC, they always denote these same things in similar fashion. But also, if with Saturn and Mars posited in the DSC, the Moon is posited in the ASC, they denote these same things in similar fashion.[2]

77. If the ASC is found with the Sun in Gemini, and the Moon is posited in the MC, i.e. in Pisces, but Mars posited in the IMC, i.e. in Virgo, . . .[3] holds the DSC angle, so that posited in duplex signs they hold [all] the angles of the nativity, they will make epileptics by this relationship.

78. If Jupiter posited in a duplex sign holds the MC angle, and Saturn posited in the IMC aspects it by opposition, and the Moon is joined to Saturn by conjunction, having been adopted by non-relatives, they seek their fortune by the title of inheritance, so that, by the laws of those [people], they are made to be children for those for whom nature has denied children [of their own].

79. If Mars and Saturn and Venus are conjoined in an equal association of degrees in the MC, and Mercury testifies to them as a fourth,[4] they will produce whores, who, to the detriment of bought modesty and for the sake of prostituting their body, seek a miserable profit day by day. But if this was the nativity of a male, he will be involved with the ardor of effeminate passion in the feminine vices of lusts.

80. If the Sun and Mars are found together in the ASC, and Saturn posited in the IMC aspects them by square, but the Moon posited in the MC [aspects] Saturn by opposition, but she aspects the Sun and Mars by square, it always incites parricidal hatreds of the parents among the sons.

81. If Mars is posited in the ASC, and Jupiter is posited in the 6th house from the ASC, and the Moon with Mercury and Venus possess the MC degree with an equal association of conjunction, the insignia of a very famous nobility are denoted by this configuration.

---

[1]That is, a mutable sign—three of which (Gemini, Sagittarius, and Pisces) are also bicorporeal.

[2]Reading **ratione* 'fashion' instead of *radiatione* 'aspect'.

[3]Ziegler notes that several words are missing in the Latin text. Probably the other planet is Saturn.

[4]Bram takes *quartus* 'fourth' to mean *ex quadrato* and translates it as 'in square aspect', but I disagree.

82. If the ASC is found in Aries, and Mars, Saturn, and Venus <are posited> together there, and also the Sun <posited> in the same sign <is joined> to them <by conjunction>,[1] it denotes a serving-maid, or an old woman as his wife, or certainly a humble woman devoid of all the protection of dignity. But if Mercury approaches them posited thus, they bring public whores to the marriage bed. But if, with all of these posited just as we have said, the Moon is found in the MC, they compel those persons, possessed by an incestuous ardor of passion, to come to having sexual intercourse with their own daughters.

83. If Mars and the Sun posited in a tropical sign are found in the DSC, and Mercury joins them as a third in that same house, they will make an armed robber, but one who, exercising his robbery in foreign places, is stained with human blood. But this same person, detected in that same crime by that association of stars, is struck down by a severe judicial sentence.

84. If Mercury and the Moon and Venus are posited together in the 11th house from the ASC, and it is a sign of the feminine gender, and Mars aspects them by trine, they will make musicians who always strike the strings of the lyre or the lute with a sweet melody.

85. If Mercury and Mars and Venus and the Moon are posited together in the ASC, or in the MC, they will make dancers [or] pantomimes adorned with the grace of charm. But if Jupiter makes a fortunate aspect to them posited thus, it bestows fame upon those same persons by popular judgment, especially if Saturn adds a good testimony to those same [stars] posited thus.

86. If the Moon is found in conjunction with the Sun in the 11th house from the ASC, and Jupiter is posited together with them, but Saturn and Mars make different aspects to the ASC, one by square and the other by opposition, and one of them, i.e. either Saturn or Mars, is posited in an equinoctial sign, they denote a lengthy and daily illness of elephantiasis down to the last day of his life.

88. If the Moon was found in the Pleiades[2] of Taurus, or in the Nebula of Cancer,[3] or in the Forehead of Scorpio,[4] namely from the 8th de-

---

[1]Ziegler adds the words in angle brackets to fill the lacunae in the Latin text.

[2]Reading *pleiadibus* with **Γ** (*pliadibus* **Δ**) 'Pleiades' rather than Skutsch's conjecture *pedibus* 'feet' (which is accepted by Bram and Prof. Monat). In Ptolemy's Catalogue of Stars (+2°20), these stars are in 4°30-6°00 Taurus.

[3]Praesepe or ε Cancri is in 12°40 Cancer.

[4]The stars βδπ Scorpii in 8°00-8°40 Scorpio.

gree up to the 10th, or in Sagittarius, or in the Spine of Capricorn,[1] or in the Line of Pisces,[2] or in the Head of Aries,[3] and it has little light—i.e. when all its light has been expended—and either Mars or Saturn makes any aspect to it, it will make persons who are blind. But if it holds any angle of the nativity in those signs and in those houses that we have mentioned, with all the substance of the eyes dissipated, it brings about the miserable danger of blindness. But if the Moon is full of light or is still receiving increases of its splendor, it will not make blind persons, but it always inflicts either a bodily defect, or an illness, or a scar or a mark on the face, so that it disgraces the face with an ugly appearance.

89. If Jupiter and Mars are found partilely in the MC, and Mercury and Venus are conjoined in a equal society of degrees in the 3rd house from the ASC, but Saturn holds the 8th house from the ASC, and the Sun is in Gemini, and moreover the Moon is posited either in her own domicile or in her exaltation, this decree will make a man who is a hero, strong, and a killer, who with his victorious right hand[4] makes heaps of foes in an exceptional massacre of them.

90. If the ASC is found in either one of the tropical signs, and the Moon is posited in the 12th house from the ASC, but Jupiter and Mars conjoined in an equal association of degrees hold the angle of the IMC, [and] Mercury and Venus with equal degrees possess the angle of the MC, this nativity displays the mind of a malicious whore, to whose sexual intercourse she invites many for the sake of sexual pleasure. But this woman is led through foreign places, and she will be involved in frequent accidents, and in frequent and great accusations. She will also be placed in public custody, and she will suffer frequent annoyances, and more frequent injuries; she will also abort twin children.

91. But she [will practice] these occupations, and because of lust she will also defame her own honor with two brothers, and she will likewise invite her own father to sexual intercourse and also her son; for she will perform all of these things because of the ardor of lust and her unrestrained desire for money. But when she has entered the time of middle age, then she will return to her homeland, and she will associate herself

[1]The stars ε κ Capricorni in 25°40 and 27°20 Capricorn.

[2]There are 15 of these stars running from 13°20 Pisces to 3°00 Aries

[3]Probably Hamal or α Arietis in 13°00 Aries.

[4]*Cf.* Lucan, *Pharsalia*, i. 3.

on the marriage bed with an unworthy, poor, young foreigner; and, joined to him by the vows of matrimony, she will come to the last day of her life in miserable want.

XXXII.

1. Since we have set forth all those things that the mixture of temperaments shows, and have composed them in diligent fashion, the discussion, my dear Mavortius, hastens toward the end of this Book. But there is [still] that which is required for the full substance of this work, which I shall now show you with the truest explanation. For otherwise, we cannot come to the secrets of astrology, which the Seventh Book will have, and to the Barbaric Sphere, which the body of the Eighth Book shows to you, unless all those things that pertain to the fundamentals of the whole science shall first have been collected in diligent fashion.

2. We shall therefore show what you ought to look for in each house[1] and to what extent. For neither does the Fourth House from the ASC show the parents and the life of the parents, nor the Seventh the marriage partner, nor the Fifth the children, nor the Third the friends,[2] nor the Sixth illness. Therefore, because we have promised that we are going to relate everything, accept the method that is full of truth and faith, so that you can collect everything by a careful method—lest, occupied by general definitions, you should lose the integral faith of truth. Therefore, you will always find the House of the Father especially by this method.

3. **The House of the Father.**[3] If you want to collect the House of the Father by the method of degrees, and it is a diurnal nativity, you should

[1]Here, Firmicus begins his discussion of a procedure similar to that used for finding various Lots, but instead of having as its goal the determination of the *degree* in which the Lot falls, its goal is to determine the *sign* in which that degree falls, and he calls that sign the "House" as he is about to explain. He then goes on to say that you cannot judge the father, the wife, etc., from the usual celestial houses, but you must calculate these special "Houses" that pertain to them. And once you have done that, you must consider the placement of the sign in the chart and the aspects to it. Thus, instead of finding the Lot of the Father, for example, you are to find the sign that constitutes the House of the Father. And you must then consider the planetary ruler of that sign, which would of course be the ruler of the House.

[2]This should read 'or the Third the brothers' or else 'or the Eleventh the friends'.

[3]The Teubner editors bracket the chapter titles here and below, but I have kept them as a convenience to the Reader, even though they may not have been present in the archetype.

compute the whole number of degrees from the degree of the Sun up to the degree of Saturn, viz. of all the signs which are from the Sun up to Saturn, and when you have made the complete sum of the number, then beginning from the degree of the ASC, you will divide that number, which was obtained, among all the signs, assigning thirty degrees to the individual signs; and in that sign in which the last degree has fallen, that same sign shows you the House of the Father. But in a nocturnal nativity, you will compute from the degree of Saturn up to [the degree] of the Sun, doing the same thing.

4. And so, when by careful computation you have found the Sign of the Father, you will figure the personal wealth of the father from the nature of that very sign. Also, look to see to what extent that same sign is adorned with the rays of the benefic stars. For if there were benefic stars in that very sign, or if they aspected it with a fortunate aspect, the good fortune of the father is found. But if malefic stars did that same thing, they proclaim to us [that] everything about the father is contrary.

5. Also, look at that same sign [to see] whether it is [the sign] of a benefic star or a malefic one, and how the ruler of that sign is situated in the nativity, or in what sign or in what terms it is, and whether it is standing in primary or in secondary angles, [and] whether it is in those houses in which it rejoices or in disjunct and dejected ones. For from all of these things you will find what sort [of person] the father of the nativity was.

6. If, therefore, it was a sign of Jupiter in which the House of the Father was found, and Jupiter is posited in that very sign, or in those signs in which it is exalted, or in the primary angles, or in the 5th or the 11th house, and it is adding to its numbers,[1] and it is posited in its matutine rising, and it sees the house by trine or by sextile, it shows the father to be decorated with the fortunate insignia of dignity. But if Jupiter was found in the secondary angles, or in dejected and disjunct houses, or it was retrograde, or hidden by the rays of the Sun,[2] it shows the father to have been of middling status.

7. But if Venus was the ruler of this sign in which the House of the Father was found, it must be sought out in which [celestial] house the star of Venus is located. For if it was either in that very house, or in the primary

[1]That is, it is direct.

[2]That is, it was under the Sun beams.

angles, or in those signs in which it rejoices, or in which it is exalted, or in the 5th from the ASC or in the 11th house, and if it is in its matutine rising, but adding to its numbers and being posited in those houses or signs, it sees the House of the Father with a fortunate aspect, it denotes the greatest insignia of honesty and the greatest charm of grace for the father. But if it was in dejected houses, and in those signs in which it is humiliated, or if it was retrograde, or hidden by the rays of the Sun, it shows us a middling father.

8. But if the House of the Father was found in a sign of Mercury, seek out in which house Mercury was posited. For if it was either in that very same house, or in its own exaltation, or in its other domicile, or in its own degrees and in those very angles and houses in which it rejoices, and if it is in its matutine rising, and it is adding to its numbers,[1] it will make the father to be involved in all the activities of business affairs, and a person on whom the greatest profits are frequently conferred, and who always cherishes his sons with tender affection.

9. But if a fortunate aspect of the benefic stars strikes Mercury—i.e. the ruler of the House of the Father—he will obtain greater increases in those things that we have mentioned. But if Mercury is in dejected houses, or in those angles in which it does not rejoice, or in its own fall, or if it is retrograde, or it is hidden by the rays of the Sun,[2] the preceding decrees of good fortune are changed, and all those things that we have mentioned are conferred skimpily and [only] moderately on the father.

10. But if the House of the Father was found in a sign of Saturn, look to see in which house of the nativity Saturn is posited. For if it was a diurnal nativity, and Saturn was found in that very house, or in his own degrees, or in his own signs, or in those degrees in which he is exalted, and in those houses in which he rejoices, and he is in his morning rising, and he is adding to his number,[3] and if Jupiter views him with a fortunate aspect, it will make the father to be serious, modest, mature, [but] terrifying with calm severity, a cultivator of fields, and one on whom from their produce the greatest supports of personal fortune are conferred, and one who is elevated by great promotions.

11. But if it is a nocturnal nativity, and Saturn is in dejected houses, or in dejected angles, or in his own fall, and if he is retrograde, or hidden by

---

[1]That is, it is direct.

[2]That is, it is under the Sunbeams.

[3]That is, it is direct.

the rays of the Sun, it makes the father to be over-worked, sordid, horrible, sad, struggling always with sluggish efforts, a slave, or a person defiled with servile habits or the squalor of servitude.

12. If the House of the Father was found in a sign of Mars, and it is a diurnal nativity, but Mars itself is either in that same house, or in the angles, or in the 5th, or in the 11th house from the ASC, or in the 9th, or in the 3rd, and if he is in his morning rising, and going on by the correct stepping forward of degrees,[1] it will make the father to be severe and thoughtless, involved in various kinds of toil and various dangers—a short-lived person—always involved in absurd desires.

13. But if Mars posited thus aspects the House of the Father by square or by opposition, it makes him die violently. But if it is a nocturnal nativity and Jupiter and Venus make a fortunate aspect to the House of the Father or the House of the Mother, those things that we have mentioned are mitigated in some part, and it makes the father to be an upright, severe soldier, whom arms and iron always [bring] delight; and according to the measure of the nativity it makes . . . . or a general.[2]

14. If the House of the Father is found in the Sun's sign, and it is a diurnal nativity, look to see in which sign or in which house of the nativity the Sun is posited. For if the Sun is either in that very sign, or in his own exaltation, or in the principal angles, or in the 5th or in the 11th house from the ASC, it shows the father to be wealthy with abundant riches, and decorated with the greatest insignia of dignity, and winning the fame of great good fortune.

15. But if the Sun is in dejected houses, or in the second angles, or in its own debilities, and an aspect of the malefic stars attacks it, [while] bereft of [support from] the benefics, all those things that we have said are for the greatest part diminished, especially if it is a nocturnal nativity; for then it ruins the father—among other things too, by a quick death.

16. If the House of the Father is found in the sign of the Moon, look to see in which house of the nativity the Moon is posited. For if she is either in that same house, or in those signs in which she is exalted, or in the principal angles, or in the 5th or in the 11th house from the ASC, and she is

[1]The Teubner editors say that they don't understand this phrase. I suppose that Firmicus merely means that the planet is direct and not retrograde, but this may not be correct.

[2]Some words are missing in the Latin text. Edition **a** supplies the words *<aut principem> aut ducem* '<either a chieftain> or a general'.

full of light, and it is a nocturnal nativity, and benefic stars make a fortunate aspect to her, and she is separated from all association with the malefic stars, it will make the father to be famous, distinguished, affluent, and one on whom wealth and dignity are always bestowed.

17. But if the Moon is in dejected houses, or in the second angles, or in her own debilities, and an aspect of the malefic stars attacks her [while she is] devoid of the protection of the benefic stars, and it is a diurnal nativity, and she has little light, and Saturn aspects her, or Mars [if she is] full, everything that we have said before is diminished to the greatest extent, and the father is either made an exile or a person dying violently,[and a person] with erratic behavior, – not knowing the right way of life.

18. But also in [considering] this House, as we have said before, you ought always to inspect the mixtures, sects, and aspects of the stars in a diligent manner, so that having mixed everything together and composed them with the combination of a sagacious blending, you may be able to explain the House of the Father with true opinions.

19. You ought also to follow this scheme of astrological influences in the following houses. For in the Houses of the Mother, and the Brothers, and the Wife, and of the Children, and Illnesses and Bodily Defects, you should blend everything together with the wisest logic, so that, having looked at the aspects of all the stars, and having collected the power of the houses and signs, and also of the degrees (i.e. the terms), you may be able to explain everything with true opinions.

20. But in the case of the other Houses, these same things also are the significations [that] we collect <for> the House.[1] Generally, moreover, in nativities the Sun is put for the House of the Father, but we have found the procedure by degrees to be better.

21. **The House of the Mother.** If you want to determine the House of the Mother by the method of degrees, and if it is a diurnal nativity, beginning from the degree of Venus and proceeding through the following signs, count all the degrees up to the degree of the Moon, and having collected the sum of all the degrees, distribute all the degrees beginning from the ASC, and in whatever degree the last degree comes to, that sign shows you the House of the Mother in a diurnal nativity.

22. But if it was a nocturnal nativity, beginning from the degree of the

[1]Reading *sint apotelesmata <pro> locum collegimus*. Firmicus is saying "follow the same procedure for the other Houses."

Moon collect the degrees up to the degree of Venus, and you will treat the rest in similar fashion. Therefore you will collect this House with a degree method, looking for[1] everything thus, just as we have said that you ought to search for it in the House of the Father, namely the aspects of the benefic and the malefic stars, also the powers of the houses and signs, and also the mixtures and proper blending of the aspects. Which, when you have brought together everything with an even-handed comparison, you will be able to explain the House of the Mother with true opinions.

23. **The House of Brothers.** If you want to find the House of Brothers by degree, and it is a diurnal nativity, beginning from the degree of Saturn, compute up to the degree of Jupiter, and however many are computed, distribute that same sum through the following signs beginning from the ASC degree, and in whatever sign the last degree of the total number comes to, that sign shows you the House of Brothers. But if it is a nocturnal nativity, you will compute the whole number of degrees from Jupiter to Saturn in a similar manner, and so, beginning from the ASC you will complete [the calculation] in a similar fashion.

24. When, therefore, you determine the House of Brothers by that method of degrees, look at that same House to see to what extent the malefic and benefic stars aspect it. See also the power of the sign and in what house of the nativity that sign is seen to be posited.

25. For if benefic stars are either found in that same sign, or if they are posited in fortunate houses of the nativity and in those signs in which they rejoice, or in which they are exalted, or in their own domiciles, they denote a group of many and good brothers. But if malefic stars do that same thing, devoid of the testimonies of the benefic stars, they do the contrary.

26. But if [both] benefic and malefic stars aspect that same House with an equal power of association, they both give brothers and take them away. But you will deal with this according to the kinds of stars. For masculine benevolent stars will give males, but feminine benefic stars females. The malefic stars do this same thing. So all things are done in accordance with the power of the individual stars. But in general, just as we said in the Book of Fundamentals,[2] the 3rd house from the ASC shows brothers. But we should inquire [about them] in particular.

---

[1]Reading *requirens* 'looking for' with MS **N** rather than *requires* 'you will look' with **Γ**.

[2]Book II.

27. **The House of the Spouse.** If you want to find the House of the Spouse by degree, compute from the degree of Saturn up to the degree of Venus, and whatever sum the computation has made, beginning from the ASC, distribute that much through the following signs, and in whatever sign you find the last degree, that degree shows you the House of the Spouse in a diurnal nativity.

28. But in a nocturnal nativity, beginning from Venus, you will compute to Saturn, and beginning from the ASC you will similarly divide the collected degrees, and in whatever sign the last degree comes to, that sign shows you the House of the Spouse in a nocturnal nativity. Others, [however], compute from the Sun to the Moon both in a diurnal and a nocturnal nativity, computing similarly in both a man's and a woman's nativity, and we have proved this in many nativities.

29. When, therefore, you have determined the House of the Spouse by this method that we have stated, first look at the power of the sign, whether it is solid, or duplex,[1] or tropical. Secondly, look at this – in what house of the nativity the ruler of the sign is located. Thirdly, take note of this same house, i.e. in which the ruler of the terms is, [and] to what extent the benefic and malefic stars aspect it. For when benefic stars possess that same sign in which the House of the Spouse is found, [and] they are posited in fortunate houses of the nativity, and debilitated by no humility, and when they have followed the power of their own sect, they will give famous rich wives, whom the [Natives] always espouse with harmonious ties.

30. But the marriage of many wives is not denoted. For whatever one they allotted, she will remain in the marriage up to the last day of his life with the charm and delight of [her] beauty. But you will define the manners of the wives from the nature of the signs; for from the difference of the signs you will be able to find the kinds of marriages.

31. But if the malefic stars make this same [configuration], they will make everything contrary to the [foregoing]. For then they denote commonplace wives who are not famous, then dissensions in marriage, bitter quarrels of disagreement, then the miserable confusion of separations is carried out, then sterile or adulterous wives. But you will be able to explain all these things according to the powers of the stars.

32. But if you want to find the **House of the Husband** in a woman's nativity, and it is a diurnal nativity, [compute] from Mars to Venus, <but

---

[1]That is, *mutable*.

in a nocturnal>[1] [nativity], you will do this same thing in similar fashion. <Beginning> from the ASC, <you will divide>[2] that amount <through the following signs>,[3] and in whatever sign the number of the last degree comes to, that sign shows you the House of the Husband. And so, what kind of person the husband is, you will be able to gather in a fashion similar to that which we have stated about women in the nativities of men. Moreover, you ought to remember that Venus generally shows the wife, [and] Mars always shows the husband.

33. **The House of Children.** Venus and Mercury always show us the House of Children. Whichever one of them is posited first in the nativity, beginning from that one, you will compute up to the other one; and beginning from the ASC, you will divide the collected sum of all the degrees through the following signs, and in whatever sign the last degree comes to, that shows you the sign of the House of Children.

34. Moreover, how it may be that we have said one of them is *the first*, we shall explain with this example. If Venus is in Taurus and Mercury in Gemini, Mercury is found first; therefore, beginning from Mercury you will compute up to Venus. But if in a similar manner Venus is before and Mercury in later signs, you will give the beginning to Venus.

35. But if they were [both] placed in one sign, beginning from the one <that was in the earlier degrees of the sign>,[4] you will come to the other one that was found in the latter degrees in that same sign. But if they were found in the same degrees, beginning from that one whose minutes are first. But if they were in the very same (identical) minutes, then having passed over that [procedure], you will compute from Jupiter to Mercury in a diurnal [nativity], in a nocturnal [nativity] from Jupiter to Mercury in the same way.

36. Therefore, when you have found the House of Children by the method of degrees, look[5] in a similar fashion to what extent the benefic and malefic stars aspect that same House, but also [after] having studied

---

[1]Adds Edition **a**.

[2]Adds Ziegler.

[3]I have added these words.

[4]Adds Ziegler (apparently rightly) to fill in a lacuna. But note that the direction of measurement here is reversed to the direction just stated for whole signs in the preceding paragraph. This appears to be inconsistent.

[5]Reading with the Teubner editors and MSS **D²N²** *inspice* 'look', instead of *in Piscibus* 'in Pisces'.

the sects of the stars with the most diligent care, and also both the nature and power of the sign. For if benefic stars, posited in favorable houses of the nativity and in favorable signs, aspect that house, they denote children according to the power of the houses and the signs.

37. But malefic [stars] do the opposite. But also those very malefic stars, if the nativity is of their own sect, do denote children—that is Saturn in a diurnal [nativity], and Mars in a nocturnal one. Moreover, children are denoted in accordance with the nature of the signs. We of course ought to remember that if the House of Children was found in a duplex sign, a man will have children from two wives, but if it is a solid sign, from one wife; but a woman will have children from one husband.

38. But if [both] malefic and benefic stars aspect the House of Children equally, at the same time they both give and take away the progeny of children, or if the power of the benefic stars prevails, [yet] some debility from the inimical aspects of the malefics is inflicted on the children that are born; or they surely separate the children from their parents by a great quarrel.

39. Therefore, both in the case of this House and in that of all the rest, you will examine the mixtures and combinations of the stars in a diligent manner, also the nature of the signs, but also the proper powers of the houses from the ASC. Generally moreover, the 5th house [from the ASC] shows the House of Children, and the ruler of its sign, and the nature of that sign, and the testimonies of the benefic and malefic stars.

40. **The House of Bodily Defects and Illness.** If you want to find the House of Bodily Defects and Illnesses by degree, in a diurnal nativity at any rate beginning from Saturn, you will compute up to Mars, and that amount from the ASC, but in a nocturnal one beginning from Mars you will compute up to Saturn, and that amount from the ASC, and in whatever sign the last number of degrees comes to, that sign shows you the House of Bodily Defects and Illness.

41. But generally the 6th sign from the ASC shows the bodily defects. And so in the first place defining bodily defects and illnesses from the sign in this house—for we have said in the Book of Instruction which parts of the body the individual signs possess—you will inspect in the second place to what extent the benefic and malefic stars aspect this same house.

42. For if they aspect the house with a fortunate aspect when they are located in their own domiciles or in their exaltations, they will free the man from every attack of illness. But if the malefic stars aspect this house with a threatening aspect, they denote bitter bodily defects of illnesses with a wretched calamity.

43. But you will perceive these bodily defects according to the nature of the signs and their power. For Mars denotes blows, minor body wounds, falls, and collapse of buildings, and demises from these same instances of wretched wounds. But Saturn denotes spasms, tremors, and troubles and wretched dangers from waters and things similar to these. But if . . . the malefic stars, they are denoting bodily defects for the testicles.[1]

44. But if this house is possessed by malefics [and] remains bereft of all aid from the benefic stars, they denote perpetual bodily defects of illnesses, and deadly outcomes of calamities. Moreover, Mars will do its harm within 15 years, Saturn within 30 years, and the Sun within 19 years. But if there are two of them doing harm, computing the years of both of them to define the time, expect the onset of the bodily defect or the illness at both times; moreover, the kinds of the bodily defects is denoted by the individual nature of each star.[2]

45. If you want to find the **House of Desires** by degrees, in a diurnal nativity of course, compute from the Part of the Daemon up to the degree of the Part of Fortune, and [cast] that much from the ASC. But in a nocturnal [nativity] you will compute from Fortune up to the Daemon in very similar fashion, and [cast] that much from the ASC, and when you have determined the House by the method of degrees, all the craving of desires will be shown to you by the sign and the testimonies of the stars. But you may find the House of Fortune and the House of the Daemon by the method we have stated in the Fourth Book.

46. **The House of Necessity.** If you want to find the House of Necessity by the method of degrees, you will of course compute from the Part of Fortune to the Part of the Daemon, but in a nocturnal one from the Part of the Daemon to the Part of Fortune, and [cast] that much from the

[1]The Latin is incomplete and possibly corrupt, but this is perhaps its meaning. Prof. Monat agrees. Bram has "These maladies are definitely attested if malefic planets are in aspect."—thereby taking *testes* to mean 'witnesses' (whence, 'attested') instead of 'testicles'.

[2]Accepting Ziegler's emendation and addition to the lacuna in the MSS.

ASC,[1] and when you have determined this same House by this method, you will define everything about this House in accordance with the quality of the signs and the stars.

47. **The House of Honors.** If you want to determine the House of Honors by the method of degrees, you will compute from Jupiter to the Sun,[2] and [cast] that amount from the ASC, and whatever sign receives the last degree, that one shows you the House of Honors, and from its own nature and from the testimonies of all the stars [you will define the honors].

48. **The House of Military Service.** If you want to determine the House of Military Service by degrees, you will always compute from Mars to the Sun, and [cast] that amount from the ASC, and in whatever sign the last degree comes to, that sign shows the outcome of military service to you in accordance with its own nature and the testimonies of the stars.

49. **The House of Travel.** If you want to find the House of Travel, you will always compute from the Sun to Mars, and [cast] that amount from the ASC, and in whatever sign the last degree comes to, that sign shows the result of travel to you in accordance with its own nature and in accordance with the testimonies of the stars.[3]

50. **The House of Fame and Reputation**. If you would like to check the Fame of Reputation by the method of degrees, you will compute from the Sun to the MC, and [cast] that amount from the ASC, and in whatever sign the last degree comes to, that sign shows you by its own nature and by the testimonies of the stars the fame of his reputation.

51. **The House of the Strength of the Body**. If you want to find the Strength of the Body by degrees, you will compute from the Moon to Jupiter, and [cast] that amount from the ASC, also doing the rest in similar fashion, for they will show everything by the nature of the sign [and] the testimony of the stars.

---

[1]Note that the procedure for determining this House is the reverse of the procedure for determining the House of Desires.

[2]The Latin text has *a IX . . . ad Solem* 'from the 9th . . . to the Sun', but the Teubner editors would emend *IX* to *Iove* 'Jupiter', and this is correct. *Cf.* Heliodorus, *Commentary on Paul*, Chapter 22, where the Lot from Jupiter to the Sun is the Lot of Wealth or the Lot of Dignity.

[3]Again, the procedure for finding this House is the reverse of the one for finding the House of Military Service.

52. **The House of the Substance of Possessions**. If you want to collect the Substance of Possessions by the method of degrees, you will always compute from Mercury to Jupiter, and that much from the ASC, and in whatever sign the last degree falls, from the nature of that sign and from the testimonies of the stars you will find the class of possessions.

53. **The House of Accusations**. If you want to find the House of Accusation by the method of degrees, you will always compute from Mars to Saturn, and that much from the ASC, and in whatever sign the last degree falls, that sign, in accordance with its own nature and in accordance with the testimonies of the other stars, shows you the result of the accusation.

54. **The House of Adversaries and Enemies**. If you want to find the House of Adversaries and Enemies by the method of degrees, you will compute by day from Mars to Mercury, but by night from Mercury again to Mars, and that much from the ASC, and in whatever sign the last degree comes to, <that sign> shows <you>[1] enemies from its nature and from the testimonies of the stars.

55. **The House of Friends**. If you want to find the House of Friends by the method of degrees, you will in fact compute by day from Jupiter to Mercury, but by night from Mercury to Jupiter, and that much from the ASC; in whatever sign the last degree comes to that sign will show you friends from its own nature and from the testimonies of the stars in very true fashion.

56. **[The House of Glory.]** [The House] of Glory by night from Venus to Jupiter, by day the reverse. [**The House**] **of Nemesis** by night from **Fortuna to the Moon. [The House] of Power by night from Saturn to the Sun. [The House**] **of the Basis** by night from Fortuna to the Daemon.[3] But if Venus has more than 30 degrees, either by day or by night, [do the reverse].[2]

---

[1]Added by the Teubner Editors.

[2]Bram omits this House and also the corrupt sentence that follows.

[3]The Latin text of II.189.24-25 *Si vero Venus XXX partes excesserit, sive in nocte, sive in die*, †*inter contra inter d. contra diu contra* is meaningless as it stands, but possibly Firmicus instructed us to reverse the previous direction of measuring (from Venus to Jupiter) if Venus was found <to be> more than 30 degrees <from the Sun?>. Some necessary words are obviously missing from the sentence.

57. **The House of Slaves**. If you want to find the House of Slaves by the degree method, you will always compute from Mercury to the Moon, and that much from the ASC, and in what ever sign the last degree comes to, that sign shows you slaves according to its own nature and according to the testimonies of the stars.

58. **The House of Burial**. If [you want to find the House] of Burial . . . it shows the outcome of <burial>.[1]

XXXIII.

1. We have begun to intimate to you, Mavortius all the secrets of astrology with the truest statements, but the Seventh Book shows the fullest treatise of all these, so that you may be able to find everything without any difficulty by the most convenient and truest inquiries. But for the completion of this book, let this that I shall demonstrate to you be added—i.e., which star is with the Ruler of Times, and that one will divide the whole amount of the 10 years and 9 months [period] between itself and the rest of the stars—what it denotes, and by what reason. Moreover, the Ruler of the Times, which the Greeks call the *chronocrator*, may be found as we have shown in a clear manner in the Book of Instruction—which thing you should diligently investigate, so that you can find the sequences and outcomes of dangers.

2. If Saturn is made the Ruler of the Times, he takes for himself 30 months of the [total] time, just as we have said in the Book of Instruction. Look, therefore, how it is posited in the nativity, and whether it is a diurnal nativity or in fact a nocturnal one, and whether it holds the angles of the nativity, and what it denotes from the nature of the sign or from the power of the house. When you have collected all of these things in a careful manner, then you will find what it may do when it is the Ruler of the Times.

3. For if dangers were decreed by it in the nativity, then there will follow whatever it had previously decreed. If it denotes childlessness in the nativity, then it overtakes the miserable offspring of children with a cruel power. If it had decreed that he would be a widower, then it dissolves his marriage either by death or by divorce. If it decreed accusations, then it stirs up plots by ene-

[1]Most of this paragraph is missing in the Latin text. I have added the words in square brackets, and the Teubner editors added the word 'burial' at the end. But Bram omits the entire Paragraph 58.

mies. If it decreed illnesses, then it inflicts the defect of a miserable disaster. If it decreed losses, then it harasses the assets with various kinds of squanderings. But if it was well posited and denotes anything fortunate in the nativity, having followed the power of its own condition, it then delivers whatever it had promised previously, especially if it has the well disposed rulership[1] of the nativity, and if it is a diurnal nativity.

4. If Saturn was made Ruler of the Times, it allots 12 months of its own time to Jupiter. Therefore, if Saturn is badly posited in the nativity, and either danger, or illness, or loss, or misfortune was decreed by it, then all the threats of dangers are mitigated by the powers of that salutary God. But if well posited in the nativity it decreed the times to Jupiter, it bestows increases of the greatest good fortune, especially if it was a diurnal nativity, and, posited in good signs or in good degrees, it is joined to Jupiter by a trine aspect.

5. If Saturn, made Ruler of the Times, had allotted the times to Mars, it allots 15 months of its own decade to it.[2] But when Mars receives the time allotted to itself from (the times of) Saturn, with all its malice happily lulled, it denotes a time of joy, for they mutually mitigate each other by reason of their contrary powers.

6. If Saturn was made Ruler of the Times, it allots 19 months of its own decade to the Sun. Therefore, when the Sun has received the time allotted to itself by Saturn, it stirs up lawsuits and contentious rivalries with quarrels. But these lawsuits for the greater part are brought about properties of houses or buildings, especially if it is a nocturnal nativity. But it also denotes danger to the father, and it makes a loss of dignity.

7. If Saturn was made Ruler of the Times, it allots 8 months of its own decade to Venus. Therefore, when Venus has received the time allotted to itself by Saturn, it will make a pleasant time and one separated from all misfortune, so that the danger of the preceding misfortune that the malice of another star had perpetrated, is corrected by a salutary remedy. But if it had decreed marriage, then the Native is coupled in the matrimonial bond with a widow.

8. If Saturn was made Ruler of the Times, it allots 20 months of its own decade to Mercury. Therefore, when Mercury has received the time allot-

---

[1]Reading *dominium* 'rulership' with **A′**, rather than *dominum* 'ruler'.

[2]Accepting Kroll's suggested emendation of *eidem* 'to it' for the *quidem* 'indeed' of the MSS.

ted to itself by Saturn, it revives the dormant hostilities of old lawsuits, and it will make secret quarrels or disputes to be reinstituted along with renovated lawsuits.

9. If Saturn was made Ruler of the Times, it allots 25 months of its own decade to the Moon. Therefore, when the Moon has received the time allotted to itself by Saturn, it will stir up illnesses from corrupt humors, or it brings about the greatest crisis of danger from water, or it will make the Native to be disturbed by the warning of new lawsuits, so that this whole time always indicates various kinds of dangers and various kinds of anxieties. But these things [occur] if the Moon was full of light; [but] if it had little light and was struck by an aspect of Saturn in the nativity, it denotes the misfortune of death along with miserable calamities.

XXXIV. Jupiter.

1. When the order of times has come to Jupiter, 10 years and 9 months are also conferred upon it. But all that time is also distributed by it in a similar manner. And so it must also be examined—since it is the ruler—how it is posited in the nativity, and in what signs and in what degrees it is located, and whether it is placed in the primary angles or in the secondary ones, and whether it is in favorable houses of the nativity, or whether in truth it is in dull and dejected houses, and whether it is a diurnal nativity or whether it is a nocturnal one.

2. For, from all of these things when it is Ruler of the Times, we find the efficacies of its decrees. For whatever in the nativity was decreed by Jupiter, it does deliver when it gets the rulership of the times. But you will [also] have to observe this in all the other stars. For whatever we have said about Saturn and about Jupiter, you should conclude in the case of the other stars in similar fashion. For whatever all the stars have decreed in the nativity—whether it is favorable or evil—will be accomplished when they get the rulership of the times.

3. When 10 years and 9 months have been conferred upon Jupiter, he claims first for himself 12 months from all of that time. And so in those 12 months that Jupiter has reckoned for himself, he denotes fortunate events, fame, joys according to the measure of the nativity, especially if he was the Ruler of the Nativity. Then for every nativity, either marriage or children are decreed, if the [Native's] time of life will allow it; also, when he is Ruler of the Times, he will bring about fame in the greatest

fashion, and he also bestows honors and increases in personal wealth, just as we have said, according to the measure of the nativity.

4. If Jupiter is made the Ruler of the Times, he allots 30 months of his own decade to Saturn. Therefore, when Saturn has received the time allotted to itself by Jupiter, it will always make men to be blunted by dull association, so that in all their actions they run short with a dull listlessness of cold; but these things [will occur] if it is a nocturnal nativity, and if Saturn is not well posited in the nativity.

5. If Jupiter is made Ruler of the Times, he allots 15 months of his own decade to Mars. Therefore, when Mars has received the time allotted to itself by Jupiter, it changes all the order of his life and business affairs; and whatever is being handled by a previous arrangement of business affairs, will be transferred to another order of life, so that at this time those things established by a previous obligation are abandoned; or it will certainly bring harm along with various crises.

6. If Jupiter is made the Ruler of the Times, he allots 19 months of its own decade to the Sun. Therefore, when the Sun has received the time allotted to itself by Jupiter, it will make all the secret things of life to be made public, and it changes all of his actions in some different way, and it induces his mind to various considerations through different anxieties. It also destroys whatever was previously put together, so that, with everything disturbed and thrown into disorder, the mind is divided by different kinds of anxieties;. But these things are lessened in a diurnal nativity, and <increased>[1] in a nocturnal one.

7. If Jupiter is made the Ruler of the Times, he allots 8 months of his own decade to Venus. Therefore, when Venus has received the time allotted to itself by Jupiter—that is in a nocturnal nativity—if it is the Ruler of the Nativity, or if Jupiter is the ruler, it makes marriage, and it denotes fortunate times, and also the conveniences of good fortune. But in a diurnal nativity, it indicates middling but incessant attractions of love, especially if the nature of the house or the sign impairs Venus.

8. If Jupiter is made the Ruler of the Times, he allots 20 months of his own decade to Mercury. Therefore, when Mercury has received the time allotted to itself by Jupiter, it denotes actions from which the greatest conveniences of profits are obtained, and it bestows the protections of very many persons and the greatest friendships, and it assigns increases

[1] Added by the Teubner editors.

of fortunate promotion to all his official duties, so that fortunate advantages in both wealth and good fortune are conferred [on him] by all of his actions.

9. If Jupiter is made the Ruler of the Times, he allots 25 months of his own decade to the Moon. Therefore, when the Moon has received the time allotted to itself by Jupiter, it denotes the quiet of tranquil serenity and the greatest increases in good fortune—namely, in accordance with the substance of the nativity. For then the sorrow of preceding misfortunes is mitigated with various kinds of relief; then the restrictions of poverty are relaxed; then good health restrains the defects of illnesses; then the fears of dangers are suppressed by fortunate supports; then in all contests and court cases [favorable] opinions are rendered for them; then sorrow is broken down; then anxiety is altered. So that, with the roughness of preceding misfortunes wiped away, a pure and clean time of good fortune comes, especially if Jupiter makes a fortunate aspect to the Moon [when she is] full of light in the nativity.

XXXV. Mars

1. When the rulership of the decade has come to Mars—i.e. [a period] of 10 years and 9 months—this whole time is also divided by it in these same ways. But <also in the case of>[1] this [star], just as in the case of Saturn and Jupiter, you should investigate everything in a similar manner—the sign, the degree, the sect, the house, and the testimonies, so that you are able to find everything with clear inquiries. And so, when Mars is made Ruler of the Times, he retains 15 months of his own decade for himself. In these 15 months, it denotes actions that are indeed the greatest in accordance with the substance of the nativity with a greater disorder, so that in these actions, of whatever sort they are, a crisis of dangers may arise, especially if he is the Ruler of the Nativity and if it is a diurnal nativity.

2. If Mars is made Ruler of the Times, he allots 30 months of his own decade to Saturn. And so when Saturn has received the time allotted to itself by Mars, it imposes the weight of sluggish delay on all associations [with others], so that all business affairs are always inhibited by slowness; and it makes the time ineffective, dirty, squalid, and devoid of all actions.

---

[1]Adds Ziegler.

3. If Mars is made Ruler of the Times, he allots 12 months of his own decade to Jupiter. And so, when Jupiter has received the time allotted to itself by Mars, it denotes all the conveniences of prosperity, and it will always make business affairs to be concluded with a fortunate outcome. It also bestows profits and all the offices of business affairs, and it gives peace to those who are laboring, health to the sick, security to those who are troubled, a return to wanderers, a [favorable] end to those involved in lawsuits, and an abundance to those in need.

4. If Mars is made Ruler of the Times, he allots 19 months of his own decade to the Sun. And so, when the Sun has received the time allotted to it by Mars, it denotes the greatest crises of dangers from continual disaster; and it always disturbs the whole order of life with miserable change; and it rouses up riots and brings about insurrections; and it denotes pains in the eyes with the greatest continuation of illness. It also shatters the whole life with the greatest dangers and with the greatest attacks of losses, And the dangers will be inevitable, unless the good testimony of Jupiter resists all of them.

5. If Mars is made Ruler of the Times, he allots 8 months of his own decade to Venus. And so when Venus has received the time allotted to herself by Mars, it certainly makes a fortunate time, and one separated from every crisis of dangers. But a hidden scandal from intercourse with many women is always brought about during those months. Because if they were square to each other in the nativity, they will cause adultery to be perpetrated at that time, but with the testimony of Jupiter they conceal that crime; [but] with the testimony of Mercury and the Sun, they make it public with a miserable crisis in the Native's life.

6. If Mars is made Ruler of the Times, he allots 20 months of his own decade to Mercury. And so, when Mercury has received the time allotted to itself by Mars, it will make dangers to be stirred up by some sort of writings; or it always inflicts a miserable loss from theft; but it will make enemies to be dispersed in repeated ways. But if they are found conjoined to each other by square or opposition, they indicate the crime of evil-doers or of counterfeiting,[1] especially if Mercury was found in the terms or in the domicile of Saturn.

7. If Mars is made Ruler of the Times, he allots 25 months of his own decade to the Moon. And so when the Moon has received the time allot-

[1]Accepting Kroll's emendation of *adulteratae* instead of *adulterae*. Cf. i.253.2-3. Counterfeiting was a capital crime under Roman law.

ted to herself by Mars, it will always make the greatest series of dangers to be brought about, especially if the Moon was full of light. For then, dangerous periods of time are denoted; then flights; then exiles; then miserable series of dangers are stirred up; then men are placed in confinement or in public prisons[1]; then fires; then fevers; then a serious loss with miserable damage to assets is denoted; then a case of serious illnesses always occurs. But if they were in square or opposition in the nativity without the testimony of Jupiter, then without doubt they will make either a bloody, or lamentable, or sudden death. But if Saturn is found with the Moon in the nativity, and the Moon has received the time allotted to herself by Mars, then demises by a bitter death are occasioned by the preceding dangers—which dangers are allotted according to the varieties of the signs.

XXXVI. The Sun.

1. If the Sun is the Ruler of the Times, that is when the time of 10 years and 9 months has been assigned to it, you ought to examine with care everything that we have also said about it in connection with the rest—the mixtures of temperaments, the house, the sign, the degrees, so that from a consideration of all of these you may find the whole arrangement of the decrees. But this [period of] time will also be divided by it in very similar fashion. And so, when the Sun is made Ruler of the Times, it will retain 19 months from its own decade. And so in those months we should hope for nothing fortunate from it, but all kinds of misfortunes. But all of these are mitigated to some extent in a diurnal nativity, but they are also lulled by the testimony of Jupiter, and they are increased by the testimony of Saturn and Mars, especially if it was badly posited in the nativity.

2. If the Sun is made Ruler of the Times, it assigns 30 months of its own decade to Saturn. And so, when Saturn has received the time assigned to it by the Sun, in a nocturnal nativity to be sure it threatens a baleful and deadly demise; but in a diurnal nativity it denotes increases of the greatest good fortune according to the substance of the nativity, if it was well posited for the decree.

3. If the Sun is made Ruler of the Times, it assigns 12 months of its own decade to Jupiter. And so, when Jupiter has received the 12 months assigned to it by the Sun, it denotes the conveniences of a tranquil good

[1]Reading with **Δ** *homines in custodiam aut publicis carceribus *accipiuntur*.

fortune with the greatest joy of life, so that, with the vestige of all evils wiped away, a whole time of good fortune may render him prosperous. Then losses are eased; then health is restored; then they are freed from the preceding difficulties.

4. If the Sun is made Ruler of the Times, it assigns 15 months of its own decade to Mars. And so, when it has received the time assigned to it by the Sun, either in a diurnal or in a nocturnal nativity, and when his personal assets have been dissipated by miserable losses, it indicates the straits of extreme poverty,. But it also stirs up frequent harassments by lawsuits; it will also make frequent pains in the eyes; and it indicates a severe incident of danger; and it disturbs [the Native] with a constant continuation of losses.

5. If the Sun is made the Ruler of the Times, it assigns 8 months of its own decade to Venus. And so, when Venus has received the time assigned to it by the Sun, it certainly denotes a fortunate outcome in all business affairs, but it always inflames the mind of the wife with a certain conflict of malice, so that the secret mind of the wife then both betrays and reveals itself; or, if there was no wife then, a danger is indicated from a woman; and because of that it stirs up public lawsuits and judicial quarrels, and with riots roused up, but minor ones.

6. If the Sun is made Ruler of the Times, it assigns 20 months of its own decade to Mercury. And so, when Mercury has received the time assigned to it by the Sun, it denotes business affairs, frequent actions, and the continuing conveniences of profits, but these profits are [only] conferred with the greatest efforts and with the greatest dangers.

7. If the Sun is made Ruler of the Times, it assigns 25 months of its own decade to the Moon. And so, when the Moon has received the time assigned to it by the Sun, it always throws the whole life of the man into confusion with an unstable and an inconstant diversity, so that whatever was acquired at that time is taken back by later[1] actions; and at that same time he will be changeable due to various inequalities, so that his financial straits are relieved by sudden riches, and again the financial straits of poverty follow closely upon [the periods of] riches.

[1]Accepting Kroll's and Ziegler's suggested emendation *posterioribus* 'later' rather than the *potioribus* 'more powerful' of the MSS.

XXXVII. Venus.

1. The space of 10 years and 9 months is also conferred upon Venus. And so, when Venus is Ruler of the Times, you ought to examine everything both in her [situation], and in like fashion those things that we have shown that should be observed with the rest [of the stars]. And so, of all [that time], at this time she gets only 8 months for herself. And so, during this whole time, the greatest grace of charm increases conjugal affections,[1] but it also denotes joy with the greatest freedom from anxiety, especially if she is the Ruler of the Nativity.

2. If Venus is made the Ruler of the Times, she assigns 30 months of her own decade to Saturn. And so, when Saturn has received the time assigned to him by Venus, it stirs up serious indignations of conflict either <with his wife, or>[2] with a woman. For then, these persons are separated from their wife either by death or by quarrels.

3. If Venus is made the Ruler of the Times, she assigns 12 months of her own decade to Jupiter. And so, when Jupiter has received the time assigned to him by Venus, it certainly denotes a good and happy time; but it will cause some scandals.

4. If Venus is made the Ruler of the Times, she assigns 15 months of her own decade to Mars. And so, when Mars has received the time assigned to him by Venus, it denotes many evils and frequent inconveniences of sorrow. For then it always disturbs the mind with various allurements of love affairs; and because of the harsh torments of love, it always imposes severe sorrow upon the mind; so that, on account of these faults of an errant mind, dangers of lawsuits frequently occur. Also, riots and dangers occur on account of very bad wives or [perpetrated] by very bad wives; also, the crime of adultery rises up, or love conceived by an impure thought.

5. If Venus is made the Ruler of the Times, she assigns 19 months of her own decade to the Sun. and so, when the Sun has received the time assigned to it by Venus, it always makes the Natives to flee from their own wives; and they bring this about with capital danger and always with the loss of [the Native's] personal assets. But if there is a fortunate aspect from Jupiter, they are separated by the necessities of travel.

---

[1]Accepting Wikström's emendation *coniugales affectus*.
[2]Adds Wikström.

6. If Venus is made the Ruler of the Times, she assigns 20 months of her decade to Mercury. And so, when Mercury has received the time assigned to him by Venus, it will make all business affairs to be completed with a fortunate result; it also denotes frequent delights of joy; and it will make the greatest profits to be bestowed, and suitable foundations of wealth.

7. If Venus is made the Ruler of the Times, she assigns 25 months of her decade to the Moon. And so, when the Moon has received the time assigned to her by Venus, she indicates disturbance to the mind from hidden jealousy. But if the Moon is full of light in the nativity, and if Venus has assigned the times to it, it will harm [the Native] in the greatest things, stirring up all the defects [resulting from] misfortunes.

XXXVIII. Mercury.

1. The space of 10 years and 9 months is also conferred upon Mercury; and in this [period of time] we ought also to combine everything in similar fashion, just as we did with the rest of the stars. And so, when Mercury is the Ruler of the Times, he reserves for himself 20 months of his own decade. And so, during all that time, i.e. 20 months, all good things are denoted from continuing good fortune; and it makes all actions to have fortunate outcomes, especially if Mercury is the Ruler of the Nativity and is well posited.

2. If Mercury is made the Ruler of the Times, he assigns 30 months of his own decade to Saturn. And so, when Saturn has received the time assigned to itself by Mercury, it denotes the deaths of members of the household from continual calamities of misfortunes, the deaths of parents, relatives, and patrons, and [in general] those who are customarily helpful to us.

3. If Mercury is made the Ruler of the Times, he assigns 12 months of his own decade to Jupiter. And so, when Jupiter has received the time assigned to itself by Mercury, it certainly denotes a quiet time and one separated from all the noise of business affairs; but, during this same quiet time, it brings about the greatest conveniences of praise and the joy of delights. It also denotes in every case [the birth of] children for those not having any, if the scheme of the nativity permits this.

4. If Mercury is made the Ruler of the Times, he assigns 15 months of his own decade to Mars. And so, when Mars has received the time as-

signed to itself by Mercury, it raises up enemies, brings in accusations, and it denotes lawsuits from injurious summonses—all of which a good testimony of Jupiter mitigates.

5. If Mercury is made the Ruler of the Times, he assigns 19 months of his own decade to the Sun. And so, when the Sun has received the time assigned to itself by Mercury, it always indicates the greatest losses to his personal assets, and the greatest mental anxieties.

6. If Mercury is made the Ruler of the Times, he assigns 8 months of his own decade to Venus. And so, when Venus has received the time assigned to herself by Mercury, it denotes good conveniences from continual good fortune.

7. If Mercury is made the Ruler of the Times, he assigns 25 months of his own decade to the Moon. And so, when the Moon has received the time assigned to herself by Mercury, it denotes the greatest illnesses and the greatest defects of weaknesses; and, according to the nature of the house and the sign, it adds a cold numbness of mind to the inconveniences of the defective weakness. But Jupiter will always mitigate these things with a good testimony.

XXXIX. The Moon.

1. The space of 10 years and 9 months is also conferred on the Moon; and in this, therefore, just as with all the other stars, you ought to consider everything with careful reasoning. And so, the Moon reserves 25 months of this decade for herself. And so, during that time in which the Moon assigns the space of 25 months to herself, if she is thus posited so that she applies to Saturn with little light, or when full [of light] to Mars, she indicates all kinds of death. But if she is full of light and adorned with the testimonies of the benefic stars, she denotes moderate increases in personal assets [but] with the greatest efforts. For the times of both the Sun and the Moon have bad outcomes, especially if the malefic stars aspect them with a menacing aspect.

2. If the Moon is made the Ruler of the Times, she assigns 30 months of her own decade to Saturn. And so, when Saturn has received the time assigned to itself by the Moon, if she has little light, she denotes miserable outcomes from corrupt humors, or from waters, or from shipwrecks, and miserable deaths. But if she is full [of light], she certainly makes those same things, but she [also] gives a means of evading them.

3. If the Moon is made the Ruler of the Times, she assigns 12 months of her own decade to Jupiter. And so, when Jupiter has received the time assigned to itself by the Moon, it denotes all good things with joy and with cheerfulness, especially if the Moon was full of light; then dangers, then fears, then illnesses are lulled; then increases in good fortune come forth in accordance with the measure of the nativity.

4. If the Moon is made the Ruler of the Times, she assigns 15 months of her own decade to Mars. And so, when Mars has received the time assigned to itself by the Moon, if she is full of light, it denotes the greatest civic disturbances and the greatest insurrections; and if she is so posited in the nativity that she is aspected by Mars by square or opposition, she denotes a bloody and lamentable outcome of calamity.

5. If the Moon is made the Ruler of the Times, she assigns 19 months of her own decade to the Sun. And so, when the Sun has received the time assigned to it by the Moon, it indicates conflagrations, illnesses, and miserable spells of weakness from raging fevers. But the fortunate testimony of Jupiter mitigates all of these things.

6. If the Moon is made the Ruler of the Times, she assigns 8 months of her own decade to Venus. And so, when Venus has received the time assigned to herself by the Moon, if it is a diurnal nativity, it denotes some disturbance arising from jealousy.[1] But if it is a nocturnal [nativity], it bestows the greatest increases in wealth, especially if the Moon has little light.

7. If the Moon is made the Ruler of the Times, she assigns 20 months of her own decade to Mercury. And so, when Mercury has received the time assigned to itself by the Moon, it denotes chilling illnesses along with bodily weakness.

XL.

1. In this way, my dear Mavortius, the total of the times is divided. But I do not want that isolated sentences should be quoted[2] in dealing with these definitions. For frequently, if a benefic star has received the time assigned to itself, and if it has with it a temporary malefic star,[3] or if one

[1]Accepting Wikström's emendation, *stridorem zeli.* But the text is uncertain.
[2]Bram renders the sense of this aptly: "quoted out of context."
[3]The rare word *temporalem* 'temporary' I take to mean a transiting planet.

aspects it by square or opposition, the decree of its goodness is dismissed by the power of the malefic star.

2. You will discover this same thing in similar fashion in the case of a malefic star. For if a malefic star has received the time assigned to it, and then a temporary benefic, either posited together with it or configured with a fortunate aspect, mitigates it, the whole decree of the malefics is mitigated by the salutary help of the benefic star.

3. These things are made known to you so that you may understand[1] the instruction of the completed work, and there is not yet anything else that may be required. For in an easy discourse we have described in detail everything that we ought to teach to unskilled minds. Now, we who[2] have been initiated in the preliminary ceremonies may approach the very threshold of the secrets; [and] with an intent mind we ought to hear the rest, lest with our ears set in disdain and rejecting those things that are said,[3] we may fail to make known the outstanding[4] opinions of the treatises on the wandering [stars].[5]

4. And so, having completed the Sixth Book, all our task of discourse will be transferred to the secrets of the Seventh Book.

---

[1]Reading *intelligis* 'you may understand' with MS **N**.

[2]MS **N** has *modo* 'only' instead of *nunc* 'now', and all the MSS have *quia* 'because' instead of the Teubner editors' conjecture *qui* 'those who'. So perhaps the sentence should read "Only because we have been initiated in the preliminary ceremonies, may we approach the very threshold…"

[3]This perhaps refers to the fact that a number of the chapters of Book 7 describe sexual indiscretions and perversions that might seem offensive to some readers.

[4]†*pereuntes* 'passing away' is plainly corrupt. Perhaps we might read *praestantes* 'outstanding', or *perennes* 'unfailing'.

[5]The following two books contain very many statements about the configurations of the planets. The word *errantium* should therefore be taken to mean 'wandering', an epithet of the planets, rather than 'erring' as Bram and Prof. Monat have done. Bram translates *errantium tractatuum* as 'false writings', and Prof. Monat has 'erroneous treatises'.

Book VII.

I.

1. When Orpheus made known the ceremonies of sacred things to unknowing men, he required nothing else from those whom he was initiating at their first entrance but the necessity of an oath with the terrifying authority of religion—lest the religious principles found and arranged might be made known to profane ears. But Plato also frequently spoke to . . . . ,[1] lest the comments of secret disputations that ought to be venerated should ever be passed on to inexperienced ears. For all of these things suffer a loss when they are thrust upon profligate and reckless minds. Pythagoras too, and our Porphyry,[2] think that our mind is dedicated to a religious silence.

2. Wherefore, I too,[3] having followed the law of these men, say to you as an oath, my dear Mavortius, by God the Maker of the World, who perfected everything with the necessity of perpetuity; who shaped the Sun and the Moon; who arranged the courses and orders of all the stars; who

---

[1]The Latin text is corrupt: *Platonici meum perpetuum a se eum frequenter convenit.* The Aldine edition conjectured *Plato Timaeum perpetuum apud se frequenter convenit*, which might be rendered 'Plato frequently spoke to Timaeus who was always in his own circle'. Bram has 'It is generally agreed that Plato also was concerned...', which is not what Firmicus said, but it is perhaps somewhat similar to what he had in mind. Prof. Monat shows a gap in the text and confines the words of Edition **a** to a footnote and notes that "the Timaeus does not contain any special recommendation on this subject."

[2]The phrase "our Porphyry" would seem to indicate that Firmicus had been personally acquainted with the famous philosopher, who died about 304 A.D. . But Bram points out (End Note 81, p. 312) that in the *De errore* Firmicus disparages Porphyry vehemently.

[3]And with these words Firmicus launches a classic periodic sentence of 24 Teubner lines that Cicero himself might well have been proud of.

compressed the waves of the sea within certain limits of the land; who kindles the fire for the eternal substance of divine perpetuity; who maintains the earth placed in the middle [of space] with equated moderation; who created with the divine majesty of workmanship all men, wild birds, and all kinds of animals; who waters the land with everlasting springs; who makes the blasts of the winds to be varied with some moderation of necessity; who perfected all things for the fabrication of all things composed with the diversity of the four elements from contrary and incompatible things, and the rising and the setting †of earthquakes. . .[1] of all; through the descent and ascension of the mind; and through the immortal order of eternal perpetuity.

3. Let not these venerable comments be made known to profane or unskilled ears, but [only] to those whom an uncorrupted mind has adorned for the right order of living with a pure and chaste guardianship of mind; whose unimpaired faith, whose hands are separated from every sin of crimes; so that the whole knowledge of divination might be made known to those who are honorable, modest, sober, chaste, and with a pure splendor of mind. Receive, therefore, everything composed with careful reason. And because we have spoken to you with the religion of an oath, receive that which we promised you with the greatest trepidation of mind.

II. Children who are Exposed and not Reared.[2]

1. Whosoever's ASC the benefic stars do not aspect, and whose Moon is posited in any angle, with Mars and Saturn posited in the 7th house from the ASC, i.e. in the DSC, those persons born [thus] are quickly exposed by their mothers. And if the ASC is in those signs that have short

[1]Some words are missing here. Némethy suggested *<corporum> *terrenorum omnium* 'of all the terrestrial bodies', which does not seem to be satisfactory. Skutsch would have merely inserted *<astrorum>* 'of the stars' and left the corrupt word *terraemotum* 'of earthquakes' as is, followed by a lacuna. Bram improves that by deleting *terraemotum* 'of earthquakes' and inserting *<astrorum>* 'of the stars'. But perhaps we could also read *<per> *terrae motum <astrorum> omnium* 'of all the stars by the motion of the Earth'.

[2]Since effective birth-control methods were not generally available in early Mediterranean society, it was evidently a common practice to "expose" unwanted infants—that is, to carry them out beyond the city limits and abandon them. And evidently some Greek astrologer had collected a number of cases of infants who were exposed.

[rising] times, and Mars is in the 7th house from the ASC, i.e. in the DSC, and in addition the Moon with little light applies to Saturn, or full of light applies to Mars, the new-born infant will similarly be exposed.

2. But also if the ruler of Fortune, i.e. the ruler of that sign in which the House of Fortune is found, and the ruler of that sign in which the ASC degree is found, are hidden by the rays of the Sun;[1] or, posited in those signs of which we have made mention before, but Saturn or Mars is posited in the DSC of the nativity, the new-born infant will be exposed. But also if the Moon is found in the ASC or in the DSC of the nativity, and Mars and Saturn are conjoined in opposition aspect, or if one malefic is found with the Sun in the conception chart, he who is born will be exposed.

3. But also if the Sun and the Moon aspect each other by opposition, or if they are in square, in such a way that they make this configuration in angles, and malefic stars are posited together with both of them, i.e. if the Sun was in the ASC and the Moon in the DSC, or the Moon in the ASC and the Sun in the DSC, and Mars was with one of them and Saturn with the other, [then] while placed in the narrow birth passage he is extinguished by suffocation. But if the malefic stars, made superior, aspect the Moon with a menacing aspect, the mother also incurs grave danger of death in that birth.

4. If the Sun is found in the ASC, and the Moon full of light in any sign applies to Mars, but Saturn is posited in any angle, he who is born, having been exposed, will die. But also if the Moon is found with Mars in whatever angle, and in the opposite [angle] the Sun is posited with Saturn, and if the testimony of Jupiter is lacking to all of them, he who is born will either be exposed, or he will quickly die along with his mother.

5. If the Moon is found in any angle, and Mars aspects that same one from another angle by opposition, or is found with her in the same degree, and Saturn holds another angle of the nativity, or is posited in the *anafora* of the angles, he who is born will be exposed. But if the star of Jupiter is found in any angle, and Mars aspects it from a superior house, it will make those who are exposed to be either found or brought back, especially if Venus makes any aspect to Mars.

6. If the Sun is found with Saturn in the ASC, and the Moon is posited in the MC, but Mars posited in the IMC aspects the Moon by opposition, he who is born will be exposed. But also if, with the Sun posited in the

[1]That is "under the Sun Beams" or, as the moderns would say, "combust."

ASC and the Moon in the MC, Saturn is in the DSC and Mars is in the IMC, he who is born is exposed and will quickly perish, or his mother will even die together with him. But also, always—something that it is proper to observe in general—if both Mars and Saturn make opposition aspects to the Sun and the Moon posited in some of the angles, or to one of them by opposition and the other by square, the Natives will either quickly perish or their mother will perish with them in a miserable demise.

7. If Mars and Saturn are found in any angle, or, with one of them posited in an angle, the other is posited in the *anafora*, but the Moon is struck by one of them by either an opposition or a square aspect, or is posited together [with one of them], he who is born thus will be exposed. But if with them posited thus, a benefic star receives the conjunction of the applying Moon, those exposed are recovered by others, and having been returned free [from exposure], are reared as their own children.

8. If the Moon is found in the ASC, and Mars is in the 12th house from the ASC, but Saturn posited in the *anafora* of the ASC makes any aspect to the Sun, the fetus will be brought forth by the physicians cut apart limb by limb among the viscera of the mother. But if with these arranged thus, Jupiter is not in the angles, the mother engaged in that birth will die. If the Moon was posited in such a way that it has a malefic in the preceding sign, and another in the following sign, and the star following the Moon makes any aspect to the Sun, he who is born will either be exposed, or as soon as he is born, he will die.

9. If the Ruler of the Nativity or the ruler of the sign in which the House of Fortune is found is found in the 12th from the ASC or in the 6th, or in the 2nd from the ASC or in the 8th, and no one of the benefic stars makes a fortunate aspect to them, and the Ruler of the Nativity is not posited in his own terms, he who was born will immediately be exposed. But also, if any malefic star aspects either the Moon or the ASC, and all of the aspects of the benefic stars are lacking, those exposed will be torn to pieces by dogs.

10. If the Ruler of the Nativity is found in tropical signs, and located in those signs it is posited in dull and dejected houses, and if the Moon aspects it by opposition, and also the malefic stars are joined in equal association of degrees[1] with the Moon, either by square or by opposition,

[1]That is, in partile aspect.

those who are born will die immediately from having been thrown either into the sea or into a river,. But if the benefic stars provide their testimony, . . .[1] having been nourished for a few days, they will be thrown into [water].

11. When the Sun and the Moon in any sign possess the 30th degree, he who is born will have no time of life.[2] But if the malefic stars aspect the Sun and the Moon posited in the 30th degree either by square or by opposition, he who is born and exposed, is killed mangled by dogs. But also if the Moon and the Sun are found posited together in the 12th house from the ASC, and the benefic stars do not make any fortunate aspect either to them or to the ASC, he who is born will be exposed. But if the malefic stars aspect them, when he has been exposed, he will be eaten by dogs. But if they are posited just as we have said [but] in tropical signs, without the testimony of the benefic stars, the Native will perish in water.

12. If in the nativity the benefic stars do not make a fortunate aspect to the Sun or the Moon or the ASC or the House of Fortune, he who is born will be exposed. But if there is an aspect from the malefic stars, the [child] exposed will be eaten by dogs. If no one of the benefic stars is found with the Sun and the Moon, or in the ASC, or in the MC, or in the 5th from the ASC, or in the 11th, or in the 9th, or in the 3rd , or in the 7th , or in the 4th, but in these houses only the malefic stars are located, then he who is born will be exposed.

13. If in the nativity the benefic stars are hidden by the rays of the Sun,[3] but the malefic stars are in their morning rising, he who is born will be exposed. But also, if the Moon is conjoined to the Sun thus, so that she loses all the substance of her light, and no other benefic star makes a fortunate aspect with her, he who is born will be exposed. But also if a malefic star aspects the Moon posited thus, either they will be born dead, or those that are born will be torn apart by dogs.

---

[1]The Latin text is corrupt or defective. Most MSS have the words *aut horoscopus* 'or the ASC' where I have indicated an ellipsis after 'testimony'. MS **N** has *aut homine* 'or by a man'. Brackman conjectures *aut horis paucis aut paucis diebus* 'either for a few hours or a few days'. Wikström conjectures *aut <Lunae aut> horoscopo* 'either <to the Moon or> to the ASC. But we could simply add the word *<post>* 'after' and get most of the meaning, '...<after> having been nourished for a few days, they will be thrown into [water].'

[2]The logic seems to be that the 30th degree is at the end of the sign, so the person it represents is at the end of his life when he is born.

[3]That is, they are *under the Sun Beams*, or, as moderns would say, they are *combust*.

14. If all the stars are located with the Sun and the Moon in the 6th or in the 12th house, he who is born will be exposed. But if with the rest of the stars posited in those houses that we have mentioned, a single benefic star is found in any angle, the child that is exposed is collected by someone and will be reared. But that benefic star denotes a lesser space of its own time for him to live.

15. If the Moon is joined in equal degrees with Mars posited in the same sign, or, if located in opposition [to each other], they hold equal degrees <in the MC and>[1] in the IMC, and if no benefic star aspects them, but Saturn makes any aspect to the Moon posited thus with Mars, their mothers will die in childbirth. But if any benefic star aspects the Moon posited thus with Mars, with the infant cut up and brought out in pieces, the mother will be freed from the danger of death.

16. If the Moon is found in the DSC, and Mars is either found with her in the same degrees, or is posited partilely in the ASC, and it is a diurnal nativity, he who is born will be exposed. But also if Jupiter posited in another angle aspects them posited thus, or if Venus does the same thing, the supports of life are bestowed on the one that is exposed by another person—namely, so that having been collected by that one he is reared. But also, if the Moon <is> in the anafora of the ASC <and Saturn> posited <in the 8th > house from the ASC aspects <her>[2] by opposition, and Mars aspects either the ASC or the Moon by square, and not any benefic star aspects all these, he who is born will be exposed and he will immediately perish.

17. If the Moon is found in one sign with Mars and Saturn, so that she holds a middle place between both of them,[3] and no benefic star aspects her—if indeed she is located thus in the middle—so that the benefic stars are distant from her,[4] and they are not joined to it by close association, he who is born will be exposed. But if both of the malefic stars are so located that they cling to the near sides of the Moon, and not any testimony comes from the benefic stars, he who is born will immediately die along with his mother.

[1]Adds Kroll.

[2]Adds **N**, a line having been omitted by **Ψ** due to homoeoteleuton (…*horoscopi* | … *horoscopo*)

[3]That is, if the Moon is *besieged* by Mars and Saturn.

[4]Reading **benivolae stellae* instead of *maleficae stellae*. (*Cf.* the next sentence.) This is the least alteration of the sentence that will make sense.

18. If the Sun is found in the MC, but the Moon is found in the DSC, i.e. in the 7th house from the ASC, but Saturn and Mars are so posited that one is joined to the rays of the Sun and the other to those of the Moon, he who is born will be exposed. But if the benefic stars make a fortunate aspect to them located thus, the child that is exposed is collected by another person, and he will be reared.

If Jupiter is found in the *anafora*[1] of the ASC, and he makes an aspect to the Moon afflicted by an opposition from Mars, [then when] exposed and nourished they are entangled in the traps of slaves. But also if the Sun is found in the DSC, and Saturn is with it, or in the ASC, but Mars is in either the *anafora* of the ASC or the *epicataphora*, i.e. in the 8th house from the ASC, and no benefic star holds any angle, he who is born will be exposed.

19. If the ruler of the sign in which the ASC is located is found in the *anafora* of the ASC, and the ruler of the *anafora* is posited in the 12th house from the ASC—with the Sun in a diurnal nativity, but with the Moon in a nocturnal one—he who is born will be exposed. But with all of these arranged thus, i.e. in the *anafora* and in the 12th house from the ASC, just as we have said before, if the Sun and the Moon are not joined to themselves in any aspect, he who is born will be exposed, and he will immediately perish.

20. If the Moon is found in the 3rd house from the ASC, and the Sun in the 11th <or the 6th>,[2] but the rulers of those signs in which the Sun and the Moon are located are posited in the 9th house from the ASC, he who is born will be exposed. If the Sun and the Moon were posited in the DSC, i.e. they were located in the 7th house from the ASC, <but Mars and Saturn were in the 8th>[3] house, but the rulers of both signs were posited in the 6th house from the ASC, he who is born, having been exposed, will be torn to pieces by dogs. If the ruler of the sign in which the ASC is located is found in the MC, and a malefic star is located in the ASC, and there is no aspect of any benefic star to the degree of the ASC, he who is born will be exposed, and he will be torn to pieces by dogs.

21. If the sign of the Giver of Life is that which is located in the *anafora* of the ASC or in the 6th house from the ASC, but the Giver of Life it-

---

[1]That is, the 2nd house.

[2]Adds **N**. But I think "the 11th" is wrong, since the 11th is a favorable house. Probably we should read either "the 12th" or "the 8th."

[3]Adds **N**.

self is located together with a malefic star in the MC <or in the IMC>,[1] he who is born will be immediately torn to pieces by dogs. But also if the Giver of Life is the ruler of the sign in which the *anafora* is placed, but the Giver of Life itself is located in the 6th house from the ASC, and no benefic star is found in any angle, he who is born will not be reared.

22. If the Moon and the Sun were so located that they neither aspect themselves nor the ASC, he who is born will not be reared. But it must be known that in general if anyone has all the stars in the *anafora* of the ASC, or in the 6th house from the ASC, or in the 8th, or in the 12th, he will either be exposed or he will not be reared.

23. But if any one star—certainly either the Sun by day or the Moon by night—is either in an angle or is in the 5th house from the ASC, with the others posited just as we have said, he who is born will be reared, but he will be short-lived and unfortunate. But also if Mars and Saturn are located together in the *anafora* of the ASC, and neither the Sun nor the Moon are found in their domiciles, he who is born will be exposed.

24. If the ruler of the sign in which the House of Fortune is found is in either the *anafora* of the ASC or in the 6th house from the ASC, but the House of Fortune is in the MC, and no benefic star is found in the angles of the nativity, he who is born will not be reared. But also, if the House of Fortune is found in the IMC, and the malefic stars possess that same House by partile aspect, but the ruler of that sign is either in the *anafora* of the ASC or is hidden by the Sun's rays,[2] he who is born will not be reared.

25. But if the House of Fortune is found in the 7th house from the ASC, but the ruler of its sign is either in that sign or in the MC hidden by the rays of the Sun, he who is born will not be reared.[3]

26. But also if the House of Fortune is found in any sign, but the ruler of that sign, posited either in the *anafora* of the ASC or in the 6th house from the ASC, does not aspect the house of Fortune, he who is born will not be reared. But also if the House of Fortune is found in the *anafora* of the ASC, but the ruler of that sign is in the MC[4] hidden by the rays of the Sun, he who is born will not be reared.

---

[1]Adds **N**.

[2]That is, it is *under the Sun Beams*, or *combust* as the moderns would say.

[3]I know of one instance where the infant was born under this configuration and did not breathe initially, but was brought to life by physical manipulations and did survive.

[4]**N** has 'in the MC <or the IMC>'.

III.

1. **The Birth of Twins.** If Jupiter and Mercury are posited partilely together in the ASC, and the ASC itself is in a duplex sign, with the Moon too posited in any angle, but the Sun is in that sign in which it has an application to another star, either the nativity is that of twins, or whoever is born thus will have twin children.

2. It certainly must be observed, that a malefic star made superior does not aspect one of these. For if it does aspect one of these, whichever one of the twins was conceived first will either die at birth or will be ejected before that time. But also if the Moon is not found in the angles, and is not in a duplex sign, but Jupiter and Mercury, just as we have said before, are found posited together in a duplex sign in the ASC, but the Moon or the Sun is conjoined with any star, twins will be born.

3. If the Moon is found either with Mercury or with Jupiter, and the Sun has another star applied to itself, and posited in duplex signs, they mutually make any aspect to each other, but also if the ASC is found in a duplex sign and it has any star applied together to itself, twins will be born.

4. But also if the Moon is found in the signs of Jupiter or Mercury, but Jupiter and Mercury are posited in the ASC or in the DSC from the ASC, twins will be born. If the Moon is found in a duplex sign, and the Sun posited in an angle possesses the 2nd sign from the Moon, or it certainly holds a duplex sign posited with Mercury or with Jupiter, twins will be born, or they will have twin children.

5. But whether they will be born of the masculine gender or the feminine one, we determine in this fashion. For if, with the Sun and the Moon and the ASC posited in masculine signs, there is testimony from masculine stars, that is from Jupiter, Saturn, and Mars, males will be born. But if Venus alone has made that same [testimony], posited in feminine signs, twins of the feminine gender <will be born. But if she has done this same thing posited in a masculine sign>[1] and feminine stars are joined to the Sun and the Moon and the ASC in that way that we have said, twins of different sex are produced.

6. If Mars and Saturn posited in their own domiciles aspect the Sun and the Moon and the ASC, and there is no aspect from the benefic stars, they

[1]Ziegler suggests this addition to fill the obvious lacuna after 'feminine gender'.

will either be ejected prematurely, or, having been born, they will immediately perish. But if with all of these located in the fashion just as we have said, both benefics and malefics aspect them, whichever one of the twins that comes forth first will die.

7. If the Moon is found in any angle, namely in a fertile sign, and a benefic star is posited together with her, and the ASC is in a duplex sign, or in a fertile one, or is with Jupiter, or with Mercury, either three or five [children] will be born. If the ruler of the sign in which the House of Children is found partilely, and found in a duplex sign, but the 5th house from the ASC is located in a duplex sign, and Jupiter and Mercury make any aspect to the Moon posited in a duplex sign, or if they were found with her, twins will be born.

IV.

1. **Servile Nativities.** If Mars or Saturn aspects the Moon by opposition, or one aspects her by opposition and the other conjoins itself to the Moon by square, a slave will be born, especially if the Moon is found in the IMC or in the DSC. But if Jupiter aspects them posited thus with a good aspect, he will get the awards of liberty.

2. If the Sun and Mercury are posited together in the MC, and a malefic star aspects the Moon by opposition, with it posited in the *cacodaemon*,[1] the Native will be subject to a female servant. But if Jupiter makes a fortunate aspect to those that we have mentioned, he will be subject to a free-born woman. If the House of Fortune is found partilely in the sign of a malefic, and Mars is found in that sign, this nativity will be that of a slave.

3. But if Mars is found in his morning rising in the above said House with Saturn, <he will be an unfortunate slave. But if Mars in that House that we have mentioned is found with a benefic star>[2], it will make fortunate slaves.[3] But also if the House of Fortune is partilely found either in Libra, or in Sagittarius, or in Aquarius, or in Gemini, and Mars is posited partilely in those same signs, it will make slaves.

---

[1]The 12th house.

[2]II 220,22 *infelix*—24 *inventus* two lines omitted by Γ due to homoeoteleuton (...*inventus* | ...*inventus*).

[3]This entire sentence is omitted by Bram.

4. But if the ruler of the sign is found posited in the same sign with Mars, or with another benefic star, [after] having been in a servile state, they will acquire the benefits of freedom.

5. If the Sun and the Moon are found in angles, and Mars and Saturn are either posited with them in the angles, or they aspect them from other angles, with none of the benefic stars located in angles, a slave will be born. But also if the Moon is found in the IMC or in the DSC, and Saturn aspects her by a dexter square, and Mars aspects these same by the same square or by opposition, they will make slaves.

6. But also if Saturn aspects the Moon partilely conjoined to Mars, namely with the Moon generally posited in an angle, it will make slaves; but if no benefic star aspects that conjunction, it will make hard-working and miserable slaves.

7. If Mars and Saturn aspect the Moon by opposition, and no benefic star aspects the Moon, and the Moon does not conjoin herself to a benefic star in the same sign, it will make slaves, and those who are alienated from their own parents. But also if the Moon is in the IMC, but Mars makes any aspect to the Moon, it will make slaves.

8. If the Sun and the Moon are found in the 12th house from the ASC, or in the 6th, and Saturn provides his testimony to them by whatever fashion, and the benefic stars do not aspect the Sun and the Moon, they will make slaves. But also if the Moon is found in the IMC, and Saturn is with her, but Mars aspects them either by square or by opposition, they will make slaves.

9. But also if the Sun is found in the 12th house from the ASC, and the Moon in the *anafora* of the ASC, and there is no benefic star posited in the angles, in a similar fashion slaves are born. But also if the Sun is found in the 12th house from the ASC, and the Moon in the 8th, and no benefic star makes a fortunate aspect to them, they will make slaves.

10. If indeed in a nocturnal nativity the Moon is found in the MC, but the Sun is posited in the 6th house from the ASC, but the rulers of both signs, i.e. of the one in which the Moon is and the one in which the Sun is, are posited in the 8th house from the ASC, they will make slaves.

11. But if the rulers of those signs in which the Sun and the Moon are posited are partilely posited either in the ASC or in the MC, with the rest of the stars posited just as we have said before, a slave will indeed be born, but, when he is established in the first age of life, he will get the re-

wards of freedom. But if these same are posited in the ASC or in the MC, just as we have said, or in the IMC, or in the DSC, or in the 5th house from the ASC, or in the 11th, he will be freed more slowly.

12. If the Sun is found in the IMC, but the Moon is posited in the 6th house from the ASC, and Jupiter is posited in the MC, but Venus afflicts either Mars or Saturn, or if they are certainly posited in dejected houses, those born as slaves will be freed. But also if the Sun and the Moon are partilely posited in the 6th house from the ASC, but the rest of the stars are found in the MC, they make [the Natives] to be transferred from slavery to freedom.

13. If the Moon is found in the 6th house from the ASC, and Mars posited in the upper parts of the *Caelum* aspects the Moon by square, and the rulers of those signs in which the Sun and the Moon are posited are [themselves] posited in the 3rd house from the ASC, but Saturn is partilely posited in the ASC, it makes them to remain slaves until the last day of their lives.

14. If the Moon is found in the IMC, but the Sun is posited with Mars in the DSC, but Saturn and Jupiter are posited in the 6th house from the ASC, or in the 8th, they will make hard-working unfortunate slaves, and those who are always oppressed by the burden of slavery. But also if Jupiter is found with the Sun in the 6th house from the ASC, but the Moon is posited with Mars in the DSC, and Venus is posited in the IMC, and Saturn holds the 3rd house from the ASC, in a similar fashion slaves will be born.

15. If Saturn is found in the 12th house from the ASC, but Mars is posited in the *anafora* of the ASC, and the Moon is partilely posited in the ASC, but Jupiter is posited in the 8th house from the ASC, and the Sun is posited in the 3rd house from the ASC, slaves are procreated in a similar fashion. If Mars is posited in his own fall, i.e. in the sign in which it is humiliated, and the Moon with little light is moving toward him, but Saturn is posited in the 3rd house from the ASC, and the Sun[1] is posited in the IMC, but benefic stars are posited in the 6th house from the ASC, it will make unfortunate slaves.

16. If the Moon with little light and posited in that sign in which she is humiliated is posited partilely with Saturn in the 7th house from the ASC,

[1]'The Sun' is a conjecture by Ziegler; **N** has 'Mars or the Sun', and the rest of the MSS have 'Mars'.

but Mars is in the 6th house from the ASC and the Sun is in the 3rd, in similar fashion a slave will be born. But also if the Sun is found in the 3rd house from the ASC with a malefic star, or in the IMC, but the benefic stars are posited in dejected houses, and the Moon with little light is posited in a similar manner in a dejected house, it will make feeble slaves.

17. But if with the rest [of the stars] arranged just as we have said, with the Moon posited with Mars in the 12th house from the ASC, but the star of Saturn is found in the IMC, lunatic slaves will be born. If the Sun is found in the *anafora* of the ASC with either Mars or with Saturn, but the Moon is posited in the 12th house from the ASC, and the benefic stars are posited in the 3rd house from the ASC, they will make unfortunate slaves. But if with these arranged just as we have said, Jupiter is found in the MC, they will get the rewards of freedom after many years.

18. If all the benefic stars are found in the 6th house from the ASC, but the malefics are posited either in the 9th or in the 8th, and the Moon is also posited in the 3rd house from the ASC, miserable slaves are born, making no progress[1] [toward freedom] and short-lived.

V. The Number of Masters: So that you may find how many Masters a Slave will have.

1. Moreover, if the Moon is found in the 2nd, or in the 5th, or in the 8th, or in the 11th house from the ASC, in a masculine sign, but the ruler of the Moon's sign is found either in its own fall or in dejected houses, but the Moon in a higher position aspects Mars by square; [then] on account of this—because Mars is posited in the 4th sign from the Moon—the one who is born thus will serve four masters. But if any star is found in the middle between the Moon and Mars, another master will be added to the preceding number.

2. But also if the Sun in a diurnal nativity has receded by any number of signs from Mars, and is dejected either by sign or by house, it will give that many masters. But in a nocturnal nativity with the dejected Moon distant from Mars or from Saturn by any number of signs, you count from it down to the last one, [and] you will find that number of masters—[and] you count duplex signs as two masters.

[1]Or perhaps we should translate *aprocopi* (απροκοποι), literally 'not progressing', simply as 'ineffective'. Bram renders it as 'retarded', and Prof. Monat renders it as *sans vigueur* 'listless'.

3. If the Sun and the Moon are dejected in a servile nativity, but the rulers of the signs in which the Sun and the Moon are located are posited in angles of the nativity, or in alien signs, or in their own humilities, slaves of powerful masters are made. But if Jupiter makes a favorable aspect to those that we have said are posited in the angles, [once] having acquired their freedom, they get the greatest insignia of fame.

4. If the Sun and the Moon are either in the *anafora* of the ASC or in the 6th house from the ASC or in the 8th or in the 12th, either partilely or apart, and they are posited in their own falls, and they have the malefic stars in the preceding degrees in the same sign, they will make feeble blind slaves, who, dejected in public places, sustain their life by beggary.

VI. Instruction as to whether the Native is born of a Slave or a Free Person.[1]

1. When Jupiter and Saturn are posited together in the MC, and the Sun is in the 6th house from the ASC, say that the father was a slave. But also, if Venus is found in the IMC, and the Sun is posited with Mars in the 3rd house from the ASC, it similarly shows the father to be a slave. But also, if the Sun is found in a domicile of Saturn, and Saturn is in the 6th house from the ASC, it shows the father to be a slave.

2. If the Moon is found with Mars in equal degrees in alien signs in the ASC, without doubt it will make the mother to be a slave girl. But also, if the ruler of the sign in which the Moon is found is in either its own humility or in dejected houses, in similar fashion it shows the mother to be a slave girl. But also, if the Moon with little light is found with Mars in the ASC, and Saturn is in the *anafora* of the ASC, it will make the mother to be a slave girl.

3. But also, if the Moon is <found> in the IMC <with little light, and she is conjoined with a malefic star in the same sign, it will make the mother to be a slave girl. But also, if the Moon> is posited <in the IMC>[2] and the ruler of that house is found in the 6th house from the ASC, it shows the mother to be a slave girl.

[1]This is the chapter title in **N**. The other MSS have ‘How you may find whether the parents are slaves’.

[2]Adds **N**, two lines having been omitted by **Ψ** due to homoeoteleuton (…Luna in IMC | …Luna in IMC).

4. If you see the Sun and Jupiter in dejected houses, either together or separated, and one of them is in the 12th house from the ASC, and the other in the 6th, say that the father is a slave. But also if you see the Moon in similar fashion with Venus in dejected houses, or one is in the 6th house from the ASC, say that the mother is a slave girl.

5. If the Moon and Venus are found in the DSC, i.e. in the 7th house from the ASC, namely in a tropical sign, and a malefic star is in the 6th house from the ASC, and another is in the 8th, and Jupiter is not in the primary angles or aspecting the primary angles by trine, it shows the mothers to be slave girls, and those to whom the custody of doors is entrusted.[1]

6. If the Sun and the Moon are found in the 6th house from the ASC, and the ruler of that sign is together with them, the parents of these [Natives] are weighed down by the burden of slavery and misfortune. But if the benefic stars are found in the angles, some good fortune will afterwards be conferred upon the parents.

7. If the Sun and the Moon are found in dejected houses from the ASC, and Saturn aspects Venus posited in any angle by opposition or square, or if he is found with her, they make slaves. But also, if Mars is with Venus just as we have said, the same thing is caused in similar fashion.

8. But also if the Sun and the Moon are located in dejected houses, and the malefic stars are posited either in the same sign or in the one that is the House of Fortune, or in the ASC, or in the rest of the angles, or in the *anaforas* of the angles, they make slaves in similar fashion. But also, if Saturn is found in the 8th house from the ASC, or in the *anafora* of the ASC, and the Moon is in either the *anaforas* or the *epicataphoras*, but Venus is hidden by the rays of the Sun, or is in the 12th house from the ASC, it will make captive slaves.

9. If with the Sun and the Moon located in dejected houses, one of the malefics is partilely posited in an angle, but the other one is either posited in the *anaforas* or in the *epicataphoras*, they make slaves. But if, with these located just as we have said, the benefic stars received the conjunction of the waxing Moon, if they are found either partilely in an angle or in the *epicataphoras*, those who are born slaves will get the prize of freedom, or they will be reared in place of [their master's] children.

[1]That is, 'door-keepers'.

10. If the Sun and the Moon are not in dejected houses, but Saturn or Mars is posited partilely in any angle, but the other one of them is posited either in the *anaforas* or in the *epicataphoras*, and both of them, i.e. Saturn and Mars, make any aspect to them, they make captives.

11. But if a benefic star, posited either in thc angles, or located in the *anaforas* of the angles, makes a fortunate aspect to all of them, they are freed from captivity by some fortunate assistance. But if more benefic stars—and those located in higher houses—receive the conjunction of the waxing Moon, with the rest [of the stars] located just as we have said, while coming into the dangers of that captivity, they will be freed.

VII. Wild Animal and Quadrupedal Nativities.

1. If the Moon is found in twisted or in wild beast signs, i.e. in Taurus, or in Cancer, or in Scorpio, or in Capricorn, or in Pisces, and the ruler of the sign in which the Moon is found is not conjoined in partile aspect with the Moon, and another malefic star aspects her either by opposition or by square, or is posited together with her, and if a second malefic star is in the *anafora* of the ASC, and it aspects the ruler of Fortune, quadrupeds are born from a quadruped, especially if the ruler of the ASC and the ruler of Fortune was found in those signs which we have mentioned.

2. But if the ruler of Fortune or the ruler of the ASC is found in a human sign, namely in the 6th house from the ASC, with all the others posited just as we have said, a monster will be born from a human. If malefic stars are posited partilely in the angles, or in the *anaforas* of the angles, but the Sun and the Moon posited in the angles strike each other with an opposition aspect, and the benefic stars are neither posited in the angles nor in the *anaforas* of the angles, or they are hidden by the rays of the Sun, either quadrupeds or a monster will be born.

3. But if Mars aspects either the Sun or the Moon or the ASC, either by square or opposition aspect, and if a quadruped is born, it will be designated for public sacrifices.. But if, with the rest [of the stars] arranged just as we have said, Jupiter and Venus posited beyond an angle, aspect either the Sun or the Moon or the ASC, the quadruped that is born will either be worshipped by men, or it will be designated for consecration either in temples or as images.

4. But all these things are plainly intimated to you by the orthogonal trine in that book that we have written *On the End of Life.*[1] For in it the scheme of the rectangular triangle,[2] which by some Greeks seems to have been wrapped in circumlocutions of ambiguity, is explained in very clear and brief interpretations.

VIII. Blind, Weak, and Physically Defective Persons.

1. If the Sun is found in the ASC, and the Moon in the MC, but both of the malefics are divided in such a way, that one holds the *anafora* of the Sun and the other the *anafora* of the Moon, and the benefic stars are unrelated to them, they will produce blind persons or those with defective vision. But also, if the Moon is joined with the Sun in a synodic aspect,[3] and they are posited in the *anaforas* or *epicataphoras* of the angles, and Saturn and Mars are partilely posited in the angles, the defect of blindness is caused for the eyes.

2. But also always in general, if the Sun and the Moon are posited in an *anafora* of the malefics, they make a defect to be caused in the eyes. If the Sun and the Moon in synodic aspect are located in any angle, and Mars posited in the same house, is conjoined to them by partile aspect, the defect of blindness is caused for the eyes.

3. But also if the Sun and the Moon are found in the ASC, and Mars is posited in the . . .[4] house from the ASC, and the benefic stars do not make any aspect to the Sun and the Moon, a defect in the eyes is caused. But also if the Sun is found partilely with Saturn in the ASC, and Mars aspects them either by square or opposition, similarly a defect in the eyes is caused.

---

[1]A book by Firmicus that has unfortunately not come down to us.

[2]This same phrase occurs in Hephaestio of Thebes, *Apotelesmatics*, ii.1.29. "And again, having known the ASC sign and the degree on the ASC of the synod previous to the conception, just as we also ascertain [it] in the ninth month, we form the rectangular triangle from that sign, namely [the sign] of the ASC, having it from the east into the leading [signs], they extend the first side of 150 degrees with which the sloping away [is] 120, and let the remaining side be 90 of the remaining degrees of the circle for the completion of the 360 degrees of the zodiac." As Firmicus says, these words (probably quoted by Hephaestio from an earlier work) are ambiguous.

[3]That is, either at New Moon or Full Moon.

[4]The house number is missing. Edition **v** has '7th'; edition **a** has '4th'.

4. But if the benefic stars from a higher house aspects them arranged thus, the blindness will be cured either by the assistance of divinity or by the intervention of medicine. If with Saturn located in the ASC, the Moon is posited in the 8th house from the ASC, or if with the Moon located in the ASC, Saturn is posited in the 8th house from the ASC, it blinds the eyes with the defect of cataract.[1]

5. But also, if the Sun is with Mars or with Mercury in the 7th house from the ASC, they make one-eyed persons, but for some of them it sometimes causes the crime of homicide. If the Sun is partilely located in some angle, with either Mars or Saturn posited in its *anafora*, the right eye will be afflicted. But if the Moon is located in the angle, and Saturn or Mars is in its *anafora*, the left eye suffers the same thing.

6. But if the Sun and the Moon are found posited together in an angle, or if they are located in different angles aspecting each other either by opposition or by square, and the malefics possess the *anaforas* of both of them, that is of the Sun and the Moon, it causes the defect of blindness in both eyes.

7. But if, with these <located> just as we have said, <Mercury is posited either in the angles or in the *anaforas* or in the *epicataphoras* of the angles, it makes weak captive persons dying violently. But if with these> located <just as we have said>,[2] Saturn or Mars aspects Jupiter from a higher house, they make gladiators, but those who having been condemned are transferred to that demise.

8. **Epileptics and Paralytics.** If Mars is partilely located in any angle, and Saturn is posited either in its *anafora* or in another angle, and both of them aspect the Moon either by square or by opposition, or if she is conjoined with one of them in the same sign in equal degrees, either lame or paralytic persons are made. But also, if Saturn is located in any angle, but Mars is posited in its *anafora*, but either Mars or Saturn aspects the Moon, they produce the same thing in similar fashion. For, having fallen down either from a high place or from [the back of] a quadruped, or involved in dangers of that sort, they suffer bodily damages.

---

[1]The Latin word *suffusio*, lit. 'flowing down' is the equivalent of the Greek word καταρράκτης 'cataract.'

[2]Adds **N**, three lines having been omitted by **Ψ** due to homoeoteleuton (... *ut diximus* | ... *ut diximus*).

IX. How You may Find Which one of the Parents Dies First.[1]

1. In whatever nativity the Sun is badly posited, or the ruler of the sign in which the Sun is found is badly posited, the father will die first; but if the Moon experienced this, the mother will die first. What we say is like this. If the ASC is found in Aries, and the Sun in Aquarius; and Saturn is in Pisces or in signs square to Pisces, [then] the ruler of the sign of the Sun—that is, Saturn—is debilitated, and because of that the father of that nativity will die first, because the Sun has fallen into the domicile of a debilitated and malevolent and killer [star].[2] If this happens for the Moon, we say that the mother will be the first to die.

2. But if, with these arranged just as we have said, Mars aspects Saturn by square, the father will die a violent death by the order of, or from the anger of, a prince. But if, with these arranged just as we have said, Jupiter is found in the angles, the misfortunes of the father are mitigated, but [only] if it aspects the Sun in a diurnal nativity, but the Moon in a nocturnal one. For if in a nocturnal nativity the Moon has experienced that which we have said, the mother will die similarly. But also these evils are then more strongly strengthened, with these arranged just as we have said, if the benefic stars are either in dejected houses or hidden by the rays of the Sun.

3. If Mars aspects the Sun located in any angle either by opposition or by square, or if it is posited with it in the same sign with equal association of degrees,[3] the father will die a violent death by order of the prince. But if Saturn, with the same aspect as Mars, is conjoined to the Sun arranged thus, the father will die either in water, or from humors, or from poison. But if the Sun is found in the *anafora* of the ASC, and Mars aspects it by square, the father will die throwing up blood.

4. But also if the Sun is found in the 6th house from the ASC or in the 3rd or in the 12th, and the malefic stars aspect it by square, or if they are found with it, it causes the demise by a bad death for the father. But if—with the Sun arranged just as we have said—it has a square aspect from Saturn, or if Saturn is found with it, the father will also die from hid-

---

[1]*Cf.* Rhetorius, *Astrological Compendium*, Chapter 102.

[2]That is, the Sun is in the domicile of Saturn, and Saturn is an evil star and is also afflicted by being posited in the 12th house.

[3]That is, if they are conjoined in the same degree.

den and concealed illnesses—i.e. from dysentery or pneumonia[1] and from other illnesses of that sort.

5. But also if the Sun is found in the DSC, and Mars and Saturn in the IMC, they do the same thing to the father in similar fashion. But if the Moon is arranged just as we have said the Sun is, and she is afflicted by that aspect from the malefic stars, the mother will experience a similar demise. But in all these combinations we ought to check the aspects of the benefic stars in similar fashion.

6. For if Jupiter and Venus, with the other stars arranged just as we have said, posited either in the angles or in the fortunate houses of the nativity, make fortunate aspects to the Sun, the preceding misfortune of the father is mitigated, [or] if [they make them] to the Moon, that of the mother is mitigated. But if with a benefic star helping and posited thus just as we have said, the ruler of the sign in which the benefic star is located is found with the malefic stars or with the Sun, namely in the preceding dejection that we have said, the aforesaid misfortunes for the father or the mother are strongly strengthened.

7. But frequently when the temporal[2] Jupiter has come to Mars in the nativity, or if it aspects him by square, the death of the father is brought about. The temporal Saturn will do this same thing if it aspects the Sun posited in the nativity by square or opposition. But if the temporal Saturn does this to the Moon, the mother will die; but this does not always [happen], but [only] when the scheme of time demands it, in accordance with the rulership of the stars, which we have discussed previously.[3]

8. But if you want to find this precisely, <this is the method>[4] to study, for it was hidden from you, and they show it proved in many nativities. If

[1]The Latin has *phthisi*, which could be translated by the more vague term '(those suffering from) consumption'. But it seems to me that it could also include lung cancer, which might be caused by the frequent inhalation of wood smoke, just as tobacco smoke sometimes causes it today.

[2]It is not certain what the word *temporalis* 'temporal' means here. It might refer to a transiting position, although Firmicus more often uses the phrase *transitum facit* 'it makes a transit', but it may refer to the planets active in the Time Periods discussed in Book VI.

[3]These words refer to the Time Periods discussed in Book VI.

[4]Some words are missing in the Latin. Kroll suggests 'you <ought> to study <the *Myriogenesis*>, and Bram accepts that. But it seems to me that Firmicus is merely referring to the method that he is about to state. So probably we should simply read **haec est ratio* 'this is the method' or something similar.

it is a diurnal nativity, compute from the Sun up to the Moon all the signs that are placed in order, and whatever the number of signs that is collected, compute again that number from the ASC,[1] and if the number of the last sign is found in a masculine sign, the father will die first, but if it is in a feminine sign, the mother will die first.

9. In a nocturnal nativity, this same thing is collected in reversed order. And so, if it is a nocturnal nativity, compute beginning from the Moon all the signs similarly that are placed in order, and whatever is the number of the signs, count that much beginning from the ASC, and if the last number is found in a feminine sign, the father will die first, but if it is in a masculine sign, the mother will die first, for it shows one way in a diurnal nativity and the other way in a nocturnal one.[2]

10. But also if the Sun and the Moon are found in masculine signs, with the ASC placed in a masculine sign, but either Mars or Saturn holds the MC, the father will die first. But if the Sun and the Moon and the ASC are similarly placed in feminine signs, and Mars and Saturn are found in the MC, the mother will die first. But this is disproved[3] both by us and by many others! But that which is collected from the preceding computation shows the death with true reasons.

X. Children Inimical to their Parents.

1. If in a nativity Mars or Saturn is found in the 7th house from the ASC, but the Sun is in the 8th house from the ASC, either the Native will be alienated from his father, or they will have serious quarrels from dissension. But also if Mars is found in the *anafora* of the ASC, or in the *anafora* of the MC, this same thing is produced in similar fashion. But also if Mars is found partilely in the ASC or in the MC, but the Sun is posited in either the DSC or the in the IMC, this same thing is produced in similar fashion.

2. But if there were those configurations of the malefic stars that we have mentioned in connection with the Moon, quarrels from enmities are

---

[1]This is the original way of computing the House of Fortune for a diurnal nativity.

[2]This the original way of computing the House of Fortune for a nocturnal nativity.

[3]The Latin has *improbatur* 'is disapproved', but Bram mistakenly transloates it as 'has been proved', and Prof. Monat renders it as 'we approve'.

aroused between the mother and the children, especially if Saturn aspects the Moon posited thus. But also, whoever has the Sun in the terms of Mars in a diurnal nativity, but in [those] of Saturn in a nocturnal nativity, and certainly Mars by day, but Saturn by night, aspects the Sun by square or by opposition aspect, and an aspect of the benefic stars does not mitigate all of these, the children will kill their own fathers; but if the Moon was found thus, they will kill their mothers.

3. If the Sun in the terms or in the domiciles of the malefic stars is posited in the 6th or in the 12th house from the ASC, and a malefic star aspects it posited thus by square or opposition, it will make children to be disinherited by their fathers. But if a benefic star from any part [of the nativity] aspects the Sun posited thus, the severity of the paternal punishment is mitigated. But if the Sun is found in the *anafora* of the ASC or in the 8th house from the ASC, he will indeed not be disinherited by his father, but it will make his father's property to be destroyed in some manner.

4. But if benefic stars aspect the Sun posited thus just as we have said, few things of the paternal property will perish. The Moon will accomplish this same thing in connection with their mothers or with the maternal property; and this [will be done] more so if she is thus posited, so that she holds either the 15th or the 17th degree in a tropical sign and malefic stars aspect her by square or by opposition, [for then] the maternal property is destroyed.

5. But if benefic stars make any kind of aspect to the Moon posited thus, some portion of the maternal property is preserved. But also if the Sun and Mars are together in any angle in a tropical sign, they will make the paternal property to be destroyed. But if a benefic star aspects them posited thus, some portion of the paternal property is preserved. The Moon posited thus accomplishes this same thing in a mother's nativity.

XI. Those Who are made Orphans by the Death of their Parents.

1. When the 7th house from the ASC is found in a duplex sign (but the sign of Libra is also added to the duplex signs), but Venus is found in any angle, with the parents separated by divorce, the children are left alone. But also if a duplex sign is similarly in the DSC, and the ASC is in a du-

plex one, but Saturn is posited in any angle, but the Sun and the Moon are posited in the signs of the malefic stars and posited in dejected houses from the ASC, both of the parents will die from quick deaths.

2. But if only the Sun was posited thus just as we have said, only the father will die; but if [it is] the Moon, only the mother will die. But these events are found up to the 15th and 16th year. Within that time, the stars arranged thus just as we have said, announce to us the deaths of the parents. Moreover, you will find the time of their deaths when the temporal Saturn has come to those places that we designated in the previous explanation.

3. But also if the angles are in duplex signs, and the Sun and the Moon are in the DSC or in the MC, and the Ruler of the Nativity is also in either the DSC or in the IMC, the parents will die in the first age of the children. If the MC is found in a masculine sign, the mother of that nativity is allotted two husbands, so that this [Native] is born from the second husband; but if in a feminine [sign], he will be born from the second wife, especially if the MC is found in duplex or in tropical signs.

4. **Those who are Adopted.** But if Venus is found in Gemini or in the signs that are in trine to Gemini, or in Pisces, or in Taurus, it will make [them] to be adopted. But [when she] is in Pisces—and also in Taurus—if she was not in the angles, it will do this same thing; but in those other [signs] that we have mentioned, when she is found to be angular, then it will make [them] to be adopted.

5. **Brothers.** Compute from Saturn to Jupiter, and the same amount from the ASC, and in whatever sign the last number has come to, that sign shows you the number of brothers. If malefic stars aspect this House, the brothers will die, or they will make mortal enemies; if benefic [stars aspect], they will be increased [in number].

6. But also if Saturn is found partilely in the ASC, and its degrees are indeed those of Saturn, all his brothers will die within the first years of his age. Other [astrologers] count from Mercury to the Sun, and the same amount from the ASC, and they define the House of Brothers thus, saying the rest [of the things] about this House in similar fashion. This procedure also has the greatest efficacy in astrological decrees.

XII.

1. **Those who marry many Wives.** In all nativities, if Saturn is found with Venus in the same sign, and if indeed Saturn has more degrees, it denotes one wife; but if Venus has more degrees, many wives are denoted. You will find this same thing in the nativities of women. Venus posited in the DSC, i.e. in the 7th house from the ASC, will give a wife who has been debauched by others, or they will live together without marriage papers. If Mars aspects <Venus>,[1] they are allotted wives known [to have committed] adultery. But if Venus is thus configured in Taurus or in Libra, it will give free-born wives, but low-born ones in other signs.

2. **Those who are Allotted their own Sisters or Relatives as Wives.** In the nativity of a man, count from Saturn to Venus if it is a diurnal one, and count the same amount from the ASC; in a nocturnal one, do the opposite; and just as we have frequently said, this sign shows you the House of the Wife. Again, compute the House of Brothers from Saturn to Jupiter, and the same amount from the ASC. If, therefore, the House of the Wife established by degree[2] falls in the House of Brothers, computed thus just as we have stated, sisters or their own kin are allotted [as wives]. You will also ascertain similarly in the nativity of women.

3. But also, if Venus is found together with the Ruler of the Nativity in the same sign, it denotes wives who are either sisters or kin. But also, if the House of the Spouse computed by degree is found in the maternal or paternal signs, they are allotted wives who are their mothers, or step-mothers, or their own nurses. You will also ascertain similarly in the nativity of women, especially if Mars, Venus, or Mercury aspect these same Houses.

XIII.

1. **Incestuous Marriages.** Because we are about to speak about incestuous marriages, other omitted things should be brought up here now. If in a nativity Saturn is found in a sign of Jupiter or in the terms of Jupiter,

---

[1]The Teubner editors put a lacuna between 'If' and 'Mars' and suggest the following addition to fill it: <'this one so posited by an opposition or square aspect'>, which may be appropriate, but I think it is sufficient merely to insert <Venus>. Bram merely renders it as, " If Mars is in aspect."

[2]Latin *partiliter* 'partilely', whence 'by degree'.

but Jupiter and Venus in those of Saturn, but Mars and the Moon aspects those [stars] posited thus by a square aspect, they will mate either with their mothers or with their step-mothers. But if Mercury was connected with them, they will mate either with sons or daughters or with step-children.

2. But also if the Moon is found with Jupiter and Saturn and Mars in a domicile of Saturn, they will secretly mate with either their mother or their step-mother or their father. But if all of these are found just as we have said in the 6th house from the ASC, then, after the death of his father, it allots his own mother as his wife; or after the death of his mother, it will make a daughter[1] to be the wife of the father. But if Mercury is found with them, women are allotted their own sons [as husbands], but men are allotted their own daughters as wives.

3. But also if the Moon posited in the last degrees of Cancer applies to Jupiter, or if she is in a domicile of Saturn, but Venus is found similarly in a domicile of Saturn, but Saturn is in a domicile of Venus, this same thing is caused.

4. **Those who are Allotted many Wives.** In all nativities, if Venus is found in duplex or in tropical signs,[2] and the rulers of those signs in which Venus is posited are similarly found in duplex or in tropical signs, they certainly denote many wives for men but many husbands for women. But if the Moon similarly aspects Venus posited neither in tropical nor in duplex signs, certainly [only] one wife is denoted for a man, but one husband for a woman. But if Venus posited in tropical or in duplex signs aspects the Moon, it denotes many wives for men, and many husbands for women.

XIV.

1. **Those who Kill their Wives.** If Venus is in a domicile of Mars or in the terms of that same Mars, and Mars located in a domicile of Venus or in the terms of that same Venus, aspects the Moon full of light posited in his own signs or in his own terms by an opposition aspect, husbands kill their own wives with their own hands; if Mars is in the angles, . . .[3] it makes

[1]Reading **filiam* instead of *filia*.

[2]That is, in *cardinal* signs.

[3]Ziegler indicates a lacuna here. But perhaps it merely contained the single word *fuerit* 'is'.

[them] to die by the sword. But if in the nativity of a woman, Mars posited in his own domicile or in his own degrees is found in the MC, and he aspects Venus by opposition, the husbands will perish, slain by their wives; but they do these things [if they are] without the testimony of Jupiter.

2. If the House of the Wife, found by degree—namely, by that method that we have shown in the preceding Book—was found in a sign of Jupiter, he will be a man separated from all the lures of lustful desires. But if Jupiter itself aspects that same House, posited in a sign of Jupiter, or if it is found in that same house, the grace of chastity is more strongly strengthened. But if it is in a domicile of Saturn, it will make lustful persons. But if Saturn aspects this House, it makes men who are austere around women.

3. If it is found in a sign of Mars, and Mars or Jupiter aspects this same House, or one of them is in that same House, and the other aspects it, it will make men who always esteem their own wives with faithful affection. But if this House is found in a sign of Mercury, and Mercury aspects this House, or if he is located there, it will make passive lovers; the Sun will make royal ones; the Moon will make pleasing and lovable ones.

4. If the Moon is found with Mars in a domicile of Mars, and Saturn aspects them by square or opposition, it will make effeminate men without a wife, without children, and consumptive. If Jupiter is found with Venus in the DSC, men will willingly have sexual relations with older women, but women with old men.

XV. Lovers of Boys.

1. Mercury and Mars posited together in the ASC make lovers of boys; nevertheless they make this lust to grow stronger if they were located in the domiciles of other [stars]. But also, if Venus is posited in a domicile of Mercury, but Mercury is badly posited in the nativity, they always impel [the Natives] to sexual relations with boys due to a perverted love. But so that this may be more clearly understood, when Venus is in a domicile of Mercury, namely if Mercury is in the IMC, or in the DSC, or in the 8th house from the ASC, or in the 6th, or the 12th, or in the *anafora* of the ASC, or in their own dejections, i.e. in those <houses>[1] in which they are humiliated, then that which we have said is done.

[1]Adds edition **a**.

2. If the House of the Spouse, computed by degree, falls in a domicile of Mercury, but Mercury is located in an angle in a masculine sign, it will make lovers of boys, but of the sort who never desire sexual intercourse with women, or at least with <little>[1] desire. But also, if Mars and Mercury have exchanged their own domiciles—namely, so that Mars is in a domicile of Mercury, and Mercury is in a domicile of Mars—they will make lovers of boys, especially if, posited thus, they are located in a dejected house from the ASC. They do that same thing too if they are together in a domicile of Mars.

3. But also if Mercury is in a domicile of Mars, and Mars aspects it by square or opposition, it makes lovers of boys. Similarly, if Mars is in a domicile of Mercury, and Mercury aspects it by square or opposition, this denotes the fault of [that] lust with similar power. But also if the Moon is found in a domicile of Mercury, or in the terms of Mercury, <but Mercury>[2] is in the domicile of the Moon, it will make lovers of boys.

XVI.

1. **How you may find how many Wives Anyone Marries.** If Venus is found in the MC, and the Moon aspects her by trine, and she also has the testimonies of the rest of the stars, it denotes one wife. But if she is found in any other house, compute from Venus herself up to that sign in which by degree the House of the Spouse is found, and however many signs there are from Venus to the Sign of Marriage, that many wives are denoted. So also in feminine nativities you will find out about [the number of] husbands. Let others prove this method—it is not proved by us!

2. **Those who marry Public Whores as Wives, or who Commit Adultery with such Persons.** If Venus is found with Mars in the 6th house from the ASC, it will make both men and women to be adulterers. But if they are in a domicile of Saturn, and Saturn himself is conjoined in partile association with them in the same sign, namely in the 6th house from the ASC, in the nativity of women, they will make public whores; but in the nativities of men, they will make it so that they will either have whores for wives, or they will be joined together with public sodomites by an impure lustful desire.

[1]Accepting Ziegler's emendation *vel <modica> 'or with little'.
[2]Adds edition **v**. But **Δ** has *vel* 'or', which may be correct.

3. **How you may Find out how many Marriages Anyone is Allotted.** If you have found the House of the Spouse, and the ruler of that sign is found in the same sign, then when the first years of that sign have been completed, marriage is denoted. But if the Ruler of the Sign is posited thus, so that it does not make any aspect to the House of the Spouse—that is, to its Sign—and another star is posited in that same sign, then when the first times of that star which is found in that same sign—that is, in the House of the Spouse—has been completed, marriage is denoted. But if no star is located in that Sign, a wife is denoted after the *anafora* of that sign.

4. But there is also another more subtle method composed in partile fashion. Compute the substance of all the stars, and make a total of the whole number, and divide this same total among the rest of the signs—beginning from the sign in which the House of the Spouse is found by degree—so that you give 30 degrees to each of the signs, and in whatever sign the last number comes to, when Jupiter comes to that sign, then marriage is denoted.

5. What I say is this—for because it was said more obscurely, I shall explain this same thing to you again more clearly. Compute 19 of the Sun, 25 of the Moon, 30 of Saturn, 12 of Jupiter, 15 of Mars, 8 of Venus, and 20 of Mercury; all of this computed makes 129. All this number,[1] beginning from that in which the House of the Spouse is found by degree; divide among all the following signs, and give 30 to each, and in whatever sign the last number comes to, when Jupiter comes to that sign after its second circuit,[2] then it denotes a stable marriage; for before that, if any [marriage] was allotted, either the marriage is dissolved by divorce, or it is divided by death without any fruit [of offspring], or certainly up to that time they disagree with various quarrels.[3]

XVII.

1. **Those who do Away with their Wives.** If Mars and Venus and Jupiter are found in the DSC, i.e. in the 7th house from the ASC, and the

[1]Beginning with this word (*numerum* at II 245.5), MS **N** adds 16 Teubner pages (ending at II 261.6) of text that is found in none of the other MSS, but is also found on handwritten sheets written by someone unknown and inserted into a copy of edition **a** in the Wolfenbüttel Library. As previously, its readings are denoted by the siglum **W**.

[2]Here Firmicus is definitely talking about transits.

[3]Bram's translation omits nearly all of this paragraph.

ruler of that sign in which they are posited is found in the MC, the husband kills his wife. But also, if Mars is found alone in the DSC, and Venus in the MC, but the Moon is found either in the ASC full of light or in the IMC, the wife will die slain by the hands of her husband.

2. If in a man's nativity, with Jupiter and Mars posited in any house, and the rulers of those signs in which Mars and Jupiter are posited are so posited that one is in the DSC and the other in the IMC, the death of the wife is denoted similarly. But if Venus is found <in the IMC>[1] and Jupiter in the DSC of the nativity, that same thing is produced. But if with Venus posited in the DSC, the ruler of that sign in which Venus is posited is found in the IMC, that same thing is denoted.

3. If Venus and Jupiter are found in the 7th house from the ASC, but the ruler of that sign is in either the IMC or is posited together with them in the DSC, the wife's death is denoted. But if, with these arranged thus, the Sun, Saturn, and Mars are posited in either the 6th or the 8th house from the ASC, the wife will perish slain by the hands of her husband.

XVIII.

1. **Those who are Allotted Older Wives.** If Saturn and Venus, posited in different signs, have equal degrees, or if they are posited in the sign [of the House] of the Wife, and indeed in the same degree, or if Venus is in the terms of Saturn, and Saturn is in [the terms of] Venus; but also if they are not in aspect and they hold each others terms, wives of advanced age are certainly denoted for men; but for women, husbands of advanced age are denoted.

2. **Those who are Allotted Wives from their Maternal or Paternal Kindred.** If Jupiter and Venus and the Moon were posited together in any sign, or if they aspect each other by opposition or square, especially if Jupiter was found in the terms of Venus, and Venus in [the terms of] Jupiter; and if both, or one of them, aspects the Moon by opposition, it denotes a wife from the mother's kindred. But if the Sun is configured either with Venus or with Jupiter, and with the Moon just as we have said, a wife from the father's kindred is denoted.

3. **Those who are Allotted their own Sisters as Wives.** If the Sun and the Moon are found together, and with them Venus or Jupiter, or if they

[1]Added by Kroll.

are aspecting each other by square, so that Venus is in the terms of Jupiter, but Jupiter is in the terms of Venus, brothers will marry their own sisters.

4. **Those who Marry their Mothers.** If Saturn and Venus are in the same degree in one sign, or if posited in opposition or in square they have the same degrees, and the Moon either gives testimony to them or is posited with them, but Jupiter posited in the terms of Venus makes any aspect to them, they make the mother and her sons to contract matrimony.

5. But in the nativities of women, with the rest [of the stars arranged] thus just as we have said, if the Sun is found in that place in which we have put the Moon, daughters will have intercourse with their own fathers for the sake of marriage. But also if Venus is found in the terms of Jupiter, and Jupiter in the terms of Venus, and Mars aspects them either by square or opposition, they compel daughters to have intercourse with their fathers.

6. **Those who Marry their Step-Mothers.** If Jupiter and Venus, posited in the angles and having equal degrees, aspect each other by square, and the Moon aspects them by either square or opposition, they allot them their step-mothers as wives. But women lie with[1] their step-fathers, if with Venus and Jupiter posited thus, the Sun was posited thus, just as we have put the Moon in a man's nativity.

7. **Those who Have Intercourse with a Father and a Son <or with a Mother and a Daughter>.**[2] If Venus, the Moon, and Jupiter are located together in the angles, or if posited in the angles they aspect each other by square or opposition, and Saturn is so posited that he makes some aspect to all of them, they make [them] to have intercourse with a mother and with a daughter. But if Saturn aspects the Moon and Venus alone, this crime is committed secretly; but if he aspects all of them, they will be allotted both of the women as wives publicly.

8. But in the nativity of a woman, if the Sun is found where we have put the Moon, she will have intercourse with both a father and a son. But if Mercury was in the terms of Venus, and Venus in the terms of Mercury, and if thus posited, they aspect each other by square or opposition,[3] but

---

[1]Accepting Ziegler's emendation of **concumbunt* for the *qui nubunt* of the MSS.

[2]I have added the words in angular brackets, since both combinations are discussed in this section.

[3]The word 'Mercury' is added only by MS **W** and may not be correct, for while Mercury and Venus could be in signs that are in square aspect to each other, they

Jupiter aspects them either by square or opposition, it will make the sons to suffer the stain of feminine lust from their fathers.[1]

9. **Adulterers.** If Mars and Venus are found together, or if Mars posited in the terms of Venus and Venus posited in the terms of Mars make any aspect to each other, they make adulterers. But if Mercury aspects them by square or opposition, possessing degrees equal to them, it will make them to be apprehended in crimes of that sort. But we have very frequently spoken about this topic in the preceding books.

XIX.

1. **Sterile Women.** If the Sun and the Moon are in masculine signs in the ASC, but Saturn is either in the DSC or in the IMC, women will not procreate children, especially if the ASC is found in Leo, or in Virgo, or in Capricorn, or in Pisces, or in Scorpio, or in Cancer, or in Taurus. But if with these arranged just as we have said, a benefic star is found in the primary angles, one or two children that are born will be reared.

2. But also if the Moon is either found in a masculine sign, or certainly in Leo, or in Virgo, or in Capricorn, and the Sun is in a masculine sign, or in those signs that we have mentioned, but Saturn is either posited in the angles or in the 12th house from the ASC, neither for a †virgin nor for a woman are <children>[2] denoted. But if Jupiter located in the primary angles makes a favorable aspect to those [stars] arranged thus, it will make one child to be denoted.

3. But also, if the Sun and the Moon are in feminine signs, and the ASC is located in a feminine sign, but Saturn is posited either in the 7th house from the ASC or in the MC, and no benefic star is found in an angle, children are not denoted.

---

cannot be in signs that are opposite each other. We should perhaps read 'Moon' instead of Mercury.

[1]That is, the fathers will have sex relations with their sons.

[2]The Latin text has *nec †virgini nec mulieri decernuntur* 'neither for a virgin nor for a woman they are denoted', which does not make sense. Kroll suggests *nec *pueri <nec puellae> mulieri decernuntur* 'neither sons nor daughters are denoted for the woman'. But I have accepted Wikström's suggestion *nec virgini nec mulieri <liberi> decernuntur*. This is perhaps the least alteration of the text that makes sense. But the word *virgini* 'for a virgin' is still suspicious. Bram translates it as 'a young woman', but I believe Firmicus only uses it in the sense 'virgin'.

4. If Saturn and the Moon,[1] located in the angles and having the same degrees, aspect each other by square, and they are also posited in duplex signs, and Jupiter does not make any aspect to them and it is not located in the angles, children are not denoted. But also if Jupiter and the Moon are posited together in the 7th house from the ASC or in the IMC, and Saturn, posited in another angles, aspects them by square or opposition, it will make no children to be denoted.

5. **Those Who do not have Intercourse with Women.** If Venus and the Moon are located together, and Saturn posited in his own[2] terms aspects them by square or opposition, and the testimony of the Sun is added to them, with Saturn posited in his matutine rising in a diurnal nativity, and with Venus either posited in the angles but in a masculine sign, or posited in her vespertine rising in a nocturnal nativity, they will never be allotted wives.

6. But if, with all of them arranged just as we have said, Saturn and the Moon and Venus were posited in Leo or Virgo, in those degrees which we have said, they will in short never mate with women. But also if no star aspects Venus posited in the terms of Saturn, but with the Moon posited either in Leo or in Virgo or in Capricorn in the terms of Saturn, they will never mate with women.

XX.

1. **Frail Persons, Epileptics, Blind Persons, those with Bodily Defects, and Lunatics.** If the Sun and the Moon posited in duplex signs are located in the angles, and Mars and Saturn aspect them posited thus by square, they will produce frail persons and lunatics. But also if Mars is found in the ASC, and Saturn is in the MC, but the Moon is either posited with them or is posited in square aspect, it will produce that same thing in similar fashion. But also if Saturn is found in the MC, and Mars is in the IMC, the same thing is produced similarly.

2. If with the Sun and the Moon conjoined in synodic aspect, the stars of Mars and Saturn were applied, and if they are conjoined to both of them—i.e. to the Sun and the Moon—with equal association of degree,

[1] There is a lacuna here. Ziegler suggests <*Luna*>, 'the Moon; MS **W** has <*Venus*> 'Venus', but I have accepted Ziegler's suggestion.

[2] Accepting Ziegler's addition *in finibus* <*suis*>.

the defects of this misfortune are imposed in their first age. But if only Mars is found, blindness of the eyes is inflicted by some violence; but if only Saturn is found, it is afflicted from a catarrh. But if they aspect the Moon by square, the same thing is brought about in similar fashion.

3. If Saturn is found in the 12th <house> from <the ASC> . . . <in>[1] the MC, and Mars is posited together with him, or in the *anafora* of the MC, they extinguish the light of one eye. But if both of them, i.e. Mars and Saturn, are posited in the 8th house from the ASC, and they are retrograde, but they aspect the Moon by square, they make persons who are both feeble and blind. But if they aspect the Moon from the dexter side, they blind the right eye, and they weaken the right side parts [of the body]; but if from the sinister side, they do the same thing for the left side parts [of the body].

4. If there is a malefic star in the middle between the Sun and the Moon, or in their synod, or certainly in the same sign, or with the Sun and the Moon located in different houses, a malefic star is posited in the middle of those signs, blindness is caused for the eyes. But if a benefic star makes a fortunate aspect to those posited thus, the dangers of that misfortune are mitigated. But in particular, whatever persons have the Moon in either the 3rd degree of Sagittarius, or in the 16th of Leo, or in the 14th of Cancer, or in the 5th of Taurus, are made feeble.

5. If Mars is located in the 7th house from the ASC, and the Moon in the 8th, a part of the body will be amputated or broken apart, in accordance with the nature of the sign in which Mars is found. If the Moon is found in tropical signs, i.e. in Aries, in Cancer, in Libra, and in Capricorn, but Mars aspects her by square, it will either amputate a foot or a hand.

6. But if the Sun makes a square aspect to them posited just as we have said, or Saturn strikes them either by square or by opposition; or if one of the lights is posited in the 7th house from the ASC, or certainly if Saturn is in that same house, it will make those having stomach disorders. But also if the Sun and the Moon and Mars and Mercury are located in the 6th house from the ASC, and Saturn aspects them by square, or with those located in the 7th house, Saturn is posited in the ASC, it will make lunatics with a distorted face and an impediment of the tongue.

[1]The additions and the indication of a lacuna are from Ziegler. But the ellipsis might merely contain *aut* 'or'.

7. But also if Mars is conjoined by square to Saturn posited in the 7th house, it will make insane persons. But if[1] [with] Mercury also posited in the ASC, Mars in the DSC, and Saturn either in the DSC or in the MC, it will make insane persons, but those to whom the crime of homicide is also added. If Mars and Saturn are found together in Capricorn, or in Pisces, or in Aries, or in Taurus, they will amputate a part of the body according to the quality of the sign.

8. Saturn and Mars posited together in any sign make pains in concealed and hidden parts of the body. But if they aspect [each other] by opposition when they are posited in solid signs—either when one is in the ASC, and the other in the DSC, or when one is in the IMC, and the other in the MC—they make epileptics. But if when posited in tropical signs they make that aspect to each other, they make epileptics, but those who can in no way be cured.

9. But if when posited in duplex signs they make that aspect to each other, they will make, along with those defects that we have mentioned, irreligious, cruel, and captive persons. But if a benefic star aspects those posited thus, the captives will be returned to their native land. But if the malefic stars are found in their stations in those signs that we have mentioned, they will be more strongly harmed; but if they are benefic stars, they will be more strongly benefited.

10. If Saturn and Mars posited in the angles aspect each other by opposition, and they aspect the Moon located in another angle either by square or by opposition, especially in the last degrees of Libra and Capricorn and Aries, they will cripple the feet. If Mars located in alien signs is partilely posited in the ASC, it will harm them either in their private parts or in their ears. Mars and Saturn, posited in tropical signs and afflicting the Moon by square aspect, make persons [afflicted] with dropsy.

11. But also, if Mars and Saturn aspect each other by opposition, they make those throwing up blood. Mars posited in Cancer, or in Scorpio, or in Capricorn, or in Pisces, if he aspects the Moon by opposition will cause impetigo, jaundice, and leprosy. If Saturn makes an opposition aspect to the Moon—located neither in the domicile of the Moon nor in the domiciles of Saturn—they make those suffering from hemorrhoids or

[1]The MSS have *ipsi* 'these same' **N** and *is si* 'if the one' **W**, but **si* 'if' seems sufficient. Bram agrees. And both Skutsch and Ziegler would insert <*Venere*> 'with Venus' before Mercury, but I don't think that is appropriate.

from an illness involving an ulcer. Mars posited in angles will also do this same thing if it aspects Venus by opposition.

12. If Mars and Venus and the Moon posited in tropical signs aspect each other by opposition, and Saturn, located either in Leo, or in Taurus, or in Sagittarius, or in Pisces, aspects them by night, it will make persons suffering from gout, but if by day, those suffering from elephantiasis. But also, if the Moon is found in Taurus and Saturn in Scorpio, or the Moon in Scorpio and Saturn in Taurus, and no benefic star aspects the Moon, those who will suffer from elephantiasis will be born.

13. If Mercury, located either in Virgo or in Pisces, is partilely posited in the ASC, and Saturn and Mars aspect it by square, they will make insane persons. If Mars and Saturn are in the *anafora* of the ASC or in the 8th house from the ASC, they will make blood to be emitted through the nose or through the mouth or through the anus. If Mars and Saturn are so placed that one of them is in the MC and the other in the IMC, they make a corrupting illness from irregular humors.

14. But if Mercury aspects them by square, health is provided for them by the aid of the Gods. But if they are posited in these houses conjoined by partile aspect, so that they possess equal degrees, they make insane persons, but those who can never be freed from the dangers of insanity. But if they are posited in their own terms, or if Saturn is in the terms of Mars, and Mars is in the terms of Saturn, and they are located in those houses that we have mentioned, they are freed from the defects of insanity after the 15th year of Mars or the 30th year of Saturn have been completed.

15. But also, if Jupiter and Mars aspect each other similarly, they will make epileptics. But if they are posited just as we have said in their own degrees, and either Jupiter is in the terms of Mars or Mars is in the terms of Jupiter, they are freed from this illness in its beginning; but when the first times of the star have passed, i.e. either the 15 years of Mars or the 12 years of Jupiter. But if Mercury has combined <with them, posited as we have said>[1] either by opposition or by square aspect, and posited in the same degrees, it will make a man who gives responses in temples.

[1] I have added these words to fill the lacuna noted by Ziegler.

XXI.

1. **Those who are Bald.** When the Moon is posited in the angles in those same degrees of the signs that are without hair, or when the Moon is posited in Sagittarius, but malefic stars are either in solid or in tropical signs, in which the House of Bodily Defects and Illnesses is found by degree, they will make bald men. <The Sun will make>[1] this same thing when it is afflicted by the aspects of the malefic stars; but also, if Venus posited in her own domicile holds the MC partilely, it will make those who are bald. But Saturn, posited between the Sun and the Moon, will make those born to have grey hair in their first age.

2. **Bodily Defects and Illnesses.** If Mars is found in Cancer, or in Scorpio, or in Capricorn, or in Pisces, or in Taurus, and posited in those sign it is posited in any angle of the nativity, and placed thus it aspects the Moon by square or by opposition, or if it is found with her, it will produce badly hunch-backed, or twisted, or crippled persons, or those paralyzed in some part of their body.

3. If Mars and Saturn are in either the 6th or the 12th house from the ASC, or at least one of the two [is there], and that sign is either duplex or tropical, or in that sign the House of Fortune is found, defects of both body and mind are denoted, especially if they aspect the Sun or the Moon by square or opposition. But if posited thus, Mars and Saturn are either posited in angles, or just as we have said in the 6th or 12 house from the ASC, they aspect the Moon . . .[2] or synodically posited, [then] either they make bodily defects due to these humors, or they produce insane epileptic persons.

4. But always if malefic stars aspect the Moon posited in the 7th, or the 11th, or in the 6th, or the 12th house from the ASC by square or opposition, or if they were found with her, they make contorted limbs and spasmodic motions,[3] or they twist up the face in various ways,[4] especially if the ASC and the House of Fortune are located in the signs of the malefics. But we find these bodily defects in accordance with the kinds of the

[1]Adds Brakman.

[2]Kroll says that either some words are missing here or else the following word *aut* 'or' should be deleted. Possibly we should read "...the Moon, <either full of light> or synodically posited." i.e. either the full Moon or the new Moon.

[3]Probably a reference to spastic persons.

[4]This sounds like the facial contortions that sometimes occur in *le petit mal* type of epilepsy.

signs. For this configuration denotes stomach trouble [and] epilepsy for some, insanity for others, leprous patches for others, impetigo for others, dropsy for others, tuberculosis for others, and elephantiasis for others.

5. But if a benefic star makes a fortunate aspect to these stars arranged thus, these bodily defects are alleviated. But if there is no testimony from the benefic stars, and the malefic stars make a strong aspect to the House of Bodily Defects located in a fixed sign, the decreed bodily defects are strongly strengthened. But if the benefic and malefic stars aspect this same house with equal powers, the bodily defects both leave off [and] at the same time increase.

6. But if with a malefic star attacking, the testimonies of the benefic stars were stronger, and if the benefic stars received the conjunction of the Moon, they are liberated from these crises of dangers by certain divinities. But if with a benefic star receiving the conjunction of the Moon, malefic stars make a stronger aspect to the House of Bodily Defects, they get a temporary respite from the bodily defects by the assistance of some divinity.

7. But if, with the benefic stars being stronger, Mercury receives the conjunction of the applying Moon, they are freed from these crises either by incantations, or medicines, or by amulets. But if, with the benefic stars being stronger, Mars makes any aspect to them, the bodily defect that was decreed will be cured by means of medicine. If Saturn was found in the 7th house from the ASC, and, posited in this house, he makes any aspect to the Moon posited in another angle, they will be operated on by physicians in hidden places [of the body].

8. But if the Moon has little light, and Jupiter is not in the angles and makes any aspect to the Moon, they will die after having been operated on by physicians. But if, with the Moon and Saturn arranged just as we have said, Mars conjoined in partile association with Mercury, and posited in tropical signs, is joined in any aspect to the Moon and Saturn, they will make insane epileptics and those who fall down.[1] But if with these arranged thus, Jupiter aspects Mercury from a superior house and receives the conjunction of the Moon, [after] having been operated on for an abscess, they are freed [from these ailments].

9. But if Mars is found in the 6th or the 12th house from the ASC, and the Sun and Saturn aspect him posited thus, they denote illnesses and

[1]Those who suffer from *le grand mal* type of epilepsy.

bodily defects with miserable damage. But if Mars posited thus and located in a masculine sign makes a square aspect to the Sun and Moon from a superior house, it will make a serious bodily defect in the sexual parts. But if it is the nativity of a woman, it always indicates serious dangers from abortion and the giving of birth, with the infant having been dissected among the viscera and thus brought forth, it will cause continual pain in the uterus.

10. If Jupiter is found in the ASC, and Mars posited in opposition to it, makes any aspect to the Sun and the Moon, it will either make insane persons or lunatics. But also if either the new Moon, or the full Moon, posited in an angle aspects Mars by square, and Saturn is joined to him by square or by opposition, these same bodily defects are denoted.

XXII.

1. **Royal Nativities.** If the Sun and the Moon are posited in masculine signs in the first angles of the nativity, with the benefic stars posited in such a way that they certainly protect the Sun in their morning rising, but in a nocturnal nativity they protect the Moon in their evening rising, they will make kings who are terrible, powerful persons subjugating [whole] regions or the greatest cities. But if they were posited in the MC, just as we have said, they will also subjugate foreign nations and exterior regions by the unlimited power of their strength.

2. But if with all of these arranged just as we have said, Mars is found in their *anafora*, but Saturn is posited in another angle, having been cast down from their own imperial position, they will be subjugated by others. But if Jupiter, placed higher [in the chart], makes a fortunate aspect to Mars and Saturn, and it receives the light of the waxing Moon, then after [a time of] captivity, they are returned to authority, so that afterwards a [still] greater heap of good fortune and dignity comes to them.

3. If the Sun is found partilely in the MC or in the ASC, and it is in a masculine sign, but the Moon is found in an *anafora* to the Sun, but benefic stars protect the Sun in their morning rising, kings are born in a similar manner. But if, with these arranged thus, Mars is found in the MC and Jupiter in the IMC, they will be dangerous, terrible, effective persons, possessing rulership over the whole world.

4. If the Sun is found posited in the principal angles of the nativity in a masculine sign, and the Moon posited in the principal angles of the nativity possesses a feminine sign, or certainly if one of them is found posited thus in the first angles just as we have said, they will make famous, noble, and powerful persons, and those to whom the defense of cities is entrusted. But if, with these arranged thus, the testimony of Jupiter is added, the army is entrusted to him by the decree of the Emperor.

XXIII.

1. **Those Dying Violently.** If the Moon is found full in the angles or in the *anaforas* or *epicataforas* of the angles,[1] but Mars posited in the *anaforas* or *epicataforas* is either found with her, or aspects her by square or opposition; [or if] she is posited just as we have said but with little light, and Saturn, similarly posited in *anaforas* or in *epicataforas*, aspects either Mars or the Moon posited just as we have said; or if Saturn aspects the Sun by square or opposition, those dying violently are born.

2. But also if Saturn and Mars aspect the Moon posited in any other house by square or opposition, without the testimony of the benefic stars, they make those dying violently. But also if Mars is found in the angles, and with the Moon posited in the *anaforas* of the angles, with Jupiter being unrelated or hidden by the Sun beams, and with Saturn posited in the angles or in the *anaforas* of the angles, or with it making any aspect to the Sun, those dying violently are born.

3. But also, if Mars posited in the angles or in the *anaforas* of the angles, aspects the waxing Moon by square from a superior house, and there is no aspect from a benefic, in a similar manner it will produce a person dying violently. And just as we have frequently said, the manner of death is denoted in accordance with the difference of the signs. For in human signs, death is caused by the sword, or by armed robbers, or in battle, or by some exercise of power. But in earth signs, it will similarly make [him] to die in deserted places, or certainly to be involved in various types of calamities.

4. In water signs, he is drowned in storms, shipwrecks, tornados, and rivers, so that a bitter end is always brought about by water. In fixed

[1]This presumably means in any one of the *anafora* houses.

[signs], it will make [him] to die by a fall from a precipice, or by being cast down from high places. In fire [signs], it hands him over to blazing flames, either exposed to them by accident, or committed [to them] by the order of some power. In humid [signs], it will make [him] to die either by indigestion, or by tuberculosis, or by black bile, or by the throwing up of blood, or by some festering illness.

5. If Mars is found in any angle, or is in the 11th house from the ASC, or in the 8th, and Saturn aspects him posited in these houses by opposition, or if with Mars posited thus Saturn is found in the 7th house from the ASC, they will make [him] to die violently after [suffering] many dangers to his life, especially if Jupiter does not aspect Mars from a superior house, and is not found with him. But death is denoted in accordance with the variety of the signs.

6. But if, with these arranged thus—namely, without any testimony from Jupiter—Mercury is found with Mars or with Saturn, or if they aspect it by square, with the Moon posited either in an angle, or in an *anafora,* or in an *epicatafora*, they will make fraudulent forgers, evildoers, counterfeiters, so that because of these crimes they are punished by a severe judicial sentence.[1]

7. But also if Saturn is found in the 4th or in the 11th, and Mercury is with him, or is joined to him by a square aspect; but Mars is either with them or is making a square or opposition aspect to them; or if, with them posited thus, Mars posited in a domicile of Saturn aspects the Moon posited in the angles by square or by opposition, it denotes demises resulting from the preceding crimes.

8. But if, with these arranged thus, Jupiter makes a fortunate aspect to Mars from a superior house, or if it is found with him, or if it receives an aspect from the full Moon, those accused of these crimes are freed by a fortunate decree. If the Moon is found in the DSC, and Mars and Saturn are posited partilely in the ASC, or, with one of them posited in the ASC, if the other malefic star is found in the MC, those who are born die violently.

9. But also, if the Moon is found in any other angle, and either Mars or Saturn is partilely posited with her in the same sign, or if one of them aspected her by opposition or square, but the other one aspects Mercury by square from a superior house, or if it is joined to him by an opposition

[1]Under Roman law, these were capital crimes.

[while] posited in either angles or in the *anaforas* or *epicataforas* of the angles, it will make those dying violently. But this evil is more strongly signified if Mars or Saturn aspects[1] the Sun by square or opposition.

10. If the Sun is found in water signs, and Mars is partilely posited with the Moon in the same sign or house, or if it is posited together with the Moon in the 12th or in the 6th house from the ASC, those dying violently will be born; for they will either perish suspended by a noose, or they will come to the final exit of death drowned in waters. If the Moon is found conjoined with Saturn in partile association in the 8th house from the ASC, and no benefic star is found in an angle, death is brought about by an excessive effusion of blood.

11. But if, with these arranged thus, a benefic star is found in any angle, after having been despaired of by the remedies of medicine, they will [still] get well. But if the Moon is found in the 7th house from the ASC with Mars, it will make [them] to die from hemorrhoids. But generally Saturn in a nocturnal nativity, or Mars in a diurnal nativity, posited in the 7th house from the ASC will make hemorrhages, i.e. effusions[2] of blood. But also, if [it is] in the signs in which[3] the 7th house from the ASC or the House of Fortune is found, they will get some defect of illness from having been cut by iron.

12. But if, with all of these arranged thus just as we have said, a benefic star gives a fortunate testimony to them by aspect, they will be freed from that illness [caused by] having been cut by iron. But if both of them, i.e. Saturn and Mars are posited in the 7th house from the ASC, with the ASC or the House of Fortune posited in those signs which we have mentioned, i.e. in [a domicile] of Mars, or in [a domicile] of Saturn, or if one of them is posited in the 7th house from the ASC, [and] the other aspects it by square or opposition, [then after] having been cut by physicians, they will die.

13. But if the Moon is found in the DSC, and Mercury and Mars are posited conjoined in partile association in the MC, they will produce murderers and parricides, or those who are stained with fraternal blood

---

[1]With the word *respiciat* (261.6) 'aspects' the lengthy addition of MS **N** leaves off, so that beginning with Paragraph 10, all the MSS continue with the text.

[2]Reading *effusiones* 'effusions' with the **Δ** family of MSS rather than *eruptiones* 'eruptions' with the **Γ** family and the Teubner editors, although the difference is slight.

[3]Reading **quibus* 'in which', rather than the †*eius qui* of the MSS.

by a criminal impulse of fury. But they will make those who, struck by the ill-will [resulting from] these crimes, and struck by a threatening accusation, die from judicial sentences.

14. If the Moon and Mars are posited in the 9th house from the ASC, but the Sun and Mercury are posited in the 3rd house from the ASC, they will make sacrilegious persons, despoilers of temples, but those who are punished by a severe judicial sentence because of that crime. But also, if the Sun is posited with Saturn and Mars and Mercury in the 11th house from the ASC, and the Moon is posited in the 3rd house from the ASC without the testimony of Jupiter, it will make [them] to die a violent death because of the aforesaid crimes.

15. If the Sun is found in the ASC, but Mars and Saturn are joined in equal degrees in the 12th house from the ASC, and they aspect the Moon posited in the 6th house from the ASC by opposition, they will make slaves dying violently. If the ASC is found in a sign of Saturn or in a sign of Mars, or certainly if the House of Fortune [is found there] ...[1] But if it[2] is posited partilely in the ASC, and Mercury is joined with it in an equal association of degrees, but Saturn and Mars are posited in the 7th house from the ASC, they make epileptics—but those who die violently.

16. If the Moon is posited partilely in the MC, and Mars is posited partilely in the ASC, but Saturn is posited in the [house] *anafora* of the Moon, they make those who die violently. But also if the Moon is found with Mercury in the 8th house from the ASC, and Mars is posited with Saturn in either the 6th or the 12th house from the ASC,[3] they will make those who die violently. But also, if Mars and Saturn aspect each other by square, with Mars posited in any angle, and one of them aspects the Moon either by square or by opposition, or if it is found with her, they will make those who die violently.

17. But also, if the Moon is found with Mars in the 8th house from the ASC, and the Sun in the 7th, but Saturn is in the MC or in any other angle, it will make those who die violently. If Mars and Saturn are found in the 11th house from the ASC, or if one of them is posited in that same house,

[1]The result of this configuration is missing in the Latin text, one or more lines having probably been omitted either by **Casinensis 361** or by the archetype itself.

[2]It is uncertain what *it* refers to—possibly the Sun.

[3]The Latin text has the 5th and the 12th houses, but I have accepted Kroll's and Ziegler's suggestion of the 6th and the 12th, which seems reasonable.

but the other is posited with the Moon, or it aspects her by square, and Mercury is joined to ...[1] or Mars by any aspect, it will make persons who are insane, epileptic, [and] who die violently. But this will be worse if Mars is found in the 11th house from the ASC and Saturn in the 5th.

18. But also, if the Sun is found in the 8th house from the ASC, and the Moon is partilely posited in the MC, and the ASC or the House of Fortune is in the Sun's sign, or in the Moon's sign, it will make insane persons who die violently. If Mars and Saturn are found together in the House of Desire,[2] and that same house is posited in any angle of the nativity, but those [stars] that we have mentioned make any aspect to Venus, they will make deaths from gonorrhea[3]; but if they also aspect the Moon, they make lunatics; but if they also aspect Mercury, they make those who have been apprehended for fraud or counterfeiting money to die violently. But if Jupiter aspects all of these posited thus, they are freed from all these dangers.

19. If Mars and Saturn are found in the ASC, and the Moon is posited in their *anafora*,[4] having lost their sight, it makes those who die a violent death. But also if the Moon and Sun are in the ASC, and Mars and Saturn in their *anafora*, they similar make those having lost their eyesight to die violently. But also if the Moon is found with Mars in the ASC, and Saturn is posited with the Sun in the MC, they make spastics, or epileptics, or insane persons, and their demise by a violent death. But also if the Moon and the Sun are found in the angles, and Mars and Saturn stand with those lights, or they are posited in the other angles, they make those who die violently.

20. If Mars or Saturn is found in the House of Fortune, and their conjunction is found in the 5th or in the 11th house from the ASC, they cause a violent death. If Mars is posited with the Moon in the 12th house from the ASC, but Saturn and the Sun are found in the 2nd house from the ASC, i.e. in its *anafora*, it makes [the Native] to die by a violent death. But frequently also in their very origin they are brought forth cut from the viscera of the mother, especially if all [those stars are] in the same degrees.

---

[1]Ziegler thinks something is missing here; if so, I would conjecture *Saturno* 'Saturn'. but Kroll would simply delete *aut* 'or' before Mars.

[2]Accepting Kroll's deletion of *id est cupiditatum* 'i.e. of desires' following 'the House of Desire'.

[3]A venereal disease of some sort, characterized by a serous discharge, but not necessarily the disease we call gonorrhea, which is painful and debilitating but not usually fatal.

[4]That is, in the 2nd house.

21. If the Moon is found in the MC or in the IMC, but one malefic star is posited in another angle, and another malefic star aspects the Moon by opposition, or if it attacks[1] the ASC similarly, or if it is found in the 5th or in the 11th house from the ASC, they produce those who die violently. For those who are born thus are either thrown down [from a high place], or they bring about their own death. But also in accordance with the nature <of that star which is opposed and in accordance with the nature>[2] of the sign, the diversity of deaths is accomplished.

22. If the Moon is found in the 8th house from the ASC, but Mars, posited in its own domicile, is posited partilely in the ASC, and with it Venus and Mercury and the Sun—all conjoined in equal or neighboring degrees—but either Mars or Saturn receives partilely the conjunction of the Moon, they will perish torn to shreds by the bites of wild beasts. If the Moon is found with little light in the 8th house from the ASC, <and Saturn makes any aspect to it, or is found with it>,[3] it will make those dying violently, but those are of the sort who incur a miserable demise of death from having been drowned in the waves.

23. If the Moon is found in the DSC, but Saturn is in the 6th house from the ASC, or the House of Fortune is in a domicile of Saturn or of the Moon, they make those who die of dysentery. If the Moon is found in the ASC, but Saturn is posited with Mercury in the 7th house from the ASC, they make foolish, indifferent, silly, epileptic persons. But also, if with these arranged thus, Mars is found in any angle, they make silly epileptics, but those who die violently.

24. If Saturn is found in the 3rd or in the 9th house from the ASC, and Mars aspects it by square, they make persons in charge of great things or great actions, but whatever personal wealth has been accumulated by them is dissipated. They will also have the greatest illnesses, and, while located in foreign places, they are caught up in many evils; they cripple the relatives and fathers of some persons, or they certainly make them to die violently. But if Mercury is found with one of them, and the Moon is either with them or aspects them by square or opposition, it will make sacrilegious persons, despoilers of

---

[1]Reading **attentat* 'attacks' instead of *attendat* 'notices'.

[2]Adds **N**, one or two lines having been omitted by **Ψ** due to homoeoteleuton (*...secundum naturam* | *...secundum naturam*).

[3]Adds **N**, a line having been omitted by **Ψ** due to homoeoteleuton (*...fuerit inventa* | *...fuerit inventus*).

temples, leaders of armed robbers, murderers, but it will make them to perish from a bad death.

25. If the Sun and Saturn and Mercury are found in the MC, they make the dangers of accusation to be lodged [against them] because of concealed documents, or from falsified public documents, or from counterfeited money. But if Mars aspects these by square or opposition, or if it is found with them, they make armed robbers, murderers, exiles indeed and fugitives.

26. But if, with these arranged thus, Jupiter is found in any angle, then having been freed after a time from these calamities, they are transferred to the status of great power. But if, with all these posited thus, the Moon is found in any angle, or in *anaforas* or *epicataforas*, after all these things they will die a violent death.

27. If Mercury and Saturn are posited in the 6th or in the 12th house from the ASC, they are put in charge of ineffectual and miserable financial operations, but they perform these same [tasks] in every detail—always being slow and listless. But if Mars aspects them by square or opposition, they produce wicked persons, armed robbers, perjurers, informers, and betrayers of their own people. But some of them are delivered to dangers or confinement on account of slaves, or on account of condemned men, especially if Mars makes any aspect to the Moon.

28. If Saturn is found in the 8th house from the ASC, or is posited in the *anafora* of the ASC, but the Moon is posited in *anaforas* or *epicataphoras*, and Mars is found in the 7th house from the ASC, they will be separated from every concern of religions. But if, with all these arranged thus, Saturn and the Moon are found in houses that are in square or opposition to them, they produce despoilers of temples, but those who are punished by a public death because of this. But if, with these arranged thus, Jupiter and Venus are found with them, they produce priests, prophets, [or] temple-keepers, but they also suffer violent death.

29. If the Moon is found with Mars in the DSC, so that Mars precedes in the degrees, but Saturn and Mercury are posited together in the IMC, they produce those dying violently. But [the kind of] death is also recognized from the nature of the signs. Posited in tropical or water signs, they perish from dropsy, or it makes them to be drowned in waves and rivers, but posited thus, just as we have mentioned, in duplex or in fixed signs, they make epileptics, but ones perishing by a violent death. But if Jupiter and Venus aspect these from any place [in the chart], the danger of the preceding misfortune is lessened.

XXIV.

1. **Those who are Condemned.** If the House of Necessity is found in a domicile of Mercury, but the Moon is found in a domicile of Saturn or Mars, but Mars or Saturn aspects Mercury by a square or opposition aspect, or if they are posited with it in any angle, or if they are in the *anaforas* or the *epicataforas* of the angles, or if they are posited in the ASC, or in the House of Fortune, or in the House of Necessity, they make persons who are condemned in some fashion.

2. But if the House of Necessity is found in a domicile of Mercury, or in the domicile of the Moon, or in a domicile of Mars, or in a domicile of Saturn, and that House is posited by degree in any angle of the nativity, and of all these stars of which we have made mention, any one of them is found in *anaforas* or in *epicataforas*, they will make perons who are condemned in similar fashion.

3. Moreover, the sentences are to the mines,[1] public works, exile, and to the [gladiatorial] games. But also if the House of Necessity is found in the domiciles of those stars of which we have made mention, and if some of them are in *anaforas* or in *epicataforas*, but others are in the angles, they will make the danger of a just condemnation to be imposed. But if, with all of these arranged just as we have said, Jupiter posited in the MC combines with the malefic stars by a fortunate aspect, it will mitigate the dangers of all the condemnations. For then, freed after a certain space of time from the aforesaid condemnations, by a decree of the Emperor they will be restored to both their own [former] dignities and their native land. But if the testimony of Jupiter is denied to all of these, then justly condemned, they will be subjected to a severe punishment.

4. If the ruler of that sign in which the House of Necessity is found is posited in a domicile of Mars, or of Saturn, or of Mercury in the ASC, or if it is posited in the House of Necessity, it will make them to be condemned. But also, if the House of Necessity itself is with its own ruler in the aforesaid places, it will make them to be condemned.

5. If the House of Necessity is found in a domicile of Mercury, and Mercury is located in any angle, but Mars and Saturn are posited in the *anaforas* or in the *epicataforas* of the angles, then having been condemned, they will die a violent death.

[1]Since working in mines was very dangerous, criminals were sometimes condemned to become miners.

6. Similarly, if the House of Necessity is found in a domicile of Mercury, and Mercury is found posited in a domicile of Saturn or in the *anaforas* or in the *epicataforas* of the angles, with Mars and Saturn partilely located in the angles, and with Jupiter not being associated with them, a sentence of just condemnation and one with the will of everyone will be rendered.

7. If the House of Necessity has fallen into the House of Fortune, or the ruler of the House of Necessity is located in the House of Fortune, they will make a sentence of just condemnation to be brought in.

XXV.

1. **Eunuchs and Hermaphrodites.** If the Sun and the Moon are found in feminine signs, either posited together, or posited in different houses, and Venus in a feminine sign is posited in any angle, but the Moon and Mars are located partilely in any angle, they will make either eunuchs or hermaphrodites. But if the Sun and the Moon were located in masculine signs in the same manner that we mentioned, and if Venus is posited in a masculine sign, and if this is the nativity of a woman, women will be born who, equipped with a masculine spirit, desire to have intercourse with women in the manner of men.

2. If Venus is found in a domicile of Mercury, and Mercury in a domicile of Venus, or if they have made this same [configuration] in their own terms, and in fact the Moon is posited in Virgo, or in Capricorn, or in Taurus, or in Leo, and the other masculine stars are in feminine signs, but the feminine stars are in masculine signs, double-formed persons and hermaphrodites are born.

3. **Indecent Persons.** If Mercury and Venus are posited together in the 19th degree of Aries, they produce those who are indecent in their mouth. But also if Venus and the Moon hold the 30th degree of any sign and aspect each other by square and opposition, they will cause these same faults to be exercised secretly. But if the rulers of those signs in which the Moon and Venus possess the 30th degree make any kind of aspect to those same signs, they will exercise those same faults in public without any concern for shame.

4. **Sterile and Homosexual Persons**. If Mars and Venus, located in their morning rising were posited together in a masculine sign, they pro-

duce women who are viragos and sterile. But in the nativities of men, if they were located together in feminine signs in their evening rising, and Saturn makes any aspect to them, they will make homosexuals, serving by singing in temples. But if that conjunction is in Aries or in Capricorn, those same faults of lusts are denoted. Consider [this] also, if it[1] aspects Venus by opposition or by square, and the testimony of Jupiter is denied to all of them—at least in feminine <nativities>[2]—then pronounce the women to be prostitutes,[3] but in the nativities of men, you will say that they are castrated priests of Cybele and sodomites.

5. If the Moon aspects Saturn by opposition, but Mars is so posited that it aspects them by square, but Venus by opposition, and all four of these have exchanged their own domiciles, they certainly make women to be sterile and viragos. But they make males to be sodomites. But also if Saturn is posited with the Moon in one sign, located in the same degree of the sign, it will make sodomites.

6. Also, the Moon and Venus posited in the same degree, makes sodomites; also, Venus and the Sun posited in the 8th house from the ASC make sodomites. But also, if Mercury and Venus are located in the domiciles of the malefic stars, but Mars and Saturn are in a domicile of Venus, they do that same thing in similar fashion.

7. But I shall show concisely how you can check this by the degree method. Compute from the Moon to Venus and [cast] the same amount from the ASC. If the number falls in a feminine sign, and the Moon is located in a feminine sign from the 25th up to the 30th degree, you will find male sodomites, but those who exercise this fault secretly, but women in similar fashion will be whores.

8. But, with the preceding number existing, compute from Venus to the Moon and [cast] that much from the ASC, and if the number falls into

---

[1]Reading *Considera etiam si Venerem aspexeriti* **Δ** 'Also, consider that if it aspects Venus' instead of *Sed et si* * * * *Venerem aspexerit* 'But also if [lacuna] aspects Venus' with the Teubner editors. Prof. Monat. Kroll suggests adding 'Saturn or Mars' to fill the lacuna, but I think the **Δ** reading is sufficient. Bram has 'But if Venus is in opposition or square aspect'.

[2]Adds Ziegler.

[3]The Latin text has †*mali post dici pronuntia* 'pronounce of evil after it is said'?, which does not make sense. Skutsch would emend it to **mastropos nasci* 'procuresses are born'. I suggest **mulieres prostitutas* 'women [to be] prostitutes' (*cf.* viii.24.11). Bram has 'women will be born with masculine character'. Prof. Monat simply leaves a blank space.

a feminine sign, say that men are detected in their lusts. You will pronounce that same thing in the case of women. And if, with the two numbers determined just as we have said, the Moon and Venus are posited in feminine signs and located in the last degrees of the signs, with the preceding numbers found in feminine signs, they make these disgraces [to occur] with public notice.

9. But if Venus was not with the Moon, but she was in her vespertine rising, and located in the last degrees of a feminine sign, [and] she aspects by square the Moon posited in the last degrees of a sign, it will makes the males to be sodomites, and the women to be whores, those who always exercise these lusts secretly. But if you have found feminine signs from the preceding number, and these are just as we have said, and Saturn, located in a feminine sign, aspects the Moon and Venus by square, it will make misshapen, poverty-stricken sodomites.

10. But if, with all of them arranged just as we have said, Mars is found with Saturn, it will make castrated priests of Cybele. But if, with these arranged just as we have said, and both numbers having been determined by the degree method, Venus located in the last degrees aspects Saturn and Mars, it will make fortunate sodomites, to whom temple duties are entrusted, or it will make noble women to be involved in the faults of whoredom.

11. If Mars and Mercury and Venus and the Moon are either together in tropical sigsn, or if they aspect each other by square, they make whores, but their inclinations are altered according to the variety of the signs. For if they are in feminine signs just as we have said, they make whores, but if they are in masculine signs they make viragos.

12. If the Moon is found with Mars and Venus in the ASC, and the Sun is posited in the 12th house from the ASC, but Saturn aspects the ASC by square or opposition, it will make castrated priests of Cybele to be sodomites; but then [only] if the testimony of Jupiter is lacking to all of them. If Venus and Saturn are either together, or if they aspect each other by square, or if they are hidden by the rays of the Sun, and the Moon is posited in feminine signs, with the ASC located in a feminine sign, they make secret sodomites.

13. But if Saturn and Venus are located in their matutine rising, they make them to be made known in that disgrace of lusts. But if Mars posited in his vespertine rising, aspects them by square or opposition, it will make public sodomites. But if, with all of these arranged just as we have

said, Mars is found in the angles, it will make castrated priests of Cybele. But if it is a feminine nativity, and all of these stars are located just as we have said in masculine signs, they make a lustful virago.

14. Generally of course, if the Moon and the Sun and the ASC are in Capricorn, or in Aries, or in Taurus, or in Leo, so that they are in the face of these signs or on the back,[1] they denote the indecencies of all these lusts along with an extreme effeminacy of the body. In every nativity, if the Moon is found in the Tail of Leo,[2] it will make sodomites, beating kettle-drums for the Mother of the Gods.[3] But if it is found in the Face of Leo, or in the Face of Capricorn, or in the Face of Aries, or in the Face of Taurus, it drives both women and men to all the faults of indecency.

15. But if Saturn and Venus, posited together, namely in the 7th house from the ASC, aspect the Moon in those signs by square, they make sodomites. But if Mars conjoins himself to them by any aspect, they make public sodomites. Also, if Mars and Saturn make any aspect to Venus posited in Taurus, or in Leo, or in Virgo, or in Capricorn, they make sodomites in similar fashion.

16. If in a nocturnal nativity the Moon is found in the 12th or in the 6th house from the ASC, but in a diurnal nativity the Sun is located in those same houses, and if in fact the Moon in a nocturnal nativity is posited in the terms of Venus, but the Sun in a diurnal nativity is posited in the terms of Venus, but Venus is located in the 7th house from the ASC or in the IMC in her own terms, sodomites are born. But if Mars aspects those [stars] arranged just as we have said by square or opposition, it will make castrated priests of Cybele. And yet, in every case look for the testimony of Jupiter, for if it is there, these faults are to some degree either mitigated or concealed.

17. **Eunuchs.** If the Moon is found in sterile signs, and Saturn is partilely located with her, but Venus makes some aspect to them, and moreover if Saturn is in the terms of Venus, and Venus is in the terms of

---

[1]Here, and in what follows, the references to parts of the body should refer to the stars in the constellation figures. But the reader could conveniently refer to Book VIII, Chapter 4, where the bodily parts are given for each sign.

[2]According to what Firmicus will tell us in Book 8, Chapter 4, the Tail of Leo is located in the 30th degree of that sign. But if the reference is to an actual star, Ptolemy says that the star Denebola or β Leonis is in the Tail.

[3]Reading **matri deorum tympana pulsantes* with Ziegler and MS **N**. The priests of Cybele marched in religious processions beating kettle-drums and other noise-makers.

Saturn, and Jupiter does not make any aspect to the Moon, eunuchs are made. But if the Moon is with Saturn in earth signs, just as we have said, and similarly there is no testimony from Jupiter, eunuchs are made, but those who lie with women.

18. **Discovering Homosexual Persons**. Now I shall impart to you the House of Lusts by degree, so that you can find with true methods the faults of all [kinds of] lusts. Compute from the Moon to Saturn, and whatever number of signs is found, compute that many again from the ASC, and in whatever sign the last number comes to, that sign shows you the House of Faults and Lusts.

19. If, therefore, it is a feminine sign in which the House of Lusts falls by degree, and a malefic star aspects that same House either by square or by opposition, but Venus is posited in any angle, homosexuals will be born, but secret ones. But if the house of Lusts, located by the degree method, is found in the dejected houses from the ASC in a feminine sign, it will make those defiled by every disgrace of indecency. But if, located in that house just as we have said, the Moon is either in the first degrees of Pisces or Capricorn or Leo, or in the last degrees of Taurus, it will make those who are involved in the indecent faults of lusts.

20. But if, with the House of Lusts located in dejected houses, and afflicted by the testimonies of the malefic stars, the Sun and the Moon are in dejected houses from the ASC, or in the signs of the malefic stars, or if they were found in their own humilities, they make public sodomites involved in the indecent vices of all [kinds] of lusts. Moreover, these things will be stronger if the house of Lust is either in Capricorn, or in Aries, or in Taurus.

21. If Venus is found to be the Ruler of the Nativity, and having [that] rulership with Mars located together [with it]—namely in a feminine sign, and in dejected houses from the ASC—but Saturn is posited in a masculine sign, and it aspects her[1] indeed by trine **. . .** but by square, located in their own signs or in their own degrees, and the Moon is posited in dejected houses, sodomites will be born. If the Moon, Venus, Mars, and Saturn are located in feminine signs, namely in dejected houses from the ASC, and they are either posited together or in square, they make public sodomites. But if one of all of those is well disposed, it will make men exercising these vices secretly.

[1]Accepting Ziegler's emendation *horam 'that one', which I take to be a reference to Venus, rather than the original textual emendation *horoscopum 'the ASC'. And some words are missing after 'trine'.

22. If Venus and Saturn located in a feminine sign are posited in the 7th house from the ASC, but the Sun and Jupiter, and the Moon, and Mars, are posited in dejected houses from the ASC, they will doubtless make sodomites. But if, with all of these located just as we have said, Jupiter alone is located in the primary angles, they do indeed make sodomites, but those who are established in the greatest glory of honors, and those to whom the duties of the royal taxes are entrusted. But if, with all of these located just as we have said, the Moon is found in the primary angles, it will make rich sodomites.

23. Venus and Mars posited in tropical signs, if they aspect each other by square or opposition—namely, in feminine signs—make sodomites, but those who are secretly involved in these vices. But if, located in their stations, they possess those signs that we have mentioned without the testimony of Jupiter, they make women indeed to be whores put up for sale, but they make men to be public sodomites.

XXVI.

1. **Experts in Letters.** If Mercury and the Sun were located together, and posited in one sign they are joined together with an equal association of degrees, and the Moon does not make any aspect to them, or is certainly not posited in the ASC, it will make experts in letters.

2. **Famous Gladiators**. Jupiter posited in the terms of Mars in any sign, and Mars in the terms of Jupiter, if posited in the angles they aspect each other by square or opposition, and if the Sun is in dejected houses in a diurnal nativity, but the Moon in a nocturnal nativity, famous gladiators will be born.

3. **Athletes**. If Mars was found in the terms of Mercury, namely in any sign, and Mercury similarly in the terms of Mars, but Venus makes any aspect to both of them, athletes will be born. But if they were posited in the angles, athletes will be born who are victors in every clash of contest. But if the testimony of Venus was lacking to Mercury and Mars, *hoplomachi*[1] will be born, or masters of a wrestling-school or of athletes, but who never commit themselves to such contests.

4. But if with Mars posited in the terms of Mercury, and Mercury again in those of Mars, there is testimony of Jupiter and Venus by any sort of

[1]The Greek name of heavily-armed gladiators

aspect, they will be boxers; and if Venus alone offers testimony, she will make couriers. But these [indications] will grow stronger if the House of Fortune and the House of Action found in an angle are joined with the preceding association of stars.

5. **Trial Lawyers**.[1] If Mercury is found in its own terms, or in those of Mars, and is posited in dejected houses, and Mars, posited in a domicile of Mercury or in Mercury's terms, makes any aspect to it, it will make trial lawyers. But if Mercury, posited thus just as we have said, is not in dejected houses in a diurnal nativity, and Mars, posited in the angles, in those degrees that we have mentioned, makes a fortunate aspect to him, it will make great and famous orators.

6. **Physicians**. If Mars and Venus are partilely joined in square aspect aspecting the House in which Action is found, physicians are born. But if their own terms are changed, if Mars, moreover, is in the terms of Venus, and Venus is in the terms of Mars, and the fortunate testimony of Mercury is made to them, talented physicians will be born. But if Mercury is not attached to them, cooks will be born.

7. **Musicians**. If Mercury posited with Venus, either by night or by day, is found in his own terms or in those of Venus, it will make musicians playing the organ with sweet control. But also, if they are not posited together, and indeed Mercury is in the terms of Venus, but Venus is in the terms of Mercury, they will make the same thing in similar fashion. But if Venus is in the terms of Mercury, and Mercury is in the sign of another [star] or is posited in the degrees of another, they will have the sound of a musical voice, but they will be obscure, downcast in some low position.

8. Moreover, in all **Occupations**, find the House of Fortune, then the [House] of Occupation, and the House will be found in the *anafora* to [the House of] Fortune.[2] And so, when you have found the House of Occupation, see also in which house the Ruler of that same Sign is posited. But also inspect in similar fashion the Ruler of the Sign in which the House of Fortune is posited, and see in which house it too is posited. And when you have found these in a careful manner, see which one of these is posited the

---

[1]The Latin has *De causidicis oratoribus*. A *causidicus* was an attorney, and coupled with *orator* 'an orator' it designated an attorney who plead the client's case forcefully and eloquently in court; hence, I have translated it as 'trial lawyer'. Certainly, an artful legal speaker is meant.

[2]Since the 2nd house is the house of income, the 2nd house from Fortuna might indicate the source of that income.

more fortunately, i.e. which of them is posited in that same sign; and if both are found in one house, see which one is posited the more opportunely.

9. But if they are not in the House of Fortune, see if they are not posited in the House of Occupation; and if they are found together in that house, see which one has fallen the more opportunely. But if they are not in that house, see which one of them makes a cardinal aspect to the ASC, and then from that consideration you will be able to explain the art of the occupation.

10. For if Venus is found thus, it will make painters, plasterers,[1] goldsmiths, silversmiths, musicians—namely, in accordance with the variety of the signs. But Jupiter will produce businessmen, farmers, money-lenders, and ship captains; and similarly too it [will act] in accordance with the variety of the signs. Mars, will produce physicians, barbers, and those whose art is either had from iron or from fire. Mercury will produce those who have duties with a pen,[2] or with the tongue, or from eloquent speech. Saturn will produce those involved in hard work, divers, and ship captains, but those who are weighed down by every kind of misfortune. But all of these things you will define, just as we have frequently said, in accordance with the variety of the signs.

11. Moreover, so that you may know whether they persevere in the decreed arts, I shall show you in a short way. See in which sign Mercury is posited, and seek out the ruler of that sign, and when you have found it, see if it is well posited. For if it is well posited, they remain in the arts, and from those they acquire the greatest profit; but if badly [posited], they will work by carrying out the duties of their own art without [gaining any] fruit, and, having been worn out, they abandon those same arts.

12. These things, my dear Mavortius, we have explained to you in a detailed manner, so that the mediocrity of our skill might set forth for you all the secrets of this divine art with clear interpretations. But, having explained them, the whole discourse is [now] transferred to an exposition of the Barbaric Sphere.

[1]The exact meaning of the words *pictores, emplastratores*, lit. painters, plasterers' is here uncertain. The word *pictor* refers to an artist who paints pictures of people or of decorative scenes, and Cumont, *L'Égypte des astrologues*, thinks that the plasterers were artisans who laid down a thin layer of plaster prior to creating a mosaic. Hence, the two words together may refer to mosaic artists.

[2]The Latin word *canna*, lit. 'reed', can denote a sort of flute (as Bram and Prof. Monat translate it), but Mercury is the patron of writing, not music, so here it must mean 'pen'.

Book VIII.

I.

1. Nothing else should be worked on in this brevity of life, my dear Mavortius, except that, when a blot of the terrene body has been purged, and *all* faults have been removed if it can be done—or certainly *most* of them—we may render to our author, God, an uncorrupt divinity of soul and one not polluted by any contagion of crimes, lest we lose our soul—if it is unmindful of its divine fabrication, and implicated in depraved snares—just like someone cast down from a precipice.

2. For this is what the earthly body does day-by-day, so that it can always connect its own divine spirit to its own perishable fragility, which is both occupied with depraved pleasures of desire, and deceived by fawning incitements, so that a depressed and sunken soul can never find the principles of its own origin, but being always cast down into darkness and into the dirt, it blushes at the origin of its own majesty with some agitations of dissimulations.

3. For we should think about nothing earthly, especially since we know that God our Maker has made us with divine moderation of artifice, so that, with the right form of body, and removed from every dejection of humility, we may see nothing else first with the opened up sight of the eyes except the Sun, Moon, stars and the most beautiful and immortal home of all of these—namely, the World above.

4. For Nature has constructed the other living things, so that, sunk down to the earth and downcast with some fallen humility, both in soul and in body, they always cling to earthly actions. But it has perfected us with a certain great moderation of necessity, so that the fragility of the body accomplishes one thing for us, and the divinity of the immortal soul

accomplishes something else—namely, that the body, which we seem to have in common with beasts, while serving the soul, would always be subjoined to the command of its divinity.

5. Considering, therefore, the principles of our origin, and that our soul is strengthened by the protection of its majesty, we ought to instruct ourselves in such a way so that the soul, with its very own self harmonized by the authority of its own divinity, may both always think about and do something worthy by its own authority; so that thus instructed and shaped, it may find the right and incorruptible path of immortality to return to its own origin—and not be returned by errant steps, and with tottering and doubtful paces with constant errors to the faults of earthly fragility.

6. And so, my dear Mavortius, look at the sky with open eyes, and let your soul always contemplate that most beautiful fabric of the divine work. For then our mind, shaped by the recollection of its own majesty, is freed from the depraved attractions of our bodies, and having laid aside the inconveniences of mortality, it may press forward with hurried step to its own progenitor, and it may always search with sagacious and ever-vigilant inquiry for nothing other than divine things through all the moments of the hours.

7. And so, these instructions will give us some small notion of divine knowledge and guide us toward the secrets of our origin. For being always occupied with divine considerations, applying our soul to the celestial powers, and introducing it to divine ceremonies, we are separated from all longings for depraved desires.

8. Which things that accomplishes in great measure, so that, having despised everything that in human affairs is either thought to be evil or fortunate, we may transfer our soul composed of natural virtue and authority—uncorrupted and unimpaired—to its own origin. For when we have learned of the coming inconveniences—the fear of imminent evils—from this we will have learned that with an upright courage of mind we can disdain those things that are going to come, and, we do not have a horror of the foretold dangers of evils.

9. If our soul has shaped itself to receive these things with the recollection of its own majesty, and we are neither seized by the inconveniences of misfortune, nor are we elated by the insignia of dignity, since we shall have known all of this that is promised for us by the declaration of the decree. So then, composed with stable reason, we can always be neither oppressed by misfortunes nor raised up by the joy of good fortune.

10. And so, I shall take care to explain that which I believe is remaining for these books. For I have reserved another time for me to explain the *Myriogenesis*.[1] Now in the beginning of this book we shall explain which signs see each other, <which ones hear each other, and in fact which ones neither see nor hear>.[2] For all of this will pertain to the interpretation of the Barbaric Sphere.[3] We shall also state the measures of the degrees. And we shall also add which degrees are looked for in the bodies of the signs, and also what the 90th degree does, which by the Greeks is called *enencontameris*. So that, having thus explained everything we may more easily grasp the [meaning of] the Barbaric Sphere and the power of the effective license of the bright stars.

II.

1. **The Ninetieth Degree**. And so, I shall first discuss the *enenecontameride*, i.e. the ninetieth degree. Which matter, unknown to many, seems to have been treated lightly by a few; for even Petosiris, just as it seems to me, wanted to conceal its explanation with an envious hissing. In every nativity, the ninetieth degree ought to be carefully examined with sagacious inquisition. For from those degrees, the end of life, death, misfortune, dangers, good fortune, and the whole substance of the nativity is collected.

2. And so, having set out from the ASC through the other signs, look to find the 90th degree,[4] and when you have found that degree, see in which

---

[1]If Firmicus ever did this, his book has not come down to us.

[2]Adds MS **N**, a line having been omitted in **Ψ** due to homoeoteleuton (…*videant* | …*audiant*).

[3]The Barbaric Sphere refers to the non-Greek constellations in the sky. However, they really have nothing to do with the seeing and hearing signs.

[4]Unfortunately, Firmicus does not tell us which way to measure the 90° from the ASC. Bouché-Leclerq (*L'Astrologie grecque*, p. 412) refers us to a passage in which Pliny, *Natural History* VII, Section 160, says: "Also the theory handed down by Petosiris and Nechepso is still extant (it is called the Theory of Quarters, from its dividing up the Zodiac into groups of three signs)… These thinkers declared that nobody exceeds the ascendant measure of 90 degrees (what is called 'risings')…" (Rackham's translation) Pliny thus seems to relate the measure to the *rising time* of the ASC degree. This can be calculated precisely from the formula: $RT = \arccos(-\tan\delta \tan\varphi)$ where δ is the declination of the ASC degree and φ is the geographic latitude of the place. Pliny says the maximum is 124 years for Rome, but the formula would give 113 for the beginning of Cancer as the ASC in the latitude of Rome. And yet, Firmicus may have simply intended

sign it is posited, that is whether it is found in the domicile of a benefic star, or a malefic one. See also how the ruler of that sign is posited in the nativity; also, diligently consider to what extent the benefic and the malefic stars aspect that degree.

3. For the individual [stars] aspecting that degree do everything in accordance with their own nature; and if the malefic stars are alone, they will give the worst; if the benefic ones [are alone], they denote the greatest insignia of good fortune; and if both the benefic and the malefic ones aspect it together, that which was decreed by them individually is mitigated. Look also to see in whose rulership and power that degree is, i.e. in whose terms, and in which house the ruler of the degree is posited; and thus, from the nature of the star and from the power of the house, you will perceive all things. For <the mixtures of the stars> do everything, both evil and fortunate, in accordance with the nature of the sign <in which the ninetieth degree is found>.[1]

4. You will look for this same thing in the case of the Moon; and having set out from that degree in which the Moon is found, you will look for the ninetieth degree. For you will also collect everything in connection with that degree in similar fashion; i.e., what sort of sign [it is in], what sort of degree, who is the ruler of both the sign and the degree, in which house or in which signs the rulers are posited, in what way the malefics, also in what way the benefics aspect that degree.

5. And if the Moon is waxing, see to what extent Mars or Saturn aspects that degree, and similarly if it is waning. For they do everything in accordance with the power of their own nature, if either the malefic stars make a menacing aspect to the ninetieth degree, or the benefic ones support it with a fortunate testimony. Thus you will find the exit of death, thus the order of life, thus the entire substance of the nativity.

---

for us to count 90° in the clockwise direction, which would come to the MC degree of the Equal House System. And this is Bram's conclusion. However, I am doubtful, for the words 'the end of life', and 'death' sound like the IMC rather than the MC, while 'good fortune' sounds the other way around. Prof. Monat rightfully says one does not know which way the measurement should be made.

[1]The words in angle brackets are added by MS **N**, two lines having been omitted by **Ψ** due to homoeoteleuton (...*natura* | ...*mixturae*).

III.

1. **The Seeing and Hearing Signs.**[1] Now I shall explain which stars see and which ones hear. Aries does not see Leo, but it hears it. Leo sees Aries, but it does not hear it. Cancer does not see Aries, but it hears it. Taurus both sees Leo and likewise hears it; similarly, Leo Taurus. Gemini sees Virgo and lightly hears it. Virgo sees Gemini lightly, but very fully hears it. Cancer both sees and also hears Libra. <But Libra does not see Cancer, but [only] hears it.>[2] Leo neither hears nor sees Scorpio. But Scorpio both hears and also sees Leo.

2. Virgo views Sagittarius sideways, but it does not freely hear it. Sagittarius both hears and also sees Virgo. Libra both hears and also sees Capricorn, and it is both heard and also seen by Capricorn. Aquarius does not see Scorpio but hears it. In a similar fashion also Scorpio does not see Aquarius but hears it. Sagittarius neither sees nor hears Pisces. But Pisces both sees and also hears Sagittarius. Pisces does not see Gemini but hears it. Capricorn and Aries neither hear nor see each other. Aquarius and Taurus view each other sideways and hear each other. . . .[3]

3. Gemini sees Libra and also hears it. Similarly, Libra both hears and sees Gemini. Sagittarius and Leo both hear and see each other too. Virgo certainly views Capricorn, but it does not hear it. Similarly Capricorn sees Virgo but does not hear it. Libra sees Aquarius, but it is not seen by Aquarius; yet they also hear each other in turn.

4. Scorpio certainly sees Pisces but does not hear it. But Pisces sees Scorpio but does not hear it. Sagittarius and Aries are so placed that they can neither see nor hear each other. But also Capricorn and Taurus can neither hear nor see each other. Aquarius and Gemini certainly see each other, but they are entirely separated from hearing. Pisces and Cancer certainly do not see each other but they hear.

---

[1]This chapter gives peculiar relationships between pairs of signs. More commonly, the *seeing signs* are signs that are equidistant from the solstitial signs Cancer and Capricorn, such as Gemini & Leo, Taurus & Virgo, Aries & Libra, Pisces & Scorpio, Aquarius & Sagittarius. The *hearing signs* are those that are equidistant from the equinoctial signs, such as Taurus & Pisces, Gemini & Aquarius, Cancer & Capricorn, Leo & Sagittarius, and Virgo & Scorpio. *(See* Paul of Alexandria, *Introduction to Astrology*, Chapters 8 and 9).

[2]Adds MS **N**, one line having been omitted by **Ψ** due to homoeoteleuton (*...audit* | *...audit*).

[3]Cancer's relationship to Scorpio is missing.

5. So that you may receive the whole forms of the order and know how the signs are disposed in the zodiacal circle, for this reason we have discussed the secrets of this matter. For neither by a certain order nor by a certain degree are these twelve signs located, nor are they so posited that those that are arising from a later place are always in aspect to the preceding or following signs. So in order that I would show you not [just] by arguments but by the very thing itself, we have edited this treatise taken from the books of Abraham, so that that which we have said, our speech may impart to you with clear interpretations.

IV.

1. **The Division of Aries.** Now I shall take care to inform you which degrees you should look for in which signs. For all 30 degrees are distributed through all the bodies of the signs. Therefore, so that you may know where the first degree is, where the second is, and where the rest are, I shall indicate all of this for you briefly. The 1st and 2nd degrees of Aries are located in the horns; but 3 and 4 and 5 in the head; but 6 and 7 in the face; but 8 and 9 and 10 in the mouth; but 11 and 12 in the breast; 13 and 14 and 15 in all of the neck; 16 and 17 in the heart; 18 and 19 in the right arm; 20 and 21 and 22 <in the left arm>[1]; but 23 and 24 and 25 in the belly; finally, moreover, the 26th and the 27th degrees have the feet; but 28 and 29 are in the kidneys; and in the tail, the 30th degree. Thus, the 30 degrees are distributed through the whole body of Aries.

2. **The Division of Taurus.** The 1st and the 2nd degrees in Taurus are located in the horns; but 3 and 4 and 5 in all the face; 6 and 7 in the neck; 8 and 9 and 10 in the forehead; 11 and 12 in the heart; but 13 and 14 and 15 in the shoulders; 16 and 17 are arranged in the front feet of Taurus; but 18 and 19 and 20 in the belly; 21 in the knees; 22 and 23 and 24 and 25 are located in the rear feet; but 26 and 27 are in the sexual parts of Taurus; but 28 and 29 in the hips; but the 30th degree alone is found in the tail. Thus the number of degrees is distributed through the whole body of Taurus. But the Barbaric Sphere has made another order of the degrees.

3. **The Division of Gemini.** The 1st and 2nd degrees of Gemini are located in its head, which looks to the north; but 3 and 4 and 5 <are in the

---

[1]Adds edition **a**.

face of that same Twin; 6 and 7>[1] are in the heart of that same Twin; 8 and 9 and 10 in the breast; 11 and 12 in the hands; and 14 and 15 in the feet. But in that Twin that looks to the south, we will find these degrees. But first we ought to know that that space that is between both of the Twins has the 16th and 17th degrees; 18 and 19 and 20 are located in the head of the southern Twin; but 21 and 22 and 23 in the face; but 24 and 25 and 26 under the belly; moreover, 27 and 28 and 29 are in the knees; and 30 alone in the feet.

4. **The Degrees of Cancer** are distributed thus. The 1st and 2nd degrees of Cancer are located in the head; 3 and 4 and 5 in the neck; 6 and 7 in the jaws; but we find the following 3 in the eyes. Here is the nebula of Cancer about which we have frequently spoken. but 11 and 12 are in the back; moreover, the three following are extended from the stomach up to the breast[2]; the three following we find in both arms of Cancer; moreover, the seven following are located in the right feet of Cancer; moreover, 26 and 27 are in the left feet of Cancer; but 28 and 29 are in the last feet; and 30 alone in the tail.

5. **The degrees of Leo** are distributed thus: the 1st and the 2nd degrees are located in the head of Leo; the three following in all of the face together and in the nostrils; another three following are posited in the mouth of Leo; but <three>[3] altogether in the heart; three in the shoulders; three in the feet; the two following in the belly; but the 20th, 21st, and 22nd we find in the back; we investigate 23 and 24 for the chest; the three following remain in the knees; 28 is in the genitals of Leo; 29 in the kidneys; and 30 alone is found in the tail.

6. **The degrees of Virgo** are distributed thus: the 1st and 2nd degrees are located in the head of Virgo; but the three following degrees in the face; but 6 and 7 in the hands; but the following three <in the spine; but 11 and 12 in the shoulders; but those> three <following>[4] in order in the

---

[1]Adds MS **N**, one line having been omitted by **Ψ** due to homoeoarchon (*in eiusdem*… | *in eiusdem*…).

[2]The Latin text has *pectinen* 'comb', but this word does not occur elsewhere in the *Mathesis*, and Skutsch suggests that we read *pectus* 'breast' instead.

[3]Reading totidem <*tres*> to make the total come out right. However, the MSS assign 6 to the feet (3 is Ziegler's emendation), in which case the number available for the heart would be 0. We would expect 1 in the heart. Another possibility would be to assign 2 to the heart and 4 to the feet (reading IV rather than VI). The text is evidently corrupt.

[4]Adds MS **N**, a line having been omitted by **Ψ** due to homoeoteleuton (…*vero sequentes* | …*sequentes vero*).

chest; but 16 and 17 in the right breast; but the three following are located in the right foot; . . .[1]; 26 and 27 are located in the left foot; but 28 and 29 in the kidneys; and 30 alone in the genitals.

7. **The degrees of Libra** are distributed thus: the 1st and 2nd degrees are located in the head; but 3 and 4 and 5 in the left part of the scale; but 6 and 7 are located in the right part of the scale; 8 and 9 and 10 are located in . . .[2]; but 11 and 12 are found in the left part of the yoke; but we find the three following in the right part of the yoke; 16 and 17 in the heart of Libra; the four following in order are recognized in the right hand of Libra; 22 and 23 are located in the chest; the three following are in its kidneys; 27 and 28 down to the last ones extend to the feet. In these degrees, i.e. in the latter ones, the ground is said to be put.

8. **The degrees of Scorpio** are distributed thus: the 1st and 2nd degrees are located in the head of Scorpio; the three following in the forehead; 6 and 7 in the face; the following three in order are set in the neck; the two that follow these are put in the back; after <three found>[3] . . .[4]; but in the right hand are located the three following in order; in the left hand, two; but the two following are arranged in the right feet; in the left feet, three; but in its sting that extends to the north, the latter five are located.

9. **The degrees of Sagittarius** are distributed through its whole body thus: the 1st and 2nd degrees are located in the head of Sagittarius; but the three following in order are put in the face, but the two that follow the preceding degrees are located in the mouth of Sagittarius; the three following in order are put in the neck of Sagittarius; but the two following in the left hand; three others in the bow; in the feet, two; and 3 others are located in the back; in the equine belly, two; but in the hind feet up to the hooves the three that follow are located; but 26 and 27 are located in the genitals of Sagittarius; but the following two are put in the right hand; and the 30th degree alone is located in the tail.

10. **The degrees of Capricorn** are distributed through the whole body thus: the 1st and 2nd degrees of it are located in the horns; the three following, in the head; 6 and 7 are put in the face; the three following in order are set in the mouth of Capricorn. If anyone has the Moon in those degrees that are in the mouth of Capricorn, even if it is adorned with the

[1]The location of degrees 21-25 is missing.

[2]The location of degrees 8-10 is missing.

[3]Adds **N**; *tres invenit* 'three it has found' **DG**; **A** indicates a lacuna.

[4]The location of these three is missing.

testimonies of the benefic stars, it will make men who are impure in their mouth, polluted with the disgrace of womanly passions. Women too, if they have the Moon in those degrees, will be possessed with every fault of indecent impurity. The 11th is located in the heart of Capricorn; 12 and 13, in the neck; the following two in the shoulders; but the following three in order are located in the right hand; the two that follow, in the back; the three following in the belly; but the four that follow are put on either side; and the last three in order are located in the tail, down to the last fin of Capricorn.

11. **The degrees of Aquarius** are distributed through all of his body thus: the 1st and 2nd degrees are located in his head; the following three, in the face; 6 and 7, in the back; the three that are after those in order are located in the chest; but 11 and 12 are put in the right hand. The three that are after these are located in the water of Aquarius[1]; 16 and 17 are put in the left hand; the two that follow them, . . .[2]; two others are put in the belly; but the three following down to the last ones, extend to the feet; another three in the kidneys; but we find the last three in Aquarius's Pitcher.

12. **The degrees of Pisces** are distributed through all of their body as follows—but we ought to know that one Fish faces to the north, the other one to the south. Therefore, the 1st and 2nd degrees are located in the mouth of the southern Fish; but the 3rd and 4th and 5th are put in the head of that same Fish; two in the jaws; the three that follow in order are located in the neck; but the 11th and 12th are discovered on the very spine; but the following three in order receive the back of that same Fish. We find 16 and 17 and 18 in the line [joining] the Fishes.

13. But in that one that faces to the north, 19 is put in the head; but the three following in the chest; but the three others that follow, in the neck; and the two last ones are located in the tail. But an obscure darkness always beclouds the three latter degrees of Pisces, which are between Aries and Pisces. For that reason, if anyone has the Sun or the Moon in those degrees, without the testimony of the benefic stars, he will be oppressed by either perpetual blindness or by some miserable debilities in the eyes.

14. When you begin to look for the location of bodily defects and illness from this division of the degrees, you will be able to find all of this

---

[1]The figure of Aquarius, the Water Carrier, is represented as pouring a stream of water out of a pitcher.

[2]The MSS do not give the location, but edition **a** supplies *in lateribus* 'in the sides'.

most manifestly and easily. But that divine Nechepso <used> this location to find the remedies of illness. And very carefully—just as the divine talent of such a man was able to do—he explained [everything] in clearly written treatises.[1] I shall take care, my dear Mavortius, to impart the interpretation of those books to you at another time.[2]

15. Now I shall explain the measures of the individual degrees. From that interpretation you will be able to find the entire measure of the zodiacal circle.[3] I shall also explain to you the measure and the size of the signs, so that you may know that attention to the divine mind leads to all the secrets of divinity.

16. For the immortal mind, having recorded these principles of its own majesty, did not learn but [merely] acknowledged [them]. Therefore, <that which was said in one sign>,[4] you will compute through all 12 signs. Which, when you have done it, the whole measure of the zodiacal circle will be shown to you. One degree of one sign has 21 thousand and 40 stadia. Which, you may learn from that computation, if it has been computed for 30 degrees, <makes> the space of one sign to have 631 thousand and 200 stadia.[5]

V.

1. Now, my dear Mavortius, you will receive the fullest teaching of this art, [hitherto] unknown to many Greeks and to all Romans, to which until today's date no one's talent has aspired.[6] For neither those divine

[1] All of which are unfortunately lost.

[2] Another book that Firmicus may have written that has not come down to us.

[3] Here the MSS insert a title: "The Measure and Size of the Signs."

[4] Added by MS **N**.

[5] The ancient unit of length, the *stade*, was the length of the footrace in the stadium at Athens, said to be about 600 feet, so there were 8.8 stades to the modern statute mile. Hence, Firmicus's measure of 1 degree was equivalent to about 2,391 miles, and 1 sign was equivalent to 71,727 miles. Consequently, the total circumference of the circle was equivalent to 860,727 miles. If we divide this by 2π, we get 136,989 miles for the distance from the earth to the zodiacal circle, which was supposed to lie upon the surface of a great sphere enclosing the solar system. Firmicus evidently found this speculation in one of the Greek treatises that he used. To us, with our knowledge that even the Moon is roughly 250,000 miles from the Earth, the number seems ridiculously small. But to the ancients, it was a very large number.

[6] It was noted by modern Latin scholars, that the information that Firmicus is about to relate agrees closely with that given by Marcus Manilius in Book V of

men and high priests of the most sacred religion, Petosiris and Nechepso, one of whom . . .[1] <and the other> held the reins of empire, since they explained everything that pertains to the discipline of this art with the most detailed and true interpretations. We are going to give out what they were able to discover. And in order that lengthy talk will not extend our declaration, I shall briefly impart to you the promised secrets of their work.

2. Twelve signs comprise the zodiacal circle, just as we said in the Book on Fundamentals. Other stars are adjacent on the sides of these signs, but stars which never abandon by an erratic course the places assigned to themselves; but—holding to the places recorded for them—they revolve in the present-day world with an unchanging movement. Placed in the neighboring regions of the signs, these arise with the 12 signs and then set with them, keeping always an immutable order of their own course.[2]

3. But antiquity appointed names for these stars from the old fables.

---

his *Astronomica*. It therefore appears that Firmicus had a copy of that part of Manilius's work; but if so, why didn't he mention Manilius? He may have deliberately omitted his name in order to claim the honor of being the first to write about the influences of these stars in Latin. But it seems more likely that he only had that fragment of Manilius's work (for he quotes nothing else from Manilius), and that it did not contain the name of its author.

[1]Several words are missing here, such as 'was a great and renowned priest."

[2]He means that, while they revolve with the daily motion of the celestial sphere, they maintain their traditional positions in the zodiac. This is approximately true for a fixed zodiac, but their longitudes slowly increase when referred to the tropical zodiac. Since this section of the *Mathesis* is very similar to the Fifth Book of Manilius's *Astronomica*, the Greek source must have been not later than the first century B.C. Hipparchus's *Catalogue of Stars* was made in the late second century B.C. and could have been the source of the coordinates of the stars. Consequently, in the notes that follow, I give the calculated degree of the tropical zodiac in which the star rose in 129 B.C. in 31N12 the latitude of Alexandria, Egypt. (See the complete table in Appendix 4.) To reduce these degrees in the tropical zodiac to degrees in the Alexandrian fixed zodiac of that epoch, 7.5 degrees should be added. The reader will see from my notes that most of the degrees mentioned in Firmicus's text are wrong—some of them very wrong! As mentioned in a previous note, he used Manilius's *Astronomica* (see G. P. Goold's edition in the Loeb Classical Library), which was completed around 20 A.D. Consequently, most of the degrees that Firmicus gives are the same as those given by Manilius. Evidently the original Greek source had many errors. Either the person who determined the rising times was astronomically incompetent, or else his text was badly miscopied before it reached Manilius (and from him, Firmicus). Neither of the Roman writers bothered to check the rising degrees (probably neither of them knew how to make the calculations), so they merely repeated the faulty figures given in the Greek source.

The most eloquent poet Aratus also related the number of these stars in Greek,[1] and Caesar and the ornament of eloquence Tullius[2] did so in Latin. But these [writers merely] set forth their names and risings, but not the authority of their astrological influences, so that it seems to me that this was not any knowledge of astrology; but—inspired by the poetic license of pleasant speech—they have [merely] brought them forth in a literary work.

4. But having examined the theory of all the astrological influences, we have also found out for ourselves that these stars attest to much in the nativities of men. Hence, that which we have promised, we shall explain. We shall state both the places [of the stars] and their names, so that thus the whole truth of their astrological influences may be acquired. Then, what things the stars denote, if, posited in their matutine rising, they have [a relationship to] the ASC or the DSC.

VI.

1. The *Ship* arises <on the right side, namely in the 4th degree of Aries>.[3] If, therefore, anyone was born with this degree rising, that is if in its rising it burst through that degree, he will be the skipper of a ship, [or] a ship owner, but one who throughout the whole space of his life chooses always to be involved in marine activities.

2. On the left side of Aries, Orion rises, namely in the 10th degree of Aries.[4] Therefore, if Orion is partilely in the ASC or in the MC, it makes

[1]Aratus (c.315-c.245), *Phaenomena*, a popular poem on astronomy and weather, based on Eudoxus and psueudo-Theophrastus.

[2]Marcus Tullius Cicero.

[3]The *Ship* is presumably the large constellation Argo, now subdivided into Vela, Puppis, and Carina. The words in angle brackets are supplied by Skutsch from Manilius, *Astronomica* v, 36-39 *Argo a dextri lateris...consurgit...quattuor in partes cum Corniger* 'Argo from the right side...rises in four degrees with the Horned One (Aries)'. G. P. Goold points out that Argo is a southern constellation and rises on the *left*, but not with Aries. The brightest star is Canopus or α Carinae, which rose with 24 Leo. Here, as in what follows, it seems likely that Firmicus has used Manilius and consequently Manilius's Greek source—errors and all—for the risings and some of the significations of the fixed stars. However, the reference may be to the constellation Ship of the Barbaric Sphere, whose location is unknown. Much useful information on the constellations and stars is given by Goold in his edition of Manilius in the Introduction, pp. xcv-xcvii, and in his notes to the text of Book V of the *Astronomica*.

[4]Another mistake! Orion, which is a large and conspicuous constellation, does

men who are seen to display swift mobility of body, and those whose mind involved in various kinds of difficulties is always seething with watchful thought. They will always diversify their domiciles, they will change their houses and abodes, and they will always fly about the entrances of all with morning greetings.

3. Auriga[1] rises towards the north in the 15th degree of Aries. He who was born in the rising of this will be either a charioteer or a horse-tamer, or one who crosses a four-horse chariot with a leap, or one who, standing on the back of horses, supports himself with marvelous control, and especially when carried on a horse he exercises military equipment. Both Salmoneus and Bellerophontes[2] are said to have been born with this star rising.

4. In the 20th degree of Aries towards the north arises *Haedus*,[3] whom Auriga bears. Those who were born with this constellation rising promise one thing with their appearance, but they conceal another secretly in their behavior. For they are serious in their face, with a spreading beard, resolute in appearance, so that in short they seem to imitate the way of life of Cato. But they feign all this with an artificial mood. For by nature they are impudent, lustful, always involved in depraved desires[4] and sensual pleasures, and who are always secretly burning with amorous desires.

5. They will also be separated from every duty of virtue, timid weak persons, and those who shudder at every danger of fights. These, frequently seized by depraved passions, and involved in acts of perverted love, are caused to bring about their own death. There are also born from

---

not rise with Aries, but rather with Gemini. Its brightest stars are Betelgeuze, Rigel, and Bellatrix or α β and γ Orionis, which rose with 14, 18, and 9 Gemini respectively. The belt star Alnilam or ε Orionis, mentioned below, also rose with 17 Gemini.

[1]A northern constellation, whose brightest star is Capella or α Aurigae, which rose with 17 Aries. The rising degree is thus approximately correct, but in Paragraph 7 below Capella is said to rise with the 30th degree of Aries.

[2]Mythological figures connected with horses. Salmoneus, a son of Aeolus, rashly imitated lightning by hurling burning torches from a horse. This annoyed Zeus, who knocked him off his horse with a genuine thunderbolt, so that he fell into Tartarus. Bellerophon was a hero, who mounted the flying horse Pegasus and slew the monster Chimaera, but he also ultimately annoyed Zeus, who punished him severely.

[3]Actually, *Haedi* 'Kids', since there are two stars, ζ and η Aurigae, which rose with 23 and 24 Aries.

[4]Reading *desideriis* 'desires' with the **Δ** family of MSS rather than *desideriorum* 'of desires' with the Teubner editors and the **Γ** family of MSS.

this constellation shepherds of sheep, but who play the tunes of rustic song on a pipe.

6. In the 27th degree of Aries the Hyades[1] rise. Whoever was born in the rising of this constellation will be restless, turbulent, popular, and one who will always incite the people with turbulent insurrections, inflaming the minds of the common people with noisy and furious struggles, an enemy of peace and quiet, and one desiring internal and domestic wars with a furious mental desire. But various occupations with continual anxieties are often produced for him. This constellation also makes ploughmen, cowboys, and shepherds of sheep.

7. In the 30th degree of Aries, which degree always shows the whole sign above the earth, there arises the *Goat*,[2] which the poets of legend say gave sustaining nourishment to Jupiter. Those who were born with this constellation rising will be troubled with too much consternation of mind, and a continual tremor always attacks their body. These persons are oppressed by minor excitements and are disturbed with a serious attack of fear by minor news items. They will also be curious about everything, and those who, whatever new was mentioned, long for it with impatient desire, so that they always seek out whatever is new with a curious desire of longing.

8. Therefore, because we have said what these stars do in their rising, it should also be said in the following place what they denote when placed in their setting. For just as shadows are contrary to light, so is death contrary to life. Life, therefore, will be sought in the rising, death in the setting. If, therefore, the rising is in the ASC, just as we have frequently said, the setting is in opposition to the ASC, i.e. in the 7th house from the ASC.[3]

[1]The *Hyades* or 'Rainers' consist of six stars in the constellation Taurus, of which the brightest is Prima Hyadum or γ Tauri; it rose with 14 Taurus.

[2]Capella or α Aurigae, sometimes called Amalthea. It rose with 17 Aries. This Goat was said to have given suck to Jupiter as a child.

[3]Firmicus, or rather the authority that he is summarizing, mistakenly assumed that if a star *rose* with a particular degree, it would also *set* with that same degree. But this is only true for stars with zero latitude. Since most stars have latitude, the degree with which they set will be different—sometimes surprisingly different—from the degree with which they rise. For example, Capella actually rose with 17 Aries, but it set with 3 Gemini! I will give the degrees with which the stars set in the notes that follow (again, as said above, for the tropical zodiac and the epoch 129 B.C.). See also the list in Appendix 4.

9. If the *Ship* was in the DSC,[1] or if the DSC falls partilely in the Ship, and malefic stars aspect this house by square or opposition, they denote the bitter inconveniences of shipwrecks. But if Saturn was posited in that star, i.e. in the Ship, they will perish by bitter deaths submerged in rivers.

10. If Orion was found in the DSC of the nativity,[2] men of such a sort are born, whose minds are always disturbed by various kinds of concern. These, sent by their own cities along with a legation, die abroad while on that trip, bearing to the lower regions the light consolation that by their own fellow citizens perpetual honors, pictures, inscriptions, and the honors of statues are denoted for them.

11. If Auriga was found in the DSC of the nativity,[3] and an aspect of the malefic stars strikes it, then thrown from chariots, they are destroyed by miserable lacerations, so that with a broken body they experience the bitter inconveniences of death. Or, struck by a thunderbolt they are overwhelmed by the sudden ruin or downfall of death; or they are crucified; or their legs are broken by [order of] a public sentence.

12. If *Haedus*, which Auriga bears, was found in the DSC,[4] and Saturn aspects it by square or opposition, the Natives die at the very moment [of the beginning] of life. Or, placed on the very threshold of birth, they are strangled by the declining strength of the mother. Or, by the swelling narrow [birth] channel, a bitter demise of death is caused for them. But if Mars is found with that same star in the DSC, devoid of all testimony from the benefic stars, it will make them to †embrace. . .[5], or to be sacrificed on the altar of some fearful religions.

13. But if the Hyades were in the DSC,[6] and an aspect of the malefic stars attacks that house, the sudden and unexpected demise of death is denoted. For, they will die, thrown down by rioters or popular uprisings and [with their bodily members] scattered by the common hands of the populace, so that the [individual] authors of their death can neither be discovered nor ever be named.

---

[1]Canopus set with 28 Aries. But the reference may be to the Barbaric Constellation called Ship, whose location in the sky is not known.

[2]Alnilam or ε Orionis, the middle star of the Belt of Orion, set with 17 Taurus. For its rising, see below.

[3]The principal star in Auriga is Capella, which set with 3 Gemini.

[4]The Haedi set with 26 and 27 Taurus respectively.

[5]Kroll indicates a lacuna here.

[6]Prima Hyadum set with 5 Taurus.

14. If Capra[1] is in the DSC, they will get their supply of personal assets from plunder. But these persons will be severely battered by ill-fame on account of insults to religion. They will also have personal property that is either collected from shipwrecks or gotten out of a river.

VII.

1. The Pleiades[2] are found in the 6th degree of Taurus. If any persons are born with these rising, they are always involved in luxurious and lascivious pleasures. The faults of petulance always raise them up smeared over with ointments and given over to excessive violence, so that in convivial situations and human association their alien faults strike with the charms of bitter speech. They will certainly be applied to every crime of lust, and they will be those who are accustomed to rouse up laughter among men with biting sayings of witty speech.

2. They will always have a neat, polished appearance and one brought out with stylish clothes, and those whose waved hair is always twisted into ringlets, so that frequently with the added hair of others[3] they feign a false and constructed beauty, softening the form of their whole body with various kinds of cosmetics. These persons, having removed all their body hair, transfer their own body into the image of a feminine body, and their clothes are also altered to the likeness of womanly attire. These persons, walking about daintily, suspend their own characteristics with a certain delicate control.[4]

3. But ambition bothers them, and that disease so attracts them, that from it they think they can arrive at virtue for themselves and the greatest joy of good fortune. They will always be in love, or they will pretend to be in love, and it will be a regret for them that they were born men. If a malefic star strikes this house with a strong aspect, they will be oppressed by sudden blindness.

4. With the Pleiades setting, i.e. in the 6th degree of Taurus,[5] if this de-

---

[1]Capra is another name for the star Capella in the constellation Auriga.

[2]The famous asterism Pleaides consists of a cluster of 6 easily visible stars, the brightest of which is Alcyone or η Tauri; it rose with 26 Aries.

[3]Evidently a reference to wigs or swatches of hair.

[4]The subject is female impersonators or would-be transsexuals.

[5]But this is incorrect for the reason stated in a previous note. Alcyone actually set with 2 Taurus.

gree was aspected by malefics, those who were born will perish in a shipwreck. But if benefic [stars] together with malefic ones aspect this same house with equal aspects, a pleasant death will come to them without any weeping—either from sexual pleasure, or from too much food during banquets and drinking—but without any lamentation a delightful death will come to them.[1]

5. If the ASC is in the division of the Hoof of Taurus,[2] and one each of the benefic and the malefic [stars] aspects this same house with equal aspects, they will make a painter, but one whom this occupation will make celebrated with famous honor. But if, without the testimony of the benefic stars, only the malefic stars make a menacing aspect to this place, famous gladiators will be born, but those who, after many prizes and innumerable victories in that occupation of fighting, die from a threatening sword with great applause and favor from the spectators.

VIII.

1. Lepus[3] arises in the 7th degree of Gemini. Those who were born with this constellation rising will have such lightness of body, that when they begin to run they seem to surpass birds. If Mars aspects this place, it makes those who race in the stadium; but if the Moon is with Mars, it makes boxers [or] *pancratiasts*[4]; if Mercury aspects, it makes jugglers or those playing with balls[5]; if Venus aspects, it makes pantomimists or actors in pantomimes[6]; but if Venus and Mercury [are] together, they perform new arts with the exercise of excessive diligence, especially if

---

[1]Bram appends Paragraph 5 to Paragraph 4.

[2]Not mentioned by Manilius.

[3]A southern constellation, the brightest star of which is Arneb or α Leporis; it rose with 30 Gemini.

[4]Accepting Wikström's emendation *<pam>macharios*. 'pancratiasts'. These were contestants in a sport in which both boxing and wrestling was allowed, perhaps something like the "free-style" or "universal style" that is becoming popular today. *Cf.* viii.27.6.

[5]The Latin has *pilis ludentes*, which could be translated either as 'playing with balls' or 'playing with javelins'. Bram translated *pilis* as 'javelins', but I think here it means 'balls' – probably jugglers are meant. Prof. Monat translates it as 'dice'.

[6]The Latin has *pantomimos aut mimologos*; *pantomimos* are certainly mimes, but *mimologos* could be either actors in a pantomime play or writers of that kind of play.

Jupiter aids by making a fortunate aspect to those same [stars] in all those decrees that we have mentioned.

2. But if Saturn aspects this house by square or by opposition, it will make fugitives, who with a headlong inclination of anger desert their own homes, migrating to distant regions. But if Lepus was found in the DSC,[1] and it has aspects from the benefic stars, just as we have said in the preceding significations, they get their life's support with great labor. But if it only receives the testimony of the malefic stars, they die eaten and torn to shreds by wild beasts.

IX.

1. The *Iugulae*[2] arise in the 1st degree of Cancer. The one who was born with these rising will surely be irreligious and treacherous, but dedicated entirely to the pursuit of hunting. He will capture wild beasts with nets, or he will ensnare them in pitfalls, or he will hunt them with various kinds of frightening things and iron, or he will search the secret places in the woods with dogs in order to capture wild animals. But also if a woman is born thus, with the spirit of a virago she will also pursue these same activities with similar motives. But if Mars along with the benefic stars makes any aspect to this same place, she will do these things.

2. But if Saturn has done this same thing, they will also be attached to every kind of activity of fishing, so that they also capture large sea creatures by that same fishing.[3] But if that constellation[4] that we have mentioned is in the DSC, and the benefic stars aspect that very house, he who is born thus will die in his sleep. But if Mars aspects this place, he will certainly frequently incur all [kinds of] dangers, but while sleeping he will have his throat cut in a bitter death.

3. Procyon[5] arises in the 27th degree of Cancer. Those who are born with this rising will surely be those who are separated from every occupation involving hunting, but actually they will either make or prepare

---

[1]Lepus set with 10 Taurus.

[2]The *Iugulae* are the three stars δ ε ζ Orionis that form the Belt of Orion. Of these, the middle star, Alnilam or ε Orionis, rose with 17 Gemini.

[3]Accepting Kroll's emendation *ex istis* 'from that' rather than *exquisitis* '(from) excellent'.

[4]Alnilam set with 17 Taurus.

[5]Procyon or α Canis Minoris; it rose with 7 Cancer.

weapons for hunters, i.e. nets, hunting-spears, arrows, and whatever pertains to the equipping of that occupation. They will also raise dogs that hunt out the lairs of wild animals, those lying hidden and their lairs, by the presentiments of their nostrils.

4. But if this constellation is in the DSC,[1] and Mars aspects that place by square or opposition, [and it is] devoid of fortunate testimony from Jupiter, then lacerated by the bite of a rabid dog, they will perish from a similar insanity of madness, so that avoiding the [very] sight of water, and dreading every drink from a cup, with their throats drying up, they have a horror of always wanting water. Or certainly, while preparing traps for wild animals, they are destroyed—torn apart by their bites.

X.

1. Canicula, which is called Sirius[2] by the Greeks, arises in the 1st degree of Leo. Those who were born with this constellation rising will apply their frenzied spirits to every action of preposterous crime. They will also be separated from every grace of humanity, and those who willingly pursue all actions of violence—frantic, irascible, frightening, threatening persons, and those whom all men both hate and also fear.

2. They will also be lively and always puffed up with a verbose fluency of speech, and those whom incautious speech always impels to every sort of invective, thereby stirring up new and unheard of quarrels. Their hearts throb with frequent agitations, and their voices, from drying throats, imitate the howling of dogs, so that, unsettled by impulse and frenzy, either their teeth chatter or they always grind them.[3]

---

[1]Procyon set with 18 Gemini.

[2]Sirius or α Canis Majoris; it rose with 12 Cancer.

[3]The Latin has *aut dentes quatiant aut *attritu semper exacuant*, lit. 'either they shake their teeth or they always sharpen them by *rubbing'. The meaning is unclear. The verb *quatio* usually means 'shake'; but the usual verb for 'gnash' is *frendo*. Manilius, *Astronomica* 5,255, has *morsibus et crebris dentes in voce relinquit*, lit. 'with frequent bites he leaves the teeth in his voice'. Goold translates this as, 'constant gnashing imparts the sound of teeth to their utterance'. Bram translates Firmicus's words simply as, 'they gnash their teeth'. Prof. Monat has 'ils se brisent les dents ou les usent en les frottant sans cesse les unes contre les autres'.'. But I think we should keep **Δ**'s reading *attritos* 'rubbed' and understand *aut dentes quatiant aut attritos semper exacuant* to mean something like what I have put above.

3. But if Mars aspects this place, those things that I have said are made stronger. These persons never fear the secrets of the woods, but they scorn the bites of all the wild animals with an inherent boldness; and frequently dangers are caused for them both from wild animals and from fires.

4. If the malefic stars aspect this place, with the Moon also aspecting Saturn, there are born hunters, combatants in the amphitheater, and reckless persons who fight with wild animals in cages under the gaze of the people. Gladiators are also made. They will also be endowed with that bodily swiftness that [enables them to] catch a rabbit in its flight.

5. But if this constellation was found in the DSC,[1] and Mars was either found in that same place, or if it aspected that same place with a threatening aspect, it will make [the Native] to be eaten by wolves or by dogs, or to be consumed by wild animals with a miserable tearing apart.

6. Crater[2] arises in the 30th degree of Leo. Whoever was born with this constellation rising will love well-watered fields and springs or streams, or he will lead off rivers from their own river-bed to other places. He will be both a lover and a cultivator of vineyards, and one who will graft live shoots by inserting them into unfruitful trees, or who, by trimming boxwood trees, shapes them into large animals,[3] or who makes the greenery of the colonnade into a circle with winding vines. He drinks wine with pleasure without any admixture [of water]. But if an aspect of the benefic stars decrees actions for him, he will trade in wet goods.

7. But if this constellation was found in the DSC[4] without the testimony of a malefic, he who is born will die in middle age in the course of banquets and drinking bouts. But if there is an aspect from the malefic stars, he will be found dead submerged either in a large wine container or in a well, or in a river, or in a lake, or in a marsh, or in the sea, or certainly in a fish-pond, or in a tub.

---

[1]Sirius set with 28 Taurus.

[2]A dim southern constellation (no star greater than 4th magnitude). The only named star is Alkes or α Crateris; it rose with 30 Leo.

[3]That is, he trims the trees into topiary shapes.

[4]The star α Crateris set with 30 Cancer.

XI.

1. Corona[1] arises in the 5th degree of Virgo. Whoever was born with this constellation rising will be occupied with various pleasures of whimsicality, devoted to the tasks of feminine arts, a designer of flowers and crowns, and one who clings to the pleasant delights of gardens, longing with a studied desire for scents, unguents, perfumes, and adorning his own body with a meretricious ornament of beauty, secretly committing debauches and adulteries, but hastening to sexual intercourse with beautiful virgins and boys, with a bold inclination to lust.

2. But if this constellation is found in the DSC,[2] and Saturn is either in that same place, or from another house casts a menacing aspect to that same degree, it denotes a demise by death in the first [age] of youth.[3] For, struck down by a public sentence, it makes [his body] to be thrown out unburied to be torn apart by the bites of wild animals, or dogs, or birds.

3. Spica[4] arises in the 10th degree of the sign Virgo. Whoever is born at the rising of Spica will always be involved in rural occupations and devoted to the cultivation of fields with patient labor, and one who produces renewal of the crops with new seeds year after year; for his life's support, he preserves many crops in storehouses. Also, according to the testimony of other stars, it makes bakers[5] of sweet goods and similar occupations.

4. But if this constellation is found in the DSC,[6] they will be disturbed either by too much fervor of anxieties, or by the scantiness of support,[7] or

---

[1]The principal star is Alphecca or α Coronae Borealis; it rose with 5 Libra.

[2]Alphecca set with 13 Sagittarius.

[3]Accepting Ziegler's suggested deletion of *malivolae stellae* 'malefic stars'.

[4]Spica or α Virginis; it rose with 25 Virgo.

[5]Not 'millers' as Bram translates it. Prof. Monat has correctly 'bakers of pastries'. The bakers formed a prominent and influential guild in Roman society. Bread was the principal item in the diet of the ordinary citizen. Cf. Matthew 6.11 *Panem nostrum supersubstantialem da nobis hodie*. 'Give us today our bread on which we subsist.'

[6]Spica set with 22 Virgo.

[7]Bram translates this as, 'stricken with fever, or suffer imprisonment', and Prof. Monat has 'constrained by the excessive ardor of hot spells…', but I disagree. *Cf.* iii.3c.22 (121,7) …*faciet penuries angustias aestus turbas seditiones pericula* 'it will make penury, want, anxieties, disturbances, revolts, [and] dangers'.

by an attack by demons.[1] But if Saturn makes a menacing aspect to this place, it will make him who is born to be weighed down by the miserable burden of poverty, so that throughout the entire space of his life [he will be nearly] nude, with badly hanging shreds of clothing; and it leads him down to his last day to be asking for food from the support of public compassion, so that with torment of mind and also his body's debt he completes the duty of life.

5. But if Mars aspects this place, then struck down by severe ill-will on account of stolen or badly distributed public provisions,[2] or those taken away by his fraudulent desire, he will be torn apart by the madness of the raging people, and his scattered members demonstrate examples of a bitter death that must be feared.[3]

XII.

1. Sagitta[4] arises in the sign of Libra in the 8th degree. The one who is born in this sign will be a shooter of arrows, one who strikes flying birds with a special control of his skill, or he calmly pierces fish with a trident or a spear within the spaces of the waves But if this constellation is in the DSC,[5] and the benefic [stars] along with the malefic ones aspect this place with equal aspects, then placed in the army and put on the line between a harsh mass of the enemy, they die gory with the endless blood of the enemy, cut down also by the right hand of that enemy.

2. But if Mars alone, with the testimony of Mercury, aspects this place, or if it is in this place, it makes the kind of people who sell themselves on account of the will for another's favor for the spectacle of death by the loss of their sold blood. But if Saturn does this, they are assigned to the

---

[1]Accepting Kroll's addition of *daemonum* 'demons' before *incursione* 'attack.

[2]This refers to the regular public distribution of bread to the citizens, an early form of public welfare.

[3]The Latin is corrupt. Perhaps we should emend it to read ... *gravi pulsatum invidia insanientis populi *rabie *dissipabitur et popularibus manibus *lacerati *artus metuenda acerbae mortis exempla demonstrant*, 'struck down by the anger of the raging people, his limbs lacerated, he will be torn apart by madness and the hands of the people; they show the fearful examples of a bitter death', where the first two emendations are mine and the last two are Ziegler's.

[4]A dim northern constellation, whose principal stars γ and δ Sagittae rose with 11 and 13 Sagittarius respectively. It was a gross error to put them in Libra.

[5]The stars γ and δ Sagittae set with 25 and 28 Capricorn respectively.

games by the sentence of a judge.[1] The [River] Styx is said to be in this degree[2]; {then there is no doubt that there is another Styx, which, having fallen down from the sky, is applied to the preservation of earthly bodies. [But] the celestial divinities, fearing punishment, have a horror of it in their mind}.[3]

3. *Haedus*[4] arises in the 15th degree of Libra. Whoever was born with this sign rising will be of various mind and always disturbed in consideration, who, involved in various plans, never really enjoys the grace of quiet composure. He will also be assigned to the service of magistrates—a record clerk, handling the duties associated with public revenues—but a person with lewd habits and one tied up with perverted desires of love; devoted to wine and banquets, and one who prefers the grace of parties to public things; good at dancing, and learning the scenic arts by heart with a studious interest.

4. But if this sign is found in the DSC, and the malefic stars make threatening aspects to this place, either they will be thrown down from a precipice, or, exercising a leap, are broken by the miserable ruin of a hanging body in a troublesome death; or hunting sexual relations with girls in the dead of night, and possessed by too great ardor of impatience for arousing unknown places, or lying in wait in the house while the husbands are asleep, they die thrown down from a precipice. But if the benefic stars are in aspect, they die from difficulty of breathing.

---

[1]Persons condemned to death were sometimes executed by putting them in the arena where they were killed (and even eaten) by wild animals.

[2]Bram omitted the text following after 'The River Styx is said to be in this degree'.

[3]Here again the Latin text of viii. 12, 2-3 is faulty. Housman (*Astronomicon,* 2nd ed., Preface to Book V, p. xliv) emends it as follows: *inde alteram Stygem esse nulla dubitatio est, <quae de caelo lapsa terrenorum corporum sustentationibus applicatur>. caelestia numina, exemplum timentes animo perhorrescunt [quae...applicatur].* Bodily parts dipped in the Styx were said to be imperishable. And the gods feared to violate an oath sworn by the River Styx.

[4]*Haedus* 'The Kid' is mentioned by Manilius, *Astronomica*, v, 311, as rising with Libra, but he gave no degree, so Firmicus assigned it to the middle of the sign. No one knows what star this *Haedus* corresponds to or whether it was simply some kind of mistake (two *Haedi*, ζ and η Aurigae, were already said to rise with Aries). See Housman's edition of Manilius (Cambridge: Cambridge University Press, 1937. 2nd ed.), vol. 5, pp. xliv-xlv for a discussion of the problem.

XIII.

1. Ara arises in the 1st degree[1] of Scorpio. Those who are born with this constellation rising, with the testimony of the benefic stars, will be priests, prophets, or temple-keepers, high priests of some very sacred religion, expounding some divine arts with very learned interpretations.

2. But if this constellation was in the DSC,[2] and Mars or Saturn aspect that place with a menacing aspect, they will be punished by a public sentence. But if there is testimony from Jupiter, either sacrificed to the Gods, or cut down on account of some religion, they are consecrated to everlasting ceremonies.

3. Centaurus[3] arises in the 12th degree of Scorpio. Whoever was born with this rising will either be a charioteer or a feeder and caretaker of horses, or certainly a trainer or a veterinary surgeon, or certainly a groom. But if Mars makes a fortunate aspect to this place, it will make him to serve in the cavalry. But if Mercury aspects this house, it will make herb-doctors, who keep herbs they have collected with expert skill for remedies for suffering cattle.

4. But if this constellation was in the DSC,[4] and malefic stars aspect this place, he will die, either from being thrown down from a high place, or from the charge of a quadrupedal animal, or from the kick of a horse, or from being thrown down off a horse, or having been thrown out of a chariot and dragged by the horses, he will be torn apart in a miserable death.

XIV.

1. Arcturus[5] arises in the 5th degree of Sagittarius. He who is born with this sign rising will be of the sort who guards the secrets of his friends with faithful taciturnity. The royal wealth is entrusted to him,[6] or the

---

[1]Manilius, *Astronomica*, v. 339, has it rise in the 8th degree of Scorpio; but the principal star α Arae actually rose with 9 Sagittarius.

[2]The star α Arae set with 12 Libra.

[3]The principal star is Rigel Kentaurus or α Centauri; it rose with 19 Scorpio.

[4]The star α Centauri set with 8 Leo.

[5]A particularly gross error; actually, Arcturus or α Bootis rose with 20 Virgo.

[6]Beginning with 'or the State treasury' and continuing to 'entrusted to them' MS **N** omits two lines due to homoeoteleuton (… credentur | … credetur)—a rare error for **N**.

State treasury, or public buildings. But if the malefic stars aspect this place, either the care of the people is entrusted to them, or they are door-keepers of the royal residence, or those who are entrusted with the duties of admitting or greeting [callers] at the palace.

2. But if this constellation was found in the DSC,[1] and Saturn along with Mercury make any aspect to that same place, it will make those struck by the infamy of a serious crime and handed over to a public prison, shackled with chains; and those who die with miserable tortures.

3. Cygnus[2] arises in the 10th degree of Sagittarius. He who is born with this constellation rising will either capture birds, or he will trade in birds, or with ingenious care he will insert the sound of the human voice into birds,[3] or he will raise doves or pigeons[4] carefully. But if this constellation was found in the DSC,[5] while they are preparing the foundations of wealth for themselves by the help of others, they are overwhelmed by the burden of captivity by enemies. Or, on account of their theft of the spoils of war, they are punished by a public sentence.

XV.

1. Ophiuchus[6] arises in the first degrees of Capricorn. Those who are born with this constellation rising will be Marsi,[7] who rear[8] poisonous snakes, having put them to sleep and pacified their stings But if this con-

[1]Arcturus set with 14 Scorpio.

[2]The principal star of the constellation Cygnus is Deneb or α Cygni; it rose with 11 Sagittarius. Manilius, *Astronomica*, v. 365, says it arises "in three times the 10th degree of Sagittarius." Firmicus missed the "three times" and simply put it in the 10th degree instead of the 30th,, thereby accidentally coming close to the truth.

[3]That is, he will teach birds to talk. Cf. Manilius, *Astronomica*, 5, 378 ...*linguas hominum sensusque docebit* 'he will teach them the languages and meaning [of words] of men'. Pliny, *N.H.*, 10, 116-124 describes several kinds of talking birds, including parrots.

[4]Reading *columbas* 'doves or pigeons' with MS **N;** *palumbos* 'wood-pigeons' **ΓD.**

[5]Deneb set with 28 Aquarius.

[6]The brightest star, Ras Alhague (Arabic for 'Head of the Serpent-charmer') or α Ophiuchi rose with 12 Scorpio!

[7]A people of Latium who were reputed to be wizards and snake-charmers.

[8]Accepting Némethy's emendation of *nutrient* 'rear' for *mitigent* 'soothe'. Cf. *Mathesis* viii.28.6 (345,9).

stellation is found in the DSC,[1] and <Mars>[2] makes any aspect to that place, they die from the bite of a venomous serpent.

2. Delphinus[3] arises in the 8th degree of Capricorn. Whoever is born with this constellation rising will have a job involving swimming, but with the testimony of Saturn he will be a diver; but with [the testimony] of Mars or Mercury, they will be vaulters, jumpers, those skilled in dance-wrestling, tumbling,[4] or certainly sailors discernible by the mobility of their walk. But if this constellation is found in the DSC,[5] and Saturn makes a menacing aspect to that place, he will be drowned in the sea or in a river by storms and tornados.

3. Lyra[6] arises in the 10th degree of Capricorn. Those who are born with this constellation rising will be just, upright, and ambitious, apt for every duty of justice, avengers of crimes, and those to whom judgments and legal questions are entrusted. But if Saturn makes any aspect to this place, they will be torturers [or] executioners, who persecute evil men with the enthusiasm of a firm desire. But if this constellation is found in the DSC,[7] they will perish torn apart by public tortures, or burnt up in fires, or tortured by a lawful criminal inquisition, especially if Mars or Saturn aspects this place.

4. Cepheus[8] arises in the 15th degree of Capricorn. Those who are born when this constellation is rising will be grave and austere—persons to be feared because of all the authority of their severity—always displaying a countenance of moral integrity, but who by disposition follow the stoic sect. People of that sort were among the old Catos; such a one in

---

[1]Ras Alhague set with 26 Sagittarius.

[2]There is a lacuna after 'that place'. MS **D**[2] adds 'Mars', which I have chosen; edition **a** adds 'malefic stars'.

[3]The brightest star is β Delphini, which rose with 24 Sagittarius.

[4]The four strange Latin words, *petaminarios, efelmatores, orchestopalarios*, and *petauristarios*, derived from the Greek, signify performers who entertained with various kinds of acrobatics and gymnastics, perhaps using ropes and springboards.

[5]The star β Delphini set with 1 Aquarius.

[6]Manilius, *Astronomica*, v. 337, says that Lyra rises with the 26th degree of Libra, but he also speaks of a star he calls *Fides* 'The Lute' that rises somewhere in Capricorn, and it is only the latter that Firmicus adopts and calls Lyra. The star in question is Vega or α Lyrae, which actually rose with 15 Scorpio! See A. E. Housman. Manilius, *Astronomicon*, vol. 5, 2nd. ed., xliii-xlv.

[7]Vega set with 1 Aquarius.

[8]The brightest star is Alderamin or α Cephei, which rose with 28 Scorpio.

our own times was Tullianus,[1] who also attained the insignia of ordinary consulship by the merit of his severity. But if Venus and Mercury were giving testimony in this house, either they recite poems of the tragic art, or they compose them. But if this constellation is found in the DSC,[2] they will die from a miserable fall of their body onto rocks which at some time they had ventured on[3]; or, when they are born, they will immediately perish; or they will be punished by public decree on account of incest, so that the demise by a new and unheard-of death is caused for them.

XVI.

1. Aquila[4] arises in the 12th degree of Aquarius. Those who were born when this constellation was rising will have their life support from the slaughter of men or from the spoils of war. They will also capture wild animals and at the same time domesticate them. Moreover, they will be strong soldiers, by whose valor and support those fearful of the impulses of wars are soothed. They will indeed be of such valor, that they go after the enemy bare-breasted, as they believe it hastens[5] them to [achieving] their own praise if they seem to have despised death with unconcerned courage.

2. But if the benefic stars make a fortunate aspect to this place, they will liberate their native land and also found other cities; and they will triumph over conquered and subjugated nations. But if Mars or Saturn aspects this place, it will make administrators, tribunes, imperial ministers, or associates of kings, and those to whom the care of the empire or the custody of troops is entrusted. But if this constellation is found in the DSC,[6] it will make the Natives to be strangled.

3. Cassiopeia[7] arises in the 20th degree of Aquarius. Those who are born with this rising will be goldsmiths, goldbeaters, gilders, plasterers, and pearl-setters, carrying on all these arts with talented skill. They will

[1]The reference is to Aurelius Tullianus Symmachus, who was consul in 330 A.D.

[2]Alderamin set with 4 Aries.

[3]This happened to King Albert I of Belgium (1875-1934), who was killed by a fall while rock-climbing on 17 February 1934. He had the sign Aries in his DSC, and the star Alderamin was there at 11°04 Aries.

[4]The brightest star is Altair or α Aquilae, which rose with 15 Sagittarius.

[5]Accepting Brakman's emendation of *se properare* for *prospere*.

[6]Altair set with 19 Capricorn.

[7]The principal stars are Schedir, Caph, gamma, and Ruchbah or α β γ and δ Cassiopeiae, which rose with 21, 10, 17, and 23 Capricorn respectively.

have very great income from these arts. But if this constellation was found in the DSC,[1] those who were born will perish either from the collapse of a building, or they will die murdered.

XVII.

1. Andromeda[2] arises in the 12th degree of Pisces. Whoever was born with this constellation rising will always attack men with a cruel savagery. Moreover, he will be either the deliverer of public punishments, or a prison guard, or an executioner to whom the duty of killing men is entrusted.

2. But if a benefic star joined with a malefic one aspects this place, it makes those in charge of convicts or metals. But if this constellation is found in the DSC,[3] and the malefic stars aspected that place, it will make [those] thrown to wild beasts or those hung on a cross. But if the favor of the benefic stars approaches the malefics arranged thus, they will make these persons to be assigned to the [gladiatorial] games, or to be perpetually bound in bonds of chains.

3. Equus[4] arises in the 21st degree of Pisces. Those who are born with this constellation rising will be in charge of racers, charioteers, drivers, horsemen, dispatch-riders, scouts, and sometimes physicians, but those who compound remedies from herbs for men and cattle. But if this constellation is found in the DSC[5] with the malefic stars, they will be badly injured,[6] either by a kick from a hoof, or from being thrown down [from a horse] or it will make them to die from an overturned carriage, and shattered with a miserable injury to the body.

4. In the last degrees of Pisces there arises *Ingeniculus*, who is called *Engonasin*[7] by the Greeks. Those who were born with this constellation

---

[1]The stars Schedir, Caph, gamma, and Ruchbah set with 18, 17, and 27 Aries, and 1 Taurus respectively.

[2]The brightest stars are Alpheratz, Mirach, and Almach or α β γ Andromedae, which rose with 12 Aquarius, 24 Aquarius, and 1 Pisces respectively.

[3]Alpheratz, Mirach, and Almach set with 19 Pisces, 5 Aries, and 20 Aries respectively.

[4]The constellation of the Flying Horse, Pegasus; its stars Markab or α Pegasi and Scheat or β Pegasi rose with 3 Aquarius and 25 Capricorn respectively.

[5]Markab and Scheat set with 29 Aquarius and 6 Pisces respectively.

[6]Accepting Skutsch's emendation of *lacerabitur* for *curabitur*.

[7]*Ingeniculus* is a Latin translation of the Greek *Engonasin* (i.e. *en gonasin*), which

rising will be wise, crafty, versed in various kinds of trickery, liars, those who approach men with various plots, and who always proceed with unrestrained boldness. But with the testimony of Mars and the Moon, they will be tight-rope walkers, *calobatae,*[1] [or] rope-dancers. Those who were born with this constellation in the DSC[2] will be in danger from various kinds of treachery. If Mars aspects this place, they will be burned alive.

5. In the last degrees of Pisces on the left side there arises *Belua*, which is called Cetus[3] by the Greeks. Those who are born with this constellation rising will be fishermen but of large fishes. For these persons will catch seals, sea-dogs (sharks), sword-fish, tuna, and crocodiles. They will also have jobs that are from the seas or from salted fish or from fish-sauce,[4] and they will trade in these things. But if this constellation is in the DSC,[5] and if Mars aspects this house, while swimming in a river or in the sea, they will be eaten by crocodiles or by [sea-]dogs and sea monsters of that sort.

6. With the rising of *Septentrio*,[6] which is between Pisces and Aries, that is between the beginning and the end of the world, which, fixed in one place and placed in the very vertex of the world, turns about the axis of the world with a ceaseless speed. And so with this sign rising, those who are born will be tamers of wild animals, i.e. those who associate bears or bulls or lions rid of their wildness with human society. But if *Septentrio* was found in the DSC with Mars bearing witness [to it], they will be killed by wild beasts.

7. Outermost is the *Snake*,[7] which, placed between the two *Bears*,[8] glides along in the manner of a river with sinuous windings. Whoever

---

means 'on [his] knees' and refers to the constellation Hercules, where the hero is represented as being on one knee. Its principle star is Ras Algethi (Arabic for 'Head of the Kneeler') or α Herculis, which rose with 7 Scorpio.

[1]This is from a Greek word that means 'tight-rope walker', the equivalent of the preceding Latin word *funambuli*, which means the same thing.

[2]Ras Algethi set with 23 Sagittarius.

[3]The Latin *Belua* means 'beast' or 'monster' as does the Greek Cetus (*kêtos*), a 'sea-monster' or specifically 'a whale'. The brightest star is Deneb Kaitos (Arabic for 'Tail of the Whale') or β Ceti, which rose with 6 Aries.

[4]The famous *garum*, a fish-flavored sauce that was much used in Roman cookery.

[5]Deneb Kaitos set with 29 Aquarius.

[6]The constellation Ursa Major or the Big Dipper as we call it. Being circumpolar and consequently always above the horizon (in northern latitudes), it cannot rise or set.

[7]The constellation Draco.

[8]The constellations Ursa Major and Ursa Minor.

was born with this constellation rising will be Marsi,[1] who are accustomed to prepare beneficial remedies from poisons and the pigments of herbs. But if this constellation is found in the DSC, they will perish struck by the bite of serpents, or surely by having drunk poison.

8. Lygnus[2] also belongs to a part of this sign. Those who were born with this constellation rising will be finders of metals who hunt for hidden veins of gold and silver with skilled searches. They will also be coin-makers. But if this constellation was found in the DSC, and Mars was in that same house, or in opposition or square, they will either be burnt up in their burning home or they will be burned by public sentence in avenging flames.

9. We ought also to know this—that if in that hour in which a birth is completed, there was either an earthquake, or if the sky thunders, whoever was born will always be unsteady with a trembling body, and who, with a doubtful tread and with hesitant foot-steps through all the moments of the hours, would expect and fear the collapse of overhanging roofs.

10. The eyes will sparkle for this one, and they have a horror of everything with a glowing edge, and they do not use words in a certain order, but rather a hindered sound of their voice whispers out a tremulous murmur—or with their jaws clenched—their words always fail to exit. They will always think it is going to thunder, always that there is going to be an earthquake, always that everything is going to come to a collapse, and, agitated by fleeting errors, they will lose the order of correct conversation.

11. These, my dear Mavortius, are the principles of the Barbaric Sphere.[3] This is learning from a Chaldean work.

XVIII.

1. Now I shall transfer the whole discussion to the following parts of the Barbaric Sphere, which emulates the *Myriogenesis* to some extent.

---

[1]A people of Latium who were reputed to be wizards and snake-charmers.

[2]In Greek *Lychnos* 'Lamp', apparently a non-Greek constellation of the Barbaric Sphere, whose location in the sky is unknown today.

[3]But this is a misnomer, since the constellations and stars mentioned in this chapter are mostly those known to the Greeks.

For whatever the *Myriogenesis* pronounces about the individual *minutes*, we shall make this [to say] about the individual *degrees*. And so the correct determination of the ASC must be made, so that the true degree obtained by careful computation may make the astrological significations to be declared faithfully.[1] But if it is [done] otherwise, all that which was promised will be overshadowed by faults and lies. Now, therefore, we shall set forth the individual forces of the degrees and their astrological significations according to the Barbaric Sphere,[2] beginning from Aries.[3]

XIX. Aries.

1. Those who have their ASC in the 1st degree of Aries, if there is an aspect from the benefic stars, will be born kings [and] generals, always leading the army successfully. Those who have the ASC in the 2nd degree of Aries will be stubborn thieves, and those who always prowl about with a perverted frenzy, transferring their own residence to foreign regions. But if with this degree in the ASC Mars offers his testimony, and, if it aspects the Moon by square or opposition, then having been detected in these crimes, they are punished by a public sentence.

2. Those who have the ASC in the 3rd degree of Aries will be deaf, one-eyed, and afflicted with a dull stupidity of silliness. Those who have

[1]It should be mentioned, however, that the classical astrologers were usually unable to determine the ASC degree with certainty due to their inability to determine the time of birth much closer than plus or minus a half hour. This alone would inject an error of 5 to 10 degrees into the determination of the ASC degree. Hence, by setting forth the significance of individual degrees, the astrologer might be able to rectify the stated birth time by choosing a degree that seemed more appropriate for the client.

[2]The Barbaric Sphere refers nominally to the non-Greek constellations recognized by the Alexandrian astrologers who invented Horoscopic Astrology in the second century B.C. But it seems that it actually contained both the Greek constellations and the non-Greek constellations. There must have been a star catalogue that gave the longitudes of the fixed stars in those constellations referred to the Alexandrian fixed zodiac, and that catalogue was used by the early Greek astrologers.

[3]In what follows the degrees are referred to the Alexandrian fixed zodiac, which in the year 2000 began at about 8° Pisces in the tropical zodiac. They were possibly based at least in part on the positions of the fixed stars in that fixed zodiac, as well as upon actual nativities. Hence, about 22° could be added to the figures given by Firmicus to reduce them to the zodiac in current use. Or 22° could be subtracted from current tropical longitudes before consulting Firmicus's figures. However, some astrologers may prefer to use them as they stand without any correction.

the ASC in the 4th degree of Aries will be thieves, who are killed when caught during their crime. The one who has his ASC in the 5th degree of Aries will rule over a great people, and it will indicate the greatest things, and he will be above all of his own people by the merit of his dignity. He will be just, virtuous, temperate, and one who keeps his national religions with the greatest veneration. But adorned with every commendation of goodness, he will die a natural death.[1]

3. Whoever has his ASC in the 6th degree of Aries will be a friend of kings and of the greatest powerful judges, adorned with the distinguished ornaments of dignity and carrying with him all the ornaments of fame. The merits of some art will commend one person; and another person will be in charge of military affairs; but they die a natural death. Whoever has his ASC in the 7th degree of Aries with the testimony of Jupiter will be an athlete, but with the testimony of Mars he will be badly hunch-backed, and he will die a violent death.

4. Those who have their ASC in the 8th degree of Aries with the testimony of the malefic stars will be athletes, but those whom the merits of their famous abilities ennoble. But, after many awards, these perish by a violent death. But if there are aspects from the benefic stars to this degree, they will be prophets displaying the greatest signs of divinity in their mind. Those who have their ASC in the 9th degree of Aries, will die a violent death in their first age.

5. Those who have their ASC in the 10th degree of Aries will be treacherous, irreligious, perjurers, but who will die in their first age oppressed by various illness resulting from bodily defects. Whoever has his ASC in the 11th degree of Aries, with Jupiter either posited in that same degree or conjoined to it by a partile trine, will be powerful, displaying the insignia of a magnificent dignity, one whom the trusty connection of friendship joins them to kings or powerful men. He will be a rich person, abounding in wealth, possessing a great extent of lands and possessions, a famous general loaded down with every honor of dignity, and decorated with fortunate testimonies of fame.

6. Whoever has his ASC in the 12th degree of Aries, with Jupiter and Venus posited in that degree along with the testimony of the Moon—or if the Moon makes a trine aspect to that same degree—will be distinguished, and decorated with the insignia of nobility; and he will die in old

[1]The phrase *morte sua morietur* 'he will die by his own death' means that he will die naturally.

age. Those who have their ASC in the 13th degree of Aries will be sterile persons to whom desired offspring are always denied. But these persons will die in middle age.

7. Whoever has his ASC in the 14th degree of Aries will be a business-man, but one provided with abundant riches, a money-lender collecting great reserves of riches from public banking—a person known to all and always famous. This place [in the zodiac] also makes weavers, or those who handle wool and fine cloth; they will die in old age. Whoever has his ASC in the 15th degree of Aries will be polluted by the shameless disgrace of lusts, and is always involved in indecent vices—a sodomite condemned by public scandal. But if it is a woman, the lust for a similar indecency will strike her.

8. Whoever has his ASC in the 16th degree of Aries will be tortured by continuous pains in his intestines, but he will die with these torn apart. But if it is a woman, the gift of life will end finally[1] in childbirth. Whoever has his ASC in the 17th degree of Aries, will be a hunter of birds, or a breeder of birds or wild animals. But if Mars provides testimony to the ASC, he will be torn to pieces by wild animals or by dogs, and he will die.

9. Whoever has his ASC in the 19th degree of Aries will be a mule-driver or a mule-herder; but he <will perish> from being stung by a small, little animal, i.e by a spider or by a sand mouse, or by a scorpion.<But if Mars makes a menacing aspect to the ASC> he will die <from being eaten by a wolf>.[2] Whoever has his ASC in the 19th degree of Aries will die in the first threshold of age.

10. Whoever has his ASC in the 20th and 21st and 22nd degree of Aries, if Jupiter makes fortunate testimony to that degree—or if Jupiter is located in that degree—will be rich and endowed with many and famous offspring of children, or he will be protected by the guardianship of many brothers. But the merits of faithful[3] friendship will unite this same person to kings or to powerful men. He will be a worshipper of the Gods, adorned with every commendation of goodness, a good person, benevolent, just, long-lived, fortunate in his old age, and one who dies a natural death.[4]

---

[1]Accepting Kroll's emendation of *extremum* 'finally' for *extremae* 'extreme'.

[2]Adds **N**, two lines having been omitted by **Ψ** due to homoeoteleuton (*...percussus* | *...comestus*).

[3]Accepting Ziegler's suggested reading of **fidae amicitiae merita* 'the merits of faithful friendship' rather than *fida amicitiae merita* 'faithful merits of friendship.

[4]Again, the Latin has 'he dies by his own death', which means 'by a natural death'.

11. Whoever has his ASC in the 23rd degree of Aries will be afflicted with strumae[1] [and] possessed with an ulcerated spot of blemishes, or certainly elephantiasis. <Whoever has his ASC in the 24th degree of Aries . . .>.[2] Whoever has his ASC in the 25th degree of Aries will be a goldsmith, a goldbeater, or a marble worker or a [worker] similar to those. Whoever has his ASC in the 26th degree of Aries will be timid, so that through all the moments of his hours he is terrified by groundless suspicions.[3]

12. Whoever has his ASC in the 27th degree of Aries will be a wool-worker, a silk-worker,[4] or a weaver. Whoever has his ASC in the 28th degree of Aries will always clean latrines and sewers, or he will be condemned to public work by a judicial sentence. Whoever has his ASC in the 29th degree of Aries will be a barber. Those who have their ASC in the 30th degree of Aries, i.e. in the end of the tail, will be insane, epileptics, delirious, [and] short-lived.

XX. Taurus.

1. Whoever has his ASC in the 1st degree of Taurus will be a prophet divinely inspired, but who is accustomed to prophesy in temples. Those who have their ASC in the 2nd degree of Taurus will carry out manure; they will clean latrines and sewers. Those who have their ASC in the 3rd degree of Taurus <will be farmers, ploughmen. Those who have their ASC in the 4th degree of Taurus>[5] will be celebrated actors who get the insignia of crowns in sacred games.

2. Whoever has his ASC in the 5th degree of Taurus, with Mars posited there or making a menacing aspect to it, will die from severe offenses. Those who have their ASC in the 6th degree of Taurus will be *exoleti*,[6]devoted to every vice of indecency—sodomites who practice

---

[1]These are swellings characteristic of scrofula or goiter.

[2]Adds edition **a** followed by the editor's own invention of the signification.

[3]Today, he would be called *paranoid.*

[4]Not 'a dagger-maker' as Bram translates. Prof. Monat has *ouvrier...de la soie* 'a worker in silk'.

[5]Adds **N**, one line having been omitted by **Ψ** due to homoeoteleuton (*...horoscopum* | *...horoscopum*).

[6]The word *exoleti* most commonly means 'grown ups', i.e. 'adults', but I believe that here it is either a corruption or else it must have some sexual connotation. It does not occur elsewhere in the *Mathesis*. Bram translates it as 'adolescent per-

irrumation,[1] but those whom a serious scandal always strikes. Whoever has his ASC in the 7th degree of Taurus will be a *haruspex*, an *augur*[2] a conjurer. Whoever has his ASC in the 8th degree of Taurus, after having advanced to new and unexpected honors, will die suddenly.

3. Those who have their ASC in the 9th degree of Taurus will be disgraceful, disreputable persons, dishonored by the stigma of all the vices. Those who have their ASC in the 10th degree of Taurus will be evil, malign, malicious persons, and who are struck by all the inconveniences of misfortune. But these will always die by a violent death. Those who have their ASC in the 11th degree of Taurus swell up in a body afflicted by malign humors, and they will die of dropsy.

4. Those who have their ASC in the 12th degree of Taurus will perish burnt up in fires. Whoever has his ASC in the 13th degree of Taurus will be in charge of athletes or will be the master of a wrestling-school. Whoever has his ASC in the 14th degree of Taurus will have a body possessed of foul odors, so that the miserable reek of a goat-like stench is always emitted. Those who have their ASC in the 15th degree of Taurus will be liars and devoid of all faith of truth. They will also be gluttons serving the lusts of the gullet and the belly.

5. Those who have their ASC in the 16th degree of Taurus will be persons defiled by every vice. Those who have their ASC in the 17th degree of Taurus will be blacksmiths. Those who have their ASC in the 18th degree of Taurus will always be slaves, persons of low degree, bakers.[3] Those who have their ASC[4] in the 19th degree of Taurus will be sterile, and those for whom children are always denied. But if Mars is in that degree, they will die either from falling from a high place, or from falling into a wet place or into water.

---

verts', and Prof. Monat has 'debauched persons'. Possibly it might even be from the rare verb *exoleo* in the sense 'to give out a bad smell' and mean something like 'smelly persons'with a reference to sodomites.

[1]Reading **irrumatici* 'those who practice irrumation' instead of *reumatici* 'rheumatic persons'. Ziegler agrees, saying it refers to *qui se inrumandos praebeant.* Edition **a** has *irrumatores, which amounts to the same thing. Prof. Monat keeps *reumatici* but translates it as 'lovers of fellation', which is less explicit.

[2]A *haruspex* was a diviner who inspected the livers of sacrificial animals, while an *augur* was a diviner who interpreted the flights of birds and other occurrences that were believed to be omens.

[3]But MS **N** has *pictores* 'painters' instead of p*istores* 'bakers'.

[4]*Habuerint horoscopum* **Γ**, *nati fuerint* **N** *habuerit horoscopum quicunque nati fuerint* **D** *habuerint horoscopum* **D**[2]

6. Those who have their ASC in the 20th degree of Taurus will be dishonored by foul indecency—sodomites serving their miserable lusts. But if this is the nativity of a woman, she will be prostituted publicly in a whorehouse. Those who have the 21st degree of Taurus in their ASC will die thrust through by a spear. Those who have their ASC in the 22nd degree of Taurus will be badly hunch-backed, ridiculous persons, and dying violently.

7. Those who have their ASC in the 23rd degree of Taurus will be hoarse-voiced pimps, sodomites, always defiled by the stain of scandal. But if the benefic stars are either in this place or if they aspect it by trine, they will be tragic actors, comic actors, [or] heralds.[1] Those who have their ASC in the 24th degree of Taurus will be musicians. But if the malefic stars aspect that same place, they will die a violent death.

8. Those who have their ASC in the 25th degree of Taurus will be fullers, or certainly barbers. Those who have their ASC in the 26th degree of Taurus, with one eye having been put out, will also be made deaf. Those who have their ASC in the 27th degree of Taurus will be pantomimists[2] or sodomites. Those who have their ASC in the 28th degree of Taurus will possess many things, having acquired boundless profits, [so that] a heap of riches comes to them. But in the latter part of their life they will be miserable.

9. Whoever has his ASC between the Horns of Taurus will be a king or a general. <Moreover, whoever has his ASC in the right Horn will be a prince or a general>,[3] great, famous, and terrible, and one to whom the naval command is entrusted, or one who leads the infantry. He will subjugate some cities and liberate others. But offspring are forever denied to him. Also, quite fortunate eunuchs will be born here, and those to whom the defense of the kingdom is entrusted. They will provide many things for many people. Images[4] along with titles are denoted for them, but afterwards, having offended the prince, they will die a bad death.

---

[1]Accepting Wikström's interpretation *ceryces* 'heralds' for the meaningless *ceruces* **AD** or *cerutes* **G**, or the emendation *truces* 'fierce persons' of edition **v**.

[2]The Latin word *pantomimus* means a pantomimist, who acted out a part on stage; but followed here by the word *cinaedus*, it probably indicates one who performed an obscene pantomime.

[3]Adds **N**, a line having been omitted by **Ψ** due to homoeoteleuton (...*vel dux* | *vel* ...*dux*).

[4]That is, statues.

10. The Ship also arises with Taurus.[1] Those who have their ASC here will be businessmen, always merry and cheerful. But if a benefic star was there, they will be powerful ship-owners. But if there is also the testimony of Mars and of the Moon, they will lead the army both through the sea and through the lands, being in charge of the cavalry and the foot-soldiers. But these persons will die because of the wrath or indignation of the prince. Moreover, those who have their ASC in the Ship, will be sailors, pilots, businessmen, or builders, or architects of ships.

XXI. Gemini.

1. Those who have their ASC in the 1st degree of Gemini, <if Saturn is found in that degree or if Saturn>[2] makes any aspect to it, they will be powerful, great, principal men of their own province, feared by their own fellow-citizens with the greatest horror[3]; but they will die from the greatest indignation of their prince.

2. Those who have their ASC in the 2nd degree of Gemini, with Jupiter posited there with Saturn,[4] especially if the Moon, full of light and located in a fortunate house of the nativity, applies to them, will be a general who leads the army of cavalry and foot-soldiers, [and] to whom the naval command is entrusted. He will subjugate very many people; he will see places [previously] unknown to him, so that the insignia of power will be given to him even in far-away places. He will indeed be just, pious, giving many things to many persons. Having begotten children, he will die naturally.

3. Those who have their ASC in the 3rd degree of Gemini will be priests, or princes or kings of the sacred ceremonies. Those who have

---

[1]But in viii. 6 above the Ship is said to arise with the 4th degree of Aries. And if the star Canopus or α Carinae is meant, it actually rose with 24 Leo. Perhaps this is the Barbaric Constellation called Ship, whose location in the sky is unknown.

[2]Added by Skutsch and Ziegler. Possibly a line omitted by the archetype due to homoeoteleuton (...Saturnus | ...Saturnus).

[3]Accepting Skutsch's suggested emendation *horror* in place of *honor*.

[4]A conjunction of Jupiter and Saturn occurred in early Gemini in 384 B.C. and again in 324 B.C. The signification would suit Ptolemy I Soter fairly well, but he is said to have been born about 367 B.C. The Seleucid King Antiochus I Soter was born around 324 BC (d. 262 or 261). However, I doubt that the Alexandrian astrologers would have tried to cast horoscopes for rulers born before the invention of Horoscopic Astrology in the second century BC. So, possibly a famous general born in 147 BC or 88 BC might have been the subject of this reading.

their ASC in the 4th degree of Gemini will be very attractive with exceptional beauty of body—those whose bodily beauty recommends them to kings, so that the desires of the king always glow with love for them. Those who have their ASC in the 5th degree of Gemini will be nobles and those elevated with a haughty spirit of arrogance.

4. Those who have their ASC in the 6th degree of Gemini will be divinely inspired prophets. Those who have their ASC in the 7th degree of Gemini will be in prisons, and overseers of guards in prisons. Those who have their ASC in the 8th degree of Gemini, if Mercury has its place in that degree, will be musicians; if Mars, they will be trumpeters. But these will die in war. Those who have their ASC in the 9th degree of Gemini, with Mars present, will be workmen, porters, weighed down by the unending burden of misfortune.

5. Whoever has his ASC in the 10th degree of Gemini will die of a pain in the lungs.[1] Those who have their ASC in the 11th degree of Gemini will be *hoplomachi*.[2] Whoever has his ASC in the 12th degree of Gemini, with Mars present, will die from the point of a missile; but women will die in childbirth. Those who have their ASC in the 13th degree of Gemini, with their belly inflated will die of dropsy.[3] Those who have their ASC in the 14th degree of Gemini, with Mars present, will die a miserable death from having fallen down from a high place.

6. Those who have their ASC in the 15th degree of Gemini will be bath-superintendents, [or] bath-attendants.[4] Those who have their ASC in the 16th degree of Gemini will be pantomimists, but those whose evident beauty of body always brings about their love by many. But they will have a soft and delicate body. Those who have their ASC in the 17th degree of Gemini—their beauty and size of body will make them outstanding. They will certainly be modest, and on account of that, friends of kings.

7. Those who have their ASC in the 18th degree of Gemini will be trainers of athletes, always assigned to service in wrestling-schools. Those who have their ASC in the 19th degree of Gemini, with Mars pres-

[1]This could be pneumonia or lung cancer.

[2]*Hoplomachi* were heavily-armed gladiators, or trainers of such fighters.

[3]Dropsy is an abnormal collection of serous fluid in some part of the body—in this case, the belly.

[4]These were attendants who poured water over the bathers. See also viii.25.3, where the same phrase occurs.

ent, will die by iron. But if Saturn is in that degree, they are weakened by perpetual labors drawing water. But if, with the Moon posited full of light in scaly signs, she applies to Mars; or, with little light to Saturn, those suffering from elephantiasis are made.

8. Those who have their ASC in the 20th degree of Gemini, with Mars present, will have the governorship of the people, and judgments affecting the people are entrusted to them. But they will die a violent death.[1] Whoever has his ASC in the 21st degree of Gemini, if Saturn is in the same place, and if the Moon is well placed, will be abounding in plentiful riches, noble, a friend of kings, the father of few children, or the brother of few brothers. But he will die in old age.

9. Whoever has his ASC in the 22nd degree of Gemini will be a singer who accompanies himself on the lute, displaying the greatest insignia of nobility from this; and one whom the connection of friendship binds to kings. Whoever has his ASC in the 23rd degree of Gemini will be energetic in valor, noble in war, and one whom the fortunate testimony of fame commends to everyone. But this one will die without children.

10. Those who have their ASC in the 24th degree of Gemini <will be couriers and those who are weighed down by the burden of continuous labor. Those who have their ASC in the 25th degree of Gemini>,[2] with Mars posited there, or aspecting it either by opposition or by square, will perish from having fallen down from a high place, or they will die from having been torn apart by wild beasts.

11. Those who have their ASC in the 26th degree of Gemini will be priests, *haruspices*, or prophets, but joined to kings by faithful friendship. But if Saturn is in that degree, it will make sodomites, but those who die because of the indignation of the king. Those who have their ASC in the 27th degree of Gemini will be temple-keepers and temple guards, or those who are assigned to duties involving sacred things, or temple slaves.

12. Those who have their ASC in the 28th degree of Gemini will be epileptics, insane persons, and short-lived persons. Those who have their ASC in the 29th degree of Gemini will be litigious, contentious persons,

---

[1]This and the preceding sentence are put at the end of Paragraph 7 in Bram's translation.

[2]Adds **N**, two lines having been omitted by **Ψ** due to homoeoteleuton (... *habuerint horoscopum* | ... *habuerint horoscopum)*.

who are always engaged in lawsuits and court actions. But if Mars is in that degree, or if it makes a square or opposition aspect to that place, then having been torn to pieces by dogs, he will die without children.

13. Those who have their ASC in the 30th degree of Gemini, with the Moon being in that degree, will be well-known nobles, but they will die placed in their first age. But if the ASC is on the last line of Gemini, and Mars is found in that same place, having been struck by a beast or by a viper, they will lose a foot or a thigh.

XXII. Cancer.

1. Those who have their ASC between the Eyes of Cancer[1] will be blind or one-eyed. Those who have their ASC in the 1st degree of Cancer, with the Moon located in that same degree, will be businessmen, or nobles; with Saturn aspecting, sailors, fishermen, inn-keepers, shop-keepers,[2] and those with occupations similar to those—always common and low-born persons. Those who have their ASC in the 2nd degree of Cancer will be famous for excessive power and nobility, violent persons who take possession of the property of others with crafty greed. They will certainly go through endless journeys, but they will die by a sudden death.

2. Those who have their ASC in the 3rd degree of Cancer will be hard-working businessmen not staying in [one] place. Those who have their ASC in the 4th degree of Cancer always attack their own enemies in every kind of way, and they are always made the winners in every struggle. Those who have their ASC in the 5th degree of Cancer, their eyes will be clouded by wounds from gravel.[3] Those who have their ASC in the 6th degree of Cancer, their eyes are always turned awry in their sight.[4]

---

[1]In *Tetrabiblos* i. 9, Ptolemy mentions the two Eyes of Cancer, but in the *Syntaxis* he does not mention them. We may suppose that the stars ν and ξ, which were at 16°20 and 19°20 Cancer were the Eyes. They are mentioned in the text below as being in the 8th degree of Cancer or 4 degrees farther along than the nebula Praesepe, which is said to be in the 4th degree. It was actually in the 12th degree, so that would put the Eyes around the 16th degree.

[2]The words 'and those ... low-born persons' are omitted by **Γ** due to homoeoteleuton (*...caupones* | *...ignobilesque*)

[3]Reading with MS **N** *calculosis vulneribus nubilabuntur*. It is uncertain whether this refers to an actual wounding of the eyes by gravel or whether it is a condition such as granular conjunctivitis or *trachoma*.

[4]The words *perversa semper acie vertentur* probably refer to the eye problem *strabismus* or squint, where one eye is perpetually 'turned sideways', or some-

3. Those who have their ASC in the 7th degree of Cancer[1] will have lumps on their head. But if the Moon applies to the ASC, they will be crafty, irreligious persons. But if Mars makes any aspect to the Moon and the ASC, they rage with cruel savagery as armed robbers. But they are either crucified, or they will perish in a public execution.

4. Those who have their ASC in the 8th degree of Cancer will be blind. This degree is between the Eyes of Cancer. The Nebula about which we have very frequently spoken is in the 4th degree.[2] Those who have their ASC in the 9th degree of Cancer will be sailors [or] pilots who guide ships through every sea with the control of a skilled master [navigator]. Those who have their ASC in the 10th degree of Cancer will complete everything with effective cooperation . . .[3]

[The significations of degrees 11-24 are missing.]

5. Those who have their ASC in the 25th degree of Cancer, with the Moon there or in aspect, will be advanced with every kind of good fortune. But those persons will defile themselves with debauches and adulteries; their youth is praised, but their later age is brought into disrepute. This degree denotes the same thing in the nativities of women . . .[4]

[The significations of degrees 26-30 are missing.]

XXIII. Leo

1. Those who have their ASC in the 1st degree of Leo will be hoarse-voiced, foul-mouthed pimps. This is also done in similar fashion in those degrees that are in the Mouth.[5] Those who have their ASC in the

---

times, as Bram translates it, they are 'cross-eyed'.

[1]The words 'will have—ASC' om. **Δ** due to homoeoteleuton (…horoscopum | …horoscopum)

[2]But there is some error here, because the stars identified in an earlier note were in 16 and 19 degrees of Cancer, and Praesepe or ε Cancri was in 12°40 Cancer.

[3]Here there is a sizable lacuna containing the degree significations of degrees 11-24. Perhaps a single page of the archetype was lost or was accidentally not copied. The editor of Edition **a** invented replacement text.

[4]Again there is a sizable lacuna, the significations of degrees 26-30 being lost. But the editor of **a** again supplied his own text to fill the gap.

[5]Presumably the 'Mouth of Leo' is the star in Ptolemy's Catalogue described as the star "in the opening of the mouth" or λ Leonis, which was in 23♋ 30. But this seems too far distant from the beginning of Leo. And in viii.4.5 above , the Mouth is assigned to degrees 6, 7, and 8 Leo.

2nd degree of Leo will be powerful kings. But whenever Mars or Saturn has come to that same place, grave battles of war are stirred up for them. In this degree there is the bright star about which we have spoken in the preceding [chapters].[1]

2. Whoever has his ASC in the 3rd degree of Leo will be a king possessing a double kingdom,[2] bringing many provinces into association by the powers of his own strength. But that same star also shows its rays in this degree. Whoever has his ASC in the 4th degree of Leo will be a hunter. Whoever has his ASC in the 5th degree of Leo will be a master or an anointer of athletes. Whoever has his ASC in the 6th degree of Leo will be born an athlete.[3]

3. Whoever has his ASC in the 7th degree of Leo will be a hymn-singer. Whoever has his ASC in the 8th degree of Leo will be famous and renowned for some skill if the benefic stars <aspect this place. But if the malefic stars> have done the same thing, they will be sodomites and pantomimists. But women [with this configuration] will be whores who sell their own honor for passive actions of lust.

4. Those who have their ASC in the 9th degree of Leo will be midwives, rearing the children of others. But if the Moon is in the ASC increasing in light, with the testimony of benefic stars, they will rear the children of kings or powerful persons. Whoever has his ASC in the 10th degree of Leo will be a general, [or] a renowned archer. But if Mars aspects the ASC and the Moon, they will be gladiators . . .[4]

[The significations of degrees 11-30 are missing. The editor of edition **a** composed his own material to fill the gap.]

XXIV. Virgo

1. Whoever has his ASC in the 1st degree of Virgo, if the Moon is full of light, or if it provides fortunate testimony to the ASC, will be conspic-

---

[1]Regulus or α Leonis that was mentioned in vi.2.2, although here the degree is slightly different; but in viii.31.4 the star is identified and said to be in the 2nd degree of Leo.

[2]That is, he will be the king of two different territories. See the note to viii. 31. 4 below.

[3]MS **N** inverts the significations of the 5th and the 6th degrees of Leo.

[4]Following this, there is a large lacuna, so that the rest of the degree significations of Leo are lost. Perhaps one or two pages of the archetype were either lost or not copied. The editor of **a** composed his own material to fill the gap.

uous with great fame; and then he will be [associated] with a king or with a queen, and made well-known by his literary merit, he will have power over many people. But if Mars has aspected this place, he will be a sodomite. Moreover, he will die in wet places. Those who have their ASC in the 2nd, 3rd, 4th, 5th, or 6th degree of Virgo will be handsome, priests, prophets, *haruspices*, conspicuous for their great fame, religious, powerful, and having the greatest insignia of divinity.

2. Those who have their ASC in the 7th degree of Virgo, with the Moon waxing or posited in the ASC, will be priests, *haruspices*, soothsayers, powerful persons, always crushing down their adversaries with the greatest authority. But if Jupiter and Mars aspect that same place, they will be generals, but those who lose when they are leading the army against the barbarians. But if Mercury furnishes his testimony, they will be in charge of treasuries, [or] they will be money-lenders.

3. Moreover, whenever Saturn comes to that place, they will be put in great financial straits. If Jupiter is alone in that place, all the insignia of good fortune are denoted. If the Moon increasing in light combines her rays with [those] of Jupiter, faithful ties of friendship will join them to powerful persons by the merit of their personal beauty. But if Venus is in that place, it will make women to be prostitutes. But if the ASC is under Spica itself, they will be bakers, but those who hold the first place among their colleagues. But if the ASC is only close to Spica, they will be unfortunate persons, wretched paupers.

4. Those who have their ASC in the 8th degree of Virgo, i.e. in Spica itself,[1] will be religious, just, conspicuous with great fame, adorned with abundant riches and who rejoice in the fortunate offspring of children. But these persons will die in advanced age. Those who have their ASC in the 9th degree of Virgo will be wrestlers, but those who attain the insignia of crowns in all contests. Those who have their ASC in the 10th degree of Virgo will be armed robbers, always soiled with unrestrained greed.

5. Whoever has his ASC in the 11th degree of Virgo will be an athlete, but one who attains the insignia of a glorious fame. He will be a rich man and the husband of rich women; but one who will die a violent death.

[1]Spica was not in the 8th degree of Virgo, but rather in the 26th degree, but there is a similar error above in viii.11.3, where it is said to rise with the 10th degree of Virgo. Perhaps some other star in the constellation of Virgo was mistakenly equated to Spica or α Virginis; or else the longitude was reported wrongly.

Those who have their ASC in the 12th degree of Virgo will be just, religious persons, winning the greatest insignia of rank. They will be prophets, or priests. They will be rectors of the great temples either of cities or of provinces. Moreover, they will have the greatest sorrows from the misfortunes of their children.

6. Those who have their ASC in the 13th degree of Virgo will be lute-players or hymn-singers. Those who have their ASC in the 14th degree of Virgo will be musicians. Those who have their ASC in the 15th degree of Virgo will be elegant persons who seek out sexual intercourse with virgins. They will have a defect in their thigh, and a thickening of the blood will frequently bother them with harmful humors. Those who have their ASC in the 16th degree of Virgo will be important persons handling many business transactions. But they will die a violent death.

7. Whoever has his ASC in the 17th degree of Virgo will be a gladiator assigned to public entertainments. Those who have their ASC in the 18th degree of Virgo will be fortunate and principal priests, learned friends of kings, and those who are always loved by women. But if Mars is in this degree or in the DSC degree, they will be punished by a public death because of a woman.

8. Whoever has his ASC in the 19th degree of Virgo will be an architect, a builder of walls, or a marble-worker. Those who have their ASC in the 20th degree of Virgo will be musicians, lute-players, singing songs with a sweet modulation of voice. But these will be among the clients of patrons, always procuring favor for themselves by the services of love. Those who have their ASC in the 21st degree of Virgo, that is in the outermost foot,[1] will be men who involve themselves in many kinds of business transactions. But judgments are frequently entrusted to these persons. Some of them will aim at friendships with judges.

9. Whoever has his ASC in the 22nd degree of Virgo . . .[2]

[The significations of degrees 23-29 are missing. The editor of edition **a** composed his own material to fill the gap.]

<Whoever has his ASC in the 30th degree of Virgo>,[3] which degree is at the last of the line, will be attacked by a Demon. But if Mars is either in

[1]This would probably be the 4th magnitude star μ Virginis, which was in the 12th degree of Libra!

[2]The remainder of this sentence is missing.

[3]Adds MS **N**.

that degree or in the DSC degree, then captured by pirates, they will be killed on the sea.

XXV. Libra.

1. Whoever has his ASC in the 1st degree of Libra will be adorned with a beautiful body and with the grace of amiable charm. But if Saturn is in this degree, he will be sound in his whole body. In the 2nd degree of Libra, there are many stars, of which some are masculine and others are feminine. Those who have their ASC in the masculine stars will be famous hymn-singers (to the Gods), to whom the secrets of the Gods are entrusted. But those who have [their ASC] in the feminine stars will be sodomites, always notable for their pleasing refinement.[1]

2. Those who have their ASC in the 3rd degree of Libra will be priests, just and long-lived. Whoever has his ASC in the 4th degree of Libra will be a lute-playing musician adorned with a sweet-sounding voice. Those who have their ASC in the 5th degree of Libra will be rich, affluent persons, but who are always involved in trials. Those who have their ASC in the 6th degree of Libra will be rich, handling great duties of business affairs.

3. Those who have their ASC in the 7th degree of Libra, with Mars[2] posited in that degree, will die a cruel death having been captured by pirates, or they are torn to pieces by large beasts. Whoever has his ASC in the 8th degree of Libra will be bath-superintendents [or] bath-attendants. Whoever has his ASC in the 9th degree of Libra will be a gambler, conspicuous in public recognition. Moreover, this degree always makes those strongly skilled in letters.[3]

4. Whoever has his ASC in the 10th degree of Libra will be a public sodomite, battered by scandal. But if this is the nativity of a woman, she will be prostituted to the passive desires of lust. Whoever has his ASC in the 11th degree of Libra will die of dropsy. Those who have their ASC in the 12th degree of Libra will be involved in legal judgments that are noticed by everyone. Whoever has his ASC in the 13th degree of Libra will be religious and just, one to whom public judgments are entrusted, and

---

[1]Reading *grata...urbanitate* with MS **N**.

[2]Mars-ASC om. **A** due to homoeoteleuton (*...horoscopum* | *...horoscopum*).

[3]This refers to individuals who are very skilled in reading and writing documents of any sort.

whom a king always loves with friendly affection. But this one will die naturally at an advanced age.

5. Whoever has his ASC in the 14th degree of Libra will be a sculptor, and one who makes images of the Gods with a marvelous splendor of construction. Whoever has her ASC in the 15th degree of Libra will be a short-lived queen without any children; she will die a violent death. Whoever has his ASC in the 16th degree of Libra will be a businessman, but one who always carries foreign goods.

6. Whoever has his ASC in the 17th degree of Libra, namely in the northern part, if the Moon well posited and full of light is moving toward the benefics, it will make literary men and royal secretaries, or those to whom the duty of dictating is entrusted,[1] and persons who are conspicuous with a great honor of nobility. Whoever has his ASC in the 18th degree of Libra will be raised up on a cross by order of the Emperor, or he will be tortured in the presence of the Emperor, or he will be hung by the Emperor's order, but only when Mars is found in that degree.

7. Whoever has his ASC in the 19th degree of Libra will be captured by a sudden assault of the enemy. Those who have their ASC in the 20th degree of Libra, namely in the northern part, will be physicians, well-known with a celebrated fame of skill. But if Mars is found in that degree, they will have actions [involving] weights and measures; but they will die without children. Those who have their ASC in the 21st degree of Libra will be short-lived geometers.[2]

8. Those who have their ASC in the 22nd degree of Libra, if Mars is found in that degree, they die a cruel death, having fallen or been thrown down from a high place. Whoever has his ASC in the 23rd degree of Libra will be either a king or a queen. But he will die by iron with many survivors left behind. Those who have their ASC in the 24th degree of Libra will be businessmen who carry foreign goods in ships. But if Mars is in that degree or in the DSC, they will die captured by pirates.

9. Whoever has his ASC in the 25th degree of Libra will be a blacksmith or one who handles things made of metal. Whoever has his ASC in the 26th degree of Libra will be a weaver,[3] but one whose mind is often

[1]Probably private secretaries to kings are meant.

[2]Probably, land-surveyors, or any occupation requiring a practical knowledge of geometry.

[3]The Latin text has *textor gerdius*. The word *textor* is the usual Latin for 'weaver'.

disturbed by insanity. Whoever has his ASC in the 27th degree of Libra will be a dealer in paints or a dealer in frankincense. Those who have their ASC in the 28th degree of Libra will be rich priests.

10. Those who have their ASC in the 29th degree of Libra will be religious, just, kindly, and embellished with all goodness. Those who have their ASC in the 30th degree of Libra will be liars, wordy, and filled up with an abundance of speech. But if benefic stars were placed there, they will be great physicians, travelers, and those dying violently. Those who have their ASC in Boötes will be divine astrologers, skilled in the Chaldean art.[1]

XXVI. Scorpio.

1. Whoever has his ASC in the 1st degree of Scorpio will be an enchanter who eases hidden pains with the power of words.[2] Those who have their ASC in the 2nd degree of Scorpio will be indecent persons, often defiled by the squalor of whoredom. Those who have their ASC in the 3rd degree of Scorpio will be dwarves, badly hunchbacked persons, [and] jesters. Those who have their ASC in the 4th degree of Scorpio will be dwarves assigned to the entertainments of kings or Emperors.

2. Those who have their ASC in the 5th degree of Scorpio, with the Moon well disposed, will be nobles, just, religious persons, furnished with a distinguished association by relationship. They will have many children. But they will have their means of life from teaching or interpretation. They will be royal secretaries handling the duties of correspondence. The faithful friendship of kings will ennoble them. Those who have their ASC in the 6th degree of Scorpio will be rich priests having many children. But they will frequently die from the anger of the king.

3. Whoever has his ASC in the 7th degree of Scorpio will die from [attacks by] wild beasts. Those who have their ASC in the 8th degree of Scorpio will be craftsmen. But they will die from having been struck ei-

---

The word *gerdius* is very rare in Latin. It was not found in classical Greek, but it was apparently everyday Greek for 'weaver'; as Cumont, *L'Égypte des Astrologues*, p. 87 n.1, says it is fairly common in the Greek papyri.

[1]This sentence is inappropriate here. The stars of the constellation Boötes rise with Virgo. And if catalogue positions are referred to, only a few mostly faint stars are in the early degrees of Libra.

[2]Possibly a practitioner of hypnosis.

ther by an asp or by a viper. Whoever has his ASC in the 9th degree of Scorpio will be a gardener [in charge] of gardens, always employed in agriculture. Whoever has his ASC in the 10th degree of Scorpio will die in his first age. Whoever has his ASC in the 11th degree of Scorpio will be a divinely inspired priest giving responses to Querents.

4. Whoever has his ASC in the 12th degree of Scorpio will be a temple-slave or someone assigned to the services of sacred things. Those who have their ASC in the 13th degree of Scorpio, with the Moon located in any angle, will be judges bearing celebrated insignia of dignity, judging on the sentences of other judges,[1] [and] having the maximum power of life and death.

5. But that power is [only] denoted for them from their 30th to their 35th year. But they are also allotted wives, and they will beget children. They will have climacterics and dangers in their 27th and 48th and 58th year; those dangers—if they occur in their 66th year—then they will die. But they will die from some bodily defect, or by the sword, or by iron, or by some force,[2] or suddenly. Those who have their ASC in the 14th degree of Scorpio. . .[3]

6. Those who have their ASC in the 16th degree of Scorpio will be bakers.[4] But if the Moon is in any sign with a bright star,[5] they will be judges with the greatest power of authority. But if Mars is found in dejected houses, they will be spies,[6] but their necks will be cut off with a sword Whoever has his ASC in the 17th degree of Scorpio will be a goldsmith, a gilder, [or] a gold-beater.

7. Whoever has his ASC in the 18th degree of Scorpio will die torn to pieces by wild beasts. Whoever has his ASC in the 19th degree of Scorpio, with the Moon well disposed, will be adorned with a great power of

---

[1]That is, they will belong to a higher order of judges. Perhaps like our Appellate Court judges.

[2]Reading *vi aliqua* with MS **N** rather than *in aqua* 'in water' with the **Γ** family of MSS.

[3]This sentence omitted by **Γ**; **Δ** has the sentence and indicates a lacuna (which would include the signification of the 14th degree and the entire sentence for the 15th degree).

[4]MSS **GN** have *pictores* 'painters' instead of *pistores* 'bakers. It is uncertain which reading is correct.

[5]Reading *in quocumque signo *cum clara stella*.

[6]**Δ** has *speculatores* 'spies' instead of *spiculatores* 'executioners'. Bram prefers 'spies', but Prof. Monat prefers 'executioners'.

good fortune; he will have the greatest power of life and death. But if Jupiter makes any aspect to the ASC, his power will also be such as may be compared to royal command. But in public affairs he will be too negligent. He will die from having offended his principal.

8. Whoever has his ASC in the 20th degree of Scorpio will be a general, a powerful warrior, who leads the army fortunately. He will have victories without number; his virtue and glory may be compared to royal commands. Exalted by too great an increase in good fortune, he will carry on by trying his command with a rebellious plan. He will be bold and rash, leaving behind sons. He will die from fire or from having offended the king.

9. Whoever has his ASC in the 21st degree of Scorpio, <in the first>[1] right foot of Scorpio will be a fisherman, but one who collects marine sponges. The one who has his ASC in the second foot will die from some wild beast or from a quadruped. Those who have their ASC in the third foot will be <gardeners. Those who have their ASC in the fourth foot will be>[2] sodomites, but women will be whores with their decency prostituted.

10. Whoever has his ASC in the first left foot of Scorpio will be a gardener; in the second foot he will die from wild beasts; in the third they will be barbers; in the fourth[3] he will be killed by pirates, or he will die from [attacks by] wild beasts in wet places. Whoever has his ASC in the 23rd degree of Scorpio, if the Moon, Venus, and Mars were posited in that degree, will be powerful, rich, and long-lived, for whom augments of good fortune in advanced age are denoted.

11. Moreover, he will have many offspring of children. Those who have their ASC in the 24th degree of Scorpio will kill their own brothers because of an instinct of greedy desire and the madness of parricidal fury;

---

[1]Added by Kroll and Skutsch.

[2]Added by **N**, one line having been omitted by **Ψ** due to homoeoteleuton (*...horoscopum erunt* | *...horoscopum erunt*).

[3]Here, and in the preceding paragraph, we have a clear indication that the author of these degree readings did not use the Hipparchus/Ptolemy Catalogue of Stars. For that catalogue does not mention any feet for the constellational figure Scorpius. Only legs and joints of the body are mentioned (aside from the forehead and the sting). But the image of Scorpius on the Barbaric Sphere evidently had four legs on each side, and in fact the image on the round zodiac of Dendera shows Scorpius with that number, so the Alexandrian catalogue may also have shown individual stars for four feet on each side of the body.

but they themselves will die a violent death. Whoever has his ASC in the 25th degree of Scorpio, if Mars is found in that very degree or is joined to it by opposition or by square, will be burnt up in a fire.

12. Those who have their ASC in the 26th degree of Scorpio will be orators, lawyers, or physicians, but those whom their talent in their profession will make famous. With the testimony of the benefic stars, a mission for their country will be entrusted to them. But they will die from having offended the king. Whoever has his ASC in the 27th degree of Scorpio, with Venus and Jupiter being present, will be rich, just, lovable, and long-lived, brought to the fore by the love of many women. But with the passage of time augments of good fortune will come to him. In his own country he will acquire the greatest augments of glory and dignity.

13. Those who have their ASC in the 28th degree of Scorpio will be squint-eyed, but the good grace of charm will adorn their squinting eyes. They will certainly be careless. But if Mars is in that same degree, they will suffer an outpouring of blood. Some of them will be [suffering from] elephantiasis; some will be madmen. But if the Moon, full of light,[1] moves toward Mars, ...[2] Those who have their ASC in the 29th degree of Scorpio will be learned lawyers. But if a benefic star is found in that same degree, they will be sent as legates to the military commander, and they will accomplish all of those things that were entrusted to them in their commission. They will get gifts, but they will have some defect in their genitals.

14. Those who have their ASC in the 30th degree of Scorpio will be Marsian[3] snake-charmers selling poisons for the murder of men, so that from that occupation they kill many people. They will certainly be liars, and evil, malicious persons. But if Mars is found in that same degree, they will be hunters, but dying a violent death. Adjacent to Scorpius on the right are [the constellations] Ophiuchus and Vulpes,[4] on the left Cynocephalus and Ara[5]. Those who are born in Ophiuchus will be bold,

---

[1]MS **A** has *plena* 'full', but **Δ** has *minuta* 'with little light'.

[2]MS **D** indicates a lacuna here.

[3]The Marsians were a people of Latium, ancient enemies of the Romans, and were celebrated wizards and snake-charmers.

[4]Ophiuchus (Greek for Snake-holder) and Vulpes (Fox), now called Vulpecula are Greek constellations.

[5]Cynocephalus 'Dog-headed' is a constellation of the Barbaric Sphere., probably the Baboon. One or more figures of this sort are seen on the round zodiac of Dendera. Ara (Altar) is a Greek constellation.

divinely inspired, knowing the future by a predictive inspiration of divinity.

15. Those who are born in Vulpes will be clever, fraudulent, defrauders, very wise, having their life support . . .[1] seeking from the cultivation of the earth. But if Saturn is found in this same house, they will be custodians of monuments. Moreover, they will die through trickery. Those who are born in Cynocephalus will be madmen, valetudinarians, childless, long-lived. Those who are born in Ara will be priests having their life support from sacrifices, but perjurers and perishing by a bad death.

XXVII. Sagittarius.

1. Whoever has his ASC in the 1st degree of Sagittarius will be famous, religious, just, and one on whom the greatest insignia of fame are conferred. But if a benefic star is found in this same degree, it will make kings or those close to kings, who complete all things effectively. Those who have their ASC in the 2nd degree of Sagittarius will be frenzied, perjurers, and sacrilegious persons. Those who have their ASC in the 3rd degree of Sagittarius will lose one eye in some way.

. Those who have their ASC in the 4th degree of Sagittarius will be custodians of monuments. Those who have their ASC in the 5th degree of Sagittarius will be impure, shameless, wretched, and dishonored with the stigma of disgraceful scandal. Those who have their ASC in the 6th degree of Sagittarius will be bowlegged with their legs wide apart,[2] and dying a violent death. Whoever has his ASC in the 7th degree of Sagittarius will be by name just and religious, and one to whom public judgments are entrusted, so that he will judge about the sentence of others.

3. Those who have their ASC in the 8th degree of Sagittarius, if Jupiter is found in that same degree, will be long-lived, and they will be the first among their relatives to beget children. They will be interpreters for kings, and master secretaries, handling duties involving sacred writings. But with the passage of time the insignia of good fortune will be bestowed on them; [and] they will die a good death. Those who have their ASC in the 9th degree of Sagittarius will be divinely inspired astrologers

[1]The Teubner editors indicate a lacuna here or else they would delete the word *quaerentes* 'seeking'.
[2]Reading *vatii tibiis *varicatis* instead of *vatii tibiis varicosi.*

and worshippers of the Gods. Whoever has his ASC in the 10th degree of Sagittarius will be an athlete [or] a *hoplomachus*.[1]

4. Whoever has his ASC in the 11th degree of Sagittarius will die struck down in war. Those who have their ASC in the 12th degree of Sagittarius will be involved in dangers. They will be rash, and persons who freely embark on every [kind of] crime because of a perverted passion of greed. Whoever has his ASC in the 13th degree of Sagittarius, while possessed by a parricidal <madness of rage>, he kills <his father>[2]; and he himself will die a violent death. Those who have their ASC in the 14th degree of Sagittarius will be lute-players and singers, devoted to the public pleasure; they will have a defect in one eye.

5. Whoever has his ASC in the 15th degree of Sagittarius will be a machinist who makes the necessary instruments of war; he will also die in a war. Whoever has his ASC in the 16th degree of Sagittarius, if Mars is found in that same degree, will die from having been lanced; but a woman will die in childbirth. Those who have their ASC in the 17th degree of Sagittarius will be athletes; if Mars gives testimony, they will be hunters; if Jupiter gives testimony, they will be horse breeders.

6. Whoever has his ASC in the 18th degree of Sagittarius will be a thief, a lying, malicious, ill-natured person; and childless, he will die a violent death. Whoever has his ASC in the 19th degree of Sagittarius will be a childless *pancratiast*.[3] Those who have their ASC in the 20st degree of Sagittarius will be dwarves, hunch-backs, and jesters. Those who have their ASC in the 21st degree of Sagittarius will eat a lot and will refuse foreign things.[4]

7. Those who have their ASC in the 22nd degree of Sagittarius, if Jupiter is found in that same degree, will be great men, powerful, possessing a limitless space of land, and those to whom [the commands of] both the infantry and the cavalry [branches of] the army are entrusted. Frequently too the naval command is entrusted to them. They will fight many wars; they will subjugate the barbarians; they will restore some cities and de-

---

[1]The Latin has *athleta oplomachus*. Again, the Greek word *hoplomachos* can mean either a person fighting in heavy armor or a trainer of such persons.

[2]Added by Ziegler.

[3]A *pancratiast* is an athlete who participates in *pancration*, a combination of boxing and wrestling—today he would be called a 'free-style' or 'universal fighter'. See viii. 8.

[4]Presumably, they will not eat foreign foods.

stroy others. They will have wives and children, but their wives will have defects or scars in their genitals. But these persons will die in battle in foreign places.[1] Those who have their ASC in the 23rd degree of Sagittarius will die from [attacks by] wild beasts in deserts and remote places.

8. Whoever has his ASC in the 24th degree of Sagittarius will be a trainer of horses or a charioteer. But if Jupiter is in this same house, he will be a royal mule-driver or charioteer, but one who acquires great insignia of fame on account of that [occupation]. But with Mars testifying, he will die a violent death. Whoever has his ASC in the 25th degree of Sagittarius will be an intoxicated drunkard, especially if Mars is found in that same degree. But if Venus offers her testimony, he will be a sodomite, but one who is condemned by public scandal; but women become whores.

9. Those who have their ASC in the 26th degree of Sagittarius will be dishonored by the contagion of vices, but the women will be shrews, whores, and devoted to every crime of passion. Those who have their ASC in the 27th degree of Sagittarius <will die>[2] in deserted places. But if Mars is found in that same degree, they will be short-lived, unfortunates, who will die of the plague.[3]

10. Whoever has his ASC in the 28th degree of Sagittarius will be an ass-driver, [or] a mule-driver, and one who is involved in continual labors. Whoever has his ASC in the 29th degree of Sagittarius will be a dwarf, a hunch-back, a captive. Those who have their ASC in the 30th degree of Sagittarius will be envious, and consumptives without any charm, but their death will be from [attacks by] wild beasts. But if Mars is found in that same degree, they will be short-lived [and] childless.

11. But if the ASC is <found>[4] in the last line of Sagittarius, that is above the tail, potters will be born; but if it is underneath the tail, they will be one-eyed, squinting, very fast runners, always subjugated to the powers of others, and unsettled in their blood.[5] They will have a pleasing face, and they will die from a quadruped.

---

[1]Cumont cites this passage in his *L'Égypte des Astrologues*, p. 211, where he remarks that very few names of the Ptolemaic admirals are known, so it is not possible to identify this particular individual.

[2]Adds **N**; the other MSS indicate a lacuna.

[3]Accepting Kroll's conjecture **qui de* 'who of' instead of *quidem* 'certainly'.

[4]Adds **N**.

[5]This perhaps means that they will have fluctuating blood pressure.

12. On the right side of Sagittarius, the Ship Argo rises, on the left side the Dog.[1] And so, those who have their ASC in that Ship will be skippers, pilots, businessmen, but those who sail to the west. But if Mars aspects this same place, they will be killed by pirates when they are returning to the east. Those who have their ASC in the Dog will be quarrelsome, noisy persons. But if Mercury is found in that same place, they will be lawyers of the best quality and friends of kings. But those who have their ASC in the Mouth of the Dog will be a person of a disgraceful life with a filthy mouth, but proud of the empty verbosity of his speech.

XXVIII. Capricorn.

1. Whoever has his ASC in the 1st degree of Capricorn will be a king [or] an Emperor. Those who have their ASC in the 2nd degree of Capricorn will be field commanders,[2] and those to whom the disposition [of forces] in battles is entrusted. But these persons will die a violent death. Those who have their ASC in the 3rd degree of Capricorn, if Mars is found in that same degree, but with the Moon placed with him, will be great, powerful persons, and having the greatest power of the sword, but who always exercise their decisions severely and cruelly. They will be cruel, clever, always bold, and those who kill many people. They will be leaders of a great army, but they will die in battle.

2. Those who have their ASC in the 4th degree of Capricorn, if Mercury is found in that same degree, it will make musicians or artisans, but those who pursue women with perverted desires of lusts. They will certainly be careless. But if the Moon is well disposed, it will make high-born secretaries, but those to whom the duties of great offices are entrusted. They will certainly be rich, just, and religious. But they will die in old age. Those who have their ASC in the 5th degree of Capricorn will be dishonorable and vile, devoted to every kind of lusts.

3. Those who have their ASC in the 6th degree of Capricorn will be afflicted with elephantiasis. Those who have their ASC in the 7th degree of Capricorn will be ingenious artisans, but those whom the excellence of

---

[1]These are not the Greek constellations Argo and Canis Major or Canis Minor, but rather the constellations of the Ship and the Dog on the Barbaric Sphere.

[2]Reading *ductores campi* 'field commanders' with **AD²N** rather than *doctores campi* 'field teachers'. Prof. Monat renders that as *maîtres de camp*. Bram translates it as 'army doctors', which is not right.

their craftsmanship recommends [so that they become] friends of kings. But <with the testimony of benefic stars>[1] in this place, physicians will also be born. With the testimony of malefic stars . . .[2]

4. Those who have their ASC in the 8th degree of Capricorn, if Venus is found in that same degree, will have the insignia of the greatest nobility. But if the Moon is well disposed, they will be doing many things, and they will handle all the duties of business. Some of them will be in charge of the public taxes. Those who have their ASC in the 9th degree of Capricorn, if Mars is found in that same degree, will die in their first age. But if Mercury offers testimony, they will be rich money-lenders; but they will die because of money.

5. Those who have their ASC in the 10th degree of Capricorn, if Mars is found in that same degree, it will make adulterers, but with the likeable grace of charm. But these persons will seduce the wives of their own friends with a perverted desire of love; but truly, never having been caught in that crime, [their adulteries] are not made public. The greatest life support is bestowed on them because of some [personal] skill; but they will be allotted wives known for adultery. They will die a sudden death. Whoever has his ASC in the 11th degree of Capricorn will be a goldsmith. Whoever has his ASC in the 12th degree of Capricorn will be an athlete of great prowess, [but he will] die a violent death.

6. Those who have their ASC in the 13th degree of Capricorn, if Mars is found in that same degree, will be those who will engage in every crime of cruelty for the sake of profit. But they will be Marsians selling poisons, who raise serpents with their fangs milked of venom.[3] Many will die because of them; they will be perjurers, counterfeiters, <adulterers, evil, malicious persons, or procurers of sex>.[4] With a refined voice they pleasantly recite the measures of poetry, deceiving all men with their false innocence; foul-mouthed, noisy persons,[5] who do not get any

---

[1]I have added *<*cum testimonio benivolarum stallarum*>. Alternatively (but in my opinion, less likely) we could read *Sed <cum testimonio malivolarum stellarum> in hoc loco, nascentur et medici.* 'But, with the testimony of malefic stars in this place, physicians will be born.' Thus combining and rearranging the two sentences.

[2]Kroll indicates a lacuna here, since the signification is missing; but see the preceding note.

[3]The Latin has *sopitis venenorum aculeis*, literally 'with their fangs of poisons lulled to sleep'.

[4]Adds **N**.

[5]These words are contrary to the first words of the sentence. Something would

joy from either their wife or their children. Truly, with the passage of time, they will be lame in their feet. But they will have their life support from commercial activities or from the public.

7. Those who have their ASC in the 14th degree of Capricorn, if Jupiter or Venus is found in that same degree, will be rich ministers of kings, to whom and to whose faith the defense of the greatest things is entrusted[1]; and they will handle the affairs of their own rulers among their own people. They will certainly be negligent, and those who enjoy many banquets. But if Mercury is found in that place, then advanced by their personal excellence, they will come to the notice and friendship of kings. Those who have their ASC in the 15th degree of Capricorn will be dwarves, hunch-backs, and jesters.

8. Those who have their ASC in the 16th degree of Capricorn will have six fingers [on each hand][2] and will be hunch-backs. Whoever has his ASC in conjunction with the Backbone and the Neck,[3] with Mars posited there, the Moon offering testimony and conjoined by a good aspect, will be long-lived nobles, parents of noble children, and friends of kings. They will die a violent death. Whoever has his ASC in the 17th degree of Capricorn <will die from a puncture of the spine.

9. Those who have their ASC in the 18th degree of Capricorn>,[4] if Mars and Venus and Mercury are located in that same degree or in the same sign, will kill their own wives, but they themselves will also suffer a public punishment. Whoever has his ASC in the 19th degree of Capricorn, if Mercury is found in that degree, will be a secretary always devoted to royal affairs. He will die in wet places, or he will die eaten by wild beasts.

---

seem to be missing before them. Bram adds the words <but they are really>. Or possibly, the phrase 'But if Mars is found in that same degree' has been omitted.

[1]The Teubner editors have *<quorum fidei maximarum rerum> tuitio credatur*, 'to whose faith the defense of the greatest things is entrusted'. MSS **ΓD** have simply *quibus tuitio credatur* 'to whom defense is entrusted. Wikström suggests *quibus <civitatum> tuitio credatur 'to whom the defense of cities is entrusted'*. But **N** has *quibus <et quorum fidei maximarum rerum> tuitio credatur* 'to whom and to whose faith the defense of the greatest things is entrusted', which I have chosen.

[2]This condition is called polydactyly. It occurs in a few births per thousand among whites, but it is much more common among blacks.

[3]These are presumably the stars θ, ι, ε, and κ Capricorni that were in 19°00-27°20 ♑.

[4]Adds **N**, two lines having been omitted by **Ψ** due to homoeoteleuton (...habuerit horoscopum | ...habuerint horoscopum).

10. Whoever has his ASC in the 20th degree of Capricorn will be devoted to records and public duties. Whoever has his ASC in the 21st degree of Capricorn will be noble, a friend of kings, and one on whom many things are bestowed from the imperial largesse. He will be loved by the people (truly, those insignia of dignity will be bestowed on him in the middle space of life), easy to anger, and one who expresses his angers with the greatest impulse of power. But misfortune will come to him from an accident to his children. He will die a suicide.

. . . .[1] [The indications for the 22nd and 23rd degree of Capricorn are missing.]

11. Those who have their ASC in the 24th degree of Capricorn will be sluggish in mind and sluggish in their senses, and they will frequently be attacked by insanity. Whoever has his ASC in the 25th degree of Capricorn will die eaten by wild beasts. Whoever has his ASC in the 26th degree of Capricorn will be a pantomime famous for his pleasing grace. Those who have their ASC in the 28th degree of Capricorn will be just and powerful, judging on the sentences of other judges,[2] and friends of kings. But for these persons the greatest anxieties of sorrow from the misfortunes of their children are denoted. Whoever has his ASC in the 28th degree of Capricorn. . . .[3]

12. <Whoever has his ASC in the 29th degree of Capricorn>[4] will be a cruel tyrant, ready for every kind of crime, subject to dangers, and rash, but one for whom death is brought about by many hands. . . .[5]

[The indication of the 30th degree is missing.]

XXIX. Aquarius.

1. Whoever has his ASC in the 1st degree of Aquarius, if Jupiter and Saturn together are found [there], or if they aspect the ASC by trine, and if the Moon is well placed, will be a king, great, glorious, long-lived, possessing the circle of all lands. But with the passage of time the greatest power is denoted for him. But he will die in water. Those who have their

---

[1]**N** indicates a lacuna here.

[2]Perhaps like our Appeals Court judges.

[3]**N** indicates a lacuna.

[4]Adds **N**.

[5]**Δ** indicates a lacuna here.

ASC in the 2nd degree of Aquarius will have an artistic skill that pertains to decoration or to pictures; they will die with sons surviving.

2. Whoever has his ASC in the 3rd degree of Aquarius, if Jupiter is found in that same degree, or if he makes any aspect to it, will be great, powerful, and possessing much land. But he will suffer the loss of his own inheritance, and yet the greatest foundations of wealth will be conferred on him through his own efforts. He will subdue his own nation, and he will be ready for every crime of cruelty, and one who rejoices in the slaughter of many men. He will also have sons from house-maids, but he will lose them at an early age.

3. He will certainly be separated from all sadness; [but] he will displease everybody; and he will withdraw from everybody, so that because of that all of his friends will avoid him. He will be gluttonous, taking much food, possessing much land. But with the passage of time all the insignia of power will be bestowed on him. But when he has entered the threshold of old age, he will cultivate his field with a weakened body. Whoever has his ASC in the 4th degree of Aquarius will be a worshipper of the Gods, just, judging on the opinions of other judges. But he will die a violent death.

4. Whoever has his ASC in the 5th degree of Aquarius will hang himself with a noose. Whoever has his ASC in the 6th degree of Aquarius will be weighed down with wretched labor drawing water. Whoever has his ASC in the 7th degree of Aquarius will be a noble athlete.[1] <Those who have their ASC in the 8th degree of Aquarius>,[2] with Venus joined to it by any aspect, will be long-lived, rich, just, and those who make progress in old age. But they will die with children surviving.

5. Whoever has his ASC in the 9th degree of Aquarius will be a builder, a sculptor, [or] an architect. Whoever has his ASC in the 10th degree of Aquarius, if Mars is conjoined [to it] by any aspect, it will make bath superintendents who will die in their first age. Those who have their ASC in the 11th degree of Aquarius will die in watery or damp places. But if the ASC is in the vertex of the Urn, they will be physicians. But if Saturn is conjoined [to it] by any aspect, they will be un-

[1]Rearranging the order of words in the Latin text of Vol. II, p. 348, lines 21 and 22. (the phrase 'he will be a noble athlete' cannot logically follow the phrase 'weighed down with wretched labor drawing water').

[2]Adds **N**, one line having been omitted by **Ψ** due to homoeoteleuton (...habuerit horoscopum | ...habuerint horoscopum).

dertakers' assistants[1] and undertakers, to whom all the duties of burial are entrusted.

6. Whoever has his ASC in the 12th degree of Aquarius will be a fisherman deriving his life support from the sea. Those who have their ASC in the 13th degree of Aquarius will be gardeners, or those who clean out sewers; but if Mars offers his testimony, bath superintendents; if Saturn does, drawers of water. Those who have their ASC in the 14th degree of Aquarius, if Mars offers his testimony to it, it will make divers or sailors, but those who will be weighed down with the task of all kinds of labor. Those who have their ASC in the 15th degree of Aquarius <will be hard-working workmen living in damp or watery places.

7. Whoever has his ASC in the 16th degree of Aquarius will be>[2] an indecent sodomite, but one who exercises this vice of lust secretly. Whoever has his ASC in the 17th degree of Aquarius, if Mars is conjoined to it by any aspect, will die from being lanced. Whoever has his ASC in the 18th degree of Aquarius. . . .[3]

8. Whoever has his ASC in the 19th degree of Aquarius will suffer pains in his lungs. Those who have their ASC in the 20th degree of Aquarius will die from dropsy. Whoever has his ASC in the 21st degree of Aquarius will be a goldsmith. Whoever has his ASC in the 22nd degree of Aquarius will be beautiful of face [and] attractive with a beautiful body, but he will die in his first age. Those who have their ASC in the 23rd degree of Aquarius will be rich dealers in paints.

9. Whoever has his ASC in the 24th degree of Aquarius, If Jupiter makes any aspect to this degree, will be handsome, attractive with a big body, [and] amiable. Moreover, if Venus is conjoined to it by any aspect, he will be the friend of a king, favored for the beauty of his body, [and generally] fortunate, but he will die in his first youth.[4] Those who have their ASC in the 25th degree of Aquarius will be sterile without children, always burning with erratic desires for love affairs.

---

[1]Those who wash corpses and prepare them for funerals.

[2]Adds **N**, two lines having been omitted by **Ψ** due to homoeoteleuton (...horoscopum erunt | ...horoscopum erit).

[3]**N** indicates a lacuna.

[4]And example of this would be the Emperor Hadrian's handsome favorite Antinoüs (c.110-130), who was accidentally drowned in the Nile. Hadrian deified him and caused numerous temples and statues to be erected in his honor throughout the empire.

10. Those who have their ASC in the 26th degree of Aquarius will have their life support from the cultivation of the land or from herbs. But these persons will be weighed down by incessant labors. They will certainly be long-lived and undistinguished. Those who have their ASC in the 27th degree of Aquarius will be *hieroduli* or temple slaves,[1] reciting hymns in sacred ceremonies.

11. Whoever has his ASC in the 28th degree of Aquarius will be gouty. Whoever has his ASC in the 29th degree of Aquarius <will be killed in desert places, torn apart by wild beasts.>[2] If Mars is found in that same degree or is conjoined to it by any aspect, cast down from a high place he will be made lame; but if Saturn is in aspect, he will die.

12. Those who have their ASC in the 30th degree of Aquarius, if Saturn is in any aspect to the Moon nearby, namely to the ASC degree, they will be long-lived nobles, but those on whom all the insignia of good fortune are conferred with the passage of time. Some of them will cross the sea because of some important business affair. They will certainly be without children; they will have their own step-children in place of children.

13. Beyond the degrees of Sagittarius there arise [the constellations] Falx, Lupus, Aquarius Minor, and Ara.[3] Whoever has his ASC in Falx will be a ploughman, who, while cultivating his fields, collects a great abundance of grain. Whoever has his ASC in the Mouth of Lupus will be a dancer; but with Mars testifying, he will be eaten by dogs. Those who have their ASC in that same Lupus will be deceitful, thieves, cruel homicidal persons, who strike down both their own people and others with the cruel atrocity of savagery. But having died a violent death, they will be thrown out unburied. Those who have their ASC in the Left Foot of Lupus, with Mars testifying,

[1]The word *hieroduli* is the Latin transcription of the Greek *hierodouloi*, which means 'temple-slaves'. Firmicus has simply given the Greek word and then a Latin equivalent.

[2]Adds **N**, one line having been omitted by **Ψ**.

[3]More constellations of the Barbaric Sphere: Falx is the Scythe; Aquarius Minor, the Lesser Waterman; and Lupus, the Wolf. There are Greek constellations named Thêrion, the Wild Beast (now called Lupus) and Ara the Altar. But Firmicus mentions the feet and mouth of Lupus, and the Greek constellation of Thêrion has a fore and hind leg but no feet or mouth, so the Lupus Firmicus mentions must also belong to the Barbaric Sphere. On the round zodiac of Dendera there is an animal above the figure of Aquarius, which may be the Wolf, and another smaller human figure between Aquarius and Pisces, which may be Aquarius Minor, the Lesser Waterman.

having been struck down by armed robbers, their feet will be dislocated.[1] Those who have their ASC in the Right Foot of Lupus, they will die as madmen in the first time of their life.

14. Whoever has his ASC in the Head of Aquarius Minor will wander about much while making his way through desert places, and he will be turned about in deserts.[2] Those who have their ASC in the Right Hand of Aquarius Minor will be masters of the horse. But if benefic stars provide testimony, they will be charioteers or mule-drivers for the king. Whoever has his ASC in the Belly of Aquarius Minor will be a gardener, a hard-working money-lender,[3] and one who dies violently. Whoever has his ASC in the Right Foot[4] will die in watery and damp places.

15. Those who have their ASC in Ara will have their life support from sacrifices; but they will die burnt up. Whoever has his ASC in the Outpouring of Water will be rich and a possessor [of property] from his first age, and he will demolish his paternal inheritance with various [kinds of] extravagance. He will be generous, but many people will frequently be ungrateful to him. But with the passage of time, he will have increases both in his personal property and in his dignity; and he will see his own enemies subjugated to him on all sides.

XXX. Pisces.

1. Whoever has his ASC in the 1st degree of Pisces will be a qualified postal inspector,[5] having his life support from royal funds. But this person will beget children by the corruption of his sisters or his relatives. Whoever has his ASC in the 2nd degree of Pisces will be a suspicious, jealous person of a screeching disposition. Whoever has his ASC in the 3rd degree of Pisces will be involved in indecent vices of lust and defiled

[1]Reading pedes *luxabuntur, since the phrase *luxabunt pedes* 'they will dislocate [their] feet' seems to be corrupt. But the verb *luxo* does not occur elsewhere in the Mathesis, so it may be entirely in error.

[2]This probably means that he will become lost.

[3]This combination of occupations seems to be discordant. Perhaps some words have dropped out of the Latin text.

[4]Prof. Monat has 'the left foot' by mistake.

[5]An officer in charge of maintaining the integrity of the Public Post, a service that provided transportation for official correspondence and also the transport of high officials. They were called *curiosi* 'inquirers' and held both investigative and enforcement authority.

in whoresome squalor—a person whose public life will always be battered by scandal.

2. Whoever has his ASC in the 4th degree of Pisces will be a sodomite with effeminate habits. But if it is a woman, she will prostitute her own modesty with a passive trafficking in lust. Whoever has his ASC in the 5th degree of Pisces, if Mercury and Venus are conjoined to it by any aspect, he will be rich, noble, long-lived, having his life support from some art. He will become familiar to the king, and, having advanced to a good old age, he will die well with surviving children.

3. Whoever has his ASC in the 6th degree of Pisces will die eaten by wild beasts. Whoever has his ASC in the 7th degree of Pisces, if Mars is found in that same degree, he will be torn apart by wild beasts, or torn apart in water by fish, and so he will die. Whoever has his ASC in the 8th degree of Pisces . . . .[1] Those who are born <with their ASC in the 9th degree of Pisces>, with Venus and Mercury present <in that same degree>[2], will be religious, just, long-lived, and handling duties [involving] documents. They will be royal secretaries, known to kings. They will die with surviving children.

4. Whoever has his ASC in the 10th degree of Pisces, if the Moon is well disposed and Venus is located in the ASC degree, will be a big person, powerful, known to all, connected with kings, traversing much land, sailing the great sea, in charge of Liburnian galleys.[3] Naval command will be entrusted to him; he will be superior in battle and a victor; he will have the greatest charm in love; he will be just and religious, but always impatient in sexual relations with women—a person performing great things and achieving everything. Moreover, he will die either from the wrath of the king, or because of his hatred. Whoever has his ASC in the 11th degree of Pisces will lose his genitals[4] from [the bites of] wild beasts in desert places, or in damp places; or he will certainly die a violent death in his first age without children.

5. Whoever has his ASC in the 12th degree of Pisces will be a mad fisherman, and he will die in his first age. Whoever has his ASC in the 13th degree of Pisces, with Venus and Jupiter being present, will be rich,

[1]The signification of this degree is missing.

[2]I have added these and the preceding additional words.

[3]A type of fast sailing ships used by the navy and also by pirates.

[4]The Latin has *naturam perdet*. Kroll would emend the text to read *vitam perdet* 'he will lose his life', but Bram and Prof. Monat and I prefer the MS reading.

noble, and having his life and his means of living from some art. But if Mercury is conjoined to it by some aspect, he will be a businessman, a dealer in paints, rich, and fortunate; he will die with surviving children.

6. Those who have their ASC in the 14th degree of Pisces will have the greatest insignia of dignity conferred upon them. They will die in watery places or in damp ones or by pirates. Those who have their ASC in the 15th degree of Pisces, with Mars being present, will go through the deserted places of earth, and they will sail through unknown seas. They will be tossed about, and they will always have their life aboard ship. Whoever has his ASC in the 16th degree of Pisces will be rich, long-lived, and always the first among his relatives.

7. Those who have their ASC in the 17th degree of Pisces will sing songs with sweet melody. But if Mars is found in that same degree, they will hang themselves with a noose. Whoever has his ASC in the 18th degree of Pisces will be bold, consuming much food, and sickly. Whoever has his ASC in the 19th degree of Pisces will be an orator, a lawyer, endowed with the eloquence of learned speech. But if a benefic star provides testimony, he will be in the royal household, controlling many things with the modesty and seriousness of his manners, always endowed with honest association.

8. Those who have their ASC in the 20th degree of Pisces <die strangled in their first age. Those who have their ASC in the 21st degree of Pisces will be fishermen laboriously plucking sponges; and they die in their first age. Those who have their ASC in the 22nd degree of Pisces>[1] will wander about <through many spaces of lands and>[2] through many nations. But if Mars offers testimony, they will be captives from their first age.

9. Whoever has his ASC in the 23rd degree of Pisces will be a bird-catcher having the means of life from birds. Whoever has his ASC in the 24th degree of Pisces will die in the sea. Whoever has his ASC in the 25th degree of Pisces will be a goldsmith, an engraver, [or] a painter. Those who have their ASC in the 26th degree of Pisces, with Mars and Saturn offering testimony, will be bath-superintendents [or] bath-attendants, sailors, and unfortunate persons; those who die a violent death, and those to whom the duties of organ mechanics are entrusted.

[1]Adds **N**, three or more lines having been omitted by **Ψ** because of homoeoteleuton (*...habuerint horoscopum* | *...habuerint horoscopum*).

[2]Adds **N**, still another line having been omitted by **Ψ**, this time because of homoearchon (*per multa...* | *per multas*)

10. Whoever has his ASC in the 27th degree of Pisces will be a fugitive wandering through many lands. But he will die from having been struck in the back. Those who have their ASC in the 28th degree of Pisces, if Mars is found in that same degree, they will die in damp or watery places, having been torn to pieces by wild beasts. Whoever has his ASC in the 29th degree of Pisces, if Jupiter and Venus are located in that same degree, and the Moon is well disposed, will be noble, rich through all time, [and] fortunate. He will die a natural death.

11. Whoever has his ASC in the 30th degree of Pisces will have his life in the sea; he will always be involved in laborious occupations. <But if Mars is conjoined [to it] by any aspect, he will be a Marsian, a mage, [and] dying violently.>[1] Moreover, whoever has his ASC at the end in the Tail, i.e. in the line that divides Pisces and Aries, will be a castrated person with his male organs cut off.

12. In the Northern Fish there arise Cervus[2] [and] Lepus; in the Southern Fish, Cetus, i.e. the Marine Monster. And so, whoever has his ASC in the Horns of Cervus, if Mars is found in the same degree, will be in charge of military arms; he will lead armies; he will fight abroad; he will die in battle. Those who have their ASC in the Mouth of Cervus will be Marsians, tracking and catching serpents, [and] dying violently. Those who have their ASC in the Feet of Cervus, wandering about much, they will die a violent death.

13. Those who have their ASC in Lepus will be skilled pilots. Those who have their ASC in the Tail of Cetus, if Mars is found in that same degree, will die torn to pieces by wild beasts. Whoever has his ASC in the Second Part of Cetus, with Venus and Mercury being present, will be subject to powerful persons, and by profiting from them they will acquire increases of life. Some will be slaves coming into great dignity from the honest and gentlemanly merit of their servitude. Those who have their ASC in the Third Part of Cetus will sail and circumnavigate many lands. But if Mars is found in that same degree, they will die from pirates.

---

[1]Adds **N**, one or two lines having been omitted by **Ψ** due to homoeoteleuton (…inplicatus | …biothanatus).

[2]Cervus, 'The Stag', is a figure of the Barbaric Sphere. See Boll, *Sphaera*, pp. 255-257.

XXXI.

In which Degrees of the Signs there are Bright Stars.

1. In the Sixth Book,[1] we said that in several signs there are bright stars, shining with royal majesty of light.[2] I shall, therefore, take care to explain what ascendants denote in those degrees in which the bright stars are found (which we stated about the Moon in the Sixth Book).[3]

2. In the 11th degree of Aries there is a bright star[4]; and so, whoever has his ASC in this star, with Jupiter there or conjoined with a trine aspect will be a great general, powerful, a friend of kings, possessing much and vast land, exalted by the honest testimony of fame. But he will die a natural death.[5]

3. In the Horns of Taurus in the 30th degree there is a bright star.[6] And so, whoever has his ASC in these Horns of Taurus will be a king or a general. But the one who has his ASC in the right Horn[7] will be a great prince, and one to whom the command of naval forces and foot-soldiers is entrusted, frightening and hard-working, freeing many cities from the besiegement of wars. He will be an only child without children. For him, public titles and pictures and statues are denoted, but afterwards he will die from having offended kings. The Sixth Book already shows you in which star of Taurus these same things are denoted <or that the Moon denotes these same things>.

---

[1]Book 6, Chapter 2.

[2]These stars are said to be in 15, 27, and 30 Taurus, 5 Leo, 7 Scorpio, and 20 Aquarius. And these were probably Aldebaran, El Nath, and Al Hecka, Regulus, α Centauri (or Antares or α Scorpii), and Fomalhaut (in Aquarius, not in Pisces), but if so, some of the degrees given by Firmicus are wrong. And the list that follows here in Book 8 is somewhat different from the one given earlier—perhaps taken from a different Greek source.

[3]The words in parentheses are omitted by Bram.

[4]The identity of this star is uncertain. Perhaps α Cassiopeiae is meant, it would have been at 13°10 Aries (adding 2°20 to the longitudes in Ptolemy's Catalogue of Stars, as I did in the notes to Book 6).

[5]The Latin *morte sua morietur* 'he will die by his own death' means that he will die naturally. The same phrase occurs in viii.19.2 above and elsewhere.

[6]The star Al Hecka or ζ Tauri, was actually on the tip of the South Horn of Taurus, as was mentioned in the note to Book 6. The star El Nath is brighter and is on the tip of the other Horn. See the following note.

[7]Firmicus calls one of these stars the "right" horn whereas in the catalogues they are called the North and South Horn. The Bull Taurus is generally represented as facing toward Gemini; hence, we might assume that the South Horn is the one on

4. In the 2nd degree of Leo a bright star is found.[1] Whoever has his ASC in this star will be a powerful king possessing a double kingdom,[2] but whenever Saturn and Mars come to that same star, the greatest wars are aroused against him.

5. In the 13th degree of Scorpio there is a bright star.[3] If the Moon, found in that star, possesses the ASC partilely, those who are born in it will be powerful, great persons having the power of life and death, and those to whom the greater part of the empire is entrusted.

6. In the 19th degree of Scorpio there is a bright star.[4] And so, if the Moon is well posited, [and] if the ASC is posited in that degree, he will be powerful. But if Jupiter is conjoined to it with a fortunate aspect, he will be the closest to the king, possessing divine honors, standing forth good, but negligent. Death will come to him because of the indignation of the king.

7. In the 22nd degree of Sagittarius there are bright stars.[5] Whoever has his ASC in these stars, with Jupiter posited in the same sign, will be great, powerful, possessing much land; he will lead the army, both the foot and the cavalry; but command of the navy is also entrusted to him. He will be a victor in all his battles; and he will subjugate the barbarians. But he will restore some cities and destroy others. He will have a wife having a bodily defect in the necessary parts[6] of her body. He will have surviving children, but he will die in battle.

8. There is a bright star in the 3rd degree of Capricorn.[7] If Mars is found in that same sign, and the Moon is well posited, whoever is born in it will be great, powerful, having the greatest power of life and death, but

---

the right. If so, then the star on the tip of that horn is Al Hecka or ζ Tauri, which would have been at 30°00 Taurus. And if the sequence of degrees that Firmicus mentions is approximately correct, then Al Hecka is the one Firmicus had in mind, since it is closer to the end of the sign than El Nath or β Tauri, which is on the tip of the Northern Horn.

[1]Regulus or α Leonis, which would have been in 4°50 Leo.

[2]The *double kingdom* may have been Upper and Lower Egypt, but see Cumont, *L'Égypte des Astrologues*, pp. 214-216, where some other possibilities are discussed, including the territories subject to Ptolemy VII Physcon (c.180-117 B.C) and Antiochus IV Epiphanes (c.200-164 B.C).

[3]Probably α Scorpii or Antares, which would have been in 15°00 Scorpio.

[4]This may be the star Wei or ε Scorpii, which would have been at 20°50 Scorpio.

[5]Presumably α Sagittarii or Rukbat and α Lyrae or Vega, which would have been at 19°20 and 19°40 Sagittarius respectively.

[6]That is, in her genitalia.

[7]Probably Altair or α Aquilae which would have been in 6°10 Capricorn.

he will be cruel, and one who rejoices in much slaughter; he will lead the army, and he will be talented, great, and bold; and he will die in battle.

9. In the 1st degree of Aquarius there is a bright star.[1] And so, whoever has his ASC there, with Jupiter and Saturn conjoined to it with fortunate aspects, will be a king [who is] great, famous, religious, just, long-lived, but on whom the greatest command of power is conferred with advancing age.

10. In the 10th degree of Pisces there is a bright star, namely in the Southern Fish.[2] And so, if Venus is found with the ASC in this star, whoever is born in it will be great, powerful [and] known to the king; he will travel through many lands; he will sail through the great sea. A warship and naval command is entrusted to him. He will be the victor in battles. He will be loved by everyone. He will be just, religious, inclined nevertheless to having sexual intercourse with women, responsible for many things, and obtaining better things. He will die because of the king's wrath or hatred.

XXXII.

1. To be sure, the Barbaric Sphere pronounces these things about the individual degrees. But a nativity cannot be wholly explained unless everything from the equated mixtures of the stars and their aspects has been compared—which as you recall we have very frequently said. For since the cold of some constellations is opposed to the heat of others, and the chill of cold is tempered by the flagrant fire of heat, a mixture of temperaments is also made.

2. And so, everything must be collected in accordance with the powers of the houses and the stars. For it is plain that a star is allotted the loss of its own power when it is located in dejected houses or when it is in its own humilities. And it is allotted its greatest power of denoting when it has come to the power of freedom of action—either from a house, or from its own exaltation. Moreover, the stars rejoice, just as we have very

[1]There is no bright fixed star at that location. The longitude must be in error.

[2]The constellation Pisces has a northern fish and a southern fish, but there are no bright stars in either of them. This then may refer to the 1st magnitude star Fomalhaut or α Piscis Austrinus, but it would have been in 9°20 Aquarius rather than in 10° Pisces. Perhaps the wrong sign was written down due to the mental association of Fish with Pisces.

frequently said, in the first place in their own exaltation, in the second place in their own terms, in the third place in their own domiciles.

3. Therefore, when all these things have been assembled by degrees, we ought to inspect the whole body of the nativity, so that, collecting the fates of men from the powers of all the stars—whatever was decreed—we are able to explain those fates with true statements.

XXXIII.

1. Receive, therefore, my dear Mavortius, that which with the greatest trepidation of mind we promised you—these seven Books—composed according to the order and number of the seven stars. For the First Book only received an advocacy of defense; but in the rest of the Books we have handed down to the Romans the learning of a new science..

2. But you—having agreed to the preceding admonition, and reminded by the religious authority of an oath—should guard these Books with a pure spirit and a pure mind, lest the knowledge of this work be disclosed to unskilled ears and sacrilegious spirits. From the beginning it has wanted itself to be kept secret and hidden, but the nature of divinity has hidden itself by means of these and [even] more concealments of things, lest they should be easy of access; nor should it have been exposed to everyone by the revealed origin of its own majesty.

3. This too it would be fitting for us to do in these Books, so that the reading of them may explain things to religious persons, [but] it should always be denied to profane and sacrilegious persons, lest we dishonor the venerable comments of the ancients in a way with sacrilegious editions. And therefore, hand them down to your sons, because you have instructed them from their first age in every duty of virtue; and hand them down to your friends—but to those whom the faithful necessity of love joins to you, to those whom you know copy the examples of your own virtue.

4. It is sufficient that for you alone we have performed the composition of these Books, which we entrust to you. You, the faithful interpreter, you the religious high priest, you alone by the merit of your virtues will be able to adorn that which we have completed with watchful care and labor—equally of mind and body—with the greatest anxiety and trepidation.

[The translation was finished at 2:42 PM Sunday 13 August 2006]

APPENDIX 1.
THE ALDINE VERSION OF THE SIGNS OF THE ZODIAC

Book II, Chapter 12 (16).

Here I give a translation of the Aldine version of the chapter on the Signs of the Zodiac to show what the editor Pescennius Franciscus Niger added. The words of Firmicus that he does include are shown in bold in the sections on the signs Aries and Pisces. The words that are not in bold are that editor's own additions. And everything in the sections about Taurus through Aquarius is his own addition, since the Latin text that has come down to us lacks them (possibly some leaves had fallen out of the archetype, or its scribe had accidentally failed to copy some leaves of his exemplar).

The Natures, Forms, and Qualities of the Signs.

We have spoken about the boundary and the kinds of the signs; **now, we ought to explain about their nature, forms**, and qualities, subject to *anaforas*, **so that we may explain the entire knowledge of this art** to you **with the clearest explanations**.

♈ is a sign in the *Caelum* that is masculine, equinoctial, regal, hot, strong, truthful, **quadrupedal**, semi-**bodied, with feeble eyes, erratic, which by the Greeks is called** *κριός*, **untamed, vocal, odd**,[1] **lustful; the domicile of Mars**, the detriment of Venus, **the exaltation of the Sun around the 19th degree, the fall of Saturn around the 20th degree**,[2] **the triplicity by day of the Sun, by night of Jupiter**. Moreover, it is for this reason **said to be equinoctial, because in this sign** the Sun **ar-**

[1]The text has *impurum* 'indecent', but this is probably a mistake for *impar* 'odd', as of an *odd* number.

[2]Firmicus has the 19th degree, but Dorotheus has the 21st degree.

ranges the hours of night and day with equal moderation, and therefore **by the Greeks it is called *τροπικον ισημεριον*,**[1] **for when the Sun is in Aries, it arranges the diurnal and nocturnal hours equally**, namely **so that the day has 12 hours and the night also 12 hours**; moreover, **it is therefore called *κυριος*[2] by the Greeks, because when the Sun is in it, it judges between day and night, which is called *κρινειν*,**[3] **and because in this sign, placed between winter and summer, it will again be judged. But it is said to be tropical for the reason that with the Sun located in this sign, it makes the spring time. For spring begins then when the Sun has entered the first degree of this sign. Finally, it is said to be hot for this reason—because whoever** has this sign in his ASC is inclined to fire and a choleric nature. Moreover, this sign is placed in the wind Aquilo.

♉ is a sign in the *Caelum* that is feminine, northern, of earth, melancholic, fixed, single-bodied, quadrupedal, tame,[4] defective, of few children, lustful, of little voice, flourishing in the south, oblique, heavy, single-minded,[5] even,[6] irrational, handy, and with cut-off members. The domicile of Venus, the detriment of Mars, the exaltation of the Moon around the 3rd degree, the triplicity by day of Venus, by night of the Moon. Moreover, this sign is placed in the Southern wind; it also signifies a bitter flavor, a green and white color, quadrupedal animals, those with cleft hooves, the fifth clime, cultivated lands, moderate men; and all illness of the neck.

♊ is a sign in the *Caelum* that is masculine, common, bicorporeal, bipedal, rational, with a beautiful voice, sterile, flourishing in the west, intermediate between light and heavy, of dual purposes, odd, northern, getting and losing; the domicile of Mercury, the detriment of Jupiter, the triplicity by day of Saturn, by night of Mercury; moreover, this sign is placed in the *Subsolanus* wind[7]; it also signifies a sweet flavor, a mixed color and temperament, rational animals, also apes and all birds of omen. The sixth clime, but all elevated places and sunny ones where fowling is

---

[1]*tropicon isemerinon.*

[2]*Crios.*

[3]crinein Kroll *criminon* **A**

[4]Latin *domesticum* 'domestic' or 'tame', since the opposite in this text is *silvestre* 'of the forest', but rather 'wild'.

[5]Latin *unius nogocii*, lit. 'of a single business'.

[6]As of an *even* number, since it is the second sign.

[7]The East wind.

practiced. Principals too, and astronomers; and all annoying illnesses of the shoulders.

♋ is a sign in the *Caelum* that is feminine, mobile, half-bodied, irrational, many-footed, wild, voiceless, defective, of many children, nocturnal, flourishing in the north, of water, phlegmatic, single-minded, intermediate between light and heavy, even, northern, solstitial, shipwrecked, lying, and weak; the domicile of the Moon, the detriment of Saturn, the exaltation of Jupiter around the 15th degree, the fall of Mars around the 28th degree; the triplicity by day of Venus, by night of Mars,. Moreover, this sign is placed in the *Afric*[1] wind; it also signifies a sharp and salty flavor, a white and whitish color, aquatic animals and serpents, the seventh clime, swampy places or those with flowing water, moderate men; and all illnesses of the heart and the midriff.

♌ is a sign in the *Caelum* that is masculine, fixed, single-bodied, quadrupedal, irrational, intermediate between tame and wild, lustful, flourishing in the east, of fire, choleric, of medium voice, light, single-minded, odd, diurnal, northern, direct, truthful, strong; the domicile of the Sun, the detriment of Saturn, the triplicity by day of the Sun, by night of Jupiter. Moreover, this sign is placed in the Northern wind. It also signifies a bitter and sharp flavor, a yellow color and one inclining to reddish, wild animals, and ferocious ones, the fifth clime, but all worthy places, those of difficult ascent, and castles, grand and royal buildings. Also, princes, dukes, powerful and rich men; and all illnesses of the chest and stomach.

♍ is a sign in the *Caelum* that is feminine, common, bicorporeal, rational, bipedal, of a beautiful voice, winged, sterile, flourishing in the south, heavy, of dual purposes, of earth, melancholic, even, northern, honest, beautiful, generous, handy, direct, nocturnal, lying, and feeble[2]; the domicile of Mercury, the detriment of Jupiter, the exaltation of Mercury around the 15th degree, the triplicity by day of Venus, by night of the Moon. This sign is placed in the Southern wind. It also signifies an astringent flavor, a white, purple, and whitish color, rational animals, and birds, the fifth clime, all cultivated and blooming places. Wise men, industrious ones, and jokesters; and all illnesses and sufferings of the belly.

♎ is a sign in the *Caelum* that is masculine, mobile, half-bodied, ratio-

[1]The South-west wind.

[2]Latin *ebileque*, a mistake for *flebileque* 'feeble'. Cf. the same phrase in the section for Scorpio.

nal, tame, bipedal, of a beautiful voice, of few children, flourishing in the west, intermediate between light and heavy, of air, bloody, single-minded, odd, southern, equinoctial, direct, diurnal, strong, and truthful; the domicile of Venus, the detriment of Mars, the exaltation of Saturn around the 20th degree,[1] the fall of the Sun around the 19th degree, the triplicity by day of Saturn, by night of Mercury. The sign is placed in the *Subsolanus* wind. It also signifies a sweet flavor, a green and a whitish color, flying creatures and especially big ones, the fifth clime, all places sown and cultivated on the summit of mountains. Also, merchants, and judges, also divines, and obliging men; and all illness of the kindneys and the vertebrae.

♏ is a sign in the *Caelum* that is feminine, fixed, single-bodied, irrational, wild, many footed, of many children, voiceless, flourishing in the north, of water, phlegmatic, single-minded, even, southern, direct, nocturnal, heavy, lying and weak; the domicile of Mars, the detriment of Venus, the fall of the Moon around 3 degrees, the triplicity by day of Venus, by night of Mars. Moreover, this sign is placed in the *Afric* wind. It also signifies a salty and insipid flavor, the color green, red, and whitish, reptilian and venomous animals, similarly sea creatures, and water creatures, the third clime, sometimes gardening and horticultural places, but sometimes stinking and deserted ones, also physicians, but false and unlearned ones, and moderate men; and all illnesses of the genitals.

♐ is a sign in the *Caelum* that is masculine, common, bicorporeal, of which the first part is rational, and the other is irrational, of beautiful voice, quadrupedal, lustful, of few children, flourishing in the east, but its second part is one of diminished voice, with plague, of fire, choleric, strong, of dual purposes, odd, southern, direct, diurnal, truthful, partly tame, partly wild; the domicile of Jupiter, the detriment of Mercury, the triplicity by day of the Sun, by night of Jupiter. Moreover, this sign is placed in the Northern wind. It also signifies a bitter flavor, a red or yellow color, rational animals, also horses, birds, and serpents, the second clime, all well-watered places, mountains, and gardens, and whatever contains any delightfulness in itself. Judges, especially worshippers of God, wretched men, interpreters of dreams, and prophets; and all illnesses of the thighs.

♑ is a sign in the *Caelum* that is feminine, mobile, half-bodied, irratio-

[1]Dorotheus has the 21st degree.

nal, quadrupedal, tame, defective, of few children, chaste, of diminished voice, oblique, of earth, melancholic, flourishing in the south, heavy, single-minded, even, southern, solstitiale, handy, nocturnal, lying, and weak; the domicile of Saturn, the detriment of the Moon, the exaltation of Mars around the 28th degree, the fall of Jupiter around the 15th degree, the triplicity by day of Venus, by night of the Moon. Moreover, this sign is placed in the Southern wind, it also signifies a bitter flavor and an astringent one, the color black or whitish, quadrupedal animals, and a part of the aquatic ones, the first clime, gardening places and watered ones, and springs, and rivers, sometimes also pastures, animal pens, also the domiciles of ignoble men. But men who are common and of low degree, but some of deep intellect, and melancholics; and all illnesses and pains in the knees.

♒ is a sign in the *Caelum* that is masculine, fixed, single-bodied, rational, bipedal, of a beautiful voice, of few children, flourishing in the west, intermediate between light and heavy, odd, single-minded, southern, oblique diurnal, truthful, strong, of air, and bloody; the domicile of Saturn, the detriment of the Sun, the triplicity by day of Saturn, by night of Mercury. Moreover, this sign is placed in the *Subsolanus* wind. Also, it signifies a sweet flavor, the color green, citron, and whitish, rational animals, and creatures of the air. The fourth clime, places with flowing water, and standing water, springs, seas, lakes, and mountains. Also princes, clever, crafty, shape-shifters, prophets, especially mages, sophists, oracles too, and archivists, or dispatch-runners, and those who announce the business of princes; and all annoying illnesses and pains in the shin-bones.

♓ is a sign in the *Caelum* **that is duplex, moist, watery, double-bodied,** fertile, **scaly, spotted, bent, mute**, common. **But one ♓ bears to the south**, the other to the north. **Moreover, it is the domicile of Jupiter**, the detriment of Mercury, **the triplicity by day of Venus, by night of Mars, the exaltation of Venus around the 27th degree, the fall of Mercury around the 15th degree. Moreover, this sign is placed in the Afric wind**. The seventh clime, ruined places and moist ones, also fishermen and sailors; and all illness of the feet.

[translated 4-2-2006]

APPENDIX 2.

Rhetorius's Secondary Significations of the Moon in Houses 4 to 9, as given in his *Astrological Compendium*,[1] Chapter 57.

4th House

The Moon [being] there in sect makes the mother honored, and it increases the Native's standard of living; but out of sect it makes the mothers low-born but wealthy; and they become involved in exchange,[2] if indeed the Sun is not in the ASC. But if the Sun is in the ASC, they are thought worthy of praise and presidency and sovereignty or of a kingdom, with Saturn or Mars by day and also by night with the Sun moreover being absent from the ASC.[3]

5th House

The Moon there by night will be most gracious. For she makes leaders, fortunate, illustrious, presidents, [and] those having good things from their parents, if indeed she is not aspected by Saturn or Mars. But by day she denotes foreign travel, estrangement of parents or orphanhood, but with the passage [of time] [the Native] will become fortunate.

6th House

[The influence of the Moon in the 6th house is missing.]

---

[1]See my translation, Rhetorius the Egyptian, *Astrological Compendium* (Tempe, Az.: A.F.A., Inc., 2009).

[2]Literally, 'in giving and taking', or 'selling and buying', referring to some sort of business transaction.

[3]The last part of this sentence appears muddled. MSS **A** & **V** have 'with the Sun either in the ASC or absent [from it]'.

7th House

The Moon there by day [makes] foreign travel and dangers either from wet places or from robbers or who are ill-treated by slaves or sickly persons, especially if it is also joined to a malefic, for then the evils become unavoidable. The Moon [there] by night makes changes of place and foreign travel and increases in assets with the passage of time.

8th House

[The influence of the Moon in the 8th house is missing.]

9th House

The Moon in the 9th by night [makes] notable persons who live abroad; some of them benefit [in some way] from the temples of the Gods, some others are entrusted with the business affairs of women, good businessmen, god-fearing. But by day [it makes] inglorious persons who live abroad, having their lives [disturbed] by wandering and dangers; some of them too dwell ingloriously in temples or [they are] temple-servants or those devoted to the Gods and those who confess, especially if Mars and Saturn are in aspect.

APPENDIX 3.
TABLE OF THE FIXED STARS MENTIONED BY FIRMICUS

Deg.	*Text*	*Text Name*	*Star Name*	*Cat. Name*	*Ptolemaic* Long.*	*True Long.†*
4 ♈	viii.6.1	Ship	(unidentified)			
10 ♈	viii.6.2	Orion	(unidentified)			
11 Ari	viii.31.2	Bright Star	Hamal	α Ari	13♈ 00	13♈ 03
			Schedir	α Cas	13♈ 10	13♈ 25
15 ♈	viii.6.3	Auriga	Capella	α Aur	27♉ 20	25♉ 02
20 ♈	viii.6.4	Haedus		ζ Aur	24♉ 20	24♉ 04
				η Aur	24♉ 30	24♉ 52
27 ♈	viii.6.6	Hyades	Prima Hyadum	γ Tau	11♉ 20	11♉ 09
30 ♈	viii.6.7	Goat	Capella	α Aur	27♉ 20	25♉ 02
6 ♉	viii.7.1	Pleaides	Alcyone	η Tau	6♉ 25	5♉ 25
15 Tau	vi.2.3	Royal Star	Aldebaran	α Tau	15♉ 00	15♉ 11
27 Tau	vi.2.3	Royal Star	Capella	α Aur	27♉ 20	25♉ 02
			El Nath	β Tau	28♉ 00	25♉ 45
30 Tau	vi.2.3, viii.31.3	Royal Star	Al Hecka	ζ Tau	30♉ 00	27♉ 58
7 ♊	viii.8.1	Lepus	Arneb	α Lep	28♉ 10	27♉ 16
1 ♋	viii.9.1	Iugulae	Alnilam	ε Ori	29♉ 40	28♉ 52
27 ♋	viii.9.3	Procyon	Procyon	α CMi	1♋ 30	1♋ 34
1 ♌	viii.10,1	Sirius	Sirius	α CMa	20♊ 00	19♊ 53
2 Leo	viii.31.4	Bright Star	Regulus	α Leo	4♌ 50	5♌ 23
5 Leo	vi.2.1	Royal Star	Regulus	α Leo	4♌ 50	5♌ 23
30 ♌	viii.10.5	Crater	Alkes	α Cra	28♌ 30	29♌ 32
5 ♍	viii.11.1	Corona	Alphecca	α CrB	17♎ 00	17♎ 24
10 ♍	viii.11.3	Spica	Spica	α Vir	29♍ 00	29♍ 17
8 ♎	viii.12.1	Sagitta		γ Sge	12♑ 30	12♑ 33
15 ♎	viii.12.3	Haedus	(unidentified)			
1 ♏	viii.13.1	Ara		α Ara	28♏ 40	0♐ 23
7 Sco	vi.2.6	Royal Star	Antares	α Sco	15♏ 00	15♏ 12
12 ♏	viii.13.3	Centaurus	Rigel Kentaurus	α Cen	10♏ 40	7♏ 55
13 Sco	viii.31.5	Bright Star	Antares	α Sco	15♏ 00	15♏ 12

19 Sco	viii.31.6	Bright Star	Wei	ε Sco	20♏50	18♏51
5 ♐	viii.14.1	Arcturus	Arcturus	α Boo	29♍20	29♍40
10 ♐	viii.13.3	Cygnus	Deneb	α Cyg	11♒30	11♒11
22 Sag	viii.31.7	Bright Stars	Lyra	α Lyr	19♐40	20♐35
			Rukbat	α Sgr	19♐20	22♐01
1 ♑	viii.15.1	Ophiuchus	Ras Alhague	α Oph	27♏10	27♏45
3 Cap	viii.31.8	Bright Star	Altair	α Aql	6♑10	6♑52
8 ♑	viii.15.2	Delphinus	Rotanev	β Del	20♑50	21♑49
10 ♑	viii.15.3	Lyra	Vega	α Lyr	19♐40	20♐35
15 ♑	viii.15.4	Cepheus	Alderamin	α Cep	19♓00	18♓43
1 Aqu	viii.31.9	Bright Star	(unidentified)			
12 ♒	viii.16.1	Aquila	Altair	α Aql	6♑10	6♑52
20Aqu	vi.2.3	Royal Star	Fomalhaut	α PsA	9♒20	9♒02
20 ♒	viii.16.3	Cassiopeia	Schedir	α Cas	13♈10	13♈25
10Psc	viii.31.10	Bright Star	Fomalhaut	α PsA	9♒20	9♒02
12 ♓	viii.17.1	Andromeda	Almach	γ^1 And	19♈10	19♈44
21 ♓	viii.17.3	Equus	Markab	α Peg	29♒00	28♒59
30 ♓	viii.17.4	Ingeniculus	Ras Algethi	α^1 Her	20♏00	21♏32
30 ♓	viii.17.5	Belua	Deneb Kaitos	β Cet	8♓00	7♓45
	viii.17.6	Septentrio	Ursa Major			
	viii.17.7	Snake	Draco			
	viii.17.8	Lygnus	(unidentified)			
30 ♏ ?	viii.26.14	Vulpes	Vulpecula ?			
30 ♏ ?	viii.26.14	Cynocephalus	Baboon			

* Ptolemaic Longitude + 2°20 (= Hipparchus Longitude + 5°00)
† True Longitude for 1 Jan 72 (= True Longitude for 24 September -128 + 5°00)

Notes:

1. 1. In the Degree column, if the sign symbol is used, it represents the stated *rising degree* of the sign; but if the sign name abbreviation is used, it represents the stated *longitude* of the star.

2. For the Pleiades I have shown Alcyone or η Tauri, which is the star in the middle of the asterism, and I have taken its "Ptolemaic longitude" as the mid-point of the figures Ptolemy gives for the two sides of the asterism.

3. In the case of 11 Aries, 20 Aries, 27 Taurus, and 22 Sagittarius there are two possible identifications, so two stars are shown..

4. Between stars rising with 6♉ and 7♊, Firmicus mentions the Hoof of Taurus. He does not give a specific rising degree, and Manilius does not mention that star, so I have omitted it from the Table.

4. Most of the degree numbers given in the Latin text are wrong—some of them very wrong. Evidently the Greek source was faulty.

APPENDIX 4.
TABLE OF THE PARANATELLONTA MENTIONED BY FIRMICUS

For Tropical Longitude of
24 September -128 and 31°12 North Latitude

Constel. Name	*Princial Stars*	*Longitude*	*Latitude*	*Rises with*	*Sets with*	*Modern Name*
Argo	α Car	15♊37	76S07	23♌14	27♈13	Canopus
Orion	α Ori	29♉09	16S19	13♊57	23♉31	Betelgeuze
	β Ori	17♉12	31S24	17♊37	8♉	Rigel
	γ Ori	21♉21	17S05	8♊08	16♉20	Bellatrix
	ε Ori	23♉52	24S47	16♊41	16♉18	Alnilam
Haedi	ζ Aur	19♉04	17N56	22♈58	25♉36	
Haedi	η Aur	19♉52	18N03	23♈40	26♉36	
Hyades	γ Tau	6♉09	5S58	13♉23	4♉50	Prima Hyadum
Capella	α Aur	22♉16	22N50	16♈26	2♊05	Capella
Pleiades	η Tau	0♉25	3N50	25♈14	1♉11	Alcyone
Lepus	α Lep	21♉46	41S20	29♊21	9♉26	Arneb
Iugulae	ε Ori	23♉52	24S47	16♊41	16♉18	Alnilam
Procyon	α CMi	26♊34	15S36	6♋27	17♊41	Procyon
Canicula	α CMa	14♊53	39S08	11♋52	27♉31	Sirius
Crater	α Crt	24♌32	22S42	29♌18	29♋10	Alkes
Corona	α CrB	12♎24	44N32	4♎52	12♐54	Alphecca
Spica	α Vir	24♍17	1S55	24♍32	21♍34	Spica
Sagitta	γ Sge	7♑32	39N25	13♐00	27♑16	
	δ Sge	3♑56	39N09	10♐45	24♑37	
Haedus						(unidenti fied)
Lyra	α Lyr	15♐35	61N51	14♏43	0♒51	Vega
Ara	α Ara	25♏23	26S14	8♐34	11♎29	
Centaurus	α Cen	2♏54	41S50	18♏26	7♌25	Rigel Kentaurus

Arcturus	α Boo	24♍40	32N11	19♍38	13♏47	Arcturus
Cygnus	α Cyg	6♒11	60N01	10♐11	27♒20	Deneb
Ophiuchus	α Oph	22♏45	36N15	11♏53	25♐29	Ras Alhague
Piscis Notius	α Psa	4♒02	20S50	4♓52	24♑31	Fomalhaut
Fides						
Delphinus	β Del	16♑49	32N09	23♐56	0♒41	Rotanev
Cepheus	α Cep	13♓43	68N55	28♏04	3♈49	Alderamin
Aquila	α Aql	1♑52	29N23	14♐45	18♑04	Altair
Cassiopeia	α Cas	8♈25	46N29	20♑47	17♈46	Schedir
	β Cas	5♈33	51N20	9♑44	16♈25	Caph
	γ Cas	14♈34	48N38	16♑43	26♈30	
	δ Cas	18♈22	46N19	22♑54	0♉18	Ruchbah
Andromeda	α And	14♓50	25N44	11♒07	18♓43	Alpheratz
	β And	0♈52	25N54	23♒04	4♈34	Mirach
Andromeda	γ And	14♈45	27N39	0♓56	19♈32	Almach
Equus	α Peg	23♒59	19N29	2♒03	28♒08	Markab
	β Peg	29♒48	31N07	24♑07	5♓49	Scheat
Engonasin	α Her	16♏32	37N32	6♏28	22♐45	Ras Algethi
Cetus	β Cet	2♓45	20S45	5♈18	28♒20	Deneb Kaitos
Helice						
Draco	B Dra	12♏06	75N32	9♎42	18♒14	Rastaban
Auriga	α Aur	22♉16	22N50	16♈26	2♊05	Capella

APPENDIX 5.
INDEX OF OCCUPATIONS[1]

[1]In this and in the three following Indexes, there are undoubtedly some errors and omissions. I apologize in advance for these.

APPENDIX 6.

INDEX OF THE CAUSE OF DEATH

APPENDIX 7.
INDEX OF PERSONAL CHARACTERISTICS

Learned persons, i.Pref.6,i.Pref.8,i.6.3,i.10.2,ii.16.6,ii.30.1,iii.3c.27,iii.3d.22, iii.3f.11,iii.3f.25,iv.7.28,viii.24.7,viii.26.13

Liars, viii.20.4, viii.25.10, viii.26.14, viii.27.6

Long-lived persons, viii.19.10,viii.26.10,viii.26.12,viii.26.15,viii.27.3, viii.28.2,viii.28.8,viii.29.1,viii.29.4,viii.29.10,viii.29.12,viii.30.2,viii.30.3, viii.30.6

Loved by many, viii.21.6,viii.31.10

Loved by the people, viii.28.10

Loved by women, viii.24.7,viii.26.12

Lovers of boys, iii.3e.20,iii.3e.23,iii.3e.28,iii.3f.14,iii.8.17,vi.31.39-40, vii.15.1-3

Low-born persons, viii.22.1

Madmen iii.7.3,iii.7.12,iv.3f.3,viii.26.13,viii.26.15, viii.29.13,viii.30.5, viii.29.13,viii.30.5

Malicious persons, i.2.4,i.3.8,iii.3a.7,iii.3d.22,iii.3d.25,iii.3f.12,iii.3f.16, iii.3f.18,iii.3f.26,iii.5.6,iv.2f.3,iv.3c.4,iv.7.5,viii.26.4,viii.26.14,viii.27.6, viii.20.3,viii.28.6

Merry persons, viii.20.10

Miserable persons, iii.3f.4,iv.2a.2,iv.2d.1,iv.3.2,iv.3b.11,iv.3c.4,viii.20.8

Modest persons, i.Pref.1,i.Pref.8,i.7.2,ii.31.11,iv.3h.3,viii.21.6,viiii.30.7

Negligent persons, viii.26.7, viii.28.7

Nobles, i.2.2,ii.31.6,iii.3b.1,iii.3b.7,iii.3d.9,iii.3d.20,iii.3d.37,iii.3d.38,iii.3e.3, iii.4.6,iii.9.7,iii.9a.6,iv.2e.1,iv.3a.2,iv.3a.7,iv.3b.6,iv.3d.2,iv.3e.1,iv.3e.8, iv.3f.16,iv.4.8,iv.7.6,iv.7.9,iv.7.17,iv.11.5,iv.14.5,iv.14.10,iv.14.11, viii.19.4,viii.19.6, viii.25.6,viii.26.2,viii.28.4,viii.28.8,viii.28.10,viii.29.4, viii.29.12.,viii.30.2, viii.30.5, viii.30.10

Noisy persons, viii.27.12, viii.28.6

One-eyed Persons, viii.19.2, viii.20.8, viii.22.1, viii.27.11

Parricides, iv.3f.9,viii.27.4

Paupers, iii.3a.5,iii.3b.23,iii.4.12,iii.5.8,iv.3.3,iv.3f.3,iv.3f.15,iv.3g.3,iv.3g.6, iv.3g.7,viii.24.3

Perjurers, iii.3d.16,iii.7.14,iv.3f.7,iv.7.8,viii.26.15,viii.27.1,viii.28.6

Perverts, iii.3b.11,iii.3e.22,iii.3e.29,iii.7.9,iv.2e.3,iv.2e.4,iv.3d.1,iv.3d.3, viii.19.1

Pious persons, i.10.13, iv.7.17,viii.21.2

Polydactyly persons, viii.28.8 note

Poor persons, iv.7.17,iii.3d.11,iii.7.5,iii.9.13,iv.3.1,iv.12.4,viii.24.3

Publicly punished persons, viii.28.9

Quarrelsome persons, viii.27.12

Rash persons, i.Pref.7,i.3.6,i.3.7,i.3.8,i.7.9,iii.7.3,viii.26.8, viii.27.4,viii.28.12

APPENDIX 8.
INDEX OF PERSONS

[1]*See* also the names of the individual editors.